Natural Cures "They" Don't Want You to Know About

Natural Cures "They" Don't Want You to Know About

KEVIN TRUDEAU

Alliance Publishing Group, Inc.

RRD

Contents

All of the author's royalties on the sale of this book are being used to help fund the mission of educating people about natural health care and exposing corporate and government corruption.

Disclaimer

It is unbelievable to me, in this day and age, that the world has come to this. It pains me that I must write a disclaimer at the beginning of this book. Imagine, a person who is supposed to be allowed to express his opinions under the banner of "free speech" must still put a disclaimer as a preface to his words, thoughts, and opinions. Heaven forbid someone reads these words and claims to be adversely affected by them, thus ensuring a barrage of lawsuits filed under the guise of protecting the unknowing victims who were stupid enough to read this and believe it! In reality, these lawyers are squashing the rights of people, like myself, from freely expressing their ideas. So with a figurative gun to my head I write these words:

Before you read this book you had better check with your medical doctor, your friends, your politicians, your priest, your rabbi, your psychic, and anyone you feel is smarter than you, and see if you can get permission to read what I have to say.

You must know that everything I say in this book is simply my opinion and that there are many people who violently disagree with my conclusions. If you do anything I recommend without the supervision of a licensed medical doctor, you do so at your own risk. The publisher and the author, the distributors and bookstores, present this information for educational purposes only. I am not making an attempt to prescribe any medical treatment, since under the laws of the United States only a licensed medical doctor (an MD) can do so. How sad!

So this book is only my opinions, my thoughts, and my conclusions. Again, it is for educational purposes only, and you and only you are responsible if you choose to do anything based on what you read.

Kevin Trudeau

Acknowledgments

I would like to recognize, acknowledge, and applaud all the people around the world that helped make this book and this mission possible. I cannot name you all by name, but you know who you are. I salute you and I am honored to serve with you on this noble mission of educating the world about the evils of greed and the benefits of using natural methods to prevent and cure disease.

I would like to specifically highlight and mention those individuals who were directly instrumental in the writing and publishing of this book: Enrique Espinosa, Felipe Correa, Pamela Farley, Reno R. Rollé, Neil Sant, and Lisa Liddy.

It is ironic, but I would also like to thank the Federal Trade Commission and the Food and Drug Administration for being a direct inspiration to me to write this book and expose the corruption in both of these organizations. Your personal attacks on me, and hundreds of other innocent people whose only objective is to help society, shows to the world just how corrupt you are and that you must be stopped. You have inspired me like Goliath inspired David, and like David, with my measly slingshot I vow to the world that I will personally help stop the needless suffering of millions of people that you are directly causing. Your organizations and the individual people involved will be exposed, disgraced, and defeated.

Read This First!

I congratulate you on having the courage to read this book. By purchasing this book you have shown that you are either sick and are looking for natural cures for your illness or you are concerned about getting sick. You may be also concerned about the health and well-being of your family and friends. In order for you to get the most benefit out of the information in this book it is absolutely essential that you read this book from start to finish, cover to cover. You must start at the beginning and read this book in its entirety in the order in which the material is presented. Do not jump ahead, and do not jump around the book looking for an immediate answer to a question you may have regarding your health. All the information in this book is presented in a very specific order for a very specific reason. Please be assured that if you start at the beginning of this book and read it in its entirety, by the time you finish you will understand the cause of your disease and you will know categorically, absolutely, with a hundred percent certainty that there is a natural cure for your disease and you will know exactly what to do to cure yourself of your disease and remain healthy for life—all without drugs and surgery.

Please note that there are many important and vital concepts that I discuss in this book. Because these concepts are an important foundation to everything else that I discuss, in many instances I repeat over and over again these basic concepts. This is done for a reason. This is done purposely. I have found from experience that in order for you to benefit from this information you must absolutely KNOW the basic foundation principles. Therefore, I repeat over and over again the basic foundation principles. My goal is for you to "get it" and be able to cure yourself of your disease without drugs and surgery. So let's begin the journey together, and when you conclude this book I promise you one thing...you will never be the same!

Yours in health,
Kevin Trudeau

Introduction

Bill Gates, the richest man in the world, was interviewed on *The Larry King Show*. When asked by Larry about his incredible wealth and success, Bill Gates said "Larry, I was at the right place at the right time, and luck has a lot to do with that."

You now are reading this book. I believe in my heart that you are at the right place at the right time. Maybe luck has something to do with it.

Bill Gates continued, "But Larry, there were a lot of people at the same place I was. One difference was I had vision. I saw the potential that was there."

Folks, I believe you are at the right place at the right time by reading this book. As you read this book, will you see the potential in the material presented? Will you see the potential that utilizing this information can have on your own health, well-being, and vitality? Do you have the vision that you can prevent and cure almost all illness and disease with natural methods, without drugs and without surgery?

Mr. Gates was not through. He continued, "But Larry, there were a lot of people at the same place I was, and a lot of people had the same vision. The big difference was I took massive and immediate action."

Folks, I believe you are at the right place at the right time. I hope that you have the vision and see the potential of how this material can positively impact you. But the real question that I cannot answer is that upon completion of this book, will YOU take MASSIVE AND IMMEDIATE ACTION by implementing the suggestions and recommendations in this book. If you do, you will succeed in your quest for longevity, health, and vitality.

There are natural cures for virtually every disease. There are non-drug and nonsurgical methods to prevent and cure almost all illness. The drug companies, the government, and a host of other organizations do not want you to know what these natural cures are. This book will give you the reasons why, and give you the answers.

It is important to note that I wrote virtually every word in this book. I did not have this book edited or written by a professional; therefore, it is written in common language and plain English. It is designed to be easy to read and understand. Since I first published this book I have received virtually tens of thousands of pieces of correspondence from people all around the world telling me how utilizing the information in this book has changed their life for the better. I hope this book will have a positive impact in your life as well.

You will be learning some very new and exciting things in this book. The concepts are logical and easy to understand and filled with common sense. However, the conclusions go against conventional wisdom. For you to fully grasp this information it is important that you ask yourself now just how "teachable" you are. There is in fact a "teachability index," which will determine just how easy learning new concepts will be for you. The teachability index consists of two variables. The first variable is your willingness to learn. I believe that by you purchasing this book, spending your own money, and spending the time to read this book, that you, on a scale of one to ten, probably have a pretty high willingness to learn. However, the second variable will really determine just how teachable you are. The second variable in the teachability index is what is your willingness to accept change. If you have a ten on willingness to learn, but a zero on willingness to accept change, ten times zero is zero; therefore, your teachability index is nonexistent. You must have a high willingness to accept change if you are to fully grasp and understand these concepts and benefit from them. I sincerely hope that you have a high teachability index.

As you go through this book please consider another important factor on fully utilizing this information in your daily life. Information is only useful when it is used. It can only be used when it is fully internalized, when you don't have to "think about it." The four stages a person goes through when learning any new information, such as the material presented in this book, are:

1. unconscious incompetence—this is the stage where you don't know that you don't know;

2. conscious incompetence—this is the stage that you KNOW YOU DON'T KNOW;

3. conscious competence—this is when you know that you know, but you have to consciously think about it;

4.   unconscious competence—this is when it is second nature; this is when the information is part of you; this is when you know it just as easily as you know your own name; this is when it is fully internalized and is just automatic.

When you read this book you will go through the first three stages. When you finish this book you will have to implement the information in this book for a period of time before you will reach level four. When you do, you will live a life, in my opinion, that is healthy and disease free, and you quite possible may never get sick ever again—a hard thing to say right now, but something to at least consider as a possibility. So let's start the journey.

I Should Be Dead By Now

> *Great spirits have always encountered violent opposition from mediocre minds.*
>
> —Albert Einstein

I was driving down the Tri-State Highway outside of Chicago, Illinois, in my brand new Corvette enjoying a beautiful sunny day. Suddenly I felt an enormous ripping pain in my chest. I could barely breathe; the pain was excruciating. I immediately pulled off to the side of the road. My life virtually flashed before my eyes and I thought, "Oh my god I'm having a heart attack and I'm only twenty-one years old!"

Just as quickly as the pain came, it vanished. I was dizzy, disoriented, and in a state of shock and disbelief as to what had just happened. I looked down and noticed my new car phone, an invention that had just come out in the Chicagoland area. I picked up my phone, called my secretary, and said "I think I just had a heart attack."

Luckily for me, within a few moments I felt fine. I concluded that if it was a heart attack, it certainly didn't cause any major damage. But something was obviously wrong.

Over the next week I was examined by three of the top heart specialists in America. Through use of the most advanced medical diagnostic devices, it was concluded after days of testing that I had been born with a deformed heart, a severe *mitral valve prolapse* which would cause me major medical problems the rest of my life. There was no cure.

These top medical minds recommended experimental drugs or risky surgery, both of which I was told had little promise. My life expectancy was to be very short. I struggled with coming up with an

1

effective plan of action that could solve my medical dilemma. I was twenty-one years old and had my whole life in front of me. I had to do something!

Months earlier I had attended a lecture where I heard about a Harvard medical doctor named Yiwen Y. Tang, founder of the Century Clinic in Reno, Nevada, who, during the Korean War, was a MASH surgeon. (Today the clinic is called Sierra Integrative Medical Center.) This MD had decided that standard medical procedures, drugs, and surgery were not the best way to cure and prevent diseases. He instead was using a diagnostic device developed in Germany by a Dr. Reinhold Voll called the *Dermatron* machine. Allegedly, in a matter of minutes, it could diagnose medical problems in the body. When the diagnosis was complete, homeopathic remedies were given to correct the imbalances and reverse and cure the disease.

At the time it sounded like hocus-pocus. The words homeostasis, holistic healing, homeopathic remedies, acupuncture meridians, energy frequencies, imbalances, and the like were used in the lecture, replacing what was, to me, the standard vernacular of germs, bacteria, viruses, drugs, surgery, and genetics. Skeptical, yet open to new ideas, I flew to Reno, Nevada, to meet this great Dr. Tang. What did I have to lose?

Upon my arrival, the doctor asked me why I was there. I looked fit and healthy, and being so young, he was slightly puzzled by my desire for diagnosis. Most of his patients were old and had severe medical problems. Wanting to see if this *Dermatron* machine was legitimate, I simply said, "I feel great. I just want a basic checkup."

Immediately he tested me with his magic machine. Within two minutes he had touched my heart meridian with the probe and the machine registered very low energy. The doctor looked at me, slightly concerned, and said, "Son you have a heart problem." I was shocked at how quickly the diagnosis came. Just as quickly he stated, "Let me find out where it is."

He began to touch other meridian points. When he got to the mitral valve, the machine again registered very little energy. He looked at me and said matter-of-factly, "You have a mitral valve prolapse."

Needless to say, I was quite impressed. The expert medical doctors took days of diagnostic testing to determine that I had a severe mitral valve prolapse. This "energy machine" diagnosed the problem within minutes. I looked at the doctor and said, "Yes I know, and I understand it is incurable." His response startled me. "Yes, in America it's incurable, but there are natural treatments in other countries that can reverse this problem in a matter of weeks. Unfortunately the FDA has not approved these treatments. So, yes, in America it is incurable." He then went on to explain a procedure of live cell injections—available in Switzerland or Mexico but not accessible via legal treatment in the United States—that would correct the problem by actually rebuilding the heart, ensuring that it would never return.

Quite frankly, I couldn't believe my ears. Natural treatments *that work* that are not approved by the FDA? Impossible!

This event happened over twenty years ago. The treatment I received was inexpensive, all-natural, painless, quick, and it worked! And still to this day, that therapy is illegal in America. The most amazing part of this story is, after I received the natural treatment that was forbidden in America, I went back to the medical doctors who originally diagnosed my heart problem and asked to be tested again. My request was met with indignation; I was told that being tested again was a waste of time and money because it was impossible for the medical condition to change in two months. Nevertheless, I demanded a readministering of all the tests anyway. The doctors humored me and were stunned when they found I no longer had a mitral valve prolapse.

I was so excited to share with them information about the treatment I had received which had cured my problem. Certainly these doctors would want to know about an all-natural medical treatment that could cure the incurable! Imagine my shock when I was told that the treatment I received could not have cured my disease but, rather, I must have been misdiagnosed in the first place and never had the heart deformity to begin with. I could not believe my ears! These medical doctors would not accept the facts: I had a severe mitral valve prolapse—the pictures confirmed it; and now I do not have a mitral valve prolapse—the pictures confirm it.

I began to think of all of the people that would come to these medical doctors and be told the bold-faced lie that their medical condition was incurable and could only be treated with drugs and surgery. It sickened me to know that the truth about natural cures would be hidden from millions of patients. The knowledge that the established medical community would deny the existence of natural cures, thus allowing millions of people to suffer and in many cases die, enraged me.

That event started me on a lifelong mission: searching for natural remedies that do not include drugs or surgery and natural treatments that can prevent and cure illness and disease. It also exposed me to the organizations, companies, and government agencies that do not want you to know about these cures.

Today I live a full, healthy, dynamic life. I take no drugs and have had no surgeries. I haven't had a prescription or nonprescription drug in over twenty years. Additionally, I virtually never get sick. Colds, flus, and all illnesses seem to pass me by. I have had hundreds of blood tests and other diagnostic tests performed on me every few years, just to make sure everything is within the normal range. The medical professionals who have examined and reviewed these results are stunned and amazed at the level of health that I enjoy. Am I lucky? Is it just genetics? Or are there some specific things that a person can do to have a disease- and illness-free life and enjoy dynamic, vibrant health? Is it possible for you to go week after week, year after year, and never get sick? I strongly believe the answer is yes. This book specifically outlines the following things:

- Yes—there are all-natural, nondrug, and nonsurgical cures for most every illness and disease.

- Yes—there are organizations, government agencies, companies, and entire industries that are spending billions of dollars trying to hide these natural cures from you.

- Yes—*every* single nonprescription and prescription drug has adverse side effects and should virtually never be taken (with exceptions that I will explain later).

In this book, it's important to note that I am oversimplifying everything. The reason is that I am not writing this book for the medical community, the scientists, researchers, or MDs. They are not going to believe or agree with anything I say anyway. I'm writing this book in plain English so that you can understand it.

Let me point out a couple of things. Everything I say in this book is my opinion. Everything stated is what I believe to be true. All my conclusions and statements of fact are, in most cases, opinions.

It's interesting to note that medical science always presents things as fact when actually what they are really presenting is not fact at all. It's only an *opinion,* based on the information they have at the current time. Throughout history, medical "facts" have been proven not to be true over and over again. Therefore they are not facts at all; they are simply *opinions.* Medical science has stated things to be true and, in most cases, years later those things have been found not to be true. Medical science is almost always wrong, yet they present things as factual, as if they "know" the truth.

The medical industry presents itself as the only source of truth when it comes to health, illness, and disease. They use words like *credible scientific evidence, scientifically tested, scientifically proven.* The fact is that what they are really presenting are theories, and these theories constantly change. Here is an example of "medical facts" that have been proven to be wrong:

- Bloodletting was once proven to cure most illnesses. Now it is considered totally ineffective.

- Margarine was considered much healthier than butter. Now research suggests that the exact opposite is true.

- Eggs were considered very bad because of high cholesterol. Now research suggests that they are not bad at all, and they are actually healthy for the body.

- Alcohol in all forms was said to be 100 percent unhealthy and therefore should not be consumed. Then the medical community said that red wine is actually healthy for the heart but not other forms of alcohol. Now "medical science" says that all alcohol in moderation actually has health benefits.

- Chocolate and oily foods were touted to be a cause of acne. Now research suggests that they do not contribute in any way to acne.

- Homosexuality was once classified as a disease.

- Medical doctors touted that baby formula was much better than breast milk for children. Now the exact opposite is shown to be true.

- Milk was recommended for coating the stomach and alleviating stomach ulcers. Now it is discouraged and has been found to aggravate ulcers.

- Medical science stated that diet had absolutely no effect on disease or illness. Now we are told that diet has a huge effect on the prevention and cause of disease.

- Medical science once had scientific evidence that the removing of tonsils and appendix improved health and should be done to virtually everyone. Now the medical community has reversed that theory.

- Children with asthma were told to stay in enclosed pool areas because the humidity was good for their asthmatic condition. Now research suggests that the chlorine in the air from the pools actually aggravates and makes the asthma worse.

- The most obvious example of all is the fact that there are thousands of drugs that have been approved by the FDA because they were scientifically proven to cure or prevent disease, in addition to having been touted as safe. Then, years later, they have been taken off the market because they had been newly proven to either not cure or prevent those diseases as originally thought, or those drugs were found to have such terribly adverse side effects that they are simply too dangerous for people to use.

The point is, what we are being told by the medical community as "fact" is simply not fact at all. It is the "current theory" and "thought of the day," which historically is often shown to be not true. It saddens me when I see doctors on TV stating things as fact when they should be qualifying their comments with such phrases as *"it appears, based on the current research we have; it seems that; we believe this to be true, however, we also know that as more research and observations are evaluated this may change in the future."* This is not happening. Medical doctors are still looked on as gods. Whatever they say is taken as absolutely true. No one else can say anything about health, illness, or disease with the credibility of a medical doctor. That simply is wrong. Medical doctors are trained to do only two things: prescribe drugs or cut out parts of a person's anatomy (surgery). They are not trained at preventing disease and, most important, they have little to no training in or exposure to any treatment other than drugs or surgery.

Another example of medical facts reversed is the diet industry. First, a low-calorie diet was said to be the only way to lose weight. Then experts said, "It's not the calories, but the amount of fat you consume that will determine your weight." Now the rage of the day is "It's not the calories and it's not the fat, it's the carbohydrates that cause obesity."

The fact is, nobody really knows. Imagine the government's highest medical authority making this statement: "Today we have more information and knowledge about the cure and prevention of disease than ever before in the history of mankind. The advancements that have been made in just the last few years have given us new insights about the treatment and prevention of virtually all illness and disease, making it safe to reach two major conclusions:

1. Even though just ten years ago we thought we knew the proper treatments of illness, we now know just how little we knew back then.

2. With these revolutionary breakthroughs in technology, virtually all illness and disease should be wiped out in America within the next ten years. We are on the verge of entering a phase where a person will never be sick. And if you do get sick, your doctor will be able to cure you of your illness in a matter of days. We have virtually reached the pinnacle of medical knowledge."

Sounds exciting, doesn't it? Wow! We have reached the pinnacle of medical knowledge. We know all there is to know about the cure and prevention of disease. Wow! In just ten years, because of medical science, sickness will be eliminated in America. Well, even though it sounds exciting, there is a downside: Imagine that the speech was given in 1902. Interesting, isn't it? In 1902, the people of the day believed they knew all there was to know about the cure and prevention of disease. We look back at them and are in awe at just how little they knew. Now here is the hard part for us to imagine. Twenty years from now, people will look at us and be in awe of how little we know about the cure and prevention of disease. Today we laugh at the thought of bloodletting curing a disease. Well, fifty years from now people will laugh when they look at some of the archaic and horrible treatments that we are using today in an attempt to cure illness.

As you read this book, imagine me prefacing everything I say with *"It seems" or "It appears based on current observations and current research ..." "I believe this to be true."*

I know that, of everything I say in this book, as more research and data becomes available, there is an excellent chance that many of these theories and opinions may be altered, modified, improved, or changed completely. Please just note this: *There are virtually no medical facts.* There are only medical opinions. You need to choose the opinion that makes the best sense for you.

How did I come up with my opinions? I have traveled over five million miles to bring you this information. I have been in all fifty U.S. states and traveled to countries all over the world. Over the last twenty years I have talked with thousands of health-care providers. I have listened to tens of thousands of people who have had serious medical conditions cured by natural therapies, many after drugs and surgery had failed them. I have personally seen with my own eyes, heard with my own ears, and experienced firsthand so much information that I believe I have the unique perspective necessary to come up with my my bold conclusions. The biggest acknowledgment I must give is to the tens of thousands of dedicated health-care professionals around the world who refuse to use drugs and surgery, yet routinely see their patients cured of diseases and who go on to live vibrant healthy lives. These natural health-care providers see people cured of cancer, diabetes, heart disease, chronic pain, headaches, arthritis, allergies, depression, and the list goes on. The question is no longer whether diseases can be prevented or cured faster and more effectively without drugs and surgery. The real question is why are health-care providers, who do not use drugs and surgery, being prosecuted as criminals because they cure people of cancer, AIDS, and hundreds of other chronic diseases? Natural therapies work. Natural therapies can work better than drugs or surgery. People who are using natural therapies to cure and prevent disease, and have a higher success rate with no adverse side effects than drug or surgery-type treatments, are being prosecuted for breaking the law. The question is, why are inexpensive, all-natural, safe, effective treatments being suppressed? Let's find out.

CHAPTER 2

What's Wrong with Health Care in America?

Medical science has absolutely, 100 percent, failed in the curing and prevention of illness, sickness, and disease. Consider the following startling bits of data:

- More people get colds and flus than ever before.
- More people get cancer than ever before.
- More people have diabetes than ever before.
- More people have heart disease than ever before.
- More people have multiple sclerosis, lupus, muscular dystrophy, asthma, migraine headaches, joint, neck, and back pain than ever before.
- More people have acid reflux, ulcers, and stomach problems than ever before.
- More women have menopause problems than ever before.
- More women have more frequent PMS and more severe PMS than ever before.
- More kids have attention deficit disorder and hyperactivity than ever before.
- More people have chronic fatigue than ever before.
- More people have insomnia than ever before.
- More people have bad skin, acne, and dandruff than ever before.
- More people suffer from depression, stress, and anxiety than ever before.

- More men and women suffer from sexual dysfunction and infertility than ever before.
- More people suffer from allergies, arthritis, constipation, fibromyalgia, cold sores, and herpetic breakouts than ever before.
- More men suffer from prostate problems than ever before.
- More women suffer from yeast infections than ever before.

Yet surprisingly enough...

- There are more people going to visit doctors than ever before.
- There are more people getting diagnostic testing, such as blood tests and X-rays, than ever before.
- More people are taking nonprescription and prescription drugs than ever before.
- Not only are more people taking drugs, but each person is taking more drugs than ever before.
- There are more surgeries performed than ever before.

What does this tell us? It tells us that standard medical science is failing. More people are getting medical treatment, taking more drugs, having more diagnostic testing and having more surgeries than ever before in history. Yet more people are getting sick than ever before in history. Medical science is failing! According to *Fortune* magazine, we are losing the war on cancer. The percentage of Americans dying of cancer today is the same as it was in 1970 and even 1950! Over $200 billion has been spent since 1971 trying to prevent and cure cancer. Yet today you have a higher chance of getting cancer than ever before in history, and you have the same chance of dying as you did in 1950. I would call that a miserable failure. Americans spend over $2 trillion a year on health care, yet the American infant mortality rate is higher than twenty other developed countries. People in thirty other countries live longer than Americans, yet Americans consume over half of all the drugs manufactured in the world. There are over 200,000 nonprescription drugs on the market; there are over 30,000 prescription medications. Doctors write over three billion prescriptions each year. The average American has over thirty different prescription and nonprescription drugs in their medicine cabinet. The bottom line: The only winners in the cure and prevention of disease are the drug companies and the health-care companies themselves. The drug companies' profits are at an all-time high. Medical science has failed unequivocally in the prevention and curing of virtually every illness.

As an example, let's look at the "Diet Industry":

- More people are on diets than ever before.
- More people take more diet products than ever before.
- More people exercise than ever before.
- Yet more people are fat than ever before. Over 68 percent of the people living in America are overweight. It's been increasing virtually every single year. Not only are more people fatter than ever before, more people are dangerously obese!

Who are the winners in the war on obesity? The corporations that sell diet food, diet pills, and other weight-loss aids are making more money than ever before.

An ideal scenario would be never having to take a single drug and never getting sick. An ideal scenario would be waking up in the morning full of energy and vitality, content, and feeling absolutely great. You go throughout your day with energy, a bounce in your step, a smile on your face. You don't feel stressed, anxious, or depressed; you don't feel tired, you have no headaches or pain in your body; you are not overweight and you don't get colds or flus or sickness. You don't get diseases, you have no pain, you're not ravenous with your appetite, you eat what you want and you are never that hungry. You don't deprive yourself of the foods you enjoy. You go to sleep at night and you sleep soundly and peacefully and get a wonderful whole night's rest. Your sexual desires are healthy and strong, and you are capable of both giving and receiving sexual pleasure. Your skin, your hair, and your nails look healthy and radiant. You have strength and tone in your muscles. Your body is fluid, graceful, and flexible. You are firm, strong, vibrant, and feel great!

This is the description of a healthy person. A healthy person never has to take a drug. A healthy person never has to have surgeries. A healthy person has no cancer, diabetes, or heart disease. A healthy person lives without illness, sickness, or disease. Most people have no idea how good their body is designed to feel. We have been brainwashed into believing that it is natural for a human being to get colds and flus, have aches and pains, and have major medical problems like cancer, diabetes, and heart disease. We are also brainwashed into believing that it's "natural" to take drugs. We are programmed to believe that it is normal and natural to take drugs and that we "need" drugs in order to be healthy. Consider this—animals in the wild, such as chimpanzees, do not get sick! They do not get diabetes, cancer, heart disease, asthma, heartburn, arthritis, etc. Animals in the wild also do not take drugs. Animals in the wild don't go to the health club to work out. Yet without drugs, medical visits, surgeries, or formalized exercise routines, animals in the wild have virtually no disease or illness and live three to five times longer than humans. The point is, you do not have to get sick. Being sick is not "normal," it is abnormal. Most people think they are healthy, but they really have no idea just how good they could feel.

Is there a place for surgery and drugs? The answer is absolutely yes! Medical science has done a very good job at addressing symptoms. However, the treatment of a symptom has two flaws. First, the treatment itself usually causes more problems which will have to be treated later. Second, the cause of the symptom is usually never addressed. When you do not address the cause, you are allowing for problems later on. With this said, if you are in an emergency situation such as that caused by a sudden accident of some sort, drugs and surgery can save your life. However, drugs and surgery have failed at preventing illness and they do not address the cause of illness. Nevertheless, they do work well in emergency crisis situations. The bottom line is, if you fall off a ladder and puncture a kidney, you want to be rushed to the closest emergency room and have a trained medical doctor use drugs and surgery to save your life. But if you want to stay healthy and never have disease, drugs and surgery are not the answer. I will explain this in more detail in a later chapter.

So if trillions of dollars in scientific research has failed in producing ways to prevent and cure illness and disease, and all-natural inexpensive prevention methods and cures do exist, why aren't we hearing about them? The answer may surprise you.

CHAPTER 3

It's All About the Money

Profit is not a four-letter word, but rape is against the law.
—Author Unknown

My contention is that there are all-natural cures for virtually every disease and ailment. These cures are being suppressed and hidden from you by the pharmaceutical industry, the Food and Drug Administration, and the Federal Trade Commission, as well as other groups. The question that arises most often when I make these statements is, "What is the motive for such a thing to occur?" The answer is simple: money and power. Most people have no idea just how powerful a motivating force money and power can be. Money does indeed make the world go round. The love of money, which is the definition of greed, is in fact the root of all evil. Think about some obvious facts. Ninety percent of all people in prison today are there because of a money-related crime. Interesting, isn't it? Money is such a powerful force people will risk going to jail for it. Seventy-five percent of all murders are committed for money. People's insatiable desire to have money actually drives them to kill another human being!

All publicly traded corporations have a legal responsibility to increase profits, it's the law! Think about it: With rare exception, every single business has one objective—to make more profits. The only way companies make more profits is by producing their product at the lowest possible cost, selling it at the highest possible price, and

13

selling as much as they can. Every decision a company makes is to increase profits.

Companies, however, are run by people. People have two motivations—first, to make more money for themselves personally; and, second, to increase their power, prestige, or influence. Therefore, the individuals who run companies will always make decisions based on what can personally enrich themselves. Very few individuals are concerned about the good of mankind, the environment, or achieving some spiritual nirvana. To varying degrees, decisions are based on the answer to the question, "What's in it for me?"

In business, is everything always about the money? Yes. Throughout the history of big business, *planned obsolescence* has been standard operating procedure. This is when a product is manufactured in such a way so that it will wear out or need to be replaced. The product could have been made to last a very long time; but in order for the company to ensure future profits, it knowingly manufactured an item that was inherently flawed. Thus it planned for the product's obsolescence, all in the name of profit.

In today's business environment, companies only do things that either increase sales, decrease the cost of the product, or guarantee a higher price for the product. A simplified example of this can be seen with restaurants that are located in airports. The restaurant has a monopoly, there is no competition. Since the restaurant knows it is not relying on repeat business, it does not have to give good-quality food, good service, or a fair price. Have you ever gotten a great meal with great service at a great price at an airport restaurant? I sure haven't. Why? Because they don't have to. Giving good service and a good product at a fair price will not increase profit at an airport restaurant because they are not relying on repeat customers. Another example is outsourcing. Why are hundreds of companies laying off millions of American workers and outsourcing this work to people in other countries? Because it's cheaper! Remember, the corporate officers and directors of publicly traded companies have a legal responsibility to increase profits. If they don't, they will lose their jobs. Big business will always make decisions based on profit, not what is good for the employees, what is good for the customer, what is good for the environment, what is good for society, or what is good for mankind.

Let's look at the drug industry. Let's say you sell insulin to diabetics. Would you be happy if someone discovered an herb that when taken cured a person's diabetes so that they never needed insulin again? Of course not. You would be out of business. As an interesting note, there is such a cure for diabetes. The person who discovered it was offered over $30 million by a major pharmaceutical company *not to market it!* It's all about the money.

Health care, defined as the treatment, prevention, and diagnosis of disease, is the most profitable industry in the world. As long as people are sick, billions and billions of dollars in profit are made every year. Think about it. There are enormous amounts of money to be made as long as people stay sick. A healthy person, on the other hand, doesn't spend any money on the health-care industry. A healthy person does not need to buy drugs, does not get medical treatment, and is a liability to the corporations involved in health care. If every person was healthy and disease-free, the drug companies and virtually the entire health-care industry would be out of business. To the drug companies and virtually all the corporations involved in health care, you are nothing more than a customer. As long as you are sick you are potentially a good customer. There is no financial incentive for the health-care industry in having people live disease-free. There is no financial incentive to prevent or cure disease. Rather, the entire health-care industry is driven by one overshadowing motive: to make money! The entire health-care industry is run by individual people in the form of officers and directors of the publicly traded corporations that make up the industry. These people are, with rare exception, some of the most ruthless, wealthiest, and greediest people on the planet. Is this true? Let's examine a fictitious— or maybe not so fictitious—scenario.

• • •

Imagine there is a scientist working in a lab somewhere. He makes a breakthrough discovery: A small plant is found in the Amazon that, when made into a tea and consumed, eliminates all cancer in the body within one week. Imagine this researcher proclaiming that he has given this tea to one thousand cancer patients and that every single one of them, within one week and without having undergone surgery, was found to have absolutely no cancer in their body. Eureka! A cure for cancer! A simple, inexpensive, all-natural cure with no side effects. Just a simple plant that you make into a tea and drink. It has absolutely no side effects at all. It's pure, all-natural, and costs just pennies.

Imagine this scientist announcing his discovery to the world. Certainly he would win a Nobel Prize. Certainly the world medical community would be rejoicing. No more cancer! Every cancer patient could drink this tea and in one week be free of all their cancer. Every person who lives with the fear of getting cancer could now know that they could simply drink a few cups of this tea, which costs them only a few pennies, and they could avoid ever getting cancer. My, my, the world would be a better place.

Unfortunately, you'll never hear this story. Not because the story is not true, but because if this simple herbal tea which cures all cancer was allowed to be sold, there would be no need for the American Cancer Society. There would be no need for any of the drug companies that are manufacturing and selling cancer drugs. There would be no need for any additional cancer research funding. Cancer clinics around the world would close, hundreds of thousands of people would be put out of work, entire industries would shut down overnight and billions and billions and billions of dollars in profit would no longer be funneling in to the kingpins who control the cancer industry.

So when this person makes this discovery, what happens? In some cases these people simply vanished. In other cases these people were given hundreds of millions of dollars for their research. In still other cases the federal government raided these researchers' offices, confiscated the data, and jailed the researchers for practicing medicine without a license. Is this fantasy or is this the truth? Well, the health-care industry has a dirty little secret, and I am blowing the whistle on it.

The conversations I've heard, the meetings I have attended, the papers that I've read, and the inside information that I have received about the health-care fraud going on in this world has made me mad as hell—and I'm not going to take it anymore. I've been dubbed "the Whistleblower" because I am blowing the whistle on the most profitable industry in the world: health care. I'm exposing the lies, the frauds, and the scams. I'm letting the cat out of the bag. Like other industries, once the truth is made known, things begin to change.

Is it true that the health-care industry is holding back natural, inexpensive cures for disease and illness? Could it be true that the only motivation in health care is profits? Let's just look at recent history.

We've all heard the stories of the inventors who had carburetors that would make automobiles run a thousand miles to a gallon of gasoline. We've heard that the automobile industry paid off those inventors with millions of dollars to secure the patents and then buried those patents and never used that technology. Why? Because it would cost the automotive industry billions of dollars in profits.

We all know the story of how the big three automobile manufacturers purchased the Redline Train System in California, only to dismantle it to make sure that more automobiles were sold. Most people don't know that a lawsuit was filed regarding this obvious antitrust issue and the "big three" were found guilty! Corruption runs deep. In this case it was evidenced by the judge awarding the plaintiffs an insulting $1 in damages! That's right, just $1! The big three automakers obviously paid off the right people to make sure that there were no consequences to their illegal actions.

Most recently, many of you have seen the movie *The Insider* or read the book about how for years the tobacco industry lied about their knowledge that the ingredients in cigarettes were highly addictive. Finally, an insider blew the whistle and told the truth. He exposed, finally, what we all assumed was true, that the research was conclusive, cigarettes are addictive, and that the manufacturers of cigarettes knew this for years and years and years but lied before Congress and said that they "have no knowledge" or "credible scientific evidence" that cigarettes are addictive. It was a flat-out lie. Why did they lie? Money. It's all about the money!

I happen to be a capitalist and an entrepreneur. Throughout my life I have been motivated to make money. Money itself is not bad. Making money and profits is not bad. It becomes bad when it becomes greed. Making money becomes very bad when you "love money." Making money and making profits is very bad when you hurt your employees, lie and deceive your customers, destroy the environment, exploit workers, illegally drive competitors out of business, and purposely sell inferior products and services. When you put money above everything else, that is when making money is a problem. Money should be *used* and people *loved*. The problem is that money is *loved* and people *used*!

We have heard the phrase, "The love of money is the root of all evil." The more multimillionaires I talk to, the more billionaires I talk to, the more Wall Street insiders I talk to, the more CEOs of major corporations I talk to, the more big business corporate directors I talk to, the more politicians I talk to, the more I believe that the love of money is indeed the root of all evil. I can tell you from firsthand experience that the majority of officers and directors of major publicly traded corporations are greedy beyond belief and corrupt beyond belief! Making money becomes an addiction. Making more money becomes the all-consuming compulsive motivator of these people. Making money becomes the most important thing in these people's lives. Making money and doing whatever it takes to make more money becomes the chief motivation in virtually all their decisions and actions. If making more money means lying, stealing, defrauding, falsifying, or harming other people, it's okay. If making more money means breaking the laws, destroying the environment, or seeing other people suffer, it's okay. Don't believe me? Let me point out a few examples.

Did you know there are thousands and thousands of millionaires, multimillionaires, and billionaires in prisons all around the world? Why are they in prison? Because even with their millions, they had such greed that they were willing to break the law to make more money. You may think these people are the exceptions. Consider this: For every drug dealer that was caught and is in prison, there are probably one thousand drug dealers on the streets that were not caught! I can tell you firsthand that for every millionaire or corporate officer or director that is in prison for breaking the law out of greed, there are hundreds if not thousands of officers, directors, and wealthy stockholders who are defrauding the public motivated by personal greed. Do you know what the number one motive for murder is? Money! That's right, money. The love of money and greed are such strong motivators that they are the number one reason people kill other human beings. It most definitely is true: Greed, defined as the love of money, is indeed the root of all evil.

We see it on TV with Enron and WorldCom and Martha Stewart. Individuals who have tens of millions of dollars in their bank accounts and are so greedy they want more. They will lie and defraud, cheat and effectively steal money from shareholders and employees for their own personal gain. Their ethics have been thrown out the window. They've sold their soul to the devil. There are thousands of people in every aspect of business and government that commit illegal acts all because they want more money. It's always all about the money. Just watch reality TV! Do you know that the producers of most reality TV shows are hoping that the real people on these shows have their lives ruined on national television? The producers make money with great ratings. If a person is physically hurt or has an emotionally traumatizing event happen, the ratings soar and the producers make more money. The more "bad" that happens to the individual the more money is made. It's like feeding Christians to the lions. Why are people so happy when another person's life has been destroyed on national TV? Because when you are so interested in money, even voyeuristically, you stop caring about other people's lives.

I've been in the corporate boardrooms of major corporations all around the world. I've listened to these people talk. I've heard first-hand, so I know that what I am saying is true; and most important, I have been there myself. Greed motivated me to break the rules, and I spent two years in federal prison because of it. Believe me, I know firsthand what I am talking about. Why haven't you heard this before? Well, for decades what went on in the Mafia was a secret. No one even admitted that La Cosa Nostra existed. Finally, one person, Joe Velacci, came forward and blew the whistle on the inner workings of organized crime. Since that time, dozens of former mafiosi have come forward to share the secrets that went on behind closed doors. In a similar fashion, the inner workings of the tobacco industry have been shrouded in secrecy. Finally, a man with a conscience came forward at the risk of his own life to blow the whistle on the greed, lies, and deceit that was directly responsible for the deaths of hundreds of thousands of people. Think about it. Where are weapons of mass destruction? They are in every package of cigarettes! Today, I am one of the first to come forward from the inside and tell you the truth about the people who run "big pharma." You may be under the illusion that drug companies have officers and directors whose sole passion in life is to prevent and cure disease for the benefit of mankind. But I am pulling back the curtain and exposing the great Oz for the fraud that he really is. You may hear the cry "pay no attention to the man behind the curtain," but do not be deceived. The officers and directors of the big corporations that make up the health-care industry are not benevolent, wonderful people with compassion and a desire to rid the world of illness. When the curtain is pulled back and the true identities are revealed, we see outrageously wealthy people whose greed, insatiable desire to make more money, and contempt for humanity is startling and mind-blowing. If you'd had the chance to shake these people's hands and look into their eyes, you would no longer feel safe.

Just remember that health care is the most profitable industry in the world and as long as people are sick, people are making billions of dollars in profits.

The bottom line is this: The health-care industry has no incentive for curing disease. If the health-care industry cured disease they would all be out of business. Their focus, as unbelievable as it sounds, is to ensure more people get sick and more people need medical treatment. That ensures profits. It's all about the money! Hospitals, drug companies, and the entire health-care industry should really be called the "sick care" industry. This money machine does not make their profits by keeping people healthy but rather finding a sick person and then selling them their outrageously expensive drugs, surgical procedures, and other medical procedures. And they make over $1.3 trillion annually doing it. Folks, I've been in the boardrooms. I've listened to these people. I've heard CEOs of major pharmaceutical companies say things such as this: "I don't care how much liver damage this drug causes, get it approved by the FDA. Pay whoever you have to pay, get the lobbyists that you have to get, but just get this drug approved. Do it, and our stock price goes up threefold. We sell our stock and move on. And five years from now, when they find out about the liver damage, they'll take the drug off the market. But who cares, we'll have our money. Just do it." That is why I am mad as hell, and I am not going to take it anymore.

Is it always just about the money? Are natural remedies and cures being suppressed and hidden from us just because greedy people and corporations want to make more money? Is it true that money makes the world go 'round? Yes! You must understand the number one motivator in the world is making money. We read about it every day. So let's look at who's involved...

CHAPTER 4

Who Are "They"?

The thing that bugs me is that the people think the FDA is protecting them. It isn't. What the FDA is doing and what the public thinks it's doing are as different as night and day.

—Herbert Lay, M.D., former FDA Commissioner

Drugs and surgery are being promoted as the only answer to the prevention and cure of illness and disease. Natural cures are being suppressed and hidden from the public. So who is involved in this "great lie"? Let me expose the culprits.

- **The Pharmaceutical Companies.** These include not only the companies that sell drugs, but also the companies that research and develop drugs. It also includes all of the suppliers in the health-care industry of such things as syringes, gauze, medical tape, tubing, plastic bottles, tongue depressors, etc. There are over 10,000 individual pharmaceutical pieces of equipment that are used up and have to be resupplied on an ongoing basis. The profits are astronomical. The money this group of companies makes is mind-boggling.

- **The Food Companies.** You may ask: how do food companies get involved in health care? Well there is a huge correlation between food and health care. I'll explain this in detail in a later chapter. Keep in mind many food companies are directly or indirectly involved in the pharmaceutical industry through corporate ownership, affiliated business transactions, or by the officers and directors personally owning stock in the pharmaceutical companies. Food companies include the companies that actually manufacture and sell food directly to us but also includes fast-food restaurants and the suppliers of the food industry, the actual growers of the food.

- **The Trade Associations.** The number of associations involved
  in the health-care industry is enormous. Keep in mind, these
  associations are not in place to eliminate disease or keep people healthy. When you read their charters you find that they
  are there to *promote* the disease, in an effort to get additional
  funding and protect its members, which are the drug companies and doctors! These associations include:

  Alzheimer's Association
  American Academy of Allergy, Asthma & Immunology
  American Academy of Child and Adolescent Psychiatry
  American Academy of Facial Plastic and Reconstructive Surgery
  American Academy of Family Physicians
  American Academy of Neurology
  American Academy of Ophthalmology
  American Academy of Orthopedic Surgeons
  American Academy of Otolaryngology
  American Academy of Otolaryngic Allergy
  American Academy of Pediatrics
  American Academy of Physical Medicine and Rehabilitation
  American Association of Clinical Endocrinologists
  American Association of Gynecological Laparoscopists
  American Association for Geriatric Psychiatry
  American Association of Immunologists
  American Association of Neurological Surgeons
  American Association for Respiratory Care
  American Association for the Study of Liver Diseases
  American Board of Medical Specialties
  American Board of Ophthalmology
  American Board of Psychiatry and Neurology, Inc.
  American Cancer Society
  American College of Allergy, Asthma and Immunology
  American College of Cardiology
  American College of Chest Physicians
  American College of Gastroenterology
  American College of Obstetricians and Gynecologists
  American College of Physicians
  American College of Rheumatology
  American College of Surgeons

American Congress of Rehabilitation Medicine
American Diabetes Association
American Gastroenterological Association
American Geriatrics Society
American Health Information Management Association
American Heart Association
American Liver Foundation
American Lung Association
American Medical Association
American Medical Women's Association
American Neurological Association
American Neurotology Society
American Orthopedic Society for Sports Medicine
American Otological Society
American Osteopathic Association
American Pharmaceutical Association
American Prostate Society
American Psychiatric Association
American Red Cross
American Rhinologic Society
American Society of Clinical Oncology
American Society for Gastrointestinal Endoscopy
American Society for Head and Neck Surgery
American Society of Pediatric Otolaryngology
American Society for Reproductive Medicine
American Urological Association
Association of Telehealth Service Providers
Catholic Health Association of the United States
The Endocrine Society
Gerontological Society of America
Leukemia & Lymphoma Society of America
National Alliance for the Mentally Ill
National Association of Psychiatric Health Systems
National Board for Respiratory Care
National Stroke Association
Society of Gynecologic Oncologists
Vestibular Disorders Association (VEDA)

This list is just the tip of the iceberg. These associations are incredibly powerful. Remember, these associations are not organizations with a goal of curing and preventing disease or protecting the consumer. These associations do not represent you, they represent their members: the companies, the corporations, and the people that are making the money. Associations such as the American Medical Association have no interest in what benefits the consumer. They only have an interest in what benefits their members. And the people that run these associations have an interest in keeping their high-paying cushy jobs.

- **Charities and Foundations,** These organizations sound great, but have you met the people who run them? The officers and directors of most charities and foundations have huge salaries and enormous expense accounts. They fly first-class and sometimes on private jets; they stay in the most expensive hotels and eat in the finest restaurants—all with your donations. Some foundations and charities have been found to spend over 40 percent of all of their donations on "administration costs." Think about it. If a foundation used the money it received to cure a disease, there would be no need for the foundation and the fat cats would lose their prestigious jobs and all the perks that go along with them. Yes, it's always about the money. But consider the second most powerful motivator for people is the combination of power and prestige. Think about that when you ask yourself: "Why are natural cures being hidden from us?" Consider this: The Jerry Lewis Telethon has raised over $1 billion for muscular dystrophy, yet more people have muscular dystrophy today than ever before.

- **Lobbyists.** This is the hidden, secret group of people in Washington that most of you have no idea even exists. These people on average make between $300,000 to $400,000 a year, plus hundreds of thousands more in perks. Their job is simply to walk up to a congressman or senator and try to persuade them to a certain line of thinking, or to pass a certain piece of legislation, or vote a certain way. Now how do they do that? Well, the lobbyist can't walk up to a member of Congress and say "Please vote a certain way on this bill and I will give you $200,000." That would be called a bribe. But what the lobbyist can do is say, "Do you have a son or a daughter, Mr. Congressman? You do? Fantastic! You know, I know your son or daughter has absolutely no experience whatsoever, but we would like to give your son or daughter a job for $200,000 a year. And the best part is they don't even have to show up for work. Oh, by the way Mr. Congressman, can you please vote a certain way on this particular piece of legislation which helps who I represent?" Lobbyists also bribe members of Congress, although Congress has passed laws that make them legally not a bribe, by doing other things. Lobbyists may make huge donations to a congressman's favorite charity or school or hire companies that the congressman is affiliated with in some way. Folks, that's what is happening in Washington. Lobbyists absolutely bribe and pay off congressmen. But according to the law it is not called a bribe or payoff, it is technically legal. And who makes the law? The congressmen. Hmm, pretty interesting, isn't it? They make a law to make sure that what they do is legal. Can you begin to see why I'm mad a hell and I'm not going to take it anymore?

- **Government Agencies.** Primarily the Food and Drug Administration and the Federal Trade Commission. Isn't it surprising that it's the Food AND Drug Administration? (Why not two separate agencies?) This organization is one of the most powerful organizations in the country. They use Gestapo-like tactics to put natural cures out of business. They act as judge, jury, and executioner. They raid companies unannounced to seize products such as bread, herbal remedies, vitamins and minerals, computers, files, research data, and equipment. They conduct these raids with armed agents with guns drawn. They seize harmless products, papers, documents, and computers, like the Gestapo did in Nazi Germany, without provocation, with no customer or consumer complaints, and without warning.

There have been several outstanding books and articles written about how the FDA operates. But in the end, the FDA is the agency that approves drugs. And when a company gets a drug approved, it's like putting billions of dollars in profits in the bank. So companies will do *anything* to get the FDA to approve drugs. It's interesting to note that of the last twenty FDA commissioners, twelve of them went to work directly for the drug industry upon leaving the FDA and were paid millions of dollars. Let's be honest, that's a payoff. It should be illegal; it's a conflict of interest, and it's wrong. More on the FDA in a later chapter.

Ok, now let's go though each of these organizations and let me show you that it is all about the money.

- **The Pharmaceutical Industry**. Virtually every pharmaceutical company is a publicly traded company, which means that the officers and directors have a legal responsibility to increase shareholder value. That means that the officers and directors of virtually every pharmaceutical company have a legal responsibility to increase profits. The only way they can increase profits is to sell more of what they sell and produce those products at a lower cost. Drug companies, therefore, have one goal, and that is to sell more drugs and produce those drugs at the cheapest possible cost. Think about that. A drug company's objective is not to cure disease. A drug company's goal is to sell more drugs. You are their customer. They want you to use more drugs every single year. They want to produce those drugs at the lowest possible cost and they want to do whatever they can to make sure that they can sell those drugs at the highest possible price. That's why there is a huge debate about people buying pharmaceutical drugs from other countries. The FDA makes up this silly excuse that a country like Canada doesn't produce drugs under the same safety guidelines as America. How arrogant!

The fact is that American pharmaceutical companies want a monopoly. They do not want anybody competing with their sales; therefore they have managed to coax the federal government into forbidding any American to purchase a pharmaceutical drug outside of America. They are in effect stopping free trade and stopping competition, which would result in lower prices. Why is the FDA doing that? As I mentioned to you before, the drug industry gives millions of dollars to the commissioners when they leave the FDA. It's a payoff!

Remember: Drug companies do not want people to get well. A drug company's goal is not to cure disease. If everyone in the world was healthy, the drug companies would be out of business. A drug company only wants to sell you more drugs. So here is how the cycle works.

The drug industry gives billions of dollars to medical schools. Why? So that their drugs can be put in the textbooks and doctors are taught to prescribe certain pharmaceutical drugs, thus guaranteeing sales of those drugs by the pharmaceutical company. Remember, in medical school doctors are taught two things: to prescribe drugs and to cut out parts of a person's anatomy, which is surgery.

When a doctor comes out of medical school, most people don't know that the pharmaceutical industry then pays that doctor to prescribe certain drugs. Often, this is done through "incentives." For example, if a doctor prescribes a certain drug to ten patients, he is given thousands of dollars in cash from the pharmaceutical company. Drug companies routinely give doctors all expense-paid trips to "medical conferences"

around the world. These medical conferences are really sales presentations by the drug companies, teaching the doctor about drugs and how to
prescribe them, and giving financial incentives to prescribe those drugs.
They are disguised as medical conferences. They are not. The experts at
these medical conferences are compensated by the drug industry.

So doctors are trained in medical school to prescribe drugs and are
given incentives and additional training throughout their medical career
directly by the drug industry to prescribe more drugs.

- **Research**. In order for a drug company to get a drug patented and
approved by the FDA, it costs approximately $800 million in research
and testing. Where does that $800 million go? Well, let's just follow
the money trail. Remember, it's always just about the money!

The companies that are approved by the FDA to do certain
research, interestingly enough, are publicly traded companies. Guess
who owns the stock in these publicly traded companies? Would it
surprise you to know that politicians and members of the FDA own
stock in those companies? It wouldn't surprise me! Would it also
surprise you that the people that work for those research companies
are friends and relatives of politicians and members of the FDA? It
wouldn't surprise me!

Once a drug is approved and the pharmaceutical company has the
patent, it becomes the only company that can sell that drug. Getting a
patented drug is an automatic billion dollars in the bank! This is why
you will never see a pharmaceutical company promoting a natural
cure. Natural cures cannot be patented! You can only make profits if
you have a patented drug. There are no large profits in selling a natural cure that cannot be patented. When you have a patented product
you are the only company that can sell it. You have no competition.
You can sell it for an outrageously high price, and the profits are
guaranteed. If you are selling a nonpatented natural product, a hundred other companies could also sell the same product. You have no
monopoly. Because of the competition, the prices will come down and
the profits become incredibly small. That is why the drug industry will
only promote patented drugs, because that's where the profits are.

This is also why the drug companies gave tens of millions of dollars
to lobbyists to get the FDA to make a new "law." Listen to this very
carefully. The FDA has the power to make "laws" and enforce them.
It can make "laws" without congressional approval or debate. In order
to protect the profits of the drug industry the FDA passed the most

incredibly insane "law" of all time. The FDA has now made as "law" the following statement, "Only a drug can cure, prevent or treat a disease." This is insane. Think about the ramifications. The FDA has now guaranteed and protected the profits of the drug companies! Only a patented drug, according to the FDA, can treat, prevent, or cure a disease. First off, we all know this is flat-out untrue. The disease scurvy, for example, which is simply a vitamin C deficiency, is treated, prevented, and cured by eating citrus fruit. According to the FDA's law, however, if you were to hold up an orange and say "This orange is the cure for the disease of scurvy," you would go to jail for selling a "drug" without a license. According to the FDA, as soon as you made a disease claim in reference to taking an orange, the orange no longer is an orange, but magically became a "drug" according to the FDA. And since that "drug" has not been patented or approved by the FDA, you are selling a "drug" without a license, which is a criminal offense. You go to jail. The "drug" is obviously not a drug, it is an orange! This is how the FDA works to protect the profits of the pharmaceutical company and suppress and hide information about natural remedies.

So how do the drug companies get you to buy their drugs? Years ago, the drug companies had to basically make sure that you were sick and had a problem that the drug addressed. Second, they had to make sure that the doctors prescribed their particular drug. That still goes on. The pharmaceutical companies give huge cash incentives and information to the doctors about the drugs they make to ensure that the doctors, who are in fact legal drug pushers, get their drugs to you via prescription.

Remember, the pharmaceutical companies have ensured that you are sick. How do they do that? This is going to blow your mind, but it's true. One of the major reasons why there is so much sickness and disease is because of the poisons you are putting in your body. The number one poison you put in your body consists of prescription and nonprescription drugs! That's right. The prescription and non-prescription drugs you are taking to eliminate your symptoms are, in fact, one of the major reasons that you get sick.

The pharmaceutical companies know that all drugs have side effects. This is the dirty little secret that the pharmaceutical companies don't want you to know. Just as the tobacco industry knew that smoking cigarettes were addictive and could cause lung cancer, yet lied for decades about this fact, the pharmaceutical industry today knows that all drugs have negative side effects and can cause further illness in the body! The pharmaceutical industry knows that the drugs people are taking are actually causing or contributing to the increases in cancer, heart disease, diabetes, and dozens of other diseases. Why is the drug industry keeping this information a secret? Mainly because it's profitable. It is just like the tobacco industry. Look at the cycle: You start taking a drug to handle a certain symptom that you have. A few months later you develop another medical condition. This new medical condition, unknown to you, was actually caused by the first drug you were taking! You now start taking another drug for this new medical condition. The drug seems to work. Your condition gets better. A few months later you develop a new series of medical problems. Unknown to you was the fact that these new medical problems were actually caused by the last drug you were taking. You are given more drugs for this newest medical condition. Can you see how profitable this is for the drug industry? The drug companies are doing this on purpose.

They're making drugs that address one set of symptoms. But they know that if you use these drugs, over a period of time, they can cause a second set of medical problems. The drug companies will then produce a drug to solve those new medical problems caused by taking their first drug. This guarantees additional drug sales and profits for the drug companies.

How is this happening? Keep in mind virtually all drug research is funded by the pharmaceutical industry. In virtually every study, drugs are found to be safe and effective. However, history has proved that this is not true. Think of all of the drugs that were proven to be totally safe and effective and were approved by the FDA. Then, years later these same drugs were proven to be incredibly dangerous and to cause all types of severe medical conditions, including death. These "safe and effective" drugs were found to kill so many people that the FDA finally had to take them off the market. Interestingly enough, they were only taken off the market after the drug companies made millions of dollars in profits.

- **Advertising.** The drug industry is doing something today that it has never done before in history: **advertising its drugs directly to the consumer**. This is absolutely unbelievable! Right now close to two-thirds of all advertising in America is for drugs. It's estimated that well in excess of $10 billion a year is spent on advertising by the pharmaceutical industry. They are advertising drugs directly to you and me, the consumer. In many cases, these drug ads don't even tell you what the drug is for. They just have some celebrity, that they pay huge amounts of money to, telling you about how their life is so much better because they take this particular drug. The ads show all these beautiful happy people and give you the impression that they are all taking this wonderful drug and that their lives are so much better.

What you don't know is that virtually every single person you see in these ads has been meticulously selected by some of the top advertising minds in the world to evoke a certain emotion in you. They are paid actors; most do not use the drug they are promoting. When you see people dressed as doctors, policemen, judges, etc., you are being deceived. Even when known figures and famous actors publicly endorse a drug or foundation (usually funded by pharmaceutical companies), ostensibly because they or a close friend or relative has suffered with a particular disease, they are being paid enormous sums to do so. They are actors. These ads are not truthful. Millions of dollars are spent using technology pioneered by the CIA and KGB to produce advertising that will motivate you to not only want their drug, but feel you *need* their drug. The ads produced by the pharmaceutical industry are the most sophisticated, well thought out, brainwashing and manipulative campaigns ever launched on the American public. This advertising is trying to brainwash us into thinking that our life will be better in every way as long as we continue to take more and more drugs. This is absolutely outrageous! Doesn't it drive you crazy when you see all of these drug ads in newspapers, magazines, and television?

The amount of drug advertising is at an all-time high and continues to increase. When you listen to these ads, doesn't it make you smile or laugh when they start rattling off all the side effects of the drugs? However, the marketing techniques are so sophisticated that the drug ads are incredibly effective.

The Food and Drug Administration, the Federal Trade Commission and the pharmaceutical industry have an unholy alliance. The regulating government body should be governing and regulating and protecting consumers from the drug companies' insatiable desire to make more profits. The problem is that they work together to increase profits and power.

A law was passed in Congress with virtually no debate at all which increased the FDA's dependence on large drug companies for its funding.

You are reading this right. The FDA gets funding directly from the drug industry. It is a law that was passed in 1992 that was intended to speed up approval for new AIDS medications. But what it actually did was get the drug companies to pay for the FDA's new employees and additional funding requirements. According to an article in the *Washington Post,* the program was developed between the pharmaceutical industry and the FDA in secret meetings. It was not debated in Congress, there was no vote. It was a secret, private negotiation between the drug industry and the FDA and went directly to the General Accounting Office for review. According to the *Washington Post,* over 500 new employees to be sent to the FDA centers that actually review new proposed drugs would be paid for by the pharmaceutical and biotechnology companies themselves. There are over 1,500 people that work for the FDA who are paid by the funding of the drug industry. That means over 55 percent of the FDA's staff directly involved in the reviewing of new drug applications is in effect on the payroll of the drug industry. That's over $1.2 billion that the FDA is getting directly from the drug industry.

Just to point out how crooked these people are, over the last ten years the FDA has approved over nine specific drugs that have been proven to have deadly side effects. *The Journal of the American Medical Association* estimates that over 125,000 Americans die each year from side effects of FDA-approved drugs.

So how do the FDA, FTC, and the drug industry work together promoting drugs and surgery and suppressing natural cures? Criminologist Elaine Feuer did a thorough investigation on the FDA and found that the FDA invests the majority of its time protecting the profits of the pharmaceutical industry. The FDA suppresses the truth about natural cures and focuses on shutting down companies that sell natural remedies for common diseases. Her book, *Innocent Casualties, the FDA's War Against Humanity,* documents how the FDA specifically goes after companies that offer natural cures for diseases that make the most money for the pharmaceutical industry. Since cancer, AIDS, heart disease, and diabetes are so profitable for the drug companies, anyone promoting a natural cure for theses illnesses will be attacked by the FDA.

Drug companies also get us to use drugs through the use of the media. This is one of the scariest things I want to talk about. The drug industry, the FTC, and the FDA produce press releases, news if you will, on new super wonderdrugs. At the same time they spread negative news on natural alternatives. The industry spends enormous amounts of money with public relations firms to get news organizations on television, radio, newspapers, and magazines to do positive stories on their drugs. You'll notice when you're watching the news that many times there is a medical expert on who says something about a new drug. This medical expert never says it's his opinion, there is never an alternative viewpoint presented. The medical expert always gives the pro-drug side and it is presented as a news story. The fact is it is not news at all. The medical experts are in many cases spokespeople for the drug companies. These "medical experts" are being paid huge amounts of money to say all these wonderful things about drugs. Where is the full disclosure? When the news organization brings out their "medical expert," they never say, "By the way, our medical expert is being paid huge amounts of money to come on our show and say wonderful things about this drug." They are put on the news without any research whatsoever done by the news organization about whether the information itself being presented is factual, fair, balanced, or honest. Everyone seems to forget that a new wonder drug makes billions of dollars in profits; and everyone seems to forget the drug companies are publicly traded companies and the people that own the stock in these companies have a major incentive for the drug company to sell more drugs. So the real question is: Who owns the stock in these drug companies? Would it surprise you that many members of the FDA and FTC own stock in drug companies? Would it surprise you that many members of Congress own stock in drug companies? Would it also surprise you that members of the news media that are supposed to be impartially presenting news own stock in drug companies? And the corporations that own television networks, radio networks, newspapers, and magazines all have financial ties to the pharmaceutical industry and all have incentives for the drug industry to sell more drugs?

That's one of the reasons why you hear so much about drugs on the news and read so many positive articles about drugs in magazines and newspapers. These organizations get financial benefit from the drugs that are sold. Additionally, most news organizations do not research the accuracy and truthfulness of information when presenting news about drugs. When they get a press release from the pharmaceutical industry, it is read and presented as news without question.

The pharmaceutical industry has an automatic outlet to get billions of dollars in free advertising which is being disguised as news.

Doesn't it surprise you that the only medical experts on the news giving any information about health, illness, disease, or sickness are all medical doctors? And that the only information we are hearing is about the use of drugs? Doesn't it surprise you that you virtually never hear any positive news at all about an herbal remedy, a natural remedy, or a homeopathic remedy? Could it be that there is no profit in those remedies? Remember, natural remedies cannot be patented.

As I mentioned previously, the unholy alliance between the FDA, the FTC, and the drug industry created the outrageous and totally irresponsible regulation that only a drug can cure, prevent, or treat a disease. Remember that the FDA has the ability to enforce this "law." Anyone making a claim that anything other than a drug can cure, prevent, or treat a disease is breaking this "law" and is subject to criminal prosecution!

The FDA has set as "law" that there is not, and never will be, a natural remedy that can cure, or prevent, or treat a disease. Because if a natural remedy did, then it has to be classified as a "drug" and once it's classified as a drug it has to go through the $800 million worth of testing that the FDA requires to be approved as a new drug. This cannot be done. Why? Because a natural remedy cannot be patented and there is no company that can spend $800 million to get a natural remedy approved as a new drug because it will not own a patent for that "new drug" and therefore can't make that money back plus tenfold profits. Natural remedies cannot be patented. Therefore, they cannot go through the testing that the FDA requires. This is why the FDA and drug companies love this system. It prevents any natural remedy from being touted as a cure or prevention of disease when in fact many of them are. The FDA has colluded with the drug industry and given the drug industry a monopoly.

Think about it. The FDA states that only a drug can cure or prevent a disease, absolutely nothing else can. How insane is that? To make matters worse, what the pharmaceutical industry and the FDA have done now is decided to classify more and more things as diseases. Once upon a time, you used to get heartburn, now it's called Acid Reflux Disease. Once upon a time people used to be shy, now it's classified as Social Anxiety Disorder, which is a disease. Kids who are eating too much sugar or are a little rambunctious are now classified as having attention deficit disorder, which is a disease. If a woman has a low sexual desire, it is now classified as a disease. An alcoholic is no longer an alcoholic; he now has the disease of alcoholism. A person who is overweight is no longer overweight they now have the disease of obesity. A male who cannot get an erection is said to have a disease.

The reason more and more things are being classified as diseases is, once it is classified as a disease, legally there can be no natural, inexpensive remedy that can cure or prevent it. The FDA says only a drug can do that. The FDA has the final word on what is a "disease." Once the FDA has decided with final authority that something is a disease, any company making a claim that an all-natural product could possibly cure or prevent that disease can be legally entered by the FDA unannounced—with federal agents, guns drawn—and seize the natural product. The FDA can then shut that business down and put the people who are in charge of that business in jail for practicing medicine without a license or selling drugs without a license, even though they are not selling drugs at all; they could be selling something as benign as bread. This actually happened back in the 1970s when a gentleman named Ben Suarez sold bread that had a high fiber content. It was an all-natural bread that was high in fiber. He stated that eating a high-fiber diet could potentially lower the risk of certain cancers. At the time that statement was not "proven." But because he made that statement, he was now, according to the FDA, selling a drug without a license. He wasn't selling a drug, he was selling bread. The FDA came in, seized the bread, and destroyed it. It was enough bread to feed a million homeless people. He offered to give the bread away to homeless people. The FDA said no, and the bread was destroyed. How sick! And why was it destroyed? Because he was selling an all-natural product and was potentially tapping into the profits of one of the most powerful, profitable industries in the world. It's all about the money! Please read this incredible story about the "no hunger bread" that was and is one of the greatest weight-loss miracles of all time and how the FDA tried to destroy this man's business and life to protect the profits of the drug industry. The entire story is printed here as Appendix B.

Web sites. The pharmaceutical industry is doing a brilliant job producing all kinds of informational Web sites which appear to be consumer oriented, unbiased Web sites which give information to consumers about various illnesses, diseases, and cures. But the fact is these are not unbiased Web sites. It's a trick, it's a scam. These Web sites are paid for and put out by the drug industry. They are made to look and appear as if they are unbiased and are there to give information to the consumer and to protect the consumer. The fact of the matter is they are nothing more than Web sites owned directly or indirectly by the pharmaceutical companies to sell you more drugs. It is important to know that the pharmaceutical industry is committed to wiping out nonpatentable all-natural cures for disease. The pharmaceutical industry is spending hundreds of millions of dollars to try to get you to believe that drugs are safe and effective and all natural cures are ineffective and dangerous. The exact opposite is true. Drugs are all dangerous and cause disease and all the current research shows that drugs are generally ineffective. Drugs do not cure any disease. This fact is becoming more and more clear. Drugs in fact CAUSE DISEASE. All natural remedies are in fact extremely safe, with virtually no side effects, and all natural remedies are incredibly effective. Technically speaking, all natural remedies do not cure disease because only the body can cure itself. All natural remedies help the body cure itself. With this said, I want to emphasize that virtually every "consumer advocacy" Web site relating to health, and every "watchdog" group or Web site relating to health, and every "consumer information" Web site relating to health is in fact a front for the pharmaceutical industry. These Web sites are NOT designed to protect consumers or inform consumers about ALL OPTIONS; but rather, these Web sites are funded and/or owned by the pharmaceutical companies and have one simple mission, to spread the LIE that drugs are the only answer to curing, preventing, and treating disease and that natural remedies, such as herbs, homeopathics, vitamins, minerals, etc., are ineffective and unsafe. This is a great lie and a great deception. The Internet is becoming one of the most powerful tools that the pharmaceutical industry uses to promulgate this great deception.

Paying of Celebrities. This shocked me when I found this out. When you watch a TV talk show, or listen to talk radio, many times a celebrity is being interviewed. That celebrity may have had some kind of disease or a family member of that celebrity may have had some kind of disease. That celebrity is on that talk show talking about the particular disease that he or a family member or friends have suffered from, and they may talk about a new treatment that they've tried or a new drug that they've tried that cured them of the problem and saved their lives and how wonderful it is. It sounds oh so interesting and oh so wonderful. It appears that this celebrity is genuinely concerned about the health and welfare of other people because they went through it in their personal life. But upon further investigation we find that these celebrities, most of whom are professional actors, are doing a brilliant job of acting, because they are being paid huge amounts of money by the drug industry to tout the drug company's drug under the disguise of a normal interview. These real talk shows are becoming infomercials for the drug industry. But you and I watch them and don't know they are in fact commercials. This celebrity, under the banner of full disclosure, never says that he is being paid huge amounts of money by the drug industry to tout the drug in public. Does this surprise you? It shouldn't, because it is common in every industry. A golf club manufacturer says "more tour professionals use our driver than any other brand." When interviewed, the tour professionals say how much they love their driver. What you are not told is that these golfers are paid millions of dollars to use the company's particular driver. So do we really know if the golfers are using this driver because it's the best driver, or are they using the driver because they are being paid to? Remember, it's always about the money.

Government Mandates of Drug Use. Another technique that the drug industry uses to make sure sales of drugs continue to increase is to get the federal government to pass laws requiring people to take drugs. There are three methods employed. First, pass a law requiring that children must take a certain drug, such as vaccines. Second, pass a law requiring all federal employees and military personnel to take a certain drug. (Note the recent drives to have government employees and members of the military vaccinated against anthrax and smallpox.) Third, get the government to pay for drug usage for the poor and elderly through Social Security, Medicare, and Medicaid. When this happens...bam! Billions of dollars in profits.

Remember the anthrax scare in Washington? I believe it was a brilliant campaign to increase the sales of a certain antibiotic, Cipro. When the anthrax scare went on the air, the drug companies did a brilliant marketing campaign talking about how Cipro is the drug of choice for anthrax. Overnight the sales of Cipro skyrocketed. Millions of dollars in profits were generated by the drug companies.

This is a vitally important point. Again, what we are talking about here is how the drug companies strategically and methodically increase the sales of their drugs. Keep in mind that the drugs do not cure disease. The drugs being sold, both prescription and nonprescription, actually cause most diseases that people are experiencing. All nonprescription and prescription drugs have horrible side effects. All nonprescription and prescription drugs cause disease. There is not one prescription or nonprescription drug that cures any disease. This is a proven fact even acknowledged by the pharmaceutical industry itself. All drugs, whether they be nonprescription or prescription drugs, simply suppress symptoms and, most important, unbeknownst to you, cause you to become sick with other diseases. Again, drug companies have only one goal and that is to sell more drugs.

What I am talking about here are all the various ways that the drug companies employ to increase their profits and sell more drugs. Working with the government is a very important aspect. The pharmaceutical industry has figured out ways to get the government behind them. The pharmaceutical industry uses the FDA and the FTC to protect their profits and protect their monopolies. The FDA and the FTC are supposed to be protecting consumers from unscrupulous companies such as the pharmaceutical industry, but the pharmaceutical companies have figured out ways to put millions of dollars into the politicians' pockets, thus ensuring that the drug companies' profits are protected. When the pharmaceutical companies get politicians to require drug use or have the government buy drugs from the pharmaceutical companies as exorbitant inflated prices, the pharmaceutical companies make billions of dollars in profits and their stock prices soar. What is the incentive for the politicians to do this?

Well, I am now blowing the whistle on one of the greatest scandals in the history of American government. The members of Congress have passed a law which allows them to buy and sell stocks on, in effect, "insider information." Listen to this very carefully. I am exposing one of the greatest issues of corruption in American history. I am blowing the whistle on something that virtually no one knows about. The members of Congress have information that you and I do not have. The members of Congress have access to information that the public does not have access to. In any other venue this would be called "insider information." However, Congress has passed a law allowing themselves to buy and sell stock based on this "insider information," and these stock transactions have been made perfectly legal! You need to know that politicians in Washington are making millions and millions and millions of dollars in profits buying and selling stocks based on "insider information." One congresswoman from California, in her first four years in Congress, made over $10 million buying and selling stock on information that the public did not have access to. This should be criminal.

Think about how this works to the advantage of the pharmaceutical companies. Congress is about to vote on buying billions of dollars of drugs and shipping them overseas in the form of "aid." It is about to give the pharmaceutical companies hundreds of millions of dollars in profits. No one in the country knows this information. The congressmen, however, do have access to this "insider information." They know that once this vote is passed, certain pharmaceutical companies' stock prices will skyrocket. They then buy the stock knowing that the information about this windfall profit will be made public very soon. The congressmen have information that you and I do not have access to. They are given the right to make profits when you and I are denied that right. This should be criminal! In any other venue people would go to jail, but in Congress it is standard operating procedure. It's one of the perks of being a congressman or senator in Washington. Can you see why the politicians have such a big financial tie to the pharmaceutical industry? Can you see why the government wants to suppress natural remedies and protect the profits of the drug companies? This scandal was briefly reported on Fox News. However, it was immediately squashed and no one in the news media has picked up on it. That is appalling! This is one of the biggest scandals and exposés of corruption at the highest levels in government. In effect, congressmen have voted that they have the right to buy and sell stock on insider information even though such activities are illegal for any other person. Can you see how the pharmaceutical companies and the money brokers in Washington are working together?! Remember, it's always all about the money.

This happens with the FDA as well. The FDA approves drugs. A company's profitability hinges on whether the FDA approves drugs or not. Pharmaceutical companies use their political connections, funnel millions of dollars into lobbyists, and actually put people on the FDA drug approval boards that are on their own payroll, all in an attempt to get drugs approved by the FDA so that they can increase their profits and stock price. This happens even though the pharmaceutical companies know that the drugs that they are trying to get approvals on do not work and actually cause disease, but they don't care. It's always all about the money. Members of Congress talk to the FDA and know IN ADVANCE whether a drug is going to be approved or not. If the drug is going to be approved, members of Congress simply buy the stock based on this "insider information" and make millions of dollars in profits. The drug industry is a money-making machine for the politicians in Washington. This is why the FDA and the FTC and big government want to suppress information about natural remedies; it simply will cost them money. Remember, it's always all about the money. Can you see why I'm mad as hell and not going to take it anymore!?

Use of Books. Another way drug companies increase the sales of their drugs is to pay millions of dollars to doctors, alleged experts, who in fact, are paid spokespeople for the drug companies. These experts then write books about the health benefits of certain drugs. Go into any bookstore and you can see book after book after book promoting drug use by "an independent medical expert." The fact is the drug companies are paying the expert to write the books. The book is nothing more than an ad for the drug.

Among other methods used by the government in tandem with the drug industry:

Censorship of Opposing Ideas. This is scary. We live in America. It's supposed to be the land of free speech. Well, speech is not free. If your speech happens to threaten the profits of big business, you are going to be bound and gagged, ridiculed and persecuted. Here's what happens.

There are hundreds of books written about the drug industry, the FDA, the FTC, and the collusion between the associations, the corporations, the lobbyists, and certain government regulators and how they work together to suppress all-natural, inexpensive ways to prevent and cure disease. These books and these authors never see the light of day. Why? Publishers won't publish these books. If a publisher publishes a book that is bashing the pharmaceutical industry, certain government agencies, or big business, the publishing company may be blacklisted and have its other books taken out of distribution. Publishing companies fear that the publishing of these books will in fact cost them millions of dollars in profits. Additionally, many of the officers and directors of these publishing companies own stock in many pharmaceutical companies, and they do not want to do anything that will adversely affect their own personal portfolio. Remember, it's all about the money!

There is also censorship of advertising. Think about this very simply. Let's say that you are the president of a major television network. The particular network that you are the president of is owned by another multinational company that owns or has huge interest in a drug company. Your network gets two-thirds, or close to 70 percent, of its advertising revenue directly from the drug industry. Now imagine a guy comes to you and says, "I'd like to advertise on your network my

book entitled *How the Drug Companies Are Ripping Off America*."
Would you, as the president of that company, run that ad? If you run
that ad, your boss could fire you. Because by running that ad, you could
have a negative impact on the sales and profits of the drug companies
in which your boss has a major equity position. That means it is costing
your boss money. You may in fact own stock yourself. Think about it
this way: If you run that ad for that book, how are your other advertisers going to feel? What if they called you up and said, "Hey, if you run
that ad for that book, we're not going to run any of our drug ads next
month." Your sales are going to go straight down and you'll probably be
fired. Folks, this is what is happening. It's all about the money.

This actually is happening to me. When this book first came out
no one in publishing or the media thought much of it, but it became a
runaway bestseller. In just the first few months this book has sold over
one and one-half million copies and became one of the fastest selling
books in publishing history. However, because this book is exposing
the truth about the news media, the television networks, the reporting
at magazines and radio stations, the collusion of the pharmaceutical
industry with the FDA and FTC, many networks have stopped running
ads for this book. Television stations all around America have pulled
the advertising of this book. They do not want my message being heard.
They are in effect suppressing my free speech. Many news networks
have actually done very negative stories on me and my book.

Think about it. A news network is sponsored by the drug companies and food industry. The news network then gets approached
by its biggest advertisers, the drug companies and the food industry.
These big advertisers tell the news network that they had better stop
Kevin Trudeau and bash him anyway they can. The news network is
in fact owned by the sponsors! All television, newspapers, radio, and
magazines are owned by the sponsors! Do you understand how that
works? The sponsors pay TV stations, radio stations, newspapers,
and magazines. The sponsors are the source of income to these news
organizations. The news organizations always succumb to the whims
and wishes of their sponsors. Since the pharmaceutical industry and
the food industry sponsor most all news organizations on TV, radio,
newspapers, and magazines, these news organizations can never be
trusted to give unbiased information.

It was reported recently, and a lawsuit was filed, about a group of
independent reporters who did an exposé story on the drug company

Monsanto, exposing the growth hormone that Monsanto sells used in dairy cows. This news story exposed that this growth hormone was making the animals sick and making the milk and dairy products from these cows deadly poisonous. However, the news organization categorically refused to run the story. Why? Because Monsanto put pressure on the news organization! To read about this incredible story, go to www.foxbghsuit.com. Do you see that the sponsors control the information you are hearing about? Do not be misled into thinking that when you are listening to the news on television or radio, or reading the news in magazines and newspapers, that it is unbiased objective reporting. It absolutely is not!

The information you see and hear on TV and radio, and read in newspapers and magazines, is in effect coming directly from the sponsors of those media outlets. The majority of money received by these media outlets is from the pharmaceutical industry and the food industry. Folks, you are being brainwashed; you are being lied to; you are being deceived. A good example of this is I had an ABC news crew come to my house at 7:00 a.m., unannounced. They banged on my door, and they made it appear that I was unwilling to answer the door and answer their questions or give them an interview. This was categorically untrue and false. ABC News specifically tried to mislead the public into believing that I would not answer the door and give them an interview. The fact is they never mentioned to the viewers that they were banging on my door at 7:00 in the morning and I was asleep. They never mentioned to the viewers that I told ABC News that I absolutely would give them a live interview. They deceived the public. Folks, this is ABC News! You have to know that you cannot trust or believe what you are reading in newspapers and magazines, seeing on television, or hearing on the radio. These outlets are simply the pawns of the pharmaceutical companies and the food industry. These media outlets are simply an extension of the sponsors. Remember, the sponsors always control the content and the information that you are being exposed to. Remember, it's always all about the money. Can you see why I'm mad as hell, and not going to take it anymore!

Debunking Natural Remedies. In an actual government memorandum, the U.S. federal government states that one of the most effective tools to get people to believe the government's opinion is to put together a well orchestrated debunking campaign. What this means is there is a coordinated effort between the FDA, the FTC, the health-care associations, and the entire pharmaceutical industry—as well as some major news organizations—to produce scare stories about natural alternatives and suppress the truth about the ineffectiveness and dangers of drugs. There is a long list of inexpensive, highly effective natural cures that are being labeled as "snake oil" or simply hidden from the public.

The FDA has led the way in this battle against natural cures. In the 1970s the FDA attempted to make vitamin supplements prescription drugs. The FDA claimed that vitamins are so dangerous they should be prescribed only by doctors. The public was outraged and Congress rejected the idea. In 1993 the FDA tried to classify certain minerals and amino acids as prescription drugs. Again, a public outcry caused Congress to act. Recently the FDA has been going after companies that sell natural remedies via the Internet. It claims these companies are selling "drugs" without a license.

In the book *The Assault on Medical Freedom,* secret documents from the medical industry have been exposed proving the FDA, the pharmaceutical industry, the AMA, and even insurance companies are working together to discredit natural medicine. The documents show how the FDA worked with the pharmaceutical industry directly, producing the "public service, anti-quackery campaign," which is designed to make people believe alternative natural remedies are ineffective, a waste of money, and even harmful. This "public service campaign" is simply a front of the pharmaceutical industry. The author claims that this collusion between the government and the pharmaceutical industry has created "nothing less than an enforced totalitarian medical-pharmaceutical police state."

The FDA targets natural remedies one at a time. Their debunking campaign begins by warning the public that these substances have not been properly tested, are potentially dangerous and should not be used. Even when double-blind studies prove the effectiveness or safety of the remedies, the evidence is debunked, suppressed, or ignored.

There are thousands of studies that prove not only that natural remedies are effective, but they can be more effective than any drug counterpart. An example is vitamin E. In major double-blind studies, vitamin E was found as effective or more effective as a blood thinner than its drug counterpart. But why aren't we given vitamin E instead of the drug? The facts are clear: Natural remedies could financially devastate the pharmaceutical industry.

Virtually every day we hear about "warnings" relating to the usage of dietary supplements. The news organizations that report this information, for the most part, do virtually no research into the accuracy or truthfulness of these warnings. There are different standards used in what is classified as news and advertising. If information is presented by a politician or government agency, such as the FDA or FTC, news organizations present that information as 100 percent factual. Any press release submitted to a news reporting organization by a politician or government agency is reported as 100 percent fact. The news reporting agency rarely if ever investigates the claims or allegations, or seeks out an opposing viewpoint. The government has the ability to influence the masses at will without opposition. So, the first standard set is that anything a government agency or politician says is true and evidence is not required to support their claims.

The next standard set is for "big business." When large publicly traded corporations send out press releases to news organizations, very little verification is done on the accuracy and truthfulness of what is presented. The information is reported as news, but because it is coming from business and not the government, occasionally opposing viewpoints are presented as well.

The FTC allows big business to do things in their advertising that smaller businesses would be prohibited from doing. Example: You are watching an ad on television. At the bottom of the screen there are several lines of "disclaimers." The FTC requires that these disclaimers be present. However, because it's big business, they are allowed to put the disclaimers on the screen for just a few seconds, and printed so small there is not a human being in the world who can read them! It's an absolute joke.

Additionally, big business ads are allowed to do something that small advertisers are routinely prosecuted for. If a small advertiser, let's say a company selling a piece of exercise equipment through a TV infomercial, were to have a man dressed up as a doctor making wonderful statements about the product, that man must be a doctor, cannot be a paid spokesperson, and must not be reading a script. However, in big business advertising when you see doctors, judges, business executives, policemen, etc., making statements about how wonderful the company's products are, you are being deceived and lied to. These people are paid actors reading a script! If a small company selling a product on an infomercial did the same thing they would be shut down and prosecuted for false and misleading advertising. The bottom line is the government and politicians can say anything on TV, and it is never challenged and it is presented as 100 percent truth. Big business can do almost anything on TV and produce false and misleading advertising without the FTC preventing them.

Small businesses or companies threatening the profits of "big business" are the ones routinely attacked by the FTC, the FDA and other regulatory agencies. It is surprising to note that the majority of actions taken by the FTC and FDA are against small- and medium-sized businesses. They rarely if ever go after big business. For example, the FTC's Field Manual states that agents should not go after "big business" because they have deep pockets and will fight back against the FTC. It instructs its agents not to go after very small businesses because they have no money. It states to go after medium-sized businesses that will settle quickly out of fear. It's shocking to note that the Federal Trade Commission does not take action against companies based on consumer complaints. Rather, the FTC succumbs to political pressure on who to go after and makes its decision based on the amount of money that can be extracted from that company.

Did you know that when the FTC charges a company with false and misleading advertising and then collects money for "consumer redress," it never gives the money to the consumer? The FTC keeps the money! This agency is supposed to protect the consumers, yet the vast majority of actions filed by the FTC are against companies where there are no consumer complaints.

The FTC and the FDA also work together to spread misinformation and lies about all-natural remedies. Think of the millions of dollars that are poured into public relations campaigns specifically designed to debunk and make natural remedies appear foolish. So-called consumer advocate associations, or watchdog groups, have sprung up with fancy names that sound like they are looking out to protect the consumer when in fact these particular organizations are nothing more than a front for the pharmaceutical industry to promote their products, increase drug usage, and increase the nation's perception that natural remedies don't work and are dangerous.

A good example of this is ephedra. Ephedra is a compound most commonly found in the herb ma huang. This herb has been used for centuries around the world, most notably in China, as a very effective herbal remedy for various types of illness including obesity and asthma. It is safe and incredibly effective. Ephedra was a substance used in diet aids to increase metabolism and decrease appetite. It did an outstanding job. If you took massive amounts and did not follow the instructions on the bottle, you may have had some adverse effects, such as nervousness or the jitters similar to drinking twenty cups of coffee. In a very well orchestrated debunking campaign, the FDA has banned the use of ephedra stating it is dangerous. This was a very coordinated effort to get people to believe that a natural herbal supplement could be dangerous. This campaign is designed to encourage Congress to ban more natural remedies, as well as require supplements as harmless as basic vitamins and minerals to be classified as drugs and be sold by prescription and manufactured by the pharmaceutical industry. This is being touted under the guise of safety. Safety has nothing to do with it. Why?

Ephedra was banned because 153 deaths have been linked to taking ephedra. Now, millions of people were taking ephedra. If you take any group of ten million people, over a year, there's a good chance that 153 people in that group will die. The FDA said there is a "link" between ephedra use and those deaths. There is absolutely no conclusive evidence that ephedra caused those deaths or even had any remote association with those deaths. However, the FDA keeps saying how dangerous ephedra is. Every single nonprescription drug is dangerous! If you went into your medicine cabinet, took a drug, and took more than what the label said, there is a high probability that you could die. Every single drug is incredibly dangerous. This is not about danger, it is about who controls these products. The scary part is whatever the FDA says, it is presented as truth and no opposing opinions are allowed to be heard.

Think about this. Two thousand people die every year by simply taking aspirin. Not overdosing on aspirin but by taking aspirin in the recommended amounts. Wow! It appears that aspirin is not safe. Yet, I don't see aspirin being banned. Do you see where this is going? This debunking campaign includes two things: getting news organizations and various publications to do positive stories about drugs, falsifying or misrepresenting research data on drugs while at the same time spreading any type of negative information about a natural remedy and natural holistic healers.

Another perfect example of this debunking campaign was a headline that said "Saint John's Wort Not Effective for Treating Depression, Study Concludes." The article—written in a national newspaper—stated that a recent study was conducted and proved that Saint John's

Wort, the herbal remedy touted as a depression alleviant, was found to have absolutely no effect on depression. This article went on to talk about how many herbs are used to treat various illnesses and disease without any research whatsoever to back up the effectiveness of those herbs. The article then went on to state that people should not take any herbs or natural substances because they could be unsafe and are probably ineffective.

The article was ridiculous, one-sided, and outrageous. Why do I say that? Because when you actually look at that particular study they were referring to, Saint John's Wort was tested in addition to Prozac in the exact same study. And the study showed that Prozac and Saint John's Wort both had no effect on depression in the patients in the study. But the news organization never mentioned that Prozac was also proven to be ineffective. It also failed to mention that there are dozens of studies that show that Saint John's Wort is, in fact, effective. But obviously this study was flawed. The fact is that you can create a study to show virtually anything you want, but the news media chose only to talk negatively about the herbal, all-natural supplement and didn't have anything negative to say about the drug. Debunking by use of studies is very common. Most "studies" are funded by the drug industry. The researchers are given very specific parameters and objectives. Since these studies are funded by the pharmaceutical industry, the objectives are to show that drugs are effective and safe, and all-natural treatments are ineffective and dangerous. These researchers are given financial incentives to produce these results: millions of dollars in additional grants, funding, future contracts, as well as luxury perks like vacations and cars. Imagine how this works. Any research results a pharmaceutical company wants, it can get; all it has to do is buy it!

Here's an example, parents were concerned that their children were eating too much sugar, causing hyperactivity, learning disabilities, and behavioral problems. The sugar industry was concerned that kids would be eating less sugar, thus cutting into their profits. (Remember the role of the food companies in all this from our discussion at the beginning of the chapter.) The sugar industry associations indirectly funded a study, which was to prove that sugar consumption had no effect on hyperactivity or learning abilities. They got the study with the results they wanted. In a national newspaper, the headline read: "Sugar Has No Effect on Hyperactivity or Learning and Behavioral Problems in Children." The article stated that a study was conducted with two groups of children. The first group was given a "controlled diet." The second group ate the exact same controlled diet but 30 percent more sugar. The hyperactivity level, learning abilities, and behavioral actions were found to be the same in both groups. This concluded that sugar did not increase hyperactivity or cause learning or behavioral problems in children.

Here is what they didn't tell you. The study had only a few children in it! Certainly not enough to have any accuracy on the study results. (This happens routinely. Studies are conducted with just a few people just so the results the companies need can be achieved.) Second, you were not told that the controlled diet contained lots of sugar in it. It actually contained enormous amounts of sugar. The controlled diet contained the sugar equivalent of eating twenty-five doughnuts, drinking three dozen sodas, and eating ten candy bars. So all the kids were so hyped up on sugar that when you added 30 percent more, there wasn't any change! Can you see how outrageous this is? Can you see you are being lied to and misled? Can you see why I'm mad as hell and not going to take it anymore? I can give you dozens of examples of studies that simply are false and misleading. You can create any "credible scientific evidence" you want if you just pay the right people.

Drugs are not the answer for the prevention and curing of disease. Natural methods work better in the long term, and are much safer than drugs and surgery. "They" don't want you to know the truth. "They" use television, radio, newspapers, and magazines, including the use of paid celebrities, paid experts, and false and misleading advertising to convince you that drugs are good and natural remedies are bad.

Lawsuits. The industry uses lawsuits as a tool to spread negative information about natural remedies and also to put out of business anyone that is challenging the profits of the pharmaceutical industry. Keep in mind the pharmaceutical industry is the most powerful, profitable business in the world.

Some of you remember the movie *The Fugitive*. Well, that was more fact than fiction. Some of you may remember that the whole reason Dr. Kimble, played by Harrison Ford, was found guilty of murdering his wife was because a doctor was falsifying research on a new drug and stood to make tens of million of dollars if the drug was approved by the FDA. Folks I can tell you that happens! It's scary but true. The industry has so much money, has such deep pockets, they can afford to file outrageous, frivolous lawsuits against small independent people and companies and virtually drive them out of business or bring them to their knees.

One particular case was with the American Medical Association. Keep in mind the AMA is a union for its members, not a government organization with the mandate of solving the medical problems of America. The American Medical Association has no interest in you and me, we are simply customers. The American Medical Association is a union designed to protect its members, which are the medical doctors and the medical industry. But it is always being presented as an independent, unbiased body presenting medical facts to the world, with a goal of curing disease, which simply is not the case. Just read their charter.

The history of the AMA is fascinating. The AMA was founded in 1847 in Philadelphia. While there were many state medical associations at the time, the need to establish a national association that would look after the interests of medical doctors nationwide was determined to be paramount one year earlier at the New York medical convention. At the time, doctors were not the majority of heathcare practitioners in America dealing with the cure and prevention of illness and disease. There were vast amounts of homeopathic and other practitioners using natural remedies. The very next year after being created, the AMA began its organized assault on debunking natural remedies and discrediting any health-care practitioner who was not a medical doctor. At the same time it set out to establish the laws governing patent medicine. This practice has continued ever since, thus establishing the health-care monopoly for the medical doctor as these continued to expand into the areas of drug manufacturing and medical research. Today, the American Medical Association stands as the largest and most powerful health-care association in the world. It has amassed enough power and influence to create laws that help expand the business of its members while at the same time eliminating any competition that might threaten their outrageous profits.

From this position of power, the AMA filed a lawsuit against the chiropractors in Illinois. Chiropractors at the time were saying that chiropractic adjustments can alleviate pain. Many people were going to chiropractors instead of medical doctors. The AMA, in order to protect its members, filed a lawsuit against the chiropractors. The chiropractors fought back and fought back big time. The chiropractors won. It was proven in court that chiropractic treatments were better at eliminating or reducing pain than anything that medical doctors could offer. But the travesty is that the case got almost no press at all. Can you see why? That was a huge landmark case but got virtually no press whatsoever.

Another huge case which got virtually no press whatsoever was when a doctor, who was treating people through all-natural methods, was saying that his all-natural nondrug methods were curing people of AIDS. He was immediately sued by the FDA. The case went all the way to the New York Supreme Court and the doctor was found not guilty. It was proven that his treatments were more effective than those offered by any medical doctor, and he was using no drugs or surgery, only all-natural methods. Did you read about this in the newspapers? Of course not. Did you hear about it on any of the TV news stations or radio news stations? No. Did you read about it in any major front page articles in magazines? Absolutely not.

Make sure you understand what I just said. A licensed health-care practitioner was curing people of AIDS without drugs and surgery. He was using all-natural methods. His cure rate was higher than anything that medical doctors could offer. He had a higher cure rate than anyone using drugs and surgery and had absolutely no side effects. This is a miracle. This man should be given a Nobel Prize. He was and is curing people of AIDS without drugs and surgery! This was proven to be true at the New York Supreme Court level. Why isn't this man and his methods front-page headline news all around the world? Why aren't his methods being employed all around the world to cure AIDS? His all-natural methods were proven in court to work better than any drugs and surgery! Doesn't this cause you outrage? Doesn't this cause you disbelief? Doesn't this cause you to be mad as hell?

The "powers that be" do not want his inexpensive all-natural AIDS cure known even though it was proven in court to work! The "powers that be" only want profits. This goes to the highest levels of government.

It has been reported that former President Bill Clinton is making millions of dollars exporting pharmaceutical drugs around the world. No one can make big money on all-natural remedies; therefore, they are being suppressed and debunked at every chance. There are virtually hundreds of lawsuits filed against health-care practitioners who are curing people of disease without drugs and surgery. Their only crime is that they are curing people of disease WITHOUT drugs and surgery! The government and pharmaceutical companies do not want people to know that all-natural inexpensive treatments work better than drugs and surgery and have absolutely no side effects. News organizations will not run these stories because of the pressure they are under by their sponsors, most notably the pharmaceutical companies and food industry. This is suppression of the free flow of information; this is suppression of people's First Amendment right of free speech; this is suppression of opposing views and alternative ideas, all in the name of profits. Remember, it's always all about the money.

Again, I want to reemphasize this fact. Lawsuits are routinely filed against individual health-care practitioners who are curing people without drugs or surgery. Not only are civil lawsuits filed against them, but many of these honest, dedicated, health-care providers are being prosecuted criminally for curing people's diseases. They are being charged with practicing medicine without a license or dispensing drugs without a license. Their only real crime is curing disease through natural methods and not using drugs and surgery. Lawsuits are also routinely filed against companies that sell all-natural products that can prevent or cure diseases. These lawsuits are filed primarily by the FTC, the FDA, and watchdog groups, which are really fronts for the pharmaceutical industry and medical associations. These suits are filed even though there are no consumer complaints! Remember, when these lawsuits are filed, the allegations are presented as facts by the news media. Also remember that virtually all television networks, radio networks, newspapers and magazines depend on the advertising revenue they receive from the pharmaceutical industry. What you read about and what you hear about will always be influenced by the pharmaceutical industry.

These attacks via lawsuit are increasing at an alarming rate. Recently the FDA, the FTC, and several other government agencies have teamed up and launched a campaign called "Operation Cure All." The reason this campaign has been launched is said to be to protect the health of consumers against natural products that are not proven effective or safe. These government agencies are making the playing field uneven. Operation Cure All allows the pharmaceutical industry to produce their deceptive and false advertising, while at the same time setting strict rules as to what is truthful, substantiated, and allowable in advertising for natural health products. One rule is the prohibition on saying that a natural product does anything relating to the prevention or curing of a disease. Not only are you prohibited from making such a statement, even if it is true; you are forbidden to *imply* such a claim.

The amazing thing is that the courts have determined that the FTC has the authority to decide whether a claim is implied or not. This

means the FTC has the absolute final word on whether an ad is in violation of law. This ultimately means that the FTC can at any time sue a
company or individual, and they will always win.

Under the banner of Operation Cure All, telling the truth is also forbidden. A person is prohibited from telling what the product has done
for him, even though his statement may be 100 percent truthful and
accurate. The FTC and the FDA have effectively taken over the right
of free speech under the guise of protecting the public. Why are drug
companies allowed to advertise their products on television, on radio,
and in newspapers and magazines so freely? These ads are clearly false
and misleading. The testimonials you hear are fake. You are watching
paid actors who are reading a script. You are being lied to and deceived
and both the FDA and FTC take no action. Why is it that advertising for
natural products are being routinely attacked? It is obvious to everyone
that the truth about natural remedies is being suppressed.

How can America, a country that presents itself to the world as
a bastion of free speech, free expression of ideas, freedom of choice,
freedom of information and free enterprise, be faced with such draco-
nian restrictions of these freedoms when it relates to our health and
medical choices? Operation Cure All is part of a new set of rules being
implemented to restrict and limit access to health information, food
supplements, and natural therapies on a worldwide basis. The World
Health Organization, the United Nations, international banks, and
the multinational pharmaceutical industry are working together right
now, implementing these regulations. This worldwide commission is
working on restrictions that would severely limit the availability of
vitamins, food supplements, natural remedies, and even information.

It appears the actual objective of this organization is to bring natural dietary supplements under the umbrella of the pharmaceutical
industry. Is it true that the pharmaceutical industry is trying to take
over all-natural products? In America, pharmaceutical giants are buying vitamin, mineral, herbal, and homeopathic companies. Currently
there are two products being marketed on television. The ads look eerily
similar to drug ads. The packaging of the products makes them appear
to be drugs. But in this instance, they are not drugs at all. They are
natural products being manufactured and sold by the pharmaceutical
industry at outrageous prices, because it's the pharmaceutical industry, these ads are allowed to run. If a small, independent company
were running the same ad, the FTC would come in and charge them

with false and misleading advertising and making unsubstantiated health claims. The FDA would come in, seize the product, confiscate the equipment, books, records and computers of the company, and charge the officers, directors and owners with selling drugs without a license. I know this to be true because I actually transcribed these ads, changed a couple of words and presented them to both the FTC and FDA. I asked if these ads would violate any of the FTC or FDA rules. I was told that these ads violated both FTC and FDA rules and regulations. Hmm. Imagine their surprise when I informed them that these ads were being run by big pharmaceutical companies. Their response was "we'll look into it." But they assured me that if I ran these ads action would be taken against me immediately. We are supposed to have equal protection under the law. Selective prosecution is allegedly forbidden in this country. Unfortunately, that's not how it works. The bottom line here is that the government is working together with the pharmaceutical industry to take control of all-natural remedies. For example, in Germany and Norway the drug companies have virtually taken over the entire health food industry. Vitamin B1, vitamin C and vitamin E, in certain amounts, are illegal in these countries. A major pharmaceutical company now controls the herb echinacea, and sells it as an over-the-counter drug at exorbitant prices. Selling herbs as food, in certain parts of Europe, is now a criminal offense.

Am I the only voice expressing outrage? No. There are thousands of medical doctors, scientists, surgeons, and ex-pharmaceutical insiders who know the truth and are desperately trying to educate the public. Hundreds of books have been written on these subjects. I am not the only author or consumer advocate addressing these critical and timely subjects. Here is a reprint of a public notice that was placed in the New York Times in January 2005, by Mathias Rath, M.D. This shows that I am not the only person expressing this viewpoint. Please note that there are thousands of MEDICAL DOCTORS who are coming forward and denouncing drugs and surgery. Even medical doctors who have been trained to prescribed drugs and perform surgery are coming forward because they see that it is really all about the money and not about curing and preventing disease. This public announcement makes some excellent points.

NO AMNESTY FOR MAKERS OF DEADLY DRUGS!
PROTECT YOUR HEALTH! ACT NOW!

Largely unbeknownst to the American people there is a war going on that has claimed victims in every family. This war is escalating and threatens every human life. It is a war being waged in the interests of the multibillion dollar pharmaceutical industry, which is not a health industry but rather an investment business built on the continuation and expansion of global diseases. Your health and the health of every person in America are threatened in several ways:

1. **"The business with disease" as the basis of the pharmaceutical industry.** The pharmaceutical industry is a multibillion dollar investment business that has orchestrated the largest fraud in human history. It promises health, but in fact thrives on the continuation of diseases. This fraud scheme is easily unmasked. Most pharmaceutical drugs are designed to merely cover disease symptoms, but are not intended to cure or eradicate diseases. As a direct result of this multibillion dollar fraud business, no cure has ever been found for cardiovascular disease, cancer, diabetes, or any other chronic disease. On the contrary, these diseases continue in epidemic proportions, killing about 5,000 Americans every day. This compares to the annihilation of a city the size of San Francisco every year.

2. **The epidemic of dangerous side effects caused by pharmaceutical drugs.** The dangerous side effects of Vioxx, Celebrex, Lipitor, and Prozac are not the exception, they are the rule. Due to their synthetic nature, most pharmaceutical drugs are toxic to our bodies, causing organ damage and other serious side effects. According to the American Medical Association, one million American suffered disabilities from taking pharmaceutical drugs and more than 100,000 of them die as a result of this every single year.

3. **Legislation that protects the expansion of the deadly business with disease.** For decades drug companies have used their giant profits to manipulate the public and influence legislation, including that from the U.S. Congress and the White House. Now that the deadly consequences of the pharmaceutical fraud business have been unmasked the survival of this industry depends on the protectionist laws. The current push of the Bush administration for so-called medical liability reform is not about protecting gynecologists

and medical doctors from medical liability lawsuits. The centerpiece of the proposed medical liability legislation is to prohibit punitive damage awards and liability lawsuits brought by injured patients against drug companies! This medical liability legislation is being used as a cover to grant amnesty to drug manufacturers, protecting them from having to compensate millions of patients for the harm their drugs have caused. It is payback for the pharmaceutical industry, which was the largest corporate sponsor of the Bush election campaign. The people of America and their political representatives have to realize that the proposed medical liability legislation is a "Trojan Horse." Passing it means granting immunity to the drug makers, allowing them the unrestricted expansion of their deadly business with disease at the expense of patients. As the direct consequence of this law, tens of millions of Americans will suffer disability and die from preventable diseases within the next decades.

4. **Withholding life-saving information about the health benefits of vitamins and natural therapies.** A precondition for this "business with disease" based on patentable synthetic drugs is the suppression of effective and safe, but nonpatentable and therefore less profitable, natural therapies. For decades the pharmaceutical industry has strategically expanded its influence on medical education with devastating results. It has deliberately blocked any information about the essential role of vitamins and other micronutrients in maintaining health contained in every textbook of biology, biochemistry, and natural science from entering medical school teaching and medical practice. Through their strategic influence, the pharmaceutical industry has established a global monopoly on medicine. As a direct result, generations of medical doctors have not received adequate training in nutritional and other natural therapies. Doctors and patients alike have become victims of the pharmaceutical industry's efforts to monopolize human health. As a result, tens of millions of Americans have died unnecessarily over the past decades because this life-saving health information has not been available to them.

5. **Suppressing effective natural therapies by law.** Effective, safe, and nonpatentable natural therapies threaten the very basis of the pharmaceutical investment business. They target and correct the underlying cellular deficiencies of today's most common diseases, thereby preventing and even eradicating them. The elimination of

any disease inevitably destroys a multibillion-dollar drug market for the pharmaceutical industry, thus the pharmaceutical industry has launched a global campaign to protect its patent-based "business with disease" by outlawing natural nonpatentable therapies at the national and international level. This is the background for the Bush administration's attack on the Dietary Supplement Health and Education Act. The key legislation protecting the rights of the American people for free access to natural therapies and to freedom of health choice. If this fundamental human right to natural health is taken away the health of billions of people will be compromised and tens of millions of them will pay the ultimate price for generations to come.

• • •

The bottom line is that there ARE natural, inexpensive, safe cures for almost every disease. The pharmaceutical industry, the FTC, the FDA and the rest of "them" are trying to suppress this information.

The pharmaceutical industry, the drug industry, the food industry, the associations and government agencies, all have a major financial incentive to keep people sick. There are billions of dollars in profits as long as people stay sick and there are billions of dollars in profits as long as people take more and more drugs. Remember, it's always all about the money!

• • •

I must now continue to blow the whistle on how the FTC and FDA operate. The Federal Trade Commission is an agency with the primary goal of protecting consumers. It was formed to guard consumers against monopolies and ensure that small businesses were given a level playing field within which to operate. The FTC's other main goal is to make sure that consumers are not "ripped off" by companies. Yet in actual fact, the FTC has no interest in protecting consumers.

Let me give you an example from my own personal experience. This is not an isolated case. I can show you hundreds of examples proving that this is in fact the standard operating procedure of the FTC. Here is what it looks like:

I was excited about a product called coral calcium. This product is simply calcium, the source being coral sand from Okinawa, Japan. Calcium is harmless, has many proven health benefits, is an essential nutrient for the body, and has been sold for years without any issues.

I produced a TV infomercial interviewing an author who was giving his opinions about the potential health benefits of supplementing your diet with calcium. I then sent this infomercial to the FTC. I telephoned the FTC on several occasions. I wrote the FTC several letters. I sent several e-mails. I kept asking the FTC if they had any issues with my television commercial promoting the product coral calcium. I informed the FTC that if there were any concerns or questions they needed answered, to please communicate that to me as my intention and desire was to be 100 percent cooperative in every way.

The FTC responded on several occasions that they had no issues with my promotion of coral calcium. The coral calcium product was being embraced by the public. Thousands of letters kept pouring in telling of the incredible health benefits people were experiencing from taking coral calcium. The return rate of the product was one of the lowest in the entire dietary supplement industry. There were virtually no complaints, and everyone seemed to like coral calcium. Unbeknownst to me, the FTC was conducting a secret investigation into the sale and promotion of coral calcium and were coordinating their efforts with the FDA. During the entire investigation, the FTC never called us or requested any information from us at all.

Suddenly, without warning, the FTC filed a major lawsuit against me, my company, and the author I interviewed. The lawsuit stated that we were making unsubstantiated health claims about the benefits of coral calcium. They went to court and asked for an emergency ruling demanding that the company be shut down and all of my personal assets frozen.

This is the *modus operandi* of the FTC.

First, they conduct a secret investigation. No matter how cooperative you want to be, they refuse to talk to or question the company or individual that they are getting ready to pounce on. Second, they go into court and demand that the companies be shut down and all assets frozen. Unbelievable as it sounds, the FTC wins this request over 97 percent of the time. The opposing side is given virtually no time to respond and is, in effect, put out of business. It may also surprise you to know that when the FTC files suit, it is not required to go to federal court. Instead, the FTC suits are presented before an "administrative law judge" who is actually an employee of the FTC! The "courtroom" is in the FTC building itself! No wonder the FTC wins 97 percent of the time. Further research revealed that, with the exception of a few antitrust cases involving huge companies, not one single administrative judge ever ruled against the FTC.

My case is almost identical to most other FTC cases. The three most outrageous things to look at are:

1. The FTC stated that we were making unsubstantiated and false health claims about coral calcium. However, how could the FTC make that allegation when they never asked us to produce any substantiation that we may have had? Making the allegation without asking us or reviewing the substantiation that we had is in itself a false and misleading statement. The FTC is guilty of making false and misleading statements and then presenting them to the media as facts.

2. Where are all the complaining customers? If our advertising was so deceptive, customers would have complained and returned the product. The FTC's response to this is that the public is too stupid to know that the ad violated the FTC rules.

3. Why didn't the FTC contact us or respond to our multitude of letters, phone calls, and e-mails? For over a year and a half, the FTC knew about our ad. We repeatedly asked them if they had any issues. They repeatedly said no. Then the sudden lawsuit and the subsequent demand that the show be pulled off the air. Why the delay? This is standard operating procedure. If the FTC really thought that our infomercial was not fair to consumers, they could have asked us to take it off the air eighteen months earlier. Why did they wait? Because it's all about the money! The FTC routinely waits for companies to generate large amounts of sales and profits before they step in and take action. They do this because they do not care about the consumer, all they want is money. If they stopped you right in the beginning you wouldn't have any money to give them.

The FTC, in my opinion, is an out-of-control organization. It is not protecting consumers. It is in fact protecting the profits and monopolies established by major corporations. Consider this fact: How many lawsuits has the FTC filed against major corporations for false and misleading advertising? Answer: None. That's right, none, zero, not a single one. However, it routinely files hundreds of lawsuits against small companies for false and misleading advertising. Let's look at some of the ads on television. There is an ad for the drug Levitra. The woman looks into the camera and says, "My man uses Levitra..." This is false and misleading. Her man does not use Levitra; this is a paid actress reading a script. The ad is false, deceptive, and is flagrantly untrue. The

FTC takes no action. If a small independent company did the exact same thing they would be prosecuted for CRIMINAL fraud. The most obvious example of the FTC protecting the monopolies' profits is in the case of Celebrex. Celebrex advertising was deemed false and misleading by the FDA itself! That's right, the Food and Drug Administration was under so much public pressure that it had to do something in response to the flagrant, false, and misleading advertising done by the pharmaceutical company in relation to the Celebrex ad. The FDA said specifically that the ad was "false and misleading."

Now here is where the story gets interesting. The FTC is the government agency that has the job of prosecuting companies that produce "false and misleading advertising." To date, the FTC has taken absolutely no action against the manufacturers of Celebrex and the producers of this "false and misleading ad." This is an outrage. The FTC has the responsibility to protect consumers from companies that produce false and misleading advertising. Here is an ad that the FDA itself has already deemed false and misleading, but the FTC takes no action. Why? Because it is protecting the profits of the drug companies. If this was any other company the FTC would sue the company, demand 100 percent consumer redress, and demand a complete freezing of all the assets of the company and a government receiver put in charge of that company. The individual officers and directors would also be held personally responsible and their assets would be frozen. Why isn't the FTC taking any action against this flagrant violation? Because the FTC is not protecting consumers from false and misleading advertising, it is in fact protecting the monopolies' profits. This is an outrage. Can you see why I'm mad as hell and not going to take it anymore?

Another standard operating procedure that the FTC uses is when it settles a case it puts out press releases. Here is one of the most amazing discoveries. When you read the press releases put out by the Federal Trade Commission, you find that the FTC itself is the most flagrant violator of its own standards for false and misleading advertising. The press releases put out by the FTC are all, virtually all, false and misleading. The FTC purposely writes these press releases to mislead the public. Let me say that again. The FTC purposely writes these press releases to mislead the public. They have done it against me and they have done it to hundreds of other companies. This is standard operating procedure by our government. The question is not whether the press releases put out by the FTC are false and misleading, they are absolutely 100 percent false and misleading. The question is does the government have the legal right to mislead the public? This is what I mean about a debunking campaign. The government and the news organizations mislead you into believing what they want you to believe even though it's not true.

I have done the unthinkable against the Federal Trade Commission. I said enough is enough. Throughout history there were people that stood up to the Goliaths of the day and said "enough is enough." Rosa Parks said I am not going to sit on the back of a bus just because I'm black. She stood up to the powers that be and changed a nation. People like Ceasar Chavez, Martin Luther King, and Mahandas Gandhi stood up to the suppression and tyranny at the time and changed the world for the better. In my opinion, the Federal Trade Commission is an absolutely out-of-control organization that lies to the public, misleads the public, and crushes independent entrepreneurs.

The FTC, in my opinion, is one of the organizations used by government to suppress the free flow of information and to take away our right of free speech. Because of this I have decided to risk it all for the betterment of society. I have filed massive lawsuits against the government and am doing everything in my power to stop the FTC from suppressing the free flow of information. The FTC even tried to stop the sale of this book! The FTC has threatened to take my books and burn them. Can you believe this? It's an outrage and someone has to stand up for all of you so that you can get the true, unbiased information about natural remedies.

Go to the www.kevinfightsback.com and read the two lawsuits I have filed against the Federal Trade Commission. When you read those two lawsuits, as well as all of the letters I have received from the FTC and FDA, you will see and understand exactly how these corrupt organizations operate. Hopefully, your eyes will be opened to the fact that you cannot believe what you see on television, hear on radio, or read in newspapers and magazines. Specifically, you will hopefully come to the realization that you absolutely cannot believe what is being disseminated from our government. Hopefully, you will absolutely see that the government is the largest disseminator of false and misleading information, solely so that the politicians can line their pockets with the millions of dollars they make every year that you and I will never have access to. They want to keep the status quo, where the rich get richer and the poor get poorer, and it's not what you know but who you know. This has to change. There must be equality for all, and I am committed to help make that happen.

The question then is, if we can't believe our government, if we can't believe television, if we can't believe what we hear on the radio, if we can't believe what we read in newspapers and magazines, if we can't believe what we hear from professors and doctors since they are all paid spokespeople for the pharmaceutical industry, who can we believe when it comes to information about health and the treatment, prevention, and cure of disease? Well, the bottom line is you can't believe anyone if they have a financial interest in selling you something. What that means is you can't even believe alternative health-care practitioners who are trying to sell you vitamins. If a licensed health-care practitioner tells you the benefits of a vitamin, herb, or mineral and is encouraging you to buy from him at a profit, maybe he is being sincere and truthful, but also maybe there is a financial incentive so strong that you may not be getting unbiased information.

The officers and directors of vitamin, mineral, herb, and homeopathic companies have financial motivations to sell their products just like the officers and directors of pharmaceutical companies. Remember, it's always all about the money. When there is a financial incentive involved it's impossible to trust the information. That's a major concept in this book, and it's vitally important that you understand that. You need to know that the information you are getting is probably tainted. You need to know that the information is totally biased and designed to get you to make a decision that can line the pockets of certain people. So again, the question is who do you listen to?

The answer: YOU CAN LISTEN TO ME!

You probably have a big smile on your face right now as you read that, but it's absolutely true. Why? Because I saw this problem evident myself. People all around the world come up to me and ask, "Where do I go for information about health? Who can I trust? Who can I listen to? Where can I get information about the curing or prevention of a disease? There is so much information out there; much of the information is contradictory, and I just don't know where to go to find the answers." This to me is the big problem. With the advent of the Internet there is more information available than ever before, but the problem is when you go on the Internet everyone is trying to sell you something. So when you are reading the information you don't know if it's truthful and honest or just designed to get you to buy their product. *Web, M.D.* is a perfect example. This is a publicly traded company where the officers and directors have made millions and millions of dollars in profits. *Web,*

M.D., in my opinion, is nothing more than a front for the pharmaceutical industry encouraging you to buy and use drugs and expensive medical procedures. It tries to make you believe it is an unbiased source of information when this is categorically not true. How can they be unbiased when they accept advertising from drug companies? How can they be unbiased when they are publicly traded? How can they be unbiased when their only motivation is to make money?

So again, the question is what makes me different? The answer is very simple. I have decided that for my life it's NOT ALL ABOUT THE MONEY. Making money is not bad. Making a profit is not bad. As I have mentioned before, giving a good quality service at a good value is an admirable thing to do. Making a profit, making money, and enjoying a beautiful lifestyle are not bad and evil. The love of money is bad and evil. Making money at the expense of your employees, the environment, and a customer is bad and evil.

Here is how I've solved the problem. Here is why you should listen to what I am saying in this book, and in my other books and other publications: I do not take any advertising. I do not sell any product. You can listen to me because I have no financial incentive in you doing anything relating to your health. If I encourage you to buy a vitamin, or use an alternative natural treatment, I have no financial incentive to give you that advice. As far as I know I am the only health-care advocate that doesn't sell vitamins and minerals or any food supplements, I accept no advertising in any of my publications, I get no kickbacks from anyone, I own stock in virtually no companies, and I have no other goal or motivation other than to see you cure yourself of your disease and stay healthy forever. Folks, consider this: I know this stuff already. I practice this every day in my life. I don't know you. Why am I risking everything by filing suits against the Federal Trade Commission and dealing with ridicule, attacks, and criticism? It isn't about the money. I'm giving most of the profits away on the sale of this book and my other ventures to help promote natural healing around the world. It's not about the money for me. Yes, I do make good money, and yes I live a very nice lifestyle, but I can tell you I am never going to make the type of money that the directors and officers of the publicly traded pharmaceutical companies make. Here is an article that I wrote in one of my newsletters about why listen to me. I think it's an important article for you to read and also give you some insight into some of the information that is in my monthly *Natural Cures Newsletter*.

WHY BELIEVE ME

There are dozens of alternative health newsletters available today such as those by Dr. Schulze, Dr. Whitaker, Dr. Wright, Dr. Williams, Dr. Mercola, and Dr. Douglass. I receive all of these newsletters. I read them. In many cases I concur with what is being written, however, there is one major, major, major problem. All of these people sell vitamins, minerals, herbs, or other food supplements. What this means is that their newsletters are not in fact unbiased informational publications, but rather cleverly crafted sales letters designed to encourage you to buy their specific vitamins, minerals, herbs, or food supplements. This means that when you are reading their publications you can never be confident in knowing that they are giving unbiased truthful information, or if they are simply trying to sell you their own vitamins, minerals, herbs, and food supplements to make millions of dollars in profits. You just don't know. It is impossible to trust them because there is such a huge conflict of interest. Their motivation to make money could be the main overriding factor. That is why, in my opinion, you can trust what you read in this newsletter, and what you read on my NaturalCures.com Web site, and what you read in my other books and informational publications. I do not sell any vitamins, minerals, herbs, or food supplements. I sell no products at all. I have no financial interest in companies that sell products. I am not compensated in any way on any products that I recommend, endorse, or suggest. There are no conflicts of interest here.

There are conflicts of interest with every other alternative health newsletter. Not surprisingly, there are also conflicts of interests with every major newspaper, magazine, news radio station, and news TV station. That's right. There are financial conflicts with all the major media venues where information is disseminated. What does this mean? This means when you are watching the news on TV and think you are getting unbiased journalism, you are not. You are getting bought and paid for commercials, which are being disguised as news and unbiased journalism. Let me give you a perfect example. On Sunday, January 2nd of this year, I was watching the Fox news channel. On this particular news segment, the Fox news host introduced his guest, a weight loss expert by the name of Dr. Molly Gee. She was to discuss New Year's resolutions relating to weight loss. This weight loss expert proceeded to tell the audience and the host why people were fat and the best ways for people to lose weight. She did not present this information as her opinion, but rather presented it as scientific fact in the standard arrogant way that doctors do. I was not shocked to hear her then promote the Slim Fast Plan as the best way for people to lose weight, and encouraged the viewers to go to the Slim Fast Web site. This weight loss expert was virtually giving a commercial for Slim Fast. The host said nothing. The host did not ask if she was a paid spokesperson for Slim Fast. The host did not ask if she was being compensated in any way to endorse and push Slim Fast while disguising her opinions as a medical expert. The host said nothing.

I enquired further. This woman is paid huge amounts of money by Slim Fast to promote their program. This was on Fox news channel. This was not news; this was a commercial for the Slim Fast program. The problem is that it was disguised as news; it was fraudulent and misleading. This is why, when you read newspapers or magazines or listen to the news on radio and television, you can't trust the information. You have to remember, it's all money motivated. This is why you can believe my newsletter, my books, and my Web site. I have no financial interest. I am not doing this just for the money. I am passionately concerned about you, your family, your well-being and health. Yes, I do make a profit doing this, but there are no hidden agendas with me. This is why I am being so viciously attacked by the Federal Trade Commission, other agencies, organizations, and industries. The reason is I cannot be bought. I cannot be bribed.

People approach me on a regular basis offering me millions of dollars to endorse their product, to recommend their product in my newsletter, or to talk positively about one product or bash another product. It sickens me that the business world is filled with people who simply live their life for one reason and one reason alone: to make more money. As I mentioned, profit is not a four-letter word. Making profit is not bad, but making profit at the expense of employees, at the expense of the environment, and at the expense of the consumer by misleading them and selling them products that do not do what they are claimed to do is unethical. I certainly don't know all the answers, and I know that my opinions may be wrong, but there is one thing you can be fully assured and confident with; that is that you are getting from me honest intentions and honest unbiased opinions. You can always know that my intentions are pure and true. You can always be 100 percent assured that when I say something it is because I absolutely, categorically believe it is true and beneficial to you and no other reason.

I hope you get the point. Some of you at this point may really be scratching your head wondering if it's always only all about the money. I have to say to you again, absolutely 100 percent, yes it is. If you are still not convinced you need to read the book called *The Corporation: The Pathological Pursuit of Profit and Power* by Joel Bakan. Famed Harvard Law School professor Allen Dershowitz said, "*The Corporation* according to Joel Bakan is the monster that can swallow civilization, greedy, exploitive, and unstoppable. We are all its potential victims, which is why we must all understand how the corporate forum makes it so difficult to control its abuses." Noam Chomskay, Ph.D., Professor of Linguistics, Massachusetts Institute of Technology and author of *9/11* says, "Joel Bakan unveils the history and the character of this devilish instrument called *The Corporation* that has been created and nurtured by powerful modern stated (politicians). The corporation by law is a "person" that is pathological by nature and by law, and systematically crushes democracy, freedom, rights, and the natural human instincts on which a life and even human survival depend." Ray Anderson, Chairman and CEO of Interface, Inc. says about the book *The Corporation,* "Since Rachel Carson's *Silent Spring* began to expose the abuses of the modern industrial system there has been a growing awareness that profit at the expense of earth, individuals, society, and the environment is exploding at an alarming rate. This book exposes corporations and their destructive natures so that all can see." The book has also become a tremendous documentary from Zeitgeist Films. Go to www.thecorporation.com for more information. The reason I continue to hammer this point home that it's "always all about the money" is that this is the basic premise for you to understand all the rational reasons why natural cures are being suppressed and hidden from you. The majority of people around the world have no comprehension of how greedy and motivated corporations and individuals are to make money at all costs and to gain power at all costs. It is vitally important that you really understand and comprehend that money and power is the motivating force behind everything on planet earth. This must be changed. You are the victims of this abuse. When you see and understand this point, everything else in this book will make total sense. Remember, the love of money is the root of all evil. Remember, remember, remember—it's always all about the money!

CHAPTER 5

Why Are We Sick?

Health is a state of complete physical, mental, and social well-being and not merely the absence of disease and infirmity.

—World Health Organization

We spend more money on health care than ever before. We take more drugs than ever before, yet we are sicker than ever before. More people are getting sick than ever before in history. As I mentioned in the beginning of this book, there are no such things as medical facts. Everything is simply an opinion based on the information we have at the current time. Additionally, all "medical facts" that are presented are those opinions which make the most profits. If information about the prevention, cure or diagnosis of disease was found to have an adverse effect on publicly traded companies' profits (primarily the pharmaceutical industry and the medical industry), then that "medical fact" will not be presented at all, it will be debunked and it will be suppressed.

There is an underground movement which includes hundreds of thousands of health-care practitioners who treat patients every day and see people get healed every single day. These health-care practitioners do not use drugs or surgery, they use all-natural methods. The individual patients who are cured know that these all-natural treatments work. There are no complaints lodged with any government agency. Yet the FDA and other government agencies are on a mission to stamp out and wipe out all of these natural health-care practitioners. Why? Because they cut into the profits of the drug companies.

Over the years, the pharmaceutical industry has come up with different theories about why people get sick. First it was bacteria and germs. The super wonder drug of the day was antibiotics, which were touted as the method that would eliminate disease forever and cure all illness, sickness and diseases. The theory was that all disease was caused by germs, primarily bacteria. This theory has proved to be wrong. Stronger and stronger antibiotics are continually developed, yet people continue to get sicker, and sicker, and sicker. More people are getting more diseases than ever before.

The next theory was that viruses were the cause of all illness and disease. Unfortunately, few people know that antibiotics have no effect on viruses. The doctors continually prescribe antibiotics at the drop of a hat. People have been brainwashed into thinking that antibiotics are needed when they feel sick, and go to their doctors and demand antibiotics. The doctor, who unfortunately is in a business and understands his patient is really a customer, has to make the customer happy and prescribes the antibiotic. If the doctor does not, the patient (aka, the customer) will simply find another doctor who will prescribe an antibiotic. The Associated Press reported that overuse of broad-spectrum antibiotics for minor infection poses a serious health threat. The government estimates that half of the one hundred million antibiotic prescriptions written each year are totally unnecessary. Still, people continue to get more diseases, more sickness and more illness.

The current theory of the day is all sickness, diseases, and illnesses are caused by genetic defects. Of course the only answer is drugs. Drugs are now being researched and looked at to handle these genetic defects. The new method of making billions of dollars in profit is to come up with a genetic defect for every problem a person has. We hear it every day, "Oh, you're fat because you have a genetic defect, and a drug is being worked on that can solve that genetic defect and make you thin." "Diabetes is nothing more than genetics, so we'll work on a drug that will correct that genetic disposition and solve the problem." Keep in mind that drug companies really do not want to cure disease as they claim. If they came up with a cure, they would be out of business.

Think of herpes. Herpes is a virus. We hear ads on TV every day that say "there is no cure for herpes"; therefore, in order to suppress the symptoms, take our beautiful, wonderful drug every day for the rest of your life. Imagine what would happen to the publicly traded company and their stock price if they announced "Here is a cure for herpes, simply take this herb for thirty days and you will never have a herpetic breakout ever again. By the way, this herb is not patented and it only costs three dollars." That company would lose billions of dollars in profits and valuation. Its stock price would plummet. Therefore, there is no incentive to cure herpes. The incentive is to keep you brainwashed into believing there is no cure for herpes, and the only solution to the "symptoms" is drugs. Remember, the FDA and the drug companies work hand in hand. If I happen to know a cure for herpes, I cannot say so. Because if I say so I am now making a medical claim and, according to the FDA, I am now breaking the law. Even if what I am saying is true, I am still breaking the law. The FDA will then come in with their federal agents with their guns drawn, arrest me, throw me in jail, confiscate any papers I have (and any of the harmless herb), suppress the information and outlaw it because there is no "credible scientific evidence." They will then put out press releases and statements of "fact" that I am a charlatan selling snake oil and have no scientific evidence to substantiate that what I am saying is true. Unfortunately, that's how the system works.

Later in this book I will tell you how we are going to change the system by blowing the whistle on the pharmaceutical industry, the FDA, the FTC, the crooked charities and foundations, the associations, and the politicians. I am going to name names and expose the individual people whose identities have been kept a secret up until now. Isn't it strange that you are never informed of the identity of the directors or major shareholders of these organizations? These individual people hide behind corporations, trusts and a maze of legal structures so that their true identities remain hidden. If the money trail were followed, it would shock you to find that it leads to a small group of billionaires from around the world that are truly pulling the strings. Through class action lawsuits and a grassroots campaign, we will get the truth out about health care. The trend will reverse, drug use will go down and people will stop getting sick. This is my mission. I am spending my fortune to help make this come to pass. I am doing this for you; I am doing this for society in general. I am putting virtually everything I have emotionally, mentally, and financially into this mission of changing the system.

So why do you get sick? Is it germs? Is it bacteria? Is it viruses? Is it genetics? Well let's think about it. You don't catch cancer. Your body develops cancer. You don't catch diabetes. Your body develops diabetes. You don't catch obesity. Your body becomes fat and obese. You don't catch heartburn or acid reflux, as it is called today. It's developed. You don't catch headaches, you don't catch fibromyalgia, you don't catch back pain, you don't catch arthritis, you don't catch PMS and you don't catch impotence. These are all "medical conditions" that are developed in the body. You don't catch them. It's not a germ. It's not a virus. It's not bacteria. The majority of illness is in fact self-inflicted. Drugs are not the answer. You don't have a headache because you have an aspirin deficiency. The question is, why do human beings have so much illness?

First of all you have to realize that being sick is not normal and it is not the natural state of the body. Your body is not supposed to get sick. Think about this startling fact. Animals in the wild never get heart attacks. Let me say that again, animals in the wild never get heart attacks. Why do humans? Animals in the wild don't get cancer. Animals in the wild virtually never get sick. Animals virtually never get sick, except of course when they are in captivity. When animals are under human care and get vaccine injections, drugs, and human processed food, animals succumb to many of the diseases that humans are riddled with.

Think about this: Animals do not exercise and have no obesity or weight problem. Animals don't go to doctors and live to be ten to twenty times their maturity age. Chimpanzees and gorillas are great examples. They don't lose their teeth, they don't have arthritis, they don't have diabetes, they don't need insulin shots, they don't have cancer, they don't have asthma, they don't have allergies, they are not constipated, they don't have insomnia, and they live to be an equivalent of about 180 years old. Interestingly enough, they go through their entire lives without taking any prescription or nonprescription drugs.

So is there a way that we as human beings can do some very simple and easy things that can keep us disease free, illness free and full of life, energy, and vitality? The answer is: absolutely yes! Let's go back to the cause of all disease and the reason why we are sick.

Think about the fact that there are cultures around the world where the people have never had cancer or heart disease, or acid reflux disease, or prostate problems, etc. Yet when these people start living a western lifestyle, amazing things begin to happen to their health. They get fat, they start getting sick, and they begin to develop all of the common diseases we hear about today. The question is: Why do human beings living a western lifestyle have more sickness and disease than other human beings around the globe? The answer is, no one **knows**! The medical industry presents information as if they do know. They claim they have "scientific evidence" proving the truth of their theories. The fact is, what the medical industry has are only **theories**. When you investigate what is being presented as fact, you find that they are actually only theories that are nothing more than the opinions of individual people. Einstein's **theory** of relativity is presented as a fact, but people forget it's called the theory of relativity and not the **fact** of relativity.

The term "scientific evidence" is one of the greatest deceptions of all time. First, this "scientific evidence" is paid for and manufactured by the corporations that it will benefit. Rarely does an independent, unbiased third party produce any of this "scientific evidence." If the "scientific evidence" is so accurate, why are the conclusions and results constantly being disproved when new research is produced? You are led to believe that "scientific evidence" proves that something is true. This is a false assumption. Every day we hear "new research shows old research to be false." The bottom line is, you will hear the term "scientifically proven" used when the medical community claims they know the cause of disease. You will hear medical doctors make statements of fact when, in reality, they are only opinions. You are being misled and you are being lied to. You are being deceived. The truth is nobody knows why people are getting so sick, we can only guess and come up with our own theories and conclusions.

So, based on personal experience, reading thousands of pages of documents, and hearing the firsthand accounts from thousands of people and health-care practitioners around the world, I have come up with what I believe to be the cause of virtually all sickness and disease in the body.

There are only two reasons why a person becomes ill:

1. They "catch" something. This means your body picked up a "germ," generally a virus or bacteria.

2. You "develop" an illness or disease. This means there is some imbalance in the body, something is not working right, and an illness or disease develops. Common diseases in this category include heart disease, cancer, diabetes, acid reflux, arthritis, etc.

Remember, in our search for the ultimate cause of all illness and the ultimate cure for all illnesses, we must always ask the question "What caused **that**?" With this in mind, let's start with "catching something."

One may say that the "cause" of catching a germ is pretty evident. You obviously caught the germ from someone else who had it. This is where medical science stops. They claim that drugs must be developed to kill these bacteria and viruses. However, they are asking the wrong question. The fact is that we are all exposed to bacteria and viruses on a daily basis. If one person in your home or office has the flu, then every single person has been exposed to and "caught" the flu virus. When anthrax was found in the envelope, not every single person in that building got anthrax! The question is not whether you will pick up bacteria or a virus, the real question is why do some people succumb to the bacteria and virus and get sick, and other people do not?

Take two people. Expose them both to the flu virus at the same time. One person comes down with all of the symptoms of the flu and becomes very sick. The other person shows no symptoms whatsoever, stays healthy, and does not "get the flu." They both got the flu virus! One person succumbed to it and got sick; the other person did not and remained healthy. Throughout your life you will pick up thousands of bacteria and viruses. That is natural. The real question to ask is why your body does not do what it was designed to do: fight off and handle the bacteria or virus. Why did you succumb to the bacteria or virus? The answer: Your body is out of balance and your immune system is weak. If your body was in balance, a state called homeostasis, and your immune system was strong, you would never show any symptoms of any of the viruses or bacteria that you pick up during your lifetime. **You would never get sick because of a virus or bacteria.** Then the question becomes, "What is causing my body to be out of balance, and what is causing my immune system to be weak?"

I will give you the answer in a moment, but first let's go to the second reason people get sick. Remember, you get sick because you either "catch something" or something develops in the body on its own. You "catch something" because your body is out of balance and your immune system is weak. You develop something in the body either because your body is out of balance, or a "toxin" is getting into your body and causing the problem to develop. So let's walk through this nice and slow.

The reasons you get sick are:

1. You catch something and your body cannot fight it off, therefore you succumb to the "germs."

2. Your body develops something in the genetically weak areas.

In both of the above cases the causes are the same.

A. Your immune system is weak.

B. Toxins are attacking your body.

If we keep asking the question, "What caused that...", we can then conclude that all illness comes from one or a combination of four things.

1. You have too many toxins in your body.

2. You have nutritional deficiencies.

3. You are exposed and negatively affected by electromagnetic chaos.

4. You have trapped mental and emotional stress.

These are the only four reasons why your immune system could be weak or why genetically weak areas in the body can break down, thus allowing illness and disease to develop. These four things cause the body to be "out of balance."

I will address each of these four issues. Let's start with toxins.

What is a toxin? A toxin is a poison. It is a substance that if taken in large doses can cause severe illness or death.

In relation to toxins, the question is what is causing toxins to be put into our body? The answer is that we have not been educated to know what these toxins are. And secondly, these toxins are being put in virtually everything we eat without our knowledge. Now, here is the big one: The most toxic thing you can put in your body, and the number one cause of virtually all illness and disease, is prescription and nonprescription drugs!

In my opinion, probably the number one reason people are sick is because of the amount of drugs they take. The statistics show very conclusively that the more prescription and nonprescription drugs a person takes, the sicker they are. Why? Because all drugs have negative side effects. Let me say it again, all drugs have negative side effects! If you are taking a drug to suppress one symptom, that drug is causing some other major problem to start developing in your body. Even if you stop taking that drug, the wheels have been set in motion, and in a few weeks or a few months—boom—you have some more symptoms caused by the first drug you took a few months ago. You go to your doctor, and he gives you another drug to suppress these new symptoms. This new drug had negative side effects, and after you start taking it the wheels will have already been put in motion, and voila! You have new symptoms which were in fact caused by the drug you were just taking. You go to your doctor and he gives you another drug. Drugs cause medical problems!

Drugs only suppress symptoms, they do not treat the cause. It's a great business for the drug companies. If they get you taking one drug, man, they've got you. Because that drug is not only going to suppress the symptom, probably, it is also going to cause you to have another symptom in a very short period of time, for which you will be prescribed another drug. Once they get you to take one drug to suppress a symptom (keeping in mind that it is not addressing the cause anyway), the likelihood of you taking another drug, and then another drug, and then another drug, keeps going up, and up, and up. The more drugs you take, the sicker you get, simply because drugs are major poisons, drugs are major toxins. Someone says, "Drugs can't really be poison, can they?" Then why don't you take thirty of them right now and see what happens? You'll probably die! If you eat thirty apples you're not going to die. You may feel full, but you are not going to die. Think about it.

Now, I love it when somebody says, "Well, it's in such a small amount," referring to the dosage. What if I put the same amount of my urine in your food? Would you eat it? Of course not!

This relates to nonprescription over-the-counter drugs as well. Let me be very clear. All nonprescription over-the-counter drugs and all prescription drugs CAUSE ILLNESS AND DISEASE. The scary thing is the drug companies and the FDA actually know it. The drug companies know that all nonprescription and prescription drugs make you sicker. Yes, they may temporarily suppress the symptoms you are experiencing, but in a very short period of time they cause you to become sicker. A good example of this is Vioxx. Vioxx is a pain medication. It was an outrageously expensive drug that reduces pain no better than an over-the-counter drug. The drug company that sold Vioxx made billions in profits. Whistleblowers now say that both the FDA and the drug manufacturer of Vioxx knew that this drug would cause over 100,000 people to die. Whistleblowers say that the decision was made to let the people die because of the potential huge profits that could be made. In my opinion, this happens all the time. Over-the-counter drugs are some of the biggest culprits. Many of these drugs were approved by the FDA twenty, thirty, forty years ago. The FDA virtually approved everything back then. The problem is once a drug is approved by the FDA, whether it's a prescription drug or a nonprescription drug, there is virtually no follow-up research or testing to verify the long-term effectiveness of the drug and the long-term safety. We are seeing now that over-the-counter drugs that have been sold for thirty years are being looked at by some independent organizations and are being shown to be incredibly dangerous and ineffective. These are drugs that were approved by the FDA and touted as safe and effective. Now, thirty years later, these same drugs that people have been taking nonstop are being shown to be totally ineffective and incredibly dangerous. These over-the-counter everyday drugs are being shown to actually cause illness and disease. Cholesterol lowering drugs, for example, are a major contributor to illness and disease. All cholesterol lowering drugs have an adverse effect on the liver. The liver is the only fat metabolizing organ in the body. The liver is needed for proper body function. When the liver is adversely affected you are prone to diabetes, acid reflux, constipation, colon cancer, heart disease, asthma, arthritis, and dozens of other illnesses and disease. Do cholesterol lowering drugs actually, specifically, and directly cause these illnesses and disease? No one really knows for sure, but it certainly is obvious to anyone with half a brain and a little bit of logic that these absolutely 100 percent CONTRIBUTE to the development of disease in the body. The bottom line is all, I repeat, all over-the-counter nonprescription drugs and prescription drugs CAUSE illness and disease.

This is the big shocker. The industry that is promoting itself as the group dedicated to the prevention and cure of disease is actually the group causing more sickness and disease to occur than ever before. All drugs are chemicals. All drugs have negative side effects. All drugs can cause death. All drugs are poisons. An outstanding book, which I highly recommend that you read, is *Overdose: The Case Against the Drug Companies,* written by Dr. J. Cohen M.D. Did you know that 250,000 Americans die every year from prescription or nonprescription drugs? That over 2,000 people every year die from taking aspirin? That there are dozens of articles showing how prescription and nonprescription drugs are causing all illness and diseases. Drugs are not the answer to preventing and curing disease. They are the cause! Even if drugs do not directly cause a disease, drugs cause the body to go completely out of balance, and they weaken the immune system so that diseases become more prevalent. People who get sick the most often are those who have taken the most drugs.

Let's back up just for a moment. Our conclusion is that all illness is caused by four things, one being the toxins in the body. When you have lots of toxins in the body, your body goes out of balance and your immune system is weakened. When this occurs your body cannot fight off any of the viruses or bacteria that you pick up, thus you get sick more often, with more severity, and for longer periods of time. You also have an environment that is very likely to produce illness and disease. I pointed out earlier that the number one cause of the high amounts of toxicity in the body is prescription and nonprescription drugs. The amount of sickness, the increased severity and increased duration, is in direct relation to the increase in prescription and nonprescription drug use.

However, illness and disease become complicated issues when you look at the hundreds of variables that are involved. I want to generally address what you should do, and then in the next chapter I'll give you some specifics depending on your current situation (keeping in mind that I am not a medical doctor). I am not giving medical advice, and I cannot cure any disease. As a matter of fact I believe that there is not a single person or substance on the planet that can cure a disease in the traditional, medically accepted sense . The only thing that happens is a health-care practitioner can do some things, using all-natural remedies, that will help your body heal itself. No one can "cure" a disease. Only your body can cure or heal itself. I do believe that there are certain things you can do to help your body heal itself better, or cure itself of illness, sickness and disease. I do believe that there are certain things you can do that can temporarily address some of the symptoms, ultimately allowing your body to regain its natural balanced state where illness and disease cannot exist.

So let me expand on this point. The "too much toxins in the body" comes down to this:
1. What goes in the body
2. What comes out of the body
3. Exercise
4. Rest
5. Thoughts
6. What you say

So let's go through the list and address some common misconceptions, and see what you should be doing if you want to virtually eliminate any disease. Maybe some of you reading this book have a disease or know someone who does. Maybe others are concerned about getting a disease and your major interest is doing the steps necessary to prevent that disease or illness or sickness. Keep in mind the natural state of the human body is vibrant health. If you have any type of discomfort, illness, disease or sickness you are out of balance. It is not the natural state that your body was designed for. Your body was designed to be healthy and never get sick. Think about that.

The six areas listed above have a direct relation to toxicity in the body. It is interesting to note that when you are toxic, your body becomes highly acidic. Your body pH should be alkaline. When your body pH is acidic you are susceptible to illness and disease. When your body pH is alkaline, you virtually can never get sick! Every single person who has cancer has a pH that is too acidic! Let me show you how each of the above six areas cause you to become too toxic, thus more acidic, and thus more prone to illness and disease.

Let's look at what we put into our bodies. We put things in our body through our mouth, our nose, our eyes, our ears, and through our skin. Let's talk about what goes into our mouths.

I think Jack LaLane said it best. Jack LaLane is an incredible human being. He is in his nineties; he is vibrant, healthy and strong. He doesn't get sick. He is a dynamic, healthy individual. Jack says: "If man made it, don't eat it." That's basically the bottom line. What you put in your mouth should be as close to as nature intended as possible. If man made it, you shouldn't eat it. Now, if you go out and eat an apple you may think, "Ah, this is an apple; man didn't make it, therefore I can eat it." Well, we have a problem. Virtually all fruits and vegetables are, in today's day and age, man-made.

Did you know that virtually all fruits and vegetables have been genetically modified by man to become more disease resistant? You have to understand that the food industry is just the same as the pharmaceutical industry—it's all about the money.

A food manufacturer, or for that matter a farmer, is in business and has to sell more of his product and produce that product at a lower cost to make more money. So what farmers do is say, "Hmm, how can I grow the most apples or the most carrots or the most onions on my field? How can I produce them in the shortest period of time, at the lowest cost, so I can sell them at the highest possible profit?" The answer is: Mess around with mother nature and change these natural fruits and vegetables with some man-made concoction that came out of a laboratory so that they grow bigger and faster totally against the natural course of things, and are resistant to disease. "That way I can make sure I have a full crop and I can sell more of my produce and make more money." So through genetic modification, your all-natural carrot is no longer all-natural, it is really a man-made product.

But it gets worse, because that farmer has to squeeze in and produce more carrots per acre in order to make more profit. He uses chemical fertilizers and chemical pesticides and herbicides that he sprays on these natural products like carrots. When you then take that natural piece of fruit or vegetable, it is loaded with toxic chemicals. It also has much less nutritional value than it would have fifty or sixty years ago. It has been said that you would need to eat up to five times the amount of food your grandparents did just to receive the same nutritional value. That's why if you are going to eat fruits and vegetables—or any food for that matter—which I highly encourage of course, they must be organically grown. Grains such as rice and wheat are the same. You need to be buying organically grown food.

In America, as opposed to many other countries, virtually everything you put in your mouth is toxic or contains toxins. Virtually everything made by man is toxic. This does not mean everything that is natural is not toxic. There are plants that are poisonous and if consumed could kill you. But, virtually everything made by man is a poison. Today, we put more toxins in our body than ever before.

Virtually everything that you put in your mouth has pesticides, herbicides, antibiotics, growth hormone, genetically altered material, or chemical food additives. Even when you eat an apple you are taking in all the deadly chemicals that were used in the growing and harvesting of that apple. All of our fruits, vegetables, grains, nuts and seeds are grown with highly poisonous chemical fertilizers, pesticides and herbicides. Many have been genetically modified, turning them into poisonous material. Even when you consume fresh fruits and vegetables, you are ingesting small amounts of poison.

The same conditions apply in the meat industry. Like farmers and other food producers, the meat industry needs to create a lot of product cheaply and quickly, and sell it for as high a profit as possible. To that end, the industry uses growth hormones to speed an animal's growth (contributing to the record levels of obesity and early puberty in our children); antibiotics to keep the animal healthy in unsanitary and inhumane, though economical, conditions (explaining the contemporary failure of antibiotics—the wonder drug of the 20th century—in humans); feeds the animals unnatural feed diets that not only pump more chemicals into the meat, but also so upset the animals' systems that they become out of balance, and diseased, and pass those imbalances and diseases along to those who consume the meat. Many meat products are also "aged." This means the dead animal flesh is allowed to rot, permitting deadly bacteria to grow. Remember, if it's not organic, if man has made it, don't eat it!

The same holds true with dairy products. Because of the use of drugs, growth hormones, pasteurization and homogenization, dairy products today are a major health concern unless they are organic, not pasteurized, and not homogenized. There are two main things to consider when looking at dairy products, one of which is pasteurization and the other homogenization. Pasteurization simply heats the dairy product to a very high temperature to kill any bacteria. The major problem is it also kills the living enzymes that are in the milk, making it much harder to digest in the body and thus making the milk a totally unnatural product. But more importantly, and more danger-ous, is homogenization.

Do you remember the milkman? We used to have the milkman come to the house to deliver milk. Why did we have to have a milk-man? Why couldn't we just buy our milk in the store? The reason is the milk went bad very quickly. It spoiled within just a few days.

The food industry said "We're losing money by not selling milk in our stores. We can't sell milk because it goes bad too quickly." So the industry came up with an incredible solution, a process called homog-enization. When the milkman delivered our milk, you may remember that the cream separated from the milk. You had to shake up the milk before you drank it. The process of homogenization actually spins the milk at a very high rate breaking down the clusters of molecules within the milk so that you don't have any separation of the cream and the milk. Therefore the milk will not spoil within a few days, it can actu-ally last a few weeks before going bad. Now that the food industry can have milk shipped to them, they can put it on the store shelf and they can sell it, there is no more need for the milkman. The problem is homogenized and pasteurized milk, and all dairy products, are unnatu-ral. The clusters of molecules are so small that when you ingest them they virtually scar your arteries. They clog up your digestive system, making it very difficult to digest food, which is one of the major causes of acid reflux disease, obesity, allergies, and constipation. And the scar-ring of the arteries causes the LDL cholesterol to attach itself to the artery, which is one of the major causes or arteriosclerosis, which is one of the major causes of heart disease. The bottom line is pasteurized and homogenized dairy products are unnatural; raw 100% organic dairy products are natural. Organic, raw, natural dairy products are natural. Remember Jack LaLane said, "If man made it, don't eat it."

When you eat fish you are only slightly better off. Many kinds of fish are "farmed," meaning that highly toxic feed and chemicals are used to make the fish grow unnaturally fast to unnaturally large sizes. Other poisonous chemicals are used in the processing of the fish before sale to consumers. When you consume this "man-made" fish, you are also taking in all the poisons and toxins that have been used in its production. Fish in the wild are much better. However, because of the massive dumping of poisonous chemicals into out lakes, rivers, and oceans, many wild fish have been found to have abnormally high levels of toxic chemicals in them as well. When you eat ANY food that has been produced by large food manufacturers, the fact is that you are 100 percent guaranteed to be ingesting highly toxic and poisonous man-made chemicals.

I know this sounds terrible. I know you are probably wondering what do I do; how do I eat? The good news is there are some very SIMPLE and EASY solutions which I will explain in a later chapter. I am trying to point out to you here that you are highly toxic, that you are constantly loading your body with toxins, which are one of the leading reasons you develop disease and are susceptible to viruses and bacteria. When I tell people they are toxic, most have a hard time believing that they are, but the fact is you are toxic right now. An independent study on women's breast milk showed a startling fact. In virtually 100 percent of the women tested it was shown that their breast milk contained high percentages of jet rocket fuel! That's right, jet rocket fuel in virtually 100 percent of the women's breast milk tested. How can this be? Just look up in the sky. When a plane flies overhead there is a "chem trail." The chemical residues fall down from the sky and we breathe them in. They also infect the rainwater and contaminate our water supplies, which are used in the irrigation of our food. The actual chemical poisons are in the food we eat!

Let me give you some other things to consider when it comes to understanding that what we put in our bodies makes us highly toxic and susceptible to disease. Keeping in mind in the next chapter I will be giving you some very simple solutions to solve this problem and the natural cures.

What else do we put in our body through our mouth? If it's in a box, if it's in a jar, if it's in a can, it's been processed by the food industry. The food industry, keep in mind, consists of publicly traded corporations that have one objective: to make more money and increase shareholder value. And the way they do that is to sell more food, and produce that food at a lower cost. Always remember that, it's always about the money.

The food industry puts tens of thousands of chemical ingredients into the food and, in many cases, they do not have to list those ingredients on the label. How do they get away with that? Through our lobbyist friends, and by paying off politicians and members of the Food and Drug Administration. It's all about the money.

So why is that bad?

The additives being put in the food are unnatural, toxic chemicals. They adversely affect the body; they suppress your immune system making it more susceptible to disease; they make you age quicker, and they turn your body from the natural alkaline pH state to the acid pH state, which means you can easily be prone to cancer, heart disease, diabetes, allergies, etc., etc., etc.

Not only are these chemical additives toxic, when they are put into the food the processing of the food strips away much of the nutritional value. As I mentioned before, if you were to eat a regular apple, it would have only one-fifth of the nutrition of an apple fifty years ago. But once the food is processed and put in a box or a can, you're going to have to eat 100 times more to get the same nutritional value; nutrition is virtually wiped out. So in addition to having the poisons put in your system from the chemicals not even listed on the label, the food you are getting has almost no nutritional value. Plus, these food additives actually block absorption of nutrients. Not only are you not getting enough nutrients from the food you are eating, but what little nutrients you are getting are being blocked and not absorbed. This means everyone has nutritional deficiencies causing imbalance, and a weakened immune system, which makes you both susceptible to viruses and bacteria, and causes your body to develop diseases and pain.

Why are these food additives put in the food anyway? Well it's very interesting. I was actually at a health spa where there was a gentleman who was a senior executive at a major food processing company, one of the largest producers of canned goods in the world. We were talking about the food additives and, yes, he admitted that there are thousands and thousands of chemical additives put into the food, and many of these additives are not listed on the label at all. I suggested that these food additives were dangerous to a person's health and were one of the reasons why people are so sick today. He assured me that these chemicals were totally safe, and that they were in such small amounts that they would have no effect whatsoever on the human body.

I then asked him a question. I said that, if they are totally safe, if I were to give you a glass of one of these chemicals, would you drink it? He stammered and stuttered and went back and forth a few times. I must have asked him the question ten times without getting an answer. Finally he said no, he wouldn't drink it because it could potentially be a problem. He finally admitted that the ingredients were, in fact, toxic. But, he repeated that, because they were in such small amounts, they had no effect at all on the human body. I then asked him the million dollar question. I said, "If you are putting such a small amount in, and these ingredients have no effect at all on the human body, then they must have no effect at all on the food. So why do you have to put them in the food?" Again, he couldn't answer the question. After grilling this man, he finally admitted that they in fact have a **major** effect. They preserve the food and give it taste. But I could tell that there was something else that these ingredients did that he wasn't telling. I then searched through my network of insiders, my network of whistleblowers, and here is what I discovered:

The food industry, just like the tobacco industry is hiding a dirty little secret. The food industry is putting ingredients in the food knowingly and on purpose, because these secret and in many cases illegal ingredients make a person hungry, make a person fat and make them addicted to the food! Now listen and pay attention, because what I am telling you is one of the biggest news stories of the century! The food industry, an industry of publicly traded companies, is all about the money.

Imagine this conversation actually happening: A junior executive walks into the boardroom and says "Gentlemen, in order for us to increase shareholder value and the price of our stock, we need to sell more food and produce this food at the lowest possible cost. And I have the solution. There are certain ingredients that, when mixed together and added to the food, actually make people hungrier. So that when they buy our product, they actually have to eat more of it, they can't stop eating it, it makes them hungrier. There are also certain chemicals we can put in the food that will actually make a person get fatter even if they don't eat that much; and the fatter they get, the hungrier they'll get, and they will have to consume more food and they will have to buy more food. And there are certain ingredients that we can put in the food that gets the people chemically addicted to the food, so that they have to have the food, they can't stop eating it; and if they stop eating it, they will get headaches, become nauseous, they'll be upset, depressed and anxious until they eat some more of the food, very similar to opium or cocaine."

Is this crazy? Well, remember Coca Cola? Coca Cola was colored sweetened water which had cocaine in it. Coca Cola was the name because Coca referred to the coca plant and Cola referred to the cola nut. The cola nut had the caffeine, and the coca or the cocaine got the person physically addicted. It was quietly removed back in the 1920s, without much fanfare or media exposure.

Right now as you are reading this, the food industry—like every other industry—has to increase profits, and the only way they can do so is to sell you more food. Why is it that Americans are the fattest people on the planet? Remember, it's all about the money.

Oh, there are a couple of other scary things as well. Many of the ingredients they put in the food make you depressed, which is really good for the drug companies because if you are depressed, you have to go to the drug companies to handle your depression. Interestingly enough, some of the food additives which are put in the food to make you depressed are manufactured by the same companies that sell you the antidepressant drugs. It's a fantastic money-making business folks. Remember, it's all about the money.

There is another reason why chemical additives and the processing of food are bad. Food must have nutritional value for it to be used by the body, but food also has a "vibration." Food actually has measurable "life force energy." When food is chemically altered, or genetically altered, or highly processed, or contains chemical additives the energetic vibration or "life force energy" of the food is dramatically altered. At the back of the book make sure you read my article on microwaved food. Microwaving of food radically changes the energetic structure of the food. When the "vibration" of food or "life force energy" of food is radically altered by chemical additives, processing, or genetic engineering, consuming and eating that food actually causes the body to go out of balance and CAUSES disease to develop. Yes, you are reading this right. From an energetic standpoint eating a genetically altered apple that has been sprayed with pesticides actually can give you cancer, as well as dozens of other diseases!

Without giving a physics lesson, when you eat anything you are getting the energy from that thing. How do we know this is true? Well, think about it. You take a pot and you put soil in it. You put in ten pounds of soil, and you put in one little tiny seed, and every day you add some water, and at the end of a year you have this big plant. Well, take the plant out, shake off the soil from the roots and weigh the soil. Guess what? You still have ten pounds of soil. The only thing you added was some water. If you were to measure the water, you may have added about five pounds of water. Theoretically, the plant should weigh no more than five pounds if it grabbed 100 percent of the water. But the plant weighs fifty pounds. Wow! What happened? How did fifty pounds of mass and matter magically appear? It didn't eat the soil, the ten pounds of soil is still there, and there were only five pounds of water added. How did that plant appear out of virtually nothing? This is a very important point; think about it again. The plant, like all living things, was virtually created out of "energy." Energy is "invisible matter.'

Human beings are the same. If you take a little baby, and you weigh every bit of food that goes in and then subtract all the excretions that come out through the urine, the stool, and sweating through the skin, you would see that whatever goes in comes out. If tens pounds of food and water are put in, guess what? Ten pounds of stuff comes out, but the little baby grows from fifteen pounds to fifty pounds to 150 pounds. But everything that goes in, all the liquid and everything we eat, comes out. How does that happen? Well guess what? Science really can't give you an answer. The answer is that we get the energy ·from the food and from sunlight and from air; and that's how matter is manifested—it's the energy.

So if we go through everything that we put in our mouth, whatever we eat and whatever we drink, ask yourself: is it as nature intended, or has it been screwed up by some greedy individual who doesn't care about your health, who doesn't care if you get sick, who doesn't care if you're depressed, or if you get fat? The only thing they care about is making money. Remember, it's always all about the money.

So what do we eat and drink? Well, ideally you want to eat all-natural things, fruits and vegetables, and get them organic. When you cook them it destroys some of the living enzymes, so raw is better than cooked. Should you become a vegetarian? I don't know if you should be a vegetarian or not. Everyone is a little different. What works for one person may work slightly better or worse for someone else. I can tell you this. I believe that if you add or increase the amount of raw fruits and vegetables in your diet, you'll be better off.

Here's the other big problem. You can't look at food labels, you have to read the ingredients. Because if the label says all-natural, it's usually a big lie. Why? The food industry has lobbied the politicians to allow certain totally man-made ingredients to be classified as all-natural. Keep in mind that there are over 15,000 ingredients that don't even have to be put on the label. So if you see something that says "all-natural," it just means that the government has allowed them to put that on so they can sell more of the food. Ideally, if it's in a box or can, don't even eat it. Some people go into "health food stores" and assume that everything that is in the health food store is good for them. It's not, you have to read labels; and ideally, if it's in a box, if it's in a bottle or jar, don't consume it.

Which leads me to restaurants. The big question is: What can I eat in restaurants? The answer: nothing!

You may say, "Well, I can't live like that." I know it is unrealistic for you to completely change what you have been doing your whole life. But realistically, there is nothing in a restaurant that can be classified as safe. Yes, I eat at restaurants. Why? Because I'm not fanatical, and I am not asking you to be fanatical. Now I do know some people who are fanatical. They eat nothing but raw organic food, and these people are absolutely amazing physical specimens. However, I live in the real world, and so do you. Just do the best you can. Realistically, stay away from anything in the fast-food restaurant. They are categorically the worst.

Let me say this again because it is so important. There are over 15,000 toxic chemicals that are allowed to be added to food without being listed on the label. Every year, the food industry puts a higher percentage of toxic chemicals in our food. These chemicals are produced in secret laboratories where the security is higher than Fort Knox! When asked why these chemicals are put into the food, the answers are vague and ambiguous. However, from information I have received from "insiders," I can now blow the whistle on the real reasons these chemicals are being added to our food without our knowledge. Remember, it always goes back to "it's all about the money."

Remember, as I've said before, food companies have one goal: to make more money. Again, as I've said before, the only way they can make more money is to produce the food the cheapest way possible, sell it at the highest price possible, and sell more and more food. The scientists who work in these secret laboratories are developing chemicals and combinations of chemicals that are added to our food and not put on the label. This is legal because the food industry, through the lobbyists' system of legal bribery, has gotten Congress to pass certain legislation allowing this to occur. These secret poisonous chemicals are specifically designed to do the following things:

- **Preserve the food.** In order to produce food as cheaply as possible, it is sometimes required that chemicals be added to the food so that it will not spoil even after years of just sitting around. We have all heard the story of the thirty-year-old Twinkie that looked and tasted the same as it did the day it was manufactured.

- **Taste and texture.** Much of today's food is produced in such an unnatural way that is has very little nutritional value and very little taste. Chemicals must be added to make the food taste like it is supposed to taste. A major hamburger chain adds a chemical to its hamburgers to make them taste like a hamburger!

- **To make you hungry!** You are reading this right. The food industry knows that it must sell MORE food to make more money. If it can add a chemical that actually makes you hungrier, you will eat more food and they will make more money!

- **To make you fatter.** Fat people eat more food. Chemicals are being added to our food that actually make us gain weight. The more fat people there are, the more profits there are for the food industry. The most shocking part of this is one such chemical put in most "diet food." How sad that an unknowing consumer buys some food that has the word "diet" on it in the hopes of losing some weight, when actually eating the food causes them to gain weight.

- **To get the person addicted to the product!** Food manufacturers are knowingly putting chemicals into the food that cause the consumer to become physically addicted to it. We know that drugs, which are simply chemicals, can be incredibly physically and emotionally addictive. This practice is not new. In the book *The Real Thing: The Truth and Power at the Coca Cola Company*, the story of how cocaine was an important ingredient in Coca-Cola is exposed. One of the main reasons cocaine was such an important ingredient was that the consumer unknowingly became addicted to Coca-Cola. Having a person addicted to your product is good for your profits, but bad for the poor bastard who is addicted.

- **To give you disease.** As outrageous as it seems, it appears that insiders know that certain "food additives" cause specific diseases. If you knew that huge numbers of people would be coming down with a certain disease in the next five or ten years, you could invest in drug companies that are producing drugs that will be prescribed for this "new disease." When I talk about the greed of the people involved, 99 percent of those reading this have no comprehension of just how the love of money has taken almost absolute control over these people's actions, ethics, and morals. Think about Howard Hughes. He was one of the richest men in the world, if not the richest. Yet, on his death bed, up until the hour he died, he was still trying to make more money!

Obviously, what I am saying here is my opinion and my conclusions. It is vehemently denied by the food industry and the FDA, but think about the same type of denials for years by the tobacco industry. I believe time will prove me absolutely correct.

The other important issue relating to the amounts of these chemicals is that chemicals ingested in the body do not necessarily leave the body. It appears that chemical fertilizers, pesticides, herbicides, growth hormone, nonprescription and prescription drugs, and food additives such as artificial sweeteners, stay in the body and lodge in the fatty tissues. Since our brain is mostly fat, a large percentage of these chemicals accumulate there over the years. This is believed to be one of the main reasons that there is such a massive increase in depression, stress and anxiety, and learning disabilities like attention deficit disorder.

The bottom line is anything you eat or drink that has been genetically modified, processed by a large publicly traded food manufacturer, produced with herbicides, pesticides, and chemical fertilizers, or has chemical additives in it, "stresses" our body. When our body is "stressed" two things occur:

1. It suppresses your immune system, making you more susceptible to disease.

2. It can turn your body from the natural alkaline pH state, in which disease and illness and sickness cannot survive, to an acidic state in which diseases like cancer, heart disease and diabetes can thrive.

You have to ask yourself a question when you put something in your mouth: Could this have been made 100 years ago? If it couldn't, don't eat it. The reason it is being processed the way it is, is because somebody is making money. Remember, it's always about the money.

You see, the food industry is very, very persuasive. They try to make you believe that science is better than nature. Science is not better than nature. Science is only better for the food manufacturer, because it allows him to make more money. A good example of this is margarine. Margarine is produced by hydrogenating oil. What does that mean? It means taking oil and spinning it until it becomes a solid. The problem with hydrogenated oil is that it scars the arteries and causes heart disease. It's classified now as a trans fat, and finally we are hearing a little bit about the dangers of trans fats. We are finally being told that, oops! we've been saying to you that margarine is much better for you than butter; I guess we were wrong. I guess the man-made product is doing all types of damage to your health and we just didn't know about it. Or maybe they did know about it but, were making too much money and just decided not to tell anybody.

We have all-natural sugar, and then we have artificial sweeteners like saccharine, aspartame, and sucralose. You are led to believe that the chemical man-made sweeteners are so much better for your health than all-natural sugar. Nothing could be further from the truth. The artificial sweeteners are one of the major reasons that you are fat. They also cause depression. There was a great book written about this, *Exitotoxins—The Taste That Kills,* and another one called *Aspartame (NutraSweet®)—Is It Safe?* If it's made by man, don't eat it! Don't be tricked by all the advertising. Remember, it's all about the money.

The food industry has to convince you that you have to buy their chemically produced, man-made food stuffs, and that it's better than something all-natural. It's a lie! They are only trying to persuade you so they can make more money.

The processing of food causes another problem. Certain processing techniques change a natural food into an unnatural toxin. Let's go back to the dairy industry. How would you define milk? We hear a lot about milk. The dairy association obviously wants you to drink more milk. Remember, they don't care about you, they only care about the profits of its members that it represents, which in this case is all the people in the dairy industry. There have been thousands of studies on milk. Some say milk is good, others say milk is bad. Is there only one kind of milk? What kind of milk was used in the studies? If I were to tell you "milk" is good for you, do you think milk is milk is milk? There are many definitions and many kinds of milk. For example:

Is it cow's milk or goat's milk? Is the animal giving the milk injected with growth hormone and antibiotics? Is the animal giving the milk eating a natural diet of grass, or a man-made diet of genetically altered corn, ground up dead animals and other chemically produced material designed to increase milk production? Is the cow giving the milk allowed to wander and walk in the way nature intended, or is the animal confined to a pen and not allowed to move for its entire life? Has the animal been genetically modified and bred specifically for increased milk production and profits, or is it a natural animal bred according to nature? Is the animal sick and diseased, or healthy? Is the animal milked by a machine, causing blood and pus to be in the milk, or milked in a natural way without blood and pus? Is the milk heated to 220 degrees for thirty minutes, killing off all the natural living enzymes (pasteurization), or is the milk immediately put into cold storage? Is the milk immediately put in a glass bottle and delivered to your door by the milkman within four hours after coming out of the animal, or is the milk processed by adding chemicals to it, which are not listed on the label, and homogenized?

You see, if I say cow's milk or goat's milk is good for you, I mean the all-natural, raw, organic non-man-made version. Once the food industry gets involved and starts messing around so that they can make more money, everything gets screwed up and the new man-made unnatural products become toxic to the body. If it's made by man, don't eat it. Remember, science is not better than nature except when it comes to making money.

Another common food processing technique is *irradiation*. This is when foods such as fruits, vegetables, grains, meat, poultry and fish are zapped with radioactive beams of energy designed to kill any harmful bacteria, so you won't get violently sick or die when you eat it. This has been needed because the food processing system is producing food that has a higher chance of having deadly pathogens, therefore causing sickness or death. Irradiation changes the energetic frequency of the food, giving the food a frequency that is no longer life sustaining, but rather toxic to the body. This has been shown with Kirlian photography. If you take an apple and take a picture of it with Kirlian photography, you see a very beautiful pattern of energy surrounding the apple. If the apple is zapped with a microwave and a second Kirlian photograph is taken, you see the energy pattern around the apple has radically changed. The pattern is now jagged, rough, and erratic. The energy pattern is more like arsenic, a deadly poison. So, the processing of food changes food from a healthy, natural, life-sustaining fuel, to an unnatural man-made toxic poison.

If you read the labels of everything you put in your mouth, you would see the name of various chemicals. All the chemicals listed are dangerous man-made chemicals. They are poisons. If you were to take any of those chemicals and ingest a large amount at one time, you would probably die. Therefore they are in fact poisons. Think about the 15,000 chemicals that are in our food that do not have to be listed on the label. The point I am trying to make here is give you an understanding of why you get sick. Remember, you get sick because you either catch something or you develop something. Catching something is not a problem because your body is designed to fight off all infection and disease. Your body has the ability to kill viruses and bacteria. Your body does this when it is healthy and is in a balanced state; but when your body is loaded with toxins and your immune system is suppressed because of lack of nutrition or energetic frequency imbalances, you become susceptible to viruses and bacteria. You develop diseases because toxins, nutritional deficiencies, or energetic imbalances allow disease to develop in the genetically weak areas of your system. The point is we need to be aware that what we put in our bodies is actually giving us and causing us disease. It is important to understand why we have disease and illness, why we are sick, and what the causes are for us to totally understand how to cure these diseases. Most people are brainwashed into wanting a magic pill that will cure their disease. If you totally understand and comprehend why you are sick and why you get disease and why you develop illness, then you will understand the "natural cures" much more easily. As I mentioned earlier, this may sound overwhelming. Just go with the flow. The good news is I do have a SIMPLE and EASY solution. As I mentioned, there are ways where you can live a normal life and be disease free. The good news is you don't have to be a health fanatic to cure your illness and disease and live a life of health and vitality.

● ● ●

Now let's talk about what else you put in your mouth, primarily what you drink. There are two problems here. The first one is most people don't drink enough water, and the second one is the water you drink is incredibly toxic. All tap water has chemicals put in it, primarily chlorine and fluoride. The level of toxicity of both chlorine and fluoride is incredible. Drinking chlorinated water, which is virtually all tap water, causes scarring of the arteries. When the arteries are scarred, the LDL cholesterol attaches itself to the artery causing arteriosclerosis.

Most people are dehydrated, which causes all types of medical problems including pain, stiffness, arthritis, asthma, allergies and other medical issues. Dehydration means the cells just simply don't have enough fluid. It can affect your energy and your sleep, but the major thing that it has an effect on is the ability to get toxins and waste matter out of the body and out of cells. Cells can live forever in a laboratory, so long as the fluid in which the cell is living is constantly cleaned and changed. If you take a cell and basically put in fluid, the cell excretes waste matter and toxins. As long as you clean that environment and get rid of the waste matter and toxins, the cell never seems to age, and that's pretty staggering! That's why cleansing and getting the toxins out of your system is so important. It's also why putting the least amount of toxins in your body is so important.

The debate is on about the best type of water. The basic types of water you have in your environment are tap water, purified water, spring water and distilled water.

Tap water is absolutely the worst kind of water in the world because virtually all tap water is contaminated. All tap water has chlorine in it, and most tap water has fluoride in it. Fluoride is one of the most toxic chemicals in the world. It is a product that comes from the manufacture of superphosphic fertilizers, and is so toxic it can't be dumped anywhere. Through lobbying, fluoride was then sold to municipalities and dumped in our water supplies under the disguise of being good for our teeth. It's a big lie and nothing could be further from the truth. Fluoride is toxic and dangerous, and should not be consumed. Fluoride adversely affects virtually every organ in the body, primarily your thyroid gland. It can be seen that the areas in America that have the most fluoride in the water have the highest obesity rates because people's metabolisms go down. Fluoride makes you depressed and causes all types of physical problems.

Certainly spring water is better than tap water. But certain agencies and interest groups publish misleading stories about bottled water not being any better than tap water because the bacteria count in bottled water is higher than that in tap water. These stories point out that there is no bacteria in tap water because of the chlorine. The problem is, chlorine kills living organisms. We too are living organisms. Chlorine is a poison, and it is put into the water supply to kill living organisms. When we drink it, we're drinking poison. Yes, we are taking it in small amounts, but it's still a highly poisonous chemical and should not be consumed. There is nothing wrong with bacteria. We get exposed to bacteria every single day. That's how our immune systems get strengthened, that's how we live. Our body is exposed to bacteria and germs and viruses and we have natural immunities to those things. The more we are exposed to them the better off our systems are.

What kind of water do I drink? I have a reverse osmosis unit in my house. I have the water in my entire house filtered. I also have a distiller which, in addition to steam distillation, also gets rid of the energetic memory attached to the water. I do drink bottled water when I travel. I do drink bottled water that is filtered or purified. I drink bottled spring water.

Let me digress here for a moment. People are always talking about cholesterol, cholesterol, cholesterol. It's a great business for the drug companies. They get you to believe you need to lower your cholesterol. But cholesterol is not the cause of heart disease. There are people with 600 cholesterol counts that have absolutely no arteriosclerosis, no blockages and no heart disease. And there are people with cholesterol counts of 100 who have massive blockages and are dropping dead from heart attacks and need triple bypass surgeries. The amount of cholesterol in your blood is not the problem. The problem only occurs when the cholesterol attaches itself to the artery, thus clogging the artery and restricting the blood flow. When it's restricted you need bypass surgery, thus says the medical community. There are all-natural alternatives to bypass surgery as well, which are more effective, get to the root cause instead of just handling the symptom. The question, however, really is not how much cholesterol you have, but what causes the cholesterol to attach itself to the artery? The cholesterol will only attach itself to the artery when the artery is damaged. If the artery is not damaged the cholesterol just goes through the blood without any problem whatsoever, and you will never have heart disease no matter what your cholesterol count is. So the question is, what causes damage to the artery?

Primarily, there are three things that cause the artery to get scarred. And its when the artery is scarred that the cholesterol begins the attaching process, and that's how you get arteriosclerosis and heart disease.

1. **Chlorinated water.** Chlorine in the water that you drink and shower and bathe in or swim in causes massive scarring of the arteries, which in turn means, no matter how much cholesterol you have or don't have, whatever cholesterol is there will attach itself and begin the clogging process.

2. **Hydrogenated oils or trans fats.** As you look at virtually 90 percent of the food produced in boxes, if you were to actually read the label you'd see the words "hydrogenated oil" or "partially hydrogenated oil." These are trans fats. Margarine, for example, is hydrogenated oil. These trans fats scar the arteries, causing heart disease and arteriosclerosis.

3. **Homogenized dairy products.** People say, "Well I drink low fat milk or low fat yogurt." The fat has nothing to do with it. You are being scammed, you are being lied to, you are being misled. It's not the fat that is the problem. Keep in mind that when they make a low fat product, it's not a natural product, it's man-made. When dairy products are homogenized it turns the dairy products into a lethal man-made product that causes scaring of the arteries. Homogenized dairy products, whether they are yogurt, milk, or cheese, are all deadly. It is not the fat that is the problem in dairy, it's the homogenization process.

These are the three major causes of arteriosclerosis.

Now let's get back to water. The reason I brought up the whole issue about cholesterol and arteriosclerosis is that tap water has chlorine in it. One reason why heart disease is so prevalent today is because people drink tap water, bathe in tap water, shower in tap water, or swim in chlorinated pools. As I mentioned above, this is one of the major causes of scaring of the arteries which lead to clogged arteries, arteriosclerosis, and heart disease. But it's not just the water. Chlorine is used in the processing of many fruits and vegetables. It is also put in the water that is used in the irrigation of fruits and vegetables. The chlorine is a major problem. Again, I'm pointing this out to you just so you can see how all encompassing the problem is. So consider this: our water supply is loaded with toxins. These toxins are getting into our bodies by:

- Drinking the water
- Eating or drinking anything made with water

- Eating any food that was grown with the water
- Eating any meat, poultry, fish or dairy where the animal drank water
- Showering, bathing or swimming in water

Since our skin is the largest organ in the body, it has been reported that we absorb more toxins by taking one shower than by drinking five glasses of water. In a shower, not only is the water with all the toxins being absorbed through the skin, many of the most volatile and dangerous toxins are turned into a gas created by the steam. These toxic fumes in your shower are then inhaled. A shower is practically a gas chamber filled with poisonous gas chemicals. Steam rooms, hot tubs and swimming pools are places where you will absorb the highest levels of toxins. The paradox is we think of these particular areas as being the healthiest.

The poisoned water supply is another significant factor relating to how toxins get into our body. By now it won't surprise you to learn how we are being misled by the news media and government agencies about the purity and safety of our water supply. Remember that chlorine and fluoride are the two main poisons that are in our water supply and are the reason our water is so unhealthy. Yet, the government and news media rates the quality of our water based on the amount of chlorine and fluoride in it! The more chlorine and fluoride in the water the healthier it is, claims the government! They even say that tap water is better than spring water because tap water has chlorine and fluoride in it and spring water does not. This is yet another way you are being lied to, deceived and brainwashed into thinking that chemicals are better than something in a natural state.

Let's talk about other things you put in your body through your mouth via what you drink: coffee, tea, sodas, and alcohol. Remember the rule: If it's man made, don't put it in your body.

What about coffee? Well let's start with pure, clean water—not tap water. Let's take a coffee bean that has been organically grown and simply ground up. If it's organic there are no chemicals, no herbicides, no pesticides and no chemicals used in the processing. It seems pretty reasonable in moderation. It appears to be okay. Teas are the same, real organic tea. I'm talking tea leaves, not tea bags, which tea drinkers will say is nothing but flavored water when you make it.

What about carbonated sodas? I very rarely, if ever, drink them. I would never in a million years drink a diet soda because the chemical sweeteners, in my opinion, are some of the most toxic things you could put in your body. On occasion I will drink a Coca Cola from a bottle, not a can. The problem, however, with virtually all carbonated beverages is they block calcium absorption. Calcium is one of the most important building blocks of nutrition.

What about alcohol? If you come to my house I have an array of liqueurs, spirits, wine and beer primarily for guests. What's the ideal scene? Drink water and nothing else. Tea can be very therapeutic, as well as wine. Try to drink mostly pure water, then some tea, then wine, then other alcohol and everything else rarely if ever.

Ah! What about juices? I would never buy juice in bottle, a can, or a carton. If man made it, don't put it in your body. Why? If you've ever gone to see how these products are made, you would see why. People think juice is juice is juice. It's simply not true! I happen to have a juice machine in my house. I also have in my back yard some fruit trees. So when I want some juice, I usually walk out, pick some oranges or grapefruits, walk in, peel them and juice them. And I get delicious, organic, pure juice.

Well how is that different from juice you buy at the store? A couple of major differences:

Remember, it's all about the money. The people who sell these products are trying to sell more product at a lower cost. How do they do that? Well, first and foremost let's take orange juice. What will happen is they'll find the worst oranges in the world that they couldn't sell, and that's what they make their juice from. Keep in mind that these oranges have been produced in the "conventional" way, with chemical fertilizers, pesticides, herbicides and genetic engineering. That's conventional? No! That's weird, that's bizarre, that's wrong!

They then pick the fruit that can't be sold, and that's what they make the juice from. The problem is that in the processing of the juice in the plants, bacteria and mold can easily develop, contaminating the product. So by law the product has to be pasteurized, which means the product has to be heated to 220 degrees for thirty minutes to kill any amount of bacteria so you don't get sick as you drink it. This kills all the living natural enzymes and destroys the natural energy surrounding that natural fruit. It is then filtered, and in many cases sugar, which is not listed on the label, is added to make the product sweeter. If sugar is not added, the filtering process and the pasteurization process make the product much sweeter. So you are getting a product that is much, much sweeter than in nature. The best example of this is filtered apple juice. When you look at apple juice that is super clear, it is so much sweeter than natural apple juice that I make at my house on my juicing machine. It has no living enzymes, and it's virtually a massive sugar high. It's just a man-made product under the disguise of a natural, healthy product. It's not healthy; it's man made, it's tainted with chemicals and toxins, and because of the processing is just not healthy. Juice is good, but only if you make it in your home with organic fruits and vegetables, and drink your juice right away. Once you have juiced the product and air gets to it, it begins to oxidize and lose its nutritional value. So if you have a juice machine in your house, you get organic fruits and vegetables, you make juice and you drink it.

But why should you drink juice anyway? That's not natural; 100 years ago we didn't have juice machines. That's a very, very good question. The answer is this: Even if you buy organic fruits and vegetables today, because over the years the soil has been depleted of much of its nutritional value and energy, today's fruits and vegetables don't have the energy or the nutritional value that they did 100 years ago. Even organic fruits and vegetables have less than they did 100 years ago. So a good alternative is to juice them. The nutritional value and the life force energy is in the juice. The fiber in the fruits and vegetables is still needed for other bodily functions such as the elimination through the colon, so you still need to eat the whole fruit and vegetable. But you can get the nutritional value through the juice. It is much better than taking vitamin and mineral tablets if you're going to juice.

So to summarize: If it's made by man, don't put it in your body.

How toxins get in your body through your skin

The skin is the largest organ in the body. Anything put on the skin is absorbed and gets into the body. Even science admits this to be true. Drugs are administered topically on the skin. These drugs wind up in the bloodstream within minutes. Everything you put on your skin gets into your bloodstream. Our friends at the FDA have determined that many chemicals are for external use only. They are poisonous and cannot be taken internally because they can kill you. But remember, whatever you put on your skin winds up in your body. Do you understand the problem here? We put things on our skin such as lotions, moisturizers, sun screens, cosmetics, soap, shampoo etc. Virtually every one of these things contains ingredients that even the FDA says are so poisonous and so deadly that they cannot be taken internally. Yet, they are allowed to be put on your skin. The FDA knows that these poisons get into your body via the skin, yet because of the tremendous pressure by lobbyists and politicians, the manufacturers are allowed to put these dangerous ingredients in their products. A Swiss study concluded that five of the most common ingredients in sun screens cause cancer. It is no wonder why the more sun screen you use, the higher the chance that you will get skin cancer. The sun does not cause skin cancer, the sun screens do! Underarm deodorants and antiperspirants contain deadly chemicals that many people believe to be a major cause of breast cancer in women.

If you can't eat it, do not put it on your skin!

We absorb many toxins through our nose

These are primarily the poisons that are in the air. Where you live and work determines the amount of pollutants in the air. Most major cities contend that the air is filled with poisonous chemicals. We breathe every second, therefore we are absorbing toxins every second. However, there are many toxins in the air that most people are not aware of. Air fresheners are one of the worst. Talk about misleading advertising! How in the world can they claim that these products "freshen" the air? These products contain deadly, poisonous chemicals. Would you consider opening the can and drinking the air freshener? Read the label, they even tell you how poisonous the ingredients are! These products eliminate odors by having you spray a deadly poison in the air. This poison kills all of the receptors in the nose so that you cannot smell the offending odor any more. They don't eliminate odors, they eliminate your ability to smell them!

Other toxins include mold, dust, pollens, and the fumes emitted from carpeting, glue, paint, mattresses, the soaps used in the cleaning of sheets and clothing, and air conditioning units. Think about the term "air conditioning." How can putting chemicals in the air be called "conditioning" the air? Air conditioning units cool the air, but load the air with contaminants. The most important nutrient to the body is oxygen. A man can live for weeks without food, days without water, but only a few minutes without air. Any aroma that you smell means something is going into your body. Even if you lived on a farm, the smell of manure means particles of manure are entering your body.

In today's world, the fact is that we are inhaling toxins on a regular basis. It is virtually impossible to eliminate them. However, it is entirely possible to dramatically reduce the amount of toxins you are inhaling. It's also interesting to note that what you inhale has a very immediate and profound effect on such things as appetite, digestion, moods, depression, anxiety, irritability, and sleep. Reducing the toxins that you breathe can have a very profound and dramatic impact upon your health.

The eyes

Toxins get in through the eyes in a similar fashion to the skin. The eyes also, in addition to the skin, are the entry point of solar energy from the sun. The sun is not a toxin, as you are being led to believe. The lack of sun causes deficiencies in the body, leading to imbalances and disease. The major form of toxins that come in through the eyes are images that cause bad emotions. Today there are more violent images on television, in the movies, in newspapers and magazines, video games, and books than ever before. Repeated exposure to negative, ugly, disturbing images causes the body to become acidic. Today, people are being exposed to over one thousand times the amount of negative images than they were just twenty years ago; and over ten-thousand times the amount of negative images compared to seventy-five years ago.

The ears

Toxins get into your body through the ears, obviously, by anything you put in your ears as well as the sounds you hear. Sounds are vibrations and frequencies. Certain vibrations and frequencies sustain and cause life to grow. Certain vibrations and frequencies can cause degeneration and death. Certain music has been known to cause plants to grow at a faster rate, to be healthier and stronger. Other music has been shown to make plants wither and die. Think of all the sounds you are being exposed to that may have a negative effect on your physiology:

- The low hum of an air conditioner
- The computer running
- The alarm clock
- Certain kinds of "music"
- The washing machine, dryer, dish washer
- Your car engine
- Honking horns

If we stop for a moment and really listen to all the sounds that surround us, we find the majority are unnatural man-made frequencies. These frequencies go in through the ear and cause every cell in the body to be affected. If the frequency of the sound is not in tune with what nature intended, it can throw off the natural balance of the body. The simplest proof of this theory is how certain music, certain sounds and certain frequencies, cause a plant to either die or thrive. Think of the opera singer who hits a high note and shatters a crystal glass. That is how powerful vibrations, sounds, and frequencies are. Sounds can affect the body in such a powerful way that even the U.S. military uses sound as a weapon that induces serious physiological and psychological damage.

The electromagnetic field around the body

Okay, up until this point I've tried to explain in very broad strokes that you are in fact loading your body with toxins. These toxins come into the body via the mouth, the nose, the eyes, the ears, and the skin. I could give example, after example, after example of all the toxins that are in food, the water, and all the things you put on your skin. I've just touched on how toxins get in through the eyes and through the ears. I am not trying to tell you every aspect and every way in which toxins get into the body. The point I'm trying to make is to get you to at least consider the fact that you are in fact loading your body with toxins and they do come in through these various channels. This is very important. Most people I talk to do not understand or comprehend the amount of toxicity that gets into the body. When we talk about health, nutrition, disease and illness, most people only think about drugs and surgery. More "aware" people consider food. However, when people consider food they only think of calories, fats, carbohydrates, or proteins. No one ever really talks about the processing of food and the chemicals put in the food. Very few people even consider all the chemicals and toxins that get in through the skin. Very few people consider the physiological affects of what comes in through the eyes in the form of negative images on television. Almost no one considers the negative physiological affects that sound vibrations have on the body that come in through the ears. Very few people consider the toxins that are in the air that we breathe that come in through the nose. Why are we sick? The answer is, first and foremost, the massive amount of toxins that are getting into your body. These toxins are one of the major reasons why illness is so rampant today. Unless these toxins are addressed, you will continue to get sick and you will be unable to cure yourself permanently of any illness and disease you may have.

Now I want to touch on a very important element of health. This is an area that virtually no one discusses when talking about the cure and prevention of disease and illness. However, later in this book when I give you the absolute natural "cure" for virtually all diseases you will see that this is one of the fundamental basic concepts that you must understand if you want to cure your disease. As I mentioned previously, many of these things that I'm talking about, and the picture that I'm trying to paint for you, may seem overwhelming and insurmountable in terms of being able to solve or address all these issues. Please do not be dismayed at this point. I am trying to paint a picture for you so that you understand in general terms and become aware of all the toxins that are coming into your body, and all the various reasons why illness and sickness develop in the body. As I mentioned before, once you at least get a general grasp of this concept you will understand better how the cures work.

So let me talk about briefly here the very important area of the cause of disease and illness that no one ever talks about. The area is electromagnetic fields around the body. Sometimes this is called vibrational fields or energetic fields.

Medical science does not accept the notion that there is an electromagnetic field surrounding the body. However, we use electromagnetic energy, and science does admit that electromagnetic energy exists. Medical science claims there is no "scientific evidence" which proves that electromagnetic energy has any effect on the health or lack of health in the body. Remember that science has stated throughout history things that were not proven that have been later proven to be true. Science has proclaimed that there was "no scientific evidence" proving the earth was round; or that the earth revolved around the sun; or that nutrition had any effect on health; or that cigarettes were addictive. Science stated that anyone believing those things were heretics. The same is true now in relation to electromagnetic energy. Everything on this planet is made up of the same thing: atoms. All atoms resonate or vibrate at different frequencies. All atoms are made up of electrons, protons, and neutrons. Science admits that "energy" is what holds the electron in orbit around the nucleus. Science also admits that electrons, neutrons, and protons are made up of energy. Science admits that this energy cannot be seen with the human eye or any accepted scientific equipment. Science also admits that it does not fully understand, and only theorizes about, these subatomic particles, or "energy." Yet, we see the effects of this "energy" all around us. Science cannot see or explain how magnets work. However, you can easily see the effects of the magnetic field. Science cannot explain how a satellite can beam electromagnetic energy that can pass through solid steel, be picked up by a radio transmitter, and magically turn into music. Think about it. If a satellite in the sky beams down electromagnetic energy twenty-four hours a day, seven days a week, and this energy is invisible, cannot be detected, yet has the ability to pass through almost any material, and contains so much information that a "receiver" converts it into the music of an orchestra or images on a TV screen, isn't it possible that this energy is also hitting and passing through our bodies? Is it possible that this unnatural energy could have a negative impact on our bodies and our health? Something to think about. Awareness of electromagnetic energy is relatively new. It's really only been around in the last seventy-five years or so. Here are a few examples of the sources of unnatural electromagnetic energy that is bombarding our bodies every day:

- *Satellites.* There are dozens of satellites beaming down unnatural electromagnetic energy twenty-four hours a day, seven days a week.

- *Radar.* Radar stations for national defense and weather emit harmful electromagnetic energy twenty-four hours a day, seven days a week. It's interesting to note that many people believe that when these radar stations are put on maximum power during times of heightened security, a higher percentage of people feel ill, fatigued, and depressed. There is also the suggestion that those living close to these powerful radar towers have a higher chance of getting cancer, depression, and fatigue.

- *Cell phone towers.* These towers push out powerful energy waves on a consistent basis.

- *Cell phones.* When your cell phone is turned on it produces powerful unnatural electromagnetic energy, as well as drawing in all the cell phone tower energy. If the cell phone is within just a few feet of you, you are being affected.

- *High tension power lines.* These lines produce powerful amounts of negative energy affecting all living things in a large area around them.

- *Electric wiring.* Wiring encompasses our homes, our offices, our cars, any electronic device we carry, and is even buried under sidewalks and streets.

- *Computers, televisions and radios.* When these units are turned on, they emit large amounts of negative electromagnetic energy.

- *Fluorescent lights.* It is common knowledge that fluorescent lighting is an unnatural light source and can cause headaches, fatigue, and a weakening of the immune system. They also emit large doses of negative electromagnetic energy.

- *Microwave ovens.* The microwaves generated in these devices change the electromagnetic structure of whatever is in the oven into an unnatural, negative, life draining product. These devices also can leak the energy, adversely affecting those around it.

- *Other people.* Every person emits electromagnetic energy. A person's thoughts are also electromagnetic energy. The human body, especially the brain, is actually a very powerful transmitter and receiver of electromagnetic energy. This is why you feel good around some people and bad around others. Have you ever noticed that when certain people walk into a room, you can "sense" their presence? There are methods, which have not been accepted by the scientific community, which show the electromagnetic field around people and things. These technologies show the positive and negative effects of electromagnetic energy.

Another dynamic relating to electromagnetic energy is ions. There are positive and negative ions. Positively charged ions have an adverse effect on the body. Negatively charged ions have a positive, health-enhancing effect on the body. Running water such as a stream, waterfalls or the crashing waves of an ocean, emit large amounts of life-enhancing negative ions. The wind blowing through trees also emits these wonderful negative ions. This is why most people feel so much better when they are in these areas. Conversely, the wind blowing through tall buildings in cities, or an electric dryer, emits harmful positive ions. If you sit in a laundromat all day, it is very common for you to feel horrible and very fatigued. These harmful positive ions also can suppress your immune system. This electromagnetic chaos cannot be avoided. However, it can be reduced, and there are simple things you can do to counteract the negative energy you are being exposed to.

The bottom line is that today we are putting more toxins in our body than ever before in history. And the trend is increasing. As this trend continues, people will continue to increase the number of times they get sick, the number of diseases they develop, and the severity and duration of these illnesses.

What comes out of the body

Our bodies, in normal function, produce toxins. This is fine, as long as our body's ability to eliminate these toxins is operating normally. Even if you put no toxins into your body, your body would still create waste material and toxins. All toxins created by the body or put into the body must be eliminated in order for us to be healthy. When toxins are allowed to accumulate they cause the immune system to be suppressed, and the body to become acidic. Accumulated toxins that have not been flushed out or eliminated allow the body to create an environment where illness and disease can flourish. We basically eliminate toxins through:

- The nose
- The mouth
- The urinary tract
- The colon
- The skin

The nose and mouth eliminate toxins primarily by use of the lungs. Our urinary tract eliminates toxins primarily through the kidneys and liver. The colon eliminates toxins primarily through the liver, the stomach and small intestine. The skin eliminates toxins primarily through perspiration. Most people today have excess accumulations of toxins and waste material in their bodies. The two main reasons for this are: 1) they are putting huge amounts of toxins in their body on a regular basis; 2) their elimination channels are clogged, slow, and sluggish.

When you put toxins in and your body creates toxins at a faster rate than you are eliminating those toxins, you have a build-up and accumulation of poisons and toxins in the body. For example, are your nasal and sinus cavities clear and mucus free? Do you breathe fully and deeply from your diaphragm, allowing your lungs to do their job fully? Do you regularly breathe aerobically and anaerobically? Do you sweat on a regular basis? Do you drink plenty of water, which allows all elimination channels to work more efficiently? Do you have three bowel movements per day? A few common things which slow the elimination process are:

- Antibiotics. If you have ever taken an antibiotic you have dramatically slowed your elimination potential via the colon. Antibiotics kill all the friendly bacteria in the intestine and colon. This allows unfriendly yeast, most notably candida, to grow abnormally and infest your digestive system. This candida yeast overgrowth slows digestion, increases gas, bloating and constipation, and itself creates an abnormal amount of toxins.

- Lotions and creams. Most people put lotions and creams all over their skin clogging the pores and suppressing the natural elimination process through the skin. This would include sunscreens, cosmetics, deodorants, and antiperspirants.

- Lack of body movement. Have you ever noticed when you take a dog for a walk, they poop? When you move your body as nature intended, you increase the elimination process. Since most people sit all day, their elimination cycles are suppressed. You should have three bowel movements per day. When you eat food, it goes through the digestion process and ends up in the colon ready for elimination. The food in the colon begins to putrefy and become toxic. The longer it stays in the colon, the more toxic it becomes. If left long enough, these toxins begin to enter the bloodstream. This can turn into a serious medical condition resulting in death. Your body's elimination system must be working at optimal levels if you want to live without illness and disease.

Exercise

In simplistic terms, there are seven kinds of exercise:

1. *Slow rhythmic movement exercise.* This is mainly walking. The body is designed to walk, for long distances, and for long periods of time. The amount of walking in America varies per geographic area. New Yorkers tend to walk more than people living in Dallas. When you go to Europe or various other countries, people walk an average of eight to ten miles a day. In America people walk an average of close to one-tenth of a mile a day. That is unbelievable. Walking is probably the most important form of exercise you can do, and the healthiest compared to driving, which increases stress. Now let's think about this for a moment. When you drive a car your stress levels go up dramatically, which means your body becomes acidic. When you go for a walk, not only are you getting the benefits of the exercise of the slow rhythmic movement, your lymph system

is getting toxins out of your body, the body is moving and flowing beautifully, the energy is flowing through the meridians, and you are grounding your feet on the earth, allowing for the earth's magnetic energy to flow though your body, energizing your cells. You are also actually looking out and externalizing through your eyes at far away distances, which increases the electromagnetic energy in your body and makes the body more alkaline and less susceptible to disease. It also has a profound effect on your state of mind and happiness factor. The lack of walking causes the body's elimination channels to become slow and sluggish.

2. *Stretching.* Your body consists of muscles, tendons, and ligaments. If you lived in a natural setting, interacting with nature as we are designed, the natural activities you would be doing throughout your day would cause the frequent stretching of your ligaments, muscles and tendons. Americans are the least flexible people in the world. Lack of flexibility allows for negative energy and toxins to accumulate in various parts of your body, allowing toxicity to build up.

3. *Resistance exercise.* This includes any form of movement where resistance is put against a muscle, and the muscle is required to push or pull against the resistance. The most common form of resistance training is weight lifting or the use of resistance machines. This is an unnatural form of exercise. Chimpanzees, as an example, are eight times stronger than a man, yet do not lift weights. Weight training can increase the size and strength of muscles, reshaping your body and making you look great. However, it generally only works with the muscles that are seen and does not address the majority of muscles that have no aesthetic value. It also does not address the strength of ligaments and tendons. This can create an imbalance, where some muscles are strong and abnormally large, and other muscles, ligaments and tendons are weak and disproportionate in size. Weight training does not increase flexibility—it actually reduces flexibility, thus hindering the flow of energy through the body. Nevertheless, doing any form of exercise is better than doing none at all.

4. *Postures.* There are certain exercise regimes where you are put into postures that are held for a period of time. The most commonly known is yoga. Keep in mind there are many forms of yoga. Not all kinds of yoga are posture based. Some yoga techniques are fluid and movement oriented. The benefits of postures are that they seem to

help open up the natural energy channels in the body, and stimulate internal organs.

5. *Aerobic exercise.* Aerobic means "with air." Any form of exercise where you are breathing heavily but can still have a conversation is aerobic exercise. Aerobic exercise stimulates blood flow throughout the body, oxygenates the body and speeds the elimination of toxins.

6. *Anaerobic exercise.* Anaerobic means "without air." Any form of exercise where you are breathing so hard you can barely talk is anaerobic. The benefits are, generally, a tremendous stimulation of your entire system because, in effect, you are putting the survival of every cell in your body at risk because of the lack of oxygen. This is very helpful in "reprogramming the body" and allowing the body to increase its elimination of toxins and stop any cellular activity that was abnormal.

7. *Cellular exercise.* At this time there is only one form of exercise that actually affects, in a positive way, every cell in the body simultaneously. Jumping on a mini-trampoline, also known as a rebounder, has been shown to stimulate and strengthen every cell in the body. This unique form of exercise dramatically increases the movement through the lymph system, stimulates every cell's elimination of toxins, and increases the strength and vitality of every cell in the body.

The Major Benefits of Exercise Include:

- *Increase oxygen to the cells.* Oxygen is needed for life. Most people are deficient in the amount of oxygen they have throughout their bodies. Viruses and cancer, for example, cannot exist in an oxygen rich environment. An oxygen rich body is an alkaline body. An alkaline body is a body where disease and illness cannot exist.

- *Movement of lymph fluid.* The lymphatic system is an important element in the elimination process. Most Americans have a lymphatic system that is dangerously clogged and sluggish. Moving the body as it was intended increases the movement of lymph fluid through the body, assisting with the elimination of toxins.

- *Cell stimulation.* Every cell in the body produces toxic waste. Every cell in the body needs stimulation in order for the toxic waste to be eliminated. Every cell in the body needs stimulation to remain healthy and thrive in a normal way. If a cell does not eliminate the toxic waste it produces and does not receive stimulation, it can begin to act in an abnormal way. Cells could degenerate and die or begin to grow abnormally in an out of control manner, causing tumors, cancer, or the degeneration of vital organs in the body.

- *Opening of energy channels.* Energy flows through our body. Just like blood flows through the veins, electromagnetic energy flows through channels in our body. When these channels are blocked or congested, energy does not flow efficiently. This energy gives life and vitality to the cells; without it the cells do not receive what is needed, causing abnormalities, suppression of the immune system, and turning the body acidic, making it susceptible to illness. Exercise helps to keep these channels open.

- *Releasing of tension and stress.* Stress is the silent killer. Stress can be defined many ways. In simplistic terms, stress is holding on to negative energy. When negative energy is being held, it can lodge itself into various parts of the body. This can cause muscles to be tight and the body to become acidic. Exercise breaks up this stress and tension, and can allow it to leave the body.

I have mentioned that toxins in the body are a major cause of disease. I have mentioned that lack of nutrition is a major cause of disease. I suggested very briefly that electromagnetic chaos also has a negative effect on the body and can lead to and cause disease. It is important also to know that "stress" is also one of the major forces that can cause illness and disease in the body. When something stresses us, our body turns from a natural state of alkaline pH to acidic. When it's acidic, disease can grow. Stress suppresses our immune system and makes us weaker and more susceptible to infections, germs, bacteria and viruses. When our immune system is weak, we cannot naturally defend against these invaders and we get sick. So the question is, what are the stressors and how can we eliminate them? I will address this question and give you the simple solutions in a later chapter.

Rest

Without proper rest, the cells are not given the opportunity to recharge and rejuvenate. Tired cells cannot eliminate toxins efficiently. It is also during rest that most healing takes place. Most people do not get enough rest, and the rest they do get is not full and deep. There are three elements of proper rest:

1. *The time in which you rest.* The most optimum time for the body to rest is when the sun is no longer shining. Ideally, a person would rest and sleep when the sun goes down and arise when the sun comes up. This is the natural cycle. However, most people's lifestyles do not allow this. Therefore they are resting and sleeping at non-optimal times. Each week a lunar cycle occurs starting at sundown every Friday ending at sundown every Saturday. This time period is absolutely the most ideal time for the body to recharge and rejuvenate.

2. *The amount of hours you rest.* Although every person is different, it appears that every person operates better when getting eight hours of sleep. People operate worse if they receive fewer hours or more hours. The majority of people sleep less than eight hours, and then try to catch up by occasionally sleeping more hours. This practice does not allow optimal recharging and rejuvenation of the cells in your body.

3. *Rest and sleep should be deep.* Most people toss and turn at night. The ideal situation is that you virtually do not move for the entire sleep time. When sleep is full and deep, brainwave activity can occur, which stimulates the healing process throughout the body. A person who snores wakes themselves up an average of 300 times per night. A person who snores never gets into the deepest levels of sleep, and thus their body is never operating at optimal efficiency.

There is a difference between sleep and rest. The body can rest without going to sleep. Most people never take a "rest" during the day. The common pattern of waking up, working all day nonstop, going to bed late, never getting a full deep eight hours of peaceful sleep, results in a body that slowly begins to break down and never has a chance to heal and recharge. If you were to take a battery powered device and leave it on until the battery died, and compare that to turning the device on for a period of time then off for a period of time, and repeating this process several times, you would find the battery life can be as high as twice as long as nonstop usage. The body is very much like a battery. The body operates almost identically, utilizing electric current throughout. It must be given a chance to rest. If a person did nothing else but get proper rest and sleep, their energy levels would skyrocket and the amount of illness and disease they experience would go down dramatically.

Your thoughts

Thoughts are things. Your body is in fact a very powerful electro-magnetic transmitter and receiver of energy. Every thought you have can have a powerful impact on the cells in your body. Positive high vibration thoughts can rid your body of disease. Negative stressful low vibration thoughts can give your body disease. Science does not believe that thoughts can have any profound effect on your health. Medical science believes that thoughts could never alone cure or cause disease. However, it is interesting to point out that medical science cannot dispute the "placebo" effect. The placebo effect is when a person is given a "placebo," which is in effect nothing, yet their disease is cured. This occurs because the patient believes that what he is taking will cure the disease. His thoughts basically cause the cure. This happens in as many as 40 percent of the cases. Imagine, up to 40 percent of the time a person with a dreaded disease cures himself with his own thoughts! Yet, remember our friends at the FDA who say that only a drug can cure a disease!?

Thoughts can heal, but they can also cause sickness and disease. Stress, which could be defined as negative thoughts, cause the body to become acidic, thus creating the environment for illness and disease. These negative thoughts can be conscious or unconscious in nature. Many of these negative thoughts are trapped in stressful or traumatic incidences from our past. Several prominent doctors have found that the vast majority of people with cancer have an incident in their past that caused tremendous grief. Individuals who have heart attacks are found to have suppressed anger. It is interesting to note the correlation between certain emotions and certain diseases.

The stress of living in today's environment is higher than at any time in history. Driving a car, for example, raises stress levels in the body up to 1,000 times normal levels. When a person is driving a car combined with talking on a cell phone, stress levels can go as high as 5,000 times the norm. Walking, conversely, actually reduces stress. Worrying about money, arguing with relatives, friends and co-workers, watching scary gruesome movies and television shows, reading the news, all increase stress levels dramatically. The good news is this can be reversed.

Doctor Coldwell of Germany has the highest cancer success rate in the country, treating over 35,000 mostly terminal cancer patients. Without drugs or surgery, but rather by using techniques to reduce stress, (in effect correcting a person's thoughts), he has cured more people of cancer than any person in German history. Dr. Norman Cousins'

The Anatomy of an Illness documents how, by laughing and reducing stress, without drugs or surgery, cancer was put in complete remission. Earl Nightingale discovered what he called "The strangest secret": *You become what you think about.* Positive thoughts and low amounts of stress create an alkaline pH in the body, meaning you virtually cannot get sick. Negative thoughts and emotions and high levels of stress cause the body to become acidic, leading to illness and disease.

What you say

Words have power. Most people speak words that increase body stress and turn the body's pH from alkaline to acidic. Words can change the way we think and feel. Researchers have concluded that speaking the correct form of words and thinking the correct thoughts actually changes a person's DNA.

Of all the things that I've talked about in this chapter so far relating to the cause of illness and disease please do not overlook the power of how you think and what you say. These two factors contribute dramatically to stress levels. Stress absolutely causes illness and disease. Reducing stress absolutely is one of the most powerful natural cures for virtually every disease in the body. This is one of the cures that cannot be patented. No one can make billions of dollars in profits selling it to you, but simple stress reducing techniques that are effective and inexpensive absolutely have been proven to be one of the most powerful natural cures of all time. This is one of the "natural cures" that "they" don't want you to know about! I will tell you exactly how to reduce stress levels and utilize this cure in a later chapter.

If you look at people today around the world who have no disease and no illness, there are virtually no common denominators. You can't look to a person's genetic disposition. You can't look to a person's diet because they vary so greatly. Some of these people smoke, some of them eat monkeys raw, some of them eat dairy products, some of them are vegetarians, some of them do not exercise, others simply walk. They generally all do sleep very well, but the most obvious common denominator is how they think and how they talk. They are very positive, optimistic individuals, they don't take life very seriously, and they don't worry too much. They are optimistic and they are light-hearted. They greet each day in a spirit of thankfulness. Attitude really makes the difference. Thoughts do affect the body, and thoughts can dramatically affect your health.

From a biological standpoint, what does this really mean? Think of it this way. The body has what is known as the immune system. The immune system fights off any imbalance or disease, virus, germs and bacteria. If your body's immune system is strong and you happen to catch any bacteria or virus, your body fights it off and you never even notice that you were exposed or had that particular virus or bacteria or germ. When your immune system is very weak, you are susceptible to showing the symptoms of succumbing to that particular virus or bacteria. People that are the healthiest are people with very low stress levels. The common denominator of the healthiest people on the planet is how they think and what they say. The mind can cause the immune system to be incredibly strong and actually change the genetic DNA structure in your body, preventing disease. What you think and what you say can actually cure disease. Conversely, what you think and what you say, in other words "stress," can absolutely cause your immune system to be weakened and cause genetic weaknesses in the body to become active causing you to develop illness and disease. Stress, negative thoughts, negative words coming out of your mouth, all are very powerful in turning your body pH either acidic or alkaline. Remember, if your body's pH is acidic you have an environment where illness and sickness can thrive. If your body pH is alkaline you virtually can never get sick. By reducing stress, speaking powerful positive words, and thinking powerful positive thoughts you absolutely can turn your body pH to the state of alkaline and reverse—yes, that's right, absolutely cure virtually every disease in the body, all with the power of your mind.

So the summary, in very general, very simplistic terms is this:

The reason why you are sick is because you are putting more toxins and chemicals in your body. Those toxins and chemicals are not coming out of your body because you are not eliminating things like you should. We are exercising more but we are not walking, and walking is the major form of exercise that gives you the most health benefits. We are not resting enough, so our body doesn't have a chance to rejuvenate and recharge. Our thoughts are more negative because of the images we are getting from television, magazines, newspapers and movies. Think about the kids' games that they are playing and how horrific those images are. The sounds we are hearing are not life enhancing, but are actually having a powerful adverse affect on our physiology—turning our body from alkaline to acid. And we are being bombarded by more electronic chaos from cell phones, microwaves, satellite waves, electronic devices, computers, televisions, etc. We drive more than ever before and, due to that, our stress levels keep going up and up, causing our bodies to become more acidic and giving us a whole environment which is conducive to sickness and disease. Our immune systems are being suppressed and we are becoming more susceptible to illness. Specifically, the drugs that we are taking are making our immune systems weaker, and are putting so many toxins in our bodies that they are in fact causing many additional illnesses.

You'll notice that every major illness that we face today, those that most people are popping drugs for, are not in fact caused by bacteria or viruses. We aren't catching them. We develop them in our body. They are actually self-inflicted illnesses. If your body's immune system is strong and healthy, when you are exposed to the viruses and bacteria which we all are every single day, your body would simply handle them and you wouldn't even notice them. If you did have a scratchy throat, if you did have some sniffles or a cough, it would maybe last a few hours or a day at most. You wouldn't have to take any drug, your body would handle it and deal with it and become stronger because of it. That's the natural way your body reacts. We forget that many of the symptoms we have are actually our body's own defense mechanisms working properly, so we go out and take drugs and try to suppress them.

A good example is a fever. If you have a fever, the body is raising its temperature to fight off some danger. But what we do is, we go out and take something to reduce our fever, allowing the invaders to take over. The problem with medical procedures, and the problem with drugs and surgery is that they all try to solve or eliminate a symptom. They never ask, "What's the cause?" If you have a fever, don't say you need to get rid of the fever. Ask yourself what's causing the fever. Keep asking and keep asking and keep asking that question. By eliminating the symptoms, you just suppress the real cause of the problem, thus causing it to get worse. If you are driving your car and your oil light goes on, you wouldn't say "my oil light's on; I need to get my oil light to go off. Oh, I know what I'll do, I'll unscrew the bulb. Ah, now the oil light is no longer illuminated." You haven't solved the problem, have you? You got rid of a symptom. There is no more illumination of the oil light. But the reason that light went on is still there. You may drive that car for another few weeks before it seizes up on you. Your body is the same way. If you have a headache, you shouldn't say, "Let me eliminate the pain of the headache." You should ask yourself what's causing your body to do that, and find the cause. When you do this, you are addressing the root cause of problems and not just treating symptoms.

Medical science, medical doctors, drugs and surgery only treat symptoms. The question that always comes up for me is: Is there a place for drugs and surgery? And the answer is: Absolutely yes! I have to applaud the medical community because they have developed the best methods to date of keeping a person alive in the event of a trauma, accident or emergency situation. If we go with the theory that we always ask, "what's the cause," and not just treat the symptom, then we can use drugs and surgery as they should be used. Here's an example:

I'm walking in my garden and I step on a nail. I rush to the emergency room and say, "Quick, I stepped on a nail. It was a rusty nail. I'm bleeding, and I'm in pain. Help!" The doctor says that I may have some infection and gives me some ointment that will kill the bacteria to make sure I don't get an infection. He gives me some type of drug that will stop the bleeding and sews me up with a surgical procedure to handle the wound. The reason that is acceptable is because the cause of my problem was stepping on a nail. We have addressed the cause. It's not going to repeat itself. We know what the cause is. Now let's handle the symptoms.

If I was in a car crash and my kidney was ripped open by the metal of the crushed vehicle, rush me to the emergency room and handle my symptoms. Don't ask: "Hmm, I wonder what caused this? Let's go for the cause." I can tell you what the cause is. The cause is a piece of metal ripped my skin open and punctured my kidney; please use drugs and surgery and save my life. Handle the symptoms. The symptoms are, "I am bleeding profusely, I'm about to die." Handling the symptoms is good in that situation.

But if a person has cancer you don't say: "Hmm, cancer cells…let me cut them out, let me shoot them full of radiation, let me use some drugs that may kill them." Ask yourself why cancer is growing in the body. The answer is: The body is acidic. What's causing the body to be acidic? Let's find out what is going into the body, what is going out of the body, what the person thinks, how he is exercising, how he is resting and what he is saying, and let's turn this around in a very simple way and then the cancer goes away. We reduce stress, we strengthen the immune system, the body becomes alkaline, and disease can't exist.

The conclusion, then, is that people get sick because:

- We are putting too many toxins in our body and not flushing the toxins out fast enough. Meaning our body is toxic.

- We are not putting enough of the necessary nutrients into our body, and the nutrients that are going in are not being absorbed. This means we are nutritionally deficient.

- We are exposed to and negatively affected by electromagnetic chaos.

- We have trapped mental and emotional stress.

Since all matter consists ultimately of energy, in simplistic terms the cause of all disease is energetic imbalance.

CHAPTER 6

How to Never Get Sick Again

You can call this chapter: "How to Cure Every Disease"; "How to Live Healthy and Disease Free Forever"; "How to be Young Forever"; "How to Have Dynamic, Vibrant Health"; "How to Live to be 100 and Never be Sick"; "How to be a Superhero"; "How to Live Without Drugs and Surgery"; "How to Never Get Old"; "How to Look 25 Years Younger"; "How to Maintain Youth"; "How to Look Like You Found the Fountain of Youth". You can call this chapter anything you want, but basically this chapter will give you the information to potentially eliminate any illness or disease you may currently have, and prevent any illness and disease in the future. This information will also allow you to potentially slow down and even reverse the aging process. Keep in mind that I am not a medical doctor. If you are currently being treated by a medical doctor make sure they are informed as to what you are doing. I cannot diagnose or treat anyone's medical conditions. I present this for educational purposes only. This information is strictly my opinion and based on the information currently available. I believe everything to be true and accurate.

Right now, you either have some known illness or disease such as cancer, diabetes, etc., or you claim to be healthy. If you claim to be healthy, you probably still experience the normal occasional headaches, aches and pains, fatigue, indigestion, colds and flus, heartburn, etc. So-called healthy people believe that these occasional medical conditions are "normal." They are not. A healthy person has little, if any, body odor, they have no bad breath, no foot odor, their urine and stool do not smell, they sleep soundly, they have no skin rashes or dandruff, they are not depressed or stressed, they rarely, if ever, get colds, flus, heartburn, aches, and pains. Truly healthy people are full of energy and vitality, and never have to take any nonprescription or prescription drug because they never have any symptoms that would require them to take a drug. So, in reality every one of you reading this book is unhealthy to some degree. I can assure you that if you continue to do what you have always done in the past, your physical health will slowly begin to deteriorate, you will get more sicknesses and diseases, and your energy levels will continually go down.

Some people always ask me if all I say is true, how did Aunt Millie live to be eighty-five? First, I say that I would like to offer my condolences for Aunt Millie's premature death. It is sad to see someone die so young. You see, I believe that the human body, like all mammals, should live to be well over 100 years old. When you compare the life spans of virtually all mammals, they live well in excess of what would be the equivalent of 120 human years. So, dying at eighty-five to me is dying young. Secondly, Aunt Millie lived the first half of her life where the amount of toxins being put into the body was a fraction of what it is today. I hear a lot about the alleged fact that we are living longer than ever before. This is categorically not true. Yes, it is true that people lie in nursing homes and hospital beds hooked up to life support devices that keep the physical body alive for years, but realistically these people are not living. The statistics on life span are fraudulent and false.

Keep in mind that these statistics, such as most health recommendations and statistics, come from the government. Without going into a very long dissertation here I will just point out the facts. When information is presented from the government, such as lifespan, recommended daily allowances of vitamins and minerals, the food pyramid, etc., you absolutely have to know that this information is false, fraudulent, and misleading. The government puts out this information based 100 percent on how much money they have received from the various lobbying groups that want certain things to be said by the government. Remember, it's always all about the money. Corporations want to make billions of dollars in additional profits. That is why they spend tens of millions of dollars with lobbyists giving this money via the various payoff methods that I explained, to the politicians so that government can then put out reports, statistics, news, press releases, and various types of recommendations that are not true at all, but only designed to increase the profits of the special interests who gave the politicians tens of millions of dollars. That's how it works. Remember again how the money is made and always remember it's always all about the money.

One side note for you to consider is the fact that the majority of wealth developed in this country was through the use of government contracts. This means that by paying off politicians people became wealthy. What that means is your tax dollars were used by the unethical politicians and given to the insiders that are now billionaires. Government takes your tax dollars and lines its own pockets with millions of dollars and makes their friends and insiders multimillionaires and billionaires. That's how it works, folks. I hope you would open your eyes to the truth. Again, I am telling you this from firsthand information and firsthand knowledge. I am the insider who is blowing the whistle on the truth behind the corruption in the corporations and government. I can assure you, I am the one man that, the board members of major corporations around the world want to get rid of. I am the one man who the politicians absolutely want to destroy, discredit, and have vanish. But, for the sake of mankind and society and YOUR health, I am standing up and exposing the secrets that have been hidden from you for well over 100 years. I am pulling back the curtain and exposing the frauds and criminals who are taking money directly out of your pocket and purposely making you suffer and die needlessly—all so that THEY can make millions and millions more.

Now let me go back to this lifespan statistic. I have to tell you, every time somebody says that we are living longer than ever before I want to scream. Again, I want you to know that it's a lie. The government wants you to believe this because they want you to believe that drugs and surgery are doing a wonderful job, keeping in mind that the majority of money that is going in the pockets of politicians all around the world is from the pharmaceutical industry. Consider that even Fidel Castro of Cuba has an estimated net worth of $550 million, much of which comes directly from the pharmaceutical industry! This was reported in *Forbes* magazine. The bottom line is people are not living longer than ever before. It is a false statistic. More importantly, those who are in their fifties, sixties, and seventies are feeble, sickly, and barely living. The fact of the matter is a person 100 years old should be strong, flexible, full of life and energy, and have the physical capacity of what the average forty-year-old person has. It is amusing to me when you hear the American Medical Association classify someone in their fifties as being "older," and someone in their sixties as being "old." The most amazing part of this is that it is assumed that as you get older, it is normal to be on some type of medication. This simply is not true.

The bottom line is that you are either (a) very sick. (b) somewhat sick, or (c) about to get sick.

It is hard to find a truly healthy person. The good news is there is a way out. Let's examine where you are right now. You are full of toxins. You are also deficient in necessary nutrients. The energy in your body is not flowing properly. Many of your systems are not operating at optimal levels. You either notice severe symptoms, or you have mild symptoms that you classify as normal. What can we do to (a) eradicate any and all symptoms you have, thus "curing" the disease or illness and (b) prevent any illness or disease from starting, thus giving you a tremendous increase in energy, vitality, and vibrant dynamic health? The first thing I would recommend is that you seek proper health care from a professional health-care provider who does not use drugs or surgery. Since every person is different and every condition is different, you need to have a knowledgeable person examine you and give you appropriate care. Keep in mind that all health-care providers have different backgrounds and experiences, and may have different opinions about the course of action that is best for you. It is wise to get several opinions from several people.

The big question I get often is: How do I find a good alternative, all-natural health-care provider? This is an excellent question. Unfortunately, these health-care practitioners cannot advertise because the FDA is looking for people who are curing disease without drugs and surgery, and if the FDA becomes aware of these people, history shows that the FDA or FTC will drive these health-care practitioners out of business. A simple way to find someone good in your area is to go down to your local health food store and ask who they recommend. On my Web site, www.naturalcures.com, I have a private member area where you can be provided with recommendations of people in your area that have excellent track records in using all-natural therapies. Generally speaking, health-care providers who practice homeopathy, acupuncture, chiropractic medicine, herbology, and nutritional therapy are all good places to start. I myself have been treated by over 200 natural health-care providers from around the world. Is one better than the other? Yes. In many cases, they are also very different in their approach. Do they all provide some benefit? I believe so. Do some treatments and therapies work faster and more completely than others? Yes. However, the one that works best for me may not work best for you. Everyone is different, every situation and condition is different, and the same treatment may have varying results with each person. You have to take responsibility for your own health. No one knows it all. No one, including the pharmaceutical industry and medical doctors, has a monopoly on the truth. So, the first step is to seek out alternative, all-natural health-care providers, and start experiencing for yourself the benefits you'll enjoy without drugs and surgery.

In addition to the customized treatment you will receive from a licensed holistic health-care practitioner who dos not use drugs and surgery, I believe that doing the things in this chapter can potentially cure disease and illness that you may currently have (provided, of course, that the condition is not past the point of no return), and prevent illness and disease from ever occurring. These recommendations are also the best way to slow, or potentially reverse, the aging process, making you look and feel younger than you have in years.

In general terms, the way to eradicate any and all illness and disease that you may have, prevent illness and disease from occurring in the future, and slow down or potentially reverse the aging process is to do the following:

1. Eliminate the toxins that have built up in your system. You are loaded with toxins. The only question is, how much. You absolutely must get these toxins out of your body if you want to cure and prevent illness and disease. Getting the toxins out of your body can immediately increase energy, help you lose weight, eliminate depression and anxiety, and potentially reverse most illnesses and disease. The basic cleanses that you should do are (a) a colon cleanse, (b) a liver/gallbladder cleanse, (c) a kidney/bladder cleanse, (d) a heavy metal cleanse, (e) a parasite cleanse, (f) a Candida cleanse, and (g) a full-body fat tissue/lymphatic cleanse.

2. Stop, or at least reduce the toxins entering your body. In today's world it is impossible to totally eliminate toxins from entering your body, but we can dramatically reduce the amount of toxins going in.

3. Make sure our elimination systems are clean and no longer sluggish, thus allowing the toxins that we do put into our body and the toxins that develop in our body naturally are getting eliminated quickly and not accumulating.

4. Make sure we are getting proper amounts of nutrition in the form of vitamins, minerals, enzymes, cofactors, and life-sustaining "energy" and make sure our system can assimilate these vital nutrients.

5. Reduce and/or neutralize the electromagnetic energy that is attacking our body energy fields and cells.

6. Reduce stress.

7. Use our mind and words to create a healthy alkaline body pH, and actually change genetically defective DNA structures into normal healthy DNA structures.

Remember in the last chapter we talked about the cause of virtually all disease. Remember I said you will either catch something and you succumb to it, or you develop something in the body. These two things occur because you have (1) too many toxins in the body, (2) nutritional deficiencies, (3) exposure to electromagnetic chaos, (4) stress.

If those are the four causes of virtually all disease, then the way to prevent any of the disease is to make sure that in effect you don't have any toxins in the body, you don't have any nutritional deficiencies, you're not exposed to electromagnetic chaos, and you have no stress. Theoretically, if that were to occur you couldn't get sick.

Let me say this again. **If the cause of all disease is too many toxins, nutritional deficiencies, electromagnetic chaos, and/or stress, then if you did not have toxins in the body, if you did not have nutritional deficiencies, if you did not have exposure to electromagnetic chaos, and if you did not have stress, then you cannot have any disease!**

Does this make sense? Can you see why drugs are not the answer? Drugs and surgery simply address symptoms, not the cause of illness and disease. Medical doctors treat symptoms, they do not treat the whole person. Drugs simply suppress symptoms by causing the body to do UNNATURAL THINGS! Think about that. Drugs do not create normalcy or balance in the body. Drugs create a state of imbalance. This is why drugs CAUSE more diseases. Drugs do not cure anything. Drug companies that say to you that they are trying to find a cure for disease are absolutely lying. Drug companies know that drugs do not cure disease. Drug companies know the drugs only suppress symptoms and cause the body to do unnatural things and be completely out of balance. Drug companies know that their drugs cause disease, not cure disease. The drug companies are flagrantly, blatantly lying to you.

I've seen CEOs of drug companies go on television and look at the camera, reading the script that their lawyers wrote, saying, "We are working on a cure." They are not working on a cure. They are working on something to suppress a symptom and put the body out of balance. Think about this: all drug companies are researching only patentable drugs! All money that is given to charities and foundations is used to find patentable drugs! All government funding used to research the prevention and cure of every disease is only being used to find PATENTABLE DRUGS. This means all the money is being used to find a patentable drug that can be sold and make drug companies billions of dollars in profits. Not one penny is ever used to look at treating, preventing, or curing disease with natural methods.

No drug company, no pharmaceutical company, no health-care company, no association, no foundation, and no government money is ever used to research natural nonpatentable methods to cure, prevent, and treat disease! This is appalling! This should get you to wake up to the truth—that it's only all about the money. The fact of the matter is the way to prevent and cure any disease is relatively simple and inexpensive. If we look at the four basic causes for all disease and try to punch holes in it no one can. I've sat in debates for hours, and hours, and hours with people trying to show that there are diseases that are not caused by those four things. Guess what, there is not one scientist, not one researcher, not one medical doctor that can make a compelling argument against what I have just said.

There is not one doctor that can prove that every disease is not caused by one of, or a combination of, the four things I mention above. The reason you never hear about it is no one can make money if they accept the truth! The drug companies know the truth, but the truth will put them out of business. The politicians know the truth, but the truth, if exposed, will cost them hundreds of millions of dollars. The most powerful, richest people on Planet Earth know the truth, but exposing the truth will cost them their influence, their power, and their billions. It's sad, it's sick, it's outrageous, and it absolutely has to stop. The health of people on Planet Earth depends on this truth coming out. Millions of people will continue to suffer and die needlessly if this truth about the cause, prevention, and cure of disease is hidden. Millions of people around the world will remain impoverished, both physically and financially, if this truth about health care, about government, about the cause, the cure, and prevention of disease is not exposed and embraced by the masses.

What I want to do here is give you some very specific things to do that can address each of those four causes of disease. I'm going to list many, many things for you to consider doing. Do not be overwhelmed by this list. If you are reading this don't think that you must do all of these things starting tomorrow if you want to prevent and cure any disease you have. Consider going at a nice easy pace. Consider adding some things slowly into your life. Do these things at a pace and level that you feel comfortable with. Please note that this is not the complete list. It is a good starting point. I can tell you that I personally do the majority of these things the majority of the time. It is important for you to know that perfection is not doing all these things all the time. That would be fanatical and, quite frankly, impossible for most people. You need to do what you feel good about doing.

Start with one of these items and then slowly add another when you feel comfortable. Some of you will start by implementing many of these suggestions right away. Some of you will go slow. If you do these things, in my opinion, you virtually should never get sick. If you do get sick the severity and duration of the illness will be short. Remember, the body heals itself! Drugs and surgery do not heal. Doctors do not heal. No treatment heals or cures. The body in effect heals and cures itself. Think about it. If you cut your finger and you don't do anything to it, the body will simply heal. It may take a few days, it may take a few weeks, but the body will heal itself. If you cut your finger very deeply you can HELP THE BODY HEAL BETTER AND FASTER, but you can't heal the body. Only the body heals itself. This is an important concept to remember. All of these suggestions in this chapter are designed to help the body heal itself. All of these suggestions are designed to ultimately turn your body's pH from acidic, where disease and illness can develop, to the healthy state of alkaline, where disease and illness cannot exist. People always ask me the question, "How do I turn my body from acidic pH to alkaline pH?" The answer is, do the things in this chapter. This is an important concept. There is not one thing that can turn your body from acidic pH to alkaline pH. The reason is I don't know what is CAUSING your body to be acidic. It could be dehydration, it could be mental and emotional stress, it could be some particular food you're eating, it could be a particular chemical that's in the food you're eating, it could be a nutritional deficiency, it could be a genetic weakness that is being exposed because of a combination of forty different things. I don't know, and nobody knows why your body's pH is acidic. What I do believe is that if you do the things in this chapter, virtually everyone's body can turn from acidic to alkaline pH. That is one of our ultimate goals and it's one of the simplest ways to determine how healthy you are. If your body's pH is alkaline it is virtually impossible to get cancer or any other major disease.

As I mentioned earlier in this book, both the FDA and the FTC, as well as other government organizations, corporations, the news media, and other groups, routinely use censorship as a method to hide the truth about natural cures and remedies from the public. Remember, it's in the financial best interest of the politicians, the FTC, the FDA, the drug companies, the foundations, the charities, and the news media to hide the truth about natural remedies. Remember, they make money as long as you are sick and buying drugs. With that in mind, I decided to write this book. After all, this is America where we have the Constitution of the United States and the Bill of Rights. The First Amendment to the Constitution gives me, as an American citizen, the absolute right of free speech. Unfortunately, many of you may not know that the Federal Trade Commission is more powerful than the U.S. Constitution. Many of you may not know that the FDA is also more powerful than the U.S. Constitution. These two organizations are used by the administration to suppress the free flow of information and ideas. These two government agencies are routinely used by the administration, in my opinion, to suppress individual citizens' right of free speech. Remember, both the FDA and the FTC have almost ultimate power in charging people, disseminating false and misleading information about individuals such as myself, and prosecuting those individuals. Both the FDA and the FTC are in many cases judge, jury, and executioner. They make the rules, they enforce the rules, and they themselves, in many cases, decide whether you are guilty or not. And you thought we lived in a free society. You thought that we had equal protection under the law. You thought that the Constitution said that every citizen is entitled to the due process of law.

Well, wake up and smell the roses. I want you to know why I am as mad as hell, and not going to take it anymore. When I decided to write this book the Federal Trade Commission simply came in and ORDERED me not to put specific product information in this book! You are reading this right. The Federal Trade Commission came in and, in my opinion, stripped me of my First Amendment right. The FTC said that if I put specific product information in this book and tried to sell this book on television they would in effect confiscate these books and burn these books. No, this isn't fantasy. This is categorically 100 percent true. How can I prove it? If you go to www.naturalcures.com and become a private member, I have every letter to and from the FTC posted on my Web site. You will see the FTC's actual letters forbidding me to put specific product information in this book, and in effect threatening to confiscate and burn these books. Read the letters. You will see in black and white that what I'm saying is categorically 100 percent true. The United States government is trying to suppress the free flow of opinions and ideas when it comes to health care. The U.S. government is specifically trying to shut me up because I am exposing the truth about the fraud going on with the pharmaceutical industry. Think about it. If I say what I wanted to say in this book, and if I simply exercise my constitutional right of free speech, the FTC in effect said they would prosecute me, potentially imprison me, and confiscate and burn all of my books and probably all of my other research papers and information. You may be shaking your head and saying to yourself "this is impossible." Well, it's not impossible. It's true and it's happening now, and not only to me, but to hundreds of other authors, pundits, commentators, and health advocates such as myself. I know it sounds like Nazi Germany or Stalinist Russia, but this suppression is happening to people like me all over America and all over the world. You need to know that suppression by governments around the world on the free flow of information relating to health and nutrition is at an all-time high and getting worse. More people are being persecuted and prosecuted for talking about natural remedies and natural ways to cure and prevent disease than ever before in our history. This is only being done to protect the profits of those who are making millions of dollars on the weak and sick and misinformed.

Because of this FTC suppression I am not allowed to give you specific product brand names in this book. However, I do have good news. You can go to my Web site, www.naturalcures.com, and become a member, or you can subscribe to my monthly newsletter. When you become either a member of my Web site community or a subscriber to my newsletter you will have access to write or e-mail me, as well as several licensed health-care practitioners that personally treat me, and you will be able to ask any question you want and get specific answers. The Federal Trade Commission is even trying to stop what I say in private conversations on the telephone or via letter. Isn't that amazing? The government is probably analyzing my letters, faxes, and e-mails and reading them. That is how scared the government is of what I am doing.

At the back of this book there are also several organizations and licensed health-care practitioners that you can write to and get specific recommendations. I want you to have this information. I want you to have this knowledge. It's not about the money for me any more; it's about you getting healthy. As a side note, I do charge for my Web site and newsletter, but please note that I do not accept any advertising, nor do I sell any products, nor am I compensated in any way for products that I recommend or suggest you use. Please also note that a huge percentage of all the profits generated from any of my enterprises now are being used specifically to fight corporate and government corruption and to increase health-care awareness around the world. Please know that everything I am doing is from a pure heart. I am not doing this for the money. I am doing this for you and the people who need it the most. Let me say this again so there is no confusion: unlike virtually every single health-care advocate, I personally do not sell any products. I am not paid or given any compensation from companies to recommend their products. I am not compensated in any way if you choose to buy a product that I recommend. I only sell books and information, and use most of that money not for my own personal wealth creating, but rather to expand this mission of exposing corporate and government corruption, and informing people about the truth about health. I donate huge amounts of money to organizations that promote health freedoms. All this suppression that I personally am under is outrageous. The attacks that I face on a regular basis on radio, television, newspapers, and magazines are unprecedented by a health advocate. The government, the pharmaceutical industry, and the food industry are putting together what I believe to be one of the largest coordinated efforts to debunk and destroy an individual. My insiders tell me that virtually millions of dollars are being put in and coordinated with government agencies to specifically drive me out of business and discredit me.

Why am I willing to put myself out to such attacks and abuse? Because I feel it is my mission in life to blow the whistle on the corporate greed and the corruption in the boardrooms across the world and in the government agencies across the world. I believe it is my mission to help free the world of illness and disease and inform them about the truth about health, nutrition, and natural remedies. If you want to help me, I want you to know I absolutely need YOUR HELP. I am under vicious constant attacks. The point is, and in order to keep this mission moving forward, I need your support, I need your positive thoughts, and I need your help. The best way to help this mission is to become a member of my Web site www.naturalcures.com, or subscribe to my monthly newsletter *Kevin Trudeau's Natural Cures Monthly Newsletter*. More information on these two informational sources is available at the back of this book. I would encourage you to subscribe so that you can help the cause and be part of the solution. When you subscribe to my Web site community, www.naturalcures.com, or my monthly newsletter you allow me to flood politicians and corporate heads with mail and correspondence, which is one of the most powerful ways to affect change and bring back our health freedoms and allow you the freedom of getting natural cures for your disease.

Now let's look at the various recommendations for the prevention and cure of disease. Each of these recommendations could take an entire book to explain in detail. If I were to go into each one of these recommendations and try to explain to you the specific reasons to do it and benefits you will achieve, it would take hundreds of pages for EACH of these recommendations. As a matter of fact, many books have already been written for each one of these recommendations. I encourage you to read those books if you are not totally convinced of the powerful benefits that you will receive by employing these recommendations into your life. You will see how these simple and effective procedures, techniques, and treatments actually do "cure" your disease

So that is the summary. If I were to call you up and test you I would say, "What are the two main reasons you're sick?" I hope you can instantly say, "Because you catch something and succumb to the germs, bacteria, or viruses, or you develop something in your body." If I were to ask you what are the four main reasons that occurs, I hope you can say, (1) too many toxins in the body, (2) nutritional deficiencies,(3) exposure to electromagnetic chaos, and (4) stress.

At this point I hope a light bulb has gone off in your head. At this point I hope you can see the two major things I am trying to get across. The first major thing at this point that you have to understand is that health care is all about the money, that the entire health-care industry is only interested in making profit, that the entire health-care industry has no interest in curing or preventing disease. The entire health-care industry has only one objective, and that is to increase profits. The entire health-care industry includes the drug companies, every single medical and health association, every charity involved in raising money for research on disease, as well as every member of Congress, all of our politicians, the FDA, and the FTC, as well as the news media on TV, radio, newspapers and magazines.

The corruption runs deeper than you could ever imagine. All of these bigwig fat cats are making millions of dollars as long as drugs are being sold, and sold, and sold, and people remain sick, and sick, and sicker. You have to understand the power of greed and the power of the love of money. You have to understand how motivated people are for power, influence, and money. This driving force is behind the fraud and corruption in health care. You have to understand the money motive behind corporations, specifically publicly traded corporations. You have to know that all publicly traded corporations, all officers and directors of those corporations have only one objective and that is to increase shareholder value, to increase profits, to increase sales, and to get more people to use their products. You have to know that the LEGAL responsibility of corporations is to increase profits above everything else.

You have to know that publicly traded corporations routinely take advantage of their employees; take advantage of and destroy the environment; take advantage of, lie to, deceive and mislead their customers—all to increase profits. It's important to know that it's always all about the money. You have to know that politicians are making millions of dollars buying and selling stock, primarily pharmaceutical stocks, using insider information. You have to know that these politicians have passed a law allowing them to legally trade on insider information, and that if you and I did the exact same thing we would go to prison for breaking the law. You have to know that the government wants to promote and push drug use because the individual politicians in Washington are making millions of dollars in the process. You have to understand and know that the administration uses the FDA and the FTC to squash competitors, wipe out independent thinking people, and suppress people's First Amendment rights of free speech. You have to understand how massive the campaign of debunking the truth is.

You must know that this entire industry, from Washington to the FDA, to the FTC, to the drug companies, to all of the associations, the foundations, and charities, as well as the news media, are all trying to brainwash you and mislead you into thinking the big lie that drugs are safe and effective, and natural remedies are ineffective and dangerous. They want you to believe that lie because they make millions of dollars, billions of dollars in profits so long as you believe that great deception. Once you understand the motivations behind this movement, then I hope you understand the second point I've talked about up until now. I hope you understand the cause of disease.

So, basically at this point you should have a grasp on two basic concepts. First, the motivation behind the deception and the fraud trying to get you to believe that drugs and surgery are the answer when in fact there are all-natural remedies that can cure and prevent virtually every disease; and secondly, I hope you understand right now the cause of virtually every disease. If you really understand the cause of disease you can see that drugs can never cure disease; you will see the big, huge, massive exposé that I am blowing the whistle on. You will see that I am letting the cat out of the bag on one of the greatest discoveries in this century. That discovery is that one of the major causes of all illness and disease is actually the vaccines, the nonprescription over-the-counter drugs, and the prescription drugs! The drug companies themselves are causing the majority of illness and disease around the world. They are not curing disease, they are causing disease.

Now that you understand, hopefully these two basic concepts let's go on and talk about how to solve the problem, how to prevent disease, and how to cure disease. The answers are unbelievably simple and inexpensive. The answers will shock you, the solutions will amaze you, and the results will absolutely, categorically astonish you beyond belief.

Here is what I believe to be the simple all-natural, nondrug and nonsurgical ways to prevent every disease and cure every disease. These are the "natural cures." These are the techniques, procedures, and methods that in my opinion can slow down the aging process; prevent disease; reverse disease; cure disease; increase your energy; make you look and feel more vibrant, vital, and younger; and give you dynamic health.

1. **See natural health-care providers on a regular basis.**

   When you have a car that you love and cherish, you keep it clean on the inside and out. You do not wait for the car to make funny noises or stop running; instead you bring the car in on a regular basis for maintenance. This regular maintenance is designed to prevent any problems from occurring. Your body should be treated in a similar fashion. You should be seeing various natural health-care providers from a variety of disciplines, even when you don't experience symptoms. Seeing more than one person is valuable so that all bases are covered. Seeing licensed health-care providers who do not use drugs and surgery is absolutely 100 percent the most important thing you can do to prevent and cure disease. Every person is different; every condition is different; every situation is different; every individual body is different. The cause of your illness and disease is probably different than someone else who has the exact same symptoms as you. Therefore, the treatment and cure is going to be different. It is important that you not treat yourself for illness and disease. It is important that you know that you cannot read a book and treat yourself effectively for illness and disease. It is important that you understand that no one can diagnose and treat you over the phone or over the Internet. You need to see someone in person. You need to see someone who does not use drugs and surgery. You need to see someone who understands the cause of illness and disease. How do you find a good health-care practitioner? In the back of this book there is a listing of associations and organizations that can provide you with recommendations. You can go to my Web site www.naturalcures.com for a list of licensed health-care practitioners in your area. You can go to the Yellow Pages and lookup naturopath, oriental medicine, chiropractor, herbalist, colon therapist, massage therapist, etc. You can go to your local health food store and inquire. I believe it is important to be looked at by several people and get several different opinions. Even though I personally believe I know huge amounts of information when it comes to the prevention and curing of disease naturally, I also know that getting other opinions is valuable and necessary. Do not, however, in my opinion, see or be treated by a doctor who uses drugs and surgery. This step, again, is number one. This is the most important. You need to be treated by a licensed health-care practitioner, in my opinion.

Some examples I highly recommend are:

a. **Get treated by a bioenergetic synchronization technique practitioner.**

Dr. Morter invented this technique. He has trained thousands of people in this treatment. This technique is painless and takes only a few minutes. It is an incredibly effective way of rebalancing the body, reducing or eliminating pain or trauma, and it's very powerful in helping your body go from acid to alkaline. For more information go to www.morterhealthctr.com.

b. **Get a chiropractic adjustment.**

Every chiropractor uses slightly different techniques. Some are great, some are good, and some not so good. If you have never gotten a chiropractic adjustment, you need one. Because of our lifestyle, our spines get misaligned. Realigning the spine allows energy to flow throughout the entire body. I personally see a chiropractor at least once a month for a tune-up. Even if you have no pain, go to a chiropractor and get an adjustment. See if there is an introductory lecture or ask a chiropractor in your area for some literature that you can read. The adjustments are painless and most people feel absolutely energized after an adjustment. I personally get treated by several different chiropractors because each one has their own personal style and variations on the treatment.

c. **See an herbalist.**

Like all health-care practitioners, there are individuals who are excellent and whose therapy will give you tremendous, vast, and profound results. Seeing a highly-recommended herbalist allows you to be treated in a natural way where you avoid the dangers of drugs. If you have never had a consultation with an herbalist at least once, you have no idea what you are missing. When you take recommended herbs in a specific recommended dosage that is customized specifically for you, the physical benefits that you can receive are enormous.

d. **See a homeopathic practitioner.**

Homeopathy is a form of medical treatment that gently brings the body into balance and can cure physical problems. A good homeopathic doctor does not treat symptoms, but he treats the whole person. Highly recommended.

e. **See a naturopath.**

Basically naturopaths are licensed health-care practitioners who use no drugs and no surgery, but rather all-natural methods to treat the person as a whole, bringing him back to a state of balance, thus curing you or really allowing your body to cure itself of any and all diseases.

2. **Stop taking nonprescription and prescription drugs.**

If you are taking drugs of any kind, do not do this step without consulting your physician. Remember, drugs are poisons. This includes vaccines. Although opinions vary, many experts believe that vaccines are the number one cause of deaths and disease in children. Vaccines are some of the most toxic things you can put in your body.

Last year over 250,000 Americans died by taking the proper dosage of prescription and nonprescription drugs. It is estimated that millions had to receive medical treatment because of the horrible side effects from taking prescription and nonprescription drugs. It is also estimated that tens of millions will develop long-term medical conditions because they took nonprescription and prescription drugs. In my opinion, drugs should only be taken in the most severe cases. This step is so important. You have to know that if you are taking any nonprescription or prescription drugs you absolutely will get sick and develop disease! Let me say that again, and let me be perfectly clear. If you continue to take nonprescription over-the-counter drugs and/or prescription drugs you absolutely will get sick. These nonprescription drugs and prescription drugs are poisons and toxins and CAUSE illness and disease! You must stop taking them if you intend on preventing and curing any disease. You cannot cure your disease if you continue to take nonprescription and prescription drugs. You cannot prevent disease if you continue to take nonprescription and prescription drugs. In my opinion, you should clean out your medicine cabinet and stop giving your money to the criminals who run the drug companies.

3. **Energetic rebalancing.**

Frequency generators have been around for decades. Royal Rife was using frequencies in the 1920s and 1930s to cure cancer. Today there are several machines using frequencies to balance out a person's energy, thus eliminating the energetic frequency of the imbalance or disease. When the frequency of the disease you have has been neutralized, the disease goes away. These machines absolutely, 100 percent allow the body to virtually cure all diseases.

They are fast, painless, and inexpensive. They are also outlawed by the FDA. Individual practitioners using these machines never publicly claim that they cure anything for fear that the FDA will prosecute these people for using an unlicensed medical device and curing people without the legally approved drugs. These machines include the Intero, Vegatest, Dermatron, and others. The most advanced technology that I know of is used by a man in Southern California who treats many well known celebrities. His technology is so advanced that, no matter where you are in the world, he can have his computerized frequency machine monitoring you twenty-four hours a day, seven days per week, constantly balancing the energetic frequencies in your body. I personally have been using this technology for the last seven years, and I have never in that time been sick. When everyone around me had a serious cold, I got the sniffles for about two hours. When all my friends got the flu, I never experienced a single symptom. I highly recommend you read the book *Sanctuary* to get the full story on this revolutionary technology. Here's what some others have to say about this program:

Dr. Wayne W. Dyer, bestselling author of *Wisdom of the Ages*, lecturer, spiritual teacher:

"In regard to Stephen Lewis, EMC², and the AIM Program: Everything is energy. Everything and everyone has a frequency. Those frequencies that are out of balance with our natural harmony can be identified and removed. I know this to be true. I have seen the Sanctuary process at work. I practice it daily. My entire family participates in the AIM Program, and I have seen wonderful results. This is real, it is transforming, it is true healing, and it is a giant step into the inevitable future where each of us is our own personal, transcendental, and totally enlightened healer. I have found that in my higher self, and so can you. It is available now."

Linda Gray, actress, Goodwill Ambassador on Women's Issues to the United Nations:

"I have used this technology for years. It is the most glorious gift that anyone could receive."

Courtney Cox Arquette, actress:

"I've been fortunate enough to have participated in Energetic Balancing® for over three years. I don't know what I would do without it. I don't believe anyone can afford not to be a part of it."

People always want to know what the "natural cure" is for their disease, or what the best way to prevent disease is. If we stop right here and you do the three things I have just mentioned, (1) see several licensed health-care practitioners for individualized treatment; (2) stop taking all nonprescription over-the-counter drugs and prescription drugs (under the supervision of a doctor); and (3) and you get on an energetic rebalancing program, I believe you will virtually never get sick and you can cure every disease you may have, provided you are not past the point of no return. If you are past the point of no return and the degeneration or disease is in its most advanced stages, then unfortunately I know of nothing that can help you—only things that can prolong your life, but you will eventually die of that disease or illness. Can energetic rebalancing alone prevent and cure all disease? I absolutely, categorically believe yes. I have seen this technology cure people of the most horrific debilitating diseases anyone can imagine. I have seen cancer cured. I have seen diabetes cured. I have seen MS cured. I have seen virtually every disease cured by energetic rebalancing. The thousands of people that are on energetic rebalancing technology virtually never get sick. This is statistically unheard of. However, the FDA, other government agencies, and all of the groups I mentioned previously categorically do not want this technology exposed and try to debunk it and attack it every chance they can. Why? Because it will cost them virtually billions of dollars in profits if people use this inexpensive technology to prevent and cure their disease. You can go to the Internet to find various energetic rebalancing treatments. I am on two programs. One is available at www.energeticbalancing.us and www.energeticmatrix.com.

4. **Check your body pH.**

Dr. Morter discovered one of the greatest breakthroughs for health assessment in the last 100 years, yet because this discovery would not increase profits to the pharmaceutical industry it has gone by the wayside without much publicity or fanfare. Dr. Morter's discovery should have won him a Nobel Prize. Dr. Morter discovered the powerful truth that when your body pH is acidic, disease such as cancer, diabetes, and MS thrives. He also discovered that when a body's pH is alkaline, disease such as cancer, CANNOT exist! Therefore, one of the most powerful and simplest ways to test your condition of health and/or propensity for disease is to check your body's pH. Dr. Morter has written many books on this subject and I highly encourage and recommend that you investigate and read more about his incredible research and technology. Dr. Morter's Web site is to www.morterhealthctr .com. The pH testing procedure is something I encourage everyone to do on a regular basis. I check my body's pH almost every month. If it's out of the proper range I can look at the various things I am doing or not doing, allowing myself to make simple adjustments in my life to correct the out of balance pH. The reason this is so important is because it takes years and years to develop most diseases. When you are checking your pH on a regular basis, even if it goes out of balance, as long as you correct it and bring it back to balance you are never allowing your body a long enough time to develop any disease. In my opinion it's the simplest easy way to make sure you virtually can never get cancer or any other major disease. The pH testing procedure for your urine and saliva can be found at www.naturalcures.com.

The above four suggestions are what I call the basic four for the prevention and treatment of all disease. These are the very, very basic things that, in my opinion, you must do if you are serious about preventing and curing disease. However, we know that the causes of all disease are (1) too many toxins in the body, (2) nutritional deficiencies, (3) electromagnetic chaos, and (4) stress. Therefore, we must address each of these areas with specific recommendations on how to achieve (a) no toxins in the body, (b) no nutritional deficiencies, (c) no electromagnetic chaos, and (d) no stress.

Here are the specific recommendations. Doing these things will turn your body's pH from acid to alkaline. Doing these things will create a state in the body of balance known as homeostasis. Doing these things, in my opinion, will prevent virtually all illness and disease from occurring and CURE you from every illness and disease.

A. Clean Out The Toxins That Have Accumulated In Your Body

It's important that you again completely understand that from the time you were born you have been flooding your body with poisons and toxins. These poisons and toxins included everything from vaccines, nonprescription and prescription drugs, the air we breathe, the water we shower, bathe, swim in, drink, and all the chemicals put in our food supply. They also include all the toxins from carpeting, paint, cosmetics, makeup, soaps, lotions, and sunscreens. They even come from things as simple as nonstick cookware. Did you know that if you took a nonstick pan, put it on your stove and turned the heat up, a bird, if it happened to be a few feet from the pan, would die from the toxic fumes that were emanating from the pan? If you have nonstick cookware, for example, over the years you have been breathing in all of those poison toxins. The bottom line is you have loaded your body with toxins in massive amounts and these toxins do not leave the body fully. They stay in the fatty tissues; they stay in the organs; they stay in the colon, intestine and throughout your entire body. They are causing you illness and disease; they are suppressing your immune system. If you want to prevent disease you must clean these toxins out. If you want to cure disease you absolutely must clean these toxins out.

Keep this in mind: if we know that toxins in our body are the CAUSE of the illnesses and disease that we are suffering from, you must realize that if you clean the toxins out of your body, IN MOST CASES, most people experience a dramatic reduction, or in some cases a complete elimination, of their symptoms! Simply cleaning toxins out of your body could be the "natural cure" of your disease. Keep in mind, if you are experiencing symptoms or have illness and disease, it took years and years to develop. If you clean out all the toxins in your system, it may take several months after that for the body to heal itself. Please give it some time. This is why I again encourage you to be under the care of a fully licensed health-care practitioner. Here are the best ways to clean the toxins out of your system:

1. Get 15 colonics in 30 days.

Right now as you read this there is an excellent chance that you have between three and fifteen pounds of undigested fecal matter stuck in your colon. This waste matter is highly toxic, suppressing your immune system, potentially causing gas, bloating and constipation, dramatically reducing the assimilation of nutrients, and slowing your metabolism. Getting a series of fifteen colonics over a thirty-day period is one of the most important first steps in cleansing and detoxifying your body. Most people lose between three and fifteen pounds simply by doing this procedure. Your hair, skin, and nails begin to radiate and glow with health. Your energy levels can skyrocket, depression, stress, anxiety and fatigue are usually dramatically reduced or eliminated. Food cravings are reduced or vanish completely.

2. Do a complete colon cleanse.

For my personal recommendations of the best cleanses, go to www.naturalcures.com.

3. Do a liver/gallbladder cleanse.

For my personal recommendations of the best cleanses, go to www.naturalcures.com.

4. Do a kidney/bladder cleanse.

For my personal recommendations of the best cleanses, go to www.naturalcures.com.

5. Do a heavy metal cleanse.

There are products available for home use to get heavy metals out of your body. There are also clinics around the world that provide excellent treatments to remove heavy metals from your body. Heavy metal cleansing like all of these cleanses is, in fact, a "natural cure" they don't want you to know about.

6. Do a parasite cleanse.

There are many products available for home use including the "parasite zapper" that effectively eliminate parasites. Parasites like heavy metals are a major cause of disease. Doing a parasite cleanse is another "natural cure" they don't want you to know about.

7. Do a candida cleanse.

If you have ever taken a single dose of antibiotics any time in your life, you have a candida yeast overgrowth in your body. This overgrowth is most common in the intestine, but can infiltrate your entire body. This overgrowth can be a cause of virtually every symptom you can imagine—headaches, gas bloating, indigestion, heartburn, nausea, allergies, asthma, Fibromyalgia, arthritis, diabetes, constipation, yeast infections, dandruff, acne, bad breath, fatigue, depression, stress, and on and on. Doing a program that eliminates the excess candida from your body is one of the backbones of good health. The most common side effect of excess candida is the inability to lose weight. People who eliminate excess candida virtually always lose massive amounts of weight without trying. Candida also causes food cravings and can make you eat when you're not hungry. When candida is normalized, a person's appetite can be dramatically reduced so that you're just simply not that hungry. There are many excellent products that can help eliminate candida from your body. The most complete candida protocol in my opinion is discussed in the book *Lifeforce* by Dr. Jeff McCombs. www.lifeforceplan.com

8. Do a full-body fat/lymphatic cleanse.

Go to www.purification.org

9. Drink eight full glasses of pure water daily.

All tap water is poisonous. All tap water is loaded with chlorine and chlorine by-products. Chlorine scars your arteries and, along with hydrogenated oil and homogenized dairy products, causes heart disease. Most tap water also has fluoride, which is one of the most poisonous and disease causing agents you can put in your body. Do not drink or use tap water for any reason except for washing your floor.

You need to drink water, and the water must be pure. Water is instrumental not only in flushing and nourishing the body, but also in keeping it hydrated and pH balanced. I recommend drinking a minimum of eight large glasses of water per day. I recommend a specific water purifier and specific bottled waters. Not all water filters or purifiers do an equally effective job. Some are much better than others. Not all bottled waters are equally pure and hydrating. Some are much better than others. Go to www.naturalcures.com for my personal recommendations.

10. Use a rebounder (mini trampoline) ten minutes a day.

A rebounder is a mini trampoline. Simply using this device for ten minutes a day can provide more cellular benefit than almost any other form of exercise. A rebounder stimulates every cell in the body simultaneously. It stimulates the immune system and is incredibly effective at cleansing toxins out of the cells. It promotes and stimulates all major organs and glands, strengthens the immune system, and dramatically strengthens and tones the muscles, tendons, and dramatically strengthens and tones the muscles, tendons, and ligaments. A truly spectacular and incredibly quick form of exercise.

11. Walk one hour a day.

People in America are exercising more than ever before, but the amount of walking has dramatically decreased. People in most foreign countries walk between ten and 100 times more than Americans. The body is designed to walk. Walking outside reduces stress, stimulates the lymphatic system, promotes a thin, lean body, and walking while looking at the world eliminates depression and dramatically reduces stress.

12. Stretch the muscles and tendons in your body.

If your body is supple and flexible, energy easily flows and blockages do not occur. When energy flows it is hard for illness and disease to take hold and manifest. I recommend doing a yoga class, or Pilates, martial arts, or any other kind of stretching on a regular basis. Every morning I spend fifteen minutes stretching. Throughout the day, during my normal activities, I spend a moment to stretch. It feels so good.

13. Practice deep breathing.

Your lungs need to be used. Due to stress levels, most Americans breathe from high up in their chests. If you watch a baby breathe naturally you will notice that they breathe fully and deeply. Their stomach and diaphragm expand as well as their entire chest and back. Deep breathing every day stimulates the immune system, increases metabolism, reduces stress, and brings vital oxygen into the body. Most people are oxygen deficient. Increasing oxygen to the cells can eliminate a multitude of diseases. Cancer, for example, cannot live in an oxygen-rich environment.

14. Sweat with a regular dry sauna or an infrared sauna (not a wet steam).

Your body is supposed to sweat. It is a very natural way to eliminate toxins. If you don't sweat, toxins build up in the system.

15. Give yourself a dry brush massage, exfoliating the skin and allowing toxins to come out of the skin at least once a day.

16. Get a full-body Swedish and/or deep tissue massage on a regular basis.

The benefits of massage are reflected in your:

Circulatory System by:
- helping to develop a stronger heart
- improving oxygen supply to cells
- improving the supply of nutrients to cells
- elimination of metabolic wastes
- decreasing blood pressure
- increasing circulation of lymph nodes

Digestive System by:

- relaxing the abdominal and intestinal muscles
- relieving tension
- stimulating activity of liver and kidneys
- elimination of waste material

Muscular System by:

- relaxing or stimulating muscles
- strengthening muscles and connective tissue
- helping to keep muscles flexible and pliable
- relieving soreness, tension, and stiffness

Nervous System by:

- stimulating motor nerve points
- relieving restlessness and insomnia
- promoting a sense of well-being
- relieving pain

Respiratory System by:

- developing respiratory muscles
- draining sluggish lymph nodes

Lymphatic System by:

- cleansing the body of metabolic wastes
- draining sluggish lymph nodes

Integumentary System (the skin) by:

- stimulating blood to better nourish skin
- improving tone and elasticity of skin
- helping to normalize glandular functions

Skeletal System by:

- improving body alignment
- relieving stiff joints
- relieving tired aching feet

There are many kinds of massages. Each masseuse gives a different massage. You may like one and not the other. I get at least one massage a week. They are highly therapeutic, and I recommend you get as many as you can as often as you can. Use different people to experience the full range of treatments.

17. Do chi kung.

Chi kung is a series of gentle movements that stimulate strength, energy flow, increased energy, and many other health benefits. I have a friend named Peter Ragnar who lives in Tennessee and is a senior citizen. He has the body and skin of an athlete in his thirties. No one would ever guess this man's age. He practices most of the concepts described in this book. One of the things he does, which he believes is a major cause of his youthful appearance and incredible health, is chi kung ten minutes a day. Because the earth's magnetic energy is so much lower today that it was thousands of years ago, he does the simple movements standing on very powerful magnets. This technique is very effective. Practitioners usually feel a major increase in physical energy within just a few days. Sleeping is improved and people report an increased sense of calmness and well-being. This course is available on videotape. For more information go to www.naturalcures.com.

18. Do tai chi.

There are many people teaching what they call tai chi. Unfortunately, most tai chi instructors aren't really teaching true tai chi. Tai chi is a series of flowing movements designed to center oneself, relieve stress, increase energy flow, increase flexibility and strength, and promote health and well-being. I have done tai chi for over twenty years and studied with dozens of so-called masters. Not until I learned tai chi from a real Shaolin monk from the Shaolin temple in China did I experience the real thing. The good news is doing any form of tai chi has benefits. If you want to learn the most authentic, most beneficial tai chi, go to www.naturalcures.com for information on videos of the Shaolin monk teaching tai chi. For more information go to www.shaolinwolf.com

19. Do a seven to thirty day fast.

For my personal recommendations on the best fasts, go to www.naturalcures.com.

20. Get "specialized treatments" as needed.

Treatments such as reflexology, acupuncture, cranial-sacral therapy, reiki, essential oil treatments, and various other holistic, all-natural therapies have profound positive effects on health.

Obviously, when a person looks at this list their initial reaction is a little bit of overwhelm. You may feel there is no way I can do all of these things. Well, start with doing something. You will notice the very first thing I listed was doing fifteen colonics in thirty days. Start with that one first. You will feel incredibly more energetic and better than ever before. Just cleaning the colon, in the vast majority of cases, has been known to cure many diseases. Each one of these things that I have mentioned above are in fact a "natural cure," and they are cures that "they" don't want you to know about. They are natural, they are not patentable, nobody's making billions of dollars on them, and they expose the fact that the drug industry and the food industry are causing the majority of illness and disease by feeding us chemical poisons. This is a fact that the powers that be don't want you to know about, but the fact is indisputable.

Dr. Schultz, www.dr-schulze.com, has a program of cleanses called "The Incurables." It has been reported that when people simply do some cleanses, such as those listed above, that incurable diseases are miraculously cured. The fact is the reason diseases leave the body is that the CAUSE of the disease, the toxins, are being removed. When the cause of the disease is removed via the cleansing processes that are listed above, the body goes back to normal, heals itself, thus the miraculous cures of the "incurable"! However, we must remember again the FDA's rule that "only a drug can cure, prevent, or treat a disease." Therefore, if any health-care practitioner said that any of the things I mention above is a cure he would be prosecuted by the FDA and imprisoned! That's right, the FDA would prosecute, and has prosecuted, and is prosecuting people criminally! And what is their crime? They are cleaning toxins out of the body and people who have incurable diseases are being miraculously cured. The crime is that these licensed health-care practitioners are not using drugs and surgery, but rather inexpensive all-natural methods and eradicating deadly, debilitating, incurable diseases from the body.

B. You Must Stop Putting Toxins in the Body

I just gave you a list of things to do to get toxins out of the body. It is important now to at least reduce the amount of toxins going in the body on an ongoing basis. Here is a list of recommendations that, if you do them, will dramatically reduce the amount of toxins you are putting in your body. Keep in mind that all of the recommendations in this chapter have a profound affect on preventing and curing disease because they are getting right at the cause of the symptoms and disease. They also have a profound affect at changing your body's pH from acidic to alkaline. Keep in mind that these are in fact natural cures! Doing these things can in fact cure your illness and disease because doing these recommendations actually stop what is CAUSING your disease.

If you stop doing the thing that is causing your symptoms and disease, then you have in fact "cured" your disease. This is what medical science does not want you to know. They don't want you to know what is causing your disease; they only want to sell you drugs to suppress the symptoms. Imagine a guy who says, "Every time I pour gasoline all over my house and light it with a match it burns to the ground. What's the cure?" You would laugh at such a ridiculous statement, but that is in fact what people do every day in relation to their own diseases. They come in and say, "What's the cure for my disease?" not realizing that they are in fact causing the disease by what they put in their body. The toxins that you are putting in your body are giving you the symptoms and disease. A question that comes up is which one of these is more important, or will have a more profound affect. The answer is every person is different; however, generally speaking, the more powerful techniques are at the top of each list. Sometimes just making one change can cause your symptoms to vanish. You must keep in mind that it has taken you years and years to develop your symptoms and disease. They didn't develop overnight, and if you stop putting the toxins in the symptoms are not going to vanish necessarily overnight, although in some cases they do. Generally, it takes weeks or months for the symptoms to slowly diminish and vanish unless, of course, as I mentioned, you are at the point of no return.

With that in mind, here is a powerful list of things to do and things to not do that will reduce the deadly poisons from going into your body and allow you to prevent and cure illness and disease.

1. Do not eat any food produced or sold by a publicly traded corporation or is a "brand name" product.

Wow! This is a tough one. If it comes in any massed produced packaging, that means it came from a mass production processing plant. If you have ever been in a mass production food processing facility, you would understand what I am talking about. Remember that there are over 15,000 chemicals that are routinely put into the food in the processing cycle that do not have to be listed on the label. Even if you read the ingredient list on the package, there is an excellent chance that the food itself has been produced with chemicals and chemicals have been added. So, virtually all food that you buy at the supermarket that comes in a package is loaded with dangerous chemicals. Secondly, the mass production processing dramatically changes the energetic structure of the food, as proven with the use of Kirlian photography.

Mass produced food in packages is simply unhealthy. Please do not believe what the fancy packaging say. The food companies are only interested in profits and getting you to buy the food. They are allowed to lie, deceive, and mislead so that they can coerce you to buy their product. If you must buy something in a box, jar, can, or package, buy something that was produced by hand in a very small facility. Also look for the words "100% organic" and read the ingredient list. It still may not be great, but at least it's better than buying mass produced, non-organic products. Do not be deceived by the words "all-natural," "fat free," "sugar free," "low in carbs," "light," "healthy," etc. The food industry has lobbied Congress to allow these words to be put on virtually anything. They are meaningless, deceptive, and in my opinion, fraudulent.

2. Get all metal out of your dental work.

It is vitally important that you see a holistic dentist. It is absolutely vital for you to know that so many people suffer horrible debilitating symptoms that are directly caused by the metal that is in their dental work. At the back of the book under my newsletter section I wrote an article which addressed this at length. I would highly encourage you to read it. Simply doing this step, for many, many people, is the cure for their disease. It can be miraculous.

3. Stop smoking.

When I first wrote this book I had mentioned that I smoked for twenty years. I was totally addicted to nicotine and tobacco. I tried everything under the sun to quit, virtually everything! Over a hundred products and techniques, all to no avail. Last year I finally discovered a combination of things that worked for me. It was like an inventor mixing different things together and making a breakthrough discovery. What I discovered was the secret that allowed me to quit smoking absolutely 100 percent effortlessly and easily. I never had a single craving. I never wanted another smoke. I could not believe how easy it was. I was offered smokes and had absolutely no interest at all. As a matter of fact, the thought of smoking disgusted me. I felt no depravation. Smoking is a horrible practice that leads to and causes all kinds of health disorders. The Federal Trade Commission, in my opinion, is trying to stop me from telling people the method that I used to allow me to quit smoking. If you want to know the exact method that I used to quit smoking, go to www.naturalcures.com and become a private member. There you can read the exact method that I used to quit smoking easily and effortlessly. If you are a smoker you need to quit. If you have tried everything and failed, I would encourage you to read what worked for me.

4. Don't drink tap water.

All tap water is poisonous. Virtually all tap water is loaded with contaminants, toxins, poisons, and known cancer causing agents including deadly fluoride and chlorine. Drinking tap water causes illness and disease.

You must drink water. However, the water must be pure. Bottled spring water (some bottled spring waters are purer than others), water filtered using reverse-osmosis, and water purified through steam distillation, are all better options than tap water. The FTC has currently forbidden me to mention brand names in this book. For my personal recommendations of the best bottled waters and water purification products, go to www.naturalcures.com.

5. Buy and use a shower filter.

You absorb more toxins by taking one shower than by drinking eight glasses of water. Your skin absorbs the water from your shower or bath. A hot shower produces steam and that turns many of the chemicals in the water into poisonous gases. These gases are inhaled or absorbed through the skin. A good shower filter removes most of the toxins in the water. Use one and you'll never have a bad hair day again. For my personal recommendations go to www.naturalcures.com.

6. Eat only 100% organic food.

You want to eat food that has not been grown with chemical fertilizers, pesticides, or herbicides. Organic food has no chemical poison residue and has much higher amounts of nutrients.

7. Do not eat in fast-food restaurants.

Read the book *Fast Food Nation* and watch the documentary *Super Size Me!* After you have finished throwing up, be glad that you are hearing the truth now. Fast food is simply some of the most nutritionally deficient and chemically loaded "food" on the planet. If the definition of food was "fuel for the body that also encourages life," fast food could no longer be called food. It should be called "fast, good tasting poison," which is a more accurate description of what it is. Oh, and did I tell you that it's designed to increase your appetite, make you physically addicted, and purposely constructed to make you obese? If you eat fifteen meals per week in a fast-food restaurant, you have a 90 percent chance of getting cancer, heart disease, diabetes, acid reflux, obesity, and potentially dozens of other diseases. Avoid fast food at all costs.

8. Do not eat anything that comes out of a microwave oven.

Throw your microwave away. I believe that when you microwave anything it becomes energetically toxic to the body. Eating microwaved food on a regular basis (this includes food that is being reheated in the microwave) weakens your immune system and causes depression and anxiety. Parents who microwave baby formula are poisoning their children unknowingly. The baby formula itself is poison; by microwaving it, it becomes even more toxic. For more information read my newsletter article in the back of the book.

9. Eliminate aspartame and monosodium glutamate.

Aspartame goes by NutraSweet®. Both aspartame and MSG are classified as excitotoxins. There are three great books on this subject. *Aspartame, Is it Safe?* was written by a medical doctor. Based on hundreds of case studies, the doctor concludes that aspartame is responsible for many distressing medical problems, ranging from headaches and memory loss to hyperactivity in children and seizure disorders. Next, the book *Excitotoxins, The Taste That Kills,* also written by a medical doctor, examines how monosodium glutamate, aspartame, and similar substances cause harm to the brain and nervous system, and how these substances can cause Alzheimer's, Lou Gherig's disease, depression, MS, and more. Lastly, *In Bad Taste, The MSG Complex,* again written by a medical doctor, explains how MSG is a major cause of treatable and preventable illnesses such as headaches, asthma, epilepsy, heart irregularities, depression, and attention deficit/hyperactivity disorder.

10. Do not eat artificial sweeteners (including Splenda).

Artificial sweeteners are man-made chemicals. They are poisons and should never be consumed. They cause all kinds of health problems.

Use raw organic honey, organic raw evaporated sugarcane juice, or the herb stevia. All are excellent choices for sweeteners. Remember, science is not better than nature.

11. Do not drink diet sodas.

Diet sodas have been called the "new crack" because they are so addicting. Diet sodas will actually make you gain weight as well as make you depressed. Because of the artificial sweeteners used, such as aspartame, they are also giving you a variety of medical symptoms. If you want a soda, ideally, get an organic soda from your health food store. Or if you must indulge, drink a regular soda. If you were to stop drinking all diet sodas and replace them with regular soda, you would in fact lose weight. The idea that diet sodas have fewer calories, thus are good for weight control, is a lie. The exact opposite is true. Remember, all carbonated drinks block calcium absorption.

12. Do not eat hydrogenated oil.

This is classified as a trans fat. Hydrogenated oils are man-made products. They are toxic poisons. More importantly, they attack the artery walls and cause heart disease. They also attack the liver, spleen, intestine, kidneys, and gallbladder, causing the internal organs to operate much less efficiently. The bad news is that hydrogenated oil is in virtually every product you buy! The good news is that if you shop at a health food or whole food store, and if you read the labels, you can find many of the products you buy now without hydrogenated oil. This is a good example of how medical science says something is bad, and then later reverses their position. For years heart patients were told to stay away from butter because it was bad for your heart. Instead, they were told to use margarine. Unfortunately, most all margarines are 100 percent hydrogenated oil. Margarines are man-made unnatural products that are deadly poison to the body. Now we hear from the same doctors and medical community that margarine is, in fact, much worse than butter. Stay away from hydrogenated oils and trans fats at all costs.

13. Do not eat homogenized and pasteurized dairy products.

All dairy products are not created equal. Today's milk, cheeses and other dairy products are radically different in nutritional value and chemical composition than they were fifty years ago. American dairy products are also vastly different than dairy products in other countries. Have you ever noticed that butter from France tastes different from butter from America? Have you noticed that the same kind of cheese tastes different depending on what part of the country or world in which it was produced?

There are vast differences in dairy products due to multiple factors. These differences mean that the dairy products affect the body in vastly different ways. Example: raw milk that has not been pasteurized or homogenized, that came from a cow that was organically raised, was free-roaming, grass fed, and not given antibiotic or growth hormone injections, will affect the body much differently than milk coming from a genetically modified cow that has been given antibiotic and growth hormone injections, never allowed to roam, is fed chemically laced growth enhancing feed, and has been pasteurized and homogenized. The problem occurs when studies are conducted and researchers do not use raw organic milk. They use the chemically laced, pasteurized and homogenized milk. If they were to conduct the studies comparing organic raw milk versus the supermarket variety, we would see dramatically different results. The bottom line here is the standard supermarket variety of milk and dairy products are very unhealthy. Homogenization makes the dairy products scar the arteries in your body and is a leading cause of heart disease. Organic raw, unpasteurized, unhomogenized milk, cheese and dairy products are incredibly healthy. Remember, science is not better than nature. When man gets involved and changes things from its natural state to increase profits, the food is no longer "real"; it becomes a man-made look-alike imitation.

14. Do not eat high fructose corn syrup.

If you look at the ingredients of the product you are buying and see sugar as the number one ingredient, you may be concerned. In order to avoid this, food manufacturers use a variety of sweeteners such as sugar, dextrose, fructose, corn syrup solids, corn syrup, high fructose corn syrup, multidextrin, and a variety of others. If you were to add up all of the sugars, in most cases sugar would be the number one ingredient in most of these kinds of products. High fructose corn syrup is used primarily for two reasons. First, it is very inexpensive. Secondly, it makes you fatter than the other sweeteners that could be used. The food industry wants you to be fat. Fat people eat more food, thus increasing sales and profits for the food companies. The food industry has lobbied against the public campaign to "eat less, exercise more" because they do not want people to be encouraged to eat less. Doing so would decrease sales and profits. Shocking, but true.

15. Use only toothpaste with no fluoride.

16. Do not use nonstick cookware.

When nonstick cookware is heated to a high temperature it emits toxic fumes that can kill a small animal such as a bird! These toxic fumes, when inhaled by humans, lead to respiratory disease, weakening of the immune system, cancer, depression, asthma, headaches, and a multitude of other health problems.

17. Eat only organic, kosher meat and poultry.

This subject is incredibly complex. Oprah Winfrey had a show devoted to the meat industry, and was sued for expressing her opinions. She won. Any meat or poultry that is not organic and kosher is incredibly toxic. Generally speaking, here are the differences:

- A conventional animal has been genetically modified in breeding, thus becoming an animal that could never occur naturally.

- An organic animal has genetics that have not been modified by man and is in its most natural state.

- A conventional animal is injected with growth hormones and antibiotics, meaning that the meat we consume is then loaded with these drugs.

- An organic animal is given no drugs, so its meat is drug free.

- A conventional animal is not allowed to roam freely or exercise normally, thus creating an incredibly toxic animal that is unnaturally obese and diseased.

- An organic animal is allowed to roam naturally, grows at its normal rate, and is not loaded with toxins or diseased.

- A conventional animal is fed an unnatural diet of chemicals and feed that it would never eat naturally. Conventional cows, for example, are also fed ground up cow parts, pig

- A grass-fed organic cow eats grass as it would in nature, and the grass has not been laced with chemical fertilizers, herbicides, and pesticides.

parts, goat parts, and horse parts. Many of these ground up animal parts are from diseased, sick animals that are not fit or human consumption. Keep in mind the cow is a vegetarian and is not designed to be eating ground up diseased animals.

- A conventional animal is slaughtered by being shot in the head with a bolt. The animal experiences incredible pain and trauma. Adrenaline, which is highly poisonous, permeates the animal's tissue. The blood, which is loaded with toxins, also permeates the issue. The trauma causes the energy field in and around the animal to become highly negative. The animal usually dies in its own urine and feces.

- An organic animal that is also kosher is killed in the most humane way possible, by slicing its throat. The animal experiences no pain, is immediately drained of all blood, its internal organs are inspected to make sure the animal is 100 percent healthy, and the tissue is salted to draw out any blood and kill any bacteria.

- A conventional animal is usually aged, which means the animal flesh is hung in a dark room and allowed to rot. A green mold covers the rotting animal flesh. This green toxic mold is bacteria that tenderizes the meat, but also fills the meat with more toxic poisons.

- Organic kosher meat is not aged.

Many conventional meat and poultry products are sprayed with dangerous chemicals to kill bacteria. Some are irradiated, wiping out the natural life force energy and, as evidenced by Kirlian photography, leaving the energy field around the meat highly toxic to humans.

When I learned about this, I decided to eat only kosher organic meat. For thirty days, every day, I ate some kosher organic meat. I tried to monitor if I felt any difference. I could not detect anything specific or dramatic. I wasn't convinced that it was such a big deal. I decided to throw a barbeque and invited several of my friends over to my home. I went to the butcher and bought the absolute best, highest quality steaks made—conventional, Black Angus aged steaks. The best money can buy. I cooked the steaks and served them to my guests. Each person raved about how delicious and tender the steaks were. Some said they were the best they had ever eaten. I took one bite of mine and felt very odd. It was as if I was eating some "bad meat." I looked around at everyone else devouring their steaks and enjoying the delicious flavor. I asked my friend to taste my steak. He loved it. So I took another bite. As I chewed and swallowed the meat I began to feel funny. Perspiration started on my forehead, I got pale, and my stomach felt very nauseous. I excused myself, went to the bathroom and threw up.

What had occurred was that for thirty days I only ate pure nontoxic, undiseased meat. Eating this highly toxic meat caused me to get sick. Because I had eaten only clean meat for so long my body had immediately rejected the toxins. This is why people in Mexico, for example, can drink the diseased toxic water and show no signs of illness. But if an American were to drink the same water, they would get violently ill. Your body does create a tolerance to poisons.

The bottom line is, chicken, duck, lamb, beef, and goat are all fine as long as it is organic and kosher. It is hard to find organic kosher products in stores. On my Web site www.naturalcures.com you can find out where this is available.

18. Do not eat farm raised fish.

Companies produce farm raised fish to make a profit. Farm raised fish are given unnatural feed and can be highly toxic compared to their natural wild counterparts. Stay away from any fish that has been farm raised.

19. Do not eat pork.

Remember, you are what you eat. Pork is a highly toxic diseased food. A pig eats anything in its path, including its own feces. Whatever it eats turns to meat on its bones in a few hours. All pork products are laced with disease and viruses. It is toxic and unhealthy. The human body virtually goes into toxic shock by consuming pork. Massive amounts of blood and energy go to the stomach and intestines to help breakdown and digest this toxic material. Pork is never fully digested in the human body; however, the human digestive system works nonstop in overdrive for up to eighteen hours attempting to neutralize and digest pork. If you didn't eat pork for thirty days and then had some, there is an excellent chance you would be violently ill. Eliminating pork, or at least reducing it dramatically, can have a profound impact on your health and sense of well-being. Try and see.

20. Do not eat shellfish.

More people are allergic to shellfish than any other food on the planet. More people get sick from eating shellfish than any other food. More people die from eating shellfish than any other food. Any fish that does not have scales and fins should be avoided. This includes clams, mussels, shrimp, lobster, crab, squid, eel, catfish, shark, etc. The fish must have scales and fins. Catfish, for example, has fins but no scales. It is interesting that this is one of the kosher dietary laws. Today, we know that fish with scales and fins do not absorb the toxins in the water as readily as sea creatures that do not have both scales and fins.

I grew up in the Boston area. I loved my shellfish more than any other seafood. Occasionally, an algae in the water called the "red tide" would infest the local shores. When this occurred, warnings went out not to eat any shellfish, for doing so could cause sickness and death. However, you could eat the haddock, mackerel, or flounder. The fish that had scales and fins did not absorb the poisons into its edible flesh; however, shellfish or any fish that did not have both scales and fins would absorb the toxins and could cause sickness and death. All sea creatures that do not have scales and fins are loaded with toxins and should be avoided.

21. If you can't eat it, don't put it on your skin.

Your skin is the largest organ in the body. Whatever you put on your skin goes into the body. Many of the things we put on our skin from antiperspirants, moisturizing lotions, cosmetics, insect repellents, sunscreens, and perfumes are so poisonous that if you put them in your mouth you would die within minutes. I know for many of you this is unrealistic. Remember that I said that if you can't do something 100 percent, do the best you can. If you can't eliminate everything at least reduce the amount of poison you put on your skin.

22. Get an air purifier.

The air in your house is most assuredly not pure and clean. You live, work, and sleep in an environment where the air is flat-out unhealthy. I absolutely recommend an air purifier for your home, your work space, and most importantly, your bedroom. Since you are breathing all night long, it would be a good idea to be breathing the cleanest, purest air you can. Your work space is the second most important. There are hundreds of various types of air filters and air purifiers on the market. I believe some are much better than others. Some are so good that they can also eliminate all the black mold that is causing illness in many homes today. Go to my Web site, www.naturalcures.com, and in the private members area you can e-mail me for my specific recommendations.

23. Use only nontoxic 100-percent organic cleaning supplies.

Cleaning products used in the home have been proven to be a leading cause of cancer in children. The cleaning products you use do, in fact, suppress the immune system and cause disease. This occurs by inhaling the fumes or through contact with the skin.

24. Do not drink canned or bottled juice.

All canned or bottled juice you buy in the store has been pasteurized causing it to be toxic to the body. The filtering and processing used in the manufacturing of juice increases and concentrates the amount of toxic chemicals in the product. Drink only fresh juice made with 100-percent organic ingredients.

25. Do not use sun block.

This is one of the greatest frauds in history. The sun does not cause cancer. Sun block has been shown to cause cancer. The ingredients in sun block are now strongly believed to be the number one cause of skin cancer. There is no skin cancer in Africa. People stay in the sun all day long with no sunscreen. It is not the pigment in the skin, as some suggest. People with African heritage living in America have the highest rate of skin cancer, and they stay in the sun the least. You don't want to get a sunburn, so wear a hat or cover your body with light clothing. The sun is healthy for you and the sun should be on your skin. Statistics show that the people who use the most amounts of sun block have the highest skin cancer rates. This goes for tanning lotions as well. Remember, whatever you put on your skin is going in your body. If you can't eat it, don't put it on your skin.

26. Do not take vitamins.

Many companies selling vitamins are only doing so to make money. There are many grades of individual vitamins. Most companies use the cheapest grades available. These inexpensive "vitamins" in many cases are chemically produced and are not natural. Most vitamin pills have vitamins and minerals in a proportion never found in nature.

It is true that you are most assuredly deficient in vitamins and minerals. The best way to correct this deficiency is by juicing. The second best way is to take whole food supplements. These are not vitamin and mineral pills. Whole food supplements simply take organically produced vegetables and fruits and concentrate them into a convenient tablet that you can take. When you take a whole food supplement you are getting all the vitamins and minerals in the proportion that nature intended. You are also getting the enzymes and cofactors present in nature. It is interesting to note that many natural plants have up to 30 percent of their composition that defies scientific analysis. That simply means that when you take a whole food supplement not only are you getting vitamins, minerals, enzymes and cofactors in the precise proportion nature intended, you are also getting all of the things that science has not discovered yet. Again, I am forbidden to give you my recommendations here in this book. Go to www.naturalcures.com, e-mail me, and I will give you my personal recommendations.

27. Do not use antiperspirants or deodorants.

Antiperspirants and deodorants contain deadly poisons, most notably aluminum. These poisons are being put on the skin close to the lymph nodes. Anything absorbed in the skin from the armpit gets picked up by the lymph system and first travels to the breasts. I believe one of the major causes of breast cancer in women is the use of these poisonous products. A healthy person should not have an offending odor; however, if you must use an antiperspirant or deodorant, there are all-natural products available. Go to your local health food store and inquire. Don't be misled by the label. Read the ingredients. If you can't pronounce the words, don't buy it. Remember, if you can't eat it, don't put it on your skin.

28. Do not eat white processed sugar.

Sugar cane, when grown organically, pressed, and dried, creates pure, unprocessed living sugar. You can purchase this in health food stores. It is healthy and good for you. White table sugar, however, is grown with dangerous chemicals, processed, stripped of all its nutritional value and heated, destroying any living vitality that it had. White sugar is a product that has such powerful adverse affects on the body it could be classified as a drug. Real, unprocessed, raw, evaporated cane juice, which is real sugar, is good for you. White sugar is poison. The chemicals used in the growing of sugar cane are known to cause cancer in sea turtles. Those poisonous chemicals used in the growing still remain in the product you buy in the store.

29. Do not eat white processed flour.

White processed flour is similar to white sugar. It comes from grain that has been chemically treated in the growing process, stripped of all its natural fiber and nutrients, and chemically bleached to make it a pretty white. White flour mixed with water makes paste. You use it to make papier-mache. It turns hard as a rock. That's what happens when you eat it. It is an unnatural product that the body does not know how to digest. It has little nutritional value, no life force, spikes your insulin, and causes constipation. Use organic whole grain flour that has been minimally processed, or buy organic grains and grind them yourself.

30. Eat nothing that says "fat free" on the label.

Food companies want you to buy their products. Whatever the hot button is at the time will determine what their marketing people decide goes on the label. "Fat free" does not mean "healthy." When you see "fat free" on the label, be assured that the company is trying to deceive you, so don't buy it. Most fat free products are simply loaded with unbelievable amounts of sugar and chemicals.

31. Eat nothing that says "sugar free" on the label.

It if says sugar free on the label there is a good chance the product is laced with artificial sweeteners. Don't buy it.

32. Eat nothing that says "low carbs" or "net carbs" on the label.

This is the current hot button. The biggest scam going now is the term "net carbs." Manufacturers load up these products with chemicals and artificial sweeteners that they claim have negligible results on insulin levels, so they do not count these real carbohydrates in the net carb number. A product that says it has two net carbs could have as many as forty grams of real carbohydrates. Do not buy these products, as you know that the manufacturers are simply trying to take advantage of the current fad to sell you their products.

33. Do not eat "food bars."

Food bars are man-made products filled with chemicals to provide, first and foremost, good taste. They are highly processed and should be avoided. There are a few all-raw organic food bars. Check at your local health food store and read the ingredient list.

34. Do not eat diet or protein shakes.

Like food bars, these are produced by companies whose goal is to make them taste great using the cheapest ingredients possible. With rare exception they should be avoided at all costs.

35. Stay away from hot tubs, steam rooms and swimming pools.

Swimming pools and hot tubs are filled with water that is loaded to excess with chlorine. Chlorine is a deadly poisonous chemical. People think swimming in a pool or relaxing in a hot tub is healthy. The exact opposite is true. It suppresses your immune system, dries your skin, and loads your body with high amounts of chlorine, scarring the arteries and leading to heart disease. The steam pouring into the steam room is from regular tap water that is loaded with toxic poisons and contaminants. A steam room is, in fact, a poisonous gas chamber and incredibly unhealthy. Swimming is excellent in the ocean or a lake. If you have a pool or hot tub, inquire about a filtration system where no chlorine or chemicals are used. The system that I use employs ozone and oxygen to purify the water. No chlorine or chemicals are put into my pool or hot tub. I have had the water tested, and it was found to be some of the purest water that the laboratory has ever seen. If you can't drink the water, don't swim in it. Some people may say you can't drink lake water or ocean water, and that is true. Those waters, however, are living, fully-vitalized natural waters. Chlorinated swimming pools are something not found in nature.

36. Eliminate air fresheners.

Ideally, don't spray anything in the air; don't use solid air fresheners or the plug-in variety. All you are doing is putting toxic chemicals in the air. It really is insane. In my bathrooms I do have a can of organic citrus oil, which can be purchased at most health food stores. Read the labels. Use 100-percent organic essential oils or air purification systems to eliminate offensive odors. Remember, if you can't eat it don't spray it in the air.

37. Eliminate fluorescent lighting.

Fluorescent lighting makes you tired and weakens your immune system. Get rid of all florescent lighting and replace it with full spectrum lighting. Full spectrum lighting is very similar to natural sunlight, and can have incredible health benefits, the most notable being increased energy and alleviation of depression.

38. Reduce or eliminate air conditioning.

Most general air conditioning is simply not healthy. Air conditioning units as a general rule make the air unnatural, thus unhealthy. Keep in mind that air conditioning did not exist seventy years ago. We think we need air conditioning; certainly, it can make your office and home more tolerable in extremely hot conditions. Use air conditioning less and you will see a decrease in the amount of colds and flus you come down with.

39. Avoid dry cleaning.

The chemicals in dry cleaning are toxic poisons. Putting them on your skin increases risk of dozens of diseases.

40. Make your own beer and wine.

If you are going to drink beer and wine, make it yourself with pure organic ingredients. It's fun, it tastes better and it's much healthier for you. Beer and wine are not unhealthy; however, the chemicals on the grapes, the hops, and other ingredients get into the final product. The heat used in processing kills the beneficial living enzymes. It is much better, however, to drink beer or wine than sodas or canned or bottled juice.

41. Buy a good vacuum cleaner with a hepa filter.

Doing the above things will reduce the amount of toxins put into your body and they absolutely, categorically 100 percent can and do cure disease. These are in fact "natural cures." I've seen people with MS simply stop drinking diet sodas and their MS symptoms vanished. I've seen people with diabetes stop eating in fast-food restaurants and in three weeks they no longer had diabetes. I've seen people who have migraine headaches and constipation problems stop eating pasteurized and homogenized dairy products and, as if by magic, their migraines stopped and they became regular. I've seen people with horrible skin rashes and acne use a shower filter and see all of their symptoms vanish, and watch their skin become smooth and beautiful again. Don't be misled or deceived into thinking things as simple as these are not cures. These things are causing your illness and disease, and eliminating them can and does cure disease!

C. You must handle and address your nutritional deficiencies.

By now, hopefully you know that you have nutritional deficiencies. Virtually every single person on the planet has nutritional deficiencies to varying degrees. The reason you are nutrient deficient is because the way the food is grown and processed strips much of the nutritional value in the food.

Virtually everything that you buy called "food" has been dramatically depleted of its nutritional value. As I mentioned before in this book, researchers have shown that you would have to eat over five times as much food as your grandparents just to receive the same nutritional value. However, it's worse because we have more toxins in our body; therefore, we cannot even absorb the little nutrition we are getting from our food. Therefore, we are all nutrient deficient. It is also vitally important that you totally understand that many, if not all, diseases are caused at least in part by nutritional deficiencies. The example I gave earlier about the disease of scurvy is a good simple example.

Scurvy, as I mentioned, is a horrible debilitating disease. However, researchers have discovered that scurvy is simply caused by a vitamin C deficiency. If you were to eat some oranges, lemons, or limes scurvy would be cured. Therefore, an orange, lemon, lime, or even simply vitamin C in a capsule is in fact the cure for scurvy. However, as I mentioned, the FDA has the crazy law that says only a drug can cure, prevent, or treat a disease. According to the FDA, oranges, lemons, and limes, or vitamin C, cannot legally be the cure for scurvy. Even though it is the cure for scurvy, legally it is not the cure for scurvy! I know it's totally insane; I know it's wrong, but that's how it is. And again, the reason it is that way is because the drug companies want to control anything to do with the treatment of illness and disease. The drug companies' profits are at stake and they will stop at nothing to protect those profits. Remember again the millions of dollars politicians make by buying and selling stock, much of which are pharmaceutical stocks based on what anyone else would call insider information. The profits and money that are at stake are in the billions, and billions, and billions! Remember, it's always all about the money.

The bottom line is you do have nutritional deficiencies and nutritional deficiencies absolutely cause illness and disease. If you want to prevent disease and if you want to cure disease you absolutely must handle your nutritional deficiencies. Again I will tell you drugs and surgery are not the answer to prevent and cure disease. Since the lack of drugs and surgery didn't cause the disease how could they cure it? Does that make sense? I hope it does. So let me give you a list of dos and don'ts, which if you do them will handle your nutritional deficiencies, and for many of you will be the miraculous all-natural cure that you have been looking for.

1. Eat more fresh organic fruits and vegetables.

You don't have to be a vegetarian to be healthy. I have never seen any real, convincing evidence that vegetarians are healthier or live longer than people who eat animal products. However, the healthiest people absolutely eat a large amount of fresh, organic, raw, uncooked fruits and vegetables. If you were to do just one thing, I would tell you to eat four pieces of fresh fruit per day and two big raw salads full of vegetables. If you changed nothing else in your diet, but just added those two things, many medical conditions would disappear. Ideally, the fruits and vegetables should be organic and uncooked, but cooked non-organic fruits and vegetables are better than none at all.

2. Buy a juice machine and use it.

Animals don't own juice machines, but animals have not loaded their bodies with the amount of toxins we have. They use their bodies as they were designed, unlike us, and they eat raw, uncooked food full of living enzymes and packed with nutrition and life force energy. Our food supply today is dramatically depleted of vital vitamins and minerals. Organic produce has up to ten times the vitamin and minerals as non-organic, and has none of the poison residues of the chemical fertilizers, pesticides and fungicides. Even so, because the soil is so depleted, organic produce still has less nutritional value than the same produce had fifty years ago. You would have to eat ten times the amount of produce today to even come close to the nutritional value of food fifty years ago. Therefore, it is absolutely impossible to get the amount of vitamins, minerals, and enzymes that you need by simply eating food. And remember, because of all of the drugs and toxins you have ingested, your ability to absorb these nutrients is dramatically reduced. Even if you ate only raw, uncooked organic fruits, vegetables, nuts, and seeds, your body would have major nutritional deficiencies. The absolute best way to correct this problem is to buy a good juice machine and make fresh juice using organic fruits and vegetables. Drinking three to four glasses of fresh juice gives your body a huge amount of living enzymes, as well as vitamins and minerals in the natural state and in the proportion that nature intended.

3. Eat raw organic nuts and seeds.

Raw means uncooked. Stay away from roasted and salted nuts and seeds. Ideally, buy them in the shell, they retain more nutrients. There is tremendous life force in nuts and seeds. They are great to snack on throughout the day.

4. Get natural sunlight.

Go for a walk in the sun! Your body needs sunlight. Do not use sunglasses or sun screens. The sun enters through the eyes and stimulates energy in the entire body. Thirty minutes a day, minimum, in the sun promotes incredible health benefits. Remember, it is the sun that creates growth in plants. The solar energy from sun can be very alkalizing to the body; it reduces depression and strengthens your immune system. Don't be misled by the medical establishment. The sun is good for you and its absolutely needed. Go to www.sungazing.com.

5. Eat an organic apple a day.

It's true, an apple a day keeps the doctor away! This is a "natural cure" for dozens of various diseases. It is in fact a superfood.

6. Take coral calcium.

The Federal Trade Commission forbids me to say anything about coral calcium. For the truth, go to www.naturalcures.com.

7. Take all-natural Vitamin E.

There are many forms of Vitamin E on the market. There are only two companies that I know of that manufacture the full spectrum all-natural Vitamin E. These are the only two forms of Vitamin E I recommend you take. The fact of the matter is every single person is nutrient deficient. The most important mineral you are deficient in is calcium, which is why I recommend you supplement your diet with calcium. The most important vitamin you are deficient in, in my opinion, is vitamin E. Taking Vitamin E can prevent heart disease, eliminate varicose veins, improve sexual performance, reduce or alleviate depression, and a whole host of other disorders. In the back of this book in my newsletter section I wrote an article about vitamin E and I highly encourage you to read it.

8. Take liquid colloidal minerals daily.

You are deficient in minerals. Nutritional deficiencies lead to disease. Correcting these deficiencies cures disease. Listen to "Dead Doctors Don't Lie," a tape available on the Internet.

9. Drink the "magic juices."

There are several fruits that are being sold that have absolutely miraculous healing properties in the body. These fruits are from around the world and are very difficult to buy fresh and juice fresh; therefore, you must buy them in a bottle. Unfortunately, because the government requires pasteurization, these juices are in fact pasteurized. Some of them have a natural substance added to help preserve the juice; however, the positive definitely outweighs the negative. I highly encourage you to buy and drink these juices as they have been shown to virtually cure disease miraculously. The juices are noni, goji, mangosteen, aloe vera, and acai berry. I wrote an article on these juices in my newsletter and reprinted that article at the back of this book. I highly encourage you to read the article. These juices are convenient and provide you with super nutrition as well as help detoxify and cleanse the body. I personally have them in my refrigerator and drink them almost every day.

10. Take a whole food supplement daily.

Whole food supplements are not synthetic vitamins and minerals. They are "concentrated real food". They contain nutrients, living enzymes, life force energy, in the exact proportion that nature intended. Whole food supplements include chorella, blue-green algae, spirulina, royal jelly, and other types of concentrated whole herbs, plants, dehydrated juices, and/or sprouts. Remember your body is deficient in nutrients such as vitamins, minerals, enzymes, and various cofactors. This is the fact. There is no way that you can get all the nutrients you need by eating food. You would have to eat ten to twenty times the amount of food as you are now, and it would all have to be organic for you to meet your minimum nutritional needs. Nutritional deficiencies cause disease. Having the proper amount of vitamins, minerals, enzymes, and cofactors allows your body to operate as it was designed and can prevent and cure almost all disease including cancer.

11. Eat raw organic honey, bee propolis, royal jelly, and bee pollen.

Raw organic bee products and honey are super nutritious foods. Royal jelly, for example, has the highest percentage of components that defy chemical analysis. What this means is there are nutrients in royal jelly that have not been discovered by science. This is an important point. Remember, science is not better than nature. Science continually thinks that they are smarter than anyone else on the planet. Science continually believes that they know all there is to know about health nutrition or anything for that matter. But science has yet to discover all of the nutrients that we need for health. Many foods contain nutrients that defy chemical analysis. It doesn't mean we don't need the nutrients, it just means that science hasn't discovered them yet. This is why eating food in its most natural raw state is so important. These foods are some of the most nutritious and healing on the planet.

12. Get an oxygen water cooler.

For a variety of reasons, your body is deficient in oxygen. Increasing the amount of oxygen in the body to the level where it should be alkalizes the body and creates an environment where disease cannot exist. One of the best ways to add oxygen into the body is through water. Do not buy oxygenated water at the store. The oxygen dissipates rapidly and by the time it gets to the store, and you buy it, any oxygen that was added is probably gone. I have a water cooler in my house and my offices that adds the oxygen when the water is dispensed. Most people feel an immediate rush of energy and increased vitality. For information on where to get yours, go to www.naturalcures.com.

13. Take digestive enzymes.

One of the main causes of indigestion, heartburn, gas, bloating, and constipation is a lack of digestive enzymes in your stomach and intestine. Because of antibiotics, other nonprescription and prescription drugs, chlorinated and fluoride-full water, it has been shown that most people simply do not have enough digestive enzymes in their system, slowing a person's metabolism and blocking the absorption of nutrients. Your body's ability to produce digestive enzymes has been dramatically reduced. Therefore, I believe you need to take digestive enzymes for a period of time until your body is cleansed and rejuvenated, so it can produce the correct amount on its own. Taking digestive enzymes can eliminate acid reflux, heartburn, indigestion, gas, bloating, and constipation. There are many brands available containing a variety of ingredients. Go to your local health food store and inquire as to their recommendations. I give you my recommendations at www.naturalcures.com. It is interesting to note that the majority of people who start taking digestive enzymes lose between five and ten pounds in the first thirty days.

14. Use organic sea salt.

Regular table salt is poison. Sea salt is infinitely better for you. This one small change can also make you lose between five and ten pounds in the first thirty days.

15. Eat organic dark chocolate.

Okay, you need your chocolate. Chocolate is not bad. The ingredients that are put in with the chocolate can be very bad. There are several brands of organic dark chocolate bars that taste wonderful and are filled with real raw organic ingredients. Go to your health food store and inquire. Read the ingredient list. Then indulge and enjoy.

16. Take an omega-3 supplement.

There is a great book written by Dr. Gary Gordon about the benefits of omega-3s in a person's diet. The book explains how and why people today get very little omega-3 compounds in their diet. Lack of omega-3s has been specifically linked to a host of illnesses and diseases including depression.

17. Eat snacks.

Don't go hungry! What I mean by eat snacks is eat in between meals if you are hungry. However, my definition of snack and your definition of snack are probably two different things. My definition of "snack" is organic apples, pears, or other type of organic fruit, organic raw nuts and seeds, organic raw celery, carrots, cucumbers or other vegetables, some organic chicken salad, tuna salad, or other organic beef or poultry. Additionally, my idea of a snack is a glass of freshly made organic fruit and/or vegetable juice. On occasion my idea of a snack is some toast made with whole grain or sprouted bread and raw organic honey. The key is you don't want to be hungry.

Remember, you are nutritionally deficient. Remember that virtually every disease has been linked to nutritional deficiencies. Remember that the research is conclusive that when nutritional deficiencies are addressed many diseases vanish! Remember, the powers that be want you to believe that you need drugs to cure and prevent disease. This is a great lie. The fact is diseases are not caused by "lack of drugs." Remember, as I said before, you don't have a headache because you have an aspirin deficiency, but you do have a headache because of either toxins in your body, or a nutritional deficiency, or exposure to electromagnetic chaos, or mental and emotional stress! Do you understand that the headache that you have is caused by one, or a combination of, those four things? It is not caused by an aspirin or drug deficiency! Understand that point. Imagine the man who walks in the doctor's office and says, "Every time I hit my foot with a hammer it hurts. How do I stop the pain?" The answer, of course, is "Stop hitting your foot with a hammer!"

Unfortunately, in today's environment the doctor wouldn't even consider telling the person to stop hitting his foot with a hammer. The medical doctor would simply write a prescription for a drug, or cut off the man's foot. Why? Well as I mentioned, he would do that for two specific reasons. Number one, he has only been trained on prescribing drugs and cutting parts of a person's anatomy. Secondly, he has probably been given huge cash incentives from the drug companies to prescribe drugs, or he needs to make a payment on his yacht and needs the money that he will get from the insurance company or the government by performing the unnecessary surgery. Please pay attention to this because this is exactly how doctors operate. This is the insider's secret that they don't want you to know. I will say it again, and again, and again—doctors are given cash incentives to prescribe drugs, and they perform unnecessary surgeries because of the massive amounts of money they get from the insurance companies and the government to do so. It's almost always all about the money. I do, of course, have respect for those well intentioned medical doctors who are making decisions based on what they feel is best for the patient. However, the number of doctors whose decisions are skewed by the financial pressures is increasing, and increasing, and increasing, and is virtually at epidemic proportions. It cannot be overlooked or underestimated. The bottom line—can eating some raw organic honey cure a disease?

Can eating an organic apple cure a disease? Can drinking some goji juice or mangosteen juice cure a disease? The answer—absolutely 100 percent yes it can.

D. Neutralize electromagnetic chaos

As you now know, electromagnetic chaos causes your body to develop disease. We cannot eliminate electromagnetic chaos, but we can reduce our exposure to electromagnetic chaos and there are ways to neutralize electromagnetic chaos. Electromagnetic chaos is powerful and causes disease. Reducing, eliminating, or neutralizing these powerful negative frequencies can and does result in the "curing" of symptoms and disease. I have seen men with erectile dysfunction and prostate cancer be cured by simply stop using laptop computers. Why? Because in their particular case the powerful wireless devices in the laptop computers were causing their disease! I've seen people with migraine headaches, fatigue, and depression be cured by simply wearing an electromagnetic chaos eliminator because their diseases and symptoms were simply caused by sitting in front of a computer screen all day long at work. Cell phones do cause cancer. Laptop computers do cause cancer. High-definition TVs do cause cancer. Irradiating food does cause cancer when eaten. Microwaving food does cause cancer when eaten. As a matter of fact, all of these things not only cause cancer, but suppress the body's immune system and make us susceptible to all kinds of diseases. Of course, the manufacturers of these devices deny these allegations. However, even in their own literature they state that there are committees around the world whose CONSENSUS is that these devices appear to be safe! The key is the word "consensus" and the word "appear." When the word consensus is used it means that there are people who disagree. That means there are scientists and researchers who categorically state that these devices cause disease. Keep in mind that the majority of people on these "committees" are actually on the payrolls of the companies on which they are reporting. There is a major conflict of interest. Remember, it's always all about the money! So let me give you the dos and don'ts in relating to electromagnetic chaos.

1. Get something to neutralize electromagnetic chaos.

As I mentioned, we are being bombarded by electromagnetic energy from hundreds of sources, including satellites, high-tension power lines, computers, cell phones, global positioning systems in our cars, wireless telephones, remote controls, high-definition TVs, etc. We cannot eliminate the electromagnetic energy around us, we can only do things to neutralize the negative effects. There are devices which I believe neutralize these negative energies. Some can be put in your home or office and neutralize all the negative energy in the space around you; others can be carried in your purse or pocket, or worn as a pendant. Because of the censorship imposed by our government, it is forbidden for me to tell you the products that I personally use. However, go to www.naturalcures.com, and in the private member area you can e-mail me and I will tell you what I use and where to obtain them. They are inexpensive and work brilliantly.

2. Use electronic and wireless devices less.

It appears that some of the most negative effects of electromagnetic energy comes from wireless devices such as cell phones, laptop computers, as well as high-definition TVs. I know it's impossible to eliminate the use of these devices; however, you should at least be aware of their powerful adverse effects and limit their use as best you can.

3. Use a gentle wind project instrument.

Our energy fields get damaged due to traumas in our life, all the unnatural man-made electromagnetic frequencies that are bombarding us, and toxic material we put in our body. This energy field needs to be repaired and balanced, and then maintained on a regular basis. The Gentle Wind Project produces healing instruments that are believed to repair and positively influence this field. Although these healing instruments are expensive, you may use one for free. The best part is it takes only five minutes and all you do is hold the instrument in your hand. Go to www.gentlewindproject.org for more information.

4. Reduce TV time.

The television produces unhealthy electromagnetic energy. High definition televisions produce such powerful negative electromagnetic energy they have wiped out entire computer networks when turned on. The images on TV are negative and stress invoking. But the number one reason I believe you should avoid television is that virtually two-thirds of all the ads you will see are for drugs. When you watch TV, you are allowing yourself to be brainwashed into believing drugs are the answer. Do these ads work? Statistics show that over 90 percent of Americans believe that health is directly related to the amount of drugs you consume. They believe if a parent does not administer drugs to a sick child immediately, they are being a bad parent. These ads are so effective that people who have never seen a doctor are now asking their doctor for specific drugs. Don't think you are immune to the power of these ads. Remember, cigarettes used to be advertised on television. They were proven to be so effective at subconsciously motivating people to buy cigarettes that they were banned.

5. Get a magnetic mattress pad.

The earth, at one time, had a magnetic level (called gauss) of 4.0. Today the earth's gauss is .04. Sleeping on a mattress pad filled with magnets stimulates energy flowing through the body as nature intended. It has been said to alleviate pain, slow the aging process, increase energy, and helps alkalize the body. There are many good pads on the market. For my personal recommendations, go to www.naturalcures.com.

6. Use magnetic finger and toe rings.

These are inexpensive and easy to use. Simply wear this specially designed magnetic ring on the small finger of each hand, and if you want even more benefit, wear the toe brace on each foot. These are worn when you sleep. The health benefits seem to be almost unbelievable. This device appears to radically slow the aging process and, in most cases, appears to reverse the aging process; people report looking and feeling younger as time goes on. These are absolutely amazing. For information on where these are available go to www.naturalcures.com.

7. Stay away from electric tumble dryers.

These devices produce massive amounts of positive ions. Positive ions suppress the immune system, make you fatigued, and can cause depression and anxiety. Do this experiment: Go to a laundromat and sit in front of all the tumble dryers in operation, and notice how you feel after just thirty minutes. Then notice how you feel for the rest of the day. Compare this to taking a walk on the beach, near running water, or through an area with lots of trees. These conditions produce life-enhancing negative ions. The comparison in how you will feel can be absolutely dramatic. The clothes that come out of the tumble dryer are also charged with these ions that have negative effects on your emotions and physiology. You will actually feel better if you wear clothes that have been line dried in fresh air.

8. Add living plants in your home.

Real living plants add oxygen to the air, balance the energy in the space, produce life-enhancing negative ions, and are incredibly beneficial to the health of human beings. Fill your house with living plants and flowers. You will feel the difference the moment you do it.

9. Wear white.

Colors affect energy. The closer you get to white, the more positive energy you bring into your energetic field. This may not be practical in everyday situations; however, having some white or light colored clothing as your general around-the-house attire can make you feel much better.

10. Use Feng Shui in your home and office.

This ancient Oriental method of arranging things allows energy to flow better, reducing stress, increasing prosperity, and generating vibrant health.

Again, I want to emphasis the fact that doing some of these things can absolutely, 100 percent be the "natural cure" you may be looking for. It depends on what the **cause** of your disease is. If the cause of your disease is one of the above things, then eliminating it is in fact the "cure." Keep in mind that with the majority of people one thing is not the cause, but a combination of things. If you were to look at all of the items that I mentioned in this chapter, and the dos and all the don'ts, and look at all the potential combinations, there are billions of potential combinations. For many of you the reason that you have symptoms, disease, fatigue, and illness is not one specific thing but a combination of things. That is why it is important to do as many of these things as you can and understand your disease did not develop overnight, your condition did not magically appear, but your condition was developing for years and years before you noticed any symptoms. It is important for you to know that your condition is not going to reverse, in most cases, overnight, but it absolutely can be cured without drugs and without surgery, with the exception being of course if you are past that point of no return.

E. You must reduce stress.

Stress is the silent killer. Mental and emotional stress affects every cell in the body. The mind can turn the body's pH from acidic to alkaline in a matter of minutes. Stress can adversely affect the genetic makeup in your body; the mind can positively or negatively affect DNA. What you say and how you think can absolutely give you disease and it can absolutely cure you of disease. If you want to prevent disease, be happy, eliminate depression and fatigue, and cure any disease you have, you absolutely categorically must reduce stress that is in your body. It is impossible to say "eliminate all stress," but you certainly can reduce stress. Can simply eliminating stress cure a disease you may have? The answer: absolutely, 100 percent yes. Health-care practitioners around the world have proven over and over again that by simply reducing stress diseases are cured. Even medical doctors cannot deny the power of the mind in healing the body. The placebo affect has been proven by even the pharmaceutical industry! The placebo affect has shown that up to 40 percent of people cure themselves with nothing more than thoughts. That comes directly from the pharmaceutical industry's own literature. That is a natural cure they don't want you to know about. So let me give you a list of what I think are the most powerful ways to reduce stress. Keep in mind that even if you did just one of these things it could be the cure for your disease. I recommend, as always, do as many of these as you can, and start doing these things as soon as you can, and do them as often as you can! You need to reduce stress in your life to live a long, happy, healthy, disease-free life. Most importantly, if you have illness and disease now, you absolutely categorically need to reduce stress if you intend on curing your disease.

1. Listen to de-stressing CDs.

If there is one thing that I could recommend to help you eliminate stress it would be to listen to stress reducing CDs. You need headphones when you use this specially created music, and in some cases words, that are designed to stimulate the brain, release healing hormones, and dramatically release stress that has been frozen and encapsulated in the body. PH levels in the body can be radically changed in a matter of minutes with these powerful tools. The most successful practitioner of this kind of technique is Dr. Coldwell of Germany. As I mentioned earlier, Dr. Coldwell has treated over 35,000 mostly terminal cancer patients and has the highest cancer cure rate in the country of Germany. How did he cure so many people of cancer? By simply reducing stress! No drugs. No surgery. Stress levels in the body are one of the leading causes of the body becoming acidic, which means stress is one of the leading causes of virtually EVERY disease! You may contact Dr. Coldwell via his associate in Germany at drhohn@goodlifefoundation.com.

2. Do alphabiotics.

Alphabiotics is a very powerful treatment that dramatically reduces stress in the body, makes one think clearer, and dramatically reduces muscle tension and pain. It is excellent for increasing energy flow throughout the body and keeping the body's posture correct. For more information go to www.naturalcures.com. For additional information go to www.alphabiotics.com.

3. Laugh.

Laughing is one of the most powerfully beneficial things you can do. Children laugh, on average, 10,000 times per week. Adults laugh, on average, five times per week. Laughing stimulates the entire immune system, elevates depression and alkalizes the body. In the book *The Anatomy of an Illness,* we hear the amazing story of a cancer patient who, given six months to live, used laughter to eliminate his cancer! Laugh every day as often as you can even if you have nothing to laugh about. You will feel better and be healthier.

4. Smile.

There are more muscles concentrated in your face than in any other part of the body. The physical act of smiling strengthens the immune system and releases endorphins from the brain, making you feel better. The act of smiling also changes your energetic field, as evidenced by Kirlian photography. Make it a habit to notice if you are smiling or not. Smile for no reason and do it often.

5. Get and give hugs.

Human contact is necessary for life. Babies who are given all the nutrition they need but receive no physical contact grow less, cry more, and come down with all types of illness and disease. In some cases they border on death. Our immune systems are strengthened when we physically hug another human being. Ask yourself how many hugs you gave and got yesterday. You should be hugging every day as often as possible! I am lucky; coming from an Italian home, we hugged and kissed everyone. It is a good habit and provides increased health.

6. Speak powerful words.

Words create. What you say is what you get! Most people get hung by their own tongue. When you say something you energetically put the wheels in motion that will manifest it into reality. Speak positively and use words as a tool to make what you desire come to pass.

7. Don't use a cell phone and drive at the same time.

Driving is stressful enough. When you are talking on a cell phone and driving simultaneously, the amount of physical stress that your body is experiencing can be as much as ten times greater. Avoid this at all costs. When driving, it is ideal to be listening to the correct kind of music, as well as wearing an electromagnetic chaos eliminator to balance out the stressful negative effects you experience in the process of driving.

8. Sleep eight hours.

Ideally, get a full eight hours of solid, deep, restful sleep every night.

9. Rest from Friday sundown to Saturday sundown.

Each week the moon cycles are in position to promote healing and rejuvenation in the body. Resting during this time promotes the optimal rejuvenation of your cells.

10. Go to bed at approximately 10:00 p.m. and arise at approximately 6:00 a.m.

In Ayurvedic medicine it is believed that there are cycles that are the most conducive for certain activities. Going to bed at 10:00 p.m. and arising at 6:00 a.m. appears to allow the body to rest the deepest, rejuvenate the most, and gives the person the most energy throughout the day. Hormones that heal the body are released only between 10:00 p.m. and 2:00 a.m., and are only released when the body is in deep sleep.

11. Take an afternoon fifteen-minute break.

Most people wake up to an alarm clock, rush to work, stress, worry and work all day, rush to get home, eat a meal, and sit in front of the television; then they go to bed and prepare to repeat the process again the next day. A fifteen-minute relaxation break, ideally using special music or relaxation CDs, allows the body to decompress, unwind, and rejuvenate. This procedure can increase metabolism, relieve stress, anxiety, tension, and depression, allowing you to feel more centered, and providing increased amounts of physical energy.

12. Get rolfing.

Rolfing is a specific type of deep-tissue massage technique that releases the fasciae (connective tissues between the muscle and the bone) and dramatically improves posture, balance, and integrates your entire body. Rolfing is generally done once per week for fifteen weeks. Each session is like a very deep-tissue massage and takes approximately an hour and a half. You can find trained Rolfers in your area. Highly, highly, highly recommended.

13. Don't read the newspaper.

You can't fill your mind with negative thoughts and believe that your body's pH will stay alkaline. The newspaper is filled with negativity, creating worry and stress. The news printed is almost always misleading, slanted, or in some cases, completely untrue. We hear today of the dozens of journalists who have been found to be fabricating facts for their articles. These journalists, from some of the most well-respected publications, have printed things as news when, in fact, it was completely made up and full of lies. You simply cannot trust the newspaper.

14. Don't watch the news.

Watching the news fills your mind with negative pictures. My personal studies show that a person's pH can go from a healthy alkaline state, to the cancer-prone acidic state after just thirty minutes of watching a news broadcast.

15. Have sex.

Sex promotes health.

16. Commit reckless acts of kindness.

Every day make it a habit to be kind to everyone you meet. The act of showing kindness has been shown to stimulate the body's immune system and give us a greater sense of peace and centeredness. Remember, what goes around comes around.

17. Listen to nice music.

Certain music has been shown to kill plants and, in humans, dramatically suppress the immune system. Certain music also has been shown to make the body very acidic. Baroque classical music seems to promote the health and vitality in plants, and seems to encourage the same in humans. There are many CDs available whose music has been designed to promote health and even slow and reverse the aging process. Certain music also dramatically reduces stress. Go to www.naturalcures.com for my personal recommendations.

18. Get out of debt.

Stress is the silent killer. Financial pressure causes a massive increase in stress, which leads to disease. There are several organizations that can assist you in managing, reducing, and eliminating your debt. When you free yourself from financial worry you are more likely to be happier and healthier.

19. Drive less.

Driving causes massive amounts of stress. The less you drive, the healthier you could be.

20. Be thankful.

Thoughts are things. Thoughts are powerful. When you wake up in the morning, take a moment and be thankful for the day. Before you eat a meal, take a moment and be thankful for the food. Before you go to bed, reflect and be thankful for the people and experiences you have. Living a life of thankfulness creates happiness, peace, and promotes general health.

21. Get an inversion table.

Machines are available online and in fitness equipment stores that allow you to tilt your body into an inverted position or hang completely upside down. This process is believed to decompress the spine, relieve back pain, increase blood and oxygen to the brain, and potentially slow the aging process. I own one of these machines myself and use it a few times a week. It only takes three minutes and you feel absolutely fantastic. Relieves stress as well.

22. Use foot orthotics.

These promote general health and can eliminate foot, joint, and back pain.

23. Get a range of motion machine.

How would you like to get the benefits of thirty minutes of aerobics, forty-five minutes of stretching, and forty-five minutes of strength training in just four minutes? There is a machine called the "range of motion machine" which does just that. Very expensive, but highly recommended.

24. Be lighthearted.

There are tens of thousands of people around the world who live into their hundreds. Research has been conducted on these centenarians and has found that the major common denominator is that they take life very lightly. A good motto to live by is "You have to care, but not that much." Instead of being demanding, you would be better off if you had mild preferences.

25. Stay away from psychiatrists and psychologists.

Psychiatrists and psychologists do not help the people they treat. Statistics show that the majority of people who are treated by psychiatrists and psychologists actually get worse! Psychiatrists almost always prescribe drugs to their patients. These drugs are some of the most dangerous and deadly pharmaceuticals available today. Did you know that in the last ten years, virtually every violent act committed in schools was perpetrated by a person who either had taken or was currently taking a psychiatric drug? Finally, the research has become so compelling that there are warnings saying that certain psychiatric drugs actually increase the propensity to commit suicide. This is such an important issue that I encourage you to read *Psychiatry: The Ultimate Betrayal,* and if you are still not convinced that psychiatrists and psychologists should be avoided at all costs, I will personally make a donation to the charity of your choice.

26. Do not use an alarm clock.

Most people wake to the sound of a loud alarm clock. This shocks the system and starts the body in a stress mode for the day. It is important to awaken slowly and gently. There are alarm clocks that wake you with lovely gentle tones that start off very low in volume and slowly begin to increase in volume. There are also clocks that wake you up with a light that gently increases in brightness. This little change in the way you awaken can have profound effects on your emotions and your body's pH.

27. Use aromatherapy.

Smells have a powerful effect on our body. Certain smells evoke chemical reactions in the body. Essential oils have many health benefits besides giving a wonderfully pleasant aroma. Inquire at your local health food store into an aromatherapy expert to help you choose the essential oils and aromas that can give you the most benefits.

28. Use Callahan techniques for urges.

Phobias, stress, and uncontrollable urges to eat when you're not hungry, can all be eliminated by using a simple five-minute technique developed by Roger Callahan. His book is called *Tapping the Power Within*. For more information go to www.tftrx.com.

29. Get a pet.

Research indicates that having a pet leads to longer life and less disease. Pets give unconditional love and allow us a non-judgmental being to give love to. The process of being loved and giving love strengthens our immune system, reduces stress, and has a variety of emotional and physical benefits.

30. Write down goals.

Use white paper and a pen with blue ink. Write down what you want. Something magical occurs when you physically write down the things in life you want. This is one of the most powerful secrets used by the super wealthy.

31. Plant a garden.

Being in the physical universe, working with living things and creating things with our hands is incredibly beneficial. Working in a garden provides an outdoor environment, exercise, stress reduction, and many more mental, emotional, and physical benefits.

32. Cook.

When we create something with our hands we benefit emotionally and physically. When you cook food from scratch you take a much needed mental break, and you can create great tasting, incredibly healthy meals. I personally cook almost every day.

33. Don't eat late.

It is best to stop eating at 7:00 p.m.

34. Dance and sing.

Dancing and singing are great ways to release stress in the body, they are fun, and have a positive impact on our emotions and our physiology.

35. Find your life purpose.

I put this last, although it should be first. The reason it is last is because it is probably the hardest. Most people go throughout life without ever finding their true life's purpose. I can tell you from personal experience how stressful life can be when you are going day after day feeling like you're not doing what you were put on earth to do. I experienced that myself early in my career with my focus solely on making money at all costs. Today, my stress levels are at the lowest level they have ever been in my life, yet the amount of stressors that are in my life are the highest. Why? One of the reasons is I believe I have found my life's purpose, and that is to expose corporate and government corruption, and help people cure themselves of disease without drugs and surgery. My life is no longer about making money. Although I certainly am far from poor and live a very luxurious lifestyle, I no longer am motivated to make money. I am motivated to expand my mission of exposing corporate and government corruption and changing the system. My mission is to get true, honest healing information to people around the world, and to stop the insatiable greed going on primarily in the pharmaceutical companies and health-care industry all around the globe.

Finding your life purpose, I believe, can help you be happier and healthier than ever before. It is hard to do, but I encourage you to consider where you are at and what your purpose is. Maybe your purpose is to help other people achieve their purpose. Maybe your purpose in life is to make your own home and family happy and healthy. Maybe your purpose in life could be to help support me in my quest of educating people around on natural healing methods. I will gently encourage you to support me by joining my Internet community at www.naturalcures.com or becoming a subscriber to my monthly newsletter. I believe the information on the Web site and in the newsletter is incredibly valuable and will be very helpful to you in many areas of your life. I also would love for you to put positive energy and positive thoughts toward me and my mission. I am thanking you in advance for your support, and I hope the information in this book will be the miracle you have been looking for.

36. Do dianetics/scientology.

I have been exposed to virtually every self-help procedure known. In many cases, I was personally worked on by the developers themselves. In my opinion the simplest, most complete and effective system of eliminating psychosomatic illness, traumas, and emotional issues is the procedure of Dianetics and Scientology auditing.

There you have my basic list of thing to do and things to avoid that can bring your body back to a state of normalcy, where disease and illness virtually cannot exist. It would be silly for anyone to believe that a person could do all these things all the time. Ideally, do as many as you can as often as you can. Doing even a little bit is better than none at all. For example, you may not be able to eliminate something 100 percent. At least cut back or reduce, or try eliminating it for a day or two. The more you do these things, and the more often you do them, the healthier and younger you will feel.

What you have in this chapter is what I believe to be the method to cure the incurable, the secrets to a long healthy disease-free life, full of energy and vitality, and in my opinion, the fountain of youth. Since I strongly believe that the cause of all disease is too many toxins in the body, nutritional deficiencies, exposure to electromagnetic chaos, and stress, the way to prevent and cure every disease is simply eliminate toxins in your body, eliminate nutritional deficiencies, eliminate or reduce exposure to electromagnetic chaos, and eliminate or reduce stress. The specific dos and don't listed in this chapter are in fact the "natural cures" that "they" don't want you to know about. They are simple, they are effective, yet they are incredibly powerful. I encourage you to start implementing some of these things immediately, and I believe in my heart that you will start feeling better within an incredibly short period of time.

I get over 1,000 pieces of correspondence every single week. The vast majority of the people writing me are people who have started to implement many of the things in this chapter. The success stories I am hearing are unbelievable to individuals in the medical community. They simply cannot believe that people are doing some of these very simple things and reporting their symptoms diminishing or vanishing, and their diseases being cured. Individuals in the medical community cannot believe the number of reports that are coming in from people who are experiencing miraculous cures in their life. These techniques are powerful because they address the "cause" of all disease and illness.

Please write me and tell me your story. Tell me how these things are positively affecting your health, your vitality, your energy, and your life. Tell me how the information in this book is making you think differently about the news media on television, or in radio, or what you read in newspapers and magazines. Tell me how I've opened your eyes to how the money moves in this country and how the politicians and government agencies systematically and routinely mislead us as a public with false information or information that has been in fact bought and paid for by special interest groups. Tell me how exposure to this information and awareness of this knowledge is positively affecting your life.

Now, I want to specifically address a very important issue facing not only America, but people all over the world. That issue is...LOSING WEIGHT! Let's learn the truth about why you are fat and how to lose weight once and for all, and keep it off forever.

C H A P T E R   7

Why People Are Fat

If you want to get rich, write a book on how to lose weight. Americans, more than any other people in the world, are obsessed with losing weight. Americans are the fattest people in the world. Statistics vary, but it has been said that over 75 percent of people in America are overweight. This statistic has been rising decade after decade after decade. The interesting thing to note about the fact that we are so overweight in America is that we are doing more to lose weight, yet we continue to get fatter. There are more diet books on how to lose weight than ever before. More people are on diets than ever before. More people eat diet food such as diet sodas, diet prepackaged food, etc. than ever before. More people are concerned about and are eating low fat food than ever before. More people are concerned about and eating low carbohydrate food than ever before. More people are concerned about and are eating low calorie food than ever before. More diet pills and diet aides are used than ever before. More people exercise than ever before. But the fact is, with all this effort being put into losing weight, we are fatter than ever before. How can this be? Keep in mind that this is really an American problem. Although obesity is rising slightly in other countries around the world, America leads the way in people that are overweight and obese.

There is so much data I have on why you are overweight and what you can do to lose weight and keep it off that I could write an entire book about it, and probably will in the future. However, in this chapter I simply want to give you the basic fundamentals so you can understand why you are overweight and how you've been lied to. In the next chapter I will tell you exactly what you have to do to lose weight once and for all and keep it off forever.

The United States government, through various agencies, has had a standard party line on the obesity epidemic. As I mentioned earlier in the book, when experts state things they always state them as fact when, in reality, they are simply their opinions. What the federal agencies state concerning obesity has constantly changed over the years.

Years ago the standard party line was the four basic food groups: meat, dairy, grains, and fruits and vegetables. No one really questioned where the four basic food groups came from, but I saw a poster that was put up in the schools back in the sixties and had noted on the bottom that the poster was, in fact, sponsored by the American Dairy Association. No wonder dairy products had their own exclusive food group. Isn't it surprising that the dairy association, whose only objective is to increase the consumption of dairy products, would strategically put in schools a poster brainwashing kids into believing that in order to be healthy they had to eat dairy products at every single meal? It goes back to "It's all about the money."

The party line for obesity has always been "If you want to lose weight you must eat fewer calories and exercise more." However, there are experts who present information as fact that will tell you that calories are not the issue at all, and you must reduce the amount of fat you consume if you want to lose weight. But there are other experts with just as much scientific proof that claim that fat is not the issue at all; the real culprit is carbohydrates, and if you want to lose weight you must reduce the amount of carbohydrates you consume. Yet another group of experts, with their stacks of scientific documentation, proclaim that food combining is the secret to losing weight and keeping it off forever. However, there is a list of experts lined up, each holding a stack of research documents, scientific proof espousing their fact about losing weight: the glycemic index, insulin secretion, hormonal imbalances, genetics...the list goes on.

As I said in the beginning of the book, no one really knows anything when it comes to medicine, health, disease, illness, sickness, or obesity. We all look at studies, general observations, personal experience, anecdotes from other people's lives, and come up with conclusions that we think make the best sense. However, no one really knows why a person is fat or why another person is skinny. Everyone is only presenting a theory. I, too, am going to present my opinion and my theory as to why you're fat, within a system that will allow you to lose weight easier than ever before and keep it off once and for all. I could, as everyone else is doing, present this information as the absolute gospel truth, scientifically proven factual information that is indisputable; however, I am not that arrogant. I'm going to present this information to you, as I always do, with the preface, "Based on the information I have currently, it appears that this makes the most sense. However, as more information becomes available this information may be altered, changed, or 'improved'." With that said, let's look at something we all know is true.

Everyone reading this knows a person who does not exercise, who eats huge amounts of food, including the so-called fattening foods like pizza, pasta, ice cream, cookies, cakes—you name it, they eat it. We all know of a person who falls into this category, yet is as skinny as a rail and never gains a pound. I have a personal experience regarding this. When I grew up my brother could eat anything he wanted, any type of food, any amount, at any time of the day, and he never gained any weight. If I followed my brother and ate the same amount of food that he did, and did exactly the same things he did in terms of exercise, I would have blown up to 300 pounds.

So it appears that some people's bodies are genetically designed to be thin, while other people's bodies are genetically designed to be fatter. At least that is how it appears. However, I was looking through history books about Nazi concentration camps in World War II and I noticed that the people behind the barbed wire, who were in the concentration camps, were all skinny. There weren't any fat people there. I thought to myself, "I wonder if some of those people were genetically disposed to be thin and others were genetically disposed to be fat." When they came out of the concentration camps and went back to their normal routines, I wondered if some of those people remained thin and other people, because of genetic disposition, got fatter. The point here is it doesn't make a difference what your genetic disposition is; if you're not eating any food for a long period of time, you're going to get skinny as a rail. But that doesn't answer the question about why a person in America has a higher chance of being fat than a person in any other country. Based upon personal experience, thousands of scientific papers, and interviews with thousands of people in virtually every state in America over a fifteen-year period, I have come up with some interesting conclusions about why a person in America has a 75 percent chance of being fat. However, these reasons why a person is fat apply to people all over the world. Yes, it is true that people in America are fatter than people in any other country in the world. However, the problem of gaining weight and obesity is starting to creep in to societies all over the globe.

1. **Most fat people have a low metabolism.**

What does this mean? This means you can eat some food and even if you eat a small amount your body doesn't burn it off very quickly and, instead, turns it into fat in your body. If you had a really high metabolism you could eat large amounts of food and it wouldn't turn to fat in your body. So the number one reason a person is fat is because of a low metabolism.

Why is this so specific to America, as opposed to other countries? I will explain. But first, what exactly is metabolism? In simple terms, there are certain organs and glands in the body which regulate how your body burns food for fuel and how it converts food into fat. These include the thyroid, pancreas, liver, stomach, small and large intestines, and colon. When you have a slow metabolism, there is a good chance that some of these organs and glands are not working at optimal levels. Always remember, if you find a problem in the body where the body is not operating as it is supposed to, you have to ask the question, "What caused that not to operate properly?" You always have to look for the cause first. There are many causes for low metabolism, including yo-yo dieting. If you have repeatedly lost weight and gained weight I can tell you that your body metabolism is all screwed up.

So, let's look at each one of these reasons, and find out what caused the malfunction.

- *Most Fat People Have an Underactive Thyroid.*

If you have an underactive thyroid, called a hypoactive thyroid, your body's ability to convert food to energy is slow and you have a higher chance of having food that you eat turn to fat in the body. What is number one cause of a hypoactive thyroid? No one knows. Remember, I will always say that no one really knows. I will always say it appears, or it seems, or we believe based on the information we have right now. The answer is really that it appears that one contributing factor to a hypoactive thyroid is the fluoride in the water that you drink. Fluoride is not put in drinking water in other countries. This is one of the reasons why Americans have such a high propensity for an under active thyroid and a low metabolism and being overweight.

Again, its only one of the contributing factors. There is no one item that is the cause of obesity in America. It is a combination of things, and a number of things that appear to be the reason that we appear to be so fat.

- *Most Fat People Have a Pancreas that Does Not Work Properly.*

The pancreas secretes insulin. Fat people appear to have a pancreas that secretes insulin at a much faster rate than thin people. A fat person's pancreas also secretes more insulin than that of a thin person. What causes your pancreas to secrete more insulin at a faster rate? The answer: No one really knows. But based on the information that we have, it appears to be some of the food additives that are in the food served in America. Many of these food additives are not put in food in other countries. It also appears that the high amounts of refined sugar cause this pancreas problem as well. American food has more processed sugar than food from other countries.

- *Most Fat People Have a Clogged and Sluggish Liver.*

The liver is a detoxifying organ. When it's clogged up, your metabolism slows down. What causes the clogging up of the liver? The number one reason your liver is clogged and not operating properly is the nonprescription over-the-counter drugs you have taken your entire life, and all the prescription drugs you have taken. Most notably, if you take any cholesterol reducing drugs, your liver is absolutely categorically clogged. Chlorine and fluoride in the water is another cause of a clogged liver. Food additives used in processed food and fast food dramatically clog the liver. Refined sugar and white flour clog the liver. Substances such as artificial sweeteners, monosodium glutamate, and preservatives all clog the liver. The bottom line is the pharmaceutical companies clog your liver and the publicly traded food industry clogs your liver!

- *Most Fat People Have A Sluggish Digestive System (Stomach, Small And Large Intestine).*

Overweight people seem to have a problem with producing digestive enzymes. If you're not producing enough digestive enzymes your food does not get converted as energy and has a higher chance of being stored as fat. What is the reason that you are not producing enough digestive enzymes? It appears to be the food additives that are put in the American food supply. The small and large intestine in overweight people are not as healthy as those of thin people. What is the cause of this? It appears to be a candida yeast overgrowth. Why would you have a candida yeast overgrowth? The reason appears to be antibiotics. If you have ever taken just one antibiotic in your life, that antibiotic killed all of the friendly flora in your intestine and allowed for candida to run rampant, infesting your small and large intestine and colon, permeating the cell walls, and slowing down your digestion and elimination.

So, if we were to ask what is the number one reason for a slow metabolism, the answer is "What you put in your body." The poisons that you put in your body affect your metabolism. These poisons or toxins include nonprescription and prescription drugs, chemical residue used in the growing of food, the artificial food additives used by manufacturers, and the toxins in our water supply, primarily chlorine and fluoride.

There is another major reason why your metabolism is low. This has to do with exercise. The more muscle you have, the higher your metabolism. Most Americans have an abnormally low amount of muscle in their body. This means you do not burn calories as effectively as you could. The second most important issue in relation to exercise is lack of walking. The human body is designed to walk. An interesting study of thin Europeans, Africans, Chinese, and South Americans shows that the common denominator of thin, lean people is the amount of walking they do on a daily basis. Thin people walk over five miles per day. Americans, on the other hand, walk less than one-tenth of a mile! Lack of walking dramatically reduces a person's metabolic rate.

2. **The majority of people who are overweight eat when they are not hungry.**

This is caused by two factors: (a) stress or emotional eating, or (b) physiological food cravings.

Stress or emotional eating is obviously caused by stress or emotional issues. Physiological food cravings are generally caused by the toxins you put in your body, or candida yeast overgrowth.

3. **Most fat people have a large appetite.**

   If you are overweight statistics show that you find yourself physically hungry a lot of the time. This hunger is generally caused by your body's inability to assimilate nutrients due to lack of digestive enzymes and candida yeast overgrowth. Another reason that you are hungry is that certain common food additives actually increase your hunger.

4. **Most fat people have hormonal imbalances.**

   If you are overweight statistics show that there is a high probability that your body is secreting too much of certain hormones and not enough of others. This imbalance is generally caused by excess toxins in the body or lack of walking.

5. **Most fat people eat larger portions than thin people.**

   This is caused by a combination of factors: larger appetite, inability to assimilate nutrients, physiological cravings, emotion and stress issues, and the food industry's increasing the size of portions. In Europe, for example, candy bars and snack food come in packages that are over 30 percent smaller than American-sized portions. Restaurants in Europe serve portions 30 to 40 percent smaller than their American counterparts.

6. **Fat people consume more "diet food."**

   Here is a major mind blower. Most diet food actually makes you fatter. Diet products labeled "diet," "low fat," "sugar free," "low calorie," "lite," "light," "low carbs," "lean," etc., are filled with artificial sweeteners, high amounts of sugars, or chemical additives that actually make you fatter. This is the dirty little secret the food industry does not want you to know. These food additives actually can increase your appetite, make you physically addicted, and cause you to get fatter.

7. **Most fat people are highly toxic.**

   Toxins lodge primarily in the colon and fat cells throughout the body. When you are highly toxic your body demands that these toxins be diluted. This causes your body to retain water and increase its fat stores in an attempt to dilute the poisons. This is why you notice people who take lots of drugs become bloated and obese with time.

8. **Most fat people eat before they go to bed.**

   When you sleep, your body's metabolism slows dramatically. When you eat late at night the food does not get a chance to burn off and converts to fat easier.

9. **Most fat people are affected by the growth hormone put in meat and dairy products.**

   Our meat and dairy supply is loaded with growth hormones. These hormones are given to the animals to speed growth in order to increase production and profits. When you consume meat and dairy you are giving yourself massive amounts of growth hormone. This leads to obesity, and is one of the reasons why children today are maturing earlier and earlier.

10. **Most fat people see themselves as fat.**

    Remember Earl Nightingale's discovery he called "The Strangest Secret"? After years of research he discovered you become what you think about. Fat people constantly think about their weight, thus creating the undesired result.

The dirty little secret the food industry doesn't want you to know.

Here I am blowing the whistle on what I believe to be one of the greatest, most devious lies in American history. Remember, "It is always about the money."

The food industry consists of publicly traded corporations. These companies, being publicly traded corporations, have only one objective: to increase profits. The only way that a food company can increase profits is to produce their products at the lowest possible cost and sell those products at the highest possible price, and sell as much of it as they can. That's how they make money. Remember, that's their only objective.

The people that run the food companies, the officers and directors, do not care about the health and well-being of the American public. They only care about the profits. Many of you have a hard time understanding just how greedy these people can be. However, we are now seeing some of these corporate bigwigs being charged and convicted of massive fraud. We are amazed at the millions of dollars that they have, and that they will still lie, and cheat, and defraud in order to make more money. Did you know that in prisons around the world there are billionaires. Why? Because the more money you make, the more money you need to make. Making money for many of these people is an addiction. The greed that overwhelms them is unstoppable. Many of these officers and directors are so consumed with making more money they will do anything, and knowingly hurt people, just to make more money. It's sad, but true.

Imagine that the executives of food companies think only about how to increase profits, and they need to come up with ways to make their product (food) cheaper. Those ways include genetic engineering and spraying chemical poisons all over the foods, so that the crops won't be damaged by disease or bugs or insects. The soil is loaded with chemicals to make the plants grow faster, or the animals are pumped full of growth hormone to make them grow faster. These companies will do anything to get their products produced less expensively. They also want to sell these products at the highest possible price, and they want to sell massive amounts of these products. So here's what happens.

Food companies will do anything to make their products cheaper. In doing so, the products become highly toxic. If you have ever been in a mass production facility you would be appalled at how food is "made." These food companies also must continue to get you to buy and consume more food. Most food companies have chemical laboratories where thousands of chemical additives are researched and tested. These laboratories are in secret locations and have tighter security than CIA headquarters. The objective is to make the food physically addicting, make the food increase your appetite, and make the food actually cause you to gain weight. Food manufacturers, specifically fast food, are knowingly putting chemicals in the food that increase your appetite, make you physically addicted and make you fatter. Two common additives which appear to do this include the artificial sweetener aspartame and the sweetener high fructose corn syrup. Like the tobacco industry, the executives of the food industry vehemently deny these allegations. Remember, the tobacco industry denied knowingly making cigarettes physically addicting. The fact is, the American food supply will make you fat no matter what you do. This is why when thin people from other countries come to America, they all seem to gain weight even though they think they are not eating any differently than they had previously.

The food industry is so profit driven that it is lobbying against the national campaign "eat less, exercise more." The food industry does not want people to eat less! The food industry wants you fat and eating more and more food every year.

This is the reason diet products, in the form of pills, powders, food bars, and prepackaged diet foods will never work. The good news is that knowing the truth allows you to take simple easy steps to lose weight faster and easier than ever before. This knowledge also allows you to eat the foods you enjoy, never deprive yourself, and stay thin for life!

CHAPTER 8

How to Lose Weight Effortlessly and Keep It Off Forever

This is not a weight loss book. However, I want to give you the simple steps that will allow you to lose weight faster and easier than ever before, and keep it off once and for all. Space does not permit me to go into the "whys" regarding each step. I can assure you that following these steps will absolutely work. I have struggled with my weight my entire life. I was a fat kid. I tried every diet, every weight loss pill, and even hired a personal trainer, exercising as much as five hours a day. Whatever I lost, I put back on. When I was losing weight I was hungry, tired, and grumpy. I never understood what the problem was, not until I went overseas did I find the answer. While living abroad I ate everything I wanted, yet began to lose weight without even trying. This led me to the discovery of the reasons why Americans are so overweight, and an easy workable solution. Doing these steps will turn your body into a fat-burning furnace and bring your weight to its natural state. These steps also have tremendous health benefits as well.

1. Drink a glass of water immediately upon arising.
Ideally, the water should be distilled. Absolutely no tap water. This starts the body's metabolism and cleansing.

2. Eat a big breakfast.
It is interesting to note that 80 percent of the people who are overweight eat a small breakfast or none at all. Eighty percent of thin people eat a large breakfast. Your breakfast should consist of as much as you want of the following items. Everything listed should be organic: apples, pears, berries, kiwis, pineapples, grapefruit, plums, peaches, prunes, figs, rye

bread, raw butter (raw means not pasteurized and not homogenized), raw milk, plain yogurt (this means no sugar or fruit), wild smoked salmon, beef in any form as long as it's organic, chicken in any form as long as it's organic, lamb in any form as long as it's organic, tuna, sardines, eggs, tomatoes, peppers, salsa, celery, carrots, any vegetable, potatoes in limited amounts, coffee in limited amounts made with pure water (not tap water), with raw milk or cream and raw evaporated sugar cane juice or honey as a sweetener, and real tea (not tea in tea bags).

3. Drink eight glasses of distilled water each day.
People think drinking water will make them gain weight and be bloated. The exact opposite is true. If you are overweight you need to flush the toxins from your fat cells. Water is absolutely needed for you to lose weight.

4. Walk for at least one hour, nonstop, per day.
The body is designed to walk. Research shows that slow, rhythmic movement exercise, such as walking, resets your body's weight set point and creates a thin, lean body. A one-hour walk everyday will change your body dramatically in as little as one month.

5. Do not eat after six p.m.
Do the best you can on this. However, the good news is you can virtually eat like a pig all day long. And if you stop eating after 6:00 p.m., you will still lose weight!

6. Do a candida cleanse.
If you are overweight, you positively, absolutely have a candida yeast overgrowth, probably throughout your entire body. Losing weight will be hard and slow and keeping it off nearly impossible as long as this condition exists. If you wipe out the excess candida, losing weight will be easier and effortless, and keeping it off will be a breeze. You must get the book *Lifeforce,* which explains the candida cleansing process. For more information go to www.lifeforceplan.com.

7. Do a colon cleanse.
If you are overweight, I guarantee you that your digestive system is slow and sluggish. Unless you are having two to three bowel movements per day, you are in fact constipated. Cleansing the colon will dramatically increase your metabolism, and you can lose up to ten pounds by simply getting rid of the embedded toxins in your colon. There are many colon cleansing programs available. Inquire at your local health food store for recommendations. For my personal favorite go to www.naturalcures.com.

8. Consume 100% organic, virgin, unrefined coconut oil.

Read my article in the back newsletter section about how this is a miraculous weight loss miracle.

9. Use infrared saunas.

Infrared saunas increase metabolism, dramatically reduce toxins, speed weight loss, and burn fat. Ideally done on a daily basis.

10. Eat organic grapefruits all day.

Remember the grapefruit diet? Well, it appears that there actually is an enzyme in grapefruits that burns fat. Eating grapefruits all day, as many and as often as you desire, will speed the fat burning process.

11. Absolutely no aspartame or any artificial sweeteners.

Aspartame, which goes by the name NutraSweet®, will make you fat. All other artificial sweeteners, including saccharin, Splenda®, or anything else, should be avoided. If you want the full story, read two books: *Aspartame: Is it Safe?* and *Excitotoxins: The Taste that Kills.*

12. Absolutely no monosodium glutamate (MSG).

MSG is an excitotoxin. It makes you fat, causes all kinds of medical problems, and can affect your mood making you depressed. It also can be physically addicting, like aspartame, and actually make you hungrier. Unfortunately, the food industry has lobbied Congress to pass laws allowing monosodium glutamate to be put in the food and not be listed on the label. There are dozens of words that can be on the label such as spices, artificial flavoring, hydrolyzed vegetable protein, etc., that are in fact MSG in disguise.

This is why I recommend buying organic food, where everything listed in the ingredient list is something you recognize and can pronounce. Also, MSG is in virtually all fast food, including things you would never imagine, such as pizza. This is why people in foreign countries eat all kinds of food and never get fat. It's not so much the food, but the ingredients used in American food processing.

13. Take digestive enzymes.

If you are overweight there is an excellent chance your body is not producing enough digestive enzymes, causing you to gain weight, feel bloated, have gas, indigestion, and constipation. Go to your health food store and inquire. Try several kinds to see which one works best for you. For my personal recommendations, go to www.naturalcures.com.

14. Absolutely no diet sodas or diet food.

Diet sodas have been called the "new crack" because they appear to be so physically addicting. They actually make you fat. The reason they are promoted so heavily is because people become physically addicted to them and they are cheaper to make than regular sodas. I did an interesting experiment with people who drank diet sodas on a regular basis. For two weeks they replaced their diet soda with regular high-calorie sugar sweetened soda. Amazingly, no one gained any weight. Even more shocking was 80 percent of the people actually lost weight. One person lost seven pounds! This was stunning to me. Diet foods fall into the same category. Do not eat anything that is being presented as a diet food. They are loaded with ingredients that will actually make you fatter and make you physically addicted.

15. No fast food or chain restaurants.

Any restaurant that is a chain or a franchise that sells fast food produces their food in such a way that it will absolutely make you fat. You can actually eat french fries and cheeseburgers and lose weight, provided that the ingredients that you use are all organic and contain no chemical additives. It is virtually impossible to eat food in a chain or franchise restaurant where the food has not been processed to last for years without spoiling. The food has to be produced as cheaply as possible for the companies to make money. They must add chemicals to make the food taste great and get you physically addicted. This food also has been produced to increase your appetite and make you fatter. Remember, these are businesses whose only objective is to make a profit. If the food tastes amazing, becomes physically addicting, increases your appetite, and makes you fat, the restaurant is assured of success. They are like drug dealers getting their customers hooked on their product. The customer can't get enough and becomes so addicted that they keep coming back for more. This is the sad truth of what is happening in our food industry today.

16. No high fructose corn syrup.

This sweetener makes you fat and is physically addictive. Just stop buying food at the supermarket, go to a health food store instead. In my personal opinion, do not buy food that is manufactured by large publicly traded companies. Do not buy brand name food. The profit motive is so high you can be assured that it is not good for you. The sweeteners that are used in food produced in a natural way include organic honey, organic molasses, organic fruit juice, organic dates, the herb stevia, and evaporated sugar cane juice. Simply read the labels and if you can't pronounce it, don't buy it.

17. No white sugar or white flour.
White sugar is in fact physically addicting and makes you fat. However, it is still better than any artificial, man-made sweetener. If you want to sweeten something, use the recommendations I listed above. Sugar would be your last option. Artificial sweeteners should not be an option at all.

White flour, as I have mentioned previously, when mixed with water, makes paste. Eating white flour makes you fat; it can also be addicting, and clogs up your digestive system, slowing down your metabolism. Use organic whole grain flours that have not been processed or stripped of the fiber.

18. Eat organic apples all day.
The old saying is true—an apple a day keeps the doctor away. Apples are loaded with fiber and nutrients; they normalize your blood sugar and decrease your appetite. You should eat at least one apple every day. The more the better.

19. Eat only organic meat, poultry, and fish.
One of the reasons you are overweight is because of the growth hormone put in meat and poultry. If you want to lose weight, eat as much meat and poultry as you like as long as it is organic, grass fed, ideally kosher, and most importantly, has not been given growth hormones. The fish you eat should not be farm raised.

20. Limit dairy products.
If you are going to consume milk, cheese, butter, or any dairy products, eat only organic products that have not been pasteurized or homogenized. The dairy products should be labeled "organic and raw." It may be hard to find raw dairy products in some parts of the country. The next best option is organic, not homogenized, but that has been pasteurized. Your last option is organic that has been both pasteurized and homogenized. Ideally, if you want to lose weight, reduce dairy regardless of what you are getting. Definitely, absolutely, do not consume any dairy products that are not organic because they will have growth hormone in them and slow your weight loss.

21. Do a liver cleanse.
If you are overweight your liver is most definitely clogged. There is a great book specifically regarding cleansing the liver called The Liver

Cleansing Diet. On my Web site, www.naturalcures.com, I give you some specific recommendations on the best ways to cleanse the liver. Dr. Schultz has an excellent liver and gallbladder cleanse. Inquire with your local alternative health-care provider or your health food store as to various products that are good at cleansing the liver.

22. Eat a big, huge salad at lunch and dinner.
I don't care if your lunch is a cheeseburger, french fries, and a pint of ice cream. Add to it a big, huge salad and eat that first. You'll be amazed how you lose weight. The salad can contain anything you like as long as it is only vegetables, and they are organic. The salad dressing should be organic olive oil and freshly squeezed lemon juice, or organic vinegar. If you really want to speed the weight loss process, use organic apple cider vinegar. Add some organic sea salt, fresh ground pepper, or some garlic for taste.

23. Rebound.
A rebounder, or mini trampoline, allows you to stimulate and strengthen every cell in the body simultaneously. Gently jumping up and down on a rebounder for just ten minutes a day stimulates the lymphatic system and increases your metabolism. It is very effective for health and weight loss.

24. Add hot peppers.
Anything spicy or hot will increase your metabolism and make you burn fat quicker. Imagine for breakfast having some scrambled eggs, some lamb chops, and some rye toast with organic butter. Smother the eggs with some organic hot salsa and you will simply lose weight faster.

25.Use organic apple cider vinegar.
This has some magical property which helps eliminate fat cells from the body. Take a couple of teaspoons before each meal and you will be amazed at how your clothes will become bigger in no time.

26. Breathe.
Oxygen burns fat. Most people do not breathe enough to stimulate their metabolism and fat burning capabilities. There are several great videos which teach breathing techniques that are simple and quick to do, and that can help you lose weight faster. For more information, go to www.naturalcures.com.

27. Wear magnetic finger rings.
Special magnet rings worn on the little finger of each hand while you sleep can have amazing results. For more information, go to www.alexchiu.com.

28. Get fifteen colonics in thirty days.

This process will clean your colon, making it easier for your body to assimilate nutrients. This reduces hunger and increases metabolism. Colonics also allow your body to digest food faster so that it will not turn to fat.

29. Add muscle.

Muscle burns fat. When you add muscle through exercise you are increasing your body's metabolism. The best way to do this is yoga, Pilates, Chinese kung fu, or old fashion basic exercises. There are several videos and books I recommend. Go to www.naturalcures.com for details.

30. Fast.

This should be number one, but for most people this is the hardest. Going on a proper juice fast for twenty-one days will completely detoxify your body, flush fat cells, and reset your body's weight set point. It is one of the fastest ways to lose weight, and one of the most effective ways to change the body's set point so that you will not gain the weight back. This should be done under supervision depending upon your medical condition. The best book I know is *The Miracle of Juice Fasting,* by Paavo Airola.

31. Cheat whenever you want.

You want ice cream, cookies, cakes, chocolate, french fries, pizza, potato chips? Don't deprive yourself. It's better to eat something without guilt than not eat something and feel bad about it. From best to worst, it looks like this: You are offered a piece of chocolate cake. You look at it and decide that you're full and wouldn't really enjoy it, so it does not look that appealing to you. You politely say "no thanks" and feel great about your choice. You feel no depravation. This is ideal. Next would be: You are offered the chocolate cake, and you decide that you want it even though you are trying to lose weight. You say "yes" and eat the cake with happiness and glee. You enjoy and savor every bite. You're amazed at how wonderful it tastes. You are happy that you are experiencing these incredible, pleasurable sensations of this delicious cake. This is not ideal, but it is second best. Next would be a situation where you are offered the chocolate cake and you struggle with the decision. You know you are on a diet, but you can't help but imagine how wonderful this cake would taste. Inside, a voice says that nothing tastes as good as being thin feels. You struggle some more, you really want the cake, but you also want to stick to your diet. You decide to be strong and say "no." This is bad. It is better to eat the cake and enjoy it than not eat the cake and be stressed out over it. Statistics prove that eating food without guilt keeps you thin. Not eating food and being stressed about it can make you fat. Eating food and feeling guilty and bad about it makes you obese. Lastly: You are offered the chocolate cake and you really want it. But you know you're on a diet and you struggle with the decision whether to indulge or be strong. You feel weak and become upset with yourself because the desire for the cake becomes overwhelming. You breakdown and eat the cake knowing full well that you shouldn't. You feel guilty and bad about yourself. This is the absolute worst. Remember: If you choose to indulge, absolutely enjoy it and be happy. Do not feel guilty or bad about it.

Ideally, if you are going to cheat and want to eat cookies, cakes, ice cream, potato chips, etc., do not buy these products from the super-market. Go to a health food store and buy the natural organic counter-part. If you like ice cream, you can find all-natural organic ice cream in the health food store. If you want chocolate chip cookies, you can find them in the health food store. The advantage is that if you read the ingredient list and choose wisely, you can enjoy these delicious treats without all the processing and chemicals that make you fat.

32. Reduce or eliminate the "uncontrollable" urge to eat when you are not hungry.
Remember, censorship is alive and well in America. The Federal Trade Commission has forbidden me from saying my opinions on how a person can eliminate addictions and uncontrollable urges to eat. And you thought there was free speech in America. If the First Amendment were true, I would be able to state my opinions and conclusions. I cannot. However, if you are an emotional eater and have uncontrollable urges and compulsions to eat when you are not hungry, get the book *Tapping The Healer Within: How to Instantly Conquer Fears, Anxieties, and Emotional Distress* by Roger Callahan. For more information go to www.tftrx.com.

It's amazing that little things can make a difference. When looking at this list, a good way to attack it is pick one thing on the list and do that for just one day. Then, look for another thing on the list and, while still doing the first thing, add the second thing. Do that until you feel comfortable adding something else. Keep in mind that the items at the top of the list are the most powerful and will create the fastest results. These techniques absolutely work.

It is interesting that people in America don't realize just how fat they are. I was investigating a phenomenon when people were asked to describe their physical build. The options were slender, average, athletic and toned, a few extra pounds, fat, or obese. Amazingly enough, over 50 percent of the people who picked slender were actually overweight. Ninety percent of the people who picked average were overweight. Ninety-five percent of the people who picked athletic and toned were overweight. What this means is that a person may think he has an average build when, in fact, he could be thirty pounds overweight. I had a friend from Australia who was fat. Everyone knew he was fat. He knew he was fat. He said he was fat. Whenever we went out in Australia he was always the fattest person in the room. However, when he traveled to visit Las Vegas a startling observation was made. We were standing in line at a buffet. He looked at all the people in the line, then looked at himself and said, surprisingly, "Hey, all these people are fatter than me."

Americans are fat and getting fatter. Take charge and do what needs to be done. You'll look better, you'll feel better, and you will be healthier. I am getting so much incredible feedback from people who are using the suggestions in this chapter and are losing weight faster and easier than ever before that I have made a commitment to write a book specifically on the reasons why you are fat, exposing all of the frauds and lies and myths, as well as go into great detail on the specific step-by-step procedures you can you that I believe will allow you to lose weight rapidly and keep it off forever. This new book will include recipes, exactly what to eat, and exactly how to implement the steps. If you want to be one of the first people to get this new book, please become a member of my Web site community at www.naturalcures.com, or subscribe to my monthly newsletter. Please note that when you become a lifetime member on my Web site community, www.naturalcures.com, you have access to all of my books and future books free of charge!

How to Read Food Labels

Hopefully by now you are convinced that there are many toxic chemicals in the majority of the food that you purchase in supermarkets or eat in primarily chain restaurants and fast-food restaurants. Our food supply is different than it was seventy-five years ago, fifty years ago, even twenty-five years ago. Many of you eat the exact same brand of product today as you did twenty or thirty years ago, not knowing that same product is not the same at all. Today that same product could have 100 times more chemical toxins than it did twenty-five or fifty years ago. In an attempt to produce cheaper food, make it last longer, lower costs, make you physically addicted, increase your appetite, and make you fat, food manufacturers are loading the food with chemicals and utilizing processing systems that add toxins and destroy any living enzymes in the food, wiping out much of the nutritional value. Food is simply not the same as it was years ago. Today the food is loaded with toxins, depleted of nutritional value, and energetically altered so much that food is, in fact, man-made foreign substances that the body does not know how to handle.

The bottom line is that today it is virtually impossible to go to a supermarket and buy any food that is not full of chemicals, drastically reduced of nutritional value, or energetically altered. It is impossible to go to a chain, franchise, or fast-food restaurant and get any food that is also not loaded with toxic chemicals, and stripped of nutritional value, making it virtual poison to the system. Ideally, a person would never eat in a chain or fast food or franchise restaurant, and you would never buy anything produced by a mass-production, large food company. But realistically, most people would never do that. Sure, ideally you would buy only organic fruits, vegetables, nuts, seeds, grains, beef, chicken, lamb, eggs, butter, milk, cream, cheese, herbs and spices, and make everything in your house from scratch. Sure, ideally you would eat a majority of live raw food, not cooking it and destroying the natural livings enzymes. But, realistically, most people could never do that.

So is it a lost cause, or is there something you can do to eat food that has much less toxins, much more nutrition, and not been energetically altered? The answer is yes. It may not be perfect, but it will be infinitely better than what you are doing now, and it's simple and easy. I'll give you some rules, and then I'll actually show you how to read the food labels and give you some examples.

The basic rule is when you go shopping, do not go to a supermarket. Major supermarkets are in business to make money. There is virtually nothing in a supermarket that is not loaded with toxins, stripped of nutrition, and altered energetically. When you go shopping for food, go to a farmer's market and buy organic fruits and vegetables, herbs and spices from small independent growers that you can talk to, meet and feel confident that what you are eating is good for you. You can plant your own herb garden or small vegetable garden. Remember, do not use hybrid seeds because that's a nice way of saying "genetically altered by man."

The most convenient way to shop for food is go to your local whole food or natural health food type store. Keep in mind, when you go to a health food store or an all-natural whole food type of store, that not everything in there is perfectly 100 percent okay. Remember, it's always all about the money. These stores, in some cases, are also publicly traded companies that have to make a profit, so you must read the labels. When you go to these kinds of stores, however, you have an excellent chance of finding things that are not loaded with toxins, are packed full of nutrition, and have not been energetically altered, unlike a regular supermarket where you virtually have no chance of finding any food that is not poisonous. The key to reading labels is not to read the front of the package. This is where the company does its advertising. It has its beautiful pictures, its nice names, attractive colors, and all the buzz-word phrases that the marketing department has spent millions of dollars researching that will make you think it is healthy and make you buy it. Take the box, or package, or can, or jar, and look for the ingredients. Keep in mind that there can be thousands of ingredients that have been put in this food that, by law, does not have to be listed on the label. The bigger the food manufacturer and the bigger the name brand, the higher chance that it is loaded with chemicals that are not listed. My first general rule: When shopping, don't go to a supermarket. Go to a health food store, a whole food store, or a farmer's market.

My second rule is: I never buy anything that is a brand name or produced by large publicly traded food manufacturers. I have been in these plants and I know what it's all about.

My third rule is: I look for small, independent companies from my local area that package food in small batches and make it with loving care. Although these people are in business to make a profit, when meeting them you find their prime motivation is not to get rich or make money. Their prime motivation is to provide an excellent quality product for their community.

My next rule is that I always, always, always, always, always read the ingredient list. I know there are certain things that, if they appear in the ingredient list, I immediately put the box down. Let me give you the most important words you should look for on the ingredient list, and if you see them absolutely do not buy the product.

1. Anything You Can't Pronounce

This is really easy. If you can't pronounce the word, don't buy it—it's a chemical. They can call it anything they want, they can say it's naturally derived, or that it comes from a plant, or that it's all-natural. None of this is true. Keep in mind that food manufacturers lobby Congress through virtual payoffs and bribes to get legislation allowing food manufactures to call chemicals "all-natural ingredients." So the bottom line is, if you can't pronounce it, don't buy it.

2. Monosodium Glutamate

Never buy anything with monosodium glutamate in it. If you're not convinced, read the book *Excitotoxins: The Taste That Kills.* MSG is an excitotoxin. It is dangerous and deadly; it makes you fat, increases your appetite, and causes all types of physical and medical problems.

3. Aspartame

This is also an excitotoxin. It makes you fat, it makes you hungry, it makes you depressed, and it leads to all types of medical conditions, including PMS and migraines. If you're not convinced, read the book *Aspartame: Is it Safe?*

4. High Fructose Corn Syrup
This is highly chemically and physically addicting, and makes you fat.

5. Hydrogenated Oil or Partially Hydrogenated Oil
If it's hydrogenated or partially hydrogenated, don't buy it. This is a trans fat. It's deadly, it causes heart disease, makes you fat, and causes a whole host of other medical conditions.

6. Sugar
The sugar used in processing is the most refined white powder you can imagine. They have taken natural sugarcane and turned it into a drug. It's put into food because of its sweetness, but also for its chemically addicting qualities. It is also laced with the chemicals used in the growing of sugarcane. This should be avoided at all costs.

A nutritional comparison between white sugar and whole raw sugar:

	White Sugar	Whole Raw Sugar
Sucrose	99.6	88 – 91
Glucose	0	2 – 6
Fructose	0	3 – 6
Potassium	3 – 5	600 – 1,000
Magnesium	0	40 – 100
Calcium	10 – 15	80 – 110
Phosphorus	0.3	50 – 100
Vitamin A	0	120 – 1,200
Vitamin B1	0	.023 - .1
Vitamin B2	0	.06 - .15
Vitamin B6	0	.02 - .015
Niacin	0	.03 - .19
Patothenic	0	.34 – 1.18

These comparisons are based on 100 grams. Nutrient amounts will vary due to variations in harvest and growing conditions. This is a comparison not based on just comparing white sugar to whole raw sugar, but is indicative of the nutritional differences between any processed food and its whole raw counterparts.

7. Natural and Artificial Flavors
If it says natural or artificial flavors on the label, know this is where food industry lobbyists have done a magnificent job allowing the food industry to lie and deceive the public. There are thousands of man-made chemicals that are put into foods to make you hungry, to make you physically addicted, and to make you fat. They are also put into

foods to make it last for years without spoiling, and make it so incredibly appealing to the taste buds that you can't stop eating it. Much of the food in today's high-tech processing loses most of its nutritional value, is energetically altered, and virtually tastes like nothing. Food manufacturers then must add chemicals to make the food taste like it's supposed to taste.

Imagine buying an apple, eating it blindfolded, and not knowing what fruit it is. Imagine food manufacturers having to inject the apple with chemicals so that the apple actually tastes like an apple again. That is actually happening today. The reason the apple doesn't taste like an apple is because the growers have depleted the soil so much over the years, used so much chemical fertilizers, pesticides, and herbicides, and the food has been irradiated by some of the most powerful electromagnetic energy known to man, that the final product, the apple, no longer has any flavor. Compare this to an organic apple that actually tastes like an apple. Just because it says "natural flavors" doesn't mean it's natural. The food industry has lobbied Congress to pass legislation allowing chemicals that are not natural at all to be called "natural flavors." This is fraud.

However, this is what's going on. Artificial flavors are treated the same way. When you see the word "natural flavors" or "artificial flavors," if you were to ask the food company to individually list the natural and artificial flavors, they would absolutely refuse. My insiders tell me that if they were to list the natural or artificial flavors used, the list could run to hundreds of chemicals put into that food under term "natural flavors" or "artificial flavors." The other major problem with chemical additives in the food is a single chemical may not have major immediate negative effects. But when you combine two or three chemicals together, just like in chemistry class, new chemicals are formed. Scientists at the food companies know this. What these new chemicals do is incredibly dangerous and incredibly powerful—so stay away.

8. Spices

This is the other great fraud that the food industry is perpetrating on the American public. Spices sound wonderful and healthy, but they are not. The food industry has lobbied Congress to pass legislation allowing chemicals to be called spices. They are not spices. They are man-made, deadly chemicals, but legally they can be called spices.

When you ask what spices they use, they won't tell you. If it was just organic, all-natural spices, why are they afraid to tell you the two or three different spices they are using? The reason is, they are not using two or three real spices that you may be familiar with. They are using hundreds of chemicals and putting it in the food, but on the label they only have to use the word "spices." So imagine you buy a can of some product and it says "spices" on there. You think they may have put in some basil, some salt, some pepper, some oregano, or something like that. But in fact they have probably put in one or two hundred different man-made chemicals that have been researched diligently in the secret chemical laboratories that the food industry uses to make this food taste like something, and have other desired benefits for the food company. If they don't list individual spices, but just use the generic term "spices," stay away. Also, monosodium glutamate can now be classified as a spice.

9. Artificial Color
Any dyes at all, stay away from. They are simply chemical poisons.

10. Palm Oil
A deadly oil that is incredibly cheap to manufacture, and causes all types of physical problems.

11. Dextrose, Sucrose, Fructose
These are, in fact, chemically made sweeteners. Stay away.

12. Sucrulose-Splenda®
This is one of the newest, hottest man-made chemical sweeteners. In my personal opinion, it is very deadly, poisonous and makes you fat. It was produced so that the food industry could capitalize on the low-carbohydrate craze. Now, products can have "no carbohydrates" or "low carbohydrates" and still taste sweet. The problem is that it's unnatural, it's artificial, and these man-made artificial sweeteners do in fact increase your appetite, make you depressed, cause all types of symptoms (including migraine headaches, PMS, depression, fibromyalgia, allergies), and most importantly, make you fat. So stay away. www.thetruthaboutsplenda.com.

13. Enriched Bleached Wheat Flour, and Enriched Bleached White Flour
Remember, stripped down white flour or bleached wheat flour has virtually no fiber. It has been totally depleted of all nutritional value and produced in a highly chemical environment, and is actually turned into such a highly refined product that it has many of the same properties as drugs in terms of how the body physically reacts when it is

ingested. Really the only kind of flour you want to see is organic wheat flour or organic other types of grain flour, such as rye, millet, etc.

14. Soy Protein Isolate

This is a common ingredient in protein shakes and protein or food bars. Stay away from this. You will virtually never see organic soy protein isolate. The reason is that in the processing of soy protein isolate, hexane is often used, which is a petroleum solvent similar to gasoline. Certainly these chemicals, or residues of these chemicals, remain in the food, but they are never listed on the label.

These are the main things to stay away from, but the good rule of thumb is to simply read the label. If the ingredients are not things that you could have in your own kitchen or if the food is something you couldn't make yourself, stay away from it—it's man-made and it is dangerous. In an ideal world you would make your own food from scratch. It tastes better, you don't feel bad after eating it, your energy levels stay high, and you don't get depressed or constipated or have gas and bloating.

A good example is ice cream. I have an ice cream maker in my house. I make ice cream every so often for myself, or when I'm having friends over. I buy raw, organic milk and cream made from cows that are grass fed. Remember, raw means the milk and cream have not been pasteurized or homogenized; it has no pesticides or antibiotics, and is incredibly pure and healthy. For a sweetener I use whole organic sugar, which has never been separated or bleached, or I use organic maple syrup. Depending upon the kind of ice cream I'm making, I may use organic vanilla beans, organic strawberries or blueberries, organic chocolate, organic nuts like walnuts, and maybe a pinch of organic sea salt. That's it. One of my favorite ice creams is maple-walnut, and it is also the simplest. I simply follow the recipe and use the milk and cream, a pinch of organic sea salt, organic maple syrup, and some crushed-up organic walnuts. When people eat this they all say it is the best ice cream they have ever eaten. Well, not only is it the best tasting, but it is also the healthiest. People forget how much fun it is for the entire family to spend time in the kitchen adding love to the food that you eat. Buying food already prepackaged and made by major food companies means you are buying food where no love has been added. The energy a person adds to food by preparing it himself actually causes the electrons in the food to spin in different directions, causing a much healthier product for the body.

But I know you don't have time, and you want something that's fast, easy, quick, and convenient. Okay, fine. Go to the store and buy your prepackaged food, but at least go to a health food store or a whole food type store, and please, please, please read the ingredients and make smart choices. It may not be perfect, but it will be infinitely better than what you're doing now. Let me point out just how radically different the food from a regular supermarket is when compared to the exact same kind of food purchased at a local health food store. Keep in mind that these products are almost identical, but the basic differences are these: The food from the health food store will have fewer ingredients, the ingredients will be organic, and there will be virtually no chemicals in the food at all. The food has not been processed so it has not been stripped of all its nutritional value, and it has not been energetically destroyed in the processing plants of the major food producers. The food from the health food store also tastes better because it is made with whole food ingredients. When you eat it you do not feel bad, you do not get constipation, bloating, or gas. Most people eat less because of the incredible increase in nutrition and, because it is assimilated into the body so much easier, you don't crave as much. Keep in mind, most food producers want you to crave their food and eat more. That's how they make more money. So the bottom line is, the food from the health food store, generally speaking, will have more nutrition, nothing energetically destroyed, taste better, and have virtually no toxins in it. So let's go through some products and I'll show you side-by-side differences on the labels.

A. Pancake Syrup

Health Food Store

Product name: Organic maple syrup
Ingredients: 100 percent raw, unprocessed, unfiltered maple syrup

Supermarket

Product name: Aunt Jemima Original Syrup
Ingredients: Corn syrup, high fructose corn syrup, water, cellulose gum, caramel color, salt, sodium benzoate, ascorbic acid, artificial flavors, natural flavors, sodium pecsameta-phosphate

B. Bread Crumbs

Health Food Store

Product name: Bread crumbs
Ingredients: Organic wheat flour, water, evaporated cane juice, organic palm oil, sea salt, yeast

Supermarket

Product name: Progresso Bread Crumbs
Ingredients: Enriched flour, malted barley flour, niacin, ferrous sulfate, diammonium nitrate, riboflavin, folic acid, high fructose corn syrup, corn syrup, hydrogenated vegetable oil, water, yeast, salt, brown sugar, honey, molasses, sugar, wheat gluten, whey, soy flour, whole wheat flour, rye flour, corn flour, oat bran, corn meal, rice flour, potato flour, butter, mono- and diglycerides, sodium, stearyl lactylate, calcium stearyl lactylate, sodium lecithin, calcium carbonate, ammonium sulfate, calcium sulfate, monocalcium phosphate, vinegar, nonfat milk, buttermilk, actic acid, calcium propionate, potassium sorbate, sesame seeds, salt, parsley flakes, spice, colors, onion powder, natural flavors, garlic, sugar

C. Potato Chips

Health Food Store

Product name: Potato chips
Ingredients: Organic potatoes, organic sunflower oil, sea salt

Supermarket

Product name: Pringles Potato Chips
Ingredients: Dried potatoes, corn oil, cottonseed oil, sunflower oil, yellow corn meal, wheat starch, malto-dextrin, salt, dextrose, whey, buttermilk, dried tomato, dried garlic, partially hydrogenated soybean oil, monosodium glutamate, corn syrup solids, dried onion, sodium casonate, multicacid, spices, annatto extract, modified corn starch, natural flavors, artificial flavors, disodium inosinate, disodium guanylate

D. Mayonnaise

Health Food Store

Product name: Organic mayonnaise

Ingredients: Expeller pressed soybean oil, organic whole eggs, water, organic egg yolks, organic honey, organic white vinegar, sea salt, organic dry mustard, organic lemon juice concentrate

Supermarket

Product name: Miracle Whip Mayonnaise

Ingredients: Water, soybean oil, vinegar, high fructose corn syrup, eggs, sugar, modified food starch, salt, mustard flower, artificial color, potassium sorbate, paprika, spices, natural flavors, dried garlic

E. Salad Dressing

Health Food Store

Product name: Salad dressing
Ingredients: Water, expeller pressed canola oil, balsamic vinegar, vine-ripened dried tomatoes, sea salt, garlic, oregano, basil, parsley, black pepper

Supermarket

Product name: Kraft Fat Free Salad Dressing
Ingredients: Water, tomato paste, high fructose corn syrup, vinegar, corn syrup, water, chopped pickles, modified food starch, salt, malto-dextrin, soybean oil, egg yolks, xanthangum, artificial color, mustard flower, potassium sorbate, calcium disodium, EDTA, phosphoric acid, dried onions, guar gum, spices, Vitamin E acetate, lemon juice concentrate, yellow dye #6, natural flavors, oleoresin turmeric, red dye #40, artificial flavors, blue dye #1

F. Granola

Health Food Store

Product name: Granola

Ingredients: Organic rolled oats, organic honey, organic safflower oil, organic sunflower seeds, organic whole wheat flour, organic spiced almonds, organic nonfat dry milk, organic sesame seeds, organic raisins

Supermarket

Product name: Kellogg's Granola

Ingredients: Whole oats, cold grain wheat, brown sugar, corn syrup, raisins, rice, sugar, almonds, partially hydrogenated cottonseed oil, glycerin, modified corn starch, salt, cinnamon, nonfat dry milk, high fructose corn syrup, polyglycerol esters of mono- and diglycerides, malt flavoring, alphatocopherol acetate, nicinamide, zinc oxide, sodium ascorbate, ascorbic acid, reduced iron, guar gum, BHT, cryodypyridoxine hydrochloride, riboflavin, Vitamin A palmetate, folic acid, thiamin hydro-chloride, Vitamin D, Vitamin B_{12}

G. Sugar

Health Food Store

Product name: Whole organic sugar

Ingredients: Whole unrefined evaporated cane juice, squeezed dry and ground. Contains the whole dried juice of sugar cane. Dried in its whole state, it is a living food and an excellent source of energy because of the balanced carbohydrates. The molasses is not separated from the sugar streams.

Supermarket

Product name: White sugar

Ingredients: Sugar (Even though the ingredient list from the supermarket simply says "sugar," this is a lie. The food industry has lobbied Congress to allow them to use the word "sugar," when in fact they should say: "Sugar that has beengrown chemically, highly processed, using dangerous chemicals, stripped of all its nutritional value, bleached with highly poisonous chemicals to make it look beautifully white and turned into this white crystal powder, which should be classified as a dangerous addictive drug.")

H. Cheese

Health Food Store

Product name: Raw sharp cheddar cheese

Ingredients: Made with raw milk, produced without hormones, antibiotics, or pesticides, salt, natural enzymes

Supermarket

Product name: Cheddar cheese

Ingredients: Milk, salt, enzymes, yellow dye #6

(Even though the ingredients seem very similar, they are two dramatically different products. There is a huge difference between unpasteurized, unhomogenized organically produced milk used in the organic cheese, and the pasteurized, homogenized milk which is loaded with growth hormones, antibiotics and other chemicals.)

I. Chocolate

Health Food Store

Product name: Organic chocolate
Ingredients: Organic cocoa beans, organic evaporated cane juice, organic cacao butter, organic non-genetically modified soy lecithin

Supermarket

Product name: Dark chocolate
Ingredients: Sugar, cocoa butter, cocoa processed with alkali, milk fat lactose, soy lecithin, artificial flavors

J. Bread

Health Food Store

Product name: Sprouted whole wheat bread

Ingredients: Sprouted organic whole wheat berries, filtered water, organic dates, wheat gluten, sea salt, organic raisins, pressed yeast, soy-based organic lecithin

Product name: 100 percent rye bread

Ingredients: Organic whole rye flour, water, sourdough culture containing organic whole rye flour and water, sea salt

Supermarket

Product name: Wonder Bread

Ingredients: Flour, barley malt, ferrous sulfate, niacin, thiamin-monotrite, riboflavin, folic acid, water, high fructose corn syrup, yeast, soybean oil, salt, calcium sulfate, wheat gluten, soy flour, sodium stearyl lactylate, calcium dioxide, calcium iodate, diammonium phosphate, dicalcium phosphate, monocalcium phosphate, mono- and diglycerids, ethoxylated mono- and diglycerides, calcium carbonate, datem, yeast nutrients, ammonium sulfate, ammonium chloride, wheat starch enzymes, tricalcium phosphate, calcium propionate

K. Chocolate Chip Cookies

Health Food Store

Product name: Chocolate chip cookies

Ingredients: Organic unbleached flour, organic evaporated cane juice, organic palm shortening, organic chocolate chips, organic brown rice syrup, walnuts, vanilla, nongenetically modified soy lecithin, organic molasses, baking soda, unsweetened cocoa, sea salt

Supermarket

Product name: Chips Ahoy Chocolate Chip Cookies

Ingredients: Wheat flour, niacin, reduced iron, thiaminmonotrate, riboflavin, folic acid, sugar, chocolate dextrose, cocoa butter, soy lecithin, sugar, partially hydrogenated soybean oil, high fructose corn syrup, baking soda, ammonium phosphate, salt, whey, natural flavors, artificial flavors, caramel color

L. Food Bar

Health Food Store

Product name: Food bar

Ingredients: Organic almond butter, organic date paste, organic aguava nectar, organic brown rice protein, organic raisins, organic flax sprouts, organic sesame seeds, organic brown rice crisps

Supermarket

Product name: Marathon Energy Bar

Ingredients: Corn syrup, soy protein isolate, peanut flour, whey protein isolates, calcium caseinate, sugar, cocoa butter, chocolate, lactose, skim milk, milk, milk fat, soy lecithin, artificial flavor, corn syrup, sugar, partially hydrogenated soybean oil, skim milk, milk fat, glycerine, lactose, caramel, salt, artificial flavors, peanuts, rice, oats, brown sugar, sugar, wheat, sugar, salt, barley malt, rice, sugar, salt, barley malt, brown sugar, glycerine, high fructose corn syrup, chocolate, salt, barley malt, Vitamin A, palmatate, tricalcium phosphate, magnesium oxide, ascorbic acid, Vitamin E acetate, niacinimide, D calcium, pantothenate, ferrous funarate, zinc oxide, pyridoxina hgl, riboflavin, thiamin monotrite, folic acid, biotin, cyanocabalamin

Product name: Advantage Atkins Bar

Ingredients: Soy protein isolate, hydrogenised collagen, whey protein isolate, calcium, sodium caseinate, glycerine, polydextros, cocoa butter, cocoa powder, water, natural coconut oil, soy nuggets, soy protein, rice flour, malt, salt, cellulose, olive oil, natural flavors, artificial-flavors, lecithin, decaffeinated coffee, multidextrine, guar gum, citric acid, sucrolos, tricalcium phosphate, calcium carbonate, magnesium oxide, Vitamin A, Vitamin C, thiamin, riboflavin, prydoxine cyanocovalamin,

Vitamin E acetate, niacin, biotin, pantothenic acid, zinc, folic acid, chromiumkelate, Vitamin K, selenium

M. Fig Bars

Health Food Store

Product name: Fig bars

Ingredients: Organic whole wheat flour, organic figs, organic honey, grape or pear juice, canola oil, corn starch, molasses, malt syrup, sea salt, cultured whey, lecithin, baking soda

Supermarket

Product name: Fig Newtons

Ingredients: Wheat flour, niacin, reduced iron, thiaminmonotrate, riboflavin, figs preserved with sculpture dioxide, sugar, corn syrup, high fructose corn syrup, whey, partially hydrogenated soybean oil, maltic acid, salt, baking soda, calcium lactate, yellow corn flour, soy lecithin, potassium sorbate, artificial flavors, malted barley flour

N. Protein Powder, Shake, or Meal Replacement

Health Food Store

Product name: Protein powder

Ingredients: 100 percent raw certified organic hemp protein powder

Product name: Meal shake

Ingredients: Organic spuralina, organic blue-green algae, organic chlorella bokensel algae, barley, alfalfa, organic wheat grasses (barley grass, alfalfa grass, wheat grass), organic purple dulse seaweed, organic beetroot, organic spinach leaf, organic rosehips, organic orange and lemon peels

Product name: Protein powder

Ingredients: Organic fermented soy protein, skim milk, yogurt powder, honey

Supermarket

Product name: Slimfast

Ingredients: Sugar, fructose, cocoa processed with alkali, whey protein concentrate, soy protein isolate, gum, arabic cellulose gel, sweet dairy whey, nonfat dry milk, powdered cellulose, guar gum, soybean lecithin, carrageean, dextrox, cellulous gum, soy fiber, modified corn starch, xanthan gum, multidextrin, artificial flavors, aspartame, calcium phosphate, magnesium oxide, calcium carbonate, sodium asorbate, Vitamin E acetate, phericortho phosphate, niacinimide, zinc oxide, calcium pantophenate, magnesium sulfate, copper glucanate, pridoxine hydrochloride, thiamine mononitrates, Vitamin A palmatate, chromium chloride, riboflavin, biotin, folic acid, sodium molybdate, sodium selenite, phylloquinone, potassium iodine, choletalciferol, cyanocobalamin

I could do a hundred of these, comparing a brand name super-market product to its almost identical counterpart purchased from a health food store and manufactured by a small independent company. There are huge differences between what is available in standard supermarkets and what is available in health food or whole food type stores. Keep in mind, again, you must read the ingredients yourself. Just because it's in a health food store or a whole food store does not mean it's good. Read the labels. When you purchase wisely, you will be buying products that:

- Have almost no toxins
- Have far more nutrition
- Taste better
- Make you feel better
- Will not give you gas, bloating, headaches, spaceyness, constipation, etc.
- Will not make you hungrier
- Will not make you fat
- Will not get you physically addicted
- And you will be supporting small, independent, and in many cases local people who are trying to produce products that taste great and are good for you.

When you go to your local supermarket and buy name brand products and/or products from major publicly traded food corporations, you are supporting the multinational companies that are hurting local growers and independent farmers, and causing massive amounts of illness and disease, not only in America, but in countries around the world. It is my opinion that these large multinational corporations are exploiting and taking advantage of people through their clever use of advertising, and knowingly giving us food filled with chemicals that increase our appetite, get us physically addicted, and make us fat, all in the name of profit. Remember, I am not being fanatical in telling you to eat only raw uncooked fruits, vegetables, nuts, and seeds. I am saying to take little steps and go at a pace that is right for you.

Many of you simply are unwilling to change any of your eating habits. Some of you like your hotdogs smothered with mustard and ketchup, and nothing is going to change that. That's fine. Eat your hotdog and enjoy it. But instead of buying the buns, the hotdogs, the mustard and ketchup at the supermarket, why don't you get some incredibly delicious hotdog buns from the local health food or whole food store? It will taste better, have no toxins in it, and be packed full of nutrition. Don't buy the brand name hotdogs filled with nitrites and made from diseased animal parts that would make you sick if you saw them being processed. Instead, get an organic nitrite-free hotdog, ideally one made with prime cuts of beef instead of beef parts. Buy some organic mustard and ketchup, and then enjoy your hotdogs.

If you like your snack food, that's fine. Go to the health food store and try various kinds of snack food to munch on; many of them are very sweet and incredibly tasty. Taste will vary, so try different kinds to see which ones you like. As I write these words, I purchased five different sweet snacks at my health food store. The first one has four ingredients: pure raw carob, coconut, pure cane crystals, pure maple syrup. All of the ingredients are organic, have not been cooked, are all raw, and are real living food. They taste incredible. Another one has as its ingredients: raw organic sunflower seeds, raw organic raisins, raw organic bananas, raw organic maple syrup, and fennel. These are sweet and delicious. Another one is this incredible almond brittle made with raw almonds, pure vanilla beans and crystals of pure cane. It's simple, real, all-natural, and toxin free. And here's the great part: Last night, to see how I would feel, I ate this huge bag of this almond brittle all in one sitting. I didn't feel bloated, I didn't get a sugar rush, I didn't have a spike in moods, I felt absolutely fine, and I slept like a baby. If I had done the same thing with some almond or peanut brittle made by a large, publicly traded corporation, I would have felt horrible, bloated, gassy and would have tossed and turned all night.

Just remember that name brand products and large multinational publicly traded corporations are investing tens of millions of dollars in research to find out what the hot buttons are to get you to buy their products. Don't believe their slick, deceptive ads, and don't believe what's written on the front of the package. You simply are being deceived. Read the ingredients and remember as you read them that many toxins that were used in the processing of the food are not listed in the ingredients, and many toxins that are actually put in the food do not have to be listed on the ingredients.

It's estimated that over 95 percent of all food purchased has as many as 300 chemicals added to each product that are not listed on the label. It's scary, but true. This is the power of the food industry and the lobbyists. If you want to eliminate sickness and disease, if you want to prevent sickness and disease, if you want to be thin, then you must increase the amount of raw uncooked organic food in your diet. The only way you can do this is stay away from the supermarket. So, the general rule of thumb is to do all your shopping at a local farmers market and make sure that all of your fruits, vegetables, herbs, nuts and seeds are 100-percent organic and raw. When purchasing other food products, avoid the supermarket at all costs and buy your food products from your local health food or whole food type store. If the product is manufactured by a large, publicly traded corporation, or is a well-known brand name, avoid it. Lastly and most importantly, whenever you buy anything, read the ingredients.

Restaurants

I am often questioned about eating in restaurants. A restaurant is not a restaurant is not a restaurant. There are vast differences between the kinds of restaurants you go to. I'm not talking about the food, I'm talking about the kind of restaurant. Virtually all restaurants have the following problems:

In order to make a profit they have to buy the cheapest food available. Restaurants get their food primarily from large, bulk food suppliers that supply hundreds of restaurants in a given area. Much of the food you eat in any restaurant has not been cooked at the restaurant; rather, it has simply been finished off or heated up. It gets worse with restaurants that are vast in number, such as franchises, chains and fast food. Most restaurants use microwave ovens to reheat the food right before serving. Most restaurants, like large food manufacturers, use frying oil all day and, in many cases, for days on end. The problem with this is once you heat the oil for frying it goes rancid in a very short period of time. All the food coming out of the rancid oil is highly carcinogenic.

I went into a very nice restaurant and was about to order, but wanted to ask some questions. I love fresh guacamole. I make it at my house with all raw organic ingredients and it is absolutely delicious. I saw they had guacamole on the menu so I inquired, was the guacamole made fresh? The waiter told me yes. I inquired a little further. I asked, "So you actually take avocados and mash them up in the back or does it come in prepackaged mix?" And he said, "Oh, well we do get a mix, but we add water and make it fresh every day." His idea of fresh and homemade and my idea were two different things. You see, this guacamole was not made in the back with fresh avocados, tomatoes, lime juice, onions, etc. Instead, it came as a powdered mix to which water was added. When I asked what the ingredients of the mix were, of course he didn't know. I persuaded him to go and find the package and bring me the ingredient list. There are over three dozen ingredients on the label, including monosodium glutamate.

I asked if the salad was fresh. He thought for a moment and said "No. It actually comes in bags that have been prepackaged." The problem with this, of course, is that in order to retain freshness the "fresh salad" has to be sprayed with chemicals. I asked if the chicken was fresh, or did it come prepackaged and frozen. Not surprisingly, it came prepackaged and frozen. Virtually all the sauces, all the mixes, and all the flavoring agents used came in boxes, cans, or packages. This is the main problem with restaurant food.

So, what do you do? Basically, you can be a fanatic and not eat in any restaurant unless it's an all-natural, totally organic restaurant, or you can simply eat really well at home and stay away from chains, franchises, and fast food as best you can. When you go to a good quality restaurant, simply ask if you can tour the kitchen and see some of the food being prepared. Most managers welcome this. It will give you a chance to meet the manager and/or the owner and inquire about how the different dishes are made. You can then see which one would be using the highest quality and the freshest ingredients. You can also simply ask to eliminate things. Example: I happen to like fried chicken wings. I make them at home myself, my mother taught me how. We take organic chicken wings, lightly dust them in organic whole wheat flour with sea salt and organic black pepper, and gently fry them in a little bit of extra virgin organic olive oil. They are absolutely delicious. When I go to a restaurant, I know that most chicken wings are purchased pre-made and pre-breaded, and are simply thrown into rancid oil in a fryer in the back, then smothered in a sauce, all of which contain massive amounts of monosodium glutamate. Therefore, I don't eat chicken wings in restaurants. So basically, I ask a few questions and make some intelligent choices. And remember, you have to care, but not THAT much. You have to do what you feel good about and happy about and not be stressed out about your decisions.

I have a close friend who is not only a vegetarian, but eats only raw, uncooked food. She is not stressed out or fanatical about it, that's just what she eats. We went to a restaurant and I ordered some salmon sushi. I know the salmon was caught in the wild, and the rice is made with pure ingredients. I also liked the cucumber and onion salad they make. The fresh ginger and wasabi was also delicious and made fresh at the restaurant. Although the restaurant does not use organic ingredients, it's a matter of degree. My meal could be classified as relatively healthy. Far from ideal, but also far from something you could find in a fast-food restaurant. At least there were no hydrogenated oils, monosodium glutamate, aspartame or massive amounts of chemicals. My friend, being a vegetarian and a raw foodist, had limited options, but her attitude about what she wanted was the key. She inquired about her choices and made her selections. We had lovely conversation, and her food was secondary in nature to our discussions. She wasn't stressed, uptight, or fanatical. She wasn't judgmental or pushing her ideas and values upon me. Maybe someday I will eat only raw food too. For right now, I love my organic lamb, chicken, beef and various kinds of cooked food. The point is, knowing all this information doesn't mean you have to do it all in order to receive benefits. Do a little or a lot, based on what you feel good about. Even making some simple modifications and changes to your diet could have dramatic impact.

CHAPTER 10

Not Convinced?

This book is filled with some very basic premises from which our conclusions are built. The most basic is that there are natural nondrug and nonsurgical cures for virtually every disease. There are natural nondrug and nonsurgical ways to prevent you from virtually ever getting sick. Many organizations, including the FDA, the FTC and the pharmaceutical industry, are working diligently to prevent you from hearing or learning about this information. The news media, including newspapers, magazines, television and radio, are biased toward the pharmaceutical industry and present half-truths and outright lies in relation to health-care. If you're still not persuaded then consider these thought provoking ideas.

1. **Still not convinced "it's all about the money'? Then consider this:**

   - It has been reported that corporate corruption is at an all-time high. There is more corporate fraud going on than ever before.

   - The *Associated Press* reported that "drug companies are seeing that cancer can be lucrative." The article goes on to say how drug companies will be making billions of dollars in profits by selling cancer drugs, even though they do not work! The article exposes the fact that curing of cancer would be devastating to companies. Companies only make money as long as people have cancer and are convinced that they need to be taking drugs. The article also exposes the fact that absolutely no research is being done on natural remedies for the treatment of cancer, and absolutely no research is being done on PREVENTING cancer. The big

money for these companies is making sure that more people
get cancer and more people are brainwashed into buying
their outrageously priced ineffective and dangerous drugs.

- *USA Today* reports that biotech stock prices soar after good
cancer drug news. This article points out the fact that publicly traded drug companies have only one goal: to increase
profits, which means selling more drugs. The article never
mentions if the drugs are effective at preventing or curing
cancer, but only talks about how much money the companies will make by selling the drugs.

- Hotels are increasingly using self-service check-in kiosks to
reduce costs and increase profits. Again, a publicly traded
company's only objective is to increase profits; it is not about
customer service or providing good quality products to you the
customer.

- *The Wall Street Journal* reported that oil companies are
reaping huge cash windfalls from the rise in oil prices. This
points out an interesting fact. Oil prices continue to rise,
not because costs are rising, but simply because the oil
companies demand more profits. *The Wall Street Journal*
exposes that the oil companies are reaping windfall profits
at the expense of the consumer. This is an obvious violation
of antitrust laws and a violation of business ethics—all at the
expense of you and me, the consumer.

- The *Associated Press* reports that there is a transfer of wealth
of historic proportions toward the oil producers. Simply put,
the oil companies have a monopoly. They can charge whatever
they want and we have to pay. It's like medieval times when
the lords could simply tax the peasants anytime they wanted
more money. This is happening today. The oil companies, like
the pharmaceutical companies, can simply charge whatever
they want and bring in as many billions of dollars in extra
profits anytime they want. This is greed in its purest form.

- *The Wall Street Journal* reported how pharmaceutical
companies routinely raise prices at will to increase profits. Since insurance companies pay for the most expensive
drugs and the government pays as well, this is easily done at
the expense of the consumer. The article exposed Celgene

Corp., which originally priced a drug at $6.00 then jumped the price to $29.00.

- *Reuters* News Agency reported that when the FDA rejected a medical device for depression the company's stock plummeted over thirty-seven percent. I wonder how many politicians made millions of dollars "shorting" the stock, thus benefiting from the price drop.

- Congress passed a law allowing banks to use new and faster processing for clearing paper checks. This will make the banking industry as much as $3 billion a year, or more, in profits! However, you don't have access to the money and it ultimately costs consumers billions more.

- Police departments had to drop suits against Ford because of pressure from Ford that it would stop selling them cars. This is obviously extortion. Big corporations always use their power to squash the little guy.

- Dozens of companies have been found guilty of failing to recall dangerous products. Most recently, Graco children's products agreed to pay a record $4 million penalty for hiding negative information about problems with their car seats, highchairs, strollers, and other products that resulted in hundreds of injuries and at least six deaths. This is an outrage. The corporate officers and directors should be held accountable for the murder of six people. These individual people made the decision to let people suffer and die so that they could make more money. This goes on all the time in business. For every company that is caught there are hundreds of other violations that are not exposed. Other companies have done the same thing and have paid fines as well, including baby product maker Cosco and sister company Safety First. Imagine, a company that calls itself Safety First was found guilty of not reporting safety defects in their products, resulting in the injury and potential deaths of thousands of people. It's always all about the money.

- I was offered $50 million to recommend certain products in this book. The individuals that made this offer even came up with a very sophisticated plan on wiring money to numbered Swiss bank accounts. Folks, I can assure you that these types of bribes and payoffs are going on on a regular basis in the news media on television, radio, newspapers, and magazines. I have been offered time and time again huge amounts of money to recommend and endorse products and services. I have been offered positive stories on major news stations and in magazines and newspapers if I spend huge amounts of money in advertising. This type of corruption is rampant.

- Think of all of the advertising shown at movie theaters before movies now. Think of the ads you're seeing when you rent a DVD. Consider that millions of dollars are given to movie companies and television producers to incorporate companies' products into the movie or TV show. Corporations do anything and everything overtly and secretively to brainwash you into buying their products. Remember, it's always all about how much profit they make.

- Corporations do not want to provide good quality products. They want to get your money. One way to do this is to manufacture products that have low quality and are guaranteed to break. This way, manufacturers can sell you outrageously priced extended service plans. Consider when you buy an electronic device such as a computer. Sixty percent of all electronic devices break down in the first year. The amount of profits made by the retailers and the manufacturers in the repair and reselling you new equipment is astronomical. This is done purposely. Where is the Federal Trade Commission? Again, the FTC is not protecting us the consumers; it is protecting the profits of the large publicly traded corporations.

- Reality shows are at an all-time high in terms of viewership. The producers make money by helping to create as much pain and misery for the contestants as possible. As one of the biggest producers of reality TV has been quoted as saying "There is appeal in other people's misery." All in the name of money and greed, do these producers victimize the participants of reality TV. In many cases, these contestants leave the show permanently emotionally scarred from their experience. The producers do not care. All they care about is how much money they will make at the expense of other people. It seems very similar to ancient Rome, when people were entertained by watching other human beings being fed to the lions. It is a sad state of affairs that greed seems to be at an all-time high in America.

- Communities make so much money on speeding tickets that the government refuses to put speed limiters on cars, even though they know that it would save over 100,000 people a year from death or injury. But it would also cost the oil companies huge profits. They have a law that says you have to wear your seatbelt. Therefore, cars have to have seatbelts installed. There is a law limiting the amount of emissions cars can give; therefore, cars have to put catalytic converters and do things to limit emissions. There is a law that says that you can't, under any circumstances, exceed the national speed limit. Why, then, are cars not required to have limiters so that they don't go that fast? The answer: It would cost the communities huge amounts of money in profits from speeding tickets, and the oil companies enormous profits in gasoline. It would also reduce huge amounts of money spent on car repairs and would save all types of money for individuals on hospital costs, injuries and missed work, as well as save lives. You see, the government does not care about people's lives, it cares more about protecting its own revenue and the profits of the oil industry. It's always all about the money.

- E-mail spamming could be stopped instantly. All Congress would have to do is pass a law forbidding credit card companies to process payments from spam e-mail. Any credit card company that processed a payment from a spam e-mail would face severe fines or loss of the right to process any credit cards, or jail. The credit card companies then would take the responsibility of knowing their customers and finding out how business was generated. E-mail spamming would stop. The policing action is simple. All the government has to do is order a product from some spam e-mail and then charge the credit card company with the violation. The reason this is not being done is because the credit card companies make tens of millions of dollars in processing business from spam e-mail. Since they've lobbied Congress,

Congress will not pass laws to hurt the companies that are giving them money. Again, our politicians do not care about you. They only care about protecting the profits of the big corporations that poured the millions of dollars into their campaigns and increased their personal wealth. As always, it's only all about the money.

- Self-serve gas stations were set up so that the corporations can make more money.

- When calling a company, many people have experienced not having the phone answered by a person, but rather a voice activated system with several menu options. Many people know that you can call a company and be asked a series of questions about the nature of your call, and if the reason for your call is a specific reason push 1, if it's another reason push 2, yet another reason push 3. Then when you get there, there is a new list of options, push 1 for this, 2 for this, 3 for this. Then when you do that, there's yet another list of options; there can be as many as ten different menus you go through. Why is this being done? It's all about the money. It saves the company huge amounts of money knowing that the majority of people will get frustrated and hang up; therefore, they don't have to take the call and spend the money on customer service. You see, big corporations don't care about the customer, you. Big corporations only care about the bottom line, and how much money they can make. Big corporations have one legal responsibility and that is to increase profits at all costs. That means you always wind up the loser. Corporations by law have one senior objective, and that is to increase profits. They do this at all costs and at the expense of the customer, the environment, their employees, as well as at the expense of honesty, integrity, and ethics. It's always all about the money.

- The pharmaceutical industry focuses more time and money on marketing than on the development of new drugs. The pharmaceutical industry is categorically not interested in curing or preventing disease. The pharmaceutical industry consists of publicly traded corporations that have only one legal responsibility and that is to increase shareholder value, which means they must increase sales and profits. The only thing drug companies want to do is sell more drugs and increase profits. They do not want to cure and prevent disease. They do not care about your health. They do not care about finding the truth about why people are sick and the best ways to prevent sickness and cure illness. Drug companies only want to develop and sell patented drugs. This is evidenced by the fact that the majority of their money is now being spent on marketing and convincing you that you need drugs and you must buy drugs. The pharmaceutical industry is not spending money on verifying their drugs actually are effective, or verifying their drugs are actually safe. They only care about SELLING drugs and MAKING PROFITS.

- Donald Trump is reported as saying "All trading done at the highest levels is illegal. It's all insider trading."

- Time Warner reported that banks lie to you in order to make more money, and recently reported that there are ten secrets or ten specific lies that banks tell customers on a regular basis that cost the consumer money and make the bank more profit. The government does nothing about this! Why? Because the banks have lobbied Congress, which means the banks have poured millions of dollars directly into the politicians' pockets to make sure that their own profits are protected at the expense of you, the customer. Again, it's not about ethics, honesty, or integrity; it's not about giving good quality service to you, the customer; it's all about making money at all costs and above everything else. It's always all about the money.

- Newspapers, magazines, television and radio commonly talk badly about all-natural products, while at the same time running ads for products that they are not bashing. This is done purposely. This occurs most blatantly on Web sites. It is important to note that there are virtually no negative reports ever done on companies or products that are the sponsors of those TV stations, radio stations, newspapers, magazines, or Web sites. The bottom line is when companies provide advertising revenue to the "news organization" that "news organization" will never run negative stories about those products or companies. Why? Because they do not want to bite the hand that feeds them. It's always all about the money.

- Health food and vitamin companies are being gobbled up and are either owned directly or indirectly by the pharmaceutical industry. This is so the drug companies can control all natural vitamins and minerals. When the pharmaceutical companies control this industry they will either raise the prices dramatically and start charging you exorbitant prices for all-natural herbs, vitamins, and minerals, or they will simply take them off the market since they will control them, therefore, making it impossible for you to have natural options to drugs. This is being systematically done so that the pharmaceutical industry can control and monopolize health care. This should be a violation of antitrust laws. The politicians do absolutely nothing. The Federal Trade Commission, the agency entrusted with protecting consumers against antitrust violations and monopolies such as this, does absolutely nothing. This is corruption at the highest levels of government.

- Many "newsletters" or books promote certain supplements. Most people do not know that the owners of these newsletters or books are the same people that actually sell the supplements. This is misleading and fraudulent, but very profitable for the big corporations. Magazines and newspapers commonly run positive articles on products if those companies commit to large advertising contracts. This is fraud, and it happens virtually all the time. What it means is you can't believe anything you read in magazines and newspapers, because you don't know if the article is really a payoff for the large amounts of advertising the publisher receives.

- Companies routinely shift jobs overseas. The main reason: It has been reported that it is twenty-five times more expensive to hire an American worker compared to his Asian counterpart. Companies are only in business to make money and will continue to shift jobs in production overseas where it is less expensive to produce the goods and services.

- Drug companies categorically lie when they say they are concerned about your health. They are publicly traded companies that legally have only one responsibility and that is to increase profits. The fact is if they were concerned about your health they would stop selling drugs and be involved in looking at natural ways to prevent, as well as cure, disease. If a drug company really was concerned with health, it would be violating its legal responsibility to the shareholders. It is a flagrant, blatant lie.

- The United Nations has now been shown to have been involved with major corruption and fraud in the Oil for Food program and potentially other humanitarian programs conducted around the world. Individual people at the U.N. are now being investigated for pocketing potentially billions of dollars that were supposed to go directly to needy people around the world.

- Almost every multimillionaire that I know is only concerned about how much money they make. Any time they have a conversation their first two questions are always how much time is this going to take me and how much money am I going to make. There is never any concern about whether the product is good or whether people will benefit from what is being offered. It's always only all about the money.

- When dealing with billionaires the conversation is almost always about how do we create a monopoly. Billionaires are ruthless and want to eliminate all competition, create a monopoly, and establish a perpetual moneymaking machine. That is really their only interest—money, money, money, money, money!

- In dealing with billionaires, they know that in order to make guaranteed profits they must get the government involved to pass a law ensuring sales. Getting government contracts, which are paid for by increasing taxes, guarantees billions in profits.

- All corporate business meetings discuss how to cut costs. In American business the easiest way to cut costs is to out-source manufacturing and most corporate activities overseas. In countries like India, the Philippines, and throughout Asia there are very little rules, even more government corruption than in America; workers have no workman's comp, no benefits, no insurance, no health care, they work fourteen-hour days, their pay is next to nothing, thus increasing profits to the corporation.

- It has been reported that the quality of products manufactured today is lower than ever before in history. Years ago products actually worked and lasted longer than they do today. Over 90 percent of products purchased break down and fail to meet the consumer's expectations. This is done purposely by the manufacturers. Low quality products cost less to manufacturer, thus increasing profits to the companies and also guarantee that consumers have to repurchase products more frequently. Isn't it sad that when we buy a product today we almost always know that it will break or not work properly within a very short period of time?

- There are thousands and thousands, that's right, thousands and thousands of individual people in corporations around the world that are convicted of fraud and corruption. For every person that has been convicted, there are probably a hundred or more that have not been discovered. Corporations are by nature corrupt because their only motivation, legally, is making more money. The individual people who are in charge of these corporations are inherently, generally speaking, corrupt because they have an overwhelming addiction to increase their own power, influence, and personal wealth. All you have to do is look at WorldCom, Enron, Martha Stewart, and corporation, after corporation, after corporation that is in the news. This type of corruption has been around for hundreds of years, but it seems to be increasing at an expediential rate.

2. Not convinced that the FTC and FDA, as well as maybe TV, radio, and news organizations, are suppressing and censoring information? Then consider this.

- CBS refused to air a thirty-second commercial from a group that was critical of the Bush administration. CBS also did not air the mini-series "The Reagans" because of pressure from conservative groups and advertisers.

- I just received an e-mail stating "Print publishers depend on drug companies for a huge part of their advertising, and may be reluctant to take an ad that antagonizes their best customers." All bets are off if the companies themselves actually apply pressure.

- Disney will not distribute a film critical of President Bush because it could jeopardize the massive tax breaks it gets on its Florida theme parks. Remember, President Bush's brother is governor of Florida. It was reported that an industry insider was quoted as saying, "Should this be happening in a free and open society, where the moneyed interests essentially call the shots regarding the information that the public is allowed to see and hear about?"

- The natural supplement ephedra was banned, but the pharmaceutical version, ephedrine, was not banned. The natural version was taken off the market, but the dangerous chemically produced synthetic version is still allowed to be sold. This shows how the FDA protects the pharmaceutical industry.

- Drug advertising is everywhere. You see drug ads on TV, hear them on radio, and see them in newspapers and in magazines. Drug companies sponsor sporting events and fill our mailboxes with direct mail campaigns promoting their drugs. These drug ads have been deemed, in many cases, to be misleading and false, yet the FTC has taken absolutely no action against any pharmaceutical company for producing these false and misleading ads even though these ads are encouraging people under false premises to use these dangerous and ineffective drugs. Most notable is the fact that every single ad is accepted by the publication. There has never been a drug ad rejected by a television or radio station, newspaper, or magazine. However, it is interesting to note that television stations, newspapers, magazines, and radio stations routinely will not accept advertising for all-natural herbal products, homeopathic products, vitamins, minerals, or books that are critical of the pharmaceutical industry. Ads for this book, for example, have been rejected by many ABC television stations, as well as CNBC. The reason, in my opinion, is because this book is critical of the pharmaceutical industry and the food industry, and those industries put pressure on the media not to run advertising for this book. This is, and should be, classified as an antitrust violation and a violation of the First Amendment where these organizations are suppressing the free flow of information, ideas, opinions, and an individual's right to free speech. The government does absolutely nothing.

- The most obvious example that the government, as well as the news organizations, are suppressing and censoring information is the Monsanto story that was squashed by Fox. This is the story where two journalists put together a report exposing the growth hormone that Monsanto manufactures and how it was being injected into dairy cows, potentially causing all types of illness and disease and tainting the milk with deadly poisons causing humans to become sick and diseased. This true story was squashed by Fox. Why? To protect the profits of Monsanto. To read more about this incredible story go to www.foxbghsuit.com.

- It has been reported hundreds of times in the last few years that the government has been found guilty of falsifying documents and/or purposely misleading the public with false information.

- The developer of an all-natural diabetes cure was offered $30 million not to market it.

- Many times when you see an alternative health-care practitioner, they will have you sign a whole host of forms, disclaimers, release forms, and statements asserting that they are not trying to cure or prevent any disease, and that you are seeing them under your own free will. Because of our litigious society, and because of oppression by the government regulating bodies, these wonderful individuals, by risking so much, must take these measures in order to protect their ability to treat people who need their treatment.

- Vaccines are loaded with poisons. Those who get vaccines are more likely to become sick in the short-term and in the long-term than those who do not get vaccines.

- The free flow of information in America is suppressed and censored. Free speech does not exist anymore in America. When the Constitution was written the method of expressing someone's opinion was to stand on a soapbox in what was called the common areas of each city or town. The most famous is the "Boston Commons." This is the place in the center of town where everyone, young or old, rich or poor, could have the exact same platform to express one's opinion. The poor person and the rich person were given the exact same platform to speak. When the rich or the politicians did not like the speech of the commoners they were taken away from the commons so their speech was denied. This is why the forefathers wrote an amendment to the Constitution in the first Bill of Rights protecting the free speech of those individuals. It is important to note that the forefathers wrote the First Amendment to protect the free flow of ideas and opinions. It was specifically designed to protect the poorest person in town and guarantee and make sure he had the same platform as the richest man in town or the powerful politician. As time went on the venue of expressing one's opinions and exercising one's right to free speech changed from the common areas to the television and radio airwaves. Government then took control of the airways and sold licenses to rich and powerful corporations and individuals. For the first time in U.S. history, the free flow of ideas and opinions were now controlled by the politicians and the rich and powerful. This is exactly what the forefathers wanted to prevent when they wrote the Bill of Rights and the First Amendment. Now, in today's society, the platform of expressing one's ideas is primarily television, which is the most powerful medium, followed by radio, then by the print media—newspapers and magazines. The poor people and commoners in today's society are routinely excluded from expressing their views and opinions by the rich and powerful, and politicians. We are in effect prevented everyday from exercising our right of free speech, since the "commons" of today is owned by the powerful corporations and politicians. It is sad that our First Amendment has been thrown by the wayside. It is sad that people who want to express opinions are routinely denied access to television and radio at the whim of the networks. How can television and radio stations, which were granted licenses by the government, deny people to express their opinions, even people who are willing to pay full price to have their views aired? This is censorship in the most obvious way, and is totally being ignored.

- Female military recruits are held to different standards than their male counterparts. They are not required to shave their heads, nor are they required to adhere to the same physical requirements that their male counterparts are. This is virtually never reported in any news organization because it is "politically incorrect.'

- I recently talked to one of the top radio disc jockeys in America. Even a person who has one of the top-rated shows in the country is still under the thumb of the corporate executives and sponsors. He is routinely told what he can and cannot say based on the sponsor's wishes.

3. Still not convinced that the media is biased, deceiving, and lying to you about many topics? Then consider this:

- Isn't it interesting to note that there has never been a bad article written about a news organizations' sponsors? Think about television, radio, newspapers, and magazines. Look at who is running advertising on those media venues. Then try to find any negative article about any of those products, or any of those companies, or any of the executives of those companies. It just doesn't happen. This is an obvious and blatant example of how the media is totally biased and succumbs to the whims and pressures of its sponsors. This shows that the news media virtually is the mouthpiece of the large corporations that buy the advertising. Today the majority of the advertising is the pharmaceutical industry and the food industry; therefore, it is virtually impossible to hear the truth about how the food being produced by large publicly traded corporations is in fact giving us disease and making us fat, and how the drugs are in fact ineffective and giving us disease.

- Bill O'Reilly has been quoted as saying "The deception going on in the media is appalling."

- News organizations often create fake stories by putting together groups of people to yell and scream for the cameras, and the minute the cameras get turned off everyone walks away and goes home. Most events you see on television are actually staged by the news organization.

- Numerous journalists have recently been convicted of writing false and fraudulent articles. Journalistic fraud is now becoming commonplace. It is reported that many journalists are being offered financial incentives to write articles that present a certain viewpoint.

- Many news articles are actually written by individuals who are on the payroll of the companies talked about in the article. An example recently was an article with a head-line, "Despite known hazards, many potentially dangerous dietary supplements continue to be used." This particular article was written by a medical doctor who was on the payroll of the drug industry. It is not news, it is not true, it is not accurate, and it is not unbiased journalism. It is a debunking campaign put out by the pharmaceutical industry to get people away from excellent, safe and effective natural remedies, and to continue to be brainwashed into believing drugs are the only answer for illness and disease.

- Pharmaceutical companies, with the huge amounts of money they have at their disposal, set up and paid for Web sites by the hundreds debunking natural remedies. Usually, one small group of people actually runs and maintains hundreds of Web sites, so an individual consumer thinks that there are these independent organizations around the world saying how bad natural remedies are and how good drugs are. This is absolutely not the case. This is propaganda in its most flagrant form.

- The four basic food groups promoted for years was actually invented by, promoted by, and funded by the dairy asso-ciation. The food pyramid today was put into effect by our government after massive amounts of lobbying by the food industry. The four basic food groups and the food pyramid have nothing to do with health and nutrition, but are designed to brainwash people into eating a certain way for the benefit of the food industry.

- The media hides the truth about the dangers of nonprescrip-tion and prescription drugs. There are very few articles writ-ten about how lethal over-the-counter nonprescription and prescription drugs really are. However, the number of articles that have been written and broadcast stating the dangers of natural supplements such as herbs, vitamins and minerals is staggering. The fact is drugs, both over-the-counter nonprescription and prescription drugs, are infinitely more dangerous than any vitamin, mineral or herb. There are virtually no reported cases of anyone dying from taking a natural supplement in its proper dose. However, there are hundreds of thousands of documented deaths that have occurred by taking an over-the-counter nonprescription or prescription drug in its proper dosage.

- Through powerful lobbying, the Atkins and the low-carb craze is at an all-time high. I promoted the Atkins diet on television for two years, but after thoroughly researching the workings of the Atkins organization I found it to be riddled with deceptions, lies and fraud. Isn't it interesting that for years no one in the news media promoted the Atkins diet as a healthy, safe way to lose weight? All of a sudden, out of nowhere, everyone is talking about how wonderful the Atkins program is. This is one of the greatest weight loss scams of all time.

- Former producers and insiders of news networks have blown the whistle on the fact that most television, radio, and newspaper news organizations do not report the news, but rather come up with the story that they want to run in advance and then go out and manufacture and create the story to fit their editorial needs. These editorial needs are based on what the owners of the network want, the boards of directors, and/or the sponsors. Basically, they produce news that will have the most and best financial benefits.

- Journalists are repeatedly being found guilty of manufacturing stories to increase their own personal wealth via payoffs by corporations or the government, or by buying and selling stock based on how their stories will affect the company's stock price.

- Whistleblowers now report that all forms of media, including radio, television, newspapers, and magazines, are in fact owned by the sponsors. There are secret meetings with the sponsors who dictate the content of all programming and topics covered or not covered in the media outlets.

- Because of the cross-ownership of corporations, and the massive amount of stock owned by the executives of corporations, and how many members of the boards of companies are also members of the boards of other companies, there is very little if any objective journalism and unbiased media reporting. A good example is AOL heavily promotes reality television shows on NBC. You will also notice that on the NBC news organizations they heavily promote as "news" what is going on within their other companies always in a favorable light. These are not news stories at all, but "commercials" for the company's other businesses disguised as news, misleading the public.

- All movies, books, and television programs are controlled by a small group of distributors. It is virtually impossible to actively promote an independent movie, television show, or book. This small group of "elites" virtually controls the flow of information in this country.

4. **Still not convinced that right now your body is loaded with toxins causing you all types of illness, disease, depression, stress, and anxiety? Then consider this:**

- All injections from botox, collagen, insulin and vaccines are loaded with poisonous toxins. Many of these are animal based and are filled with deadly pathogens and chemicals.

- There are so many toxins in our environment and food that even people who live in the most remote parts of the world have been found to have massive amounts of toxins in their fat cells, even though the toxins do not exist in their local environment. This is a toxic world, and no one is immune. You are filled with toxins right now.

- Because of toxicity, most people do not assimilate high amounts of nutrients from what they are eating.

- A study showed that traces of industrial strength fire retardant have turned up in wild and farm raised salmon around the world. Farm-raised salmon has been found to have troubling levels of PCBs, a known cancer causing agent. When you eat this food the toxins go inside you!

- The newspaper *The Daily Mail* reported "Ready to eat salad linked with birth defects. Cancer hazard is in packed salad." The article goes on to expose how premixed ready-to-eat salad is washed with chlorine. The chlorine is bad enough, but it combines with chemicals naturally present in lettuce to create chlorine byproducts which can be even more hazardous to your health.

- The government has found traces of rocket fuel chemical in milk, green leaf lettuce, and drinking water. The government also acknowledges that these chemicals adversely affect the thyroid, which potentially can make you fat and lead to dozens of other diseases.

- *The Associated Press* reports that flame retardant is found in Lake Michigan. The article goes on to say that the amount of chemicals found in supermarket food, and even women's breast milk, is alarming. Studies suggest that high levels of these chemicals cause liver and thyroid damage, meaning you are toxic and these chemicals cause disease.

- The *Los Angeles Times* reports that deformed frogs are showing up at alarmingly increasing levels. The deformities are linked to pesticides used in agriculture.

- *Reuters* reported that air pollution is so bad that it is adversely affecting lung function in teenagers.

- *The Daily News* newspaper reported that certain cookies are having hydrogenated oil removed since there is overwhelming evidence that these trans fats cause obesity, clogging of the arteries, heart disease, strokes, and death. This is significant because you have been eating massive amount of trans fats for the last thirty years, which is one of the major reasons sickness and disease are at an all-time high.

- Food recalls are at an all-time high. Food is recalled because it is unsafe to eat and loaded with poisons. For every recall I can assure you that there are thousands of food products being shipped that should be recalled but have not been discovered.

- *Reuters* reports that living in the suburbs can actually make you sick. Many factors were theorized, one of which is the heavy amounts of toxicity a person ingests in suburban living.

- *Reuters* reports that air around indoor swimming pools is harmful to children's lung cells. Researchers believe that exposure to chlorine byproducts in air around indoor pools harm respiratory cells.

- *Reuters* reported that mercury is being released from coal fired power plants and is one of the contributing causes of increase in autism and other health disorders. It is also believed that whether you live near a power plant or not you are still affected since mercury travels virtually around the globe.

- It has been reported that the feed that is used in U.S. cattle production may be routinely tainted with poisons and disease. The rules and regulations relating to feed are not being complied with. Cattle producers are more interested in making money than safety. They routinely break the law and do not comply with safety standards. This means the beef that we are eating is loaded with toxins, poisons, and disease causing chemicals.

- *USA Today* reports the air pollution from other countries drifts into the United States. We breathe in more toxins today than ever before in history. These toxins stay in our body and cause disease.

- William Campbell, M.D., states, "Your daily shower could be killing you softly with the same toxins used to kill lab rats and in chemical weapons." The toxic substances in most municipal water systems have been used in the past to kill laboratory animals and as a weapon of war. It may be more dangerous to shower in municipal water than even drinking it. Your body absorbs up to four times more toxins in a shower than drinking the same water. If you drink tap water, or shower or bathe, or swim in a pool you are categorically loading your body with poisonous toxins, which lead to and cause disease.

- The FDA is ready to clear genetically enhanced salmon. Genetically modified food is rampant in our food supply. It does not have to be labeled as genetically altered. Now, food manufacturers, in a quest to make more money, are changing the nature of things by genetically manufacturing animals and fish. Eating genetically modified food means we are ingesting more poisons and toxins into our system.

5. **Still not convinced that politicians and various government agencies are corrupt, out of control, and operating un-policed? Then consider this:**

- Did you know that there is a law that allows the government to walk up to you on the street and take away any money you have in your pocket, as well as confiscate any property that they want such as your car and home? Did you know that this can be done to any person living in America and you don't even have to be charged with a crime, and you don't even have to be arrested? If you want to get your money or personal property back, you then have to file suit against the government and it could take up to two years.

- Did you know that there is a law in America that allows the government to take any person living in America and, without arresting them and without charging them with a crime, take that person and incarcerate them for an unlimited amount of time, as well as forbidding that person from having any contact with any person, including an attorney? This person—who has not been arrested or charged with a crime—can be held and incarcerated, and can be denied all access to the legal system. I know this sounds like the Gestapo in Nazi Germany, but it is absolutely true, and most people just don't realize just how much the U.S. Government is becoming a police state.

- Did you know that Congress makes themselves exempt to virtually every law they pass? It's unbelievable but true. Congress will pass a law requiring handicapped access to all businesses, but makes the government exempt. It will pass a law requiring mandatory retirement, but will make themselves exempt.

- The government has changed the definitions of some of the most basic things we know. Example: There was a reported list of the healthiest states in America. Health, in this particular survey, was defined as the number of hospital beds per 1,000 people, and the percentage of children who got all their recommended vaccinations. They were defining healthiest states as the states where the most people were getting the most amounts of drugs and surgery. How insane. The definition for "spices" now includes thousands of deadly chemicals. Roast beef doesn't have to be real roast beef anymore, it can be a man-made manufactured product and still be called "roast beef."

- Did you know that if you have a child who has been diagnosed with cancer, not giving that child chemotherapy and other drugs can be a criminal offense?

- Politicians who are on the payroll spend 80 percent of their time running for re-election. This is a scam. If a person had a job and decided to run for office, he would not be allowed to take 80 percent of his time and spend it running for office. He would have to resign from his job so he could spend his time in his new pursuit. Politicians, however, stay on the payroll whether they do their job or run for re-election. It's another example of the government out of control.

- Politicians who are being paid out of taxpayer money should be doing the job that they were elected to do. Unfortunately, as I mentioned above, they spend the majority of their time actually running for re-election and not doing the job that they are supposed to be doing and are being paid to do. Did you also know that 95 percent of the aides that the politician has working for him, who are also on the payroll and paid for by our taxpayers' money, are actually "political advisors?" This means that your tax dollars are paying for staff members who work for the politicians whose only goal and objective is not to help that politician do the job he was elected to do, but rather get that politician re-elected. The majority of a politician's day is making sure that he gets re-elected. The majority of a politician's day is spent working on getting money from lobbyists and major corporations, it is not doing the job that he was elected to do and he is being paid to do. This corruption is at an all-time high. It must be exposed and it must be stopped. When we elect politicians they should be required to do the job they are being paid to do and that they were elected to do and that is protect us the voters. Politicians are supposed to be working for the voters, not for the lobbyists and the big corporations. Our Constitution says, "We the people..." It does not say "We the corporations..." Unfortunately, big business controls our politicians. We can change this, and we must.

- The government promotes watchdog groups, but no one is asking who formed these watchdog groups, who started them, who funded them, where do they get their money, what are the salary and perks of its officers and directors. Did you know that most watchdog groups, which appear to be consumer advocate groups or government-backed groups, are actually funded by big business, whose objective is to promote the industries or companies that are funding them? These are not watchdog groups at all. They are propaganda organizations used by big business and allowed to flourish by the government.

- Former Homeland Security chief, Tom Ridge, did a very strange thing when he encouraged everyone in America to buy duct tape. Interestingly enough, the largest seller of duct tape, Home Depot, made windfall profits on his comments. Now upon leaving the government, Tom Ridge has been given a lucrative job on the board of directors of Home Depot! It sounds like a payoff to me!

- President Bush bypasses Congress and during its recess fills posts at the Federal Trade Commission. This is an outrage and shows how the administration puts its puppets into various government agencies and uses these agencies like Hitler used the Gestapo and Stalin used the KGB.

- *The Associated Press* reports that members of the House of Representatives are invited to, and accept, travel overseas that is in fact improper. At least eight house members and fifteen house aides accepted trips to South Korea from a registered foreign agent despite rules prohibiting the practice.

- *The Washington Post* reported that a U.S. Indian tribe and a gambling services company made donations to a Washington-based public policy group to cover most of a $70,000 trip to Britain in mid-2000 by House Majority Leader Tom DeLay. Amazingly, that week-long trip took place just two months before DeLay helped kill legislation opposed by the same tribe and the same company. Can we say conflict of interest? Can we say payoff? Can we say bribe? Folks, wake up and open your eyes to the corruption in big business and government.

- The Bush administration paid commentators to promote certain laws! *USA Today* reports that the Bush administration paid a prominent black pundit $240,000 to promote certain

Bush policies on his nationally syndicated television show and urge other black journalists to do the same. This is outrageous! This is corruption! This is payoffs! This is independent journalists being paid money by our government to say certain things. This is why you cannot believe what you hear people say on television, and you cannot believe what the government says.

- *The Associated Press* reports how lobbyists are involved in cabinet appointees. When the president appoints cabinet members, lobbyists spend huge amounts of time and effort making sure that the picks benefit their corporate clients. The lobbyists even make selections and recommendations to the president. This is how corporate America controls government policy.

- *The Associated Press* reports how the government agency in charge of airport security, the TSA, spent almost half a million dollars of taxpayer money on a lavish party entertaining themselves. It also gave its senior executives bonuses higher than any other federal government agency and failed to provide adequate justification. These government fat cats are living the big life on our tax dollars.

- It is reported that government secrecy has increased sharply in the past few years, keeping Americans in the dark about information we should be able to access. The government is hiding more information and more documents away from public view. This is exactly what happened in Nazi Germany. Slowly but surely the people's freedoms were taken away, all in the name of "national security." This is the exact same thing that happened under Stalinist Russia.

- A former Connecticut governor has been charged and convicted for selling access to his office for personal gain! The governor of Connecticut was found guilty of accepting more than $100,000 in charter trips to Las Vegas, vacations, and repairs on his personal lakeside cottage. He even tried to hide a personal account worth over $416,000. This is the governor of the state of Connecticut committing fraud and engaging in corruption at the highest levels. I can assure you that for every politician or corporate executive that has been charged and found guilty of fraud and corruption there are thousands more committing the same kinds of fraud and corruption who have not been discovered yet.

- *The Associated Press* reports that scientists on the Yucca Mountain nuclear project have falsified documents committing egregious fraud.

- The Bush administration has been exposed for committing flagrant propaganda, a violation of our Constitution. The Bush administration produced videos that were designed to deceive news organizations and the public into believing they were independent news stories. These videos are fake news; they are not real. They are manufactured by the government and specifically sent and broadcast to mislead and deceive the public into believing they are objective news reports. This is a flagrant and blatant example of how the government commits corruption on a regular basis, lies to the public, and misleads the public systematically.

- The number of politicians being charged with unethical activities and criminal activities is at an all-time high. The number of individuals and corporations that have government contracts that are being charged with fraud is at an all-time high. I can assure you for every person or company that is charged with fraud, or criminal activity, or unethical activity, there are thousands that are doing exactly the same thing, but have not been caught.

- Politicians around the world have been convicted of accepting bribes and pressure from special interest groups, lobbyists, corporations, and wealthy individuals over the last 100 years. The wealthy controlling government is not new, however, this form of corruption is at an all-time high and getting worse. The average guy today doesn't have a chance against the wealthy and the large corporations. We are being exploited every single day by the wealthy, politicians, and large corporations. The system today is worse than ever before. The system today makes it almost impossible for the little guy to get ahead. The system today is weighed heavily in favor of the politicians, the wealthy, and the large corporations. It is truer today than ever before, the rich get richer and the poor get poorer, and it is harder than ever before for the poor to become rich. This is exploitation and corruption at its highest level. Can you see why I'm mad as hell, and not going to take it anymore? Keep in mind, I am not doing this for me. I've made hundreds of millions of dollars. I'm doing this because like many people throughout history I have "seen the light." Many of you of the Christian faith may remember the apostle Paul. Paul's original name was Saul and he was a persecutor of Christians. However, when he was struck by a light and had an epiphany, he turned around his ethics and activities a hundred percent; and instead of persecuting Christians, became the lead apostle of Christianity. I, too, have seen the light and am now fighting for the little guy, you!

- Judges are now being exposed for accepting trips paid for by large corporations, many of which have cases before those exact same judges. These are bribes and payoffs in their most obvious form, or at least a major conflict of interest.

- In the book *King of Cons: Exposing the Dirty Rotten Secrets of the Washington Elite and Hollywood Celebrities*, by Aaron Tonken, the author explains how politicians are routinely involved in fraud, corruption, misuse of power, and misleading the public.

- The *Associated Press* reports that the Transportation Security Administration misled the public. It was reported that the Transportation Security Administration illegally obtained personal information on over twelve million airline passengers, including dates of birth, credit card information, addresses, phone numbers, and other sensitive personal information. The Acting Inspector General of Homeland Security said that the TSA had misinformed individuals, the media, and Congress! Although it did stop short of saying TSA lied, anyone with two eyes can see that the TSA flagrantly and blatantly lied. Another example that the government consciously, purposely, and routinely misleads the public by putting out false information.

- I have personally seen high-ranking members of the Department of Justice lie under oath, committing perjury. I have sued various government departments and in depositions have caught these senior officials lying, deceiving, defrauding, and committing perjury, yet they are never charged for the crime of perjury even though they have blatantly and flagrantly lied. The government always protects its own.

- Political insiders are now blowing the whistle on how politics works. Report after report shows that politicians have virtually no interest in what is best for the country, the communities, or the individual citizen. Every politician has simple objectives: (a) to get re-elected, (b) to increase their political power and influence, and (c) to increase their own personal wealth. Politicians surround themselves with dozens of "political advisors" who calculate every word said by the politician, every speech made, and every vote on legislation based on not how it will positively or negatively affect the country, the communities, or the individual citizens, but rather how those actions will positively or negatively impact the politician's chance of getting re-elected, increasing their political power, or increasing their own personal wealth.

- Governments and corporations around the world have routinely abused power and are filled with corruption. Thousands of findings of such abuses of power and corruption have been reported for over 100 years all around the world. The most common form of corruption is individuals, in corporations and in political office, taking money illegally for personal gain. This practice is rampant throughout the world and rampant in American corporations and politics. Hundreds of books documenting these facts have been published with indisputable evidence; however, the majority of these books are buried and very few people ever heard about them. Alliance Publishing Group will be actively promoting and publishing these works, exposing corporate and government corruption in America and all around the world.

- State and federal employees in America are repeatedly being found not showing up for work, being asleep on the job, or simply doing in effect nothing. When interviewed privately these individuals say off the record that working for the government is the best job in the world because you don't have to do anything and you can't get fired!

- Inspectors in both federal and state agencies routinely are found to write fraudulent inspection reports when in fact no inspections have ever been done.

- Isn't it amazing that in the last fifty years there have been thousands of "suicides" and accidental deaths by public officials and politicians; however, not one murder? This means that the highest suicide rate and accidental death rate of any occupation is being a public official! Doesn't it make you think or at least suspect foul play and corruption?

- Politicians repeatedly lie about the fact that they are trying to stop illegal aliens from entering America. This is a flagrant, bold-faced lie. If you have ever been to the Mexican border there are actual holes in the fence! These holes have been there for ten years; everyone knows about them. They are there so that Mexicans can ILLEGALLY COME INTO AMERICA. The fact is the politicians lie. In every community in California there are illegal aliens working in the fields. If the politicians really had an interest in stopping illegal aliens, all they would have to do is drive up to a field, walk in to the workers picking the fruits and vegetables, and ask to see their green cards. They could virtually clean up this mess in a matter of months. In every community there are hundreds of Mexicans who stand around street corners waiting for daily work. I have asked the police personally if they are aware of this, and it's a big joke. They all know these people are illegals, but they have strict orders from "the powers that be" to leave them alone. Corporations need and want illegal aliens so that they can pay next to nothing and not be required to give benefits. These corporate fat cats put pressure on the politicians. The bottom line is everyone knows hundreds of thousands of illegal immigrants come into America every year. Everyone knows this could be easily stopped if politicians wanted it stopped. But because of payoffs by big corporations it is allowed to happen and the politicians constantly insult us by lying about it.

- Politicians and government are responsible for the majority of wealth in this country because the majority of wealth has been generated through public corporations and government contracts. Specifically, the oil industry, pharmaceutical companies, and military contracts are the main source of wealth. All of these industries are in fact controlled and manipulated by politicians and government. In relation to the drug companies, the government and the drug companies use the insurance companies to do the major funneling of money from the majority of people into the pockets of the wealthy corporations and politicians.

6. **Still not convinced that the FDA is working with big business and major drug companies allowing them to deceive the public and flood the public marketplace with dangerous products? Then consider this:**

- Cigarettes are obviously bad; however, they are the only product in America where the ingredients do not have to be listed. How can this be? Well, consider that the FDA is in charge and that the politicians who receive huge amounts of donations and lobbying by the tobacco industry tell the FDA what to do. The obvious connection between the FDA and big tobacco is exposed on the Web site www.crazyworld.com.

- Federal law prohibits the FDA from using experts with financial conflicts of interest, but the FDA has waived the restriction more than 800 times since 1998. Although the FDA does not reveal when financial conflicts exist, since 1992 it has kept the details of any conflict secret so it is not possible to determine the amount of money or the drug company involved. Two recent articles, both ran in Reuters News and *USA Today,* reported that 54 percent of the experts the FDA asked for advice on which medicines should be approved for sale have a direct financial interest in the drugs or topics they are evaluating. These financial conflicts of interests typically include stock ownership, consulting fees, or research grants. The *USA Today* article stated, "These pharmaceutical experts, about 300 on eighteen different advisory committees, make decisions that affect the health of millions of Americans and billions of billions of dollars in drug sales. With few exceptions, the FDA follows the committee's advice." The scary part is these people who are making these decisions have a direct financial interest and financially benefit based on the decisions they make.

The *USA Today* article concluded that at 92 percent of the meetings, at least one member had a financial conflict of interest. At 55 percent of the meetings, half or more of the FDA advisors had conflicts of interest. Conflicts were most frequent at the fifty-seven meetings when broader issues were discussed; 92 percent of those members had conflicts. At the 102 meetings dealing with the fate of a specific drug, 33 percent of the experts had a direct financial interest.

- The pharmaceutical industry has more influence with the FDA than anyone realizes. In the May 19th edition of the prestigious medical journal *Lancet,* editor Richard Horton claimed that the FDA has become a servant to the drug industry. An example: Even though there are multiple deaths caused by certain drugs, the FDA does not recall them from the market, but suggests adding a warning. The LA *Times* reported that the FDA has withheld safety information from labels that physicians say would call into question the use of the drugs. Since 1993, at least 1,000,000 people were killed by drugs that were approved, but never should have been. Before 1990, 60 percent of drugs submitted to the FDA were approved. Today over 80 percent are approved. *The Los Angeles Times* reported that seven killer drugs that were approved by the FDA, and were so deadly that they had to be withdrawn, generated over $5 billion for the pharmaceutical industry before the recall. Most shocking is that the FDA knowingly puts children at risk. According to the LA *Times* article, the Agency never warned doctors not to administer a drug to infants or other children, even though eight youngsters who were given this drug in clinical studies died. Pediatricians prescribed it widely for infants afflicted with gastric reflux, a common digestive disorder. Patients and their doctors had no way of knowing that the FDA, in August 1996, had found the drug to be "not approvable for children." "We never knew that," said the father of a three-month old son who died on October 28, 1997, after taking the drug. "To me, that means they took my kid as a guinea pig to see if it would work." By the time the drug was pulled, the FDA had received reports of twenty-four deaths of children under age six who had been given this drug. By then, the drug had generated U.S. sales of over $2.5 billion for the drug company.

- An FDA insider said, "People are aware that turning down a drug for approval is going to cause problems with officials higher up in the FDA. Before I came to the FDA, I always assumed things were done properly. I've now lost faith in taking any prescription medication."

- According to the *Los Angeles Times*, "Seven drugs were approved by the FDA. These seven drugs were found later to be ineffective and fatal. These seven drugs were found to be so deadly that they caused the deaths of numerous people. How the FDA approved these drugs is still a mystery. They obviously relied on misleading and/or false studies. Keep in mind all studies submitted by the FDA are always paid for and produced by the drug company which is seeking approval. These drugs were not needed. They were not miracle drugs designed to save lives. They were simply drugs designed to increase profits of the drug companies. One was for heartburn. Another was a diet pill, and a third was a pain killer. Six of the drugs were never proved to offer any lifesaving benefits and the seventh, another antibiotic, was ultimately judged totally unnecessary because there were other antibiotics available that had been already proven to be safer than this deadly antibiotic. These drugs did not have to be approved, but they were pushed for approval so that the drug companies could market them and make billions of dollars." These seven drugs have now been found to be so deadly and have killed so many people that they had to be pulled off the market. The FDA is repeatedly allowing dangerous drugs to be approved and sold because of the pressure put on it by the drug industry.

- According to the *Los Angeles Times,* in 1988, only 4 percent of new drugs introduced into the world market were approved first by the FDA. In 1998, the FDA's first in the world approval spiked to 66 percent. The reason is now it appears that the easiest agency in the world to approve a new drug, regardless of the safety, is in fact the FDA. The FDA was once the world's leading organization when it came down to the safety of drugs it approved. Now the FDA seems to be more interested in the sales and profits of the drug companies than the safety of consumers. The FDA, as an example, was the last worldwide regulatory agency to withdraw several new drugs in the late 1990s that were banned by health authorities in Europe as being dangerous. Routinely, FDA officials recommend against the approval of drugs, and advisory committees concur and also recommend against the approval of drugs, only to have the drug approved by the FDA and called "safe and effective."

- According to Dr. Kurt D. Furberg, a professor at Wake Forest University, "The patients are the ones paying the price. They're the ones developing all the side effects, fatal and nonfatal."

- One particular drug the FDA approved and called "safe and effective" was pulled within the first year because it was linked to five deaths, the removal of many of the patients' colons, and other major bowel surgeries. Other drugs called "safe and effective" by the FDA had been proven to cause heart valve damage, liver damage, pancreas damage, prostate cancer, colon cancer, impotency, infertility, heart attack, stroke.

- In the *Los Angeles Times* article, seven specific drugs that were called "safe and effective" resulted in a minimum of 1,000 reported deaths. Other experts say that number is much higher, and could go as high as 20,000 deaths. All from drugs the FDA has called "safe and effective." What is not recorded is the potential hundreds of thousands of patients who took these drugs that developed other severe medical conditions such as liver damage, heart problems, cancer, diabetes, digestive issues, etc. The most outrageous thing is that all of these new medical conditions will be treated by the medical doctors by surgeries and/or more drugs. The needless pain and suffering of hundreds of thousands of people, and the deaths of countless more, is being ignored—all in the name of profit.

- In the *Los Angeles Times* article, it is reported that more than twenty-two million Americans took the drugs that were proven to be dangerous and proven to cause major medical problems. This means there are potentially twenty-two million people who will now have other medical concerns that were caused specifically, and directly, by the drugs they took.

- Dr. Lamuel Loy, a University of Texas School of Public Health physician who served from 1995 to 1999 on the FDA Advisory Committee, says the FDA has lost their compass and forgotten who it is they are ultimately serving.

- The FDA states "All drugs have risks." Most of them have serious risks.

- *The Los Angeles Times* of Tuesday, April 6, 2004, quotes Harvard psychiatrist Dr. Joseph Glen Mullen as saying the following: "Evidence that the FDA is suppressing a report linking suicide to drugs is an outrage given the public health and safety issues at stake." The FDA has information that antidepressants caused children to be twice as likely to show suicidal behavior. The article shows how the FDA claims that there is no conclusive scientific evidence linking antidepressants and potential suicide behavior. However, the article goes on to say that there is absolute evidence that the FDA is suppressing and hiding the information so that the drug companies can continue to sell drugs.

- Nonfatal skin cancers are the number one cancer. The four other most common kinds are breast, prostate, lung, and colorectal, which is cancer of the colon. There is research and observations that strongly suggest that those who are the most prone to getting these cancers are those who have taken the most nonprescription and prescription drugs and who have eaten the most fast food, yet the FDA does nothing to inform the public of the dangers of these two activities.

- The *New York Times* reports that Johnson & Johnson's popular treatment for congestive heart failure, Natrecor, has now been shown to reduce kidney function. The drug causes disease.

- Expert says the drug Zoloft causes dementia.

- *The Associated Press* reports that prostate cancer drugs make men prone to broken bones.

- The FDA silenced Vioxx warnings. The FDA effectively silenced one of its own drug experts who exposed the safety concerns about the profitable drug Vioxx. This shows the FDA is more interested in protecting the profits of the drug companies than the safety of consumers.

- A previously unpublished internal survey of FDA scientists points to potentially dangerous gaps in the approval and marketing of prescription drugs. The internal secret survey showed that the FDA does not adequately monitor the safety of prescription drugs once they are on the market, and the majority of FDA scientists do not believe that the labeling decisions adequately address key safety concern. It also showed that an alarming percentage of FDA scientists themselves were not confident that the final decisions adequately addressed the safety of drugs. The most alarming piece of information to come out of this secret internal survey was the number of scientists that said they have actually been pressured to approve or recommend drugs despite their own reservations about safety, efficacy, or quality of the drug. This means that the senior executives at the FDA are more interested in protecting the profits of the drug companies than they are about the safety of the consumer.

- *The Wall Street Journal* reports that too many unproven drugs are getting approval by the FDA.

- The *Chicago Tribune* reports that the FDA is caught in the middle of a drug safety conflict. The article suggests that the drug industry actually controls what is happening at the FDA.

- The FDA reviewed the drug Celebrex. The FDA's advisory panel recommended that Celebrex stay on the market. The amazing thing is that the members of this advisory panel are all in effect on the payroll of the drug company that sells Celebrex! Can someone stand up, and yell and scream conflict of interest please?

- The FDA itself now admits that two eczema creams cause cancer.

- *The Wall Street Journal* reports that cholesterol drugs fail to offer benefits to patients! Cholesterol reducing drugs are the number one selling drugs in the world. They make the most profits for the drug industry, but the fact is cholesterol reducing drugs do not do anything to reduce the potential dangers of heart disease. The studies show that there were no heart health benefits after four months and no significant benefits after two years. However, it did show that continued use of these cholesterol lowering drugs actually caused illness and disease.

- *The Associated Press* reports that consumer groups blast the new cholesterol guidelines. Most of the heart disease experts who urged more people to take cholesterol lowering drugs have been exposed to have made huge amounts of money from the companies selling those medicines! "It's outrageous they didn't provide disclosure of the conflicts of interest." said Merrill Goozner with the Center for Science in the Public Interest. Folks, this happens all the time. Remember, too, that virtually all studies for new and existing drugs are paid for and funded by their own manufacturers.

- The New York attorney general sued the pharmaceutical giant Glaxo/Smith/Kline saying it committed fraud by withholding information about the dangers of its antidepressant drugs to children. This should not be the only suit filed. It is important that you know that every major pharmaceutical company withholds information about the ineffectiveness and dangers of their drugs. It is important that you know that the drug companies and the FDA know that the drugs do not work and actually are dangerous and cause disease, yet they are hiding and withholding this information from the public.

- *The Associated Press* reports that the drug Avastin increases the risk of heart ailments including chest pain, strokes, mini-strokes, and heart attacks. This means that this drug can kill the people who take it. It is interesting to note that every article that I am reporting on here that talks about drugs also has a heavy emphasis on the stock price and how this news is affecting shareholder value. I cannot emphasize enough that drug companies are publicly traded companies whose only objective is to make profit. They do not want to cure or prevent disease.

- *USA Today* reports that a grieving father spends $1 million nest egg to investigate the drug Acutane. It has been said that this drug caused Liam Grant's son to commit suicide. He has been offered, allegedly, hundreds of thousands of dollars to drop the case. The drug companies don't want you to know the truth about just how dangerous Acutane and other such drugs are.

- Reports out of London state that the drug industry has now bowed to public pressure and will disclose more trial data; however, this is voluntary. This means that the drug industry still refuses to release information it has about the ineffectiveness and dangers of its drugs.

- The Hippocratic Oath, which doctors are allegedly bound to follow, says first do not harm to the patient. This is categorically never followed. Every single doctor should be prosecuted for breaking their solemn oath every time they prescribe a pharmaceutical prescription drug, or any time they recommend that a patient take a nonprescription over-the-counter drug. Why? Because it has been proven, and even the drug manufacturers' own literature states that every single drug, without exception, causes harm to the body.

- Insiders report that for years the tobacco industry secretly paid millions of dollars to individual producers and directors of movies and television shows, making sure that cigarettes were prominently and positively displayed in their movies and programs. Did you ever wonder why? In the old movies when a person was standing before a firing squad, when asked if he had any final requests his answer was always "A cigarette?" The tobacco industry invested millions of dollars devising specific subliminal messages to be put in programs such as this to brainwash us into using their products. The drug companies are doing the same today.

- Whistleblowers have reported that internal documents at both the drug manufacturers and FDA show that drugs, both prescription and nonprescription, have no positive effects in over 70 percent of the people that use them. However, these same documents show that all nonprescription and prescription drugs have negative side effects in 100 percent of the people that use them. All nonprescription and prescription drugs are ineffective and cause disease.

I virtually have in my hand hundreds of articles which show that drugs cause disease, drugs are ineffective, the pharmaceutical companies know that the drugs cause disease and do not work yet are hiding this information, and the various government regulatory bodies around the world, including the FDA, are doing virtually nothing to protect consumers, but are actively working with the pharmaceutical industry to protect their profits. In the last five years alone it is estimated that over 100,000 individual news articles were written exposing this information. Very few of these articles ever see the light of day. They never make the front page headlines. On my Web site, www.naturalcures.com, I will be listing every one of these articles so you can read them in their totality. The evidence is overwhelming. Let me just rattle off a few more headlines to drive home the point even further.

- "Heartburn drugs linked to pneumonia."
- "Cholesterol drugs do nothing to prevent heart disease."
- "Drug maker admits fraud, but sales still flourish."
- "Merck should have pulled Vioxx in 2000."
- "FDA scientists themselves expose major problems with five deadly drugs."
- "Government finds Celebrex ads misleading."
- "Biogene voluntarily suspends drug after deaths from people who used it."
- "Interns long hours cause medical errors resulting in deaths."
- "Blood transfusions at birth almost always unneeded."
- "Merck tried to bury Vioxx concerns for years."
- "Crestor harms kidneys."
- "Pain drugs damage heart."
- "Antibiotics raise heart death risk."
- "Glaxo ordered to release negative data on its drugs."
- "Ads for controversial drugs must be changed."
- "Drug complaints reach record high."
- "Scientists see no need for pain drugs."
- "Whistleblower warns of more drug risks."
- "Attention deficit drugs have negative long-term effects."
- "Most people do not need flu vaccines."
- "Splenda claim unsubstantiated and false."
- "Broad-spectrum antibiotics pose serious health threat."
- "Scientists say road salt causes disease."

- "Seventy-five percent of Americans over fifty are pharmaceutical drug addicts."

- "The American Medical Association admits prescription drug side effects are now the fourth leading cause of death in America."

- "An FDA scientist admits Vioxx alone may have caused as many as 150,000 deaths. The FDA is virtually defenseless against similar catastrophes with other drugs."

- "Prescription drugs are now killing more people than the diseases they are supposed to be curing."

- "Crestor causes serious muscle damage and other health risks."

- "Pacemakers cause heart failure."

- "Cholesterol lowering drugs can trigger heart attacks."

I can go on, and on, and on, and on, and on.

7. **Still not convinced that the pharmaceutical industry pushes drug sales and usage at all costs, and has an insatiable desire for increasing profits? Then consider this:**

- Nurses are given gifts and money in an attempt to induce them to administer drugs from a specific manufacturer.

- Schools get $500 per month for every child they have on a psychiatric drug, including Ritalin or Prozac. This gives a major incentive for schools to get kids on drugs.

- Doctors routinely get visits from pharmaceutical sales reps. These sales reps do not tell doctors how to cure and prevent disease. These sales reps have very sophisticated presentations that are designed to tell doctors how they can increase their profits. These pharmaceutical sales reps tell doctors how they can make more money by prescribing more drugs. These presentations have almost zero information on the safety or effectiveness of these drugs. The concern is not the patient; the emphasis is how doctors can make more money.

- Doctors receive cash bonuses to prescribe drugs.

- *The Wall Street Journal* reports that professors take payments to express certain views.

- Doctors on government advisory panels make recommendations for drugs while being paid huge amounts of money by the manufacturers of those same drugs.

- Drug companies routinely sponsor foundations' research. An example is Amgen gave $150,000 for research done by the Kidney Foundation. Remember, all foundations, all charities, and all research that is conducted on drugs are almost always paid for by the drug companies themselves, and therefore guarantee the results that they want.

8. **Still not convinced that the ads that you see on television, or read in magazines and newspapers, or hear on the radio are filled with deceptions, fraudulent information, misleading data, and outright lies? Then consider this:**

- TV ads routinely use words such as "greatest," "world's finest," "best," etc. There is no substantiation to these claims.

- In virtually every ad seen there are actors used. When you see somebody telling you how wonderful their product is you are being misled. The people on the ads rarely, if ever, have used the product and are simply reading a script. When you see people dressed as doctors, policemen, or judges you are being misled as they are simply actors. It is important to note that when these ads are developed the companies specifically want to create a "net impression" that you, the consumer, will receive from the ad. These "net impressions" are always untrue. This means that a company selling a certain product wants you, the customer, to believe something that is categorically untrue. This is how ads are created. An example is a beer company, in order to increase sales, wants to produce an ad that gets the viewer to consciously or subconsciously believe that drinking their beer will actually help them lose weight. This intention is given to the media company producing the ad. The ad is then produced using sophisticated techniques to achieve the goal. This is exactly how ads are produced. They are false, they are misleading, and they should be stopped.

- In restaurants and on television food is shown giving you the impression that when you buy the product it will look like what you see. For anyone who has ever purchased anything, it absolutely never looked like that when it was shown on television, or as it appeared on the package or appeared in the restaurant menu. This is false and misleading, but is allowed to happen because of the lobbyists paying off our friendly politicians.

- In movies and on TV shows companies routinely secretly pay millions of dollars to have their products prominently displayed or used by the characters in the movies and television programs. Scripts are actually written around products to encourage you to buy them. This is done without disclosure, and to covertly brainwash you into purchasing products.

9. **Still not convinced that all over-the-counter nonprescription and prescription drugs are poisons and causing you great physical and emotional harm? Then consider this:**

- Depending on who you listen to, either the third or fourth leading cause of death in America is doctors. This is because doctors routinely prescribe drugs that kill their patients, or perform surgeries that are unsuccessful and the patients die, or the doctors misdiagnose the illness and do the wrong thing which causes the person to die.

- *The Journal of the American Medical Association,* Vol. 284 states, "Things like unnecessary surgery, medical errors, negative effects of drugs, etc., cause almost as many deaths as heart disease and cancer. Over 250,000 people in America alone die each year from physicians' activity or therapy. These account only for the deaths; they do not include people who are permanently maimed, injured, or develop serious other medical conditions due to drugs and surgical procedures. The number of people who get permanent serious disabilities or discomfort, or develop other diseases from drugs and surgical procedures could exceed over three million people per year in America alone."

- Estrogen therapy is now shown to be very dangerous.

- Lowering cholesterol will not prevent a heart attack.

- An aspirin a day can give you a stroke. New research also shows it can destroy your eyesight.

- Sunscreens don't prevent skin cancer, they cause it. Scientists say five ingredients in most sunscreens are highly carcinogenic.

- Since the invention of sunscreen, skin cancer rates in the U.S. have gone up. No one can explain this. No one can explain why the incidence of skin cancer in the tropical countries where the sun rays are the strongest are very low.

- It has been reported that over seven million Americans older than sixty-five receive prescriptions for drugs that a panel of experts deemed inappropriate for use by the elderly because of potentially dangerous side effects.

- According to a study in the *Journal of the American Medical Association,* every prescription drug has dangerous side effects, and over 20 percent of them come on the market without any warnings.

- In Ralph Nader's book *The Chemical Feast,* he talks about how the Food and Drug Administration deceived consumers and concealed important information about the safety of drugs and food additives. That was over thirty years ago. Amazingly, nothing has changed.

- It is estimated at the current rate most Americans will consume over 1,000 pounds of nonprescription over-the-counter and prescription drugs over the next twenty years. This massive increase in drug consumption is in direct proportion to the increase of major disease, the duration of every major disease, and the severity of every major disease.

10. **Still not convinced that advertising is having a major effect on what you believe and think? Then consider this:**

    - Advertising has such a profound impact at brainwashing people into believing that drugs and vaccines are so important for health, that if a person does not give their children drugs and vaccines people believe that the children are being neglected and social services can take the children away.

    - People who have never taken any drugs at all are now going into their doctor and demanding certain drugs that they've seen advertised on television.

    - An eighteen year old gets more impressions from drug ads than any other advertising. The average eighteen year old will be exposed to over 50,000 drug ads.

- Ads trying to convince people of adult attention deficit disorder are being called false and misleading, and nothing more than a marketing ploy by the drug company to convince people they need to buy their drugs. It is obviously working as the sales of these drugs skyrocket.

11. **Still not convinced that horror stories in relation to the FDA and the pharmaceutical industry don't exist? Then consider this:**

- An infant, Alexander Horwin, was diagnosed with an aggressive form of brain cancer and underwent two surgeries. The first left him unable to walk and with optic nerve damage. The second left him tumor free, but his doctors informed his parents that the disease threatened to return if he didn't receive treatment. The doctors recommended state-of-the-art chemotherapy treatment. It was the best in the world, but the risk included damage to the young infant's heart, lungs, liver and kidneys; and could lead to loss of hearing, small stature, infertility, more cancers, intellectual decline, or even death.

  Less than four months after beginning treatment, Alexander died; most probably from the chemotherapy itself. Only later did the parents learn, by reading various medical journals, that the state-of-the-art chemotherapy recommended by the doctors was proven to be ineffective for young children. Various medical journals reported that the drug Alexander was given caused seizures, dementia and death, and even caused cancer itself. This state-of-the-art chemotherapy was performed at a prestigious children's hospital.

  The parents found that there were other treatments that were potentially far less dangerous but, according to FDA rules, could not be administered. The parents also found stories of how people with the same disease as their son who received these additional treatments were healthy and suffered few, if any, side effects. The problem was, unbeknownst to the parents, the treatment their son received was part of an FDA approved clinical trial. The FDA regulation that prevented the young infant from receiving the alternative treatment is part of the Food, Drug, and Cosmetics Act, and has been upheld by various lawsuits and state codes. What this means is that Americans don't have the freedom to choose what they and their physicians believe is best. An investigative journalist stated, "Few American are aware that their treatment options, indeed their most personal medical choices, are regulated by the government and are seriously limited if they become ill." This young boy lived only five months after being diagnosed with cancer, yet his medical bills totaled almost $250,000.

• The sad story of Jack and Maryanne Kunari: Their son was diagnosed with brain cancer. Doctors recommended surgery, radiation and chemotherapy, and told the parents of the devastating side effects. The doctors claimed that young Dustin had only four months to live. The parents found an alternative health doctor, Burzynski. When the parents told their medical doctors they were thinking about alternative treatment as an option, they were warned that there was a good chance that social workers from the state could come in and force the young boy to receive the "conventional" treatments of chemotherapy, radiation, surgery and drugs. "It's unbelievable that people have to live with the stress of not only having a severe medical condition in their family, but being threatened that the state will come in, take your son or daughter away from you, and force them to receive horrible, painful medical treatments that will kill them." The FDA says patients must use approved therapies, and get no success from those therapies before going to any alternatives. That means that if a person has deadly cancer they must take the poisonous drugs, the radiation and chemotherapy, and pay hundreds of thousands of dollars to the cancer industry, even though these treatments are deadly and could potentially kill them. Luckily for young Dustin, the scenario happened before these laws went into effect, and the parents were not bound by them. The young boy received the alternative all-natural cancer treatments for four years. Eight years later, young Dustin is tumor free, healthy and off medication. You would never know he was sick, his mother said. If this young boy had taken the conventional treatment recommended by the medical doctors of drugs, surgery, radiation, and chemotherapy, the boy would have experienced an excruciatingly painful, horrible existence and probably would have died within a few months anyway.

- In order to protect the profits of big business, FDA inspectors evaluate fish safety by the unbelievable method of simply smelling the fish. Of course they only smell a small portion of fish to determine whether it's safe for human consumption. This is laughable at best.

- There are rules and regulations set up to protect consumers from contaminated food produced by food manufacturers, restaurants, and fast-food restaurants. These rules and regulations are routinely broken at alarming levels. There have been several major news stories showing the hundreds of violations that routinely exist on a daily basis in fast-food restaurants around the country. This means it's virtually impossible to eat in a restaurant, and primarily a fast-food restaurant, and eat food that is not classified as "contaminated" and "unfit for human consumption." This means that all the food in restaurants, and primarily fast-food restaurants, are full of disease causing agents. For those of you who eat this food on a regular basis, is it any wonder why you get so sick? The answer is the publicly traded corporations that own these restaurants and produce this food are making you sick, all in the name of their profits.

- The number of people who are getting sick from eating in fast-food restaurants increases every year.

12. **Still not convinced that aspartame (NutraSweet®) is one of the most dangerous food additives available today? Then consider this:**

- NutraSweet®, which is aspartame, contains methanol, a wood alcohol which is a deadly poison. Aspartame was approved based on 112 studies submitted to the FDA by the original manufacturer, Surrel Pharmaceuticals, which was acquired by Monsanto. All of these studies were paid for and funded by the drug company. Critics who look at these studies, most notably the fifteen pivotal studies that the FDA based its approval on, are astonished and amazed that anyone could deduce that aspartame is safe. It's amazing that one of the subjects in the study died within a year after taking aspartame. Some of the studies showed people who were taking aspartame were having brain seizures. Once the aspartame was withdrawn from the subjects' diets the brain seizures ceased. All the studies were very short, consisted of only a very few subjects, and the duration was only a few months. The FDA today has received more complaints from people who have consumed aspartame and have had major negative side effects than any other approved food, yet no action has ever been taken.

13. **Still not convinced that your thoughts and energy in general is important to your health, and can have a major impact on your physiology, and disease? Then consider this:**

   - The magnetic energy of the earth is substantially lower than it has ever been in history. Very few people actually stand with their feet directly on the earth, allowing them to pick up that energy. The earth's gauss, which is measurement of magnetic energy, was at one time 4.0; today it is at .04. For any organism to grow and prosper, healthy magnetism is one of the first requirements. If you take a magnet and put it under some wet straw and place a kernel of corn on top of it you will soon have a stalk of corn. However, reduce or eliminate the magnetism and you will have little to no growth. The potential kernel will die. Why? Because magnetism is essential for life to exist. Where the earth's magnetism is low, degeneration of cells develop. If you work in buildings or areas that are deprived of healthy magnetism you develop a whole host of physical disorders.

   - The mind and thoughts can have a dramatic instantaneous effect on the body's chemistry and how all organ and gland functions work. In testing people who have been diagnosed with multiple personality disorder, thought has been shown to do what is scientifically impossible. In one particular example, a person's blood was tested and found to be free of diabetes. Within minutes, when his personality changed, the blood was taken again and the person was found to have diabetes. This is physically impossible according to all scientists. It shows that the mind, or the belief system of a person, can do things to the body and change the body chemistry when science has determined that it is impossible to do so. Thoughts and energy absolutely affect a person's physiology and health.

- Exposure to electromagnetic pollution such as high tension power lines, electrical appliances, computers, fluorescent lighting, etc. reduces the magnetic field around you, increasing illness and disease.

- Exposing yourself to strong, powerful, healthy magnetic fields have been scientifically proven to change the body's pH to a more alkaline state, even dissolving calcium deposits around arthritic joints, reducing heart rate, increasing oxygenation of the body's cells, reducing pain, and increasing muscle tissue resulting in major increases of strength and endurance.

- An experiment was conducted by a quantum biologist. When DNA was added to a container the nonphysical photons lined up in an ordered way and aligned with the DNA. When the DNA was removed, the photons remained ordered and lined up where the DNA had been. The mystery is what were the photons connected to? The quantum biologist was forced to accept the possibility that some new field of energy, a web of energy, something that science has not discovered yet, exists.

- An experiment was conducted by the military where DNA was placed in chambers so that electrical changes could be measured. The donor of the DNA was placed in a room far away from the chamber where the DNA was. The donor was subjected to emotional stimulation consisting of video clips, which generated different emotions in the donor. Both the donor and his DNA, which was in a different room in the same building, were monitored as the donor exhibited the various emotional peaks and valleys. To the surprise of the researchers, the DNA exhibited the identical responses at the exact same time. There was no lag time, no transmission time. The DNA peaks and valleys exactly matched the peaks and valleys of the donor in real time. The military wanted to see how far they could separate the donor from his DNA and still get the same affect. They stopped testing after they separated the DNA from the donor by fifty miles and still had the same exact effect—no lag time, no transmission time. What does this mean? It means that living cells communicate through a previously unrecognized form of energy. This undiscovered energy field is not affected by time and distance. This is why thoughts and energetic rebalancing materials go beyond the understanding of biology and drugs, and can absolutely cure and prevent disease. Science does not want to accept this because they cannot patent it and make money.

- An experiment was conducted with DNA to determine if thoughts can affect DNA. DNA was placed in a container; it was discovered that the DNA changed its shape according to the feelings, thoughts, and emotions of the researchers. When the researchers felt gratitude, love, and appreciation, the DNA responded by relaxing and the strands unwound; the length of the DNA became longer. When the researchers felt anger, fear, frustration, or stress, the DNA responded by tightening up; it became shorter and switched off many of its codes. This could be why people feel totally shut down when they experience stress and negative emotions. The DNA codes were reversed and were switched back on when feelings of love, joy, gratitude, and appreciation were felt by the researchers. This experiment was later followed up by testing HIV positive patients. It was discovered that there was a 300 times increase in resistance to viruses and bacteria when the HIV positive patients felt love, gratitude, and appreciation. The bottom line is thoughts, feelings, emotions, and "energy" have a positive or negative effect on your DNA structure and can give you disease and can cure you of disease. Your thoughts can absolutely keep you healthy, and electro-frequency generators and energetic balancing machines and homeopathic remedies, all of which deal with energy, can categorically, 100 percent keep you healthy and disease free and cure you of disease if you do become sick.

- A major magazine had an article entitled "Miracle Cures—Tapping the Power of Make Believe Medicine." The article describes how a Harvard professor shows that a placebo

actually cures disease. Well, actually, the placebo does nothing except help the person believe that his disease will be
cured and it's his own mind and belief that cures the disease.
To point this out, it shows that placebos are moderately
effective when given as a little white tablet, but much more
effective when given as a big red capsule, and still almost 100
percent effective when the patient has to roll up his sleeve
and get an injection. In effect as the belief level goes up the
power of the mind increases and the body simply heals itself.
This shows that the mind causes the body to heal itself.

- Everything emits energy. Researchers have shown that plants
  grow much better in pots made of clay instead of pots made of
  plastic. Why? Because plastic is a man-made material which
  emanates life draining energy. Clay pots and other earthen or
  natural materials emanate life sustaining energy.

- In the book *The Hidden Messages in Water*, by Masaru
  Emoto, it is shown that the structure of water is dramatically
  affected by thoughts. Candice Pert, Ph.D. says, absolutely
  thought alone can completely change the body. This book
  shows the pictures so you can actually see how dramatically the water is changed structurally simply by thoughts.
  I highly, highly, highly encourage you to get this book and
  see the pictures for yourself. Go to www.beyondword.com
  for more information. This is also discussed in the movie
  What The BLEEP Do We Know. For more information visit
  www.whatthebleep.com.

- In research, when a person begins to worry and have
  stress, the body's pH can go from alkaline to acidic in a
  matter of minutes. Thoughts can bring on disease faster
  than any other cause.

- In research, poker players have their body functions monitored, and within a matter of seconds blood pressure and
  heart rate can dramatically change just by how a person
  thinks.

- High Definition TVs emit so much powerful electromagnetic
  energy that in one office building, turning a High Definition
  TV on wiped out entire computer systems. In addition,
  High Definition TVs can knock out a bird's natural sense of

direction. Electromagnetic waves also have adverse affects on dolphins and whales and their ability to navigate. Certainly then, electromagnetic energy is having a profound negative effect on our physiology and health, as well as our emotional well-being.

- The June 2003 issue of the *Townsend Letter for Doctors and Patients* discussed energy-based frequencies used at clinics throughout the world and how effective they are at curing the incurable diseases.

- According to researchers, electromagnetic frequencies underlie all chemical and mechanical reactions in the body. Applying a frequency that resonates with specific tissues helps the tissue regain coherence and heal. This goes against all medical theories and against the concept that drugs are the only cure and prevention for disease.

- It is actually illegal to use an electromagnetic frequency to heal patients, even though the machine causes absolutely no harm, is nonevasive and painless. However, individual people can own such machines themselves, and use them as they see fit, so long as they do not use the machines to cure a disease. How insane.

- In the owner's manual of a leading computer it says, "Wireless LAN products—like other radio devices—emit radio frequency electromagnetic energy. The level of energy emitted by wireless LAN devices are believed to be safe for use by consumers. These standard recommendations reflect the consensus of the scientific community, and are a result of deliberations of panels and committees of scientists who continually review and interpret the extensive research literature." What this means is that there are many people in the scientific community who believe that wireless based products including radios, computers, global positioning devices, cell phones, etc. emit such powerful and negative electromagnetic energy that it is dangerous for a person to be exposed to these frequencies. Unfortunately, even if you do not own them you are being exposed to these on a regular and consistent basis. It is interesting to note that this so-called warning is put in the owner's manuals of computers.

- Food has energy. The natural energy that natural organic food possesses is vital to the health of the human body. Microwaves dramatically change this energy and make food dangerous to consume. Consider that individual people also emit energy, and can emit energy into food as well. A good example was found at the world famous Rancho La Puerta health spa in Mexico. In their organic garden, half of the garden was cultivated and maintained normally. The other half of the garden was also cultivated and maintained normally, but with the addition of having the gardeners consciously emit love to the plants. At the end of the growing season, the half of the garden that was given love produced twice as much crop as the other half. There is no scientific explanation.

- A chiropractor friend of mine had two trees in front of his window. One tree he looked at and emitted love energy. The other tree he looked at and emitted hate and anger energy. In six weeks the tree that received hate and anger energy was withered and almost dead; the other tree was flourishing. Again, there is no scientific explanation.

- My mother and grandmother cooked the exact same Italian pasta with marinara sauce. It looked the same, smelled the same, and was almost identical, but you could always tell who did the cooking. I could never understand how it could taste slightly different. I watched my grandmother cook and I watched my mother cook. They did exactly the same things. They cooked in exactly the same pans in the exact same kitchen. They used the same ingredients and did everything exactly the same way. I could never understand why my mother's cooking tasted different than my grandmother's until I understood that each person emitted a different kind of love energy into the food, which affected the taste of the food.

- While fishing in Canada, our Indian guide would take our freshly caught fish and cook it over an open fire made of wood. The fish was delicious. One day it was raining heavily and we decided to cook inside over gas. The fish was delicious, but tasted different. I asked the Indian guide how that could be. He explained that wood transmitted different energy into the food than the gas flame.

- Energy fields are picked up by all living things on the planet. Whales use energy to navigate the oceans. Salmon are hatched, swim downstream into the ocean, and then have the unbelievable ability to swim back to the exact spot they were hatched to lay their eggs. Birds return to the exact spot after traveling thousands of miles. Science cannot explain this because science does not believe in or understand energy fields.

- Hospital patients who had a view which included beautiful gardens felt better and healed faster than patients without the view.

14. **Still not convinced that music has a powerful effect on physiology and your health and well-being? Then consider this:**

- The latest research confirms that music bypasses your conscious mind. It goes directly to and stimulates the part of the brain that controls your emotions and vital pulses such as heart and respiratory rates, as well as blood pressure. Music that is played at sixty beats or less per minute will slow down your metabolic responses, which not only decreases your stress level, but also increases the amount of chemical endorphins your brain releases and leads to strengthening of your immune system. The exact opposite occurs when listening to music that is against the natural rhythm of the body. Listening to special music that has been designed to work with the body's natural frequency has helped people reduce or eliminate stress, anxiety, pain, insomnia, moodiness, and susceptibility to catching colds and flus, as well as helping to eliminate and prevent many other diseases. It has also been found to turn the body pH from acidic to alkaline, where disease cannot exist. Stress reducing music such as this has been proven by health-care practitioners around the world to be a major aid in eliminating degenerative diseases without drugs and surgery.

15. **Still not convinced that research and scientific studies are filled with misrepresentations that are doctored and altered to persuade you to a certain line of thinking, and in many cases are outright lies and deception? Then consider this:**

- According to the FDA's Officer of Inspector General, medical device trials were twice as likely to violate FDA regulations as trials for drugs and biologics. Seventy-five percent of the cited violations included missing data, poor data, and falsification of data. Fraudulent statistics and fraudulent research information is rampant in the health-care industry.

- Most statistics presented by the medical community are false, misleading and deceptive. Example: In a recent experiment, 100 individuals were sent to psychiatrists for evaluation on whether or not they had attention deficit disorder. These people were incredibly focused, well-balanced, had never been on any psychiatric drugs, incredibly healthy, and maintained high grades in school. The psychiatrist did not know this. They were told simply that they were having some concentration problems and needed a full evaluation. Every single one of these people was diagnosed with attention deficit disorder and prescribed Ritalin or other psychiatric drugs by the psychiatrist. This is fraudulent and outrageous.

- Most studies conducted by the medical industry are specifically designed studies to get the results that the industry wants. Most studies have hand-selected subjects. These subjects are specifically picked out with full knowledge that they will produce the best results. In most studies, the number of subjects can be as small as only five people, and the length of time the study is conducted can be as short as a few weeks. Many pharmaceutical companies do trial studies, figuring out the best way to conduct a study to provide the results they need to get FDA approval of drugs. You simply cannot believe any of the studies or research data or alleged "scientific evidence" submitted by the pharmaceutical industry.

- Consider how "scientific evidence" is produced.

  1) All scientific evidence is bought and paid for by the company that will benefit from a particular finding.

  2) There are, in many cases, hundreds of trials that are done before the final test. The public never sees what goes on in the initial trials. This information is hidden and kept secret.

3) The initial trials show that the drugs are ineffective and dangerous, but the manufacturers are trying to find a specific profile of a person who could see some benefit.

4) By the time the final evaluation is done, the individual profile has been refined so well that you are not getting anywhere close to a true global picture of how this drug or procedure will affect the general population at large.

5) The trials are usually done with a very small group of people, which cannot give you accurate information about how this will affect large numbers.

6) The trial is usually done for a very short period of time.

7) The statistics and the results are always misrepresented in terms of their efficacy and safety.

8) The final panels reviewing this and giving their recommendations are usually always on the payroll of the company that wants the particular finding.

As you can see, this type of scientific research is in no way accurate, but is false and misleading. This is why you cannot believe any "scientific evidence."

16. **Still not convinced that the FTC is an unpoliced, unregulated independent government agency that actually is judge, jury, and executioner, suppressing the rights of Americans while protecting the profits of big business? Then consider this:**

- There are so many stories of how the FTC has attacked companies selling alternative health-care remedies that are harmless and absolutely work. Darrel Stoddard had a product called Bio-Tape that reduced or eliminated pain in over 90 percent of the subjects tried. Over 18,000 people had used this product with spectacular results. But because the pain industry is so profitable, this product was squashed by the FTC and virtually banned from the market.

- The government spends tens of millions of dollars prosecuting people and small companies who do not have the resources to defend themselves. It's David versus Goliath. If you are sued by the government, you don't have a chance.

- The FTC admits that it usually does not, and the FDA does not, receive any reports of people injured by products being sold that they attack and go after.

- David Walker was found to have cancer, and was told by his doctor he had no more than three to five years before his colon cancer would kill him. Twelve years later, Walker is cancer free. Walker cured himself. He created his own treatment, which includes herbs, enzymes, vital nutrients, detoxification and energetic therapy that recharged the depleted cells, alkalized his body and allowed his cancer to vanish. He shared his knowledge and helped hundreds of other cancer patients eliminate their disease without drugs or surgery. But the Federal Trade Commission sued Mr. Walker, citing as its basis Walker's records reporting that 14 percent of the people using his protocol died. However, the report did not include the mortality rate over the same period for cancer patients who underwent the approved cancer therapies—drugs, radiation and chemotherapy. In that group 96 percent of the people using that protocol died. When the court case ended, Walker became one of the thousands of individuals and companies whose effective alternative nondrug and nonsurgical health treatments have been stifled. You can read the entire story on www.sumeria.net.

  The article claims that an individual with breast cancer used Walker's regime and her cancer was cured. When she informed her physician, the doctor claimed to have lost $350,000 because her breast cancer went away. The Federal Trade Commission, under pressure from the FDA, then went to work. Never mind that Walker had over 2,500 testimonials from people who loved his protocol. Eighty-six percent of the people that Walker worked with survived their cancers. The government did not care. The only thing that they cared about was that he was not using approved drugs, surgery, and radiation.

- The FTC categorically protects monopolies. One hundred television ads produced by major publicly traded companies were reviewed for their accuracy. Of the 100, all 100 were deemed to be partially or totally false and misleading to varying degrees! That's 100 percent of the television ads produced by publicly traded companies that are false and misleading. The Federal Trade Commission is supposed to protect us from false and misleading advertisers. The FTC takes absolutely no action against large publicly traded companies that are giving huge amounts of money to the politicians, even though these companies are getting us to buy their products under false pretenses. This is corruption and fraud at the highest levels of government.

- Advertisements for food are made to intentionally make you falsely believe that their food is healthy and will make you lose weight. The exact opposite is true. The food industry purposely produces these false and misleading ads. The advertising agencies are under strict orders to produce ads that convey this false and misleading message. The FTC knows this but does absolutely nothing.

- The food industry tries to produce ads to make you believe that there are health benefits to their product when the exact opposite is true. The food industry's products actually cause disease. Consider that cigarettes were once advertised as being good for your health and designed to improve health. Coca Cola was also originally advertised as a drink that had dramatic health benefits.

- Go to www.kevinfightsback.com and I will show you every single letter that I have received and sent to the FTC. You will be absolutely blown away by how out of control the FTC is, and how they are flagrantly and blatantly trying to suppress the free flow of information, opinions, and ideas.

- Secret private investigations into the Federal Trade Commission and the individuals who run this corrupt organization have reported startling new discoveries of how this organization operates. These reports are being confirmed by inside whistleblowers. The shocking truth about the FTC will be published shortly, exposing the individual people. Names will be named, and the truth will be revealed. The inside information reads like a juicy novel filled with adultery, sex clubs, drugs, payoffs, secret meetings with politicians and lobbyists, and corruption at virtually every level. Alliance Publishing Group will be publishing a book on the FTC and the individual people involved. When the truth is revealed, this organization will come crumbling down, to the benefit of all American citizens.

17. **Still not convinced that organic food is much better for you? Then consider this:**

    • A February 2003 study published in the *Journal of Agriculture and Food Industry* showed organically grown berries contain up to 58 percent more polyphenolics than those grown conventionally. This means that organically grown berries have 58 percent more antioxidants than those grown conventionally.

    • A 1993 study published in the *Journal of Applied Nutrition,* showed that over the course of two years organic foods contained up to four times as many trace minerals, thirteen times more selenium and twenty times more calcium and magnesium than commercially produced produce, and also had significantly fewer heavy metals, including 25 percent less lead and 40 percent less aluminum.

18. **Still not convinced that we are losing the war on cancer and cancer is getting worse and worse every year? Then consider this:**

    • Cancer will surpass heart disease as the number one cause of death in the United States in the next few years. Every year, over 1.5 million Americans are diagnosed with cancer and the number is increasing. The probability that you will develop cancer is one in every two men and one in every three women, and it's getting worse. The war on cancer has been a total failure. Some scientists estimate that up to 70 percent of all cancers could be prevented simply by dietary change. The only legal remedies for cancer treatment are surgery, chemotherapy, and radiation. You can go to jail if you treat cancer with all-natural methods even though they are more effective than surgery, chemotherapy and radiation, and have absolutely no negative side effects. This is insane.

19. **Still not convinced that the FDA suppresses information on natural cures? Then consider this:**

    • *The California Western Law Review* published an article entitled "Why Does the FDA Deny Access to Alternative Cancer Treatments?"

    • Canadian scientist, Gaston Naessens, created an herbal blend called 714-X. This blend, as of 1991, has cured more than 1,000 people of cancer, as well as several AIDS patients. The FDA has attacked him. The story is on Web site http://www. luminet.net/~wenonah/new/naessen.htm.

- Jason Winter authored the book *Killing Cancer,* which has sold more than a million copies, about how he cured his cancer with herbs. He is quoted as saying, "I must tell you that I was scared about publishing a book talking about how herbs can cure cancer. I was not prepared to take on the billion dollar drug companies, the medical associations and doctors, all of whom would chew up and spit out anyone that would dare to say that possibly, just possibly, herbs can help." Winters outlines the typical fate of natural cancer and other cures that are advertised in U.S. publications. Usually the publication gets into a lot of trouble for printing it in the first place, and then all future publicity is stopped. The persons selling the products are usually tricked or entrapped into a phony suit about "practicing medicine without a license," or "selling drugs without a license," or selling "unregistered drugs." If the government can't stop them that way, they usually use another federal agency, the IRS, to attack them with some phony, trumped up income tax charge. Those who practice natural medicine, or sell natural remedies, live with the knowledge that they could be closed down any day.

- Registered nurse, Kathy Stevens, promotes the benefits of magnets. However, she is forbidden from using the word "pain." She must only use the word "discomfort," otherwise she is selling an unregistered medical device without a license and making a medical claim that is unsubstantiated. Kathy herself suffered from osteoarthritis pain for five years. Her brother exposed her to a nondrug solution. Being a registered nurse, she was trained only in drugs and surgery. When her brother suggested that she try magnets, she laughed and scoffed. According to the medical establishment, magnets do nothing to reduce or eliminate pain or have any other health benefits. The medical community states that there is no credible scientific evidence showing that magnets have any health benefits whatsoever. While at a family reunion, her brother had her sleep on a magnetic sleeping pad and a pillow, as well as a quilt containing far inferred technology. Kathy recounts waking up the next morning astonished that she had slept the entire night without waking. She experienced absolutely no pain for the first time in five years. She couldn't believe that she was pain free and her body was full of energy. Kathy believes, based on her own personal experience, and that of witnessing countless others, that anyone's osteoarthritis pain can be reduced or eliminated by the use of magnets. She can't tell people the truth, and she can't tell people what she has experienced for herself or witnessed. If she does, she could be prosecuted and potentially arrested and jailed. In effect, she has lost her right of free speech because her opinions go against the monopoly of the pharmaceutical industry.

- Keep in mind that the FDA wants to prosecute anyone who is curing disease without the use of drugs and surgery. The tens of thousands of alternative/natural health-care practitioners are risking their very existences—not because of riches, but because of genuine concern for people's health and well-being. It is sad to know that millions of people suffer needlessly because of the government's suppression of natural alternatives.

- It pains me knowing that people die every year because of the government's suppression of the truth about all-natural alternatives and the dangers of drugs and surgery. These doctors or health-care practitioners will generally say they do not cure anything. In many cases they say they do not treat cancer and they do not treat any form of disease, because saying so would put them in peril with the FDA. They are acting as an underground organization, doing so because of their mission for the betterment of mankind. As I mentioned before, many times when you see an alternative health-care practitioner they will have you sign a whole host of forms, disclaimers, release forms, and statements asserting that they are not trying to cure or prevent any disease, and that you are seeing them under your own free will. Because of our litigious society, and because of the oppression imposed by the government regulating bodies, these wonderful individuals, by risking so much, must take these measures in order to protect their ability to treat people who need their treatment.

- In a *New York Times* news service article, it was stated that
  more than half of all new drugs approved for marketing
  have severe or fatal side effects not found in testing, and
  not reported until years after the medications have been
  widely used. This information was found by congressional
  investigators. The General Accounting Office showed that
  between 1976 and 1985, of 198 drugs approved, over half
  of them should be taken off the market because they are so
  deadly and caused so many medical problems. This again
  shows that taking any nonprescription or prescription drug
  absolutely causes medical problems. The drugs themselves
  give you illness, sickness and disease.

- Virtually all violent acts committed by children in schools
  over the last ten years were committed by individuals who
  had been on prescribed psychiatric drugs. The psychiatric
  drugs prescribed increase the chance of suicide and dramatically increase the chance of violent acts. Prescribed psychiatric drugs are deadly and should never be consumed.

- Most drugs are physically addicting. Most notably, pain medication, as evidenced by many celebrities, including Rush
  Limbaugh, who were given drugs by their doctor not knowing the addictive nature of the drug. Unable to stop, these
  people became slaves to the drug. The drugs also caused
  major medical problems such as permanent hearing loss.

20. **Still not convinced that government agencies fight against
    individuals while allowing big business to go unpoliced? Then
    consider this:**

    - The IRS audits three times the percentage of individuals
      as opposed to corporations, small businesses, and partner-
      ships. The largest multinational corporations get audited the
      least even though they are the ones most likely of commit-
      ting tax fraud.

    - Jonathan Wright, M.D., wrote an interesting article about
      how the FDA is trying to take away our health freedoms.
      He exposes the fact that the World Trade Organization is
      getting involved with regulating natural dietary supplements
      in America and around the world. When our government
      signed on to the World Trade Organization it agreed to

commit to act in accordance with the rules of this multi-lateral body. The United States is legally obliged to ensure national laws in America do not conflict with World Trade Organization rules. The European Union set up a directive on dietary supplements. It is part of a larger forum of world-wide legislation in which the government of the United States is bound called CODEX. This will severely restrict access to natural health products in Europe and all around the world. This directive is set up by some of the wealthiest people on planet earth to guarantee and ensure their prof-its. CODEX is one of the most unbelievable set of legislative rules in the history of mankind. It, in effect, puts everything a person consumes or puts on their skin under the control of a small group of multibillionaire businessmen and multi-national corporations. This small group controls, allegedly, 80 percent of the wealth in the world. This small elite group is in effect the rulers of planet earth. They will now control every drug, every vitamin, every mineral, every herb, and every substance that you put in your body or you put on your skin. This particular group also includes many indi-viduals that come out of the Nazi government of Germany. CODEX is being virtually ignored by the U.S. media. When this goes into effect, over 5,000 products could virtually dis-appear from the American consumer. This world-wide law will classify vitamins and minerals in Europe as "medicinal drugs." This means the price of such things as Vitamin C or the herb Echinacea will rise from $1 or $2 a bottle to $150 a bottle. In order to get nutrients you will have to go to a licensed medical doctor and get a prescription. Getting such a prescription will cost you even more money. This direc-tive, for all intents and purposes, virtually makes it illegal for any person to keep themselves healthy by supplementing their own diet with essential nutrients. It will become illegal for you to be in charge of your own health. The reason that this organization is wiping out our access to nutrients is because this group controls the pharmaceutical drug indus-try around the world. This group categorically wants people to become sicker and sicker, and have more and more dis-ease. This group knows that nutritional deficiencies are one of the major causes of disease. This group is going to continue to strip all of our food supply of vital nutrients, therefore guaranteeing that people around the world continue to get sicker and sicker, and the need for drug consumption will appear to become more and more important. This group is only concerned with selling more drugs, not with preventing or curing disease. To read more on this go to my Web site, www.naturalcures.com.

21. **Still not convinced that "experts" are generally wrong when they present things as fact when they should be presenting it as opinion, or that these "experts" are paid spokespeople and have a financial interest and conflict of interest in relation to what they are saying? Then consider this:**

- Talent agents give their expert opinion as fact as to who has talent and who will never make it. However, most talent agents have been proven to be wrong more often than they are right. Examples: Britney Spears lost in her appearance in Star Search. Elvis Presley was told by a talent scout that he had no talent and should go back to driving a truck. Most major actors, actresses, and musicians were told by experts that they should give up and they had no talent.

- The president of Digital Equipment Corporation said that there was absolutely no long-term market for a home personal computer. He was obviously wrong to such a huge degree that the statement sounds insane. Surprisingly, this person made the statement in the late 1970s.

- The USDA has daily recommended allowances of nutrients. These are taken by the American public as factual and scientifically based. The USDA cannot give any scientific basis or rational reason how these numbers have been established. Throughout the last fifty years these daily recommended requirements have changed radically. The point is that just because a government agency says you need this or you don't need something else doesn't mean it's true. Generally speaking, history shows that they are wrong.

- Government agencies tell you the nutrients you need in your diet, and in what levels. However, every few years new nutrients are discovered. Just because a nutrient hasn't been discovered doesn't mean you don't need it. This is one of the major reasons why whole food supplements are so much better than chemical or synthetic vitamins. It is also the reason why studies and research done on synthetic vitamins do not necessarily show favorable results. When studies are conducted with whole food concentrates, whole food concentrates that include not only the vitamin in question, but all the cofactors and parts and elements that defy analysis, the results are always better. Remember, science is not better than nature.

- Fingerprints are believed to be infallible and an accurate way of identifying a person; however, you have been misled. The truth is that the top fingerprint experts in the world in independent testing are wrong over 50 percent of the time!

- Experts promoted Coca-Cola as a "health drink" designed to make a person's health better. This was done when Coca-Cola contained the drug from the coca leaf itself!

- In the 1920s medical experts promoted cigarette smoking as a health benefiting practice. It was said that smoking cigarettes actually was healthy for you and could benefit an individual! This was actually promoted as medical fact in the American Medical Association's own journal!

22. **Still not convinced that you are under massive amounts of physiological, energetic, and emotional stress that are affecting your health and causing your body to be acidic, which leads to virtually all disease? Then consider this:**

- I was fishing in Canada with my good friend Dr. Morter, one of the pioneers in pH research. After our third day of fishing in a stress-free environment with no telephones, no computers, no TVs, virtually in the middle of nowhere, he told me that every person has locked in stress that is adversely affecting their health. I told him I was totally relaxed and didn't think I had any stress. He then said to me, "Relax the muscles in your forehead," which I promptly did. He then pointed out if I was totally relaxed, how could I relax muscles in my forehead? You see, if I was totally relaxed the muscles in my forehead would have actually been relaxed and could not have been relaxed any further. The fact was,

I was holding them tight unconsciously. We are all under massive amounts of stress in today's living environment. This stress causes our body pH to become acidic, setting up the perfect environment for sickness and disease. It is vital that you de-stress and relax on a regular basis. De-stressing and relaxing on a regular basis has been shown to reverse virtually every disease because the state of full relaxation puts your body in a state of alkaline pH where disease cannot exist.

23. **Not convinced that you need to eat more raw, uncooked organic fruits, vegetables, nuts and seeds? Then consider this:**

- Dogs who ate standard man-made, chemically laced dog food live, depending on the breed, between twelve and fourteen years. Dogs that are fed all organic raw food, as they would eat in nature, live to be twenty-two to thirty years old.

24. **Not convinced that companies produce poisons that they call "food"? Then consider this:**

- People always ask me, "Why do food companies and restaurants put all of these chemicals into the food?" The answer is very simple, they must make the food in the cheapest possible manner. This means growing the food in an unnatural way, which produces food that virtually has no taste. The food cannot be allowed to spoil, as it would cost the company money. It is laced with chemicals to make the food last a very long time. In the processing of the food, chemicals are put in to make you physically addicted to the food, to make you hungrier by increasing your appetite, and are specifically design to make you fat. This increases sales and profits for the food companies. Companies also have to produce food that can have a shelf life of many years, so that it can be stored if it is not sold and the company can still make a profit. Real, whole, natural food virtually has no shelf life; it goes rancid, therefore is not profitable to the food companies. Remember my earlier example of how homogenization and pasteurization replaced the milkman.

  The processing of food itself turns the food from real food that nourishes and feeds the body into something that is foreign to the body, unnatural and causes the body undue physiological stress to cope. It causes disease and makes you age faster. For years, the food industry has refused to list the amount of trans fats on the label. A cost benefit analysis conducted in 1999 by the FDA itself showed savings of $8 billion per year in averted heart disease costs alone, and a saving of 5,000 American lives if trans fats were listed on the label. In fact, you could say the FDA's failure to require the food companies to list trans fats caused the death of 5,000 Americans. Maybe the FDA should be listed as a terrorist organization?

- The *Los Angeles Times* reported that sports drinks dissolve your teeth. It was also reported that the "all-natural fruit juices" sold by publicly traded corporations are not as healthy as you would think due to the processing techniques used. It was also reported that "energy drinks" really do not give you energy. Another report is headlined with "Coke Wants to Fool You With Their Bottled Water." The most shocking was the headline "Would You Give Your Toddler Seventeen Teaspoons of Sugar a Day?" This article talked about how "drinks" marketed to children by the publicly traded companies are specifically designed to get the children chemically addicted to their food by loading it up with sugars.

25. **Not convinced that all drugs are ineffective and dangerous? Then consider this:**

- Lotronex was approved by the FDA to treat irritable bowel syndrome. When the FDA approves a drug the FDA says that it is fully convinced that the drug is both effective and safe. Just eight months after the drug was approved a minimum of five people were confirmed dead and the drug had to be yanked off the market.

- The FDA approved the drug Baycol for reducing cholesterol. Again, the FDA said the drug was both effective and safe. Within months the drug caused a minimum of thirty-two patients to develop fatal kidney failure, causing the drug to be taken off the market.

- The pain killer Oxycontin is still on the market, yet there are confirmed 120 deaths.

- The most popular drugs in the world, cholesterol-lowering drugs, can actually trigger a heart attack. This is confirmed by the drug manufacturer's own research! But this information is kept from doctors, the media, and patients. The drug companies knew about these dangers thirteen years ago when it first introduced the cholesterol-lowering drugs.

- Studies confirm that people with high blood pressure will die faster if they take the drugs prescribed to reduce the high blood pressure compared to those who take no drugs at all and live with high blood pressure.

- Antibiotics are now linked to causing breast cancer, autism, asthma, autoimmune disease, recurrent ear infections, hormonal imbalances, skin conditions, Candida albacans, constipation, depression, joint pain, blurred vision, and a host of other illnesses and disease.

- Antibiotics are responsible for over 900,000 deaths since their introduction.

- *Reuters* news reported that a drug used to treat "attention deficit disorder" poses a high risk of deadly liver damage and should be banned immediately. The drug has been linked to a minimum of thirteen deaths. This drug has already been pulled off the market in both Britain and Canada, but the FDA refuses to do so.

- For more scary stories, go to www.drugvictims.com.

26. **Not convinced that natural cures are being suppressed and the standard medical practices of drugs and surgery are actually killing people? Then consider this:**

- Dr. James Walker, author of *Holocaust American Style,* says, "There should be a criminal indictment against the medical cartel led by the U.S. Food and Drug Administration, the Federal Trade Commission, and against our U.S. Congress, (who has oversight responsibility over the FDA and the FTC), for letting over one million men, women, and children die each year when most of them do not have to die. We need to expose the deadly corruption in our government that lets millions of Americans die without taking any action to put a stop to the unnecessary high medical costs, suffering, and deaths annually when several proven cures have been available for hundreds of years. Today we see our so-called "leaders" making serious decisions that affect the health and lives of millions of Americans, but basing those decisions on greed for political power for the particular politician or political party or their medical connections with no regard for the truth or what is best for the people. Worse yet, citizens are complacent with what is being done to them.

Everyone disregards the fact that the worst holocaust in recorded history of mankind is now happening in America and is being successfully covered up right out in the open, and it is conducted by a corrupt, power seeking, vicious medical cartel led by the FDA and supported by Congress. This whole medical mess was brought into existence by a powerful and corrupt monopoly known as the medical cartel consisting of the American Medical Association, National Institute of Health, National Cancer Institute, the American Cancer Society, the Memorial Sloan-Kettering Hospital, the Mayo Clinic, the M.D. Anderson Medical Center, the Roswell Park Medical Center, the big powerful pharmaceutical companies, hospitals, insurance companies, universities, and dozens of other charities, foundations, and associations, all being politically and "legally" supported by corrupt, self-serving, vicious, lying, and uncontrolled medical scoundrels at the FDA.

Since the early 1920s there have been successful natural cures for cancer, heart attacks, strokes, and other degenerative diseases, but those protocols have been aggressively and successfully suppressed by the medical cartel and the FDA. As long as these people can make vast amounts of money playing the game of "there is hope, we **almost** have a cure" they had no incentive to really help people by letting the true natural cures be introduced into medicine. In fact, they are now trying to place the control of all natural treatments, including vitamins, minerals, and natural food supplements, under the prescription control of medical doctors, all who have had virtually no training in the use of anything other than prescribing toxic chemical pharmaceutical drugs or cutting out parts of a person's anatomy via surgery. Do not believe that a cure is on the horizon. The natural cures are already here. They have been used in other countries for centuries. The medical cartel just won't let any natural, nontoxic, and economical cure to be released to the public. Instead, they dictate that deadly/painful chemotherapy (mustard gas) and radiation be used on cancer patients.

Dr. Benjamin Rush, a signer of the Declaration of Independence, said "Unless we put medical freedom into the Constitution, the time will come when medicine will organize itself into an undercover dictatorship...to restrict the art of healing to one class of men or companies and deny equal privileges to others will constitute the Bastille of medical science." We certainly have come to that point in the American medical field! Consider that modern western medicine has "searched" for the "cause" and "cure" for cancer and other degenerative diseases for well over 100 years and has failed miserably even though:

1) The mission was entrusted to the "best" researchers in the medical, academic, and industrial sectors.

2) They have private and government contracts with huge amounts of free money.

3) Many private organizations are actively gathering money for these "researchers."

4) They have a government supported monopoly on disease prevention, treatment, and cure.

5) They have illegal support from government and private agencies, including our U.S. Congress.

6) They falsify research procedures, lie about results and cover for each other.

Look at the progress report on the war on cancer. When knowledgeable researchers were asked "What do you think of the war on cancer?" here are the replies "...largely a fraud," Dr. Linus Pauling, Ph.D., twice Nobel laureate; "...a qualified failure," John Bailar, M.D., former editor of the *Journal of the National Cancer Institute*; "...a medical Viet Nam," Dr. Donald Kennedy, former president of Stanford University; "...a bunch of manure," Dr. James Watson, Ph.D., Nobel laureate, co-discoverer of DNA code.

The medical community won't tell you that according to the Merck manual chemo is mustard gas that was used during World War I to kill soldiers, and during World War II to kill millions of Jews. In fact, our own military went to Iraq looking for weapons of mass destruction, which included mustard gas. Chemotherapy shuts down your body from making white blood cells, the natural soldiers that fight diseases; then shuts down your whole immune system, leaving you with no way for your body to fight disease. Only about 3 percent of the people who take chemo survive the suffering and ordeal. These seem to be the ones whose immune systems are so that it can survive the onslaught of chemotherapy.

Dr. Walker explains the true nature of the pharmaceutical industry:

1) The natural purpose and driving force of the pharmaceutical industry is to increase their sales of pharmaceutical drugs that treat ongoing diseases, and to find new diseases or rename old diseases to market their existing drugs.

2) The eradication of any disease inevitably destroys a multi-billion dollar market for prescription drugs as a source of revenue. Therefore, deadly toxic chemical pharmaceutical drugs are developed primarily to "treat symptoms, but not cure anything." They will not tolerate a true cure being available to the public.

3) If eradication therapies for diseases are discovered and developed, the pharmaceutical industry has an inherent interest to suppress, discredit, and obstruct these medical breakthroughs to make sure that diseases continue as the basis for a lucrative pharmaceutical drug market.

4) The economic interest of the pharmaceutical industry itself is the main reason that no medical breakthrough has been made for the cure of most common diseases such as cardio-vascular disease, high blood pressure, heart failure, diabetes, cancer, strokes, osteoporosis, and why these diseases continue on an epidemic scale worldwide.

5) For the same economic reasons, the pharmaceutical industry has now formed an international cartel by the code name "CODEX," with the aim to outlaw any health information in connection with vitamins and to limit free access to natural therapies on a worldwide scale.

6) At the same time, the pharmaceutical companies withhold public information about the affects and risks of pharmaceutical prescription drugs and life-threatening side effects are omitted or openly denied, especially in the deadly mixing of drugs.

7) In order to assure the status quo of this deception scheme, many pharmaceutical lobbyists are employed to influence legislation, control government regulatory agencies like the FDA and the FTC, and to manipulate medical research and education. Very expensive advertising campaigns and PR agencies are used to deceive the public.

Remember, all companies in the pharmaceutical industry are publicly traded corporations, which means they only have one objective, and that is to increase profits. Curing disease would wipe out their businesses.

Multimillions of people and patients around the world are defrauded twice. First, the major part of their income is spent to finance the exploding profits and the dictatorial power of the pharmaceutical industry. Second, in return they are offered many toxic chemical pharmaceutical drugs that CURE NOTHING, but keep them dependent on these toxic drugs for their remaining lives. In the meantime, the medical cartel lets millions of men, women, and children die, most of whom do not have to die, while we and Congress do nothing to curb this deadly corruption and suffering. Congress has now passed a prescription drug bill to give "free" or cheap drugs to the elderly. It is estimated to cost the taxpayers over $500 billion. Nothing is "free." The government makes nothing. They can't give away anything until they first take it from someone else in the form of higher taxes. The American taxpayer has been shafted again with the big Ponzi scheme called Medicare, Medicaid, and Social Security. These are now bankrupt because when our payments go in the politicians take it out and spend it.

27. **Not convinced that "consumer groups" are in fact controlled by the pharmaceutical industry? Consider this:**

- One of the most prominent Internet based "consumer watchdog groups," Quackbusters, has been exposed in court for deceiving the public and has lost a major lawsuit in California Superior Court where the judge ruled on Quackbusters' "credibility." In effect, it was determined that the Quackbusters' Web site is misleading, fraudulent, and deceives the public.

28. **Not convinced that household cleaners are dangerous to your health? Consider this:**

    - The *Associated Press* reported that deaths show dangers of household chemicals. This article explained how ALL household cleaners are chemicals that are incredibly toxic. The all can be fatal if they get into your body. They get into your body through the skin, through the fumes that you inhale, and of course, by accidentally drinking. Most people won't die immediately by inhaling the fumes, but this article points out that several people did die immediately because they mixed several of these cleaners together, which made the concentration of the chemical toxins so severe that it caused instantaneous death. If these chemicals in high concentrations can cause instantaneous death, then using these chemicals on a regular basis obviously causes health problems, suppresses the immune system, and leads to disease. Don Imus, the famous radio talk show host has a ranch for sick children where he has only organic food and absolutely no toxic chemical cleaners as he believes that environmental toxins are one of the leading causes of cancer.

29. **Still not convinced that the food produced by publicly traded companies and fast-food restaurants are actually giving us disease and making us fat? Then consider this:**

    - *Reuters* news reported that McDonalds has agreed to pay $8.5 million to settle a lawsuit because they were putting trans fats in its cooking oil. The lawsuit was filed by an activist seeking to raise public awareness of the health dangers of trans fats in hydrogenated or partially-hydrogenated oils. Go to www.bantransfats.com for more information.

    - Kraft Foods was sued for knowingly putting dangerous trans fats in its food, most notably Oreos.

    - An investigator for an animals rights group captured video showing chickens being kicked, stomped, and thrown against the wall by workers at a supplier for Kentucky Fried Chicken.

- Beef used for hamburger patties at fast-food restaurants now contains enormous numbers of cattle which are being herded, fattened, slaughtered, and ground up together. This means meat from a single cow is not used in the hamburger patty; they are pooling bacteria from as many as a thousand different animals.

- The magazine *The Ecologist* points out that cosmetically perfect, irresistibly firm, brilliantly colored fruits and vegetables taste like nothing because they are genetically modified and contain so many toxins. The magazine claims you have been conned. The magazine goes on to say that bread routinely contains enzymes made from pig pancreases, fractionated fats, excessive yeast, and antifungal agents.

- Samples of non-organic chicken breasts were found to be only fifty-four percent chicken! The rest was in effect poisons and toxins, giving you disease.

- A Dutch additive supplier for the food industry and a German protein manufacturer were caught on video boasting that they had developed undetectable methods of adulterating chicken with waste from cows!

- It is reported that supermarkets are on a chemical treadmill. Quite simply, their demand for cosmetic perfection of fruits and vegetables forces farmers to use more pesticides than they would otherwise, as well as genetic engineering of food.

30. **Not convinced that natural remedies cure disease better than drugs, with no side effects? Then consider this:**

- In the last five years over 100,000 articles have been written around the world reporting on the effectiveness and safety of natural remedies.

- Licensed health-care practitioners who use natural remedies instead of drugs and surgery report higher success rates than medical doctors using drugs and surgery. They also report virtually no side effects compared to medical doctors who report negative side effects in virtually 100 percent of their patients.

- *Reuters* reports that herbal extracts show promise for diabetes.

- *The Associated Press* reports that walking may ward off Alzheimer's disease.

- *Reuters* reports that eating organic is shown to prevent and cure a host of various diseases.

- *Reuters* reports that acupuncture eases post-surgical ills including nausea and actually works better than drugs!

- *Reuters* reports that the herbal remedy St. John's Wort is as effective, or more effective, in treating depression than drugs.

- The FDA itself finally admits that extra virgin olive oil reduces the chances of coronary heart disease.

- The BBC news reports that eating apples wards off colon cancer, and apples prevent and can cure cancer.

- *The Associated Press* reports that walking keeps weight in check.

- *Reuters* reports that people who sleep less tend to be fat, showing the benefits of getting proper rest.

- ABC News reports that relaxation techniques lower blood pressure.

- Yahoo News reported that herbs help ease children's illnesses, such as colds, skin allergies, and sleep problems. It also reported that the herbs worked better than drugs and had no side effects.

- *Reuters* reports that green tea is identified as an anticancer agent.

- There is increased scientific validation of how homeopathy prevents and cures disease.

- Mangosteen juice, in studies, has been shown to prevent hardening of the arteries, protect the heart muscle, be beneficial in the treatment of Parkinson's disease, Alzheimer's disease and other forms of dementia, elevates mood and is an antidepressant, prevents and arrests fungus, prevents bacterial infections, fights viruses, prevents gum disease, lowers fever, prevents glaucoma and cataracts, increases energy and fights fatigue, promotes anti-aging and weight loss, lowers blood fat, has anti-tumor benefits, prevents cancer, lowers blood pressure, lowers blood sugar, and improves digestion.

31. **Still not convinced that electromagnetic energy causes disease? Consider this:**

   - Research now shows that eating microwaved food causes disease.

   - College researchers believe electric light changes hormone levels in women and makes breast cancer more prevalent. The theory is exposure to artificial, mostly florescent light, causes cellular damage leading to cancer, as well as dozens of other diseases.

   - *The Associated Press* reports that driving a car in traffic dramatically increases your chance of heart attack. The studies also conclude that driving in cars in heavy traffic dramatically increases your risk of dozens of other diseases due to the fact that you are constantly breathing in heavily polluted air.

   - A Swedish study shows that people who use a cell phone increase their risk of developing tumors in the head.

   - The cell phone industry seems to be just as harmful to a person's health as big tobacco. The similarities are eerily obvious. The cell phone industry is determined to deny or prevent any suggestion that its products might be dangerous even though years of negative research is proving otherwise. A study showed that mobile phones emanate radio waves that definitely damage the cells in the body, as well as DNA. Most shocking was the fact that the damage extended to the next generation of cells as well. The Cellular Telecommunications & Internet Association hired a man to head up a $28 million research program looking into the possible health effects from cellular phone use. Amazingly, the industry's own research showed that heavy cell phone users experience an increase rate of brain cancer deaths, development of tumors, genetic damage in the cells, as well as other negative health issues.

32. **Not convinced that cleansing and fasting actually can prevent and cure many diseases? Then consider this:**

   - Colonics were said to be a healthful practice in ancient texts dating over 2,000 years old.

- A German Nobel Prize winner discovered that fasting just three days a month caused a dramatic improvement in longevity and reduction in illness and disease.

- He also discovered that almost all diseases can be cured by fasting, as well as prevented.

- When you cleanse the colon and/or liver the body absorbs nutrients up to 100 times better than before the cleanse.

33. Not convinced that laughter can cure disease? Then consider this:

- Researchers conclude that just fifteen minutes of laughter a day can reduce the risk of heart attacks and strokes dramatically! Interestingly enough, watching violent movies was shown to actually increase the risk of heart attack and stroke.

My most recent experience of how health care is really a monopoly for the pharmaceutical industry was when I requested some blood tests be done. I walked in to a lab and asked for some blood work to be performed. I was told it was against the law to do blood work without a prescription. I was appalled how the lawmakers created this monopoly for medical doctors. I reluctantly acquired a prescription. When I had my blood drawn I paid the bill and asked when I could get my results. I was told it was against the law for them to give me my test results. It must be sent to a medical doctor. This was my blood, and I paid for the tests with my money, yet the law denies me direct access to the results. This is a good example of how lawmakers guarantee profits for medical doctors.

Some people wonder if corporate executives are as ruthless and greedy as I suggest many of them are. Consider Ford Motor Company. The executives knew that if they did not recall the Ford Pinto thousands of people would die. Yet they made the decision not to order the recall because it would cost too much money. They decided that profits were more important than people dying or being maimed for life.

Can such corruption actually be occurring in the corporate world, with politicians and government agencies, on such a widespread basis without anyone blowing the whistle? Consider the New York police officer Frank Serpico. A movie and book came out about his life. For years payoffs, bribes, and corruption were widespread and commonplace in the New York police department. It went to the highest levels. Yet for years no one exposed the truth and no one even considered that such corruption could be occurring on such a widespread basis for so long within law enforcement. However, when the truth was exposed the unthinkable and unimaginable had been occurring. Right now, this same type of corruption is occurring in health care at every level.

I could go on and on and on proving all of these points that I mention in this chapter and throughout this book. The evidence is overwhelming. The volumes of documentation, substantiation, and reports backing up everything I say would easily convince even the biggest skeptic. Can you see why I'm mad as hell, and not going to take it anymore?!

But we're not through yet...there's more!

CHAPTER 11

Frequently Asked Questions

Since this book was published, millions of people have been exposed to the fact that drugs and surgery are ineffective and cause most diseases, that the food produced by the publicly traded food corporations and fast-food restaurants, which is in effect virtually all the food that most people consume, actually causes illness and disease, and the fact that there are natural non-drug and non-surgical ways to prevent and cure virtually every disease. There are many people who are now being listened to because of the success of this book. Many health advocates and health experts who promote non-drug and non-surgical ways to prevent and cure disease, and who promote organic food not laced with the poisons and chemicals that the publicly traded food industry uses, are now becoming more mainstream. Because there are so many voices talking about the subject, there are obviously different opinions regarding natural remedies and natural health. This is good. As I mention in the beginning of this book, nobody has a monopoly on the truth—including me. As I mention in the beginning of this book, there are virtually no such things as "facts," but rather only opinions based on the information we currently have. Every health expert can therefore come up with slightly different opinions regarding what the best thing to do is in relation to health.

With that said, I would like to address in this section some of the most frequently asked questions that I get regarding health and nutrition, and the concepts covered in this book. As I mentioned at the very beginning of this book, it is important that you read this book cover to cover, word for word, in the exact order in which I present the material. Some people will get to this chapter and skip over some of the questions that they don't feel are applicable to them. I would encourage you to continue reading this book in the exact order in which this information was presented. Even though you don't think a question is relevant, I can assure you the answer may be very relevant. Keep in mind that everything I write in this book is put in this book for a reason, and the order in which the information is presented is done for a specific reason as well. It is done so that you "get it" completely and totally. Keep in mind, if you have additional questions that are not answered by the time you finish this book, I would encourage you to subscribe to my newsletter, or become a member of my Web site community. Newsletter subscribers and members of my Web site community have the ability to write me any question and get an answer free of charge. You will also have the ability to write to many of the licensed health-care practitioners that I can refer you to who will also, as a courtesy to me, give you answers absolutely free of charge. The licensed health-care providers that I refer you to are some of the providers that actually work on me directly. This way you can be assured that the information you are getting is almost the exact same as if you were talking to me directly on the telephone. Due to the millions of people that could be asking questions, I am sure that you can understand why I must limit this benefit only to those members of my Web site community or subscribers to my newsletter.

Question: My doctor says I need drugs and/or surgery. What do I do?
Answer: First, I would encourage you to stop going to medical doctors who prescribe drugs and surgery. I would encourage you to get advice from licensed health-care practitioners who do not use drugs and surgery. I would encourage you to get three or four different opinions. This way you can make a proper informed decision. Your condition may be past the point of no return, where only drugs and surgery are effective at keeping you alive a little longer. However, I believe that any person who says that you "need" drugs and surgery is misinformed, unknowledgeable about natural methods, or simply trying to make money off you.
Question: Can I ever eat a cheeseburger again or go to a fast-food restaurant?
Answer: Yes, you can eat cheeseburgers, french fries, ice cream, cookies, cakes, fried chicken with mashed potatoes and gravy—virtually everything, as long as you make it at home and all the ingredients are 100-percent organic. People always ask me what I eat. You can eat virtually anything and everything (with some exceptions) as long as it's certified organic. You can eat beef, cheese, butter, milk, cream, eggs,

lamb, chicken, duck, mashed potatoes, french fries, onion rings, ice cream, cookies, cake, chocolate, you name it—as long as it's organic. No, you can't go to fast-food restaurants. That's the one thing you categorically cannot do if you want to cure yourself of disease and remain healthy. Fast-food restaurants use chemical ingredients in the growing, processing, and manufacture of their "food." It's the chemicals in the food that are making you sick. It is also the lack of nutrients in their food that gives you nutritional deficiencies that makes you sick. It is also the outrageous amount of free radicals and other "bad stuff" in the food that is making you sick, and it's also all the energetically altered food that they use that is making you sick.

Question: How come you don't talk about calories, fats, protein, or carbohydrates?

Answer: Everyone talks about calories, fats, protein, carbohydrates, sodium, and things of this nature. The fact of the matter is they are important, but not very important when compared to the chemicals and poisons put into the food. What is more important than calories or fats and carbohydrates is the chemical fertilizers used in the food, the pesticides used in the food, the fact that the food is picked early and then gassed, the fact that the food is genetically modified and manufactured in an unnatural way, the processing methods that are used, the irradiation that was used, the actual thousands of chemicals that are put in processed food to make it taste better and give it certain textures, preserve it, or specifically designed to get you chemically and physically addicted to the food, increase your appetite and make you fat. This is what is more important than the amount of calories, or the amount of fat, or the amount of carbohydrates. That's what everyone is missing.

Question: How are you qualified to write this book—you're not a medical doctor?

Answer: My number-one qualification to be able to write this book is the fact that I am **NOT** a medical doctor! If I were a medical doctor, I would not be qualified to write this book. Think about it for a minute. If you are a medical doctor you spent virtually the majority of your life learning and being trained on drugs and surgery. How can you wake up one day and say that everything you have been taught is wrong; everything that was drilled in your head that you were forced to believe is false? It would be virtually impossible. How can medical doctors be qualified to talk about health and nutrition when they had virtually no training in natural methods of prevention and curing disease?

My qualifications are that I am logical; I use common sense; I have two eyes that can see the truth; I have traveled millions of miles around the world; I have interviewed thousands of individual patients and doctors; I have been treated by hundreds of licensed alternative health-care practitioners; I have studied volumes of books, research papers, and documents; and I have made billions of dollars in business, putting me in the corporate boardrooms all around the world dealing with the most powerful people on planet earth. I know how the inner workings of government work; I know how the inner workings of corporations work; I know about the greed; I know about the insatiable appetite people have to make money at all costs; and I know about the fraud and deception going on behind closed doors. I've been there; I've been part of it; so much so that I spent two years in federal prison. I know more about the inner workings of the money-making machines and political machines around the world than most people. I also live everything I talk about. I have experienced it firsthand and see the results in myself, my friends, and my family. Plus, I'm 156 years old and have virtually never been sick (just kidding).

Question: Are you the only person who believes this?

Answer: There are thousands and thousands and thousands of licensed health-care practitioners, medical doctors, scientists and researchers all around the world who believe what I believe relating to drugs, surgery, and natural health. These voices, however, are virtually never heard. The news media, on television, radio, newspapers, and magazines, suppress their voices. Publishers will not publish their books. Only with the Internet are we beginning to hear this huge, stifled, and suppressed collective voice. My publishing company, Alliance Publishing Group, Inc., will now be a leading publisher in getting this message out. As a publishing company, I am putting much of my fortune into promoting authors whose voices have been suppressed up until now. Hopefully you will see Alliance Publishing produce dozens of books from other authors around the world sharing more about this subject.

Question: How come I never really hear about any of this stuff on TV or radio, or read about it in the newspapers and magazines?

Answer: As I mentioned, newspapers, magazines, radio, and television are outlets that are publicly traded corporations. Their only interest is making a profit. They have no interest in providing truthful information. They make a profit by getting ratings; therefore, they will produce stories that get the most ratings. Unfortunately, they are also in effect owned by the advertisers. The sponsors of these media outlets control the message that you hear on television and radio, and read in newspapers and magazines. That is the fact. No one can deny it. Therefore, since the majority of advertisers are pharmaceutical companies and the major food companies, you will never hear the truth that the food industry is giving you disease and the pharmaceutical drugs are giving you disease.

Question: Is there a difference between fitness and health?

Answer: Yes. A person can be very fit, but very unhealthy. Jim Fixx was a well-known runner who wrote a book called *The Complete Book of Running*. He dropped dead of a heart attack. He was very fit, but very unhealthy. There are other people who are unfit, they may be slightly overweight, they may not be very strong or flexible, yet are incredibly healthy and live to be well over 100 years old. Generally speaking, there is a balance between fitness and health. In order to be very healthy you have to be at least moderately fit; but you can be incredibly fit and still be very, very unhealthy, get many diseases, and die young. It is more important to be healthy than fit, but for those who want to look good in front of a mirror or in a bathing suit, being fit is more important. I believe in a balance between fitness and health, with health taking the number-one priority. If health is your number-one priority, your fitness level will probably be better than the vast majority of the population anyway.

Question: You mention lots of products that I should get, such as colon cleansers, water filters, shower filters, electromagnetic chaos eliminators, air cleaners, etc. How do I know which products are good and bad?

Answer: The Federal Trade Commission has, in my opinion, completely stripped me of my First Amendment right to free speech. Keep in mind I do not sell any products, I am not compensated in any way on the sale of any products, but yet the Federal Trade Commission has said that if I mention a product by brand name in this book they will in effect confiscate my books, probably burn the books, and probably arrest me as well. I wouldn't be surprised if they charged me criminally with something. The FTC is on an absolute mission to put me in jail, discredit me, and get me out of their hair. They have said this on national television! The FTC has said that they are virtually on a mission to get me at all costs. This is an outrage, this is a vendetta, and this is the government simply stripping a citizen of his constitutional rights.

With that said, I am committed to giving you consumer information regarding what I believe to be the best products, and which products you should stay away from. In the future, I will be publishing various buying guides similar to *Consumer Reports*, but specifically for the health-care area. I will also be publishing all this information on my Web site, www.naturalcures.com.

On naturalcures.com, as a member you will be able to send me a product, and I will either personally review it or my staff will review it. We will write a review and place it on the Web site. My intention is to put together hundreds of product evaluators and reviewers who will be reviewing products and the companies that manufacture them and telling you which products and companies are good, and which products and companies you should stay away from because they are run by greedy people with no ethics who are misleading you. These buyer's guides, both on my Web site community and that I will publish, I believe will be the finest, most objective buyer's guides in the world because they are the only buyer's guides where there are no conflicts of interests and no financial incentives to recommend or not recommend certain products or companies.

Question: Aren't charities, foundations, and health associations good?
Answer: Unfortunately, the answer is, in most cases, no. Every charity relating to the health-care industry, every foundation relating to health or disease, and every association relating to health or disease are only interested in increasing their own profits. It is sad, but true. I have been in the boardrooms of charities, foundations, associations, and various groups of this type. These groups are in effect businesses. Their only objective is raising money. Their only objective is increasing awareness of their cause and getting more money donated. They do not want to wipe out the problem—they want to see it increase.

I was recently with the director of one of the largest nonprofit foundations in the world. This man laughed when he said his "business" was great because the problems that his foundation addresses keep getting worse and worse. He was excited that the problems were getting worse because that meant he would make more money and his organization would make more money. This is the problem with virtually every charity, every foundation, and every association. It is the problem with the American Medical Association, the American Diabetes Association, the American Cancer Society, the American Heart Association, and all the charities and foundations that are associated with illness and disease. They do not want to wipe out illness and disease. They are only concerned with raising more money. If disease was wiped out and cured, they would all be unnecessary, and all the individual people would lose their jobs, lose their power, lose their influence, and lose their huge incomes. It's scary, but it's true.

One of my objectives is to set up a group of people that will actually investigate every single charity, every foundation, and every association. I want to find out exactly how much money is being donated to these organizations, how much time and effort the individual people who work for these organizations spend on raising money, exactly how much time and effort they spend on solving the problems that they are supposed to address or curing the disease, and exactly how much money these people are getting paid and what type of perks they are getting. I am going to be the first person in history to expose these individual people. I am going to name names! I can tell you this, the charities, foundations, and associations are shaking in their boots right now because they know once they get investigated and exposed for the frauds that they are, they will lose their power, influence, and money. This is good for society because we will then know what true charities are available for us to donate to, and which ones are fraudulent. We will know which foundations are virtually ripping us off, and which associations are nothing more than fronts getting government money, taxpayer money, and individual people's money for their own personal use. I'm going to expose the corruption with all the associations, foundations, and charities.

There will be several charities, foundations, and associations that will stand out above the rest. There will be, and there are, charities, foundations, and associations that are run by sincere, honest, ethical people who really have a true mission in life for the betterment of society. These organizations will be endorsed and recommended by me. As a member of my Web site community on naturalcures.com or as a subscriber to my newsletter, you will have access to, and the knowledge of, which foundations, associations, and charities to stay away from, and which ones are good. It is going to be exciting to actually expose the individual frauds that are perpetrating this great deceit and deception on the public at large.

Question: Isn't real research being done on the cure and prevention of disease? Isn't the government spending billions of dollars on this research? Don't corporations and individuals donate money for this research?

Answer: This is one of the biggest frauds and deceptions put on the public. Yes, the government gives, and has given, billions of dollars for "research." Yes, corporations give huge amounts for "research." Yes, foundations give huge amounts of money for "research." Yes, individuals donate huge amounts of money for "research." However, the money is not being used to find a cure, or a way to prevent disease. The money is not being used to find the cause of disease. The money is only being used to find a PATENTABLE DRUG or PATENTABLE MEDICAL PROCEDURE that can be used in the TREATMENT of the disease! Researchers are not looking at the cause, and they are not looking at ways to prevent disease. They are only trying to find a patentable product that can be used to TREAT the disease! They are not looking for a cure. All the research being funded and done is so that the drug companies can own the patent on a product, sell it, and make billions of dollars in profits. There is absolutely no research being done on the real causes of disease. There is absolutely no research being done on any non-patentable natural method to prevent, treat, or cure disease! Never give money to anybody who is going to do "research" for medical purposes. You are only giving more money to the drug companies!

Question: Are all medical doctors bad and evil?

Answer: No. I believe most people who got into the medical profession sincerely and genuinely wanted to help people. The problem is once you go to medical school you are in effect being trained by the drug industry. The only thing you are being taught is the use of drugs and surgery. You get virtually no training in the true cause of disease; you get virtually no training in how toxins cause disease and drugs cause disease; you get virtually no training in how nutritional deficiencies cause disease; you get virtually no training in any method of the prevention or treatment of disease other than drugs or surgery. You have no information on essential oils or homeopathy. As a matter of fact, as a member of the American Medical Association, you are FORBIDDEN by its charter to use anything other than drugs and surgery! Once you are a medical doctor and a member of the AMA you cannot use homeopathic remedies, or essential oils, or any natural method to treat a patient! Therefore, medical doctors are caught between a rock and a hard place.

The other problem with medical doctors is that they are given huge financial incentives by the drug companies to increase their own personal wealth by prescribing drugs and performing surgeries.

As I mentioned earlier in the book, medical doctors are experts at handling emergency life-threatening situations where time is of the essence. And as I mentioned in the beginning of the book, if I'm in a horrible car accident, rush me to the closest emergency room and have a trained medical doctor use all of his skills and knowledge, and all the technology available to him, to save my life. Of course I also mentioned the downside earlier in the book that medical doctors in hospitals have virtually no sleep, and therefore make huge amounts of mistakes due to sleep depravation!

Question: You mentioned that microwave ovens are bad. What about convection ovens?

Answer: Microwave ovens should never be used. In my opinion, eating food that comes out of a microwave is one of the causes of disease. Convection ovens are standard ovens where the heat is simply moved with a fan. These are fine. Infrared ovens are also okay.

Question: How do I change my body pH from acid to alkaline?

Answer: Do all the things in Chapter 6.

Question: You say it's all about the money, but it seems like you are really rich and have been rich most of your life, and you charge for your newsletter and Web site. It seems like you are only about the money too.

Answer: My dad was a blue-collar worker at G.E. He was a welder. My mom raised my brother and me, and managed the house. I grew up in an average blue-collar, middle-class family. I did not grow up rich. I barely made it through high school, and I never went to college. I started working when I was very young delivering newspapers, shoveling snow, and doing odd jobs in the neighborhood. I got my first real job working at a bowling alley cleaning the machines. I worked as a busboy and a waiter in a restaurant. I did other odd jobs to make money. We did not have any air conditioning in our house. I grew up very "average."

When I was fifteen, I was invited to an Amway meeting and learned about the benefits of being in a business of your own and having a positive attitude. I was given several books to read, including *The Magic of Thinking Big*. These encouraged me to have a good attitude and to start my own business. I also read a book called *Seven Steps to Freedom: How to Escape the American Rat Race*, which taught you how to start your own mail-order business. With the money I saved from my paper route and other odd jobs I started my first small mail-order business at the age of fifteen. Through hard work, skill, and a lot of luck, I became very successful. In fact, I made millions very early on in my life. Just as fast as I made the millions, I lost the millions. My personal desire to make money was overwhelming and got me into major trouble. I cut corners and my ethics went straight out the window. My entire story is told on my Web site, naturalcures.com.

The bottom line is over the years I've made and lost hundreds of millions of dollars. By most accounts people would call me "rich." But please know that money is no longer my driving, motivating force. As I mentioned earlier in the book, making money is not bad; it only becomes bad when you put making money above everything else, including your employees, the environment, and society in general. Yes, I continue to make profits, and, yes, I continue to make a very good income and live a very nice lifestyle. But please know that I am using my fortune to expand my mission of educating the world about the dangers of drugs and surgery, and about the benefits of natural cures.

Question: You mentioned you were in jail. It says on the Internet that you have been a really bad person.

Answer: There are tens of thousands of Web sites on the Internet that say terrible things about me. Without exception, I have never met any of the people who write bad things about me. I have been told by my insiders that the vast majority of these "Web sites" are actually run by only a few organizations, but are made to look like there are thousands of Web sites out there. My insiders tell me that the pharmaceutical companies are actually funding Kevin Trudeau bashing on the Internet. As I mentioned, this is a technique that the drug companies and the government use to squash the free flow of information, and that is to debunk and neutralize that person's influence by spreading false, misleading, and negative information about them. My story is, I believe, a tremendous turnaround story. I believe my past and what I have done and have achieved is a great inspiration to others. I have made major mistakes in my life and have taken full responsibility for those mistakes. I have paid my price, and I have turned my life around.

Question: Why do you have to charge to be a member of the Web site, and why do you charge for your newsletter?

Answer: The reason there is a fee to join and become a member of the Web site, and the reason there is a fee to become a subscriber to my monthly newsletter is because I do not accept any advertising, I do not sell any supplements or any products, and I am not compensated in any way on any products that I talk about or recommend. It is my intention to have hundreds of people on staff providing the content and the information on the Web site, and doing the research for the newsletter. The money that you pay to subscribe to the newsletter and be a member of the Web site pays for the postage, the printing, the mailing, the telephones, the light bill, the rent, and all the employees' salaries. It is a huge expense, and I am putting millions of my own money into it. I am not running these enterprises for personal gain or to achieve personal wealth. I am running these enterprises to benefit people, and society.

Question: Why can other people write books and mention products by brand name and you are being so restricted?

Answer: There are dozens of other books, many of which I recommend in this book under the chapter "Still Not Convinced?" that say things that I am being forbidden to say. Other authors are allowed to mention products by brand name and make certain statements I am not. The reason is the Federal Trade Commission has taken direct aim at me personally. The Federal Trade Commission knows that I have over twenty million customers all around the world. The FTC knows that I have more influence on television, and on radio, than most any other author in natural health care. The FTC knows I am the person who will get the message out to the vast majority of people around the world where the other authors will not. They know that my books and publications sell in the millions, where other books only sell five or ten thousand copies. They are directing their attack on me because I am the one they fear the most.

Question: You say a lot of things in this book. Where is the documentation and substantiation?

Answer: If I gave you the documentation and substantiation for every single statement I make in this book, I would have to provide more than 500 pages of this data. Please note that everything in this book has a basis of fact for it being stated. There are more than 900 studies that back up everything I say. There are more than ten thousand articles that have been published around the world that backup virtually everything I say, and there are over one million patient- and doctor-documented reports virtually backing up almost everything I say in this book. As I mentioned in the beginning of this book, everything I say is my conclusions based on my personal experience and observation, and all the literature that I have read. If you would like to see all of this documented evidence, simply go to www.naturalcures.com, and it will be there available to you.

Question: Why is a liver cleanse so important?

Answer: Doing a colon cleanse and a liver/gallbladder cleanse are two very important things if you want to cure yourself of disease. It is important to know that the liver is the major fat burning organ in the body. The liver is the only organ that can pump fat out of the body, and the liver is the filter and cleanser of the bloodstream. Every single person, in my opinion, has a sluggish liver. If your liver is sluggish you cannot burn fat properly, you cannot get fat out of the body properly, and you cannot filter and clean your blood properly. Therefore, if you have a sluggish liver you are absolutely guaranteeing yourself illness and disease. Your liver is sluggish because of all the chemicals and toxins in the food that you eat, and all the nonprescription and prescription drugs. Most notably, if you are on cholesterol-reducing drugs, you absolutely have a sluggish liver. If you have ever taken an antibiotic in your life, the antibiotic has killed the friendly flora in your intestine, causing a Candida yeast overgrowth, which always goes and attacks the liver. When you do a liver cleanse, almost everyone feels so much better they can't believe the difference.

Question: Is fast food really that bad?

Answer: Fast food categorically, 100 percent, causes illness and disease, including cancer, diabetes, and a host of other major health problems. Fast food categorically makes you fat. Fast food is purposely produced with chemical additives that are designed specifically to increase your appetite, get you physically and chemically addicted to their food, and make you fat. The fast-food industry is in effect causing illness and disease, and knowingly doing so. Lawyers for McDonald's state that the dangers of its food are universally known! McDonald's itself stated in legal papers that it's a matter of common knowledge that any processing that its foods undergo serve to make them more harmful than unprocessed foods! An example is McNuggets. These were originally made from old chickens that could no longer lay eggs. Now they are made from chickens that have unusually large breasts, a kind of genetically altered and produced animal. The manufacturing process includes stripping the meat from the bone and grinding it up in a sort of mash. It is then combined with a host of preservatives, stabilizers, and other chemicals, pressed into shapes, breaded, deep -ried, freeze-dried, and then shipped to McDonald's. Judge Robert Sweet termed them a McFrankenstein creation of various elements not utilized by the home cook!

To point this out even further, I would encourage you to view the movie *Supersize Me*. It is available on DVD. This is absolutely a must watch by every person who eats at fast-food restaurants. In this documentary one of the most amazing things was examined. What if a person ate only McDonald's food for thirty days? What would happen? Could just thirty days of eating McDonald's food cause any medical problem? Could just thirty days of eating McDonald's food cause a massive weight gain? Could just thirty days of eating McDonald's food cause disease and illness? Certainly no doctor would believe that simply eating McDonald's food for thirty days would cause any medical or health problems. This documentary shows the truth. The man had his blood work tested before, during, and after his experiment. He had his weight checked. In just thirty days, the medical doctors were dumbfounded and astonished by what happened to this man's body. In just thirty days of eating McDonald's food this man gained twenty-five pounds. In just thirty days! But it's worse than that. He started at only 185 pounds, so he gained almost 20 percent of his original body weight. No doctor could believe it.

I can believe it because I know that McDonald's, like every other fast-food restaurant, in my opinion, is purposely putting ingredients in the food to get you physically addicted to the food, increase your appetite, and make you fat. This movie certainly makes one believe that it is absolutely true. From a health standpoint, the doctors were again astonished. His liver virtually turned to fat. His cholesterol shot up sixty-five points. His body-fat percentage went from 11 to over 18 percent. He nearly doubled his risk of coronary heart disease. He felt depressed and exhausted most of the time. His moods swung on a dime, and his sex life became virtually nonexistent. He craved this McDonald's food more and more when he ate it, and he got massive headaches when he didn't! The doctor said if kept on this diet, he would definitely develop coronary artery disease, inflammation and hardening of the liver, probably develop dozens of various illnesses and diseases, and would certainly die an early death.

The doctors who did the blood work could not believe how this man was, in effect, dying in just thirty days! They couldn't believe it because they were only looking at calories, carbohydrates, protein, fat, and sodium. They weren't considering the "trans fats." They weren't considering how the food has been genetically produced. They weren't considering how the food was energetically destroyed and was toxic to the body. They weren't considering all the food processing chemicals and additives used in this food. That's the reason why this man became so sick in such a short period of time. This is why you need to know that if you are sick and are eating food from fast-food restaurants, or from publicly traded corporations, they are in fact making you sick. It is the poisons, chemicals, additives, and energetic altering of the food that's making you ill.

Let me point out a few other things from this documentary in relation to fast food. Fast-food restaurants, like all food manufacturers, have only one legal objective and that is to increase profits. They increase profits by getting more of your money. They increase profits by selling you more and more food. One of the ways they do this is increasing the portion size. Keeping in mind that in order for any of these techniques to work they have to make the food so that it becomes chemically addicting to you; therefore, you crave it and need to eat it. They have to make the food actually increase your appetite so you eat more, and they have to make the food cause you to become obese, that way you will continue to buy more and more food.

When french fries were first sold at McDonald's there was one size. That size french fries is now the "small." McDonald's also has a medium, a large, and a super-size. The original size is still there, but no one ever orders it. The difference is the original size was 200 calories, but the super-size is over 600 calories. When Burger King first opened they sold a twelve-ounce small soda and a sixteen-ounce large soda. Today, the twelve-ounce soda is called "kiddy"; the sixteen-ounce is no longer a large, it is now the "small." They have a medium, which is thirty-two ounces, and a forty-two ounce size. This is pretty much across the board at all fast-food restaurants. In the movie *Supersize Me* it was mentioned that cars have introduced larger cup holders to accommodate those huge 7-Eleven double gulps, which are sixty-four ounces, a full half gallon, and hold anywhere from 600 to 800 calories. Just imagine, a half gallon of soda for one person. That is forty-eight teaspoons of sugar.

Fast-food restaurants also are involved in some of the most devious advertising campaigns ever put on the public. This is similar to what happened in the tobacco industry. As discussed in the documentary *Supersize Me*, a secret study by one of the tobacco companies was about brand imprinting for later acquisition in life! What this means is the tobacco companies would produce things such as toy cigarettes, so that a child at age four, five, or six would play smoke them. The theory was even though the little child had no real knowledge of what they were doing, that they were imprinting in their memory the act of smoking. Then when they get to the age where they're allowed to smoke, without even realizing it, they are going for that pack and they recognize it because they had those nice feelings when they were a kid.

The same goes with children at the playgrounds at fast-food restaurants like McDonald's and Burger King. They bring the children in, they have fun, they have warm fuzzy feelings, and then later in life they relive those feelings when they go to their fast-food restaurant. This is being done purposely by the fast-food industry to increase sales down the road. You have to understand, the fast-food industry is spending millions of dollars researching ways to get people to buy their products. Kids who eat in fast-food restaurants as little as three times a week have elevated abnormal liver function tests. Under a microscope the livers have evidence of scaring of the liver, fibrosis of the liver, and early states of sclerosis. This is all caused by fast food.

I also encourage you strongly to read the book *Fast Food Nation* so you can see just how bad fast food really is, not only for your health, but for society in general. Think about this: The average American child sees 10,000 food advertisements per year on TV alone. Ninety-five percent of those are for sugared cereals, soft drinks, fast food, and candy. It's not a fair fight. The food industry has the money and the clout to brainwash our children into buying their products, giving us disease and illness. The scary thing is when children are shown pictures of such people as George Washington, Abraham Lincoln, George Bush, and Jesus Christ, they generally have no idea who these people are. But when they are shown a picture of Ronald McDonald, every single one knows his name. And the sad part is they believe that he is a "good man" who is helping children. This is how the food industry misleads and brainwashes our kids.

Think about this, as discussed in the movie *Supersize Me*: companies spend billions of dollars making sure you know about their product. In 2001 on direct media advertising alone, that's radio, television, and print, McDonald's spent $1.4 billion worldwide getting you to buy their products. On direct media advertising Pepsi spent more than $1 billion. To advertise its candy Hershey Foods spent almost $200 million. In its peak year, the five-a-day fruit and vegetable campaign had a total advertising budget, in all media, of just $2 million—100 times less than just the direct media budget of one candy company. We are being bombarded by the food industry with lies, deceptions, and brainwashing, getting us to believe their products are healthy and good for us—and it's working. Think about the way food is marketed: tee-shirts, coupons, toys for children, giveaways in fast-food places, and placemats, and all the different ways to get you to buy food. The most heavily advertised foods are the most consumed. There is no surprise. Whoever spends the most money on advertising sells the most food.

Think about this scary fact, the majority of people tested could not recite the Pledge of Allegiance; however, almost all of them could sing the Big Mac song...two all-beef patties, special sauce, lettuce, cheese... You are probably singing it right now!

The scariest thing to me is how fast food is in effect being sold in schools. When you look at the school lunch programs, it is absolutely appalling. Again, watch the movie *Supersize Me* to get the full story. The most appalling observation is there is huge resistance from junk-food companies that make huge profits off of the schools. Junk-food companies do not want to get kicked out of the school system. They want to be there to addict the children and have them as customers for life.

This points out many things. Major food manufacturers know their foods are dangerous, and deadly, and cause harm to the body. They don't care. They are specifically targeting children because as large publicly traded corporations they have only one objective, which is to make and increase profit. Therefore, they will do anything, and hurt anyone, and destroy people's lives, and virtually give people disease and illness, all in the name of increasing profits. These food companies are demanding that soda machines and junk food be sold in schools, and will do everything they can to increase the usage of their prod-ucts by these kids; therefore, giving these kids guaranteed illness and disease. The motivation for profit is unbelievable, overwhelming, and consuming to these corporations.

Back to McDonald's, consider this—as I mentioned, McDonald's, in my opinion, is manufacturing food that is in effect like a drug. All fast-food companies and junk-food manufacturers ideally want you to be physically addicted to their food, just like a drug dealer wants you to become physically addicted to his drug. They also want you to have an increased appetite for their food. This is why, in my opinion, these companies have spent millions of dollars in secret laboratories produc-ing chemical additives that purposely are put into the food that get you physically chemically addicted to the food, increase your appetite, and make you fat.

In internal documents at McDonald's Corporation it is said to call people who eat their food at least once a week "heavy users!" If you eat at McDonald's once a week you are a "heavy user," just like a drug addict! Seventy-two percent of the people who eat at McDonald's are heavy users. They also have another category, the "super heavy user." These people eat their food three, four, five times a week and up. Twenty-two percent of the people who eat at McDonald's are super heavy users. From the movie *Supersize Me* it stated if you look at the menu at a fast-food restaurant they use all the addicting components. They'll take a slab of meat, cover it with cheese, and then serve it with a sugary soda, which has the addictive powers of sugar with plenty of added caffeine. Give this to a twelve-year-old kid and his brain is no match for that chemical combination.

I wondered about the health of the 22 percent of people who ate at McDonald's three, four, five times a week and up. In my observations I found that these people are riddled with disease. I found that people who eat at McDonalds three times a week or more have the highest chance of getting cancer, diabetes, obesity, heart disease, acid reflux, constipation, sleep disorders, depression, eczema, dandruff, and a host of other medical disorders. I'm sure McDonald's will violently disagree with my observations. I would not be surprised if McDonald's Corporation filed a suit against me, as they do against any person who says anything even remotely bad against the McDonald's Corporation. McDonald's, in my opinion, is the new "evil empire." Remember, the food industry is a massive business. As I mentioned, it uses lobbyists in Washington to make sure that no government agency ever says eat less of its products, and to make sure that the government never passes any legislation that is unfavorable or could hurt the company's or industry's profits. So the bottom-line answer to the question is absolutely never eat in a fast-food restaurant. And, again, I would encourage you to watch the movie *Supersize Me* and read the book *Fast Food Nation*.

Question: Are we really full of toxins, and will doing the cleanses really prevent and cure diseases as serious as cancer, diabetes, or heart disease?

Answer: Absolutely yes. Every single person has massive amounts of toxic poison material in their body causing illness and disease. Yes, by simply doing a colon cleanse, a liver/gallbladder cleanse, a kidney/bladder cleanse, a heavy metal cleanse, a parasite cleanse, a Candida cleanse, and a full-body fat cleanse you can absolutely prevent yourself from ever getting sick, as well as cure yourself of even the most horrible diseases. Yes, simply doing cleanses is one of the "natural cures" that they don't want you to know about.

Let's do a little test. Let me give you a questionnaire so you can see just how toxic you are. Answer each question yes or no. If you answer yes to over twenty questions, you are highly toxic.

1. I have taken antibiotics in my life.

2. I have gotten vaccines.

3. I have taken in my life aspirin, or Tylenol, or ibuprofen, or other over-the-counter pain medication.

4. I shower and/or bathe in regular tap water.

5. I drink water out of the tap.

6. I have been in a swimming pool where chlorine was used.

7. I use a cellular telephone without any electromagnetic chaos protection.

8. I use a laptop computer with a wireless device.

9. I watch TV.

10. I own and watch a high-definition television.

11. I use a wireless telephone in my house.

12. I use a remote control for my television or other electronic appliances.

13. I have a satellite television.

14. I drive in a car every day.

15. I drive in heavy traffic.

16. I use hair dyes.

17. I use fingernail polish.

18. I use makeup and cosmetics.

19. I use moisturizers, body lotions, and sunscreens on my skin.

20. I use air fresheners in my house.

21. I use bug spray in my house.

22. I use standard cleaning products in my house.

23. I use standard soap and detergent for my skin and my clothes.

24. I use toothpaste with fluoride.

25. I eat in fast-food restaurants at least once a month.

26. I eat in restaurants at least once a month.

27. I eat products produced by large publicly traded corporations.

28. I buy brand-name food products that are heavily advertised on TV.

29. I eat food that is not certified 100-percent organic.

30. I eat beef, lamb, poultry, eggs, and dairy products that are not certified 100-percent organic.

31. I eat pork and shellfish.

32. I use artificial sweeteners such as NutraSweet or Splenda.

33. I drink sodas at least several times a week.

34. I drink diet sodas at least several times a week.

35. I have less than two large bowel movements everyday.

36. I have taken over-the-counter nonprescription drugs that I purchased at a drug store in my life.

37. I have taken prescription drugs in the last five years.

38. I use nonstick pans to cook with.

39. I use deodorant and antiperspirant.

40. I do not drink eight glasses of purified water every day.

41. I have never had a colonic or enema.

42. I live near high tension power lines.

43. I live within a few miles of a manufacturing plant of some kind.

44. I live within 100 miles of an agricultural area where produce is grown.

45. I live within 100 miles of ranches where livestock, cattle, chickens, **or other animals are raised.**

This is just a quick list to hopefully open up your eyes to the fact that living a "normal life" absolutely results in mass toxins going in your body. Keep in mind this is a relatively new phenomena to the human species. One hundred years ago people were not exposed to all these toxins in our environment. One hundred years ago people were not loading themselves with massive amounts of toxins as we are today. Every single year the amount of toxins we put in our body increases. The amount of toxins in the air, in the water supply, and the food supply continually goes up. The amount of toxins surrounding our environment and our living spaces goes up. The amount of electromagnetic chaos goes up. The amount of nonprescription and prescription drugs goes up. The amount of chemicals used in the producing of our food goes up. The amount of toxins being force-fed to use by the large publicly traded corporations all in the name of profit continues to rise. So yes, you are absolutely toxic, and yes, by cleaning the toxins out you can see miraculous cures.

Question: Is there anyone in the medical community supporting you, and do you have much support with the general public and the natural health-care industry?

Answer: Yes. I am getting overwhelming positive support across the world, from people, individuals, and organizations, from all walks of life, all backgrounds, and all belief systems. I also have large numbers of critics and enemies that viciously attack me because I am exposing the fraud and corruption in health care, government, and corporations. Because my books and publications are costing the large publicly traded corporations huge profits, I am being attacked from every side.

Here is a letter from Dr. Coldwell supporting my cause.

"As you have noticed, Kevin Trudeau has had a major impact on the FDA and pharmaceutical industry. You hear daily all over the news about drugs being taken off the market and the FDA being questioned about its role in these huge scandals. Few people are saying it directly, but I believe that Kevin and his book *Natural Cures* has caused huge public awareness. I believe thousands of people took action after reading Kevin's book and called and wrote politicians, the FTC, and the FDA expressing outrage for the fraud and deceit in the drug industry, and support for Kevin Trudeau. I personally congratulate Kevin Trudeau for his personal effort to lead America to medical freedom and to protect the consumer from unknown dangers that are caused by the pharmaceutical and medical industry. Kevin needs all of our support for his valuable cause because the government powers that he has to fight are hidden everywhere. Because of Kevin's stand the government is organizing efforts to squash him anyway they can. It even extends down to putting pressure on Kevin by attacking companies that Kevin supports, such as by having their credit card processing cancelled simply because Kevin Trudeau supports their company. Watching everything that happens I cannot overlook the illegal abuse of power the government employees are using to destroy Kevin's business, source of income, and the business of those companies around him, all in an attempt to reduce his ability to fight back for you the consumer, the patient, the person who suffers. The only reason they are after his money and trying to discredit him is to shut him up and make him helpless. All of you need to raise your voice. Write or call your senator, your congressman, the FTC, the FDA, and the President. Tell them that you are outraged at this abuse of power and the actions and misleading tactics used by the FTC and the drug companies. Tell them you are as mad a hell and not going to take it anymore. Tell them you support Kevin Trudeau. Millions of people continue to die because they do not get the information on natural treatment that could save their life. I know this from firsthand experience. I am known as the leading expert for cancer, stress related illness, and depression in Europe. As far as I know, I believe I have the highest curing rate for all kinds of so-called incurable diseases. I cured my mother from liver cancer in a terminal state over thirty years ago. At that time she was told she had only two years left to live. Today, thirty years later, she is healthy, vibrant, and full of life. I was attacked from all directions for curing people without surgery, chemotherapy, radiation or drugs. In fact, the pharmaceutical industry and the medical profession did everything it could to destroy me, all because I proved that it is easy to cure cancer and other so-called incurable diseases with simple natural techniques that are inexpensive and affordable by all. I know what Kevin is going through. I've been there and I know what is to come. It is for this reason that I ask all of you to support Kevin's cause in every way you can. Subscribe to his newsletter, become a member of naturalcures.com, call and write your senator, your congressman, the FTC, the FDA, and the President. Tell them you're mad as hell and not going to take it any more, and make sure you tell them you support Kevin Trudeau. We all should be grateful for the sacrifices Kevin is making fighting this war on our behalf. It is our responsibility to support him every way we can.

Sincerely,

Dr. Coldwell, N.M.D., N.D., Ph.D.

You may contact Dr. Coldwell directly through his associate in Germany, Dr. Hohn at drhohn@goodlifefoundation.com.

Question: Can we really get disease just by breathing the air?
Answer: Absolutely, yes. The *Associated Press* reports that toxic dust is a household threat! The article states that Americans are exposed to a variety of potentially dangerous chemicals in their homes from products such as computers, frying pans, shower curtains, cleaning chemicals, bug sprays, etc. A study found thirty-five hazardous industrial chemicals in household dust samples. This brings home the fact that hazardous chemicals are in our daily lives. All of these chemicals are known to be harmful to the immune, respiratory, cardiovascular, and reproductive systems. Infants and children are especially vulnerable! The lobbying group, the American Chemistry Council, which represents major chemical companies, made the insane statement "Just because a toxic substance is found in dust or in the body doesn't necessarily mean it causes health problems." This is why you need air filters and air cleaners and you must start using nontoxic, organic cleaners and other substances in your home. This also points out one of the leading causes of illnesses in infants and children.

Question: Is it true you have given millions of dollars away?
Answer: I believe what a person does in terms of his personal giving is a private matter. When you see companies and individuals publicizing their charitable giving, please note that this is being done specifically to make you believe how wonderful they are. Corporations not only give money to charity, but usually spend more money publicizing the fact that they are giving money to charity! They do this to brainwash people into believing that they are really "good for the communities." I have never publicized my personal giving. But in direct answer to the question, yes I have given millions of dollars away. I mostly give needed items directly to those who need it. An example is my habit of driving around the streets of Chicago in the winter giving coats, gloves, hats and sweaters to homeless people I see on the street, or giving food directly to shelters that feed those in need.

Question: How do you know these insider secrets that go on behind closed doors in the big publicly traded corporations, and with politicians and government agencies?
Answer: When you make hundreds of millions of dollars you in effect become part of a "secret society." I was a member of such a society and was personally involved in secret meetings all around the world.

I have had private conversations with prime ministers and various heads of states from around the world. I have had secret discussions with military leaders and generals who were involved in major conflicts that you all know about. I have hundreds of moles and insiders providing me with information. Over the next few years more and more of these insiders will start coming forward. This is exactly what happened when the first whistleblower came forward exposing the fraud in the tobacco industry, or when the first mafia informant exposed the secret society of La Costra Nostra.

Question: Is all brand-name popular food sold by publicly traded corporations bad?

Answer: Yes. Remember, natural food, organic food, is fine. It is when the profit motive becomes the main objective those foods stop being natural and is in effect manufactured. This is when it causes obesity and causes disease. When making a profit is involved above everything else, you can be assured that the food being produced is deadly. Think about the average farmer. He wants to produce some vegetables and make a profit. The problem is chemical companies bombard him with sales pitches telling "Farmer Joe" how he can increase his yield and increase his profits by using their fantastic chemicals. So Farmer Joe first buys hybrid, genetically modified seed that he is told will produce more crops faster and be germ resistant. The problem, of course, is this is an unnatural food that when consumed by a human being actually causes disease. Farmer Joe then has to use chemical fertilizers to make the vegetables grow at an unnaturally, unhealthy fast rate. He then sprays incredibly poisonous and deadly bug killers, pesticides, and herbicides on his vegetables. These are all absorbed into the vegetables and cannot be washed off. In order to make the vegetables look beautiful and last longer, they are picked before they are ripe and put into a gas chamber and sprayed with more chemicals. They are then shipped to the grocery store where they can last for days or weeks without spoiling or going bad. You then eat them. The problem is the whole process guarantees that the product is genetically modified, full of toxins and chemicals, devoid of any nutrients and, because of the irradiation, energetically changed, causing the food to be toxic to the body.

Question: Can something as serious as multiple sclerosis be cured with natural methods?

Answer: Absolutely yes. A few months ago I met a woman who had multiple sclerosis. She had a cane and couldn't walk very well. She recognized me from television and asked if I was the author of the *Natural Cures* book. I said yes. She then said that she read the book and didn't understand how anything in the book could help her with her multiple sclerosis. As she said this I noticed that she had a diet soda in her hand. I explained to her that multiple sclerosis, like all diseases, is caused by too many toxins in the body, nutritional deficiencies, electromagnetic chaos, and/or stress. I asked her how long she had been drinking diet soda. She said most of her life. I asked her if she had a lot of dental work. She said her whole mouth was filled with dental work and various kinds of metal. I suggested that the majority of MS sufferers that I have seen have experienced tremendous results by eliminating aspartame, the artificial sweetener in diet sodas, getting rid of all the metal in their mouth, and sleeping on a magnetic mattress pad. Most also have Lyme disease, which can be cured with homeopathics, intravenous hydrogen peroxide therapy, and other natural therapies. Usually sufferers see tremendous relief in just a matter of weeks or months. She said it didn't sound like it would help, but she would give it a try. I gave her my number and told her to call me as I was curious to her results. I also let her know that I was not a doctor or a licensed health-care practitioner and could not treat her, and that she must seek professional help, but I was only giving her my opinions and was not trying to "practice medicine." Three months later she called and explained that she could not believe the spectacular results that she had experienced; she felt like a new woman and felt fifteen years younger. This is a good example of how simple "natural cures" work.

Question: Will "natural cures" work for everybody?

Answer: I believe "natural cures" will work for everyone, but the specific "natural cure" that works for one person's symptoms may not work for another. An example is not everyone who smokes cigarettes comes down with lung cancer, but 98 percent of the people that develop lung cancer smoke cigarettes. What this means is not every single person that drinks diet soda will come down with multiple sclerosis, but almost everyone who comes down with multiple sclerosis probably is adversely affected by the aspartame in the diet soda. This is an important aspect to understand. Not everyone who puts a laptop computer on their lap will develop prostate cancer or arthritis in the knees, but almost all the people that have these types of problems were probably adversely affected by the laptop computer that they had on their lap. The reason for this apparent inconsistency is that everyone's genetic strengths and weaknesses are different. The four causes of all disease affect the genetically weak areas in a person. Therefore, two people could do exactly the same things and one person could come down with a disease and another person may not. This is also why two people can do the exact same "natural cure" and one person will see spectacular results and another person may not see the same exceptional results. However, there is a "natural cure" that that second person could use that would effect spectacular results. That is why doing the things in Chapter 6 is so vitally important for prevention and curing of disease.

Question: Kevin, you seem to have knowledge of people and events that would virtually be impossible for anyone to know unless they had access at the highest levels in both U.S. government, international government, corporations and money brokers around the world. There is a rumor that you were actually an undercover secret operative working for some agency like the CIA or the international police agency Interpol. How else would you know all this insider secret information? Is this true?

Answer: Yes, there are many rumors about how I know so intimately the facts and inner workings of governments around the world, corporations, and the power money brokers that operate in this global economy. There are many rumors about my alleged secret involvement as an undercover agent for the U.S. Government. On this issue I make no comment other than the fact that what I am blowing the whistle on in this book, and in my other publications, is obviously and flagrantly true and is verified by numerous sources around the world. The FTC, the FDA, and the drug companies are scared because they KNOW that I do in fact know the truth.

C H A P T E R   1 2

Still Not Convinced?

This book contains many basic premises. Some, or probably most, of my statements may be hard to believe. Some of the things I say, such as walking being incredibly healthy, or eating more fresh, raw fruit and vegetables has many health benefits, may be easy to accept. Other basic premises that I espouse in this book, such as nonprescription and prescription drugs cause disease, may be harder to accept as true. I encourage you to educate yourself on these subjects. To help you do that, I would like to provide additional material that goes into detail on these various subjects. Much of this material is authored by, surprisingly enough, medical doctors who were trained in surgery and the prescribing of drugs. They know the truth firsthand from an insider's perspective. Other authors come directly from the industry that they are writing about. It is important that you know everything that I say in this book comes from a variety of sources. Much of the material in this book comes from my own personal experience, my own firsthand observations, interviewing thousands of health-care practitioners and patients, reading hundreds of books, and reviewing more than 900 studies from around the world. Every single basic premise that I say in this book has volumes of backup information, studies, "scientific evidence," documentation, and substantiation. Some people have asked me to put a bibliography in this book or all the references. If I did, you would have virtually over 500 pages just of the references for this book! I encourage you to go further in your search of the truth. I am in the process of putting together the entire reference library that I have used in researching and writing this book. It will be available at www.naturalcures.com.

As I mentioned, there are more than 900 studies proving the basis premises in this book. More than 900 studies proving that the chemicals put into our food supply are giving and causing us disease; that the nonprescription and prescription drugs are giving and causing us disease; that the lotions, creams, etc. that we put on our skin are giving and causing us disease; that the poisons in the air are giving and causing us disease; that the water that we drink and bathe in and shower in is giving us and causing us disease; that stress is giving and causing us disease; that the wireless devices like TVs, laptop computers, and cell phones are giving and causing us disease. There are hundreds and hundreds of studies documenting the fact that homeopathic remedies, herbs, pure water, and stress-reducing music do in fact CURE and PREVENT even the most incurable diseases! I encourage you to investigate further these basic premises and learn the truth.

I do make recommendations in this book and in my other publications. I want to emphasize again to you that I have no financial interests in anything I recommend. You must know that I am one of the only health-care advocates and authors that does not sell vitamins, minerals, or any products. I am not compensated in any way on any products that I recommend or encourage you to use. I own no stock in any company that I recommend. I have done this so that you know that my recommendations and comments are what I absolutely believe in my heart to be the best for you and that there are no conflicts of interest in my opinions and recommendations. My mission is to be a guiding force all over the world helping people prevent and cure themselves of illness and disease without drugs and surgery. I highly encourage you to investigate further the subjects that are of most interest to you. These books are available from a variety of sources, and I will encourage you to go to www.naturalcures.com if you are interested in getting more information about these books. If you become part of my Web site community you will have access to excerpts of these books free of charge, as a member, and you can also purchase the books at discounted rates. When you do purchase any of these books at www.naturalcures.com, I am compensated financially, and those proceeds are used to help fund my mission of positively impacting people all over the world.

1. **Not Convinced That Pasteurized And Homogenized Milk Is Deadly? Not Convinced That You Should Only Be Eating Organic, Raw, Unpasteurized And Unhomogenized Dairy Products? Then Read:**

   • *Homogenized Milk May Cause Your Heart Attack: The XO Factor* by Kurt A. Oster, M.D.
   (And how it can destroy your arteries, your heart, your life!)

- *Don't Drink Your Milk!* by Frank A. Oski, M.D.
  (New frightening medical facts about the world's most over-rated nutrient.)

- *Milk—The Deadly Poison* by Robert Cohen

2. **Not Convinced That Aspartame (Nutrasweet®) And Monosodium Glutamate (Msg) Are Deadly And Should Never Be Consumed? Then Read:**

   - *Aspartame (NutraSweet®) Is It Safe?* by H.J. Roberts, M.D.

   - *Excitotoxins—The Taste that Kills* by Russell L.Blaylock, M.D.
     (How monosodium glutamate, aspartame [NutraSweet®] and similar substances can cause harm to the brain and nervous system, and their relationship to neurodegenerative diseases such as Alzheimer's, Lou Gehrig's disease (ALS), and others.)

   - *In Bad Taste: The MSG Symptom Complex*
     by George R. Schwartz, M.D.

3. **Not Convinced That You Have A Candida Yeast Overgrowth Causing All Types Of Medical Problems Including Excess Weight, Arthritis, Depression, PMS, Acne, Migraines, Stress, Constipation, Bloating, Skin Rashes And More? Then Read:**

   - *Lifeforce* by Jeffrey S. McCombs, D.C.
     (A dynamic plan for health, vitality and weight loss.)
     www.lifeforceplan.com

4. **Not Convinced That Subtle Energy Therapies Can Cure Virtually All Disease? Then Read:**

   - *Sanctuary* by Stephen Lewis and Evan Slawson
     (The Path to Consciousness)
     www.energeticmatrix.com

   - *Vibrational Medicine* by Richard Gerber, M.D.
     (The #1 handbook of subtle energy therapies.)

   - *Energy Medicine—The Scientific Basis of Bioenergy Therapies* by Candace Pert. Ph.D.

5. **Not Convinced That Food Additives Are A Leading Cause Of Illness? Then Read:**

   - *Hard to Swallow* by Doris Sarjeant and Karen Evans
     (The truth about food additives.)

6. **Not Convinced The Food Industry Is Purposely Creating Foods That Make You Physically Addicted, Increase Your Appetite, Make You Fat And Give You Disease? Then Read:**

- *Fast Food Nation—The Dark Side of the All-American Meal* by Eric Schlosser

- *The Crazy Makers* by Carol simontachhi
  (How the Food Industry Is Destroying Our Brains and Harming our Children.)

- *Genetically Engineered Food—Changing the Nature of Nature* by Martin Teitel, Ph.D. and Kimberly A. Wilson
  (What You Need to Know to Protect Yourself, Your Family, and Our Planet)

- *Food Politics* by Marion Nestle
  (How the Food Industry Influences Nutrition and Health.)

- *Restaurant CONFIDENTIAL* by Michael F. Jacobson, Ph.D.
  (Think a chicken Caesar salad is perfect for your diet? Think again. Choose a tuna sandwich over the roast beef sandwich? Wrong! The startling truth about our favorite foods from our favorite restaurants, with fat, calorie and salt content.)

- *Fat Land* by Greg Critser
  (How Americans Became the Fattest People in the World.)

7. **Not Convinced That Vaccines Are Deadly, Cause Disease And Should Never Be Used? Then Read:**

- *A Shot in the Dark* by Harris L. Coulter and Barbara Loe Fisher
  (Why the P in the DPT vaccination may be hazardous to your child's health.)

- *VACCINES: Are They Really Safe & Effective?* by Neil Z. Miller

- *What Your Doctor May Not Tell You About Children's Vaccinations* by Stephanie Cave, M.D., F.A.A.F.P., with Deborah Mitchell

8. **Not Convinced That Cancer Can Be Cured Without Drugs And Surgery? Then Read:**

- *The Cancer Cure That Worked! Fifty Years of Suppression* by Berry Lynes

- *The Cancer Conspiracy* by Berry Lynes

- *How to Fight Cancer & Win* by William L. Fisher
  (Scientific guidelines and documented facts for the successful treatment and prevention of cancer and other related
  health problems.)

- *The Breuss Cancer Cure* by Rudolf Breuss
  (Advice for the prevention and natural treatment of cancer,
  leukemia and other seemingly incurable diseases.)

- *The Cancer Industry* by Ralph W. Moss, Ph.D.
  (The Classic Exposé on the Cancer Establishment.)

- *The Cure for All Cancers* by Hulda Regehr Clark, Ph.D., N.D.
  (New research findings show there is a single cause for all cancers. This book provides exact instructions for their cure.)

- *The Healing of Cancer—The Cures—the Cover-ups and the
  Solution Now* by Berry Lynes

9. **Not Convinced That Stress Causes Your Body To Become Acidic
   And, When Handled, That Virtually All Diseases Can Be Cured?
   Then Read:**

   - *Stress: The Silent Killer* by Dr. Leonard Coldwell.

10. **Not Convinced That Your Thoughts Can Make You Sick Or Heal
    You? Then Read:**

    - *Anatomy of an Illness as Perceived by the Patient*
      by Norman Cousins
      (Reflections on Healing and Regeneration.)

    - *Why Animals Don't Get Heart Attacks...But People Do!
      The Discovery That Will Eradicate Heart Disease*
      by Matthias Rath, M.D.

      (The natural prevention of heart attacks, strokes, high
      blood pressure, diabetes, high cholesterol, and many other
      cardiovascular conditions.)

    - *Head First—The Biology of Hope and Healing Power of the
      Human Spirit* by Norman Cousins

11. **Not Convinced That You Should Never Eat Any Meat Or Poultry
    That Is Not Organic? Then Read:**

    - *Slaughterhouse* by Gail A. Eisnitz
      (The Shocking Story of Greed, Neglect, and Inhumane
      Treatment Inside the U.S. Meat Industry.)

- *Mad Cow* by Howard F. Lyman with Glen Merzer
  (Plain Truth from the Cattle Rancher Who Won't Eat Meat.)
- *Prisoned Chickens, Poisoned Eggs* by Karen Davis, Ph.D.
  (An Inside Look at the Modern Poultry Business.)

12. Not Convinced That Our Food Is Loaded With Chemicals Causing Illness And Disease? Then Read:

- *The Chemical Feast* by James S. Turner
  (Ralph Nader's Study Group Report on the Food and Drug Administration.)
- *A Chemical Feast* by Harding Le Riche
  (A rational, commonsense discussion of chemicals in foods by a noted specialist in nutrition and epidemiology.)
- *Sowing the Wind* by Harrison Wellford
  (A report from Ralph Nader's Center for Study of Responsive Law on Food Safety and the Chemical Harvest.)

13. Not Convinced That Electromagnetic Pollution Is Bombarding Your Body, Causing All Kinds Of Medical Problems? Then Read:

- *Cross Currents—The Promise of Electromedicine*
  by Robert O. Becker, M.D.
- *Electromagnetic Fields* by B. Blake Levitt
  (A Consumer's Guide to the Issues and How to Protect Ourselves.)

14. Not Convinced That We All Have An Energetic Field Around Us That Is Adversely Affected By Magnetic Pollution? Then Read:

- *The Unseen Self* by Brian Snellgrove
  (Kirlian Photography Explained.)
- *Kirlian Photography—A Hands-On Guide* by John Lovine

15. Not Convinced That Drugs Are Poisons And Cause Most Disease? Then Read:

- *Over Dose The Case Against the Drug Companies—Prescription Drugs, Side Effects, and Your Health*
  by Jay S. Cohen, M.D.
- *Bitter Pills: Inside the Hazardous World of Legal Drugs*
  by Stephen Fried

16. Not Convinced That The Pharmaceutical Industry Is Purposely Selling Ineffective Dangerous Drugs, And Working Tirelessly To Suppress Natural, Effective Cures For Disease? Then Read:

- *Racketeering in Medicine—The Suppression of Alternatives* by James P. Cater, M.D., Ph.D.

- *The Drug Lords: America's Pharmaceutical Cartel* by Tonda R. Bian

- *The Big Fix* by Katharine Greider
  (How the Pharmaceutical Industry Rips Off American Consumers)

- *The Assault on Medical Freedom* by P. Joseph Lisa
  (Why American Health Care Costs So Much!)

- *Disease-Mongers—How Doctors, Drug Companies, and Insurers Are Making You Feel Sick* by Lynn Payer

- *Under the Influence of Modern Medicine* by Terry A. Rondberg, D.C.

- *The Social Transformation of American Medicine*
  (The rise of a sovereign profession and the making of a vast industry.)

- *Confessions of a Medical Heretic* by Robert S. Mendelsohn, M.D.
  (Approximately 2.4 million operations performed every year are unnecessary and cost about 12,000 lives. In six New York hospitals, 43 percent of performed hysterectomies reviewed were found to be unjustified. Historically, when doctors have gone on strike, the mortality rate has dropped.)

- *Medical Blunders* by Robert M. Youngson and Ian Schott
  (Amazing True Stories of Mad, Bad, and Dangerous Doctors.)

17. Not Convinced That Psychiatry, Psychology, And All Psychiatric Drugs Harm Patients And Actually Cause Depression, Suicide, Violent Acts, And Disease? Then Read:

- *Psychiatry: The Ultimate Betrayal* by Bruce Wiseman

- *Your Drug May Be Your Problem* by Peter R. Breggin, M.D.
  (How and Why to Stop Taking Psychiatric Medications.)

- *Talking Back To Ritalin* by Peter R. Breggin, M.D.
  (What Doctors Aren't Telling You About Stimulants and ADHD.)

- *Talking Back To Prozac* by Peter R. Breggin, M.D.
  (What doctors aren't telling you about today's most controversial drug. The only book that tells you the truth behind its testing and it's potentially frightening side effects.)

- *The Antidepressant Fact Book* by Peter R. Breggin, M.D.
  (What Your Doctor Won't Tell You About Prozac, Zoloft, Paxil, Celexa, and Luvox.)

- *The Myth of Mental Illness* by Thomas S. Szasz, M.D.
  (Foundations of a Theory of Personal Conduct.)

- *The Manufacture of Madness* by Thomas S. Szasz, M.D.
  (A Comparative Study of the Inquisition and the Mental Health Movement.)

- *Mad in America* by Robert Whitaker
  (Bad Science, Bad Medicine, and the Enduring Mistreatment of the Mentally Ill.)

18. **Not Convinced That Calcium Is A Nutrient That Most People Are Depleted In? Then Read:**

- *The Calcium Factor: The Scientific Secret of Health and Youth*
  by Robert R. Barefoot and Carl J. Reich, M.D.
  (The Relationship Between Nutrient Deficiency and Disease.)

19. **Not Convinced That If Your Body Ph Is Alkaline You Can Virtually Never Get Sick? Then Read:**

- *Alkalize or Die* by Theodore A. Baroody
  (Superior Health Through Proper Alkaline-Acid Balance.)

- *Dynamic Health* by Dr. M. Ted Morter, Jr.
  (Using Your Own Beliefs, Thoughts And Memory To Create A Healthy Body.)

- *The Acid-Alkaline Diet for Optimum Health* by Christopher Vasey
  (Restore Your Health By Creating Balance In Your Diet.)

- *The pH Miracle* by Robert O. Young, Ph.D. and Shelly Redford Young
  (Balance Your Diet, Reclaim Your Health.)

20 **Not Convinced That Magnets Can Heal, Alleviate Pain, And Cure Disease? Then Read:**

- *Magnet Therapy* by Gloria Vergari
  (The Gentle and Effective Way to Balance Body Systems.)

- *Healing with Magnets* by Gary Null, Ph.D. with Riba Koestler
  ("Study on Using Magnets to Treat Pain Surprises Skeptics" — *New York Times*)

21. **Not Convinced That AIDS Is One Of The Greatest Hoaxes And Deceptions Ever Perpetrated On The American Public? Then Read:**

    * *AIDS* by Peter H. Duesberg, Ph.D. and John Yamouyiannis, Ph.D.
      (The good news is HIV doesn't cause it. The bad news is "recreational drugs" and medical treatments like AZT do.)

    * *Inventing the AIDS Virus* by Peter H. Duesberg, Ph.D.

    * *AIDS: What the Government Isn't Telling You* by K. Steven Whiting, Ph.D.

    * *Infectious AIDS: Have We Been Misled?* by Peter H. Duesberg, Ph.D.
      (A collection of thirteen articles originally published in scientific journals that call into question the dogma of infectious AIDS.)

    * *The AIDS War* by John Lauritsen
      (Propaganda, Profiteering and Genocide from the Medical-Industrial Complex.)

    * *Do Insects Transmit AIDS?* by Lawrence Miike

    * *Why We Will Never Win the War on AIDS* by Bryan J. Ellison and Peter H. Duesberg, Ph.D.
      (Greed, power, sex, and politics have combined to create the biggest SCAM in medical history: AIDS. But now, everything you thought you knew about this "deadly epidemic" is about to change...)

22. **Not Convinced That Your Digestive System Is Absolutely Dysfunctional If You Live In America? Then Read:**

    * *Restoring Your Digestive Health* by Jordan S. Rubin, N.M.D. and Joseph Brasco, M.D.
      (How the Guts and Glory Program can transform your life.)

23. **Not Convinced That Stress, Anxiety, And Emotional Problems Can Be Cured Almost Instantly? Then Read:**

    * *7 Steps to Overcoming Depression and Anxiety* by Gar Null, Ph.D.
      (A practical Guide to Mental, Physical, and Spiritual Wellness.)

- *The Basic DIANETICS Picture Book* by L.Ron Hubbard.
  (A visual aid to a better understanding of man and the mind based on the works of L. Ron Hubbard.)
- *Scientology Picture Book* by L.Ron Hubbard.
  (Use it to understand yourself, life, and those you live with.)
- *Dianetics* by L.Ron Hubbard.
  (The Modern Science of Mental Health.)

24. Not Convinced That Pain In Any Part Of Your Body Can Be Eliminated Easily Without Drugs Or Surgery? Then Read:

- *Pain Free: An Evolutionary Method for Stopping Chronic Pain* by Peter Egoscue
- *Instant Relief: Tell Me Where it Hurts and I'll Tell You What to Do* by Peggy W. Brill, P.T.
- *Pain Free at Your PC* by Peter Egoscue
  (Using a computer doesn't have to hurt. Prevent or reverse repetitive stress injuries; cure carpal tunnel syndrome; end chronic wrist, shoulder, and neck pain; ease eyestrain; avoid surgery, drugs, and wrist braces.)
- *Natural Relief from Aches & Pains* by C.J. Puotinen
  (Alternatives to Over-the-Counter Medications for many conditions.)

25. Not Convinced That Women Are Being Exploited By The Medical Establishment? Then Read:

- *The Politics of Stupid* by Susan Powter
  (Lose the weight you want to lose forever.)
- *Hormone Replacement Therapy: Yes or No?* by Betty Kamen, Ph.D.
  (How To Make An Informed Decision About Estrogen, Progesterone & Other Strategies For Dealing With PMS, Menopause, And Osteoporosis.)
- *Alternative Medicine Guide to Women's Health* by Burton Goldberg
  (Clinically Proven Alternative Therapies for Relief From Women's Health Conditions.)
- *Male Practice: How Doctors Manipulate Women* by Robert S. Mendelsohn, M.D.

26. **Not Convinced That Tap Water Containing Fluoride, Chlorine And Other Contaminants Is A Major Cause Of Illness And Disease? Then Read:**

   - *Fluoride: The Aging Factor* by John Yiamouyannis, Ph.D.
     (How to Recognize and Avoid the Devastating Effects of Fluoride. Find Out Who's Profiting from the Chronic Poisoning of Over 130 million Americans!)

   - *Your Body's Many Cries For Water* by F. Batmanghelidj, M.D.
     (You are not sick, you are thirsty! Don't treat thirst with medications—A preventive and self-education manual for those who prefer to adhere to the logic of the natural and the simple in medicine.)

   - *Don't Drink The Water* by Lono Kahuna Kupua Ho'ala
     (The Essential Guide to Our Contaminated Drinking Water and What You Can Do About It.)

   - *Water—The Foundation of Youth, Health, and Beauty* by William D. Holloway, Jr. and Herb Joiner-Bey, N.D.

   - *The Water We Drink* by Joshua L. Barzilay, M.D.; Winkler G. Weinberg, M.D.; and J. William Eley, M.D.
     (Water Quality And Its Effects On Health.)

   - *The Drinking Water Book* by Colin Ingram
     (A Complete Guide to Safe Drinking Water. There's nothing more important than the quality of the water that you drink.)

   - *Water: for Health, for Healing, for Life* by F. Batmanghelidj, M.D.
     (You're not sick, you're thirsty! You always knew water was good for you. Now discover why it's nature's miracle.)

   - *Water Wasteland* by David Zwick with Marcy Benstock
     (Ralph Nader's Study Group Report on Water Pollution.)

27. **Not Convinced That Arthritis Can Be Eliminated Without Any Drugs Or Surgery? Then Read:**

   - *Arthritis Defeated at Last! The Real Arthritis Cure* by Len Sands, N.D., Ph.D., ACRP
     (The amazing story of CMO™—Nature's revolutionary immuno-modulator that rectifies the cause of arthritis forever!)

   - *Arthritis Beaten Today!* by Len Sands, N.D., Ph.D., ACRP
     (A revolutionary, new, natural, dietary supplement that is

restoring the quality of life of people suffering from arthritis, as well as other chronic autoimmune diseases. The CMO™ story is a scientific breakthrough that has been described as "The nutritional discovery of the 20th century.")

28. **Not Convinced That Rebounding Exercises Strengthen Every Cell In The Body, And Bring Vibrant Health And Weight Loss? Then Read:**

   - *Looking Good, Feeling Great* by Karol Kuhn Truman
     (Fifteen Minutes a Day to a New You. An easy, fun way to tone you figure, improve health, and develop total fitness!)

   - *Rebounding to Better Health* by Linda Brooks
     (A Practical Guide to the Ultimate Exercise.)

   - *Urban Rebounding™...An Exercise for The New Millennium* by J.B. Berns
     (The system known as Urban Rebounding brings together the science of the West and the philosophy and practicality of the East to form a holistic program of exercise in which people of all ages, sizes, shapes and states of physical condition can participate.)

   - *Harry and Sarah Sneider's Olympic Trainer* by Harry and Sarah Sneider
     (The world's finest total body fitness system that's easy and fun for everyone! Improves: gripping, throwing, jumping, kicking, sprinting, skiing, skating, stamina, depth perception, balance, coordination, body alignment and endurance.)

29. **Not Convinced That The FDA Is Purposely Suppressing Natural Cures For Diseases, And Allows Drug Manufacturers To Sell Ineffective And Dangerous Drugs? Then Read:**

   - *Innocent Casualties: The FDA's War Against Humanity* by Elaine Feuer

   - *Stop the FDA: Save Your Health Freedom* by Steven Fowkes (Editor)
     (Discover the FDA's hidden agenda; learn how to improve your health with supplements; discover the real reasons the FDA banned tryptophan; find out how the FDA suppresses medical breakthroughs; learn the true value of nutritional medicine; learn what you can do to save you health freedom.)

- *Hazardous to Our Health?* by Robert Higgs
  (FDA Regulation of Health-care Products.)

- *Protecting America's Health*
  (The FDA, Business, and One-Hundred Years of Regulation.)

- *The History of a Crime Against the Food Law* by Philip J. Hilts
  (The Amazing Story Of The National Food And Drugs Law Intended To Protect The Health Of The People—Perverted To Protect Adulteration of Foods And Drugs.)

30. **Not Convinced That Using Oxygen Can Reverse Aging, Speed Healing, And Potentially Cure Many Diseases? Then Read:**

- *Flood Your Body with Oxygen* by Ed McCabe "Mr. Oxygen"
  (Therapy for our polluted world.)

- *Stop Aging or Slow the Process: Exercise With Oxygen Therapy (EWOT) Can Help* by William Campbell Douglass II, M.D.

- *Oxygen Healing Therapies* by Nathaniel Altman
  (For Optimum Health and Vitality, Bio-Oxidative Therapies for Treating Immune Disorders, Candida, Cancer, Heart, Skin, Circulatory and Other Modern Diseases.)

31. **Not Convinced That Yoga Has Absolutely Amazing Health Benefits? Then Read:**

- *Ancient Secret of The Fountain of Youth* by Peter Kelder
  (Can five ancient Tibetan rites really make you look and feel years younger? The secret of youthful health and vitality.)

- *Bikram's Beginning Yoga Class* by Bikram Choudhury with Bonnie Jones Reynolds
  (Classic Illustrated Yoga Guide.)

- *Power Yoga* by Beryl Bender Birch
  (The Total Strength and Flexibility Workout.)

32. **Not Convinced That You Can Eliminate Phobias, Traumas, Addictions And Compulsions In As Little As Five Minutes? Then Read:**

- *Tapping the Healer Within* by Roger J. Callahan, Ph.D. with Richard Trubo. For additional information go to www.tftrx.com.
  (Using Thought Field Therapy to Instantly Conquer Your Fears, Anxieties, and Emotional Distress.)

33. Not Convinced That Herbal Remedies Can Potentially Cure Many Diseases? Then Read:

- *Next Generation Herbal Medicine* by Daniel B. Mowrey, Ph.D.
  (Guaranteed Potency Herbs.)

- *Herbal Tonic Therapies* by Daniel B. Mowrey, Ph.D.
  (Remedies from nature's own pharmacy to strengthen and support each vital body system.)

- *Herbal Healing: An Easy to Use A-Z Reference* by Phyllis A. Balch

34. Not Convinced That Homeopathic Medicines Are A Safe Natural Alternative To Drugs And Surgery And Can Cure Disease And Keep You Healthy? Then Read:

- *Everybody's Guide to Homeopathic Medicines*
  by Stephen Cummings, M.D. and Dana Ullman, M.P.H.
  (Safe And Effective Remedies For You And Your Family. Homeopathy is a natural, safe, inexpensive, and highly effective complement to conventional medicine.)

- *The Complete Homeopathy Handbook* by Miranda Castro
  (Safe and effective ways to treat fevers, coughs, colds and sore throats, childhood ailments, food poisoning, flu, and a wide range of everyday complaints.)

35. Not Convinced That Fibromyalgia Can Be Eliminated Naturally? Then Read:

- *The Fibromyalgia Relief Handbook* by Chet Cunningham
  (Gives a full explanation of fibromyalgia—in plain English—and why so many people suffer from it, how to get relief from fibromyalgia symptoms, and more. This book is of vital importance to anyone suffering symptoms of fibromyalgia.)

36. Not Convinced That There Are Natural Remedies For Virtually Every Disease? Then Read:

- *The Cure for All Diseases* by Hulda Reghr Clark, Ph.D., N.D.
  (New research findings show that all diseases have simple explanations and cures once their true cause is known.)

- *Encyclopedia of Natural Medicine* by Michael Murray, N.D. and Joseph Pizzorno, N.D.

- *Health and Nutrition Secrets That Can Save Your Life* by Russell L. Blaylock, M.D.
  (Harness Your Body's Natural Healing Powers)

- *The Natural Physician's Healing Therapies: Proven Remedies That Medical Doctors Don't Know About* by Mark Stengler, N.D.

- *Alternative Medicine: The Definitive Guide* by Burton Goldburg

- *The Most Common Diseases & Their Alternative Natural Therapies* by Alex Duarter, O.D., Ph.D.

- *The Most Effective Natural Medicines in the World* by Alex Duarter, O.D., Ph.D.

37. Not Convinced That You Never Have To Get Sick? Then Read:

- *You Can Be…Well At Any Age: Your Definitive Guide to Vibrant Health & Longevity* by K. Steven Whiting, Ph.D.
  (For those seeking to ensure not only the maximum number of years to their lives, but the best possible quality to those years as well.)

- *How to Get Well—Handbook of Natural Healing* by Paavo Airola, Ph.D.
  (Proven, effective solutions to your health problems—whatever they may be…An authoritative and practical manual on the most common ailments—and what you can do about them by a world-famous authority on nutrition and natural healing.)

- *Death by Diet* by Robert B. Barefoot

- *The Food Revolution* by John Robbins
  (How Your Diet Can Help Save Your Life And Our World.)

38. Not Convinced That Proper Deep Breathing Is One Of The Most Important And Beneficial Things You Can Do? Then Read:

- *Super Power Breathing for Super Energy, High Health & Longevity* by Paul C. Bragg, N.D. and Patricia Bragg, N.D., Ph.D.
  (Live Longer, Healthier, Stronger With Every Breath! Empower Yourself—stimulate your body's natural healing & brain power; Energize Yourself—39 simple exercises for a vibrant, energized body; Relax Yourself—35 calming effects of a healthier, fitter body.)

39. **Not Convinced That Your Liver Absolutely, Positively Is Clogged, Congested, And Needs Cleansing, Potentially Curing A Host Of Illnesses Including Allergies, Diabetes, And Irritable Bowel Syndrome? Then Read:**

    - *The Liver Cleansing Diet* by Dr. Sandra Cabot, M.D.
      (Love Your Liver And Live Longer.)

    - *The Amazing Liver Cleanse* by Andreas Moritz
      (A Powerful Approach To Improve Your Health and Vitality.)

    - *The Healthy Liver & Bowel Book* by Dr. Sandra Cabot, M.D.
      (Detoxification Strategies for Your Liver and Bowel. Life Saving Strategies for those with many health problems, including liver disease, bowel problems and weight excess.)

40. **Not Convinced That There Is An All-natural Cure For Diabetes, And That The Pharmaceutical Industry Offered $30 Million To Take It Off The Market? Then Read:**

    - *The Natural Diabetes Solution* by Richard Laliberte and Pat Harper

41. **Not Convinced That Juicing Is Absolutely Needed If You Want To Get The Proper Nutrition Your Body Needs? Then Read:**

    - *The Juice Lady's Juicing For High-Level Wellness and Vibrant Good Looks* by Cherie Calbom, M.S.

    - *The Juice Lady's Guide to Juicing for Health* by Cherie Calbom, M.S.
      (Unleashing the Healing Power of Whole Fruits and Vegetables. A Practical A-To-Z Guide to the Prevention and Treatment of the Most Common Health Disorders.

    - *The Ultimate Smoothie Book: Whip Up 101 Elixirs, Cordials, Tinctures and Teas to Boost Immunity and Enhance Well-Being.* by Cherie Calbom, M.S.

    - *The Joy of Juicing* by Gary Null, Ph.D.
      (Creative Cooking with Your Juicer. 150 imaginative, healthful juicing recipes for drinks, soups, salads, sauces, entrées, and desserts.)

    - *Power Juices Super Drinks* by Steve Meyerowitz
      (Quick, Delicious Recipes to Prevent and Reverse Disease.)

42. **Not Convinced That Juice Fasting Is The Most Effective Way To Lose Weight, Cleanse The Body Of Impurities, Increase Energy, And Stimulate The Immune System? Then Read:**

- *Juice Fasting & Detoxification* by Steve Meyerowitz
  (Use the Healing Power of Fresh Juice to Feel Young and Look Great. The fastest way to restore your health.)

- *The Miracle of Fasting* by Paul C. Bragg, N.D. and Patricia Bragg, N.D., Ph.D.
  (Proven Throughout History for Physical, Mental and Spiritual Rejuvenation.)

43. **Not Convinced That Colon Cleansing Is Absolutely, Positively Needed By Every Single Person, And That Doing So Can Alleviate Illness And Disease, Increase Metabolism And Potentially Slow Or Reverse Aging? Then Read:**

- *Cleanse & Purify Thyself "And I Will Exalt Thee to the Throne of Power"* by Richard Anderson, N.D., N.M.D.
  (Highly effective intestinal cleansing; removes pounds of Disease-Causing Toxins and Disease-Causing Negative Emotions.)

- *The Detox Diet: The How to and When to Guide for Cleansing the Body of Chemicals, Toxins, Sugar, Caffeine, Nicotine, Alcohol, and More* by Elson M. Haas, M.D.

- *How to Cleanse and Detoxify Your Body Today!* by Elson M. Haas, M.D.
  (Finally...You Can Look And Feel Better! A body freer of toxins, mucus, acids, dead cells and all irritants is STRONGER, HEALTHIER & more VITAL.)

- *Internal Cleansing* by Linda Berry, D.C., C.C.N.
  (Rid Your Body of Toxins to Naturally and Effectively Fight: Heart Disease, Chronic Pain, Fatigue, PMS and Menopause Symptoms, Aging, Frequent Colds and Flu, Food Allergies.)

- *The Master Cleanser (with Special Needs and Problems)* by Stanley Burroughs

- *Healthy Living: A Holistic Guide to Cleansing, Revitalization and Nutrition* by Susana Lombardi
  (Healthy Living: how fasting can save your life; how your body can rejuvenate itself, how you can achieve and maintain balanced health; how to improve your well-being; how you can

prepare delicious vegetarian dishes including soups, entrées, salads, beverages and desserts. Features delicious all-natural vegetarian recipes.)

44. **Not Convinced That Toxins Lodge In The Fatty Tissue Of The Body And Absolutely Are Causing A Host Of Physical And Mental Problems And Must Be Cleansed? Then Read:**

   - *Clear Body, Clear Mind* by L. Ron Hubbard
     (The Effective Purification Program.)

   - *Purification: An Illustrated Answer to Drugs*
     by L. Ron Hubbard.
     Go to www.purification.org for additional information
     (Drugs cause the death of consciousness and awareness, and eventually of the body itself. If you value the ability to think clearly, emotional stability and a positive attitude about your-self, then *Purification: An Illustrated Answer to Drugs* is your answer.)

45. **Not Convinced That Proper Diet Can Potentially Cure Illness And Lead To Vibrant Health And Wellness? Then Read:**

   - *The 7 Steps to Perfect Health by Gary Null, Ph.D.*
     (A practical guide to Mental, Physical, and Spiritual Wellness.)

   - *The Ultimate Healing System* by Donald Lepore
     (The Illustrated Guide to Muscle Testing & Nutrition. A Breakthrough in Nutrition, Kinesiology, and Holistic Healing Techniques.)

   - *Diet for a New America* by John Robbins
     (How Your Food Choices Affect Your Health, Happiness, and the Future of Life on Earth.)

   - *Ultimate Lifetime Diet* by Gary Null, Ph.D.
     (A Revolutionary All-Natural Program for Losing Weight and Building a Healthy Body.)

   - *Official Know-It-All™ Guide to Health & Wellness* by Dr. M. Ted Morter, Jr.
     (Your Absolute, Quintessential, All You Wanted to Know, Complete Guide to wellness, disease prevention, and nutri-tion.)

- *Living Well: Taking Care of Your Health in the Middle and Later Years* by James F. Fries
  (Easy-to-Use Decision Charts Quickly Show How to Treat Problems Yourself and When to See a Doctor.)

46. **Not Convinced That Energy Exists, And Energy Healing Absolutely Works? Then Read:**

- *The Healing Energy of Your Hands by Michael Bradford*
  (Demystifies the art of healing, beginning with a basic explanation of the nature of healing energy, illness and the role of the mind in the healing process. Offers techniques so simple that anyone, even a child, can work with healing energy.)

- *Quantum-Touch: The Power to Heal* by Richard Gordon
  (*Quantum-Touch* represents a major breakthrough in the art of hands-on healing. Whether you are a complete novice, a professional chiropractor, physical therapist, body worker, healer or other health professional, *Quantum-Touch* allows you a dimension of power in your work that heretofore had not seemed possible.)

- *Wheels of Light: Chakras, Auras, and the Healing Energy of the Body* by Rosalyn L. Bruyere
  (Explores the seven chakras, or energy centers, of the body with particular focus on the first charka, which has to do with our basic life force, our physical bodies and our sexuality.)

48. **Not Convinced That Hydrogenated Oil And Trans Fats Cause Heart Disease And A Whole Host Of Medical Problems? Then Read:**

- *Trans Fats: The Food Industry's Way of Giving You a Heart Attack* by Judith Shaw

49. **Not Convinced That Eating Lots Of Raw Organic Fruits And Vegetables Can Give You Dynamic Health? The Read:**

- *Raw Foods: The Key to Eternal Youth* by Gary Null, Ph.D.

54. **Not Convinced That Watching Too Much Television Causes The Body To Become Acidic, Leading To Disease? Then Read:**

- *Four Arguments for the Elimination of Television* by Jerry Mander

55. **Not Convinced That Lack Of Smiles, Love, Hugs, And Affection Can Cause Illness And A Host Of Emotional Disorders? Then Read:**

- *The Medical Consequences of Loneliness*

56. **Not Convinced That Your Words, What You Say And How You Say It, Have A Powerful Impact On Your Health And Success? Then Read:**

- *Should: How Habits of Language Shape Our Lives* by Rebecca Smith
- *What You Say Is What You Get* by Don Gossett
- *The Tongue: A Creative Force* by Charles Capps

57. **Not Convinced That Writing Things Down Causes Them To Happen? Then Read:**

- *Write it Down, Make it Happen* by Henriette Anne Klauser

58. **Not Convinced That The Super Rich Are Greedy And Corrupt Beyond Belief? Then Read:**

- *Perfectly Rich*

59. **Not Convinced That You Can Easily Live To Be Over 100 Years Old, Never Get Sick, And That Virtually Everything I'm Saying In This Book Is True? Then Read:**

- *How Long Do You Choose to Live? A Question of a Lifetime* by Peter Ragnar
  (Imagine never needing another doctor again, having more athletic ability at seventy than you had at seventeen, perfect mental recall, and eternal youth. If the author can show you that these are more than wishful claims, that would interest you, wouldn't it? Read this book!)
- *Power Aging* by Gary Null, Ph.D.
- *The 100 Simple Secrets of Healthy People* by David Niven
- *Stopping the Clock* by Ronald Klatz and Robert Goldman
  (Dramatic Breakthroughs in Anti-Aging and Age Reversal Techniques.)
- *The Longevity Strategy by David Mahoney and Richard Restak*
  (How to Live to 100 Using the Brain–Body Connection.)

- *Successful Aging* by John W. Rowe, M.D. and Robert L. Kahn, Ph.D.
  (Learn the surprising results of the MacArthur Foundation Study—the most extensive, comprehensive study on aging in America. Find out how the way you live—not the genes you were born with—determines health and vitality.)

- *The Okinawa Program* by Bradley J. Willcox, M.D.; Craig Wilcox, Ph.D.; and Makoto Suzuki, M.D.
  (How the World's Longest-Lived People Achieve Everlasting Health—And How You Can Too.)

- *On My Own at 107: Reflections on Life Without Bessie*
  by Sarah L. Delany with Amy Hill Hearth
  (Sarah "Sadie" Delany's tribute to Bessie, her beloved younger sister and century-long companion who died…at age 104.)

- *Having Our Say: The Delany Sisters' First 100 Years*
  by Sarah L. Delany and A. Elizabeth Delany with Amy Hill Hearth
  (The Delany Sisters on Family, Marriage, Taxes and Life…)

- *Living to 100* by Thomas T. Perls, M.D., M.P.H. and Margery Hutter Silver, Ed.D. with John F. Lauerman
  (Lessons in Living to Your Maximum Potential at Any Age.)

- *Centenarians: The Bonus Years* by Lynn Peters Alder, J.D.
  (The book addresses the social and health needs of both the centenarian and their families or caretakers.)

- *If I Live to be 100* by Neenah Ellis
  (Lessons from the Centenarians. This is a beautifully written and elegantly wise work that takes us inside the world of the very old and invites us to learn from them firsthand the art of living well for an exceptionally long period of time.)

- *On Being 100* by Liane Enkelis
  (Thirty-one Centenarians Share Their Extraordinary Lives and Wisdom.)

- *Centenarians* by Dale Richard Perelman
  (One Hundred 100-Year-Olds Who Made a Difference.)

60. **Still Not Convinced That It's Always All About The Money, And Corruption Is Permeating Corporations And Government In America And Around The World? Then Read:**

- *Conspiracy of Fools: A True Story*, by Kurt Eichenwald
- *The Informant: A True Story,* by Kurt Eichenwald
- *Serpent on the Rock*, by Kurt Eichenwald
- *Serpent on the Rock: Crime, Betrayal and the Terrible Secrets of Prudential Bache*, by Kurt Eichenwald
- *Rats in the Grain: The Dirty Tricks and Trials of Archer Daniels Midland, the Supermarket to the World*, by James B. Leiber
- *Funny Money,* by Mark Singer

All of these books are terrific. They give you more facts, more documentation, and more inside information verifying and backing up everything I promote in this book. Please buy these books from us. The small profit we make will be used in our fight against health-care fraud and corruption. If you have any questions about these books, or would like to buy them, go to www.naturalcures.com.

CHAPTER 13

The "Natural" Cures for Specific Diseases

Stop! If you just bought this book and flipped to this chapter trying to find the "magic pill" to cure your specific disease, go back to the beginning of this book and read this book cover-to-cover! If you are sick and you want to know what the natural cure is, do not start reading this chapter first because you will not "get it." You must understand how the medical system works and how you have been brainwashed. You must understand the cause of all disease and the basic ways to cure all disease and bring your body into a state of balance where disease cannot exist. This chapter is only designed to give you some suggestions on some specific non-drug and non-surgical things you can to do to potentially address some of the symptoms that you may be experiencing.

It is important to note that if you think you have a particular disease, there is an excellent chance that you are being misdiagnosed. This is a vitally important point. It has been estimated that 80 percent of diagnoses made have been proven to be wrong. If you are experiencing some symptoms, the first question that you categorically must ask is "What is causing the symptoms?" What most people do is they say "What can I do to eliminate the symptoms?" This is wrong. You must ask what is causing the symptoms. This must be asked, and when you find what is causing the symptoms, then ask what caused that, and continue asking until you find the root cause. Then you address the root cause. When you do this the symptoms vanish. You are then miraculously "cured."

As I have mentioned previously, this is the problem with standard drugs and surgery. They only address suppressing the symptoms, they never address the cause. This is good for the drug manufacturers as it makes them lots of money, but it's very bad for you because it will guarantee that you will continue to remain sick and get sicker, and sicker, and sicker.

Let me give you a good example. If a person walked up to you and said, "Every time I hit my foot with a hammer it hurts. How do I stop the pain?" You would laugh and simply say "Stop hitting your foot with a hammer." If a person said "Every time I pour kerosene all over my house and light it with a match, my house catches fire. How do I stop my house from burning?" You would say "Stop dousing your house with kerosene and putting a match to it." Do you get what I'm trying to say? If you go to a licensed health-care practitioner and say, "I have acid reflux. What to I do?" what you are really saying is, "Every time I load my body with all these chemicals that the food industry is putting in our food supply, I get a burning sensation in my stomach." Well, simply the answer is, stop loading up your body with chemicals. Does this make sense?

A man came to me and said, "I have osteoporosis, what do I do?" The answer was, "Let's come up with the cause of your osteoporosis. What is causing your body not to absorb enough calcium. Either (a) you are not getting enough calcium in your diet, or (b) there is something that is blocking the absorption of calcium. It's really pretty simple isn't it?" He said "Yes." I said, "Well, do you know the things that block calcium absorption?" He didn't know. I said, "Carbonated sodas. Do you drink a lot of them?" His jaw almost hit the ground. He said, "I drink about ten a day." "Well, if you are drinking ten a day, you are blocking your calcium absorption. It doesn't mean that is the reason for your osteoporosis, but it certainly could be." I told my friend to go see a licensed health-care practitioner and suggested that he consider stopping the carbonated sodas and maybe he would start absorbing calcium better. Interestingly enough, within a few months his problem was solved. He was "cured."

Somebody will ask, "But not everyone who drinks carbonated sodas has osteoporosis." That's true, and not everyone who smokes cigarettes dies of lung cancer, but virtually everyone who dies of lung cancer has smoked cigarettes. Get it?

So let's quickly review. You probably are experiencing some symptoms. There is an excellent chance you have been misdiagnosed. We are not trying to suppress your symptoms. Yes, we want your symptoms to go away, but we are really trying to find what the cause of the symptoms is. We also must understand that your symptoms did not develop overnight, they probably took years and years to develop; therefore, they may not vanish overnight. Like the example of the man hitting himself on the foot, or the man burning his house down, if we stop doing the thing that is causing the problem we still may have the current problem. Example: If a man comes to you and says, "Every time I hit my foot with a hammer it hurts," even if he stops hitting his foot with a hammer he may still have pain. Why? Because he hit his foot with a hammer so long he actually broke bones in his foot; therefore, there is an immediate problem that needs to be addressed. The man whose house burns down every time he douses it with kerosene and puts a match to it may say, "Okay, I won't do that anymore." In the meantime, his house is burning. He has an emergency and he has to do something to stop the burning now.

Your medical condition may be exactly the same. If you find the cause of your problem while consulting with a licensed health-care practitioner, you still have an immediate situation that needs to be addressed. That's what this chapter is really all about. Chapter 6 addresses virtually the cause of all disease. I'll say it over and over again, because if I ever meet you personally I will test you. Remember the four causes of all disease? (1) Toxins in the body; (2) nutritional deficiencies; (3) electromagnetic chaos; and (4) emotional and mental stress. If you do all the things in Chapter 6 you will address all four of those issues and virtually cure yourself of every disease, and prevent virtually every disease. However, there is an excellent chance you have done nothing positive for your health in twenty, thirty, forty, or fifty years. So there is a good chance that you have a real serious situation that needs some particular attention.

This is why I will state over, and over, and over again—go to a licensed health-care practitioner who doesn't use drugs and surgery, and ideally go to two or three different people to get different opinions. Getting personalized treatment is invaluable and there is no substitute.

Now, when you go to your licensed health-care practitioner and come up with a personalized treatment for your particular situation, you can consider some of the following things. Remember, I am not a doctor; I have no medical training; I am not a health-care practitioner; I am not prescribing medical treatment; I am not treating any medical condition; I do not treat patients; and I am not making any attempt in this book to prescribe, diagnose, or treat any illness, or treat any patient. I present all this information simply for educational purposes only. You and only you are responsible for your health. You must do what is right for you while consulting with a licensed health-care practitioner. With that said, I am now going to present to you what I believe to be the best protocol to follow if you are currently sick. This is the procedure that I would follow if I were to come down with some illness or disease. Keep in mind, because I do the things in Chapter 6, I have virtually never been sick.

1. Go back to Chapter 6 and do all the things in Chapter 6.
I cannot emphasize this enough. The things that I mention in Chapter 6, such as seeing a licensed health-care practitioner, getting energetic rebalancing, doing all of the cleanses, etc. will, in my opinion, and in most cases, cure almost all disease. Doing the things in Chapter 6 can eliminate virtually all symptoms in a very short period of time because it addresses the root cause of all illness. Simply doing energetic rebalancing, or doing the cleanses listed, can cure the "incurable." This is documented and proven. Over a million reports from all around the world have shown that this is categorically, 100 percent true. Simply doing the things in Chapter 6 can cure disease.

In addition to doing the things in Chapter 6, there are some specific things that you could do that could help your body return to a state of "homeostasis" (balance) which will allow your body to heal itself faster. Remember, there is no drug, no surgical procedure, and no natural remedy that actually cures disease. The "natural cure" for all disease is doing the things that bring your body back to balance so the body can heal itself. Only the body can heal itself. So in addition to doing the things in Chapter 6, I now present to you an A to Z list of some common diseases, and some specific additional therapies that can be done in conjunction with the things mentioned in Chapter 6.

Every single one of these illnesses and diseases can be cured, in my opinion, by simply doing the things in Chapter 6. Example: For every one of these diseases I should say "First, go to a licensed health-care practitioner." Getting individualized treatment from a licensed health-care practitioner, which could include essential oils, herbs, homeopathic remedies, chiropractic care, vitamins, minerals, etc., can cure all disease. Getting energetic rebalancing and doing nothing else can virtually cure every disease. Doing a colon cleanse, a liver/gallbladder cleanse, a kidney cleanse, a heavy metal cleanse, a parasite cleanse, a Candida cleanse, and a full-body cleanse can, in thirty to sixty days, virtually cure any "incurable" disease. Not doing these things makes trying to cure your disease, in my opinion, much more difficult and next to impossible.

Yes, you can do some things that could reduce your symptoms on a temporary basis, or eliminate them for a short period of time, but since you are not addressing the root cause they will come back, or other diseases will develop in other areas of your body that are genetically weak. Therefore, again, I cannot emphasis enough to go back to Chapter 6 and do the things in Chapter 6. If you want to cure yourself of the disease you have, you absolutely must get the toxins that are in your body out, and stop putting them in; you must start giving your body super nutrition because you are nutrient deficient; you must stop or at least neutralize the electromagnetic chaos that you are being exposed to; and you must eliminate the trapped emotional and mental stress that you are holding in your body unconsciously. Doing these things will bring your body pH from acidic to alkaline where disease cannot exist. If you do not do these things, it is virtually impossible to cure yourself of disease.

DISEASE MAIN CAUSES:	NATURAL CURES:
Acid Reflux/Heartburn/Gas/ Bloating	
Candida, parasites, nonprescription and prescription drugs, eating food that has been over processed with no living enzymes, mental and emotional stress	Raw organic apple cider vinegar with mother, drink 2-4 tablespoons before each meal; digestive enzymes, specifically with betatine hydrochloric acid; probiotics, specifically acidophilus bifidus; Candida cleanse; parasite cleanse; colon cleanse; eat more organic raw fruits and vegetables; Dr. Coldwell's stress-reducing techniques
Acne	
Hormonal imbalances; Candida; parasites; dehydration; allergies	Drink 10 glasses of distilled water daily; Candida cleanse; colon cleanse; liver/gallbladder cleanse; parasite cleanse; full-body fat cleanse; infrared sauna; Dr. Coldwell's stress reducing techniques; probiotics

ADD/ADHD	
Candida; high fructose corn syrup; food additives; allergies; heavy metal toxicity; electromagnetic chaos; essential fatty acid deficiency; sensitivity to the chemicals in dairy and meat; nitrites; artificial sweeteners; monosodium glutamate; aspartame; blocked calcium absorption	Candida cleanse; liver/gallbladder cleanse; Omega-3s; supplements; no dairy; no nitrites; no artificial sweeteners; no fast food; alphabiotics; cranial sacral therapy; Dr. Coldwell's stress-reducing CDs

Allergies	
Candida; clogged liver	Consult with a certified NAET practitioner; do all the cleanses; Dr. Coldwell's stress-reducing techniques

Anxiety/Stress	
Totally individualized. The cause of each person's stress is totally unique to that person.	Calcium and magnesium supplementation; B-Complex supplementation; exercise; rebounding; massage; Dr. Coldwell's stress reducing techniques; Dianetics; colon cleanse; liver/gallbladder cleanse; Candida cleanse; heavy metal cleanse; Callahan Techniques; organic dark chocolate; sun; rest

Arthritis	
Candida; heavy metal toxicity; parasites; viruses	CMO (Cetylmyristoleate); parasite cleanse; crocodile protein peptide; removal of all dental metal in your mouth; arnica; DMSO

Asthma	
Trapped mental and emotional stress; allergies; hormonal imbalances; Candida	Go to www.sorvinoasthmafound.org

Autism	
Viral infections; heavy metal toxicity; Candida; vaccinations; adverse effect to nonprescription and prescription drugs	Will vary on individual since the cause of this syndrome varies greatly; do the things in Chapter 6

Back Pain	
Mental and emotional stress; trauma; dehydration; viral infections	Chiropractic treatment; acupuncture; alphabiotics; Rolfing; cranial sacral therapy; deep-tissue massage; magnetic mattress pads; Dr. Coldwell's stress-reducing technology

Bad Breath	
Lack of digestive enzymes; toxic overload; Candida; parasites; heavy metal toxicity	All the cleanses; raw apple cider vinegar; probiotics; infrared saunas

Bladder Infections	
Bacterial infection; virus infection; fungi; parasites	Two tablespoons raw unpasteurized apple cider vinegar with mother, mixed with 1 tablespoon raw honey in 8 ounces of warm water, drink with meals; pure unsweetened, unpasteurized cranberry juice (up to a quart a day), do not buy cranberry juice in a bottle, make your own; watermelon juice; crocodile protein peptide; homeopathic treatments; propolis; larrea

Bloating/Gas/Heartburn/Acid Reflux	
Candida, parasites, nonprescription and prescription drugs, eating food that has been over processed with no living enzymes, mental and emotional stress	Raw organic apple cider vinegar with mother, drink 2-4 tablespoons before each meal; digestive enzymes, specifically with betaine hydrochloric acid; probiotics, specifically acidolphis bifidus; Candida cleanse; parasite cleanse; colon cleanse; eat more organic raw fruits and vegetables; Dr. Coldwell's stress-reducing techniques

Blood Clots	
Nonprescription and prescription drugs; mental and emotional stress; trans fats (hydrogenated oils) in the diet; homogenized dairy products; Vitamin E deficiency	Natural Vitamin E; nattokinase; Omega-3s; intravenous chelation; oral chelation

Cancer	
Toxins in your body; nutritional deficiencies; electromagnetic chaos; mental and emotional stress	If you have cancer you need to go to a licensed health-care practitioner! If I had cancer, I would make sure I was doing every single thing in Chapter 6. In the back of the book I give a list of reference clinics that specialize in cancer.
Chronic Fatigue Syndrome	
Candida; Epstein-Barr virus; parasites; heavy metal toxicity; hypoactive thyroid; allergies	Ginseng, chelation, homeopathy
Circulation Problems	
Blockages in the arteries due to chlorine in the water you drink and bathe in; homogenized dairy problems; trans fats (hydrogenated oils); Candida; heavy metals, allergies, and viruses	Oral chelation, in severe cases intravenous chelation; hydrogen peroxide therapy; natural Vitamin E (There is only one company that makes a pure natural Vitamin E. I am forbidden to tell you the product by brand name. Please contact the licensed health-care practitioners I recommend and they can give you the information, or go to www.naturalcures.com); nattokinase; Omega-3s.
Cold hands and feet	
See Circulation.	See Circulation.
Cold Sores/Herpes	
Viral infection	The best book on the subject is *Never an Outbreak,* by William Fharel; larrea; red marine algae; lysine; hydrogen peroxide; DMSO
Colds	
Bacterial or viral infection	Green papaya extract; enzymes; propolis; raw ginger boiled in water—drink it as a tea; cat's claw; crocodile protein peptide; homeopathic remedies; infrared saunas; the sun

Constipation	
Candida; eating food without living enzymes; too much white flour/white sugar and refined food; non-prescription over-the-counter drugs and prescription drugs; mental and emotional stress; dehydration	Drink 10 glasses of distilled water daily; eat 5 apples a day; prunes; colonics; Candida cleanse; colon cleanse; probiotics; digestive enzymes; raw apple cider vinegar with mother, hot peppers, ginger

Cough	
Candida; bacterial or viral infection; allergies	Gargle with salt water; gargle with colloidal minerals; tea with lemon and honey; propolis; homeopathics

Dandruff	
Toxic overload; allergies; Candida; parasites	Infrared saunas; dry brush massage; drink 10 glasses of distilled water a day; all the cleanses; probiotics; raw apple cider vinegar

Depression	
There is no one main cause. As with most diseases or symptoms, the causes vary by individual; Candida	Go for a walk outside one hour each day and look far away as you walk; St. John's Wart; Omega-3s; rebounding; any stretching or aerobic exercise; elimination of prescription and nonprescription drugs; elimination of aspartame; Candida cleanse; all the cleanses; the sun; Dr. Coldwell's stress-reducing techniques; Dianetics

Diabetes	
Prescription drugs; Candida; artificial sweeteners; overuse of white flour and white sugar; overuse of trans fats (hydrogenated oils)	Candida cleanse; liver/gallbladder cleanse; eliminate all nonprescription and prescription drugs; exercise; digestive enzymes; raw apple cider vinegar; a combination of herbs researched at the University of Calgary for over twenty years, called by the Asian Diabetic Association the final cure for diabetes. I am forbidden by the Federal Trade Commission to mention the product by brand name; however, the person I interviewed who told me about this was Dr. Yung Su Kim,

	a Korean living in Canada. Also most of the licensed health-care practitioners that I recommend are fully aware of this product. The FTC did concede that I can recommend you to a licensed health-care practitioner. Please go to the end of this book for my recommended licensed health-care practitioners.
Diarrhea	
Parasites; Candida; prescription and nonprescription drugs	Drink 8-10 glasses of pure distilled water every day; digestive enzymes; probiotics; Candida cleanse; parasite cleanse; colon cleanse; liver/ gallbladder cleanse
Fibromyalgia	
Like many "diseases," there is no one cause. When doctors don't know what you have they have to call it something. Diseases like "fibromyalgia" are made up to try to classify a set of symptoms where a cause cannot be completely ascertained.	Magnetic mattress pad; the sun; all the cleanses; crocodile protein peptide
Flu	
See Cold.	See Cold.
Gallbladder Problems	
Prescription and nonprescription drugs; too many trans fats in your diet (hydrogenated oils); genetic weaknesses acerbated by the chemicals in food, primarily meat and dairy; Candida	Candida cleanse; colon cleanse; liver/gallbladder cleanse; heavy metal cleanse; parasite cleanse; digestive enzymes
Gas /Bloating/Heartburn/Acid Reflux	
Candida, parasites, nonprescription and prescription drugs, eating food that has been over processed with no living enzymes, mental and emotional stress	Raw organic apple cider vinegar with mother, drink 2-4 tablespoons before each meal; digestive enzymes, specifically with betatine hydrochloric acid; probiotics, specifically acidolphis bifidus; Candida

	cleanse; parasite cleanse; colon cleanse; eat more organic raw fruits and vegetables; Dr. Coldwell's stress-reducing techniques
Gout	
Excess protein; allergies; poor circulation; viral infections	Chelation
Heart Disease	
Viral infections; parasites; heavy metal toxicity; Candida; trans fats; homogenized diary products; vaccines; prescription and nonprescription drugs; nutritional deficiencies; lack of exercise; calcium deficiency; magnesium deficiency; bacterial infection; mental and emotional stress; chlorine in the water you drink and bathe in	Oral chelation, in severe cases intravenous chelation; hydrogen peroxide therapy; natural Vitamin E (There is only one company that makes a pure natural Vitamin E. I am forbidden to tell you the product by brand name. Please contact the licensed health-care practitioners I recommend and they can give you the information, or go to www.naturalcures.com); nattokinase; Omega-3s; rebounding; crocodile protein peptide; magnesium supplementation; calcium supplementation; live cell injections
Heartburn/Acid Reflux/Gas/ Bloating	
Candida, parasites, nonprescription and prescription drugs, eating food that has been over processed with no living enzymes, mental and emotional stress	Raw organic apple cider vinegar with mother, drink 2-4 tablespoons before each meal; digestive enzymes, specifically with betatine hydrochloric acid; probiotics, specifically acidolphis bifidus; Candida cleanse; parasite cleanse; colon cleanse; eat more organic raw fruits and vegetables; Dr. Coldwell's stress-reducing techniques
Hepatitis C	
Viral infection	Hydrogen peroxide therapy; homeopathics; crocodile protein peptide

Herpes/Cold Sores	
Viral infection	The best book on the subject is *Never an Outbreak*, by William Fharel; larrea; red marine algae; lysine; hydrogen peroxide; DMSO
High Blood Pressure	
Mental and emotional stress; various nutritional deficiencies; Candida	Raw extra virgin coconut oil; flax and flax seed oil; Dr. Coldwell's stress reducing techniques; calcium and magnesium supplementation; nattokinase; natural Vitamin E; Omega-3s; the sun; 8 glasses of pure water a day; heavy metal cleanse; Candida cleanse; parasite cleanse
High Cholesterol	
Food; allergies; candida; lack of exercise; vitamin E and calcium deficiency	Vitamin E; calcium; omega-3s; red wine; mangosteen juice
Inflammation/Pain	
Dehydration; blockage of electromagnetic impulses between cells	Drink 10 glasses of water per day; acupuncture; a therapy was developed that has been used by over 18,000 chronic pain sufferers with remarkable success. The Federal Trade Commission has forbidden me to mention the product by brand name; however, it was developed by Darrell Stoddard. You can go on the Internet and search out Darrell Stoddard and find the product, or I can refer you to my licensed health-care practitioners who can make their own recommendations. MSM; magnetic mattress pads and therapy; chiropractic; Dr. Coldwell's stress reducing techniques; alphabiotics; Candida cleanse; heavy metal cleanse; chelation; ozone therapy

Insomnia	
If you were to test 100 people with insomnia you would probably find that each person's insomnia is caused by a different reason. There are virtually no main causes; therefore, the treatment will vary from person to person—more so here than in many other situations.	Dr. Coldwell's stress-reducing techniques; Candida cleanse; liver cleanse; calcium and magnesium supplementation; elimination of all nonprescription and prescription drugs; melatonin; extra virgin cocoanut oil

Kidney Stones	
Dehydration; nutritional deficiencies; Candida; nonprescription and prescription drugs	Colon cleanse; liver/gallbladder cleanse; kidney/bladder cleanse; heavy metal cleanse; parasite cleanse; drink 1 gallon of distilled water combined with the juice of 5 organic lemons and 2 cups of apple cider vinegar every day for two weeks.

Liver Problems	
Nonprescription and prescription drugs, primarily cholesterol reducing drugs; Candida; parasites; trans fats (hydrogenated oils); viral and bacterial infections	Colon cleanse; liver/gallbladder cleanse; Candida cleanse; heavy metal cleanse; parasite cleanse;

Lupus	
Like many "diseases," there is no one cause. Take fifty people with lupus and you could find fifty different causes, which means there could be fifty different treatment protocols.	Do the things in Chapter 6.

Male Erectile Dysfunction	
Nonprescription and prescription drugs; vaccines in childhood; poor circulation; mental and emotional stress; Vitamin E and calcium deficiencies; diabetes; hormonal imbalances; Candida; heavy metal toxicity	Correct diabetes with herbal discovery as discussed under diabetes section; intravenous chelation; oral chelation; exercise; Dr. Coldwell's stress reducing techniques; nattokinase; natural Vitamin E; Omega-3s; ginseng; Peruvian maca; horny goat weed; muira puama; tribulus terrestris; ginkgo biloba; Candida cleanse; heavy metal cleanse

Migraine headaches	
Dehydration; stress; hormonal imbalances; Candida; food allergies; parasites; heavy metal toxicity, allergies, and TMJ	Do all the cleanses; apple cider vinegar; must eliminate artificial sweeteners; Dr. Coldwell's stress reducing techniques; acupuncture; alphabiotics; cranial sacral therapy; chiropractic adjustments
Multiple Sclerosis	
Heavy metal toxicity; aspartame; mental and emotional stress; viral infections; Candida	Magnetic mattress pad; eliminate all artificial sweeteners and monosodium glutamate; colon cleanse; Candida cleanse; heavy metal cleanse; eliminate all metal dental work; liver/gallbladder cleanse; alphabiotics
Obesity	
Low metabolism; mental and emotional stress; Candida; hypoactive thyroid; inefficient pancreas	Colon cleanse; liver/gallbladder cleanse; parasite cleanse; heavy metal cleanse; chelation; walking; extra virgin coconut oil; apple cider vinegar; digestive enzymes; the sun; infrared saunas; fasting
Pain and Inflammation	
Dehydration; blockage of electromagnetic impulses between cells	Drink 10 glasses of water per day; acupuncture; a therapy was developed that has been used by over 18,000 chronic pain sufferers with remarkable success. The Federal Trade Commission has forbidden me to mention the product by brand name; however, it was developed by Darrell Stoddard. You can go on the Internet and search out Darrell Stoddard and find the product, or I can refer you to my licensed health-care practitioners who can make their own recommendations. MSM; magnetic mattress pads and therapy; chiropractic; Dr. Coldwell's stress-reducing techniques; alphabiotics; Candida cleanse; heavy metal cleanse; chelation; ozone therapy

Phobias	
It's anyone's guess.	Callahan Thought Field Therapy technique

PMS	
Calcium and magnesium deficiency; hormone imbalances; thyroid abnormality; heavy metal toxicity; Candida; nonprescription and prescription drugs; mental and emotional stress	Calcium and magnesium supplementation; colon cleanse; liver/gallbladder cleanse; Candida cleanse; heavy metal cleanse; parasite cleanse; Dr. Coldwell's stress-reducing techniques; extra virgin coconut oil

Snoring	
Dehydration; candida; allergies	Essential oil throat spray

Sore Throat	
Bacterial or viral infection; Candida; parasites	Gargle with colloidal silver or colloidal minerals; Candida cleanse; parasite cleanse; heavy metal cleanse; cat's claw; larrea

Stress/Anxiety	
Totally individualized. The cause of each person's stress is totally unique to that person.	Calcium and magnesium supplementation; B-Complex supplementation; exercise; rebounding; massage; Dr. Coldwell's stress-reducing techniques; Dianetics; colon cleanse; liver/gallbladder cleanse; Candida cleanse; heavy metal cleanse; Callahan Techniques; organic dark chocolate; sun; rest

Tumors	
Toxic overload; electromagnetic chaos such as cell phones or laptop computers; mental and emotional stress; Candida; viral infections	Hydrogen peroxide therapy; ozone therapy; chelation therapy; flax seed oil mixed with soy protein; shark cartilage; all the cleanses; infrared saunas; Dr. Coldwell's stress reducing techniques; energetic rebalancing machines and therapies

Varicose Veins	
Nonprescription and prescription drugs; mental and emotional stress; trans fats (hydrogenated oils) in the diet; homogenized dairy products; Vitamin E deficiency	Natural Vitamin E; nattokinase; Omega-3s; intravenous chelation; oral chelation

It is important to again emphasize that you must seek professional care from a licensed health-care practitioner who does not use drugs and surgery. It is very important for you to understand that virtually every one of these, and every disease, could be cured by simply doing one of the things in Chapter 6. An example: Did you know virtually every disease has been shown to be cured by simply getting more sun? Did you know that virtually every disease has been shown to be cured by simply doing a colon cleanse? Did you know that virtually every disease has been reported to be cured by simply doing a liver cleanse? Did you know that virtually every disease has been reported to be cured by doing simply energetic rebalancing? Did you know that virtually every disease has been shown to be cured by simply doing a parasite cleanse? Did you know that virtually every disease has been reported to be cured by simply using Dr. Coldwell's stress-reducing technology? Did you know that virtually every disease has been reported to be cured by simply taking herbs? Did you know that every disease has been reported to be cured by simply taking homeopathic remedies? Do you understand?

It is important to know that people who are looking for a specific cure for a specific disease are missing the point of this book. A disease is simply a label put on a series of symptoms. The symptoms could be caused by hundreds of different factors, or combinations of factors. This is one of the things that medical science does not want you to understand or know about. In order for the medical community to make money they must "isolate" a specific something so that they can find a drug that can be patented to treat it. This is how they make billions of dollars in profits.

The fact is each individual person must be treated individually by a licensed health-care practitioner and given personalized individualized treatments and protocols. What this means is very simply this: If you were to take 100 people who were all experiencing the exact same symptom, such as a migraine headache, it could be determined that every single person's migraine headache symptoms were caused by something different. That means every person's cause could be different. This means every person's treatment will be different. What will work for one person might not work for someone else. This is why when you say "What is the cure for 'X?', the answer is 'I don't know, and no one knows until you are looked at, analyzed, and the cause is discovered. Once the cause is determined, then the treatment that will work will be discussed. It is impossible to know what particular treatment will work for you without knowing what the cause is."

It is again important for you to totally understand that the cause for the same "disease" can vary greatly from person, to person, to person; therefore, it is virtually impossible to say what the specific treatment that will work for you is going to be. Example: If you have genital herpes, we all know the cause is a virus. What we don't know is why the virus became active in you. Everyone gets exposed to the virus, but not everyone develops breakouts and succumbs to the virus. So even though we do know that it is a virus, if you had five people who had genital herpes breakouts, each person's reason that they succumbed to the herpes virus could be different; therefore, the treatment that would work for each of the five persons could be slightly different. In one person red marine algae may completely kill the virus and you will never have an outbreak ever again. In another person it could be the herb larrea; in another person hydrogen peroxide applied to the breakout could kill the virus; in another person DMSO applied to the breakout area could kill the virus; in another person lysine could suppress that symptom. In some people, they may need to use a combination of various treatments. This is why it is important, again, to understand that individualized treatment is necessary.

When you look at 100 very sick people, all with different diseases and illnesses, you do find common denominators. Virtually every sick person is dehydrated; virtually every sick person needs a colon cleanse; virtually every sick person needs a liver/gallbladder cleanse; virtually every sick person has a Candida yeast overgrowth; virtually every sick person has parasites; virtually every sick person has nutritional deficiencies; virtually every sick person is loaded with toxins in their body; virtually every sick person has some type of emotional or mental stress that has been trapped and encapsulated in their physical body; virtually every sick person has viruses such as herpes; virtually every sick person has heavy metal toxicities; virtually every sick person has

Lyme disease and doesn't even know it; virtually every sick person has environmental and food allergies and doesn't even realize it.

This is why I always tell people who have any physical problems to do the things in Chapter 6, and then re-evaluate their condition in three to six months. It is unbelievably amazing that the majority of people see their symptoms dramatic diminish or vanish.

Just yesterday a seventy-eight-year-old woman called me on the phone. She was on five different prescription drugs and has been on those drugs for over ten years. Her symptoms continually got worse. She read my book and started applying the things in Chapter 6. She did this under the care of a licensed health-care practitioner who didn't use drugs and surgery. Within three months she got totally off all her prescription medications, and she told me that she did about 50 percent of the things in Chapter 6. All her symptoms have vanished. She says she feels twenty-five years younger. She is full of energy, full of vitality, and all of her symptoms and illness and disease have been cured—all by simply doing the things in Chapter 6.

This is not an isolated incident. These kind of "miraculous' cures are happening to thousands of people all over the world every week. It could happen for you.

I will emphasize again, and again, and again, if you are sick, you must see a licensed health-care practitioner who does not use drugs and surgery. In my opinion, you must be on an energetic rebalancing program. You must do a colon cleanse, a liver/gallbladder cleanse, a kidney/bladder cleanse, a Candida cleanse, a parasite cleanse, a heavy metal cleanse, and, ideally, a full-body cleanse. You must stop all nonprescription and prescription drugs. You must stop eating the poisons such as fast food, artificial sweeteners, and the like. You must be drinking at least eight to ten glasses of purified water every day. You must use some technology to eliminate the stress your body is holding on to. If you don't do these basic things, it's impossible, in my opinion, for you to truly get your body back in a state of balance, eliminate your symptoms, and cure yourself of disease.

C H A P T E R   1 4

NATURALCURES.COM

Your Only Source of Unbiased Health Information

The basic premise of this book is the fact that there are non-drug and non-surgical, all-natural methods to prevent and cure virtually every disease, and the fact that "they" don't want you to know about them. After reading this book I hope you at least consider this to be true. Nothing is more evident than the fact that the Federal Trade Commission, which is the U.S. Government agency entrusted with protecting consumers against primarily monopolies and fraud, is actively trying to stop me from giving you this information.

The Federal Trade Commission has repeatedly sued me, although there has never been a finding of any wrongdoing! The FTC repeatedly puts out false and misleading press releases as to my activities. I am suing the Federal Trade Commission now because of their continued retaliation against me and false and misleading press releases. The Federal Trade Commission has said on national television that they are doing everything in their power to stop me. The FTC even went so far as to threaten to confiscate and burn my books. This book is one of the only books I know of in America that has ever been censored by the U.S. Government.

I am committed to giving you the truthful information about natural cures, and exposing the corruption in government and corporations around the world. I am committed to being at the forefront of consumer advocacy and exposing the fraud and deception, and the fact that you are being misled about the truth relating to natural cures and treatments.

For this reason, I have launched naturalcures.com. This Internet Web site community is in its infancy. It is my intention to make naturalcures.com the ultimate source of truthful information relating to natural cures and remedies. This Web site will be the counter-Web site to WebMD. WebMD, in my opinion, is nothing more than a front for the pharmaceutical industry. All you have to do is look at who is advertising on WebMD and you will see that the pharmaceutical industry controls the content of that Web site. Also look at the board of directors of WebMD, as well as the officers and senior executives. Look at the tens of millions of dollars in pure profit these people have made on the stock of WebMD. It's nothing more than a moneymaking machine and pure propaganda, all designed to make money, enrich the individuals involved, and promote drugs and surgery.

Naturalcures.com will be the only health-related Web site in the world that I know of that will not accept any advertising or sell any products. Naturalcures.com will be a true, honest source of information relating to natural cures and health. Since I will not accept any advertising, or sell any products whatsoever, or be compensated in any way for any products that we talk about on the Web site, you can be assured that the information you are getting is unbiased and there are no financial conflicts of interest. When you subscribe and become a member to naturalcures.com you will have access to information about natural remedies and natural cures that are not available anywhere else. It is a private community where we will be free to talk and share information without fear of a government agency prosecuting us for expressing our opinions.

It is my intention to have the following at naturalcures.com:

- My monthly newsletter.
- Back issues of all my monthly newsletters.
- In the News" section. In this section my reporters will be investigating news reports around the world relating to the drug industry, health, nutrition, and natural remedies for diseases, as well as corporate and government corruption. I believe this will be the most comprehensive single place to find news that is being suppressed around the world. There are thousands of news reports, studies, and articles written about corruption in the corporate world and government, as well as natural remedies, which are systematically

suppressed and hidden from the public. We will find these stories, articles, and reports and publish them in this single source. Never in history has there been one place to get all the information.

- Natural Cures by Disease. In this section we will list over 100 diseases in alphabetical order. Under each disease we will put all the research data available on all the natural remedies, as well as clinics that specialize in the natural treatment and curing of these diseases. Never before has one place had a mission of being the single source of information for natural remedies from around the world.

- Health-care Practitioner Directory. It's vital that you see a licensed health-care practitioner, but how do you find one? How do you know if they are good? This area of the Web site will be a worldwide list of licensed health-care practitioners and clinics who do not use drugs and surgery. It will be categorized by location, and medical condition specialty. You will be able to find licensed health-care practitioners around the world who specialize in various treatments, or specialize in various health conditions. More importantly, you will be able to read the comments of other people who have used these health-care practitioners, and what the results were. This way, you will be able to be treated by the best.

- Talk to me and my licensed health-care practitioners. As a member of the Web site you will be able to e-mail me and my licensed health-care practitioners, and get responses to your health related questions.

- Product Reviews. It is my intention to put together a huge staff of product researchers and reviewers who will be investigating and giving thorough reviews on all products that relate to health. These may include vitamins, minerals, herbs, homeopathic remedies, supplements, as well as other products including food, meat, air filters, water filters, shampoos, toothpaste, conditioners, cosmetics, etc. It is my intention to review thousands of products and give you our personal evaluations. Our reviews will be different than anyone else's. Keep in mind, we are not compensated in any way on products that we endorse or recommend. We will be the only source of unbiased information. In addition to simply reviewing a product, we will find out who owns the company that makes the product, and visit the manufacturing facilities. We will look at every ingredient that has been put into the product, and the processing used in the manufacturing of it. We will visit the farms where things are grown and see firsthand if, in fact, these are pure and good. I can tell you this, I personally know of manufacturers that are shaking in their boots because they will be exposed for producing absolute garbage and crap. This section will not pull punches. We will tell the truth. We will tell you what products are garbage and should be avoided, we will expose the greedy corporate frauds for who they are, and we will tell you what products are produced by sincere honest people whose main motivation is not making money, but helping society. You may also send us products for personal evaluation and we will add that to the site as well.

- Message Boards. Message boards will be set up by disease and treatments. This way you will be able to communicate with other members of the naturalcures.com Web site community and share information.

- Chat Rooms. Chat rooms will be established by disease and various categories. This way you will be able to chat with other people in a free, secure environment, sharing information about natural remedies and health.

- FDA and FTC Horror Stories. I will send my investigative team in to review the files at FDA and FTC headquarters using the Freedom of Information Act. We will personally investigate the crimes and corruption being committed by the FDA and FTC. We will expose in detail how both of these organizations are using Gestapo-like tactics to suppress truthful information and are actually protecting monopolies to exist. We will investigate fully the individual people at these agencies. We will expose the corruption and crimes against humanity being committed by these individuals. We will name names. The arrogance and abuse of power will stop because for the first time the individual people will be fully and completely investigated.

- Books and tapes I recommend. There are thousands of books and tapes; which ones should you read and listen to? We will be personally reviewing books and tapes, giving excerpts, and making recommendations.

- Plus a whole lot more…

Joining the naturalcures.com Web site will give you information about health and healing that is not available anywhere else in the world. Being a member also supports the mission of educating the world about natural remedies, and stopping the corruption in government and the drug companies. Joining this Web site helps give me the funding needed to fight back and file massive numbers of lawsuits against the individual people, corporations, and government officials that are perpetrating these heinous crimes against humanity.

When I first wrote this book, I had a chapter entitled "The Cures for All Diseases." I wanted to emphasize the fact that if you did the things in Chapter 6, you could virtually cure every disease. But I also wanted to do one other thing—I wanted to list every disease in alphabetical order, and list a specific brand name product that I felt could be helpful in the treatment of that condition and/or could help in the "curing" of that condition. The Federal Trade Commission in effect censored the entire chapter. They said if I wanted to sell this book on television I could not mention a product by brand name in it. I was outraged at this flagrant censorship. I was shocked and amazed that my First Amendment rights were being taken away from me. I simply said to myself, "I'm mad as hell and I'm not going to take it anymore!" The individual people at the Federal Trade Commission and the Food and Drug Administration should be held accountable for their actions. The individual people who run the drug companies, who knowingly allow drugs to be sold when the evidence is clear that hundreds of thousands of people will DIE by taking them, are absolutely outrageous. Remember the fact as published by the American Medical Association: Prescription and nonprescription drugs kill more people than the diseases they are supposed to be curing! This cannot be emphasized enough.

If we are to effect a change, aggressive action has to be taken against these organizations. I need your support in leading that fight. When you join naturalcures.com, you are helping support the cause, and you are also getting tremendous value for your financial contribution. Go to www.naturalcures.com and please join today. I would like to reprint my original chapter entitled "The Cures for All Disease." I wrote this chapter out of complete frustration when the FTC threatened to prosecute me and burn my books. In this new updated edition I have made huge headways in the court about what I can and cannot say, but I am still being restricted in this particular forum. However, so that my original book's integrity is kept in tact, I do want to reprint that chapter as it appeared in the original version of Natural Cures.

The Original Chapter 12

There are natural nondrug and nonsurgical cures for virtually every disease, illness and physical ailment. These cures are inexpensive and have virtually no negative side effects. I am not a doctor. I do not treat patients. According to the U.S. Government, I cannot diagnose or treat disease. If I were to cure someone of cancer, I could go to jail for practicing medicine without a license. Therefore, I am presenting this information for educational purposes only.

I know that therapies such as energetic medicine, homeopathy, herbs, nutritional supplements and cleansing can help the body heal itself. What standard medicine attempts to do is to look at a person's symptoms, call it a "disease," and then prescribe drugs or surgery to suppress or eliminate the symptom. Unfortunately, medical doctors do not look for the cause; they only attempt to suppress the symptoms. If you simply suppress a symptom, you have not addressed the cause and the person will continue to get sick. Combine that with the new illnesses that are actually caused by the drugs themselves, and we find that a patient treated by a medical doctor with drugs and surgery continues to become sicker and sicker over time. A good example is a child who appears to have hyperactivity and a low attention span. He will probably be diagnosed with attention deficit disorder. Doctors will say that the child's brain chemistry is not right, and he needs a drug to fix the imbalance in the brain chemistry. The drug may have some short-term effects on balancing the brain chemistry, but the question that was missed is WHY the brain chemistry was unbalanced to begin with. What caused the chemical imbalance? If this was asked, we almost always find that food allergies, excitotoxins such as MSG and aspartame, and food additives are to blame. With simple dietary adjustments the brain chemistry becomes balanced, and the child, in a matter of days, is no longer hyperactive and his attention span is back to normal.

Another example is when a person has pain, a doctor will give a drug to suppress the pain. All the drug does is stop the pain signals from reaching the brain. The cause of the pain is never addressed; if it is, we virtually always find the pain was caused by a blockage in electromagnetic impulses between cells. The Chinese actually discovered over 2,000 years ago that with simple nondrug and nonsurgical procedures, the cause could be addressed and the pain eliminated permanently.

Imagine you are driving your car and the oil light goes on. That would be a symptom of a bigger problem. To "correct" the situation, you could simply take the bulb out. You stopped the symptom; the oil light is no longer illuminated. But you have not addressed the cause, continuing to run your car without oil, which will quickly cause major engine damage. The human body is the same way. Think about it this way: You don't have a headache because you have an aspirin deficiency.

The most important thing you can do is prevent disease and sickness. Most people wait until they have symptoms before seeking medical attention. In many cases the problem is so severe that major attention is needed. Imagine a person who never takes his car in for maintenance. One day the car starts making funny noises. The person does not immediately take the car in for service. He continues to drive the car, not realizing that the problem is getting worse and worse. The car finally stops running and must be towed in to the service station. The mechanic says all the bearings are worn out and must be replaced, a major engine overhaul. Our body is very similar. People run their bodies with aches and pains and symptoms, using drugs to suppress the symptoms without addressing the cause. One day the problem is so severe they seek medical attention and are told "Your body is riddled with cancer," or "Your arteries are almost completely clogged and they need immediate bypass surgery." This would never happen if a person did basic maintenance of their body.

The pH test, in my opinion, is one of the simplest and best ways to determine your health potential. If your saliva and urine pH is alkaline, disease and sickness virtually cannot exist. Remember, most serious medical conditions such as cancer, heart disease, arthritis and any pain in general did not develop overnight. The condition was developing for years before you ever noticed a symptom. I was asked one time what I would do if I found out I had cancer or heart disease. My response was that that was virtually impossible since I routinely check my body pH and monitor my arteries. Blocked arteries, for example, develop over years. I would know if my arteries were beginning to clog years before any major blockages. If I discovered this, I would utilize natural treatments such as nutritional therapy, and chelation. I would then review my condition to see if it stayed the same, got worse or got better. The key element is that I would know years in advance of any major problem.

The good news is that even if you do have a major problem, there are natural alternatives to drugs and surgery in most cases. I realize that what I present in this book is said to be unconventional. However, throughout history "conventional" has always been what the majority believed to be true. Those who were in the minority were classified as heretics. The conventional wisdom at one time was that the sun revolved around the earth. Anyone who thought that the earth revolved around the sun was a fool and a heretic. At one time the conventional wisdom was the earth was obviously flat, and anyone who suggested the earth was round was a fool and a heretic. At one time the conventional wisdom was man will never build a machine that can fly, anyone who thought otherwise was a fool and a heretic. As early as the 1970s, the conventional wisdom within the scientific community was food and nutrition had absolutely nothing to do with health, disease, or illness. Anyone who suggested good nutrition could play a major role in preventing and curing disease was a heretic.

I would like to give you the cures for virtually every disease; I would like to tell you the natural treatments available that can eliminate your symptoms and, at the same time, address the cause instead of simply suppressing the symptom. However, as I began to write this book the Federal Trade Commission and the Food and Drug Administration took unprecedented action. The FTC has ordered me NOT to give you any specific product recommendations, or say where you can acquire the cures and receive treatment. And you thought we had free speech in America. You thought that the First Amendment of the U.S. Constitution protected our rights to speak our opinions freely. This simply is not true. We do not have free speech in America when it comes to health care. I can write a book about how to build a nuclear bomb. I can write a book on how to be a terrorist. I can write a book filled with pornographic images. I can write a book accusing politicians and big business of corruption. I can write a book filled with bigotry, hate and prejudice. I can write a book about my alien abduction. I can write a book about how I talk to the dead and see angels. All of this is protected by free speech. But I cannot write a book and tell you how to cure your cancer without chemotherapy and surgery.

This entire chapter has been censored by the FTC. If you are as outraged as I am, you will join me in fighting this censorship. Just imagine for a moment what is happening here. I am not allowed to tell you my opinions in this book. How many millions of people will needlessly suffer and die because they are not allowed to know the truth about effective, inexpensive natural cures? However, there is a way you can get this information. If you go to www.naturalcures.com and become a private member, you will have access to all of this data. You can even e-mail me any question, and either I or my staff will give you the answers you seek. It is important for you to know that the very first step that you must take if you want to be healthy, prevent, or cure any disease is to take personal responsibility. Do not rely on the pharmaceutical industry, the scientists and researchers, the medical doctors, your insurance company, government agencies, or politicians; you must take charge and take full responsibility for your health.

A week ago I met a woman who recognized me from television. Her son was diagnosed with attention deficit disorder. He was incredibly hyperactive, and his attention span was almost nil. He failed every exam in school and was disruptive to the class. She wondered if she should take the doctor's advice and give the child Ritalin. I suggested that she see some health-care practitioners who use all-natural treatments instead of drugs and surgery. I asked what the child ate, trying to get her to be as specific as possible. I said simply eliminate all dairy products, white sugar, white flour, aspartame, and MSG. I wrote down recommended meals and educated her on how to read food labels. She became very encouraged and excited about the possibility, yet remained skeptical that such a simple change could make such a profound difference. I gave her my number and asked her to call me, as I was curious to know the results. Three days later she called. This woman was out of her mind. She told me that she absolutely could not believe the change in her child. The hyperactivity was virtually gone and the child's attention span and ability to concentrate was near 100 percent. For the first time in two years the child sat at the dinner table and ate his meal like a normal, well-mannered person. She even received a phone call from the child's teacher, who could not believe the change that had happened.

These kinds of stories happen all the time. Whether your concern is cancer, heart disease, arthritis, heartburn, PMS, headaches, pain, insomnia, acne, lupus, asthma, herpes, sexual dysfunction, yeast infections, ADD, snoring, diabetes, depression, anxiety, stress, etc., there is a simple, effective natural solution. I am sorry that I cannot list all the products by brand name in this book. The FTC and FDA have promised to prosecute me if I tell you the products by brand name to use that cure or prevent disease.

Keep in mind that I am not compensated in any way from any of the products that I recommend. I have no conflicts of interest. I only make money when you purchase the books and other informational material that I sell. I use much of this money to educate the public and continue with my research. I also use this money to fight against corruption in the pharmaceutical industry and government. Please know that you can prevent and virtually cure almost every disease without drugs and surgery. Please know that you can live a life full of energy and vitality, and virtually never get sick.

CHAPTER 15

The Solution

Over the years there have been a few individuals, such as Ralph Nader, who have done a commendable job of exposing corruption in government and big business. There have been a few pure consumer advocate groups that have been untainted by the lure and influence of big business money and government pressure.

These individuals and groups have educated people around the world about corporate and government corruption that affects our lives. They have done this education through the use of books, public appearances, newsletters, and recently, Internet Web sites. Although they have done an admirable job at trying to expose corporate and government corruption, and educate people around the world about how corporate and government corruption adversely affects our lives, two major problems still exist.

1. Even with the truth about corporate and government corruption being exposed to the public, the mainstream media has still suppressed and watered down this information.

2. These organizations and individuals, generally speaking, only attempt to EXPOSE the fraud, deception, and corruption that exists in both corporations and government, but do little to actually stop it.

I believe the only way to stop corporate and government corruption, and stop the exploitation that corporations and governments engage in against the public is the following plan:

1. The majority of people must be made aware of corporate and governmental corruption. The majority must be exposed to the truth of how "it's all about the money," at the expense of the average person. Therefore, my mission is to not only write the books, newsletters, and Web sites exposing the truth, but also to invest my fortune in promoting these books, newsletters and Web sites throughout the television, radio and print media. The challenge is already evident. The Federal Trade Commission has already taken action denying me my First Amendment right of free speech by forbidding me to publish my opinions in book form and marketing them. The mainstream media is also suppressing my ability to run advertising promoting these books, newsletters and Web sites. However, it must be done. The information must get out to as many people as possible as soon as possible if change is ever going to occur. The corrupt corporations, corporate executives, politicians and government agencies must be exposed.

2. In addition to educating the public on how they are being deceived by big corporations and the government, if change is to occur, aggressive action must be taken against the corporations, government agencies, and individual corporate executives and politicians. In addition to educating the public, it is my intention to spearhead lawsuits—specifically, class-action lawsuits—against those who are allowing millions of people to suffer needlessly through suppression of the truth about natural nondrug and nonsurgical cures. Since class-action suits have been filed against the tobacco industry, things have slowly begun to change in that area. The same will happen in health care. As of right now, no one is taking the lead in fighting the pharmaceutical industry. Together we can create a society where fewer people get sick with disease and illness, instead of the current trend where more people every year become sick with disease and illness.

3. In order for me to achieve the first two objectives listed above, I absolutely need your support. I need you to subscribe to my monthly newsletter and/or become a member of my naturalcures.com Web site. The more subscribers I have to my newsletter, and the more members I have on the Web site, the more I will be able to do in terms of educating the public worldwide about natural non-drug and non-surgical ways to prevent and cure all disease, as well as expose the corporate and government corruption that is keeping

the general public broke and sick. Additionally, the more subscribers I have to my newsletter and the more members I have on the naturalcures.com Web site, the more we will be a major political force. This means we as a group working together have enormous power at making changes in government. Politicians and corporations do not listen to one person, but when one person is backed up by millions of individual people, then a major movement is created and a voice that is so loud cannot be ignored. We individually are powerless to change things in the large corporations and in government, but together as a group we become an unstoppable force that can change the world for the better.

4. In order to stop the corruption in corporations and in government, your voice must be heard. I need you to write and/or call the President, write and/or call your congressman, write and/or call your senator, write and/or call the FTC, and write and/or call the FDA. (The addresses, phone numbers, and e-mail addresses are listed at the end of this chapter.) I need you to simply say "I'm mad as hell, and not going to take it any more! I support Kevin Trudeau." Doing this simple step will shake things up so much that we will see changes happen faster than you could ever imagine.

5. Lastly, I need your positive thoughts, and your positive prayers. This is a huge battle I am fighting for you. I am risking everything for this cause. I am risking my fortune and my own personal freedoms. I know that because I have taken this cause the government will attack me every way they can. They have already said publicly that they are looking for any way to attack me, debunk me, discredit me, and prosecute me. I am risking not only all my money and materials possessions, but I am risking my freedom for what I believe to be this noble mission. I absolutely need your financial support and encouragement. Please subscribe to my monthly newsletter and/or become a member of the naturalcures.com Web site. Please send me your success stories. Please send me your encouragement. I try to read all the correspondence that comes into my office. Your words of encouragement give me the strength to continue with this fight.

Why should you help me with this mission? Well, let me ask you a question.

Doesn't it make you mad knowing that corporate executives are knowingly and purposely putting chemicals in our food that make you fat and give you disease? Wouldn't you like those big greedy corporations to pay for their actions? I would.

Individually we are powerless against the big corporations and the government agencies that run unpoliced.

- Together as a group we can be a powerful force that will change health care for the better.

- As a group we can demand that the food we buy in supermarkets and restaurants be free of chemicals and food additives.

- We can demand that we have free access and freedom of choice regarding natural alternative treatments and therapies.

- As a group we can demand that the advertising we are exposed to no longer be deceitful, misleading and fraudulent.

- As a group we can create a society where there is less sickness and disease, where we live longer with more energy and vitality than ever before, and where we eat delicious foods and are not condemned to being fat.

- Please subscribe to my *Natural Cures Monthly Newsletter.*

- Please go to www.naturalcures.com and become a member.

- Please call and/or write the President, your congressman, your senator, the FTC, and the FDA, and tell them you're mad as hell, and not going to take it anymore and you support Kevin Trudeau.

- Please send me your success stories and positive comments, as well as suggestions on how to do things better.

I am determined to change health care in America and the world. I want to pick up where Ralph Nader and others before him left off. I want to be a true pure consumer advocate working for the betterment of society and the "little guy." My new motto is "Empowering the Powerless." Please help me and please join me. (To subscribe to my *Natural Cures Monthly Newsletter*, go to www.naturalcures.com or call (800) 931-4721.)

Putting It All Together

In order for things to change a few basic things must happen:

1. The Food and Drug Administration must categorically, 100 percent admit their mistake and change the regulation which currently

states, "Only a drug can cure, prevent, or treat a disease." This is categorically not true. This is a flagrant and obvious lie. This regulation is one of the most outrageous dictums put out by the U.S. Government. This particular regulation is one of the major reasons why illness and disease are increasing at the most alarming rate in history. This regulation simply protects the profits of the pharmaceutical industry. This must be changed. The FDA law should state "ANYTHING CAN CURE, PREVENT, OR TREAT A DISEASE." This is the most fundamental thing that must be changed. If the FDA were to allow this to be true, we would see people from all over the world come forward expressing their discoveries and their observations about how natural remedies can cure or prevent disease. The problem is instantly, virtually overnight, the drug industry's profits would plummet because tens of millions of people would stop taking drugs and start trying natural remedies. This is why the FDA is not doing it. Their defense is that there will be thousands of "charlatans and snake oil salesmen" preying on the hopes and fears of people selling them useless and potentially dangerous natural substances. This is a "sound good excuse" that the FDA is using, but it doesn't hold water. As long as there is a requirement stating that the information presented about "natural remedies" is simply the opinions of those selling it, and that "other opinions may vary," the information should be presented. As long as the people selling health-related substances require the individual purchaser to acknowledge the fact that the "proof" that these things actually work is disputable, and that they are purchasing it and using it at their own risk, then we would eliminate any major problems. These rules should also be required of the drug companies. They should be required to have the patient acknowledge that the drugs are "not proven and that the opinions and research on these drugs is disputable and other opinions vary!" It should be fair across the whole spectrum. This one change would save the lives of millions of people! This is not hyperbole. The statistics show that more people die by taking drugs than are killed by the diseases that the drugs are supposed to be curing! The drugs are actually worse than the "diseases." Simply getting people off drugs would increase lifespan and cure more disease than any other single thing; however, the profits of the drug companies would plummet, and the profits and power of the politicians would also plummet.

2. The U.S. Government should take the lead in trying to prevent and cure disease! The government should allocate money directly into funding research organizations that can look at everything EXCEPT drugs and surgery as a way to cure and prevent disease! If the U.S. Government gave money to research the prevention and cure of disease that specifically looked at things other than patentable drugs and surgical methods, we would then hear about the breakthroughs on a regular basis. Keep in mind, the information is already there, the breakthroughs are already there, the knowledge is already there, and the methods to prevent and cure disease are already there. The reason we are not hearing about it is it can't be patented, and the drug companies don't want you to know about it. If a government agency was put in charge instead of giving the money to the drug industry, then independent researchers who are not trying to find patentable, moneymaking drugs and surgical procedures would actually be allowed, for the first time, to tell the truth about the effectiveness and safety of natural methods. We would also hear the absolute truth about how the food additives are being used, and the genetic modifying of seeds and food is actually CAUSING many of the diseases and illnesses. Our food supply would dramatically change, illness would plummet, and people would be healthier and live longer than ever before.

Making these things happen for society is a big monumental job. It's going to take people, and money, and effort, and time. It will require protests, advertising, promotion, and individual politicians running for office who are willing to step forward and institute these changes. This is why I would like to gently again encourage you to become a member of the naturalcures.com Web site community and/or subscribe to my *Natural Cures Monthly Newsletter*. Not only will you get information that can personally affect you in a positive way, but your small financial contribution can make a huge and dramatic impact on this movement. Again, your support and help is needed and deeply appreciated.

We can make a change, and with your help and support it will be done!

The Simple Next Steps

There is a lot of new information in this book. There is a lot of information published about living a long, healthy, disease-free life filled with vitality, energy, and happiness. It is easy to get overwhelmed with the vast amount of data that you are being presented with. This book has been specifically designed to be easy to read and understand, using broad strokes to give you some basic concepts for you to consider, as well as give you some very specific things that you can do that can create some very spectacular and immediate positive changes in your health and well-being.

Throughout this book I repeatedly made the statement "I'm mad as hell and I'm not going to take it any more." For many people who read this book there is a feeling that I am outraged at the lies and deceptions put on people by governments around the world, various agencies such as the FDA and the FTC, and by the large publicly traded corporations, all in the name of increasing their power, influence, and money. Many people have written me saying they can feel my passion, yet wonder if my anger and lashing out is something that I actually enjoy doing! Folks, I want you to know that I am passionate about this subject. I am outraged and saddened when I see millions of people suffer and die needlessly all because federal agencies and governments around the world, and multinational corporations, repeatedly lie and deceive the public just so they can make more money and increase their power and influence.

Remember, I didn't have to write this book; I don't have to do the work that I'm doing. I know this information. I enjoy incredible vibrant health. I am doing this because I believe it is a calling. I am doing what I'm doing because I believe it's my mission to help educate people and make society a better place. I am not doing this for the money. The money generated from my ventures now virtually all gets put right back into the venture and the enterprises to increase the number of people that are positively impacted. I am not doing this to increase personal wealth. I want you to know that I truly do care about you and your health. Think about it. The constant attacks that I face because I am in the forefront blowing the whistle on the injustices, frauds, lies, and deceptions are constant and never-ending. My mission is having a positive impact on millions of people's lives, but also having a negative impact on the power, influence, and profits of the Goliaths around the world. I am in their sights for attack; I am the target. Believe me, it would be a lot easier for me if I didn't care so much about you!

I have been offered tens of millions of dollars to stop saying what I am saying. One particular organization offered me $100 million in cash if I were to stop everything I am doing and just live a quiet life, cease my consumer advocacy work, and stop blowing the whistle on the insider information that I know. I have been assured by prominent and powerful people, who will remain nameless, that if I continue my mission I will be repeatedly sued, attacked, debunked, ridiculed, and persecuted in the media, the press, and the courts. I have been threatened in every way you can imagine. All of these things simply firm up my resolve even further.

In the words of the great American patriot Patrick Henry, "Millions for defense, not a penny in tribute." I refuse to be bribed; I refuse to be bought; I refuse to cave in to the pressure; I refuse to live my life operating out of fear. I know the work I'm doing is having a huge positive impact. Every week I get thousands of pieces of correspondence from people telling me how they are off drugs and cured of their illness, symptoms, and disease. When I listen to the people tell me how their lives have changed and their lives are better, how they are saving money, and how the pain in their body is gone, I know that what I am doing is right.

Every time I speak or present information I close my eyes and make a wish. I simply ask, please let just one person be positively impacted by this information, and then I know it's all worth it. I hope you are that person. I hope this book has made the difference in your life. I hope that you start an exciting and beautiful journey. I hope that your family is happier, healthier, and wealthier because you apply the knowledge that you have from this book. We have heard the phrase "knowledge is power." It's really only half true. Knowledge is power only if you use it. The knowledge that you have and the knowledge that you will continue to gain will only benefit you and your family when you use and apply the information presented. The wonderful author Leo Buscaglia once said, "To know and not to do is not to know." Apply these techniques in your life and, as I mentioned in the beginning of the book, I know, I know, I know…that you will never be the same!

> Humbly, yours in health
> Kevin Trudeau

To contact the Federal Trade Commission (FTC):
Federal Trade Commission
600 Pennsylvania Avenue, N.W.
Washington, D.C. 20580
(202) 326-2618
Fax: (202) 326-2034

To contact the Federal Drug Administration (FDA):
U.S. Food and Drug Administration
5600 Fishers Lane
Rockville MD 20857-0001
(888) 463-6332
Fax: (301) 443-6591

To contact your congressman or senator:
Look in your local phone book—or go to one of these Web sites for
address, phone, and e-mail listings.
www.congress.org
www.visi.com/juan/congress/

To contact the President of the United States:
The White House
1600 Pennsylvania Avenue NW
Washington, DC 20500
Comments: (202) 456-1111
Switchboard: (202) 456-1414
E-mail: president@whitehouse.gov
www.whitehouse.gov

A P P E N D I X   A

Free Bonus Material: Newsletter Articles

Every month there are thousands of discoveries relating to health, longevity, and the prevention and cure of disease through natural methods. Every month there are thousands of new bits of information that come out showing how drugs and surgery are ineffective and cause disease, and how various types of natural remedies are effective at preventing and curing disease with absolutely no side effects. Every month thousands of new discoveries are made showing how genetically altered food, irradiating of food, microwaving of food, and the chemicals being put in food are causing disease and making you sick. Every month there are thousands of new discoveries showing how our food supply is becoming more and more nutrient deficient, causing massive nutritional deficiencies in our body, which are causing illness and disease. Every month thousands of new discoveries are being made showing how electromagnetic chaos from wireless devices, cell phones, TVs, laptop computers, and electric appliances are in fact causing illness and disease. Every month there are thousands of new discoveries showing that stress causes disease and the mind itself can actually change the DNA structure in the body and heal disease.

This is why I have put together a monthly newsletter called *Kevin Trudeau's Natural Cures Monthly Newsletter*. This newsletter is mailed to you, the subscriber, each month and consists of approximately ten pages of pure, unbiased information. My newsletter has absolutely no advertising. I do not sell or promote any products in my newsletter. I am not compensated in any way on any product that I recommend or encourage you to use. My health newsletter is the only newsletter in the world that I know of where you can get unbiased, unfiltered, honest information regarding health and nutrition without any financial conflicts of interest. Every other health newsletter or magazine or publication accepts advertising and/or sells supplements; therefore, you can never know if the information you are getting is pure and unbiased. Because of this I charge a small monthly subscription fee. My newsletter is also available for members of my Web site community. If you join naturalcures.com, you have access to the newsletter online, and it is not mailed to you. For those who do not use the Internet or who like newsletters in the mail, subscriptions are available where the newsletter is mailed to you.

When I first wrote this book, I started getting feedback from people who read it. There were many common questions that came up in many areas that I found that I needed to amplify and explain further. Since I wrote this book, there have been new discoveries and new breakthroughs that I wanted to share with my newsletter subscribers and Web site members. This chapter contains several articles from some recent newsletter that I wrote since the original publishing of this book. It is absolutely imperative for you to get the full understanding of this book, that you read each of these newsletter articles as they were written directly to people who had bought the book and addressed specific questions that needed clarification. So enjoy these articles, and I think you will find them to be very helpful in clarifying the book's basic premises, as well as giving you additional breakthrough health that was not available in the original publishing of the book.

Never Have a Heart Attack!
Never Have Clogged Arteries!

Heart disease is one of the top killers in the nation. Every single person reading this either has had heart disease or knows someone who is about to have heart disease. The scariest thing I can tell you is that virtually every single person reading this is at some stage in the development of major heart problems. When you are born, your arteries are open and the blood flows freely. As time goes on, plaque begins to build up on the artery walls making the openings smaller causing the blood flow to be restricted. When the arteries get so clogged, and blood flow is almost totally restricted, people experience chest pains, shortness of breath, fatigue, tiredness, poor circulation, cold feet and hands, diabetes, memory loss, mood swings, weight gain, depression, erectile dysfunction, loss of sexual desire, loss of motivation, and potential heart attack. Bill Clinton recently had quadruple bypass surgery for blocked arteries. Anyone who has bypass surgery is a victim of the food industry and lack of knowledge. Let me explain. Clogged arteries do not happen overnight. It takes years to develop clogged arteries to the point where you need bypass surgery or you have a heart attack. No one should ever develop clogged arteries to the point where surgery is used or a heart attack develops.

You have to understand, as I have said in my book, that it is always all about the money. The medical industry wants you to be sick. That's how they make their profits. If everyone were healthy, the drug companies and the entire health-care industry would be out of business. The reason your arteries get clogged is simple. In your blood, you have cholesterol. The cholesterol will only attach itself to the artery wall when the artery is scarred or damaged. One of the biggest scams perpetrated on the American public is making you fearful of high cholesterol. I will explain this later, but consider that the number-one selling drug in the world is Lipitor, a cholesterol-reducing drug. The amount of cholesterol has nothing to do with your chances of getting hearth disease, clogged arteries, or a heart attack. The cholesterol in your blood is harmless and actually healthy for you. The only time that cholesterol will attach itself to the artery wall is when the artery is damaged. The question then is what causes the artery to be damaged. The three main culprits are:

1. **Chlorine in the water.** When you drink water, take a shower, or go swimming in chlorinated water you are severely damaging your arteries.

2. **Hydrogenated oils and trans fats.** These are manmade products. Most margarines, for example, are 100 percent hydrogenated oil. Virtually everything you buy in the supermarket has hydrogenated oil in it. These trans fats are deadly to your health. They severely scar and damage your arteries. Even the FDA is finally admitting the dangers of trans fats.

3. **Homogenized dairy products.** The homogenization process, which was developed to increase profits for grocers, makes dairy products a deadly poison. The homogenization process makes the molecules in dairy products so small that they severely scar the arteries. It is not the fat in dairy products, it is the homogenization that's the problem. People are always coming up to me and saying, "Well, I drink low-fat milk or skim milk. Isn't that better than whole milk?" The answer is no. It's not better; it's worse. It's a manmade product. Remember, science is not better than nature. Whole milk is better than low-fat and skim milk, provided that it is not homogenized.

These are the three main things that cause the arteries to get scarred. Even if you have incredibly low amounts of cholesterol, the cholesterol will attach itself to the artery wall, causing blockages and all the problems associated with it as I mentioned above. The most important point I want to make here is that you should never have blocked arteries and never need bypass surgery. Why? Because it takes ten, to twenty, to thirty years to get your arteries clogged. It happens slowly over time. What is amazing to me is that the medical community refuses to mention to patients that there are simple painless tests that can be done to anyone at any time, inexpensively, to determine if your arteries are fully open or are beginning to be clogged. I recommend that every person, every year or two, get this simple inexpensive test done. There are several types of tests available and new tests are being developed all the time. These tests show the blood flow throughout your entire body, in all your veins and your arteries. If you take this test every year or two you can see what the current state of your arteries are, whether they are open of clogged, and you can see the trend. You will see specifically if over time your arteries are slowly beginning to get clogged. This way you will know fifteen years in advance whether you are on the path of blocked arteries.

If you are, you can take some simple steps to reverse the condition. The natural cure for this condition is chelation. There are two main types of chelation: oral chelation and intravenous chelation. There are many companies that sell products that are oral-chelating agents. They are all-natural, safe, and inexpensive. You simply take these tablets and they slowly begin to reopen your arteries and increase circulation. If your condition is very severe, intravenous chelation can be used as well. This way, you can virtually guarantee that you will never have clogged arteries, or any of the conditions that go along with it, and you will never need bypass surgery. Go to the Internet, type in "chelation" and you will see a whole host of products that are available. Go to Amazon.com and type in "chelation," or go to your local book store, or health food store, and ask about books and chelation products. This is urgent. Every single one of you should call your health-care practitioner and tell them you want to be tested to see how open your arteries are. I can guarantee that once you get tested you will be surprised at how clogged your arteries are, and once you open them using a chelation natural therapy, you won't believe how many symptoms that you have right now that will simply vanish. Most notably, your energy levels will skyrocket and most of you will lose weight. Go to: www.centurywellness.com

Weight Loss Tip

Walk and lose weight. Walking is by far the best exercise for weight loss. It is also the best exercise you can do for your health. The body is designed to walk. Formalized exercise is not done throughout the world. The majority of people who live to be over 100 years old and have virtually no disease do not do formal exercise. However, they do walk. People throughout the world walk an average of ten miles a day where people from America walk less than a quarter of a mile a day. If you want to lose weight, walk. The ideal way to walk to lose weight is by walking for one hour non-stop every day. This is not running, it's not jogging, it's walking. You should be walking at a pace that you feel comfortable with. Some of you will start out very, very slow. Some of you will not even be able to walk for a full hour without getting too tired and winded. Start with fifteen minutes and increase to twenty-five minutes, increase that to forty-five minutes, increase it to an hour. It may take you a month before you get to a full hour. It's sad because people all over the world can walk for hours and hours and hours. People in America can't walk for an hour without getting tired or waking up the next day with sore ankles, knees, hips and legs. That means you are in desperate need of walking. If you walk for a full hour and then wake up with any stiffness, pain, or discomfort, you are in serious trouble. You are destined for illness and disease. You are not moving the toxins out of your body, you are not oxygenating your body, your muscles, tendons, joints, and ligaments are all beginning to deteriorate and you are headed for a health disaster. You absolutely have to be walking: Walking will reverse your condition and cure you of many ailments.

The main thing that walking does for weight loss is that it seems to reset your body's "set point." Your body has a point that it sets regulating your weight. If you go above this weight, it will regulate it back to the set-point weight; if you go below this weight it will regulate it back up to the set-point weight. Your body's set point will determine what your "weight" is. This is the reason why most people have a certain weight that they stay at. Even if they lose weight, they always bounce back to that weight, or if they gain weight for a while because of an eating binge, when they start eating normally they kind of revert back to that set-point weight. By walking for one hour every day for thirty days your body will tend to reset its set point. If you do this every single day, you will start losing weight automatically and effortlessly. Plus, you will feel better, have more energy, sleep better, be less depressed and be happier. When you walk it is important not to walk on a treadmill, but walk outside. It is important not to stare at the ground while walking, but look around you. The process of looking far away at things has a profound effect on your mental state. You won't believe how much better you will feel and you won't believe how easy it is to lose weight without changing anything else.

From the Book—Rest, the Key to Rejuvenation

In my book, I talk about the importance of getting proper sleep and proper rest. It is absolutely vital to get the proper amount of sleep and have your body fully rested if you want to have optimal health, optimal energy levels, lose weight, and guarantee you can cure any disease and never get sick again. Your body needs time to rejuvenate and recharge. The optimal time to sleep is going to bed between 9:00 and 10:00 p.m. and arising at approximately 6:00 a.m. There are several reasons for this. The cycles of the earth's rotation around the sun and the moon around the earth cause the body to rest better during these hours than at any other time. This is why people who work night shifts have been shown to be more depressed, more overweight, more tired, more fatigued, and have more illness and disease than other people. It is also known that people who do not sleep a full eight hours every night are not as happy and also get sick more often. The body secretes healing hormones during the times between 10:00 p.m. and 2:00 a.m. If you are a person who goes to sleep very, very late, you are not giving your body the proper amount of hours it needs to secrete the hormones that will rejuvenate, recharge and refresh your body. The three basic important factors of rest and sleep are:

1. When you go to bed, and the times in which you are actually resting. If you go to bed late and sleep late, even though you are getting a full eight hours, you are not doing your body good because those healing hormones can only be released between 10:00 p.m. and 2:00 a.m. It is absolutely vital that you are sleeping during those times as most often as possible. So, the time in which you are getting rest is important.

    During the evening hours the majority of people are sleeping or resting. The amount of energetic buzz that people transmit by working and operating their daily lives during the day is high, at night it is much lower. This allows the body to recharge and rejuvenate much better. Many people who are used to staying up very late, or sleeping until 8:00, 9:00, or 10:00 in the morning, have interesting observations when they start going to bed between 9:00 and 10:00 p.m. and arising at 6:00 a.m. Some people notice, even from the very first night, that they have 100 times more energy, they feel better, they laugh more, their appetites are radically different, they eat less, and they are happier. Other people are so fatigued and tired for the first two or three days after starting this new sleep pattern they can't believe how tired they are. The reason for this phenomena is that the body finally has a chance to recharge and rejuvenate, and is taking this opportunity to reset the body. It may take three to four days for the body to adjust, it may take even a week, but once the body readjusts and realigns you won't believe how much more energy you have, you will be able to jump out of bed without an alarm clock, and you'll have more energy throughout the day. You will have less sickness and disease and, if you are currently sick or have any type of disease or symptoms, many people will notice that they start going away and the body is healing itself and curing itself from the illness and disease that you have because you are giving the body a chance to do the healing work it needs during the only times that it can really do the healing, which is between 10:00 p.m. and 2:00 a.m.

2. The second most important thing is the number of hours a person should sleep. Eight hours is the optimal amount of time a person should sleep. I cannot emphasize enough the fact of how important rest and rejuvenation is to your health. People come up to me all the time and say, "I have this disease, I have that disease what do I do? Kevin, I have diabetes. Kevin, I have a friend who has cancer. Kevin, I have a friend who has shingles. Kevin, I have psoriasis. Kevin, I have arthritis. Kevin, I have herpes. What do I do? What's the cure?" I always ask a few basic questions, "When do you go to sleep? Give me your eating patterns. What type of water do you drink? Are you taking nutritional supplements? Are you taking any nonprescription or prescription drugs?" People don't want to talk about these things. They don't want to change anything. They just want to know the "cure." "What pill can I take? What herb can I take? What can I do to cure my problem?" The answer is you are causing your problem. You can't continue to do everything you

are doing exactly the same way and expect a different result. The Chinese definition of insanity is to continue to do the same thing and expect a different result. If you are sick, if you have illness or disease, you have to look at everything you are doing. What are you putting in your body? How are you resting? How are you thinking? How are you moving your body? Are you walking? Are you taking nutritional supplements? These are the things that are causing your symptoms, and causing your illness, and causing your disease. There is no magic panacea or cure. Yes, there are some natural things you can do to reduce the symptoms, suppress the symptoms, or eliminate the symptoms on the short term. But if you are not addressing the true cause, these symptoms will come back or manifest themselves in some other way. You will continue to feel bad, you will continue to have low energies, you will continue to be fat and overweight, you will continue to be depressed, you will continue to have medical problems, you will continue to get sick, you will continue to be tired and fatigued. You have to make some changes. One of the simplest things people can do to boost their immune system and allow the body to heal itself is getting proper rest. Eight full hours of sleep every night is ideal, and going to bed between 9:00 and 10:00 p.m. and arising at 6:00 a.m. is the ideal scene.

3. The next question that comes up is what do I sleep on? There are two considerations here about sleeping that I want to address. The first is the type of mattress and sheets that you are using, and the second is the quality of the air that is in the room.

First, let's talk about the mattress. You spend a third of your life sleeping, but people won't invest any money and won't invest in any time in obtaining the appropriate and best sleeping system. This to me is just not a smart choice. There was an old commercial for Fram oil filters, and the commercial said, "You can pay me now, or you can pay me later." Your body is the same way. You can pay now by investing in things for your health, like a good mattress and sleeping system, good quality air and water filters, good food, good nutritional supplements, and educating yourself with knowledge, or you can pay later with cancer, heart disease, diabetes, arthritis, major surgeries, sickness, illness, disease, depression, stress, pain, and misery. Folks, think about it. You can pay now—a small amount of time and effort, or you can pay later with a life of misery and pain and an early death. Invest in educating yourself, and invest in things for your health.

What is the best mattress to sleep on? The answer is it's a personal choice. There are three outstanding mattresses that I do recommend. For years I have slept on a 100-percent natural, all-organic mattress made with all organic materials. This was very good because the materials did not emit any poisonous fumes that I would be inhaling for the entire night. Then, I invested in a $20,000 mattress. It is made with the finest cashmeres, the finest quality silks, and it is the mattress that the Queen of England sleeps on. It is an incredibly comfortable bed with mostly natural organic materials, but it is outrageously expensive. I then decided to test some other mattresses that most people could afford so I could make a recommendation. I tested the three most heavily advertised mattresses on TV. All of these mattresses are outstanding and, in my opinion, will give you a better, more restful night's sleep than other kinds of mattresses. However, everyone is different and every body is different; therefore, you should test these mattresses out yourself. The good news is these companies will send you the mattress for a free-trial period. One, for example, has a three- to six-month free trial. I highly recommend that you call these companies, get the mattress sent to you for the free trial and try each one. After the free trial is over, send it back and then try the next one. You will virtually be sleeping on the finest mattresses made for free for six months to a year before you can make your purchasing decision. You then will have tested the various mattresses to see which one you like the best.

The sheets that you use are vitally important to a proper night's rest. The material should be 100-percent organic and all-natural cotton. Other materials will emit a negative energy and a negative fume, which, although subtle, does have a slightly negative affect on your sleep. The sheets must be washed in organic all-natural soap. Do not buy laundry detergent from a large publicly traded company. They are filled with chemicals and synthetic fragrances that you will be inhaling all night causing you sleep problems. This little thing can make a huge difference. I have met people who tell me they have a hard time sleeping. I walk into their house, go into their bedroom, and just smell the sheets. It is so obvious to me, based on the fragrance that I can smell, why they are not sleeping well. I immediately changed their sheets, grabbed some organic cotton sheets that have been washed in nothing but pure organic soap with no fragrance added, no chemical softeners used, and throw them on the bed. I then tell the person, "Sleep on this sheet tonight and let me know if there is any change." Invariably, virtually 100 percent of the time, people tell me, "I can't believe it. I slept better." I'm thinking to myself, "No kidding. You were inhaling poisonous fumes all night before. No wonder you weren't sleeping well."

The air that is in your bedroom is vitally important to a good night's sleep. Today's homes are not built like they were seventy-five years ago. Before air conditioning, homes were built with natural materials, not synthetic manmade materials. Homes were designed for the windows to be opened so that air could flow easily throughout the house. Today's homes are different. We generally sleep with all the windows closed and air conditioning or heating systems in operation. The air quality in our homes is absolutely horrible and worse than ever before. Combine that with the fumes that are emanating from the synthetic materials used in the carpeting, the walls, and all the glues used in today's homes we can see that our air quality is terrible. This adversely affects our sleep and adversely affects the healing process. It suppresses our immune system and makes us more susceptible to illness and disease, and can cause everything from allergies to depression to cancer. Combine that with the fact that our houses are wired with so much electricity that we are being bombarded the entire evening with energetic frequencies that are disturbing our sleep, making ourselves go crazy, suppressing our immune system, and making us much more susceptible to illness and disease. Our sleeping environments today are not conducive to allowing the body to recharge, and rejuvenate, and regenerate, and heal. Our sleeping environments today do the exact opposite.

While they are sleeping, most people never get into a deep sleep where healing can occur. Most people don't sleep during the times when the healing hormones are released. Most people do not get the proper amount of sleep, so the body doesn't have time to recharge. Most people are in an environment where their bed itself is causing them pain, discomfort, and pressure hindering circulation, hindering healing. The air quality is hindering deep sleep, causing allergies, filling us with more toxins and poisons, suppressing our immune system, and the energetic fields around us are making our cells vibrate totally out of balance, leading us to all types of illness, disease, and even cancer.

The solution is two-fold. Number one, an electronic chaos eliminator of some sort should be in your room. There are several types of products available. These units seem to neutralize all the electronic chaos in the room, giving you an environment that is much more conducive to sleep. This is significant. Have you ever noticed, if you went on a camping trip and slept in the woods, where there is no wiring around your tent or cabin, how incredibly deep you sleep, how much rest you get, and how much calmer you feel? This is important for health.

The second thing that is vital in your sleeping environment is some type of an air-purification system. There are several. In my home, my air conditioning and heating unit has electrostatic and hepa filters built in. They are very expensive and need constant maintenance. Additionally, an ozone generator is very helpful. Basic air purifiers or hepa filters are excellent, but can be very loud. There are several brands on the market that make good air filters, but the problem is the noise is not conducive for good sleep. Also, photo catalysis units are silent and do a great job of cleaning the air. In my bedroom, in addition to the hepa filters and electrostatic filters in my entire heating and air-conditioning system, I have two ionic type air filters, plus a photo catalysis unit that I have on during sleep. I also use an air purifier with ozone that I turn on when I'm not sleeping to cleanse and purify the air, and the ozone also permeates the fabrics to make sure I'm not inhaling any poisonous or disruptive fumes while I am sleeping. People tell me that when they start using air purification systems that they breathe better, they sleep better, they have more energy when they wake up, congestion is diminished, and allergies are reduced.

A proper mattress, proper sheets, proper soap used to clean the sheets, an electronic chaos eliminator, and air filtration will not cure any disease, but what they do is provide a better environment for you to get deep sleep so that your body can recharge, ejuvenate, and heal itself. Invest in these things today or you will be laying in an operating room staring at men and women with masks who have knives ready to cut you open to save your life because of the way you have treated your body. Be good to your body and you can eliminate and prevent virtually every illness and disease.

Recommended Product
Vitamin E

Years ago, Vitamin E was a very popular food supplement. Today, the interest in Vitamin E has waned due to much more exotic herbs, minerals, natural formulas, and other breakthrough food supplements. However, Vitamin E is incredibly valuable for health. The fact is every one of you is deficient in nutrients. You are all deficient in vitamins and minerals. You are all deficient in enzymes. All of you are not getting the proper amounts of nutrients that you need for optimal body functions and optimal health. It is impossible to get all the nutrition you need from just eating food. The food supply has been so depleted that you simply can't get the nutrients you need from just eating food. Combined with the fact that many things that you are consuming are actually reducing your ability to assimilate and absorb the nutrients anyway, makes you doubly assured you are deficient in important nutrients for health, well-being, and proper body function. One of the most notable nutrients that people are deficient in is Vitamin E. When people start taking Vitamin E supplements, reports of incredible heath benefits abound.

There are many types of Vitamin E, and many brands. As always, I strongly recommend against taking any synthetic form of Vitamin E or buying any food supplement from a large publicly traded corporation. You can be assured that large publicly traded corporations have only one goal, and that is to make money. They will cut corners at every chance and generally spend more money on marketing and advertising their product than on the development and production of the best product available. Go to your local independent health food store and inquire, or go on the Internet and inquire about the various types of Vitamin E. Remember, stay away from publicly traded chain "health food stores" like GNC. Always remember the money motive. Ideally, as I mentioned in my book, it is always best to take a concentrated whole food supplement, which contains all the vitamins, minerals, enzymes, and cofactors in the exact proportion that nature intended. Most people notice when they start taking nutrients that they are deficient in, they feel better, have more energy, have fewer symptoms, less aches and pains, sleep better, get colds and the flu less often, are less depressed, feel less stressed, and in many cases lose weight. Nutritional deficiencies are one of the main causes of all disease. Vitamin E specifically increases blood flow, circulation improves, and it helps oxygen get throughout the entire body.

Products to Stay Away From
Fluoride

Toothpaste with fluoride is deadly. I categorically, 100 percent recommend that no one should be using toothpaste with fluoride in it. As always, I recommend that you stay away from any product manufactured by a large publicly traded corporation. Publicly traded corporations have only one goal, and that is to make money. They will cut corners at every chance and spend the majority of their money on marketing and packaging, not on the quality of the product. They will do everything they can to produce that product at the lowest possible cost, thus ensuring that the natural state and quality is adversely affected. Therefore, it is imperative that you stay away from toothpastes sold by large publicly traded companies, and stay away from any toothpaste that has fluoride in it.

Fluoride is a dangerous, poisonous chemical. It is so deadly that even the smallest amount, if consumed, can kill you. It causes all types of physiological problems; the most notable is fluoride reduces the ability of the thyroid gland to operate correctly creating a condition known as a hypoactive thyroid, or an under active thyroid. When your thyroid is not acting properly, your metabolism is very slow, causing you to gain weight. Fluoride in toothpaste and fluoride in the water is one of the major reasons why we have such obesity levels in America today. In communities that have the highest amounts of fluoride in their water supply, there are also the highest amounts of obesity and a host of other diseases. The link is indisputable. You should brush your teeth at least twice a day the first thing in the morning and before you go to bed, and ideally, you should brush your teeth after every meal. Keep in mind, however, that animals in the wild do not brush their teeth. Animals in the wild are eating raw, very hard crunchy material, thus cleaning their teeth on a regular basis. Animals in the wild also do not consume the manmade processed food that cause tooth decay and gum disease.

If you want a beautiful healthy smile, brush your teeth but use a toothpaste that is 100 percent all-natural and has ingredients that you can pronounce. I vary my toothpaste from time-to-time. When I finish one tube I go to the health food store, see what is available, and I read the ingredient list. If there are only two or three ingredients that I can read and pronounce and the company is a small independently owned business, I try that product. You should do the same. Even a small amount of poisons in your mouth will get into your entire system.

Repeatedly using fluoride toothpaste, or toothpaste produced by large publicly traded corporations, suppress your immune system, make you depressed, and can even make you fat.

Book Review

The 7-Day Detox Miracle

People always ask me, "Kevin, what is the best way to do a cleanse?" The answer is: there is no best way. There are many, many ways and all of them are very, very good. All of them seem to do similar things, yet different things. This book, *The 7-Day Detox Miracle: How to Revitalize Your Mind and Body with This Safe and Effective Life-Enhancing Program* has a very powerful, simple seven-day home detox program that you can do. This system can allow you to free yourself from chronic aches and pains, allow you to feel healthier, and be more energetic. The process is really called detoxification, and it stimulates your body's natural ability to cleanse itself. Remember, the major reason you are sick is because your body has too many toxins in it. You must get the toxins out. People are always coming up to me saying, "How do I cure herpes? How do I cure my diabetes? How do I cure my arthritis? What's the cure?" The answer is, in most cases, there isn't a "cure." The reason you are sick is because (1) you have too many toxins in your body; (2) you are deficient in the nutrients your body needs for optimal health; and (3) the electronic chaos and energy frequencies that are bombarding us are making you sick. Those are the three major reasons that we are all ill. You will never get well, you will never cure your disease, you will never live at optimal levels unless you get the toxins out. You are all super toxic. Getting the toxins out will improve resistance to disease, normalize your weight, and increase physical and mental stamina. It's similar to an oil change in your car. You need to clean out the sludge so your body can operate more effectively. There are many ways to cleanse, from doing colonics, fasting, raw food, sweating, etc. There are many products you can buy that will help you cleanse such as herbs, benkonite clay, fiber like psyllium seeds or psyllium husks, and wheatgrass juice. All are very good. The thing I like about this book is the program is simple, can be done at home, and only takes seven days.

Question of the Month

Q: I have herpes. How do I cure it?

A: The medical community states that there is no cure for herpes. For years the medical community has repeatedly made statements of facts, when in reality it is nothing more than their opinions. Keep in mind the amount of money made by making people believe that you cannot "cure" herpes. The amount of drugs sold in the treatment of herpes is astronomical. The profits made are astronomical. If you have genital herpes, or if you have cold sores on a regular or recurring basis, you have a herpetic virus in your system. That's what everyone seems to think is true. Most people think that once you have the herpetic virus, it will stay with you forever and there is no way you can "cure" it. The answer is no one really knows whether the virus leaves or stays in your system. No one can really see the virus. Medical science can only see the antibodies your body develops if you have allegedly been infected with the virus. Keep in mind that this is all medical theory, and none of this is "known facts." The only thing I'm concerned with is if you have breakouts, your ideal scenario is that you never have another breakout ever again. Well, if you never had a breakout ever again, I would call that a cure. I don't know if the medical community would call it a cure, but I would. So the real question is not "How do I 'cure' my herpes?" The real question is, "I have breakouts," whether they are genital or cold sore-type breakouts, "what can I do so that I don't have any more breakouts?" That is the real question. Well, I'm not sure if this treatment that I'm about to give you will allow you to never have another breakout but, from everyone I've ever talked to, most people never have another breakout and for those who do it's so rare and so short-lived that it doesn't really matter.

1. You have to cleanse and detoxify your body. The reason you have breakouts is because your immune system is suppressed and allows the virus to activate. If your immune system is low, the virus will activate. You have to do a cleanse, a colon cleanse, a Candida cleanse, a liver and gallbladder cleanse. You must do these cleanses because without the cleanses your body's immune system will always be weak and you will always be susceptible to disease.

2. You need proper nutrients. Your body is deficient in nutrients, making it incapable of fighting off the viruses and preventing the

breakouts. You need to supplement your diet with proper food supplements whole food supplements. You need to get nutrition. Ideally, juicing or taking whole-food supplements. Eating more raw fruits and vegetables are key.

3. You need to handle the energetic frequency of the imbalance. If you go to a homeopathic doctor, homeopathy deals with frequencies. If you go to the EMC², which is talked about in the book *Sanctuary,* and sign up for the AIM program like I am on, you will have your energetic frequencies balanced twenty-four hours a day, seven days a week. I highly recommend and endorse that. Go to: www.energeticmatrix.com/

4. Lysine. Lysine is an amino acid that will suppress the ability for breakouts to develop. If you eat food with lots of arginine, such as peanuts and tomatoes, you have a tendency to increase breakouts. So the best way to prevent breakouts is to take lysine daily. Go to your health food store and inquire.

5. Red Marine Algae. This appears to kill and wipe out the herpes virus. You can go to a health food store there are several brands available. The ideal scene is when you begin to feel the next breakout coming on, take the red marine algae and take it nonstop for sixty days. Just by doing that there is an excellent chance you will never have another breakout again. If you do, the moment you feel the breakout, start taking the red marine algae. You will notice the breakouts are much, much less severe and don't last as long. Continue that procedure until you never have another breakout again.

6. There is a product in health food stores called DMSO. When applied it kills the herpes virus. Also, drink liquid oxygen available in health food stores, as the virus cannot live in an oxygen rich environment.

7. Larrea. This plant is anti-viral and can kill the herpes virus in 30 days.

If you do the things I recommend, I believe that (1) your breakouts will be less frequent and less severe, and (2) there is an excellent chance you will never have another breakout again. As always, I am not a doctor. I am not giving medical advice. I am giving my opinions for educational and informational purposes only. It is vital if you are concerned about your health that you seek out proper health-care professionals in your area and get their opinions and have somebody treat you directly. Ideally, for herpes you can go to a proper herbologist or homeopathic doctor, which are probably the two best choices.

Cancer Prevented and Cured!

You have a higher chance of getting cancer today than you did in 1950. You have a higher chance of dying of cancer today than in 1950! The war on cancer has been a miserable failure. Drugs and surgery have failed. What causes cancer? How do you prevent cancer? How do you cure cancer? These are the big questions. No one knows for sure what the answers are; however, we do know some general things that cause cancer. We do know some general things that can prevent cancer. We do know some general things that can cure cancer. There is so much on this subject that a short article cannot possibly give you all the information. Over the next few months, I will be putting volumes of information on my Web site www.naturalcures.com regarding the causes of cancer, ways to prevent cancer, and what I believe are ways to cure cancer.

In this article, I want to talk about one specific potential cause of cancer. If we know what the cause is and eliminate it, you can prevent cancer and potentially reverse cancer if it has not gone past the point of no return. What I am about to say is my opinion and many people wholeheartedly disagree. I believe one of the major causes of cancer, as well as one of the major causes of multiple sclerosis, muscular dystrophy, attention deficit disorder, fibromyalgia, arthritis, lupus, and virtually all diseases, is eating food that has been in a microwave oven. You are reading this right. Let's consider that microwave ovens were invented by the Nazis. The Soviets took over the research that was started in Berlin, and looked very intently at how eating microwaved food affected the body. They found so many physical ailments that seemed to be caused directly from eating microwaved food that the Kremlin banned these machines for use.

Authors Anthony Wayne and Lawrence Newell state in their article, "The Hidden Hazards of Microwave Cooking," that the Russian researchers found microwaved food had a decreased nutritional value and a significant diminishing of their "vital energy fields" of up to 90 percent! Foods with little nutritional value and no "vital energy" have a major negative effect on the body. Food that is in a microwave, even for just a few seconds, has the B-Complex, C, and E vitamins virtually destroyed. The essential trace minerals are rendered useless. These vital nutrients are important for stress reduction and the prevention of cancer and heart disease. Eating microwaved food also causes lymphatic disorders. This is incredibly significant. When lymphatic disorders exist, certain cancers form at a significantly increased rate.

The Russians reported stomach and intestinal cancers, as well as digestive disorders were all significantly increased in people who ate microwaved food. Cell tumors were also significantly higher. Eating microwaved food has also been shown to increase high blood pressure and cause symptoms such as migraines, dizziness, stomach pain, stress, and anxiety. Other observed and reported problems included hair loss, appendicitis, cataracts, infertility problems, abnormal hormone levels, adrenal exhaustion, heart disease, memory loss, and attention disorders. Also, crankiness, depression, and poor sleep.

The Russian researchers stressed that eating microwaved food can be fatal. The energy produced in a microwave oven makes the food a poison. Consider, however, that this energy is all around us. Similar energy is in your cell phone, and the new long-range cordless phones radiating at a 2.45 gigahertz frequency is the same as your microwave oven. This microwave energy comes from computers, televisions, wireless devices, satellite transmissions, etc. This is why you **NEED** an electronic chaos eliminator.

Eating the molecularly altered microwaved food alters your blood chemistry as well. Consider this: Researchers have shown that if you eat organic vegetables that have been cooked in the microwave, your cholesterol rapidly rises. Swiss scientists have discovered that blood cholesterol is less influenced by how much cholesterol is in the food we eat, and more influenced by the molecular structure of the food itself. Any food that comes out of a microwave oven will send your cholesterol soaring. A noted researcher has stated that the effects of microwaved food can be long-term, permanent, and fatal to the human body. The minerals, vitamins, and nutrients of all microwaved food is reduced or dramatically altered. The human body gets little or no benefit from the needed nutrients, and the human body absorbs these altered, newly formed compounds that cannot be broken down and these compounds have a dramatic adverse affect on the entire physiology. This leads to cancer, heart disease, diabetes, MS, muscular dystrophy, lupus, and virtually every degenerative disease.

Dr. Mercola agrees. "Recent research shows that any food that comes out of a microwave oven suffers severe molecular damage. When eaten it causes abnormal changes in human blood and immune systems." Not surprisingly, the public has been denied details on these significant health dangers.

Don't believe me yet? Well, do this experiment at home. Plant seeds into pots. Water one pot with water that has been "nuked" in your microwave, and the other with normal filtered water and watch what happens. Surprise, surprise, surprise. The seeds soaking up the micro-waved water will never sprout. Does this scare you? It should. Throw out your microwave oven. More importantly, share your experiences for a possible class action suit against the manufacturers of microwave ovens. I believe they know of the dangers and have been hiding this information and lying about it for years all in the name of profit.

Make sure when you go to restaurants you ask them if they micro-wave the food. You will be surprised that almost all restaurant food is microwaved. Make sure they do not microwave any of your food, including sauces and gravies. This is very, very common. If you have cancer, did eating microwaved food cause it? Well, it certainly appears that it definitely at least contributed to your cancer. If you stopped eating any food that comes out of a microwave oven will you be pre-venting yourself from ever getting cancer? Well, you are at least taking one of the causes out of the equation, so you are at least dramatically reducing your risk of ever getting cancer. If you do have cancer and stopped eating microwaved food will your cancer go into remission? Well, it will certainly speed the process of your cancer going into remission. Keep in mind that eating microwaved food does not only cause cancer, but causes virtually every other condition and disease. Stop eating any food that comes out of a microwave oven.

If you feel like you have been misled by the manufacturers and are interested in joining a potential class action suit against the manufactur-ers, please write me or send me an e-mail so we can add your name to the list when, and if, a class-action suit is filed.

FTC Update

The Federal Trade Commission is out of control. Here is what they are currently saying: the FTC has said that I cannot mention a product by brand name in this newsletter. As a matter of fact, in any book I write I cannot mention a product by brand name. As a matter of fact, because of my TV infomercial, the FTC contends that anyone who would ask me any questions could be doing so in connection with that infomercial, therefore, they contend that I cannot mention a product by brand name in virtually any context. I am working hard to change this outrageous violation of my First Amendment rights. I believe this is a violation of the Civil Rights Act, and the individual people at the FTC who are involved should be held personally accountable under the law. The most outrageous new thing the FTC has done is this: I currently have over 300,000 bottles of coral calcium. The FTC has said I cannot sell this coral calcium. I then sent a letter to the FTC and asked them if I can give away the coral calcium. Can you believe that the FTC said absolutely not?! The FTC is forbidding me to give away, free of charge, this wonderful product called coral calcium. The FTC wants me to destroy the coral calcium. Can you believe how insane, insensitive, and outrageous this organization is? I am working through legal channels to try to correct this problem.

Many of you have asked me for the individual people's names at the FTC, their e-mail addresses, and phone numbers so that you can call and complain about their suppressive behavior. My attorneys advise me that at this point I should not give you the agents' individual names. However, I encourage you to write to your U.S. Representatives and Senators, and to the head of the FTC, letting them know that you are unhappy with the way this agency is acting against me and other people whose voices they are trying to suppress.

Here is another outrage. I have submitted my newsletter, where I talked about certain products by brand name, to the FTC. The FTC stated that I am not allowed to publish my newsletter and sell it if it contains products by brand name. However, in a recent letter from the Federal Trade Commission, they said I could sell and advertise a book called "The Supplement Shopper" because "The entity that publishes the book is providing objective information; the authors appear to have a basis for their knowledge in this area; the book conveys the information in an objective manner. The fact that we are not objecting to this book should in no way be interpreted to mean that the Commission would not object to other books that conveyed specific product information." Can you believe this? The Federal Trade Commission has now determined that they have the right to decide what books I can promote and sell. This is censorship in the highest form. The government is trying to say that they alone can determine what opinions can be published and sold. It sounds like Stalinist Russia or Nazi Germany. In my opinion, the Federal Trade Commission is acting like the Gestapo in suppressing the free flow of ideas and opinions. I intend to take legal action to correct this injustice, suppression of my civil liberties, and violation of the Civil Rights Act. This violation and stifling of my First Amendment right must be stopped.

Weight Loss Tip

If you want to lose weight, you have to increase your body's ability to burn fat and eliminate toxins. I can guarantee you that in your colon you have anywhere from three to fifteen pounds of undigested fecal matter. This toxic material makes it more difficult for you to absorb nutrients, it slows down your metabolism, it makes you susceptible to all types of allergies including food allergies, gives you constipation, gas, indigestion, and acid reflux, and is a breeding ground for Candida yeast. It is vital to clean your colon. There are many ways to clean your colon. If you go on the Internet and type in "colon cleanse," there are dozens of companies that sell herbal formulas or other type of ingestible-type products that are effective at helping clean your colon. One of the most effective and thorough ways to clean your colon is to purchase one of the herbal-type supplements that you take orally, while at the same time getting a series of colonics done by a certified colon therapist. Go to your Yellow Pages under colon therapy or colonics, and you will see a list of people that you can consult with who can give you a number of colonics. An effective way to do this is get one colonic every other day for thirty days. While you are doing the colonics, also be taking a colon cleanse product. It is also important to discuss with the colon therapist taking some type of friendly flora product, such as acidophilus, to replenish the flora as you are cleaning out the colon. If you do nothing else, but just do this one step for thirty days, I can almost guarantee you that you will lose a minimum of five pounds. I can tell you from personal experience that the majority of people who do this procedure lose, on average, ten pounds in thirty days. The most notable thing that occurs is the person's stomach flattens out, their energy level skyrockets, they think clearer, sleep better, and digest food much, much better. Colon health is important. A dirty, clogged colon—which I can guarantee that you have right now—can lead to colon cancer, liver disease, diabetes, and a host of other problems. Do this procedure and you will see spectacular results in a very short period of time.

Cure Anything Now

I get hundreds of e-mails every single day from people all around the world telling me their horrific health problems. No matter where I go in the world, people come up to me and tell me about their health problems. Everyone wants to know how they can cure themselves of the diseases, illnesses, and ailments that they have. For years and years and years, I would simply give people some specific recommendations of what they could do to alleviate the most problematic symptoms, and then tell them what they should do to get at the root causes of the problem so that it wouldn't reoccur and was cured on a permanent basis. It is very important for you to understand that there are two ways to handle your medical and health conditions. The first thing is to address the symptom. If you have pain, what can you do to alleviate the pain and make life more bearable? The second is, what is the cause of the pain and let's address that so that the pain doesn't come back? It is important that these things be addressed. It is more important to look for the cause than just address the symptoms.

I was recently doing a speaking tour. As I was sitting at the table signing books for the thousands of people that were in line, I would ask people how their health is. Virtually every single person in line had health problems. One particular group that I was addressing consisted of mostly people in their twenties. It was amazing to me that so many people at such a young age had so many health problems. I started asking people in line what prescription drugs they were currently taking. To my utter amazement, virtually every single person was taking at least one prescription drug. They majority were taking two or more. These are people in their twenties. The drug companies are doing an effective job getting more and more people to take drugs, and getting each person to take more and more drugs. This leads me to a very important point. If you are reading this and you subscribe to this newsletter, there is a good chance you have some medical issues. I can categorically, 100 percent guarantee that the majority of your medical conditions are caused by the nonprescription and prescription drugs you have taken over the years and are currently taking. Let me say that again. The health conditions that you have right now are caused by the nonprescription and prescription drugs you have taken over the years and are currently taking. The drug companies are killing you. The drug companies are making you sick. As I research more and more illnesses and keep asking the question, "What caused that? Then what caused that? Then what caused that?" Virtually all illnesses lead to nonprescription and prescription drugs at the end of the road. It is sickening to me that virtually all medical conditions are caused, in whole or in part, by nonprescription and prescription drugs. We are seeing it in the news right now. The drug company Merck manufactured a drug called Vioxx for arthritis pain. We are hearing the horrifying stories about how both Merck and the FDA knew five years ago that this drug caused heart attacks and strokes. We are shocked by the fact that both Merck and the FDA knew that if this drug was put on the market over 20,000 people would die from heart attacks and strokes because of this drug. People are mad as hell that the drug companies' desire to make money was more important that 20,000 people's lives. Let me say this again, and let me be very clear. I believe that the executives at Merck and the senior people at the FDA knew five years ago that if they put Vioxx on the market people would die! Yet, they still put the drug on the market. Consider this: If a person took a bomb and blew up a building and 20,000 people died, that person would be called a terrorist and a murderer. What are we calling the executives of Merck and the executives at the FDA when they put a drug on the market, Vioxx, knowing that 20,000 people would die? Can you see the dilemma we have? These executives and the people at Merck should be held accountable for the murder of 20,000 people. Unfortunately, I don't think this will happen. It is important to know that the executives of Merck and the FDA had information about how dangerous this drug was, yet they purposely hid the information. Then, to make matters worse, they lied about it over and over again. Folks, this is not the only drug. Right now, as I am writing these words, over ten other drugs are now under suspicion and more and more drugs are being looked at. It is categorically, 100-percent true that the drug companies know that the drugs that they sell cause disease and kill people, yet they are in fact hiding this information and lying about it. They are doing exactly what the tobacco industry did starting back as early as 1950. The point is, whether you have cancer, heart disease, liver disease, fibromyalgia, MS, muscular dystrophy, acid reflux, diabetes, or any medical condition, I can categorically, 100 percent guarantee that that condition is caused, in whole or in part, by the nonprescription and prescription drugs you have taken your whole life and are currently taking. The big challenge I have when people come up to me and tell me about their medical or health conditions and want to know the cure, is the fact that they have taken so many nonprescription and prescription drugs over the years and, more importantly, are currently taking one, two, three or more drugs right now. If you have a medical condition and are taking nonprescription and prescription medication right now, guess what? Those drugs are causing your disease and illness. You can virtually never get well and never cure your disease if you continue to take nonprescription and prescription drugs. This is the bombshell. This is the eye-opener. The drugs cause your disease.

Let me give you one prime example of how drugs cause disease. A little baby is born and immediately given a set of vaccinations. These vaccinations are drugs. They are poisons. They are diseased chemicals. You are injecting the little baby with viruses, drugs, chemicals, and disease. The baby's immune system begins to act in a totally unnatural way and becomes very susceptible to bacteria. Virtually every child, then, gets infections, primarily an ear infection. These infections were caused by the vaccines themselves. The doctor then prescribes more drugs in the form of antibiotics. These antibiotics are designed to take care of the ear infection, but they cause a huge problem. The antibiotics kill all the friendly flora in the intestine, causing the bad flora, primarily Candida, to overgrow. This then carries on the rest of the person's life. The Candida yeast begins to overgrow, first starting in the intestine, then in the stomach, then through all the organs the liver, spleen, pancreas, gall bladder, kidneys, up into the lungs affecting glands such as the thyroid, and even into the brain. The Candida begins to cause, or participate in the cause, of acid reflux, digestive disorders, multiple sclerosis, muscular dystrophy, thyroid problems, diabetes, liver problems, urinary tract infections, asthma, and virtually every other major disease. As these symptoms come to the forefront, doctors simply prescribe more drugs. Every drug you take, whether it is a nonprescription drug or a prescription drug, will cause you to be sicker. The drug causes illness and disease. The drugs cause body imbalances.

In my research it becomes clearer and clearer and clearer that if you put every single disease down and ask what caused that set of symptoms, and then ask what caused that set of symptoms, and then ask what caused that set of symptoms, it almost always goes back to Candida and/or nonprescription and prescription drugs. Those are the two main root causes for almost all disease. The third major root cause is your own mind. The stress and emotional challenges that you store in your mind. These are the big three. If you address these three things, virtually every single disease gets better or vanishes completely. I have seen people with muscular dystrophy, MS, acid reflux, diabetes, liver problems, chronic pain, arthritis, migraines, depression, anxiety, asthma, and the list goes on, that have been cured by handling these three things. First, cleaning out the Candida. Second, stopping all nonprescription and prescription drugs and doing the detox cleanses to get them out of your system. Third, using stress-reducing techniques such as what has been developed by Dr. Coldwell in the form of music and relaxation techniques. Don't be fooled into thinking that something as simple as reducing stress can't have a profound, powerful long-term effect on your health. Don't be fooled into thinking that the simple stress-reducing techniques cannot in fact cure even the most aggressive horrible disease. They can.

Very simple stress-reducing techniques do in fact cure the incurable. The mind is the most powerful curing mechanism you have. The placebo effect proves that the mind can cure disease more effectively than anything else on the planet. This is why when people write me and ask me what is the cure for this, or what is the cure for that, I always go back and say, "Do the things in Chapter 6 first, then come back to me in four or five months and tell me what symptoms you still have, if any." In most cases the people's symptoms are gone. When people come up to me and ask me what the cure for their disease is, what they are really asking is, "I have these set of symptoms, and I would like some natural remedy to alleviate the symptoms." The problem is, I can't give you a natural remedy if you are continuing to do what is causing the symptoms. If you are taking nonprescription and prescription drugs, if you still have Candida, or you still have stress lodged in your mind, anything to alleviate the symptom is simply not going to correct the problem in any significant way. When people come up to me and say, "I have acid reflux. What can be done?" I then ask, "How many drugs are you on?" They are on one, two, three, four or more. The answer is, "I'll tell you what. Get off all the drugs, do the Candida cleanse, and then come back in two months and tell me if you still have acid reflux." If a person were to do that, their symptoms would be gone. They don't understand that the reason they have acid reflux is because the root cause of it has not been addressed. The root causes of virtually all disease are nonprescription and prescription drugs. You must get off the drugs. The problem, though, is all the drugs you have taken since you were a baby have a residual effect. They do not leave the body 100 percent; much of the drug stays in the fatty tissues in the cells, and you must get the drugs out. That is why I recommend doing a Candida cleanse, a liver cleanse, a gall bladder cleanse, a colon cleanse, and a full body-fat cleanse. This gets the toxins out. If the toxins stay there, your symptoms will persist. You can do natural things to alleviate the symptoms on the short term, but the cause remains and the symptoms will either reappear or reappear in some other part of your body. Symptoms always appear in the genetically weak areas of your body.

Now, here is the big challenge. If you are currently on prescription medication you must get off the prescription medication under the supervision of a doctor. These drugs are so powerful that they not only cause major problems when you take them, but if you were to stop immediately, in many cases, that could also cause major problems. You must, in my opinion, get in front of a licensed alternative health-care practitioner. When you go to a licensed alternative health-care practitioner, you must understand that all practitioners are not equal. Some are excellent, some are just okay, and others are not very good.

On our Web site, www.naturalcures.com, my goal is to have the ultimate world-wide guide of alternative health-care practitioners. This is not up and running yet, but starting sometime next year, we will slowly begin to start a directory of licensed health-care practitioners who do not use drugs and surgery. You will be able to find one in your area using this directory. You will also be able to read the comments of other people who have gone to those practitioners and what they have said about them. You will be able to find practitioners who specialize in particular medical areas, or who specialize using specific types of medical treatments. Until then, a good way to find a good licensed alternative health-care practitioner in your area is go to the Yellow Pages and start with a chiropractor and ask them who they know who is a licensed health-care practitioner who uses herbs, or is a naturopath, or is a homeopath, or who uses energy work. You can also look for licensed massage therapists and ask them. You can go to the Yellow Pages and look under naturopath, alternative medicine, herbalist, oriental medicine, and headings such as that.

It is important to know that you cannot be treated by somebody over the phone or via e-mail. Every condition is different and all medical conditions can be caused by a number of different things. A good example of this is someone called me on the phone and said, "I have fibromyalgia. What's the cure?" My response was Fibromyalgia is one of dozens of "diseases" that are really just a label for a series of similar symptoms. MS, muscular dystrophy, attention deficit disorder, fibromyalgia and things of this nature are not diseases at all. They are a label put on a person who has a set of similar symptoms. If I were to take five people who have been labeled as having fibromyalgia the symptoms may be different with each person, and the causes of those symptoms may be different with each person. If you take five people who have MS, the symptoms would be different with each individual, and the causes of those symptoms are probably different with each individual. Therefore, there is not one blanket cure for these types of diseases. I have taken groups like this and continued to ask the question, "What caused that? And what caused that? And what caused that?" Invariably, in every single case, it all ended up with (1) nonprescription and prescription drugs that they have taken and are currently taking; (2) Candida; and (3) stress in the mind. Every single person, no matter what symptom they have, no matter what disease label they have, if they address those three things, invariably spectacular results are achieved. Most people do not want to believe that the cure can be this simple and easy. That is the brainwashing that you have been getting from the pharmaceutical industry. The fact is it can be that easy.

If I said it once, I will say it a million times, do not take nonprescription and prescription drugs. You have been brainwashed by the hundreds of millions of dollars in advertising that the pharmaceutical companies put in every day convincing us that we need drugs to make our life better. The exact opposite is true. We are being brainwashed by these companies to go to our doctors and demand drugs. How insane! You do not need drugs to make you healthy. Nonprescription and prescription drugs are making you sick. You must understand that. If you are on drugs now, either nonprescription or prescription, you will continue to be sick and you will get sicker, and sicker, and sicker. The amazing thing to me is that people do not even realize that they are taking drugs. NyQuil is a drug, cough syrup is a drug, Alka-Seltzer is a drug, aspirin, Tylenol, Advil, and nasal sprays are all powerful drugs. I believe Tums, Rolaids, and allergy sprays are all powerful drugs. Get off the drugs!

There is one other important thing that I am just going to touch on and that is something that I unbelievably missed in my book in Chapter 6. Chapter 6 is full of the do's and don'ts if you want to cure every disease and remain healthy. One glaring omission is "Quit Smoking." It is obvious to everyone that smoking is bad. Tobacco in any form (pipes, cigars, chewing tobacco, cigarettes) is bad. Tobacco in any form is like nonprescription and prescription drugs. It is one of the major causes of all types of disease in the body. It can lead to every disease, not just lung cancer. I smoke cigars. I have been smoking since 1986. Like most people, when I picked up my first tobacco product I did not think I would be addicted. Guess what? I got addicted. I have tried everything under the sun to quit. The longest I have stopped smoking was six months. I am currently reviewing a technique right now that appears to have some promise. I can tell you this, the moment I find the cure for smoking addiction I will let you know. If any of you have found a cure, please let me know. I will use it myself, and if it works, I will pass on the information to our readers.

If you want more information on how to do the best Candida cleanse in the world, the book *Lifeforce*, available at www.lifeforceplan.com. If you want to know the techniques that Dr. Coldwell used to eliminate stress, you may contact Dr. Coldwell via his associate in Germany at drhohn@goodlifefoundation.com. The other major cause of all diseases is nutritional deficiency. This will be discussed in an upcoming issue.

Recommended Product
DMSO and Hydrogen Peroxide

If there are two miracle products on the planet that can virtually help assisting in you curing virtually every disease it is DMSO and hydrogen peroxide. The reason you have never heard about these two products is because they are 100-percent unpatentable, and they are incredibly inexpensive. This means that no one will spend any serious money reviewing the effects of these products, and the pharmaceutical industry categorically wants these products to be off the market and the information about them suppressed. These are miracle products. These products help cure herpes, cancer, arthritis, MS, muscular dystrophy, and virtually all virus type diseases and degenerative diseases. There are volumes that can be written about these two products. Over the next few months I am going to have on my Web site, www.naturalcures.com, so much information about the use of these two products in the curing of disease it will blow your mind.

What these two products effectively do is get oxygen into your body. Nobel Prize winning author Dr. Otto Wallberg discovered that cancer and all viruses cannot live in an oxygen-rich environment. When your body Ph is acidic, there is very little oxygen in your blood and in your tissues. When you flood your body with oxygen, your body Ph goes from acidic to alkaline. When your body is flooded with oxygen, viruses instantly die, cancer dies, and your energy levels skyrocket. Using DMSO topically can rid a person of all types of diseases that are viral based, from herpes, perrones disease, shingles, warts, moles, etc. Hydrogen peroxide can be used topically and also taken orally to flood your body with oxygen. It can also be taken intravenously, and is used in medical clinics around the world that specialize in cancer. One particular hospital in Mexico has virtually a 100-percent success rate in eliminating cancer in just a matter of weeks by giving intravenous ozone and hydrogen peroxide.

I encourage you to go to the Internet and type in DMSO and start reading about its powerful effects. Also, type in hydrogen peroxide and start reading about how it is used to cure and prevent all types of diseases. Please know that most of the information is being suppressed, and the pharmaceutical industry has set up a host of front Web sites talking negatively about these two products. I can assure you that all the negative discussion is misleading and untrue. These are miracle products. They can help you cure and prevent cancer and virtually all types of medical diseases. They must be used correctly, and I advise you to use them under the supervision of a licensed alternative health-care practitioner. They can also be used very effectively in combination with essential oils, herbs, and nutritional supplements. The DMSO speeds the assimilation of these nutrients, making them work quicker and faster. They are also very effective in helping get ride of Candida throughout your entire body, as well as detox your body from toxins. These are miracle products. Let me say it again, these are miracle products. Proper use can change your life.

DVD Review

There are two movies/documentaries that you absolutely, 100 percent must see. They are *Super Size Me* and What the *Bleep Do We Know*. *Super Size Me* is a very important documentary about an individual who decided to eat only McDonald's food for thirty days. It shows clearly just how dangerous fast food is. When you watch the documentary, you will see that this man almost died in thirty days. He gained 28 pounds, and the doctors who were monitoring his health said that whatever he was doing was killing him. This points out the fact that the fast-food industry is causing disease. It's not cheeseburgers or French fries that give you disease, it's the chemical poisons that are put in the food by the food manufacturers that cause the disease. A cheeseburger made with organic ingredients is not unhealthy, but a cheeseburger at a fast-food restaurant categorically, 100 percent gives you disease. This documentary proves the point. If you have children, have them watch this movie it can save their life. If you eat in fast-food establishments, watch this DVD, it will open up your eyes to the truth.

The other DVD is *What the Bleep Do We Know*. This is an out-standing documentary, which correlates with many of the things I have talked about in my book about energetic imbalances. I highly encourage and recommend that you watch both of these DVDs. They are available on the Internet.

Question of the Month

Q: I've heard that Vitamin E, which you talked about last month, has been shown in studies to be potentially harmful. What's the truth here?

A: This is a prime example of the medical industry actively trying to debunk all-natural remedies. The pharmaceutical industry has tens of millions of dollars earmarked on a specific campaign. It uses public relations firms, and front groups that appear to be consumer advocacy groups, to get a certain message across and make you believe a certain thing. The message that the pharmaceutical companies are spending tens of millions of dollars on is to make you believe that all-natural remedies are ineffective and harmful, and make you believe that drugs are very effective and safe. The exact opposite is true. Anytime you hear about a "study" that has been done on a natural product like Vitamin E, you are being misled.

These "studies" are funded by the pharmaceutical industry or by front groups for the pharmaceutical industry. They do not use the natural derivative. What they do is they take a chemical compound, which they say is identical to the main ingredient the particular vitamin or mineral. Then they do a "study," and they give you the twisted, misleading results. The issues here are, first and foremost, that they are not using the natural compound, they are using a chemical derivative that was manufactured in the lab, it is not Vitamin E. They are using a chemical derivative that they are calling Vitamin E. The studies are manufactured and misleading.

The fact is all-natural Vitamin E is a spectacularly effective food supplement. It increases circulation and increases oxygen throughout the body. Men, for example, who have erectile dysfunction who take Vitamin E see a dramatic improvement in their condition. Vitamin E works better than the drug heprin as a blood thinner preventing clots in the arteries. Vitamin E is incredible for increasing circulation, improving memory, concentration, as well as helping healing throughout the body. Vitamin E put on wounds increases healing of cuts and sores dramatically. The all-natural

Vitamin E is a brilliant, effective, safe supplement. The synthetic chemical version is not.

Good News

This is a huge win for everyone. Although the Federal Trade Commission is forbidding me to tell you a product by brand name, they have allowed me to refer you to licensed alternative health-care practitioners. Obviously, a licensed alternative health-care practitioner is not bound by the insanity and suppression that the FTC is forcing on me. A licensed practitioner can give you the information you seek that I am being forbidden to tell you. Here's the good news. Obviously, I have traveled throughout the entire world and have been personally treated by thousands of alternative health-care practitioners. Some were excellent, some just fair, and some not so good.

How would you like to get advice from the licensed health-care practitioners who give me advice? Well, as a subscriber to the Natural Cures Newsletter you can. Most importantly, you can get their advice for free. If you have any medical questions or want specific recommendations on any health subject, please send an e-mail to the following three health-care practitioners. They will answer your questions, as well as continue to send you free updates and information. So please, if you have a specific medical question e-mail these doctors directly. If you e-mail me, I can give you general recommendations, but can't mention products by brand name. These people will give you, in effect, the same advice I would give you. Here are their e-mail addresses: (this is available for newsletter subscribers only).

Cholesterol

People write me all the time and say, "How do I cure my disease of high cholesterol?" Folks, this is one of the greatest scams perpetrated on the public. You have been misled and lied to. High cholesterol is not, I repeat, not a disease. High cholesterol is simply a condition that you have. It is not a disease. Years ago, the pharmaceutical industry decided that they could make huge amounts of profit if they convinced people that they had to lower their cholesterol. This was a great business model for the drug companies. If they convinced you that you needed to lower your cholesterol, they could then convince you that you needed to take their cholesterol lowering drugs every day for the rest of your life. This means billions of dollars in profits to the drug companies. The fact is Lipitor and all the other cholesterol drugs are the most profitable drugs on the planet. The drug companies make more by selling cholesterol-lowering drugs than anything else. It is their biggest profit moneymaker. The fact is that by taking cholesterol drugs you are being lied to about its benefits.

Most people believe that if they take cholesterol-lowering drugs and lower their cholesterol they are reducing their risk of heart attack and stroke. The exact opposite is true. The cholesterol-lower drugs do not reduce the risk of heart attack and stroke. The cholesterol-lowering drugs cause disease in the body. They cause liver damage and make you get dozens of various types of sicknesses and diseases. These cholesterol-lowering drugs do not in any way reduce your risk of heart attack and stroke. They do in fact give you more sickness and disease.

Go back and read that again. Think of how idiotic this scene is. You walk into a doctor's office and say, "Doctor, I'm concerned about clogged arteries." Your doctor then says, "Well, let's check your cholesterol. Whoops! Looks like you have high cholesterol. If you are concerned about clogged arteries, take these cholesterol-lowering drugs to lower your cholesterol. This will lower your risk of getting clogged arteries and having heart disease." You believe your doctor, walk out of the office and take these drugs for the rest of your life not knowing that these drugs do not reduce your risk of heart attack and stroke, or clogged arteries, and these drugs do in fact do give you a whole host of other illnesses and diseases. Consider this, if you walked into the doctor's office and asked, "I'm concerned about clogged arteries, arterial sclerosis, and heart disease." Why is your doctor checking your cholesterol? Why isn't your doctor simply saying, "Okay, if you are concerned about your arteries being clogged, let's do a simple test and find out if your arteries are blocked now."

Why is he checking cholesterol? Why isn't he checking to see if the arteries are clogged or not? The test is simple, inexpensive and painless. The answer is the doctors are brainwashed as well. All they want to do is to sell you drugs.

When I go into my doctor's office I don't ask about my cholesterol, I ask him "Are my arteries open?" That is the most important thing we are looking for, correct? Why are we even looking at cholesterol? Chapter 6 of my book tells you what I believe you can do so that your cholesterol will be normal. The fact is some people's natural cholesterol levels will be lower and some people's will be higher. It doesn't matter how much cholesterol you have in your body. That is not a determining factor in whether your arteries are clogged or not. Cholesterol is not the problem. Cholesterol will only attach itself to the artery wall if the artery is damaged. As I mentioned in the previous newsletter, the three major causes of damage to the arteries are (1) homogenized dairy products, (2) hydrogenated oils, and (3) chlorine in the water you drink and bathe in. These are the main culprits. Don't be scammed and misled into believing that high cholesterol is a medical condition. It is not. It is not a disease. Your real concern is your circulation. Your real concern is whether your arteries are clogged or not, not how much cholesterol you have. You absolutely need cholesterol in your diet and you need cholesterol in your body for your body to operate normally and function properly.

Cholesterol-lowering drugs are a scam. They are a moneymaking machine for the pharmaceutical companies. As I mention in my book, never stop taking drugs without the supervision of a doctor. The drugs are dangerous when you take them, but they can also be very dangerous when you stop abruptly. Do so under the guidance of a licensed health-care practitioner. I will say this again, and again, and again. If you are going to a medical doctor who simply prescribes drugs and surgery, stop going to that medical doctor. Go find a licensed health-care practitioner who doesn't use drugs and surgery.

Let me give you a good example. I had a friend who needed her wisdom teeth taken out. This is a good example of when surgery can be a wonderful thing for our health. The surgeon expertly removed her wisdom teeth. When she came out of the surgery the doctor said that she would be in excruciating pain in about three hours after the anesthesia wore off and immediately wanted to prescribe Vicodin. I told the doctor, "She doesn't take drugs." He said, "Well, she is going to be in excruciating pain." I said, "Well, is there anything she can take for the pain other than drugs?" He said, "Well, she can take Tylenol or Advil." I pointed out that these were drugs as well. The doctor thought for a minute and realized that they in fact were. He said, "Well, I don't know of anything natural to get rid of the pain." I said, "How about the homeopathic arnica and maybe icing it? And perhaps, using a healing light and some magnets?" He laughed and said, "Well, they won't hurt, but they won't do anything." I said, "Great." He also informed me that the bleeding would continue for at least an entire day and that the pain would be excruciating for at least three to four days. I said, "Fine." I asked him for a less powerful prescription in case the pain became too overwhelming. After all, she did have major surgery and there was a good chance that she would be experiencing some severe pain. He then wrote a prescription for Tylenol with Codeine. This he said would help numb the pain and make her sleep. I took the prescription in case of an emergency.

She went home and put arnica cream on both cheeks, iced both sides, and used magnets and a healing laser. To everyone's amazement the bleeding stopped in just an hour. This was absolutely unheard of. Obviously, the natural treatments we were using were making her heal much faster. In addition, she experienced no pain whatsoever. She slept throughout the entire night without any discomfort. She never had to take any drugs and she never experienced any pain. The healing was amazingly fast. This is the power of natural cures. Keep in mind that my friend adheres to most of the items in Chapter 6 of my book. Her body was clean from toxins and full of super nutrition, so her body was capable of healing much faster than a person who had a suppressed immune system, was lacking nutrients and loaded with toxins. This is the power of natural cures.

The most important point to consider here is this: Don't be brainwashed by the drug companies. The pharmaceutical industry is spending virtually billions of dollars trying to brainwash you into believing that drugs are safe and effective and will make your life better and that you need them for health. They are spending billions of dollars trying to make you believe that natural remedies are not safe and are ineffective, and actually dangerous. This is the greatest brainwashing ever perpetrated in the world. Do not be brainwashed. The exact opposite is true. The fact is all nonprescription and prescription drugs are ineffective, they are incredibly dangerous, they cause disease, and you categorically do not need them for health. They destroy your health.

Situations like being misled and lied to about the dangers of high cholesterol and being brainwashed into believing that you need to take cholesterol-reducing drugs is causing people to be sicker and sicker. Remember, all drugs, both nonprescription and prescription drugs, lead to and cause disease. If you are sick and are currently taking nonprescription and prescription drugs, I can guarantee you that the number-one reason you are sick is because of the nonprescription and prescription drugs you are currently taking, plus the residual effects of all nonprescription and prescription drugs (including vaccines) that you have taken over the years. The way to cure virtually every disease is not drugs and surgeries. In Chapter 6 of my book I tell you what I believe are the ways to cure virtually every disease.

Weight Loss Tip

If you want to lose weight, it is absolutely imperative that you eat a substantial breakfast. The facts are clear. The vast majority of people who are thin eat breakfast, the vast majority of people who are overweight eat no breakfast or a very light breakfast. People who are overweight generally have a slow metabolism. In order to get your metabolism moving, one of the most important things you can do is eat a substantial breakfast.

There are two elements here: (1) you must eat a substantial breakfast, and (2) you must eat the right kinds of food that make your metabolism go up and get your body burning fat instead of eating food that causes your body to retain fat and gain weight. Is there a best breakfast? Well, let's start with this basic premise: everything you eat for breakfast must be organic and unprocessed. It cannot, generally speaking, be out of a box or from a company that is publicly traded. If you are eating food that you have purchased from a publicly traded corporation, I can assure you that there are ingredients in the food that are not listed on the label. I can assure you that these companies are secretly putting ingredients in the food to increase your appetite, get you physically addicted to the food, and make you fat.

So, with that in mind, here are some good types of food that you can eat for breakfast:

1. **Meats**. Eat organic beef, lamb, chicken. Make sure these are real cuts of meat and not deli-type meats or any type of processed meats.

2. **Fish**. Wild salmon, sardines, tuna, etc.

3. **Fruits**. Grapefruits, apples, pears, strawberries, blueberries, plums, peaches, and apricots. Make sure the fruits are fresh and not dried. As always, make sure they are organic.

   Stay away from bananas as they have a tendency to make you gain weight. If you must have milk with your breakfast, make sure it is organic and ideally, raw milk that has not been pasteurized or homogenized.

Here are some common breakfasts that I eat:

1. Scrambled eggs with a side of smoked salmon, or lamb chops, or sardines, or a small steak.

   I make my scrambled eggs various ways. I always use fresh organic, non-pasteurized, fertile eggs. The simplest way is to gently beat the eggs, add organic sea salt and organic pepper, a little pure water and a small amount of pure organic raw cream. I heat a nonstick skillet and use a little either extra virgin olive or raw organic butter. Sometimes I add some chopped up organic green and red peppers, organic onions, organic parsley and organic mushrooms. When people come to my house and eat my scrambled eggs they cannot believe how delicious they are. The lamb chops I simply broil with a little organic salt and pepper. This is a filling, delicious high-protein breakfast, which gives me plenty of energy for the day and starts my metabolism. Sometimes I add a slice of organic rye bread. If you read the ingredients, you will notice that the bread should have only three ingredients: organic rye flour, water, and yeast. I stay away from wheat bread and sometimes eat other types of sprouted breads or wholegrain breads other than wheat. Just read the ingredients on the label. Make sure they are organic, and there should be only a few ingredients. Do not buy bread if it has honey, molasses, sugar, or ingredients you cannot pronounce. On my bread, I use a little raw butter, and sometimes I eat an apple with this meal as well. If I am in a rush, I will take some organic apples and pears and make fresh juice. I put the juice in a blender and add some fresh blueberries, a few ice cubes, some spirulina powder and blue-green algae powder, and a little organic flax seed oil. Sometimes I add a little organic non-genetically altered soy powder for some added protein. I drink this and also eat an apple or pear to get the added fiber. Depending on how I feel, I also may add a piece of toast. Sometimes for breakfast, I like potatoes. I take an organic potato, slice it up and in a nonstick skillet, with a little extra virgin olive oil, I gently sauté them with a little organic salt and pepper, organic paprika and some fresh, chopped organic parsley. They are delicious.

When people come to my home, I cook for them and show them how delicious meals can be made in less than thirty minutes. They are easy and fun, and taste absolutely delicious. People cannot believe how incredibly delicious the food is. It is better than any restaurant. Most importantly, after they eat they do not feel bloated, tired, or lethargic. The food gives them energy, which is what food is supposed to do. You will notice, when people eat, most people will get tired, gassy, bloated, constipated, and lethargic after a meal. Food is supposed to give you energy. Food is supposed to be fuel. If, after a meal, you aren't filled with energy, then there is something wrong with that food, or you are so toxic and full of Candida that the food cannot be used as fuel. Therefore, you must do your Candida cleanse and colon cleanse. Taking some digestive enzymes with your meal will prevent you from having any acid reflux or heartburn, prevents gas, and allows the food to digest better.

I love doing experiments and take people who are overweight and just do one simple thing with them for just a week to see the results. My most recent experiment was to take overweight people who didn't eat breakfast. I told them to change nothing else. Don't exercise; don't change what you eat; and don't do anything. All I wanted them to do was add a big breakfast. They were skeptical because they felt by adding additional food, calories and fat, they would gain weight. The exact opposite happened. By eating a breakfast their energy levels were higher throughout the day, they felt better, they weren't ravenous throughout the day, they had less headaches, they slept better, they weren't hungry at night, and most importantly, after one week everyone lost weight.

The body needs fuel on a regular basis. Eat a big, substantial breakfast, and eat the right kind of breakfast and you will see your weight normalize and you will lose weight.

Good Products
Gogi Juice; Mangosteen Juice; and Noni Juice

People come up to me all the time and ask what is one simple thing that they can do without changing their lifestyle that can make them feel better, reverse disease, and prevent disease. Well, there are a lot of things you could do that would provide those benefits. If we go back to our basic premise, which is you are sick because you have toxins in your body and you have nutritional deficiencies. Then let's ask ourselves what we can do that can help get rid of toxins in our body and supply us with massive amounts of nutrition. If those two things happen there is an excellent chance that you will feel better, have more energy, as well as having many medical symptoms vanish.

There are three fruits that do exactly that. The mangosteen fruit, the wolfberry (known as gogi), and the noni fruit. These fruits come from around the world, not America. We can't get them fresh. There are companies that sell bottled mangosteen juice, gogi juice, and noni juice. In most cases, unfortunately, these juices have been pasteurized, which means they have been heated and many of the enzymes have been destroyed. However, the benefits of drinking these juices outweigh the fact that they have been pasteurized. Drinking these juices seems to help detoxify the body of toxins, as well as supply super nutrition directly into the cells.

There are many other things that seem to be occurring when a person drinks these three juices. I have seen firsthand diseases and illnesses simply vanish within a few months after drinking these juices. These diseases include acid reflux, GERD, hiatal hernias, arthritis, fibromyalgia, chronic fatigue syndrome, depression, anxiety, asthma, irritable bowel disease, urinary tract infections, diverticulitis, sleep disorders, allergies, eczema, joint pain, lupus, migraine headaches, diabetes, cancers, hypertension, high blood pressure, high cholesterol, fungal infections, bacterial infections, viral infections, PMS problems, and more. It appears that these juices can equal, or even out-perform, prescription and over-the-counter drugs, including Nexium, Prevacid, Zantax, Pepcid, Allegra, Claritin, Singulare, Pregnazone, Valium, Zanax, Prozac, Zoloft, Paxil, Lexapro, Vicodin, Celebrex, Dextra, Naprosyn, ibuprofen, Lipitor, Zocor, Pravachol, Ultram, Talwin, and many, many more. These juices have been reported to reduce the risk of heart disease, help the fight against cancer, reduce the risk of diabetes, increase energy, produces beautiful skin, lowers and maintains cholesterol levels, reduces arthritis inflammation and pain, as well as relieving pain, muscle tenderness, fatigue, and sleep disturbances of fibromyalgia. There are many other reported health benefits as well. The great thing about these juices as they are not "vitamins and minerals," they are simply fruit juices, which means you are getting the vitamins, minerals and cofactors in their complete natural state and in the exact proportion nature intended. This is a good example of a whole-food supplement as I describe in my book. I would highly encourage anyone and everyone to drink these juices on a regular basis. I believe you will see spectacular health benefits.

When people come up to me, tell me about their health problems, and ask me for answers, I always say the same thing how many of the things in Chapter 6 are you doing? Do those things for three to six months, then see if you still if you still have your health problems. If you are not willing to do the things I mention in Chapter 6, which I believe are in effect ways of cleaning out the toxins, adding super nutrition, balancing out the electromagnetic energy fields in the body, which in turn turn your body alkaline, then how do you intend on curing your disease? Remember, diseases just don't happen, you give them to yourself. These are three juices that I highly encourage and recommend. There are many manufacturers of these juices. Is one manufacturer better than the other? I don't know. It is my intention to visit the manufacturing plants and make personal recommendations in the future. In the meantime, try different brands and see which ones you like the best. Please write me with your results so I can share them with others.

Question of the Month

Q: How do I do the cleanses that you recommend?

A: Every single person reading this is loaded with toxins. There is no way that you are not full of toxins throughout your entire body. If you have any illness or disease, one of the major reasons is that your body is toxic and cannot handle bacteria or viruses, thus causing you to become ill. The toxins also create an environment where you cannot fully absorb nutrients, which means your body is incapable of fighting off bacteria and viruses and you become ill. Toxins also block the energy flow throughout the body causing you to develop disease. Toxins themselves are poisons and, in fact, allow you to develop a whole host of diseases and illnesses in the genetically weak areas of your body.

As I explained in my book, you absolutely must clean out your body if you want to cure your diseases and prevent illness and disease from occurring. There is no way around it. You must realize that in order for you to be able to help cure your disease you must find out what the cause of your disease is and solve that problem. If you are sick right now with any kind of disease, one of the major causes of your illness is the fact that you are toxic. These toxins come from the nonprescription and prescription drugs you have been taking your entire life, including vaccines, the chemicals put in our food supply, the poisons in the water and the air, and the poisons you have put on your skin in the form of antiperspirants, lotions, etc., plus the toxins your body creates on its own primarily due to Candida and undigested food in your colon. There are many other causes of body toxicity. The fact is, if you are sick, one of the causes is you are sick because you are toxic.

When people come up to me with questions about their health issues, people get frustrated when I say, "Do the cleanses and come back in two months and tell me if your symptoms or disease still exist." People say to me, "I don't want to do the cleanses, I want the cure for my disease." I tell them again, "Do the cleanses and you probably will cure your disease because the toxins are causing your disease." People don't understand this. An example would be if a fellow came into my office and he said, "I have pain in my toe. What is the cure?" As I watched this fellow he proceeded to take a hammer and hit his toe with it. He looked at me and said, "I have pain my toe. What's the cure?" He then hit his toe again with the hammer and said, "Come on, Kevin, I have pain in my toe, what's the cure?" Again, he whacked himself with the hammer. I looked at him and said, "Stop hitting your toe with the hammer and your pain will be cured." Imagine if he said, "I want to continue to hit my toe with the hammer, but I want you to tell me what the cure is for the pain in my toe." Do you understand this? Are you getting what I am saying?

Most people are loading their body up with toxins every single day, and yet some people come to me and say, "What's the cure for this disease or that disease?" You can't cure any of the diseases you have if you continue to do the same things you have always been doing. You must do the cleanses. The main cleanses are:

1. a colon cleanse;
2. a liver/gall bladder cleanse;
3. a kidney/bladder cleanse;
4. a heavy metal cleanse;
5. a parasite cleanse;
6. a Candida cleanse; and
7. a whole-body cleanse.

There are many products on the market sold by many companies that help you do these cleanses. All will provide you benefits. Which one is the best? I really don't know, but I do know that doing any type of cleanse will give you tremendous value and tremendous benefit. You can go to your health food store or go to the Internet and type in "colon cleanse" and you can see a whole host of various products. These include herbs, seeds, husks, etc.

Getting colonics done by a certified colon therapist is also a very effective way to clean the colon. I would always start with a colon cleanse first. Certain juices can be consumed which help clean the colon. Since most toxins come out through the colon, it is important to clean the colon first.

I would then do a liver and gallbladder cleanse. You can go to the health-food store or the Internet and punch in "liver cleanse" and "gallbladder cleanse," and there are various companies that sell various products that are very good for doing this. These cleanses are not very difficult and take only about a week.

The two longest cleanses to do are the Candida cleanse and the full-body cleanse. There are many ways to handle Candida, but almost all Candida cleanses that are done only get rid of the Candida in the colon and not through the entire body. The absolute best, most complete Candida cleanse I know of is described in the book *Lifeforce* by Dr. Jeff McCombs.

The last cleanse is what I call the full-body cleanse. This cleanse is really a cleanse that gets the toxins out of the fatty tissue throughout the entire body. It is done by taking certain supplements and sweating the toxins out in a sauna. It provides some of the most incredible health benefits any person can imagine. It takes from three to eight weeks, depending on how toxic a person is. To get more information on this cleanse go to www.purification.org.

Everyone has different opinions on cleansing. Some people suggest an infrared sauna is an incredibly effective way to cleanse and detox the body. I believe it certainly is. Some people believe that taking a dry brush and vigorously brushing your skin helps exfoliate the skin, open up the pores, increase circulation and increase the detoxification and cleansing process. It does. Other people believe that rebounding or doing exercise such as yoga increases circulation to the vital organs and speeds cleansing and detoxification. They absolutely do. The important thing is not to be overwhelmed by all the various cleanses that you can do. Start slow, but definitely start. The sooner you get started, the sooner you will feel better.

Is there a best way to do cleanses? Are some cleanses better than others? The answers are, all cleanses are good. The key is that you start doing some of them. The fact is, we can't live in a pure environment. If you do cleanses now you certainly will continue to put toxins in your body, and your body will continue to create toxins. I personally have done virtually every cleanse in the world. I am not fanatical and realize I live in a toxic world. I go to restaurants, I travel on planes, and I am surrounded at various times by toxins.

I live in a stressful environment with my battles against the FTC and various government agencies, and my body creates toxins on a regular basis. What I personally do is, at least three or four times a year, spend a week and do various cleanses. One very powerful cleanse is, of course, fasting. You choose what is best for you. If my best friend came to me and asked me, "Kevin, friend to friend, what should I do first for a cleanse?" I would suggest getting a series of fifteen colonics over thirty days, go on as much raw food during those thirty days as possible, including lots of fresh organic fruits and vegetables and fresh organic juices, eliminate daily for a month, and go to the health food store and buy various herbal colon cleaning products. This will clean out the colon and really flush the system of almost all the toxins.

Then I would recommend to my friend to go on the Internet and find a good gallbladder and liver cleanse and do the procedure recommended. That should only take about a week.

Then I would strongly recommend that my friend do the Lifeforce Plan Candida cleanse. This is not hard at all, but needs to be done for approximately eight weeks.

Then I would suggest to my friend to do the purification full-body cleanse. At that point, my friend would be fully cleansed, more so than he has in his entire life. I believe almost any medical condition that he had would vanish or be in complete remission. At that point, he would be starting with a clean slate.

Three or four months later, I would recommend that he take one week and do some sort of colon cleanse, maybe a seven-day fast, including colonics, and either once a year, twice a year, three times or four times a year, do some type of cleanse that he feels his body needs. The Candida cleanse really only has to be done once, and the purification full-body cleanse only has to be done once. The liver and gallbladder cleanse only has to be done once every three or four years, depending on how clean you are. The colon cleanse should be done at least once a year, and I recommend two or three times a year or more. Since all toxins start in the colon and back up and start infesting the liver, the gallbladder, and the fat cells, if you keep your colon clean everything else remains relatively clean.

The most important point to remember is if you are sick, there is absolutely no way you can permanently cure your disease unless you attack the cause, and one of the most important things to attack is the toxins in your body. The most effective way to cure and prevent disease is by getting the toxins out. This must be done if you intend on living a healthy, long life without pain and illness.

I Am Right!

I have been saying over and over again, that **ALL** drugs, both non-prescription and prescription, **cause** almost all illness and disease. The facts are clear and my book is exposing the truth! Since my book came out, the drug company Merck announced that their drug Vioxx causes heart attacks and strokes and is so poisonous that it must be pulled from the market. It is estimated that 20,000 people were killed by Vioxx! Then Celebrex was exposed to be a deadly poison as well. It is estimated that over 10,000 people have been killed by Celebrex. Most recently, it has been announced that the **non-prescription** pain reliever Naproxen, which goes by the name Aleve, is killing people as well. This is **MAJOR**. Naproxen was approved by the FDA over 25 years ago. No one knows how many people have died because they went into a drug store, and bought the non-prescription over the counter pain reliever Naproxen (Aleve)!

Folks, I have said it over and over and over...all drugs, both prescription **and** non-prescription over the counter medication **cause** illness, disease and death! **STOP TAKING DRUGS!** Just because you can buy it in the store does not mean it is safe!! The FDA does **NO** follow up studies once they approve a drug! Again...all drugs cause you to be sick and **give** you disease!

DVD Review

There is a great movie that was made, actually a documentary, entitled *The Corporation*. In my book I talk about "it's all about the money." The movie talks about the fact that the love of money is the root of all evil. I talk about the fact that corporations are legally defined as individual entities. The legal responsibility of corporations is to make a profit. As a matter of fact, the law states that a corporation must, above everything else, make a profit. That means it cannot take into account its employees' welfare before profit. It cannot take into account the environment before profit. It cannot take into account anything before profit. Profit is the most important overriding thing above everything else.

Most people just have no idea of how corporations operate and how they take advantage of the public. As I mentioned, making money is not bad. Making a profit is not bad. As a matter of fact, making a profit and making money is a good thing. The key is making a profit and making money when you have an even exchange between the consumer and yourself. If you are offering a good quality product or service to a consumer and you make a profit in doing so, that is a good thing. The problem is, when people make profit while they hurt their employees, or when a company makes a profit while it destroys the environment, or when a company makes a profit while deceiving and misleading the customers, or when a company makes a profit while it bends the rules, commits fraud, or breaks the laws, that is when making a profit is bad. The big challenge is most corporations make a profit in these bad ways. When companies make profit by offering good quality services and products to the consumer, while they take care of their employees and staff, while they take care of and are protective of the environment, and while they adhere to all the laws and regulations, that is when making a profit is a good thing. It comes down to honesty, integrity and ethics. This is what is missing in the corporate world. This DVD is available on the Internet and I highly would encourage and recommend that you watch it. It is entertaining and incredibly compelling.

Vioxx Update

I mentioned in last month's newsletter the fact that the drug company Merck has pulled their prescription pain drug Vioxx from the market because it has been uncovered that when a person takes Vioxx their risk of stroke and heart attack goes up dramatically. It is important to reiterate to you the facts that the drug company Merck, as well as the FDA, knew five years ago that this drug would kill tens of thousands of people. Merck and the FDA did not release this knowledge, but in fact suppressed and hid this knowledge because the profits that would be earned by selling this drug would be in the billions. This is exactly what the tobacco industry did in the 1950's. They knew, in fact, that cigarette smoking would kill people, but they hid this evidence and lied about it before congress. The drug companies and the FDA are doing the exact same thing. Well, I am blowing the whistle on this outrageous, flagrant example of corporate and government greed and corruption. If this were happening in any other country, the U.S. Government would be claiming genocide, but because it is happening in America, virtually no action is being taken. Remember that Vioxx is a prescription drug that was given to people for pain. What is being uncovered now is the information that was suppressed and hidden for five years. This information shows many disturbing facts, the most significant fact is that both the FDA and the company Merck knew that Vioxx increased and caused heart disease and strokes. The more information that is being uncovered, shows that the situation is much worse than anyone has thought. This is exactly what I been saying in my book and in my newsletters. It is now being reported and the FDA scientists themselves actually admit that Vioxx alone has caused over 140,000 heart attacks, strokes and deaths. And the FDA is actually saying that it, as an agency, is virtually defenseless against a similar future catastrophe with another drug.

Non-prescription over-the-counter drugs and prescription drugs are in fact deadly and are killing people. The American medical association itself admits that prescription drugs are now the fourth-leading cause of death in America. Prescription drugs are actually killing more people than the disease that they are supposed to be curing. Folks, this is just the tip of the iceberg. I will say this in every newsletter over and over again; if you are taking non-prescription, over-the-counter drugs or prescription drugs you absolutely must stop taking these drugs now. However, I must warn you, only stop taking drugs under the supervision of a licensed health care practitioner. Many of these drugs are so powerful that stopping to suddenly could cause medical problems, but if you want to cure your disease, you must stop taking drugs. If you want to prevent disease, you must stop taking drugs. Remember drug companies are publicly traded corporations, which means they have only one objective and that is to make money. The only way that drug companies make money is by getting you to believe that you **need** to take drugs. Drug companies only make money by getting more people to take more drugs. If a drug company's objective was to cure and prevent disease, they would all be out of business. You must remember that. If you watch any of the financial news networks such as CNBC, Bloomberg or any of the cable stations that focus on publicly traded companies and the financial markets. You will see over and over again how drug companies talk about their business. They do not talk about curing disease and preventing disease, they talk about "market share," "profitability," "long term growth" and new blockbuster drugs that will increase bottom line profits. Read the *Wall Street Journal, Investors Business Daily, Business Week* or any financial newspaper or magazine when you read articles about the drug industry, they never talk about preventing and curing disease, they only talk about these companies ability to sell more drugs and increase profitability.

They talk about the millions of dollars being put in lobbying efforts to get congressmen to pass laws that the government itself buys drugs or supplements drugs. It's all about the money. The fact is, if you want to prevent illness and disease and if you want to cure yourself of illness and disease, you must stop taking over-the-counter non-prescription drugs and prescription drugs. These drugs are actually giving you and causing disease, the facts are clear, you will hear more and more about this, as this information becomes uncovered. The drug companies know it, the Food and Drug Administration knows it, but they are taking no action because there is too much money and profits involved. Think about this, Vioxx has been voluntarily pulled from the market by its manufacture the drug company Merck. It is categorically proven now that 100,000 people have died because they took Vioxx. It is estimated that over a million people may have had heart attacks and strokes because they took the prescription drug Vioxx. The drug company Merck knew this would happen five years ago and so did the FDA. They took no action because of the massive amount of profit involved. Here is the shocking truth, the FDA, as I write this newsletter, still has not banned Vioxx from the market! Think about that. Remember in my book I talked about how the FDA banned the herb mahaung because it contained ephedra. The FDA claimed that ephedra had been linked to 153 deaths over a ten-year period, therefore concluded that the herb mahaung was too dangerous and must be banned from the American marketplace. Remember those deaths were linked to ephedra, not proven to be caused by ephedra. But the FDA still said they believed it showed that the herb was too dangerous and must be banned. However, Vioxx is now known to have killed over a 100,000 people. Yet the FDA still has not taken any action and banned it from the market place. In the last few weeks there have been organizations now that have shown and proven that drug advertising has been false and misleading. Where is the Federal Trade Commission??? They have yet to take any action against the drug companies for producing false and misleading advertising. Where is the FDA??? They have yet to have taken any action for these drug companies producing what is now proven to be false and misleading advertising. Remember in my book how I talk about how the FDA and the FTC only pick on the little guys like myself, trying to crush us with massive lawsuits, asset freezes and smear campaigns in the press. They try to put us out of business, shut us down and shut us up. But these organizations take absolutely NO action against the drug companies even though they have categorically been proven to produce false and misleading advertising, hide information and in fact knowing kill over 100,000 people.

I just received an email that really hits the nail on the head, it said (and I'm paraphrasing) major pharmaceutical companies admitted last week that they are failing to produce new medicines, yet the industry manages to earn more than $500 billion annually due to aggressive marketing and inflated prices on prescription drugs. All the major pharmaceutical companies in the United States announced disturbing news regarding product development in the drug industry. To compensate for the lack of new profitable drugs, drug companies instead use strategic advertising campaigns specifically designed to increase sales to both patients and doctors. They also hike up the prices of prescription drugs to increase profitability. The lack of successful drug research and development has been common knowledge to the scientists and researchers involved in the industry, according to a *USA Today* report. It is not until now that the companies have actually gone public with this information. Drug companies have also publicly announced that they have concerns with the negative side effects and an alarming high number of people who use many of the most popular brand named drugs such as Celebrex. It appears that the drug companies simply are not producing any new drugs that have any effectiveness against disease. However, the drug companies seem to be remedying this situation by spending more money on marketing and advertising their drugs than on research and development of new drugs. The pharmaceutical industry is now reaping record-breaking profits, specifically because of their new slick advertising campaigns designed to convince consumers that they need to purchase drugs. "If you don't have a lot of breakthrough drugs in your pipeline and you are a drug company, you need to market the hell out of the drugs that you do have," Dr. Jerry Avorn, a professor of medicine at Harvard Medical school and author of *Powerful Medicines: The Benefits, Risks and Costs of Prescription Drugs*, told *USA Today*. Consequently people are taking popular brand name prescription drugs that have little or no effect on their medical conditions and in fact, are causing more medical and health problems. Dr. Avorn went on to explain that companies are reluctant to vigilantly monitor the side effects of drugs because if consumers learn about the negative side effects that they will experience by taking these drugs, it could cut into the sales and profits of the drug companies and could reduce sales of future drugs because customers will be concerned about their safety and be reluctant to purchase them.

As you can see, folks, from this article the fact is clear nonprescription over-the-counter drugs and prescription drugs are dangerous. Remember that there is absolutely no follow up testing on the safety of drugs once it are approved by the FDA, this is a significant point. Once a drug, both a non-prescription over-the-counter drug or a prescription drug is approved by the FDA there is virtually no follow up testing to see if the drug actually works and is safe. Keep in mind when the FDA approves a drug, it is relying on research that has been bought and paid for by the pharmaceutical companies. The committees that are reviewing the drug are usually filled with doctors that are on the payroll of the drug company whose drug is up for review. This means conflict of interest, conflict of interest, conflict of interest. Also, when big profitable drugs are approved, many of the FDA people involved in that approval process resign from the FDA and go to work directly for that drug company and are paid millions of dollars. Payoff, payoffs, payoffs! Then once that drug is approved, there is absolutely no further review on whether or not that drug actually works and is safe. This is why today more people are sicker than ever before in history yet we take more drugs than ever before in history. Drugs do not work at preventing and curing disease they cause disease.

The Cause of All Illness and Disease

I want to be very clear about what the cause of virtually all illness and disease is. If you are sick, if you have any type of illness or disease, the only way you can cure yourself of the illness or disease that you have is to understand what the causes are. All illnesses and disease are caused by the same things; (1) too many toxins in the body; (2) nutritional deficiencies; (3) electromagnetic chaos exposure; (4) mental and/or emotional stress. Let's go back to the basics: There are really only two ways you get sick. One, you catch something, or two, you develop something. If you catch something, such as a germ, a virus or a bacteria, you will only succumb to that germ, bacteria or virus if your immune system is weak. If your immune system is strong, all the viruses and bacteria that you are exposed to are fought off by the killer cells in your body. The fact is, you are exposed to hundreds of germs on a regular basis, and this is totally natural. Your body then releases killer cells, which go and attack, kill, and wipe out the various invading viruses and bacteria and germs. However, if your immune system is weak, then you succumb to that virus, bacteria or germ and develop sickness. What causes your immune system to be weak? Well, toxins in the body, nutritional deficiencies, electromagnetic chaos, mental and/ or emotional stress. The second reason you are sick is you develop something in your body such as cancer, or diabetes or clogged arteries. You don't catch these things—you develop them. Why do you develop them? Well, you develop them because of too many toxins, nutritional deficiencies, electromagnetic chaos, or mental and emotional stress. People always ask me, where do genetics play into this? We all come into this world with certain genetic weaknesses; however, if you don't have many toxins, if you have no nutritional deficiencies, if you are not exposed to electromagnetic chaos, and if you aren't exposed to mental and emotional stress, these genetic weaknesses actually correct themselves and never manifest. They only manifest themselves when you have one of the four things that I have mentioned.

People always want to know what the natural cure is for their disease, and the fact of the matter is the natural cure for every disease is absolutely the same thing. No matter what disease you have, whether it's cancer, heart disease, diabetes, fibromyalgia, allergies, asthma, acne, dandruff, eczema, herpes, acid reflux, constipation, colitis, PMS, infertility, erectile dysfunction, etc., etc., etc. The cure is the same because the cause is the same. No matter what disease or illness you have, one of, or a combination of, these four things causes it:

1. You have toxins in your body;

2. You have nutritional deficiencies;

3. You have exposure to electromagnetic chaos; and

4. You have mental and/or emotional stress.

Since that is in fact the cause of all illness and disease, the cure is simply to correct these imbalances. Let me go through each one of these and show you the simplest way to correct it. Keeping in mind the umbrella to this whole thing is when you have corrected these four issues your body pH will be alkaline, and when your body pH is alkaline, you virtually can never get sick. When these four things are affected your body pH can go acidic; therefore, you are susceptible to all disease. People always ask me, "How do I get my body alkaline?" The answer is always the same, "Go back to Chapter 6 in my book and do the things in Chapter 6." If you do the things in Chapter 6, I BELIEVE you get your body alkaline. By doing the things in Chapter 6, I BELIEVE you are in fact cleaning out the toxins and you have stopped putting the toxins in, you are correcting the nutritional deficiencies, you are reducing or at least managing your exposure to electromagnetic chaos, and you are reducing and eliminating the mental and emotional stress. When you do those four things, IN MY OPINION, you turn your body pH from acidic to alkaline, and when you do that I BELIEVE you cure yourself of every disease and you can never get sick in the future well, almost never!

So let me go through these one by one to make sure you get it.

1. **Toxins**.

You are toxic. That's factual; there is no way around it. The number-one toxin you have put in your body over the years are non-prescription over-the-counter drugs and prescription drugs. This started from the moment you were born. When your mother went into the hospital and was given drugs in the operating room when you were delivered; then when you were delivered you were pumped full of drugs by the doctors; then you were pumped full of vaccines; then you were pumped full of antibiotics all within the first year of your life. For the rest of your life you were pumped full of drug after drug after drug after drug. You were fed food from cans, boxes, and jars. All of the food has been loaded with chemicals, poisons, and toxins. The air you breathe is full of chemicals, poisons, and toxins. The water you drink, bathe, swim in, and shower in is loaded with poisons, toxins, and chemicals. You didn't know any better and depending on where you lived and what you ate, determined how many toxins were put into your body. It isn't a matter of if you put toxins in your body; it's just a matter of how much. As I mentioned, the genetically weak areas will begin to deteriorate first. That's why two people can do exactly the same thing and one person will be dead at 40 years old and the other person can live to be 100. Why is it that two people can smoke cigarettes, side by side, and one person drop dead at 40 from cancer and the other one live to be 100 and never have any cancer? They were both putting in the same amount of toxins, but one person had genetics that were strong in those specific areas and didn't succumb to the toxins in the cigarettes, and the other person had genetic weaknesses and succumbed very quickly. In order to cure yourself of disease and never get sick again you have to do two things.

A. You have to get rid of and clean out the toxins that are in your body. That means you have to do cleanses. The cleanses that you must do are colon cleanse, a liver cleanse, a gallbladder cleanse, a kidney/bladder cleanse, a parasite cleanse, a Candida cleanse, and a full-body cleanse. I mentioned this in last month's newsletter. If you haven't read it, go to my Web site. All past issues of my newsletter are there at naturalcures.com.

B. Reduce the number of toxins you are putting in your body; you can certainly reduce them. There are a multitude of ways of reducing them. For example, get a shower filter, so you are not showering and bathing in toxic-filled water. Get a water filter and drink more water. Drinking pure, filtered water will cleanse toxins out of your body. Eat only organic fruits, vegetables, and meat, therefore reducing the amount of toxins you are putting into your body. Stop taking any non-prescription, over-the-counter drugs and all prescription drugs. Get an air filter in your house, especially your bedroom. Stop eating things that are filled with toxins such as fast food, food from chain restaurants, food in boxes, packages, cans, and jars that are sold by publicly traded corporations. Buy only organic. There is a whole list of things in Chapter 6 of my book on how to reduce the amount of toxins you are putting in your body. Again, you can never stop totally, but you can certainly reduce and then every year or so you can do a cleanse to clean out the toxins that you have been putting in.

2. **Nutritional Deficiencies.**

Every single person has nutritional deficiencies. When you are deficient in vitamins, minerals, enzymes, and other nutrients your body cannot operate at optimal levels, thus causing illness and disease because your immune system cannot operate efficiently. In my opinion, the two most important nutrients you can have are Vitamin E and the mineral calcium. I believe that these are the two most important and significant nutrients that you need to be supplementing your diet with. I believe that every single person is deficient in Vitamin E and deficient in calcium. I believe that these two specific deficiencies lead to a variety of illness, and by supplementing your diet with these two nutrients you can prevent virtually all illness and disease and cure yourself of most illness and disease. However, there is a big caveat to these statements. I say in my book do not take "vitamin supplements." The reason I say that is because almost all vitamin supplements sold are sold by companies who, just like the drug companies, are only in it for the money. They are selling you vitamins and minerals that are nothing more than dirt and do little, if any, good. They are usually synthetic man-made vitamins that are not in their natural form. I have talked to the presidents of major vitamin and mineral manufacturing companies and these people, unfortunately, are just as greedy and ruthless as the presidents of the pharmaceutical companies. They are in it only for the money. They talk about market share, marketing, positioning, return on investment, what's hot in the market place, how to reduce costs, how to get away with saying things on the label because of certain rulings made by the government, etc. etc. They are all about selling you products; they are not about producing the best quality product that is the most effective. I talked to one president of a company just last week, and I asked him specifically. I asked, "Hey! I just got a mail advertisement for this new supplement." I asked him, "How good is this supplement?" He then went on to tell me that his "positioning" of this vitamin was going to create huge sales and profits for his company, and that the "market" for his product was a certain group of people. He went on to explain the massive amount of money he spent on research and development in producing the label and the advertisement that effectively sold the product. He never once mentioned how effective or good the product was. I then asked him about the ingredients. He actually laughed at me and said, "Look, we put the same crap in this as everybody else and we just make sure that we can get it at the cheapest price possible." This is what I'm talking about folks. Remember, unfortunately, it's all about the money.

When I mention that you are deficient in Vitamin E and calcium, and that you need to supplement your diet with Vitamin E and calcium and that by doing so you can prevent and cure a host of diseases, what I am talking about is taking the all-natural, real, as found in nature supplements. Synthetic, man-made, cheap versions do not work. Remember, every "study" conducted on vitamins and minerals are conducted using the cheap synthetic, man-made versions. No wonder the studies never show, or rarely show, that vitamins and minerals are effective. Also keep in mind that these studies are funded, directly or indirectly, by the pharmaceutical industry whose intention is to prove that all-natural supplements are ineffective and potentially harmful.

So let's go back to Vitamin E. Vitamin E categorically is one of the most important, if not the most important, vitamins that you need to have. Unfortunately, the processing of food today dramatically reduces the amount of Vitamin E that is available through the food that you eat. Therefore, every single one of you is massively deficient in Vitamin E. Having this deficiency will cause various problems depending on the individual, and that individual's genetic weaknesses. For example, having a deficiency in Vitamin E for one person may cause phlebitis, blood clots, varicose veins, asthma, or allergies. Deficiency in Vitamin E in another person could cause circulation problems, cold feet, cold hands, fatigue, depression, memory loss, mood swings, or male erectile dysfunction. Trying to get all the Vitamin E you need from the food you eat in today's environment is very difficult. Even if you were to eat only pure organic fruits, vegetables, and meat, it is still difficult. So it is important to supplement your diet with Vitamin E.

In all my research, I have found only two brands of Vitamin E that are actually effective. That's right, only two brands out of the hundreds and hundreds of brands of Vitamin E are actually the full all-natural Vitamin E that are effective. Because of the Federal Trade Commission's insanity and Gestapo-like tactics I am forbidden to tell you the brands of these products. But if you e-mail the licensed health-care practitioners that I currently recommend I am sure they will tell you the brands of Vitamin E that they recommend, which are the same ones that I use. The licensed health-care practitioners are at the end of this newsletter.

What you are looking for is a Vitamin E that has a natural unesterified mixed tocopherol complex containing antithrombic d-alpha tocopherol, which protects against internal blood clots and actually dissolves them. And also containing d-beta, d-gamma, and d-delta tocopherols for synergistic antioxidant protection against harmful free radical damage and perioxynitrates damaging to brain cells, and also containing tocopherols in a non-genetically modified source. You do not want the synthetic dl form and not the esterified tocopherol acetate or succinate, not the ordinary soy oil diluted mixed tocopherols or adulterated forms. You want the Vitamin E, which contains all four components for the powerful synergistic effects as nature intended. You do not want a Vitamin E with added soy oil or other oil fillers, which can turn rancid and cause harmful free radical damage. You do not want one with added preservatives, colors, or flavorings.

When you take this Vitamin E you should take one capsule for every thirty pounds of total body weight just before or with your morning meal. You take it all in one dose. The key with Vitamin E is "It's what goes over the dam that counts," so you want to take all your Vitamin E at one time. I have seen people take Vitamin E and have had blood clots dissolve in a week. I've had people who had varicose veins and phlebitis vanish in as little as two or three days. I've seen people who had manic depression had it reversed in an incredibly short period of time. Men, and even women, with sexual problems have it reversed in a matter of weeks as Vitamin E increases circulation and oxygenation to all the cells.

Vitamin E increases circulation and oxygenation to the body, thus increases the absorption of all nutrients to the cells, as well as increases the ability of cells to eliminate toxins. It is one of the master nutrients that are needed for optimum health. It prevents heart disease and clogged arteries. The list of health benefits goes on.

The master mineral that everyone is deficient in is calcium. Like Vitamin E, our food source has been depleted of calcium. Also, much of the food we consume, such as carbonated drinks and coffee, as well as prescription and non-prescription drugs, block calcium absorption. Therefore, I can categorically assure you that you are calcium deficient. Calcium, in my opinion, is the most important mineral in the body. When you are deficient in calcium, nothing else works well. Increasing calcium to the level that it is supposed to be and eliminating the deficiency does wonderful things to the body. It increases oxygen to all the cells, and increases the ability for electric energy to flow better throughout the entire body. Like Vitamin E, it allows the cells to detoxify quicker and faster, and allows nutrients to get into the cells quicker and faster. It relieves stress and is a major element needed to keep the body alkaline. Research shows that bringing calcium levels back to normal makes weight loss happen faster and easier.

Like Vitamin E, there are many kinds of calcium. In my opinion, you must get a form of calcium that is the most absorbable and useable in the body. I believe that marine grade coral calcium from Okinawa, Japan, is one of the best forms of calcium you can take. There are many brands available. If the label says marine grade coral calcium from Okinawa, Japan, you should be okay with that product. There are only a few manufacturers in America that make coral calcium. These manufacturers make the coral calcium for hundreds of various resellers. All the coral comes from Japan as long as it says from Okinawa, Japan. There are two grades available. One is marine grade, which comes from in the ocean, and the other one is non-marine grade, which comes from the sand on the beach. I believe the marine grade is better, since it has not been bleached by the sun. There is also coral calcium in sachets that you put in water that helps calcify the water. This is excellent, especially for people who do not like to take pills. Again, always look for marine grade coral calcium from Okinawa, Japan.

Those are the two most important nutrients you need to supplement your diet with, but I can categorically assure you that you are deficient in a whole host of other nutrients as well. Taking a whole food supplement, or drinking fresh organic fruit and vegetable juice, can solve this problem. The best way to relieve yourself of nutritional deficiencies is to drink pure organic fruit and vegetable juice. This way you are receiving all the nutrients in the most absorbable form in the exact proportion that nature intended. You need to get a good juice machine for this purpose. I have tried dozens of juice extractors and I believe that the best juice extractor is the one you will actually use. That means the best juice extractor is the one that is easy to use and easy to clean. I have used dozens personally, and I can assure you that if it isn't easy to use and easy to clean, it doesn't get used. Therefore, it is useless. I can't tell you the brand that I use, but e-mail the licensed health-care practitioners and ask the question and they will send you their recommendations. They use the same juice extractors that I do.

By the way, a Vita-Mix is not a juice extractor. I own a Vita-Mix and it is a very good blender and has a lot of very good uses, but it is not a juice extractor. A juice extractor extracts the juice from the fruit, separating the juice from the pulp. A Vita-Mix, being a very powerful blender, simply liquefies the entire fruit or vegetable. This is not juice; this is a liquefied fruit or vegetable. It's not bad, but it is not juice. That's why I recommend a juice extractor. For those of you who want more convenience, as I mentioned in last month's newsletter, you can enjoy mangosteen juice, goji juice, or noni juice. Although these juices are in many cases reconstituted or come from concentrate and are pasteurized, they are still packed with incredible amounts of vitamins, minerals, and cofactors and are very effective ways of handling your nutritional deficiencies.

The next-best way to handle nutritional deficiencies is by taking a whole-food supplement. Whole-food supplements are not by definition vitamins and minerals, but are in fact concentrated whole-food sources. I can't mention brand names, but I will tell you a couple of specific things. Chlorella is an excellent whole food source. It is simply a plant that is in concentrated form containing massive concentrated vitamins, minerals and enzymes in the exact proportion nature intended. Spirlina, blue-green algae, and hydrilla are all excellent whole food sources. They contain protein, enzymes, vitamins, minerals, and cofactors. Bee pollen and royal jelly are also outstanding whole-food sources.

People can't believe that they can actually eliminate such devastating diseases such as fibromyalgia, MS, muscular dystrophy, and colitis with simply cleansing their body and increasing their nutrition. By simply cleaning out the toxins and reversing your nutritional deficiencies almost all diseases can be reversed and cured. I see it happen every single day. Don't be misled into believing that it sounds too good to be true or it is just too simple to work. When you understand the cause of your disease, then you can understand the cure. Keep in mind; it took years and years and years to develop your medical condition. It is not going to reverse itself in a couple of days. It took years to develop. Luckily, it won't take the same amount of time to reverse, but it will take weeks or months. Be patient, but do these things and you will see results.

3. **Electromagnetic Chaos**

    You can't avoid electromagnetic chaos; it's impossible. It's around us, from the laptop computers, to our TVs, the satellites in the sky, cell phones, any and all wireless devices, radar transmissions, high-tension power lines, electrical lines, and fiber optic networks. We are surrounded by electromagnetic chaos. You can't avoid it. You can reduce it by eliminating all wireless devices from your home, but seriously, you may only be able to reduce it a little. Therefore, in my opinion, it is categorically imperative that you have an electronic chaos eliminator. There are several brands available, each purporting to be the best and most effective. In my initial research, I believe that they are all effective to varying degrees. Which one is the most powerful and the best? I do not know. Once I do know, I will let you know. I use several that I carry with me and have in my home, and I recommend that you e-mail our licensed health-care practitioners and inquire, and they will make their own recommendations.

4. **Stress**

    This is really powerful. Stress is defined as conscious or unconscious negative emotions that are being held in the body. It is important to know that stress can be conscious or unconscious. You may be the happiest person going, but may have some hidden locked-in negative emotions that you aren't even consciously aware of. These hidden negative emotions can be causing your entire body to become acidic and giving you a whole host of various diseases. You must eliminate conscious stress and unconscious stress if you want to eliminate disease. It is important to know that this one area is more powerful and more important than the other three areas combined. Your mind is more effective at curing yourself of disease than eliminating toxins, curing your nutritional deficiencies, and eliminating or reducing electronic chaos combined. Your mind is the number-one cause of all illness and disease. Your mind is an enormously effective tool to cure and prevent disease. Stress can be one of the major factors of suppressing your immune system and causing your body to become acidic and allowing you to develop a whole host of diseases.

There are several effective ways of reducing stress. One of the most effective in my opinion are the techniques developed by Dr. Coldwell. I discussed him in my book. I have seen personally medical miracles happen right before my eyes from people who use techniques to eliminate unconscious, hidden, trapped negative emotions. When these trapped negative emotions were released, I've seen people physically change right before my eyes and disease virtually vanish. To get information on Dr. Coldwell's technologies please e-mail licensed health-care practitioner Dr. Hohn at drhohn@goodlifefoundation.com.

If you want to cure yourself of the disease you have, you have to understand the cause of those diseases, and all diseases are caused by the same four things. When you understand that, then you will understand how your body works, why you are sick, and what you can do to correct the problem. I can absolutely tell you this, if you cure yourself of your diseases by using these techniques and you continue to use these techniques, it will be almost impossible for you to be sick in the future. If you ever do come down with any type of cold, flu, or illness, the symptoms will be mild and the duration will be very short, and the likelihood of you coming down with some serious debilitating disease is almost zero. Remember, when your body pH is alkaline, it is virtually impossible to have any disease. All these techniques are designed to get your body pH to the alkaline level. When that occurs, disease is eliminated and future disease is prevented.

The Drug Companies Are Scared of This Newsletter!

My insiders tell me that the pharmaceutical industry has put together a multi-million dollar task force to debunk all the information I put out in this newsletter. It is incredibly interesting to me to find that in my first newsletter when I mentioned Vitamin E, within weeks after my newsletter was published, there was a news story published talking about how bad Vitamin E was. My next month's newsletter talked about hydrogen peroxide and how effective that was at curing disease. Within weeks after that newsletter came out there was a major news story debunking hydrogen peroxide therapy. My insiders tell me that the pharmaceutical industry has put together a multi-million dollar debunking campaign specifically designed to debunk what I say in my newsletter. So I can assure you that whatever I talk about in this newsletter, within a few weeks there will be stories and articles written saying the exact opposite. This is what I talked about in my book. The drug companies spend hundreds of millions of dollars in publicity campaigns doing two specific things. On the one hand, they try to brainwash you into believing that drugs are effective and safe, and on the other hand they try to convince you that all natural therapies are ineffective and dangerous. This is what the drug companies, the American Medical Association, and the FDA are doing. They are spending hundreds of millions of dollars to do this.

I find it flattering to note that my newsletter is being so closely monitored and debunked so quickly. However, I want to again reassure you, my readers, that my information is unbiased, unfiltered, and there are no conflicts of interest. I say things because I believe them to be true, and I believe them to be in your best interests. When you read articles where "experts" give their opinions you have to ask yourself, are these experts paid spokespeople for the particular industry or company that they are talking about? The *Wall Street Journal* reported that the majority of university professors who give expert opinions on a particular subject are paid by that company or industry to give a specific opinion. These payments are never disclosed. These "experts" appear to be unbiased professors, doctors, researchers, scientists, or specialists giving unbiased opinions. The fact is, they are totally biased. There are massive conflicts of interests and in the majority of cases they are flat-out being paid to say specific things. You are not being told the truth. They are not giving full disclosure.

This most recent article about hydrogen peroxide was absolutely appalling to me. There is a doctor who had treated well over 1,500 patients. Two patients receiving hydrogen peroxide therapy died. This doctor was then attacked by the FDA. However, they never talked about the over 1,400 patients that were **cured** of their disease, they could only talk about the two who had died. The funny thing is, they never tell the whole story. If these 1,500 people had used conventional therapy, over **80 percent** of them would have died! Do you understand this? This is how crazy the FDA is, the AMA is, and the media is. They are categorically lying and misleading you, and trying to convince you that all-natural therapies are ineffective and dangerous. They are trying to convince you and brainwash you into believing drugs are effective and safe. Folks, the exact opposite is true. You have to know that non-prescription over-the-counter and prescription drugs are, in most cases, ineffective and incredibly dangerous. All-natural remedies, vitamins, minerals, herbs, food supplements, homeopathic remedies, essential oils, enzymes, and the like, are incredibly effective and incredibly safe. Don't be misled.

Why Organic?

You must eat organic fruits, vegetables, meat, eggs, etc. There is no way around it. You cannot buy fruits and vegetables, or canned goods, or products in boxes, jars, packages, etc. that are not organic. You have to eat only organic food. If the box does not say 100-percent organic, and if the ingredients don't all say organic, don't buy the food. Why is this so important? You have to understand one of the major reasons that you have illness and disease is because of toxins in your body. One of the major ways you get toxins in your body is from the food that you eat. When you eat food that is not 100-percent organic, what you are eating is loaded with poisons and chemicals. I talk about this all the time, but some people just have a hard time understanding.

I had a guy over to my house; we were talking about organic fruits and vegetables. He said, "Well, when I went to buy some organic apples they didn't look very good. The conventional ones looked a lot better, so I bought them." I said to him, "Don't you realize that that conventional apple is loaded with toxins and poisons, that it has been sprayed with pesticides, insecticides, fungicides, and herbicides, which are nothing but poisons and chemicals? That they have probably been injected with chemicals? That the fertilizers used in the earth are all poisons and chemicals? Those fertilizers get into the trunk of the tree and ultimately end up inside the fruit, and the fruit itself can't even bare fruit. They are made from hybrid seeds that produce fruit that can't even germinate and reproduce its own kind. It can't even sustain life. Not only is it full of poisons and toxins, but it can't even sustain life." He said, "Well, I really don't notice any difference."

As he said that, he noticed that I had in my kitchen melons, papayas, tomatoes, oranges, grapefruits, pears, apples, lemons, limes, grapes, and a host of other fresh produce. He said, "I bet all that's organic." I said, "Yes, it is." He said, "Okay. Well, why don't you give me one of those apples?" I said, "Great." So I grabbed an apple and said, "Wait a minute. Let me do a little experiment." I ran outside to my woodshed where I knew my gardener kept a can of Raid bug killer. The reason I know this, is that I saw it and specifically told him that I did not want chemical bug killers around my house, and he assured me that he would correct the situation. I took the can of Raid and I sprayed the apple in front of my guest. I then handed him the apple and said, "Here you go. Tell me if you like it." He was shocked. He explained, "I'm not going to eat that! You just sprayed it with Raid." I said, "Well, I'm confused. You eat conventional apples. They are sprayed with bug killers that are ten times stronger than the poisons used in Raid, but you eat them." He said, "But they are cleaned." I said, "Fine. I'll wash off this apple." He still wouldn't eat it. Do you understand what I'm talking about?

When you go buy conventional fruits and vegetables you are buying produce that has been sprayed with some of the most deadly, lethal bug killers known to mankind. It's like eating an apple that has been sprayed with Raid, and you are feeding this to your kids. Think about it. When you buy food in boxes, cans, jars or other packages that are not 100-percent organic, they have all been sprayed with pesticides, herbicides, and fungicides, which are ten to 100 times more powerful than Raid. Think about it. Will you still eat it? When you consider that most of these fruits and vegetables have also been doused in chlorinated water or bleach, can it get any worse? When you also consider that highly toxic poisons are used as fertilizers to make these fruits and vegetables grow, could you imagine that these chemicals are actually inside the fruits, vegetables, and produce? Of course they are. Non-organic conventional food is all full of toxins and poisons.

Report after report, after report, after report comes out showing the toxicity levels in conventional food is higher today than ever before. The toxicity levels in organic foods are almost zero. I can assure you that for many people, eating conventional food leads directly to all types of diseases and illnesses. For other people who are genetically stronger, it may not lead directly to these illnesses and diseases, but it certainly suppresses the immune system making the person more susceptible to diseases and illness. Food that is not 100-percent organic is all full of toxins. Additionally, in most cases, food that is not 100-percent organic is also genetically modified. What this means is scientists in laboratories mess around with all the genes in the food to make food that is not natural. They are creating food that is something that would never occur naturally. They are creating food that can't even produce it's own kind. They are creating food whose seed will not germinate. They are creating food that looks almost identical in shape, size, and color. They are creating food that can last for weeks, and weeks, and weeks and never go bad. They are creating food that is resistant to bugs and disease. They are virtually creating food that is not food. It is something that the body does not know how to deal with and cannot breakdown. It is not nourishing to the body. It is devoid of nutrients; it is chemically altered so that it is foreign to the body; it throws the body completely out of balance; and it's full of toxins.

There is one more thing that is terribly bad with food that is not 100-percent organic. In most cases, it is irradiated. That means that it is zapped, in effect, by microwaves. In last month's newsletter I talked about the dangers of eating microwaved food. Even if you throw out your microwave oven and you go to the store and you buy meat, grapes, pears, fresh carrots that are not organic, did you know that most of that has been zapped by a method called irradiation, which is in effect microwaving the food. It is done to kill bacteria and viruses. The problem is, it kills all the living enzymes as well, and makes the molecular structure of the food radically different. Go back and read my article on microwaving in December's newsletter.

People always ask me, "But organic food is more expensive. How can I afford it?" My answer is, "How much will cancer cost you? How expensive is it going to be to have a heart attack? What's it worth to sit in a hospital room and have your stomach ripped open by a surgeon installing a colostomy bag because you have some horrible disease?" What's the cost of good health? You can't put a price tag on it. If you learn how to cook food, you will find that fruits and vegetables, even though they are organic and cost more, are actually cheaper. I've done the math. I went to the store, I bought the Hamburger Helpers, the McDonald's food, the non-organic crap in cans, boxes, cartons, and jars, and I made three meals a day and added up the money. I didn't eat the food, but I made the food. I monitored how long it took and how much it cost. And then I did the same thing with fresh organic fruits, vegetables, grains, nuts, seeds, meat, poultry, chicken, eggs, cheese, butter, and milk, and I made three luxurious delicious meals a day and three big snacks. I ate all this food, of course. It took about 20 percent more time to make the organic food, and cost only about 5 percent more, but I can guarantee you the taste was 1,000 percent better and the quantity of food was at least twice as much. It was much more food to eat. It tasted better, was better for you and it didn't take that much more time and that much more money, but you have to know how to make the meals.

On my Web site naturalcures.com I'm going to have a whole section on recipes, and I'll have videos that you can download, free of charge to our lifetime members, where you will actually see me making all these meals and teaching you how to cook. It is interesting to note, by the way, that I offered to the Food Network on television to do a cooking show, showing people how to buy food properly in the grocery store and how to make food simply and easily at home in very short amounts of time. They had no interest in such a show. The reason is all their sponsors are publicly traded companies, such as Kraft and the drug companies, and they categorically did not want me on the air. As I mentioned to you before, the sponsors run the networks. So when you want to know what information is being presented on a TV network, whether it's a news network or what have you, simply look at who is running ads. When the drug companies are running ads on a network, you can be assured that the drug companies are dictating what is being said on that particular network. It's scary, but true especially when you note that 60 percent of all the ads on television are by drug companies. The bottom line is if you want to prevent illness and disease, and if you want to cure illness and disease, you have to start eating organic.

Now, don't be misled. Make sure you read the labels. Even companies that sell organic food try to deceive you. I went into a store and I saw some food and it said, "Made with organic ingredients." Looks pretty good, doesn't it? Well, it isn't. The label said "Made **with** organic ingredients," it didn't say, "Made with **only** organic ingredients." What this particular company was doing was putting in a few organic ingredients and the rest non-organic ingredients. In fact, the majority of this particular product was non-organic ingredients, but it was made with some organic ingredients. The key is you want to buy food that is made with **only** organic ingredients. So, read the label. Flip the label over and read the ingredient list, and look for food where everything listed is 100-percent certified organic. People ask me, "Well, I buy my food at Whole Foods or Wild Oats or Trader Joe's, isn't it organic?" No. Those stores give you a better chance of getting 100-percent organic foods, but they don't only sell organic food. Keep in mind, do the best you can. The ideal scene is to buy food that is 100-percent certified organic, but if you can't and it's **mostly** organic, well that's better than nothing. Do the best you can and you absolutely will see and feel the difference in your own vitality and health and vibrancy.

Book Review

I talked about eating organic in this newsletter. That means not just fruits and vegetables, but all food including meat. Eating organic meat is probably even more important than eating organic fruits and vegetables. There has been a second reported case of Mad Cow Disease in Canada. This is significant because I can assure you that if there have been two reported cases of Mad Cow Disease, that means that there are thousands and thousands of cows that have Mad Cow Disease that have not been reported. I believe that cows in America have Mad Cow Disease and are not being reported. The information is being suppressed and hidden from you.

If you are eating regular conventional beef, you are an absolute insane crazy person because I believe you are eating meat that is highly diseased. The meat industry in America is producing some of the most toxic dangerous substances that we are putting in our body and calling it food. Almost all meat in this country, with the exception of kosher organic, is diseased and poisoned. All meat comes from cows that have been genetically modified, which means they are something that you don't find in nature; almost all meat are fed products that are inorganic, chemically laced, and diseased; almost all of these vegetarian cows are being fed ground-up other animal parts, including horses, cows, chickens, other cows, goats, and pigs.

Much of the ground-up animal parts that are being fed to our cattle and dairy cows are in fact highly diseased and were so sick and were so diseased that they couldn't be slaughtered for human consumption, so they were in fact ground up and fed to other cows that are in turn slaughtered and fed to us for human consumption. Do you see how insane this is? Almost all of these cows are given injections of growth hormone and massive amounts of steroids and antibiotics. They are sick, diseased, and unnatural; they are slaughtered in their own feces and urine; they are aged, which means they are rotting animal flesh. When we eat this beef, it is giving us disease. Now there are people who believe that you should be a vegetarian and not eat any beef. I am not one of those people. If you want to be a vegetarian, that is perfectly okay with me, but I do eat beef. I eat organic kosher beef, chicken, lamb, and duck. It is absolutely imperative if you are going to eat beef to eat organic beef.

A new book that just came out is called *Brain Trust* by Colm Kelleher, Ph.D. It talks about the hidden connection between Mad Cow Disease and misdiagnosed Alzheimer's disease in human beings. Here is what people are saying about the book:

"Anyone who thinks the meat on their plate is safe is living in a fantasy world. When the public sees this book, there will be hell to pay."—George Knapp, Emmy Award-winning journalist

"This well-documented, accessible tale is the wake-up call that could literally safe your life."—John L. Peterson, president, The Arlington Institute

Consider this: There are 120 million adults in America, and over five million Americans have been diagnosed with Alzheimer's Disease. The most significant part of this number is that Alzheimer's Disease has increased 9,000 percent in just the last twenty years! Even scientific research believes that as high as 13 percent of diagnosed Alzheimer's cases may actually be not Alzheimer's at all, but another brain disease called CJD, which is directly linked to Mad Cow. This book exposes how Mad Cow Disease has jumped species, infecting humans in the form of CJD and may be causing a whole myriad of physical, mental, and emotional problems in human beings that are being totally misdiagnosed, including depression, fibromyalgia, MS, and dozens of other illnesses. This book is absolutely a must read. When you read this book, you will be riveted and fascinated about how the American meat industry works, how the USDA works, and how in fact that our meat supply is probably some of the worst, most diseased meat in the world. You will categorically be convinced that eating conventional meat is not only potentially dangerous to your health, but also absolutely dangerous to your health.

I can assure you that after you read this book you will be so thankful for having this knowledge and that you will only eat organic beef in the future.

It is important that you read this type of information so that you can totally comprehend the benefits of eating organic meat and how deadly poisonous it is to eat non-organic beef, poultry, eggs, etc., but 100 times worse! I had a woman write me once and say, "But organic chicken and beef is so expensive. There really can't be that big of a difference." I simply said, "If I took a steak and accidentally dropped it on the street, would you still eat it?" Of course not. If you were at a restaurant and they dropped your food on the floor, would you eat it? Of course not. That is exactly what you are doing when you are buying non-organic beef, poultry, eggs, etc. You are getting the most toxic, poisonous food you can imagine, but you think it's a bargain because it's cheap in price. Folks, don't be brainwashed and stop being stupid. Wake up, open your eyes, and pay attention. You are being brainwashed by the companies that are selling you these products and calling it food. You are being brainwashed, lied to, and misled. The reason the stuff is cheap is because it's crap! The reason organic is more expensive is because it is pure. What is your health worth? Get this book. The book is *Brain Trust*, the author is Colm Kelleher, Ph.D., the publisher is Paraview Pocket Books, and it is available on Amazon.com.

ABC's *Good Morning America* Attacks Me!

ABC's *Good Morning America* television show, at the time I am writing this article, is putting together what I believe to be a one-sided, false, and misleading story about me and my best-selling *Natural Cures* book. By the time you are reading this newsletter there is a good chance that the story may have already run. Without seeing the final story, I will give you the interesting facts as I know them up until this point. As you all know, the drug companies do not want me selling my book and exposing the fact that drugs are ineffective and unsafe, and that there are in fact natural cures for virtually every disease. The drug companies do not want you to know that they are only in business to make money and sell you more drugs.

The major food companies want my book off the market because they do not want me exposing the fact that the major food companies are secretly putting chemicals and ingredients in the food purposely to increase your appetite, get you physically addicted and make you fat. Both the powerful pharmaceutical industry and food industry are spending millions of dollars in public relations campaigns, funneling millions of dollars to lobbyists in Washington and putting pressure on Washington politicians to use agencies like the FDA and the FTC to stop me from selling my book.

The FTC uses "news organizations" and TV shows such as ABC's *Good Morning America* to spread their anti-Kevin Trudeau propaganda. ABC's *Good Morning America* show is heavily sponsored by both the drug companies and the major food industry. Therefore, ABC does not want me selling my book either. They have a major conflict of interest. Here is what I believe has happened.

The Federal Trade Commission sent out false and misleading press releases to news organizations all around the country trying to get people to run negative stories on me and my *Natural Cures* book because it became the fastest-selling book in American history. Tens of millions of people were exposed to the shocking truth and dirty little secrets about the drug industry and the food industry. Both of these industries started using the millions of dollars that they have available to spread misleading and false information about my book and me. The major television networks that get hundreds of millions of dollars in sponsorship money from both the food industry and the drug industry have pressure put on them by those industries to run negative stories about my book and me. The individual reporters doing these stories and the producers of these stories, probably own stock in fast-food companies, major food industry companies and pharmaceutical companies. My book is probably having an adverse affect on their own stock portfolios, so they have a major incentive to run negative stories about my book and me.

It appears that the FTC covertly worked with ABC's *Good Morning America*, giving them false and misleading information about my book and me. ABC's *Good Morning America* called me, asking for me to do a taped interview. We all know that when a news organization does a taped interview they have the ability to edit that interview and make you look like a complete idiot. Their selective editing also twists and misleads the facts and truth. Therefore, most prominent people do not do taped interviews, they will only do live interviews. This way, there can be no editing and you can hear the complete information in an unedited form. I told ABC News that I would be more than happy to go to New York at my own expense and do a live interview. They categorically denied my request. They only wanted to do a taped interview, so that they could butcher my comments and produce a piece that was one-sided, biased, false and misleading.

Even though they knew that I declined doing a taped interviewed, they arrived at my home unannounced at 7:15 a.m. with TV cameras and reporters. I was still in bed sleeping. At 7:15 a.m., totally unannounced, the ABC News film crew started banging on my door and ringing the doorbell nonstop for thirty minutes! How unprofessional, rude, and what an invasion of privacy. Why did they show up at 7:15 a.m.? So that they could make it appear that I was unwilling to answer the door and answer their questions. This is false and misleading.

I would like to send a film crew of my own to the individual reporters' and producers' houses, as well as to the president of the ABC *Good Morning America* show, and bang on their doors at 7:15 a.m. demanding a personal interview. I would like them to see how it feels!

The reporter started yelling through the door that my book did not contain natural cures. This is false and misleading. In Chapter 6 of my book it specifically says that the cure for every disease is doing the things in Chapter 6. The book does give you the natural cure for every disease. Any statement otherwise is false and misleading. The reporter also started yelling through the door that many people were unhappy with the book because they felt that the book did not contain natural cures. This is false and misleading also. I get over 500 emails a day. The vast majority of these people absolutely love the book and for those people who are smart enough to do the things in Chapter 6, those individuals report that they are seeing their diseases and illnesses diminish or be totally cured.

The fact is, if ABC portrays any of these false and misleading situations, I will take massive and immediate action against this organization. For example, if ABC's *Good Morning America* show tries to make you believe that I denied doing an interview or would not come to the door when they came to do an interview, this is false and misleading. I absolutely accepted doing a live interview. If ABC News does not clearly state that they came to my door at 7:15 a.m. and banged on it for thirty minutes, and they try to suggest that I was unwilling to answer the door, this is false and misleading. They woke me out of bed and, of course, I would not answer the door. These reporters were so belligerent and rude, they would not leave when requested to do so. I had to call the police and the police escorted them off the property for trespassing. If ABC's *Good Morning America* segment suggests that the book does not contain natural cures, this is flagrantly untrue, as the book does contain the natural cure for every disease and clearly says so. If ABC News suggests that huge percentages of people are unhappy with the book, this is flagrantly untrue as the vast majority of people I hear from who buy the book, who read the book cover-to-cover, absolutely love the information that is in it and are benefiting greatly from it.

You need to know that news organizations do not provide you with accurate, truthful "news." You have to know that organizations like ABC's *Good Morning America* are not news organizations giving you facts. They are propaganda machines that are in effect owned by the sponsors. ABC's *Good Morning America* show is nothing more than a propaganda machine for the drug companies and the food industry. The drug companies and the food industry hate my book and hate me blowing the whistle on their deceptions and lies. They use these organizations to stifle people's First Amendment rights. You can be assured that I am taking the leading role in this country at fighting these news organizations from false and misleading portrayals of information.

A good example of this is the boxing promoter Don King. The TV network ESPN produced a segment about Don King. This segment gave the impression that it was giving the viewer "facts" about Don King. It gave the viewer the impression that it was reporting "news" about Don King. This was not true. This segment was merely giving the opinions of the producers. It portrayed information that may have been untrue and false, and was at least misleading. It did not give you the entire true, honest, clear, balanced picture of Don King. This happens all the time in the news media. It happens in newspapers, magazines, television and radio. These news organizations are no longer presenting factual news. They are nothing more than propaganda machines for the publicly traded companies that own them. Don King was so furious that he surprised the world by filing a $2.5 billion lawsuit against ESPN. I support Don King's action 100 percent. We have to stop the television stations, the radio stations, the newspapers and magazines from having the ability to twist facts and present information that is false, misleading and deceiving. People need to know the conflicts of interests with these stations in relation to the stories and viewpoints that they express. People need to know that when a TV station says something is bad, that there may be financial incentives for that station to say that something is bad. People need to have full disclosure. Honesty, truth, and fairness in the media should be something that this country demands. If not, then TV, radio, newspapers and magazines will continue to be nothing more than the propaganda outlets of those who own them, using them for their own personal financial self-interests.

Please support me in my fight against this injustice. Write ABC's *Good Morning America,* and tell them that you love this book and you love the work I'm doing. Tell them you are upset with their one-sided, biased, unfair portrayal of my book and me. Tell them you are upset that the sponsors of their show, the drug companies and the food industry, have such an ability to dictate the content of their programming. Tell them you think it was unfair for the reporters to be banging on my door at 7:15 a.m. Tell them you're mad as hell, and are not going to take it anymore. Please know that this will not be the last battle. I thank you for your support as I fight this battle not for me, but for you. Remember folks; I don't need to be doing this. I know all this information. I have it. My family has it. We enjoy spectacular health. We don't take drugs; we don't get sick. We know this information. I'm doing this work for you, and believe me I am taking massive amounts of heat and abuse because I have chosen this mission. Please continue your support.

The Sun Can Cure Disease

In the *Natural Cures* book I talk about the fact that the sun does not cause skin cancer. The sun is needed for life. If you do not spend time in the sun you will be sick. The sun is vital for health, longevity and to be disease free. If you are sick, one of the things that you must do is get out in the sun. I can tell you this, that the sun itself can virtually cure disease. Every living thing on the planet, with rare exception, cannot live without solar energy from the sun. Virtually every living thing on Planet Earth needs the sun to survive. (There are rare exceptions to this, of course.) The human body needs sunlight to function at optimal levels and be healthy. Without sunlight, a whole host of physical abnormalities and diseases become prevalent. Without sunlight you develop diseases, including depression, lack of energy, poor sleep, poor digestion, weight gain, arthritis, constipation, bad breath, body odor, cancer, high blood pressure, high cholesterol, diabetes, attention deficit disorder, stress, headaches, susceptibility to colds, flus and viral infections, PMS, male erectile dysfunction, loss of sexual desire in women, infertility, anxiety and more. The sun can prevent all of these diseases. The sun can POTENTIALLY CURE YOU OF ALL OF THESE DISEASES. This is an example of a "natural cure" that they don't want you to know about! Why would a drug company want to you to know that the natural cure for depression is simply getting some sunlight? They don't want to you to know this truth. All they want to do is sell you drugs. Think about that long and hard. I'll say it over and over again, drug companies only have one objective and that is to sell more drugs. Drug companies do not want to cure or prevent disease. If they did, they would all be out of business.

Does the sun cause the skin to wrinkle and look old? No. One of the things that the sun does is draw out from the body toxins to the skin. It also stimulates cell re-growth, which actually makes you look younger and keeps your skin wrinkle free. Why is it then that people who spend hours and hours in the sun have a tendency to have dried-out skin and wrinkled skin and look older than they are? The reason is because they are so toxic. When your body is toxic, the sun will draw out from that body and bring those toxins to the surface. This is a good thing. It helps you cleanse and detoxify your system, keeping you young, beautiful and healthy.

However, if you are nutrient deficient, specifically in the good oils and fats that you need in your diet, excessive or prolonged exposure to the sun can cause these problems. The solution? Very simple, you absolutely need sun for health and longevity. However, unless you are pretty much toxic free, have no nutritional deficiencies, are balancing your electromagnetic chaos and are stress free, excessive exposure over a long period of time can make your skin look leathery, dry and wrinkly. Therefore, the solution is to first and foremost do the things in Chapter 6 of the book. I believe this will make sure that you are toxic free, that you do not have nutritional deficiencies, that you are balancing the electromagnetic chaos around your body and that your stress levels are dramatically reduced. Therefore, you can spend as much time in the sun as you want and it will benefit you. There is a caveat to this: Every person's pigment is different and will "burn" at a different level. Obviously, use common sense. If you are pale white and haven't been out in the sun in years, don't go out in the sun in the middle of the day for four hours. You will get sunburned, and it will not be a good thing! Build up the time in the sun.

It is important to sunbathe and get sun over your entire body. Remember: Never ever, ever use any sunscreen. Do not put anything on your skin that you can't eat. Sunscreens cause skin cancer. Every person is different, but I will give you a good way to start your sunbathing. Bathe your entire body in sunlight for fifteen minutes in the morning, within the first four hours after sunrise or in the evening within the last four hours before sunset. Fifteen minutes on both sides is a good place to start. Build up and get as much sun as you feel comfortable with.

There is also a very important additional benefit available from solar energy and the sun and that is called "sun gazing." (www.solarhealing.com) Sun gazing is actually looking at the sun. This can only be done right after sunrise or right before sunset. Other times would be too dangerous for the eyes. However, the health benefits of sun gazing go even beyond that of sunbathing. I would encourage you to go to this Web site to learn more information on sun gazing. I have seen and heard of hundreds of people that have virtually cured themselves of major diseases by simply sunbathing and sun gazing. This sounds incredible to some people. It sounds crazy and ludicrous to some people. The facts are that you can cure and prevent almost all diseases by sun gazing and sunbathing. That is why it is one of the things in Chapter 6 that I say can help you cure and prevent virtually every disease. This is another overlooked, simple "natural cure." And the best part is this natural cure is free. Don't think just because it is easy and free that it is not a natural cure. It is a natural cure for disease. Will it absolutely cure the disease YOU HAVE? I don't know, but I do know it will HELP YOU CURE OR PREVENT ANY DISEASE YOU HAVE. I do know and believe that it will make the curing and healing process happen better and faster and more completely.

What Is a Whole-Food Supplement?

I get this question all the time. In my book I say do not take vitamins and minerals. I make that statement because most vitamins and minerals sold are sold by companies who are only in business to make money. These vitamin and mineral companies are mostly publicly traded and only want to sell vitamins and minerals. They, generally speaking, are like the drug companies, they do not have an interest in curing or preventing disease, they only have an interest in getting you to buy their pills. Most of these companies spend more money on marketing, packaging and advertising than they do on researching and developing their products. They select, as a general rule of thumb, ingredients that are the most inexpensive available. They are not concerned with how effective the product is. They are only concerned about how EFFECTIVELY THE PRODUCT SELLS. Therefore, I say do not buy or use "vitamin and mineral supplements."

The other thing about this issue is most "health experts" who promote vitamins and minerals actually sell vitamins and minerals and make money when you buy vitamins and minerals. There is a financial conflict of interest here. I do not sell any products; therefore, I can give you an honest opinion. If you come to my house you will see that I have a cabinet full of nutritional supplements. I am constantly observing others and personally testing nutritional supplements on myself. I am constantly doing individual research on nutritional supplements to see how effective they are. I pick up the phone and I call these companies and talk to the presidents and CEOs and investigate how these products are manufactured, and if they do work. I see if the people selling them are passionately behind the product or they are doing it "just for the money." Here is one of the most shocking truths. Did you know that the presidents and senior executives of almost every vitamin and mineral company DO NOT TAKE THE VITAMINS AND MINERALS THEY SELL! That's right. They and their families do not even take the vitamins that they are trying to get you to buy. This is shocking, but true. However, even though I say do not take vitamins and minerals, I also say in my book that you have nutritional deficiencies. I say in my book that you are deficient in vitamins and minerals, enzymes and other various cofactors. I believe that nutritional deficiencies are one of the major causes of illness and disease. So what I say is you need to handle the nutritional deficiencies. But, you can't handle them by taking vitamins and minerals.

The best way to handle nutritional deficiencies is to clean out all the toxins in your body by doing the various cleanses that I recommend. This will allow you to absorb more nutrients and handle much of the nutritional deficiencies you are experiencing.

I also suggest that you stop eating food that is toxic and lacking nutrition, such as food from fast-food restaurants and non-organic fruits, vegetables, meat and other products.

I also suggest that you buy a good juice machine and drink one or two glasses of fresh juice a day made with organic fruit and/or vegetables. This will help eliminate or reduce your nutritional deficiencies.

Then I suggest that you take a "whole-food supplement." Simply taking a whole-food supplement can reduce or eliminate your nutritional deficiencies. When this happens you can virtually cure yourself of every disease. It is my contention that all diseases are caused by the same things, one of which is nutritional deficiencies. If you solve the nutritional deficiencies your body has the ability to heal itself. Think about it. Your body has the ability to heal itself! If you cut your finger, even if you did nothing to it, the cut would heal itself. You don't have to do anything! Your body can heal itself. However, it can't heal itself or has a harder time of healing itself if it is nutritionally deficient. When your body is nutritionally deficient you succumb to viruses and bacteria you pick up and your body begins to break down in the genetically weak areas. Therefore, it is vital to eliminate or reduce your nutritional deficiencies. Whole-food supplements are a good solution.

What are whole-food supplements? Well, I cannot give you specific product brand names. The FTC, I am sure, is secretly getting this newsletter, reading every word and waiting for me to make one mistake so that they can pounce like the Gestapo, arrest me, throw me in jail, prosecute me, and shut down my ability to inform you of the truth about health and nutrition. However, we did make a huge step forward by getting the FTC to concede that I can refer you to a licensed health-care practitioner. The licensed health-care practitioners that I can refer you to can do whatever they want. They are not under the restrictions that I am under. Therefore, if you were to ask one of the following licensed health-care practitioners any specific question, they can tell you and give you specific answers. The good news is the answers that they give you will be pretty much the same answers that I would give you.

The whole-food supplements that I routinely take include bee pollen, non-freeze dried royal jelly, chlorella, blue-green algae, spirulina, red marine algae, raw unfiltered honey, barley juice capsules, alfalfa capsules, wheatgrass capsules, capsules or tablets are made from 100-percent organic freeze dried dehydrated vegetable and/or fruit juices.

Although I can't mention the brand name, I am looking at one supplement that I take which has the following ingredients: red beet juice dehydrated root, celery stalk and leaf, carrot juice dehydrated root, goat whey, purple dulse seaweed and spinach leaf. All of the above ingredients are 100-percent organic. Other excellent whole-food supplements are capsules that include sprouts. The one I have in my hand has the following ingredients: soy sprouts, onion sprouts, kale sprouts, broccoli sprouts, fennel sprouts, bean sprouts, alfalfa sprouts and mustard sprouts. These supplements that I am referring to are in fact concentrated food. Another excellent whole-food product is called hydrilla. Can taking a whole-food supplement cure you of cancer? Absolutely, yes. Will it cure 100 percent of people who have cancer? Absolutely no. If you have cancer or any disease, one of the major reasons you have the disease is nutritional deficiencies. When you no longer have nutritional deficiencies your body can heal itself and cure itself of every disease you have. This is true for ANY DISEASE. Remember, there is not one food supplement, or food, or herb, or homeopathic remedy, or essential oil, or anything that, by law, can be said to prevent, treat, or cure a disease.

Remember, the Food and Drug Administration made the law that says, "Only a drug can cure, prevent or treat a disease." If anyone selling a whole-food supplement makes a claim that it, in fact, can treat, prevent or cure a disease, that person will go to jail and all of his products will be confiscated and destroyed by the Food and Drug Administration. This is the insanity that we live in today's health-care environment. When people come to me and say, "I have this disease, what's the cure?" I always ask them if they have done the cleanses? Are they taking a whole-food supplement? Have they addressed their nutritional deficiencies? Have they eliminated or reduced the electromagnetic chaos affecting their bodies? And, what have they done to reduce their stress that is trapped in the body? The answer is, these people have done nothing, yet they still want that "cure." I was on a radio show today and a woman called up and said, "I have headaches all the time and when I got your book I wanted to know what the pill or herb is that I can take to cure my headaches." I said, "Well, let's go through a few things first. Do you eat microwaved food?" "Well, yes, but that has nothing to do with it, Kevin." "Do you eat in fast-food restaurants?" "Well, yes, but that has nothing to do with it, Kevin." "Do you drink diet sodas?" "Yes, but that has nothing to do with it, Kevin. I want to know what I can buy and take that will get rid of my headaches."

I tried to explain to her that she needs to ask, what is causing her headaches. It could be toxins, it could be nutritional deficiencies, it could be emotional stress, it could be that her body is out of alignment and she simply needs a chiropractic adjustment. She may have a TMJ problem in her jaw that needs an adjustment. It isn't a pill that is going to solve your problem. You have to ask what is causing the problem and address that first. Taking a whole-food supplement is vital because it will help handle your nutritional deficiencies and allow you to prevent and cure yourself of virtually every disease faster than if you still have nutritional deficiencies.

Product Recommendation and Weight Loss Secret:
Organic, Unrefined, Virgin Coconut Oil

Here is an amazing product that can have tremendous benefits, as well as help you lose weight faster and easier than ever before. Unrefined, pure, organic, virgin coconut oil is a product that falls in that "miraculous" category. All you do is take one tablespoonful in the morning and one tablespoonful in the late afternoon. If you do this every day for thirty days, here is what you could find. High blood pressure can be a thing of the past. Circulation problems vanish. Mood swings, gone. Depression, lifted. Constipation, cured. Arthritis pain, reduced or eliminated. Cancer, in remission. Cholesterol, normalized. Acid reflux and heartburn, diminished or gone forever. Oh, and here is a major side effect: If you are overweight, you will probably lose ten pounds! This oil has a dramatic, positive effect on the body. The health-giving properties that it contains are overwhelming. In upcoming issues of this newsletter I will provide you with more references on this oil so you can read all the research if you are so inclined. However, I take this every day and can personally tell you that the effects are startling. When I started taking this within three days all of my pants were falling off. This happened in just three days. I didn't get on the scale so I don't know how much weight I lost, but all of my pants were falling off. They were all too big in just three days. I couldn't believe it. Try it and then write me with your success story.

I Have Sued the Federal Trade Commission

I have done the unheard of. I have sued the big, mighty and all-powerful Federal Trade Commission! Never before in history has an individual citizen decided to fight the goliath in Washington and stop the misleading of the American public. The Federal Trade Commission is one of the most corrupt political organizations in the world. It was commissioned to protect consumers from monopolies and protect consumers from false and misleading advertising, amongst other things. Unfortunately, today, the Federal Trade Commission does the exact opposite. The FTC actually actively engages in protecting the monopolies that exist and in protecting the companies who are putting out false and misleading advertising. Additionally, the Federal Trade Commission is probably the number-one violator of its own false and misleading advertising standards.

The FTC repeatedly puts out press releases that are flagrantly and blatantly false and misleading. Corruption must stop. The government must stop taking advantage of the citizens. The large multinational corporations must stop putting profit above ethics, integrity and honesty. We, as a society, are being made sick purposely so that large companies can make billions of dollars in profits. This must cease. The FTC is engaged in helping this to continue to occur. They must be stopped. The FTC is supposed to protect us; instead it is protecting the large multinational corporations.

Consider this, the Federal Trade Commission takes no action against large multinational corporations in relation to false and misleading advertising. Isn't it surprising, the large multinational corporation never engages in any false and misleading advertising even though they produce the majority of ads? The reason the FTC takes no action against the large companies' advertising is not because they are not false and misleading—they flagrantly are—but because those companies are paying millions of dollars to lobbyists and politicians who are then telling the FTC to not take action against them. The most flagrant example of this is the ad for the drug Celebrex. This ad was so blatantly false and misleading that the FDA actually said that this ad must be taken off the market because it was so false and misleading. The Federal Trade Commission is the agency that is supposed to take action against companies that produce false and misleading advertising and rip off the consumers. Here is an ad that was deemed false and misleading, and deemed to have ripped off consumers of hundreds of millions of dollars, yet the FTC remains silent. The FTC should have sued the manufacturer of Celebrex, required the company to pay millions of dollars in fines and to give 100 percent consumer redress for all the people who took that drug based on the false misrepresentations in the advertisement, but the FTC takes no action. Why? Because of political payoffs.

The FTC is not interested in protecting the consumers; it is interested in protecting the profits of the large companies. The FTC repeatedly sues people like myself who advertise truthfully and honestly, but whose products and opinions can have an adverse effect on the large companies. This is how the FTC protects the monopolies and protects the profits of the large corporations. This is wrong and must be stopped, which is why I have taken this unprecedented action on behalf of all citizens by suing the Federal Trade Commission. Here is a copy of the press release relating to this action. For more information go to www.kevinfightsback.com.

Kevin Trudeau Sues Federal Trade Commission for "False Advertising"

National Consumer Advocate and FTC Critic Seeks End to Ongoing Retaliation

Chicago, February 28, 2005, Kevin Trudeau, an author who is fast becoming one of the nation's leading consumer activists, filed today two separate suits against the United States government charging the Federal Trade Commission with publishing false and misleading information.

Mr. Trudeau is suing the FTC for very much the same reason that the FTC sues people for, in essence, a form of false advertising. According to the suits, the FTC has, by its own standards, committed a flagrant violation of the rules governing deceptive communications.

In an agreement to settle prior to litigation then pending in the United States District Court before the Northern District of Illinois, the government expressly acknowledged that "[t]here have been no findings or admissions of wrongdoing or liability by [Kevin Trudeau]."

Within days, however, the FTC issued a news release maligning Mr. Trudeau in language that directly contradicts the terms of the settlement agreement by falsely implying that Mr. Trudeau was found guilty of false advertising.

Mr. Trudeau is charging that the FTC again, to use the FTC's own articulated standard given the "net impression" in its press release that Mr. Trudeau has been found guilty of wrongdoing, is a habitual false advertiser, and was ordered to pay a fine. According to the suits, these are blatant falsehoods, which additionally rob Mr. Trudeau of any benefit of the settlement agreement.

On February 16, 2005, Mr. Trudeau, through his lawyers, wrote to the FTC asking the agency to remove the misleading news release from its Web site, issue a retraction, post the retraction, and disseminate it to all the news agencies that received the original release.

On February 22, Christian White, Deputy General Counsel for Administrative Law and Ethics, rebuffed this request by asserting that the release does not violate the settlement agreement because "nothing in the press release refers to any 'findings' of fact or law..."

Astonishingly, the FTC is thus defending its actions related to the settlement agreement by stating that its published allegations about Mr. Trudeau, which are presented in their new release as fact, are indeed unsubstantiated.

"The FTC has played fast and loose with the facts," said David Bradford, an attorney with Jenner & Block who represented Mr. Trudeau in his settlement with the FTC and in his current lawsuits against the agency. "If an advertiser manipulated the truth like the FTC has in its Web site and news release, the FTC would not hesitate to sue them for misleading the public. The FTC has disregarded their first and foremost obligation to promote the truth."

Even the headline of the release was misleading, Bradford said. It stated that Mr. Trudeau has been banned from airing infomercials, implying a total ban. In fact, there is no total ban; indeed, Mr. Trudeau is currently airing one of the most successful infomercials of all time, for a book which is critical of the FTC.

The lawsuits accordingly charge the FTC with retaliation against Mr. Trudeau. In his publications, and in a highly popular series of TV infomercials, Trudeau has bluntly criticized federal agencies and the FTC in particular, for working with the pharmaceutical industry to stifle discussion and marketing of natural food and medicine alternatives.

Mr. Trudeau is the author of *Natural Cures "They" Don't Want You to Know About*, which discusses natural remedies for common ailments and diseases that don't involve expensive drugs or high-priced medical consultation. The book has become a best-seller.

In one suit, Mr. Trudeau seeks a declaratory judgment that the FTC's news release is false and misleading, that the FTC has exceeded its authority, and that the FTC has wrongfully sought to chill Mr. Trudeau's exercise of his First Amendment rights. That suit seeks an injunctive order requiring the FTC to cease its wrongful conduct and correct its misleading statements. Mr. Trudeau's second suit seeks unspecified monetary damages for injury to his business.

"This breach of contract is so bald-faced that it can only represent a concerted attempt by the government to put Kevin out of business," said Kimball Anderson, a lawyer with Winston & Strawn who also represents Mr. Trudeau. "Their news release repeats charges that, in the course of litigation, were never adjudicated. And now (in its February 22 letter) the FTC even admits it."

The FTC news release was, the suits charge, additionally designed to maximize negative media coverage of Mr. Trudeau and his business. It is evident from media coverage that the strategy has been unfortunately successful, as the resulted coverage appears to have relied primarily, if not entirely, on the FTC release.

- oOo -

I need your support in this action. You can write the Federal Trade Commission and tell them you are outraged at how they mislead the pubic and that you back me. Send your mail to Federal Trade Commission, 600 Pennsylvania Avenue, N.W., Washington, D.C. 20580; or fax to (202) 326-2012, Attention: Consumer Response Center (CRC); or e-mail by going to www.ftc.gov and clicking on "File a Complaint."

ABC's *Good Morning America* Puts Out False and Misleading Story on Me and My Natural Cures Book

ABC's *Good Morning America* did a story on me and the *Natural Cures* book. The story was flagrantly false and misleading in the net impression it left on people watching it. This is standard operating procedure by the news media. Why would the news media do a negative story on my book? Very simple. The majority of advertising money that ABC gets is from the pharmaceutical industry and the large food companies. These are the two industries that I expose the most in my book for their fraud and corruption and how they are in fact making us sick and fat on purpose so that they can make more profits. I believe that the sponsors put pressure on ABC to put this misleading story on.

The most obvious example of how they misled the public in their story was when they showed the reporter knocking on my door and made it appear that I was unwilling to answer the door and answer their questions. What they failed to mention was that they came to my door at approximately 7:00 a.m. in the morning unannounced. This way, they knew that I could not answer the door since I was still sleeping. This is misleading. It is also misleading because I repeatedly told them that I would do a live interview at any time. They denied my request. I also repeatedly told them that I would do a taped interview provided that I could view how they edited my comments. They denied my request again. You see, it is obvious that they wanted to mislead you into believing that I had "something to hide" or was unwilling to answer their questions. I need your support. Please write ABC's *Good Morning America* and tell them you are outraged at their false and misleading representation in their story. Tell them how much you benefited from the book and my newsletters and how the information is in fact changing your health for the better. I need your support now more than ever. You can write to ABC at ABC, Inc., 500 S. Buena Vista Street, Burbank, CA 91521-4551, or call (818) 460-7477, or e-mail netaudr@abc.com.

Get The Toxins Out and Cure Your Disease

Remember, virtually every single disease is caused by the same thing.

1. You have too many toxins in your body;
2. You have nutritional deficiencies;
3. Electromagnetic chaos is adversely affecting you; or
4. Stress is causing your body to become acidic and the genetic weaknesses to be exposed and disease develop.

To cure any disease you must find out what the cause of that disease is. Do not simply try to suppress symptoms. Drugs only suppress symptoms, and they cause disease because they are toxic. It is also important to remember that no matter what disease you have, there is no one cure for a disease because what caused your particular disease may be different than what caused another person who had the same disease. Example: If ten people came to me with Multiple Sclerosis and asked, "What's the cure?" There is no one cure for Multiple Sclerosis. Each of those ten people could have the symptoms of Multiple Sclerosis, but those symptoms could be caused by different factors. One person's symptoms of MS could be caused by his laptop computer or eating microwaved food. Another person's symptoms of MS could be caused by a Candida yeast overgrowth. Another person's symptoms of MS could be caused by heavy metal toxicity. Another person's symptoms of MS could be caused by Aspartame. Another person's symptoms of MS could be caused by some prescription or nonprescription drug they are currently taking or have taken over the years. Another person's symptoms of MS could be caused by some stress or trauma in that individual's life. Another person's symptoms of MS could simply be a nutritional deficiency. So, the treatment for each person would be different. That is why I always say if you are sick or if you want to remain super healthy, it is vitally important to see a licensed health-care practitioner. I recommend seeing several licensed health-care practitioners on a regular basis to keep you healthy and not just treat you when you're sick. I believe it's important to see several people because each person looks at you from a different viewpoint and uses a different set of background knowledge and facts to give you certain recommendations to keep you healthy or cure your disease.

The fact is you must get rid of toxins if you want to remain healthy or cure yourself of disease. It is obvious that toxins cause disease, but most people that I talk to don't believe that they are toxic. Let's look at the research; let's look at the facts. Virtually every kind of food you eat in a restaurant is loaded with chemicals. The air is loaded with chemicals and poisons. The water you bathe in and shower in is load-ed with chemicals and poisons being absorbed into your body. Every lotion, cream, toothpaste, shampoo, soap is loaded with poisons and chemicals going into your body. Every nonprescription and prescrip-tion drug you have taken over your life is a chemical that has been put in your body, etc., etc., etc. These toxins and chemicals do not come out of your body; they stay in you and create a residual build-ing up effect, which causes you to be sick and prone to disease. It was recently reported that rocket-fuel chemicals were found in mothers' milk. The *Associated Press* reported, "A toxic chemical used in rocket fuel was found in virtually every sample taken in a new study of nurs-ing mothers' milk." The report went on to say that rocket-fuel chemi-cals were also found in virtually every sample of dairy milk tested that was pulled from grocery store shelves. These deadly chemicals have also been found in drinking water supplies in 35 states and also in veg-etables! This should help convince you that you are absolutely full of poison chemicals and toxins. This is why the number-one thing I say to do is to clean the toxins out of your body and stop putting toxins in your body. If you want to remain healthy, this is an absolute must.

More On DMSO

I mentioned in a previous newsletter that DMSO (dimethyl sulfoxide) is colorless, nontoxic water soluble liquid derived from wood pulp. DMSO comes in very small molecules and has the unique ability to permeate the skin and cells very quickly. It is a powerful solvent of both inorganic and organic material. Its penetrating ability is far superior to most any other substance. It comes in gel and cream form. When applied to your feet, it can within moments cause your breath to smell slightly garlic-like. This is because it penetrates so quickly and travels throughout the body so rapidly. DMSO also pulls in water at an incredible rate. It has such a powerful attraction to water that it can even pull it out of the atmosphere. When you combine DMSO's ability to penetrate and attract water you can see why it travels throughout the body so rapidly. It is important to know that DMSO is used throughout the world as a medical treatment for many afflictions, including arthritis, head and spinal injuries, infectious diseases, cataracts, asthma, sinusitis, diabetes, sciatica, cancer, stroke, herpes simplex and much, much more. It has been known to inhibit bacterial growth, viruses and fungi. At Hospital Santa Monica in Rosario Beach, Mexico, Dr. Curt W. Donsbach uses DMSO and hydrogen peroxide intravenously on virtually every cancer patient with reportedly remarkable success. This appears to be because cancer cannot survive in an oxygen-rich environment. Both DMSO and hydrogen peroxide get oxygen into the body very quickly. It helps alkalize the body's pH. As I mentioned before, the FDA will not allow the use of DMSO for the treatment of disease because it is not a patentable drug. This is done not to protect patients, but to protect the profits of the drug companies. There is a great book written by William Fharel which talks a lot about DMSO and hydrogen peroxide. It is called *Never an Outbreak*, and I highly recommend it. It is available on the Internet.

What People Are Saying

I get thousands of e-mails every week from people sharing their experiences from doing the things I recommend in Chapter 6 of the *Natural Cures* book. Here are some comments that hopefully will encourage you to do the cleanses I recommend and start getting the nutrition that you need, eliminating the electromagnetic chaos, and reducing stress.

- "I am eating more than ever before, enjoying it more, yet have lost five pounds. Great revelation."
- "After struggling for years to get my stomach flat it finally is. It's miraculous!"
- "You deserve an award for bringing this information out and restoring my good health."
- "Thanks for making me feel better than ever before. It's a shame most Americans just don't know this information."

- "My friends didn't believe it, but after doing the cleanses and losing their pouch they are all believers."

- "My skin rash went away without any drugs just by doing the colon cleanse."

- "You deserve a medal. Many of my ailments have already disappeared."

- "In less than a month my stomach is nearly flat. Thank God for information on cleansing."

- "After the cleansing my skin is now smooth and pink, just like a little child. It's amazing. I look ten years younger."

- "After the colon cleanse I lost my pot belly. It's unbelievable. It works."

- "The colon cleanse did the trick for me. My stomach is a thing of the past."

- "My whole family noticed a difference. No one could believe how flat my stomach was."

- "It's obvious why we haven't heard about this. Doctors would lose too much business."

- "It's truly amazing how everything changes with a clean colon. Less cravings, not hungry, and no more wanting bad junk or processed food."

- "Dropped two dress sizes in about four weeks."

- "I'm 91, feel better physically and emotionally. Not taking any more drugs that harm the body and that has had a great impact."

Get Rid of Your Silver Fillings

I've heard of people who have cleaned their colon, liver, kidneys, wiped out parasites, viruses, stopped eating processed foods and drugs yet still have symptoms and feel they are not at their optimal health levels. When all else fails, you must address the devastation of toxic dental metals, root canals, and mercury amalgams. This information is still being ignored by the majority of mainstream dentistry and medicine. Holistic doctors (doctors who treat the whole person and not just disease) have looked at this issue for years. It has been recognized as having a devastating impact on your health. Metal simply should not be in your mouth. Researchers in Europe have estimated that perhaps up to half of all chronic degenerative diseases and illness can be linked to the toxic dental metals in your mouth. It most notably causes symptoms like MS, Parkinson's, arthritis, headaches and lack of energy. It can also cause stress, depression, anxiety, mental confusion, feelings of insecurity, lack of concentration, irritability, kidney, cardiac and even respiratory disorders. Remember, all dental metals are toxic. They contain serious toxins. These toxins adversely affect your liver, thymus, thyroid, spleen, critical organs, and many body functions. This is one constant toxin that can breakdown the body's ability to perform efficiently, leading to disease and illness. If you are sick in any way, open your mouth and take a look. I would highly encourage you to remove all metal and root canals. Remove all dead and bacteria-infected teeth. Doing this can bring absolutely miraculous healing to many afflictions. You will see unexplained symptoms vanish. Remember, don't go to mainstream dentists, look for alternative dentistry, biological holistic metal-free, or Huggins dentists. Here is a list of references:

Scientific Health   (800) 331-2303
Referrals for Huggins dentists

International Academy of Oral and Toxology
(863) 420-6373   Metal-free dentists

Foundation for Toxic-free Dentistry
Send self-addressed, stamped envelope for more information

Box 608010, Orlando, FL 32860

Environmental Dental Association   (800) 388-8124

American Academy of Biological Dentistry
(831) 659-5385 or (831) 659-2417

Matrix, Inc.   (866) 949-4638   Huggins Office

www.talkinternational.com
Directory of mercury-free and biological Dentists

APPENDIX B

No-Hunger Bread: A True FDA Horror Story

On my Web site, www.naturalcures.com, there will be hundreds of true real-life horror stories of how the FDA and FTC persecute individuals, and how these government agencies protect the profits of big business. Rarely, if ever, are these abuses of power exposed. Most people do not realize that these agencies act as judge, jury, and executioner. The individuals and small businesses that they attack are virtually powerless against these out-of-control, ruthless agencies. When you read these stories you will begin to feel like the Gestapo is operating in America. Remember, when the citizens of this country stand up and make their collective voices heard, change will occur. Here is one such story as told firsthand by the victim himself. It is the story of a revolutionary weight-loss and health food called "No Hunger Bread." It shows how the FDA and other government regulatory agencies routinely crush individual citizens whose legitimate businesses can potentially have an adverse effect on the profits of the drug companies.

This is not an isolated story. What you are about to read will shock you, but unfortunately these type of abuses of power are happening on a regular basis to thousands of honest people every year. This particular story took place in 1977 and the situation is worse today than ever before.

The "No Hunger Bread Atrocity"
by Ben Suarez
(Reprinted with permission)

Before I married, I was on a vigorous weight program. After I married, I stopped lifting. This, plus the fact that I ate regular meals, caused me to bloom from my normal weight of 165 pounds to 200 pounds. I tried everything to lose the weight, but nothing worked. There was, it seemed, no workable diet or real diet expert, for that matter. Diet and nutrition are not specialties of a medical doctor. In fact, few people know that doctors only take a few hours of nutrition during the entire course of their education.

Most of the popular diets that I tried, such as the low carbohydrate or the protein diet, ended in disaster. The trouble with most of these fad diets is that they cause the body to expel excess fluid but not fat. Protein diets for instance overload the system with protein which is treated like a poison and the body tries to flush it out. Other diets consist of stimulants such as caffeine or direct diuretics. I managed to lose about 15 pounds of my excess 45 pounds through periodic calorie counting and fasting. However, my real weight loss came early in the '70s, not as a result of some fad diet or doctor's treatment but because, of all things, a bread my wife had accidentally invented.

It all started when a book was submitted to me for promotional purposes. The book was about a Himalayan civilization called the Hunzas, which is reported to be one of the three longest-living civilizations on earth. In reading the book, the one thing that fascinated me was that the majority of the Hunza diet consisted of various forms of whole wheat bread. I asked my wife, Nancy, to duplicate one of their bread recipes. In trying to duplicate the recipe, she made two alterations, one unknowingly. First, the bread would not rise properly, so she would let it set for six hours in order to get maximum rising, which was not called for in the recipe. Second, she had unknowingly added too much honey to the recipe because she would always let her measuring cup overflow, which did not seem significant, but later our measurements showed that this doubled and tripled the honey content.

The original purpose of the bread was to eat it for nutritional purposes. It intrigued me that this type of whole wheat bread was a staple of one of the three longest-living civilizations on earth. This, combined with two other health theories that had emerged—one, the fiber theory promoted by Dr. Reuben, and, two, the fact the U.S. Agriculture

Department had determined that the American diet needed much more 100% whole-grain bread in it to maintain proper nutrition—fueled my interest in the bread. Bread, for some reason, has become a no-no for low-calorie diets due to the ignorance of the diet inventors over the past two decades.

The bread my wife produced was a very tasty bread to say the least. We started to include it in our regular diet, and we did start feeling better, possibly from the combination of the nutritional value and the fact that a high-fiber diet aids regularity, which more and more tests are proving to be a valid factor for good health. But, unexpectedly, something else happened. For some reason, when we ate the bread, we lost our appetite. In fact, it got to the point where we did not eat the bread before meals. With this factor in mind, I started using the bread as a diet aid and, astonishingly, I lost the balance of my 30 pounds of excess weight. But that wasn't the best part. Not only did I lose the weight, I kept it off. Unlike stimulants or diets, which throw your body chemistry out of kilter, the bread was a perfectly natural, healthful addition to the diet, and it could be used indefinitely. Simultaneously several universities announced tests that concluded that whole wheat bread was indeed a food that promoted weight loss.

Also during this period of time, ITT Continental Baking Company introduced Fresh Horizons Bread, which were extra high-fiber white and whole wheat breads. They even went so far as to promote it to doctors much the same way you would promote a prescription drug. But neither whole wheat bread nor Fresh Horizons Bread worked nearly as well as my wife's bread. Because my wife's bread took a great deal of time to make; many times we ran out. We kept trying to substitute whole wheat bread or Fresh Horizons bread, but it just did not work anywhere near as well.

Then, one day we were talking to a friend who had been telling us about all the unsuccessful diets she had gone through. Then the idea hit me. Why not promote my wife's bread as a diet aid?

One drawback was that food was not in our area of expertise. But, as far as dieting and producing the bread, we certainly were more than experts. After lengthy deliberation, I felt that the good points of promoting the bread outweighed the bad points. We decided to start marketing the bread, initially by mail, of all things.

The first step mandatory to marketing the bread was to have documented tests that showed it was indeed an appetite suppressant. We knew it was. It worked for us and many of our friends. We first tried going to testing laboratories and were very surprised to find that there were few, if any, who specialized in this sort of testing. Secondly those who were willing to look into it were talking astronomical figures in the neighborhood of $500,000 to a million dollars. That was totally out of line. I had my degree in psychology, so I was well versed in statistics and testing. I knew that no such test could ever amount to that sum of money.

I decided to test the bread myself using employees from companies with whom we did business as test subjects. We didn't tell them it was our bread, but a new product someone else brought to us. The results were astounding. Test subjects reported appetite satisfaction from eating my wife's bread, of anywhere from two to 24 hours, with an average of five and one-half hours.

The bread, of course, affected each person differently and affected each individual person differently at different periods. Body metabolisms change periodically depending on stress, emotions, activity, etc.

At this point, we didn't know exactly why the bread worked, but later lab tests were to disclose many of the reasons. Some of the reasons it works still remain a mystery today.

The first known reason it works is commonly called the Ayds principle, based on a court case won by Ayds, which demonstrated that adding a quick shot of carbohydrates to the bloodstream suppresses appetite. Our bread even goes one better. The long rising process caused the bread to have a high degree of carbohydrate breakdown. Carbohydrates come in many molecular forms. But, in order to enter the bloodstream, it has to be broken down to a one-molecule carbohydrate, technically called a monosaccharide carbohydrate. Also, almost all honey is already a monosaccharide carbohydrate. The breakdown of the bread itself and the fact that it contains an excess amount of honey or a great deal of monosaccharide carbohydrates that enter the blood stream quickly reduces the appetite.

The second known reason is that being a whole wheat bread it contains a great deal of fiber. Fiber is chewy, and, once it is in the digestive tract, it expands. While it is in the digestive tract, it causes food to move through the tract more rapidly, thus decreasing calorie absorption.

A third factor that makes the bread effective is that the bread never rises properly, and it is very heavy. The most common comment about the bread, after eating it, is, "I feel like I have a brick in my stomach."

The fourth proven reason is that the bread is sweet yet wholesome tasting. It satisfies a wide range of cravings, for it contains the three basic body materials of fat, protein and carbohydrates. It is also eaten hot with a hot beverage, which is satisfying.

A fifth explanatory factory involves the baking process in which the bread is pulled from the oven after being cooked for a short time at a low temperature, just when it is going from raw dough to bread. Whatever chemical composition exists in the bread in this form produces a slight release of gas in the stomach to bring a further feeling of fullness. It is not a great deal of gas or unpleasant gas, it is just enough to create a full feeling. Other lab experts said that it could produce a pH factor in the stomach conducive to appetite satisfaction. The total scope of this factor is not totally known. There is also a trace of herbs in the bread, which could contribute something. In all, the net effect is this: it works better than any weight-loss product on the market, be it food or drug.

Before producing the bread and marketing it, we made an all-out effort to determine what laws we had to comply with. We were in a new area, and we were totally ignorant of the food business.

We assumed, as anybody would, that the best place to get this information would be the Food and Drug Administration. Therefore, we had our attorney contact the Food and Drug Administration in Washington. He described what we wanted to do, the nature of the product and asked for guidelines for the marketing and production of our diet bread. Our attorney was told by the FDA that no such guidelines existed, that, in effect, this area had a big "Fog Index," and you just had to "play it by ear."

I found this hard to believe, so I personally called the closest FDA office, which was in Cleveland. The phone was answered by a grumpy man. After talking to him for awhile, it was obvious that he didn't know much about my question. I asked him where his supervisor was, and he said the FDA regional office was in Cincinnati, Ohio, and he gave me a number to call there. I called the Cincinnati office, and, as usual, after being shuffled around to five different people, I got the same message my attorney got. There are no guidelines for the marketing and production of a new food product.

It, therefore, appeared that we were to be off on our own. I had planned to exceed any regulations anyway because I believe in taking a great deal of pride in my products. I undertook the task of supervising both the production of the bread and the marketing of it.

During the last six months that I was thinking about marketing the bread, I had been testing it myself to be sure that it was everything that I thought it was. There were periods when I could eat the bread and then not eat the bread. One of the things I noticed was that I definitely felt better during the periods I was eating the bread. In my research for writing the ad, I thoroughly read up on the civilization of Hunza in which such a bread is the main staple of their diet. I also read research papers relating the effects of high-fiber diets, plus several books by noted doctors about the benefits of high-fiber diets. These studies show there are many benefits to a high-fiber diet, which include the reduction of many intestinal tract diseases, reduction of obesity and the promotion of regularity. Some side benefits include the well-known relationship between regularity and lower incidence of acne.

The main thrust of the bread was as a diet aid. I usually don't like to complicate things in an ad. I usually stick to one main benefit. But I felt these side benefits concerning nutrition were something people should know, so I decided to put them in the ad and in the brochure that accompanied the product. Now mind you, all of this information is well documented and scientifically proven.

After writing the ad, we turned it over to our law firm for review. They made the usual suggestions. After that, they worried primarily whether what I said about the bread was true. They also said, since we were going into another field, the food field, this type of detailed and enthusiastic advertising might not fit well there. But, who cares how it fits, as long as it's 100% true. What is wrong with motivational advertising? That's what built the nation.

We placed the ad with several test newspapers that were scheduled to run just before Christmas in 1977. Then we went about the task of lining up a feasible way to get the bread produced in mass. We named the bread "No Hunger Bread."

Originally we attempted to come up with a way to bake the bread in loaves and deliver it frozen. However, this turned out to be economically impossible. The idea then hit me to sell the bread in a dry mix in which the purchaser simply added water and baked the bread at home. However, preparing such a dry mix turned out to have unbelievable complications. My wife's recipe called for real milk and real butter. In order to put together a dry mix to which you only added water, we would have to use dry milk and dry butter. The honey was the next problem. How do you get honey into a dry mix to which you just add water? The obvious solutions were dry butter, dry milk and dry honey, which we found were available.

However, before I used these dry ingredients, I wanted to make sure it would produce the same quality product.

We figured this was a good time to try to contact a supplier that had mixers big enough to blend the dry ingredients together. This turned out to be another unbelievable chore. In the entire state of Ohio, there were only two such suppliers. One was at a "mix house" of a major corporation which did not accept new products, and the only other one was at a company called Colso in Columbus, Ohio.

We contacted Colso and were referred to the production manager for whom I will use a fictitious name; I will call him Joe Palmer. I talked to Mr. Palmer by phone and briefed him on what I had in mind, and he enthusiastically scheduled the meeting for the next day. The next day my general manager, Jim DiCola, his wife, Fran, my wife, Nancy, and I drove down to Columbus to meet with Joe Palmer, Terry George, the controller for Colso and Bill Murphy, the company's marketing director. When we got there we were greeted very enthusiastically, and we soon found out why. Colso apparently had lost several major accounts and the place resembled a morgue.

We were shown through the plant and immediately got down to business. I had brought along samples of the bread and the recipe. I asked Mr. Palmer if there would be any problem in producing this dry mix with dry milk, butter, and honey. He said no problem at all. He also said that they were very eager to do business with us, that he would quickly put together a batch of the bread from the recipe, bake it, and we could come down shortly and test it.

Several days later we went back down to Colso for another meeting. We were to take home and try the test loaves of the bread.

We walked into their test lab of the kitchen where Mr. Palmer cut slices of the bread and gave each of us one to taste. Our hearts sank. The test bread did not look, smell, feel, or taste like my wife's bread. I asked Mr. Palmer what had gone wrong and he said he didn't know. He baked it exactly according to the recipe using dry milk, dry honey, and dry butter. However, upon more discussion, we soon learned that they had taken our first meeting very lightly and thought that this was ordinary whole wheat bread. They had not let it rise properly, and they had baked it the same time and temperature as ordinary whole wheat bread.

I told them this was not a joke. I said, "What makes this bread different is the type of ingredients, the proportion of ingredients and the baking procedure. You have to bake this bread at a lower temperature for a shorter baking time, and, most critically, you must pull it out as soon as the bread goes from dough to bread."

To make a long story short, I got back with Mr. Palmer, and we worked out a procedure for producing a dry mix in mass production. We also set up tests to determine the shelf life of the bread. It turned out in the shelf-life tests that honey, which is actually an antibiotic, preserves the bread.

The results of the test ad were now coming in and were unbelievable. Naturally we were very excited. Mr. Palmer said he could get ingredients immediately, so we decided to go ahead and start placing ads. We launched the first full ad campaign in the week of January 1, 1978.

We lined up a meeting for January 6 to finalize our agreement and to set up a long-term contract. The first rollout ad ran January 2, 1978. On January 3, 1978, an FDA agent out of Cincinnati showed up at our door. Also, an agent from the Ohio Department of Agriculture showed up at Colso to take samples of the dry mix. We greeted the agent cordially as we had always done with regulatory officials. Our policy had always been to give regulatory officials full cooperation and courtesy. We spent nearly a whole afternoon with him. I even took him over to my house and showed him how the bread was prepared and gave him some to eat. He asked for the formulation of the bread, which I gave him. He then said he wanted to go through the ad in detail for substantiation of the claims, which we did. The meeting was very cordial, and I assumed it satisfied the agent that we indeed had a good product, and our claims were substantiated.

That same week I got a call from a friend whom I will call Bob Gilmond. Gilmond, a direct-marketing executive, was an older gentleman who had been around and had several friends in high-level government jobs. He said it was urgent to talk to me and that he and a friend were going to fly out. At dinner the next day, they told us their horror story.

Gilmond started by saying that we had better drop the bread or we would be put out of business. He explained that the health and drug business was a well-protected field in which only an exclusive handful of people were allowed in. It made no difference if our product was good, all claims substantiated, and it was the most effective product ever produced, he insisted. If we persisted, we would be put out of business through the use of the dirtiest tricks imaginable, and he added we could not fight these forces, because they were big vested interests that were invincible. At this point I really was furious.

I said there has never been a man, a man-made organization or a man-made thing in the history of the world that has been invincible. No tyrannical son-of-a-bitch is going to take my valid product and put it off the market. Gilmond told me that other people had said the same thing, but their businesses had been destroyed permanently. I said that's other people, that's not me. And, I added, "I swear to you at this table today, should anybody unjustly try to take this product off the market, may God help them, because I will retaliate and destroy them." The entire meeting ended with everyone visibly shaken.

I received messages the next day from several other friends in the direct-marketing business who had learned of the bread, and they said the same thing. One of them told me, "Look, you are especially vulnerable right now because a new patented medicine drug is just coming on the market for which a great deal of money has been paid to the government to falsify test reports."

I asked, "Is the product effective?"

He said, "No, I don't believe the product is safe or effective. These large drug companies will do a test and come up with a meaningless small correlation between the drug and its effectiveness to do something. In this case the product is a nasal decongestant." He said that somebody noticed that sometimes antihistamines make you nauseous and decided to fudge some tests and pass it off as an appetite suppressant. Also, he thought the product was probably unsafe because it caused drowsiness, and extended use is not recommended.

I told him I would never do anything like that. "I do not sell products that do not work or are unsafe. Furthermore, I can't believe that the federal government could be involved in such a blatantly immoral scheme. I'm not naïve; I know there is corruption out there, but these guys certainly have to know that there is a limit to what they can do.

He said, "Forewarned is forearmed." Then he added, "Look, they are not going to let anything natural on the market; use your head. They only want patented drugs and, especially, oil-based patented drugs. That should make sense to you. Synthetic drugs could be patented and natural remedies cannot. This patent allows only a small group of men to control and license and get a piece of the action on everything that is sold. With natural remedies you cannot do that."

I told him, "You are making sense, but this still sounds like a script out of the movies."

We had set up the big meeting with Colso for Friday, January 6, 1978, to finalize our deal to produce the bread. At the meeting with my attorney, my certified public accountant, the owner of a fulfillment company that was going to process the orders, my general manager, and me. With Colso there were the lawyer, Tom Runyan, whom we had never met before, Joe Palmer, the production manager, and Terry George, the controller.

We had given everybody from our company a preliminary as to what had transpired before and the quoted cost per pound. We said, "They are going to ask for four or five cents. We know that the cost should be one to two cents. We want to get this first batch going. After we have leverage and it's in full production, we will get the price lowered. For right now, we will settle for two and one-half cents per pound." Before going to the meeting, we took the Colso people through our operation so they could see the orders coming in. We used WATS lines in the ads and had placed 4 million newspaper circulation ads. We had about 35 operators manning the phones, which were literally ringing off the hook. Orders were pouring in. Our entire universe of newspapers was around 30 million. We had only placed 4 million this week and were projecting that we were going to do around 40,000 orders from that 4 million. For some reason I felt edgy showing the Colso contingent all this, but Mr. Runyan was very eager to see with his own eyes the orders coming in.

After the tour we went to the corporate house, which I purchased for such occasions. We had a caterer come in and serve dinner, giving Colso the royal treatment, not knowing that soon they were going to give us the royal treatment.

We started out to order 200,000 pounds of mix for the first order. The meeting went on for several hours after the meal, and we ironed out all the details on how everything was going to be produced and packaged. The first thing that disturbed me was that Runyan did not want to get involved in the individual packages for consumers, which Mr. Palmer had shown an interest in. They had the facilities there to do it, and, in fact, had done it in the past, but Runyan said he wasn't interested in that. I was amazed that he would turn down such a revenue-producing job offer. He just wanted to mix the ingredients.

We then discussed the ordering of ingredients and determined what they would cost. Mr. Runyan said that he did not want to purchase the ingredients; he would rather have us do it and ship to him. Through all this I noticed Mr. Palmer looked visibly upset, as though he didn't know what was going on and was surprised at the turn of events.

Then came the haggling over the price. I expected Mr. Runyan to come across with a highball price of five cents a pound of mix. But, he stated, "Well, boys, I'm afraid it is going to cost you thirty-five cents a pound." Everybody looked like they had been shot, and Mr. Palmer turned red, and his jaw almost dropped to the floor.

I said, "What? Truly, you are joking!"

The bread mix that would go to the consumer was a four-pound dry-mix package, which, with water, would produce four 1-1/4 pound loaves of bread. We were already running tight. To ship the bread UPS would average about $1.50 per kit; order processing would average another $1.00 for a total of $2.50. Then packaging would be another $1.00 or more for a total of $3.50. Minimally, with a direct-mail product, the markup of goods should be three times. We were already over the $3.33 limit before paying Colso for the mix.

I said, "We already have no room in the price of this product. And you want thirty-five cents just to mix the ingredients. That would put us out of the ball game.

He said, "That's it. Either take it or leave it."

I said, "Wait a minute. I can't believe this. Mr. Palmer said this 200,000 pound initial order would take three men only two days to do. Even if you paid them $10 an hour, which I know you don't, that's $240 a day for a total of $480 for two days. I know the going rate is one to two cents per pound. At two cents per pound, that's $4,000 for something that's going to cost you $500.00. That's already a 300% markup. Now you're telling me you want to charge me $66,000 on top of that? What for?"

He replied, "The honey causes the mixers to get sticky, and we have to have somebody clean them out."

I said, "Who are you going to have clean them out, brain surgeons and nuclear physicists? Hell, at that rate you can get Johnny Carson to come in to do it for you!"

I told Mr. Runyan that we could project from our orders today that this month alone we would sell 600,000 pounds of the mix. That was only one-third of the total market on newspapers alone, which meant on our first run alone, we should sell at least 2 million pounds of the mix. That didn't count second and third runs. We are talking about a huge order here and a perpetual customer and, "You are going to treat us like that?" I asked.

Runyan said, "I'm not going to sit here and argue anymore. Either take it or leave it."

He obviously knew we needed the mix now because orders were pouring in and we would not have time to set up with an out-of-state mixer and go through all the procedures again. The process had already been set up with Mr. Palmer and his men were ready to roll. When I asked about succeeding orders, Runyan said, "I'm not interested in any succeeding orders." I said, "Well it looks like you're going to have to walk." The meeting was abruptly adjourned.

After the Colso contingent left, we all simply sat around in amazement and could not figure out what was going on. This man had us in a position to overcharge us $66,000 on our initial order, and, in effect, told us that the rest did not matter. He wasn't interested. And, on top of it, they needed the business. We projected we would be a million dollar account over a year's period of time. How could he possibly turn such business down? It made no sense to me.

We adjourned the meeting and everybody went home to do some brainstorming. We said, "This has got to be a bluff; they'll call back."

That night, Mr. Palmer called me. He said, "Ben I want to apologize. Can we still do business?"

I replied, "Look, I've got orders pouring in. Certainly, I want to do business."

He said, "For the life of me, I don't understand why Tom Runyan did that, and in fact, I'm trying to get hold of the owner right now to get Runyan taken off this project. I talked to the nephew, the president of our company, and he was infuriated."

I said, "Fine. See what you can do with the owner, and we'll talk in the morning."

In the morning Mr. Palmer called and said, "I can't tell you everything that went on. The only thing I can tell you is that the bottom line is that we will reduce the price by fifteen cents a pound to twenty cents." That was still totally out of line. These calls went on and on until finally the price was dropped five cents more, and they were absolutely not willing to drop further. Thus 15 cents represented an overcharge of approximately $27,000 on the first order. We had to have the mix produced because we had orders in-house. We lined up with another mix company in Michigan, and the price was two cents a pound, but in no way could we set up to produce the mix in enough time to fill the customers' orders on time. So we decided that for the first 200,000 pounds of mix we could go to Colso and take the balance to the Michigan mix company.

In our last phone call, Jim and I got on with Runyan and Palmer and said, "Look, let's have an understanding here. You mean you are going to take the chance of losing us as a customer by trying to over-charge us this outrageous amount? You are going to lose a million dollars over $27,000?" He said, "That's right. So we initiated the order.

Mr. Runyan demanded that money be put in escrow before the mixing, which infuriated us. Further, he steadfastly refused to sign any contract for the order and was, I thought, completely unreasonable throughout the whole proceedings. We kept wondering, "What in the world is going on? What could be behind this man's behavior?"

To top it off, in mid-January of 1978, one of the worst snowstorms in the history of the country hit and delayed our supplies for the bread by up to two weeks and further added to our aggravation.

The second week of January, the same FDA agent showed up again, this time with a female partner. Their names were Terrence Sweeney and Susan Morgan. They wanted to gather more information, precise and detailed information on where and how the bread was going to be shipped. In fact, they went into such detail it made me wonder why they would want such information. The agent also wanted a copy of an order to verify that we were doing business across state lines. I asked him specifically if there was something wrong with the ad or the formula of the bread, or anything at all for that matter, and he said, "No."

A week later he was back with his female partner. This time he wanted detailed information on the packaging. Again I asked, "Is there anything wrong? Let us know now, because orders are pouring in, and I would like to correct anything if it is." Again, he said everything was absolutely fine. I related the conversations I had with my friends in New York saying the FDA was going to put us out of business. He and his partner both shook their heads and kind of laughed and said, "Oh, no. Those people are just living in a fantasy world. The FDA wouldn't do something like that."

We were now into the latter part of January and our office had turned into a pressure cooker. We finally got the supplies for the first 200,000 pounds.

Sales continued to be incredible. We accumulated over 165,000 orders for the bread mix, totaling $1,650,000 in sales.

I stopped the advertising in order to give us time to search for a new supplier who could give us a quick turnaround time. This proved to be futile. They were available, but they were too far away for us to control and oversee. The problem was that we needed huge mixers because all the ingredients along with the honey had to be thoroughly blended.

We also had to line up some place to package the mix we were getting from Colso into the four-pound parcels for the consumer, and it had to be a place suitable for food processing. Even though the FDA said there were no such guidelines, I wanted to be sure that our customers' bread mix would be prepared in a hygienically clean atmosphere.

We searched high and low around Ohio to find such a place. The various food-processing companies in the state that we toured were appalling. There were a few that were clean and well-kept establishments, but many supposedly FDA-inspected places were filthy pigpens.

Finally we decided we would be just as well off to look in our hometown for a place. The most obvious choice was a hometown bakery. We obtained an agreement from a local bakery specializing in pastries and Italian bread called Ferraro's. The owner of Ferraro's agreed to lease a part of his building to us for the purpose of packaging the bread.

However, this still did not solve our big problem. Where would we get all of the ingredients mixed? To get it down to a feasible cost, we had to have mixers that would handle 1,000 to 2,000 pounds of ingredients at a time. One day when we were setting up Ferraro's for the packaging of the mix, an idea hit me. I saw that he had mixers there, but nothing on the scale that we would need. These mixers could hold about 200 pounds, not enough for the entire job, but maybe for a portion of it.

My idea was why not let the customer mix the two major ingredients of honey and flour themselves, and we would simply mix the dry milk, butter, and various ingredients such as herbs. The idea was great. We would only have to mix 10% of the poundage. For instance, on a 200,000 pound order, we would only have to mix 20,000 pounds. We could simply include a jar of honey, pour unmixed flour into a bag, and then put the mix of minor ingredients on top of the flour and instruct the customer to mix them all together. We had a trial production run, and it worked beautifully. Now we had everything right in our own hometown and totally under our control. Colso no longer had us over a barrel. It was my project that with the bread selling like it was, we would soon be producing finished loaves and going with national distribution to retail stores. We could even build a baking company in our hometown, Canton, and bring the area a major new growth industry.

We placed orders for the ingredients and packaging material for the remaining 400,000 pounds that was already sold. This bill came to a whopping $500,000.

Next, we prepared Ferraro's to meet our standards for sanitation. The bakery was already clean and had just passed the state health inspection, which it does twice a year, but we wanted it better than that. We gave Ferraro's the money to completely repaint the place and give it a thorough cleaning. We initiated procedures for personnel to get periodic medical checkups, and we ordered sanitary smocks and head gear to be worn while packaging the mix.

It was now the beginning of February and our ingredients finally came through for the first 200,000 pounds that Colso was supposed to produce. The 200,000 pounds was supposed to be mixed February 8 and February 9, and we would go down to pick up shipments as soon as they came off the mixing machine in order to expedite the shipping process. All during this, Runyan was in my opinion extremely antagonistic. He had to have our check in hand for every order that left the door. The order was finally completed on the afternoon of February 9, when all 200,000 pounds were at Ferraro's. The crew was business preparing the packages to go to the consumer.

The very next day, on February 10, coincidentally when Colso was completely done and had all the money (Runyan demanded cashier's checks) the FDA and Ohio Department of Agriculture showed up at Ferraro's for an inspection, even though Ferraro's had passed the same inspection several months earlier. They had trouble finding anything, but went so far as to tear apart mixers, mechanical parts included, bit by bit. The whole bakery was virtually laying in pieces. They would scrape dirt out of mechanical parts that in no remote way could come in contact with food. In their hands they had a checklist, one of the very things that I had asked for and was told didn't exist. Pushing things to the furthest stretch of the imagination, they cited Ferraro's for an incredible 27 violations, on such things as dirt in mechanical parts of gears, a missing ceramic tile in the bathroom and other ridiculous items that had no bearing on causing unsanitary conditions in foods. What made it all the more ludicrous was all the pigpens that we had seen throughout the state that supposedly passed inspections.

Upon learning this I became infuriated. Why hadn't we been given that checklist of sanitation requirements that I had asked for? Why were we told no such thing existed? I called the Cincinnati office of the FDA and asked to talk to the head man. He turned out to be a

James C. Simmons, regional director for the FDA, Cincinnati office. He was relatively new on the job and had just attained the most cherished goal of civil service workers, a permanent top-level post in his hometown, Cincinnati.

I had to wait to talk to Mr. Simmons because he was gathering the people in his office to witness the phone call. He picked up the phone and put me on a loudspeaker. I told him emphatically I wanted to know why I was not given a checklist of sanitation requirements, which I had asked for along with requirements for the advertising and marketing of the bread. He told me it was really inconsequential and that "there were serious problems with the advertising and labeling of the bread, so serious, in fact, that the bread could not be marketed, and he doubted that it could ever be marketed again in the near future, no matter what we did." In his opinion, our advertising and labeling classified the bread as a drug, and we had not taken out an NDA, or a new-drug application.

I said, "The bread is not a drug, the bread is a food."

· He said, "No, the things you said in reference to the fiber, etc., made it a drug." He said they even classify water as a drug, if you label it improperly.

As we learned, if you file a new-drug application, this gives the FDA the right to: (1) delay you almost indefinitely, and (2) arbitrarily grant or deny your application for a new drug, even though you may have volumes of test results to prove the validity of your product.

In any case, the point was the bread was in no way a drug. This was an obvious misclassification in order to suppress the marketing of the bread. What our colleagues in New York had predicted had come true. I asked Mr. Simmons what we could do to correct the problem

He said, "Get out of the business!"

In effect, Mr. Simmons had told us not to ship any of the product, or it would be seized. They were going to do everything in their power to keep the bread off the market. So there I was, I had in-house 165,000 orders totaling $1,650,000 in sales, and I had just spent the majority of that on advertising the product and supplies. Mr. Simmons said the only way we could get out of this was to mail all the people their money back, which was impossible. The corporation was in terrific financial condition before with about a $500,000 net worth, but out of the $1,650,000, we had already spent one million dollars of irretrievable money in advertising and product supplies. To send all their money back would mean we would be $500,000 short. The company would go bankrupt and a huge number of customers would be left without either money or product. I was stuck with $1.6 million worth of orders that I could not fulfill, and I did not have the cash to send the money back.

Now I thought back to how Runyan handled our negotiations. In my opinion, the best explanation I could think of for his attempting to overcharge us was that he somehow got wind of the possible action by the FDA and the ODA. From this, he could surmise we would be out of business soon. I also believe he got this information somehow from the agencies themselves, perhaps from some high-level friend who worked there. Otherwise, why else would he jeopardize our future business and insist on payment in advance. This suspicion might also explain the coincidence that inspectors showed up in Canton after our last payment to Colso. I have no hard proof of any of this occurring—one rarely does—but I believe this might have been what happened.

Another thing that made the Colso incident incredible was the rift between Runyan and the nephew. How could Runyan take a chance on blowing a deal of our magnitude? He knew that we would be able to pay a few penalties, which is the most likely thing that would happen, and be able to put the bread back on the market. If the bread flourished, he would look very bad. He had to know that we were not going to get the option of changing anything or paying penalties and that we were going to be put out of business permanently.

An Unprecedented Move—Fighting Back and Winning

I had only one recourse at this point. I had to do something unprecedented. I had nothing to lose. For the first time in the known history of the regulatory system, a victim was going to fight back After long deliberation, I felt the best way to do it was to publicize the incident right in their bailiwick, Washington, D.C. My theory was these were rats we were dealing with, and rats don't like the light.

I started to write the full-page ads that would publicize what was happening to us. Then one of my co-workers made a suggestion. President Carter was elected on the platform that he was going to curb the bureaucracy. Why don't you take him up on it? If there is any need or time for it, it's now. I thought about it for awhile. My instinct was, well, I can't call the president, that's ludicrous.

But then, I thought, the president is an elected official. He's not God, he's not royalty. In fact, with the income tax I had been paying, I figured out that I had paid half his salary for the year. He is the president of an executive branch of government of which the FDA was a part. When I have a serious problem occur, I am held responsible as the president of my company. He should be held responsible in this case. I don't know of any problem that could have been as serious. We had a major industry for our area on the verge of being destroyed, along with an existing business, which employed well over 250 people.

So I decided, rather than call the White House, which would give me virtually no chance to get through to the president, I would address the full-page ad I was planning as an open letter to him, only I would address in it details of the bureaucratic problem. I would not name the bureaucracy involved, the FDA, that is, just to give the president a chance to do something about it before it was out in the open. So I wrote the ad as an open letter to President Carter, and it ran on February 16, 1978.

Before we ran the ad, we made another last-ditch effort to settle the problem with Simmons. We had a number of these conversations with no results. To this point we had not received one piece of documented correspondence from Simmons, indicating that there was any problem. I was infuriated with our present law firm because its members had reviewed the ads and, although they had reservations, they certainly did not say categorically that anything this serious would happen. So I fired the law firm and hired what I considered another top law firm in Canton. It was certainly evident that dealing with food and drugs required special legal expertise and our area was not the hotbed of food and drugs. FDA legal experts were concentrated in Washington and New York. Through some of my New York connections, we selected a New York law firm that specialized in dealing with FDA.

We hired a top lawyer with the firm, and he proceeded to research the case. One thing he did was try to find similar cases in the past. He came up with an almost identical one that had occurred just the year before. It concerned International Telephone and Telegraph's Continental Baking Company Division. The year before, they introduced a product called Fresh Horizons Bread, which contained five times the fiber of normal whole wheat bread, which was accomplished by mixing cellulose from wood pulp into the bread. They had made benefit claims citing a research study of the benefits of a high-fiber diet, the same ones that we cited. However, they went a step further and actually distributed literature to doctors, much the same as you would a prescription drug.

Fresh Horizons Bread was put on the market before the FDA intervened. After it was on the market, the letter on the following page (obtained under the Freedom of Information Act) was sent from FDA to Fresh horizons. After four to six months of very casual correspondence back and forth, the resolution of the problem came as follows:

ITT had to change its advertising to take out the reports on the benefits of the high-fiber diet. However, get this. They were allowed to sell out all remaining stock and packaging that had been preprinted and that was it.

The New York attorneys also had on file a case that they had handled for the Ayds Diet Product, which demonstrated in court that an ingestion of carbohydrates prior to eating does indeed lower the appetite. This was one of many principles used as the basis for curbing the appetite with No-Hunger Bread.

When two opposing law firms are engaged in potential litigation, they each research the case to determine case law, that is, what decisions have been rendered in the past on identical issues. The justice system in this country revolves around reason applied consistently. Therefore, if a decision is made on an issue, judges will usually render that decision on similar issues over and over again. Attorneys get together all the court cases on a similar issue and stack up the wins and losses. They each get together with the opposing attorney and say, "Look, we won. There is no sense in going into litigation with this." Only if the stacks are equal and a point is nebulous, then litigation transpires. It doesn't work everytime. Of course, when you have a highly emotional issue one person may still be willing to take a 20% chance it will run in the court. The judge may see something different in a case and rule differently on a matter as opposed to what had transpired in a previous case.

DEPARTMENT OF HEALTH EDUCATION AND WELFARE
Regulatory Letter

CERTIFIED
M. C. Woodward, Jr., President
ITT, Continental Baking Company
Halstead Avenue
Rye, New York 10580

Dear Mr. Woodward:
Investigation on August 16, 1976, revealed that you have been marketing Fresh Horizons Breads with the label bearing the following claim: "The importance of fiber in foods-there is growing evidence to suggest that many Americans just aren't getting enough fiber (Roughage) in their diet. And now, there

is increasing scientific and medical opinion that fiber may even prevent several serious diseases." Additionally, consumer leaflets available at retail food stores bear the claim: "There is increasing medical and scientific opinion that this action of fiber in the body may be tied to the prevention of various gastrointestinal and other disorders." Inspection also discloses an advertising campaign scheduled in medical journals and mailings to physicians bearing claims that represent and suggest that breads are useful in the prevention of serious disease conditions such as but not limited to, ischemic heart disease, diverticular disease, diabetes, obesity, deep vein thrombosis, varicose veins and colonic cancer.

Such claims and statements cause these articles to be new drugs. A new drug Cannot be legally marketed in interstate commerce until the Food and Drug Administration has received and approved a New Drug Application (NDA) for the Article.

In summary, it is the opinion of the Food and Drug Administration that Fresh Horizons Breads are new drugs and as labeled are seriously misbranded and, Therefore, may not be marketed with their present labeling in the absence of an approved new Drug Application.

In view of the above and in the public interest, we request that you immediately discontinue marketing Fresh Horizons Breads as labeled at the local bakery level and immediately discontinue all distribution of promotional literature containing misbranding claims and statements.

We request that you reply with ten (10) days after receipt of this letter, Stating the action you will take to discontinue the marketing of this drug Product. If such corrective action is not promptly undertaken, the Food and Drug Administration is prepared to initiate legal action to enforce the law.

The Federal Food, Drug and Cosmetic Act provides for seizure of illegal products and/or injunction against the manufacturer or distributor of illegal products, 21 U.S.C. 332 and 334.

> Sincerely yours,
> George J. Gerstenberg
> District Director
> New York District

I had a last ditch talk with Mr. Simmons before we ran the open letter to the president ad. We had a conference phone call with a New York attorney, a local attorney, myself, my general manager, Mr. Simmons, and whoever was in his office at the time. The conversation went like this:

Our lawyers told Mr. Simmons that they did not feel that their client was guilty of any wrongdoing, and if he was guilt, it certainly was not intentional; it was done innocently. But, if the FDA did feel that there was a violation of the law, then we would be more than willing to cooperate. They told Simmons we had already stopped advertising and were willing to change the advertising and packaging as per his wishes. They cited the ITT case as an example of what the FDA had done in the past. Simmons would have no part of this and was not even willing to acknowledge that the ITT case existed. He stated he had already recommended seizing our product and that the seizure was very near. The only way that he would not seize was that if we reimbursed all of the customers and got out of the business. The lawyer told Mr. Simmons it was financially impossible for us to do so, that it certainly was not fair to tell us to get out of the business. Mr. Simmons repeated that the product could never be marketed again. Our New York attorney said, "Really, Mr. Simmons, you will never get a court of law to grant you such an injunction." (Simmons also told us not to hire an FDA lawyer.) Simmons threatened that he might file criminal charges against us. He said in the statue of the Food, Drug and Cosmetic Act the executives of a food and drug company may be tried with criminal violations on a matter, even if somebody else in the company was doing something wrong without their knowledge. This is an absurd law, which many elected officials have tried to overturn, but were overruled by more liberal elected officials. To the best of our knowledge, this law had never been enforced and this was merely a tactic on Simmons' part.

Our lawyers then told Simmons that we were willing to go even one step further. Before sending the people their bread, we were willing to send them a letter that would correct the advertising he found questionable and would ask them if they still wanted their order. Simmons would not have any of it. He said the only recourse was to send the people all of their money back and get out of the business.

Our lawyers were appalled. They said they had never witnessed an encounter like this with a regulatory agency, and it was unprecedented in their experience. Then they explained what was going to happen. The FDA is one of the most powerful regulatory agencies because it has seizure powers. That is, it can seize your personal property without your right to a defense. Seizure is an absurd law. If a regional FDA agent finds a product that, in his estimation, is in violation of the Food, Drug and Cosmetic Act, the regional director of his regional office sends a recommendation for seizure to Washington. There are three basic types of seizure alerts: red alert, which means a highly toxic or poisonous product is on the market; a green alert, something that might be mildly toxic, and thirdly, what they call an "oh shit" alert, which is a harmless and nebulous thing like misleading advertising, particularly on labeling. Ours was classified as an "oh shit" alert, and it was taking Simmons a while to get the seizure cleared through Washington. We assumed he got a lot of cooperation in Washington because we had treaded on a protected territory. Even so, the bureaucracy still worked slowly.

Once this seizure order is granted from the Washington FDA office, it is turned over to the regional U.S. Attorney. The U.S. Attorney takes a seizure order to court which is an automatic and meaningless process. The judge cannot legally turn down the seizure order. Nor do the accused have a right to defense. The accused do not have the right to even be present during the judge's deliberation or lack of deliberation. There is no legal way to stop a seizure, even if it is meant to be harassment. Even if the accused goes to court to show that the FDA is really harassing him or that there is nothing wrong with the product, the FDA arbitrarily and at its own whim and decision can keep on seizing a product and no one can stop it.

I couldn't believe this. I said, "What kind of a moron would put this power in the hands of unelected civil service workers? You mean they have the right to arbitrarily seize a man's personal property? These are the things that cause revolutions and civil wars. It's an unfair and unjust law."

The lawyers said that the law became more open to arbitrary decision by civil service workers in 1960 when the famous Kefauver Amendments were passed. Before that, the FDA only had the right to rule whether a food or drug was harmful before they could seize. However, Senator Kefauver also wanted them to decide arbitrarily whether a drug was effective, a word that opens up a wide range of nebulous, subjective interpretations. Since the Kefauver Amendment, the FDA had really become powerful. It can arbitrarily say that a product, food or drug, can or cannot be marketed. It can seize your personal property, destroy you financially, sabotage your character and business, all without your right to a fair trial. I said, "I really can't believe this. This has to be a nightmare or a horror story." They said, "It's true."

"You mean this one unelected civil service worker in Cincinnati has the power to be, in effect, enforcement officer, judge, jury and executioner?"

They said, "That's right."

In my opinion, Simmons' statements imply that he doesn't really care about elected officials and that the FDA really runs the government. He once stated, "I wish we didn't have to go through the courts." Can you imagine? What incompetence it is to put a man like Simmons in that position of authority. This man struck me as having obvious hostility to anything that exists beyond his regimented world.

After our encounter with Simmons, our New York attorney called Washington and talked with the attorney in charge of the case in the main office of the FDA. He said, "This is not a case of getting anybody to comply with the law or protecting the public, a concern for national welfare or anything of that nature. Somebody wants to put you out of business. It's that plain and simple. They are going to use every trick in the book."

I said, "Look, I'm still in a state of shock. I still cannot believe that this is going on." I knew that there were problems in government, but I still thought it was limited, and overall there was some sense of responsibility in our government workers for the general welfare of the country and its citizens. I said, "What about an internal affairs department? Is there such a thing that we can go to?"

He said, "No."

I asked, "What about going to our congressmen?"

He said, "No, that won't help. They don't have the power to stop a seizure."

"You mean nobody controls these guys?" I exclaimed. "They have complete control of the citizens, elected officials, and the courts?"

"That's right," he stated.

Disillusioned and infuriated, I went back to the drawing board to figure out how we were going to get out of this mess. The first thing that became apparent was that we had better begin generating another source of income, that is, another product line very quickly. We did have another product we were supposed to launch at the beginning of January, but it had been delayed because of the bread trouble. I had been documenting material for over eight years to write a book about how to start a direct-market business. I didn't want to write the book until I was sure that my success was not due to luck or stumbling upon lucky situations or being in the right place at the right time. Too many "How to Succeed" successful authors write books before they actually know what was behind their success. I've seen more than one entrepreneur happen to stumble upon an incredibly powerful market, then go out and make all kinds of speeches and write books on how he made a lot of money. Then the market depletes, and the business collapses, and he soon finds he did not know everything there was to know about being successful in business. But because I had been involved in selling many different products through many different media, I felt that I had more than adequate knowledge to produce an adequate degree of success. I had been working on the book off and on ever since December, but had really devoted little time to it.

We had an incredible situation now dealing with the crisis of our bread and putting out a major product, a well-illustrated, information-packed book on how to start your own business. The book was to be called *7 Steps to Freedom, or How to Escape the American Rat Race.*

The wheels were now turning rapidly in Washington to try to put us out of business. Research of more case histories showed that our situation was not unprecedented. What was happening to us was a well-systematized plan and coordinated effort. ITT got off the hook because it had Washington influence. However, the case histories show that, in most cases, when small businesses that become viable and visible trespass into a lucrative market area of vested-interest corporations, they will be systematically put out of business. There is no regard for public welfare, national welfare or gaining compliance with the law. The whole system is meant to do one thing—put the company out of business permanently.

Not all market areas, of course, fall into this situation. Some do to a larger degree than others. We were in one of the most tightly controlled and most vigorously controlled market areas—food and drugs. With the seizure laws and the passing of the Kefauver Amendments, this really made it possible for a handful of men to control the food and drug industry.

Many of the case histories that we studied involved the health food industry which was being hit by vested interests in the patent medicine industry. The people in the court cases we studied testified that the reason for the attack on natural drugs and nutrition items is that there is a vested interest in the government to promote synthetic oil-based drugs. They went on to say this is especially true with regard to cancer cures. It has been determined that the cure for cancer will come from an oil-base synthetic patent medicine, and all others will be put off the market. All research money is directed toward oil-base synthetic drugs, while research in the area of natural remedies is already all but shut off.

Studying these cases indicated there is a common pattern of how small companies that promote natural health remedies are put out of business. This system has even been used on progressive doctors who try to experiment with something different because the standard patent medicines are not working to cure cancer. Many doctors were also having their reputations sabotaged, and they were put out of business.

The FDA would be tipped off that a natural-health remedy was being used that might become a viable market item. The FDA would make the necessary arrangements to seize the product. They would then arrange to plant a story in a major news media. This occurred usually in established network media, such as one of the large TV networks, a key influential newspaper, or through the Associated Press. The FDA actually went so far as to have certain planted reporters actually working for them. The media would be tipped off when a seizure would occur and coordinate it with agents. The agents and their media cohorts would burst into the business's or doctor's office, seize the products, splash the story across TV, radio, and newspapers, all before the victim had a right to a fair trial. There was no such thing as "innocent before proven guilty."

To get ahead of our story, coincidentally or uncoincidentally, ours followed the same pattern. It all started on March 2, 1978, on NBC's "Today" show. Betty Furness did a hatchet-job story on our bread and tried to become a prophet, "predicting further action on this bread from governmental agencies."

Later she also aired a totally unwarranted news report on my book, before she even had the product in hand.

This brought up another incredible point. The FDA had made a decision to seize our bread, as Simmons admitted, without testing it and without any consumer complaints. Since it was impossible for them to come from the consumers, we contacted Mr. Simmons to ask from whom the complaints were coming. He said, "I'm just loaded with complaints."

I asked, "Are they from consumers?"

He said, "No."

I said, "Well, then obviously they are from our competitors then, right?"

He wouldn't answer me. So apparently the decision was made to seize without testing the product, without consumer complaints, but from complaints from the competition.

I had an obligation to my customers and, whether the FDA made a seizure or not, I could not sit on my orders any longer. The FTC has a 30-day rule that says you are supposed to ship orders after they are received before 30 days expire. This rule was also staring us in the face. I initiated the shipment of 30,000 orders. This would be a good test of whether the customers thought that they had been deceived. So far this deception idea was theoretical on the part of the FDA.

In direct marketing, you can tell if you have a shoddy product or if the advertising intentionally or unintentionally misled the public. You gauge this through complaints and refunds. Refunds are the best direct gauge. Many government agencies claim this is not a valid measurement due to apathetic consumers. Many people who order the product will not bother to send it back. But the truth is a majority of the public will send the product back if they are dissatisfied. In fact, case histories show a 90% return of a product that is either shoddy or misleading. Acceptable refund rates by the largest, most respected mailorder companies, such as large catalog houses, *Time/Life* books, etc., and throughout the industry range from 10% to 15%. If the product is a book, for some reason there is a built-in 4% refund rate. With books the public knows they can order books by mail and either photocopy the book or parts of it, or read it and then return it for a full refund.

So this first 30,000 shipment would measure whether we had misled the public or whether they were satisfied with the product. How true was our advertising, and how good was our product? Of those 30,000 shipped and all succeeding shipments, there was only a one-half of 1% refund request. Incredibly low. In fact, that kind of public acceptance is usually unheard; 99 ½% of the public was satisfied.

To make matters even more convincing, we produced an ad with the help of the FDA experts in New York that deleted any reference to health benefits. We changed the name of the bread from No-Hunger to Nancy's Special Formula Bread, and all the wording was done with the help of the lawyers so that in no way would it be misleading.

Even though we had proved that we had a viable product, it appeared that no government agency would step in to help us. I decided to help myself. I called the antitrust department at our regional office in Cleveland, Ohio. I talked to a Mr. Edmond Round. We sent him all the information we had accumulated, which certainly provided cause to believe that the FDA's actions were a ploy to put us out of business because we were competing with vested-interest concerns. This was a direct violation of antitrust laws. Mr. Round's attitude was nonchalant, and I could tell immediately he was not going to do anything. I followed up with him in succeeding months and still could tell nothing was being done. I gave him leads but he never followed up. Six months later, we got a letter saying he had done an investigation and could find no wrongdoing. No investigation ever transpired.

I next went to the Small Business Administration and was directed to a division of the S.B.A. that was relatively new called Advocacy. It was specifically set up to protect small businesses from unjust acts from regulatory agencies. I was turned over to an agent within this division named Jerry Lawson. My first contact was with one of Mr. Lawson's assistants, and he certainly was encouraging. He said, "Keep the faith, baby. We'll take care of you." This all sounded too good to be true, and as it turned out, it was. After many succeeding phone calls and correspondence, I learned that Advocacy was nothing but a propaganda tool. The propaganda was that it was created to protect small businesses from regulatory agencies and large, vested-interest groups, but it was given no legal power to do anything. Regulatory agencies totally ignored it and, in fact, considered it a joke.

Getting back to the ad we ran in February, the Open Letter to President Carter, we chose the *Washington Star*. The advertising department at the *Washington Star* had been very excited about the ad. It was unprecedented. They had visions of this ad giving them national publicity. Frankly, so did we. This was a first. For once, a small businessman had enough of the tyrannical rule of the regulatory agencies and was going to fight back. A classic David/Goliath battle. It was not a cheap publicity stunt. Our company was in dire need. People were depending on this action for their jobs, and it meant survival. We had documented evidence to indicate that there was probable cause that we were fighting corruption, and we had exhausted every other means to remedy the problem. Everyone, including the law firms, felt this ad would get national attention in the news media.

After the ad ran, we waited for something to appear in the news media. That night nothing happened. The next day, nothing. Nothing ever appeared anywhere. A complete blackout. The people in our company and our legal counsel could not believe it, but it became apparent how incredibly powerful this regulatory network, along with its sources in the news media, were. We were deluged with calls from people in the direct-mail industry. They said it was an incredible feat, the best thing they had ever read. They could not believe that the news media did not pick it up. This drove home the point that the news media is managed and controlled far beyond what the general public can imagine.

The day the ad ran, we received tremendous phone feedback, mostly from private citizens in Washington, D.C. The inquiries that came from government officials were merely to find out what agency was involved. Not one congressman called, including our own.

Three days later, we received a call from the White House. Not from the president, but from an aide, an aide of an aide, no less. It was from a woman named Shelley Weinstein in the office of President Carter's aide, Midge Costanza. She took down the details of what agency was involved and what our problem was. I let her know the importance of the matter, and that I had all these customers sitting on the line with hundreds of thousands of dollars worth of perishable supplies waiting in the wings. She said she would get back as soon as possible.

Days went by, and no one called. I called back and asked what the status was. She hem-hawed around. I tried to get specific. I asked, "What have you done?

She replied, "Well, we turned it over to this person and that person."

I inquired, "What person? And what are they doing exactly?"

At this point she started to get flustered. She said, "Oh, you mean you really wanted us to do something?"

I said, "Are all you people insane there? Why the hell do you think I spent $6,000 on a full-page ad in Washington? Did you think it was my hobby or something?" She really became unglued at this point and said she could no longer discuss the matter, that somebody would be in touch with me.

The next day I got a call from a Mr. Wishman. He said President Carter had a policy of not getting involved in regulatory actions, that there was nothing he could do.

I said, "Well, what do you mean you don't get involved in regulatory actions? That's a promise he made to the voters and one which everybody expected him to carry out. He said he was going to reduce the bureaucracy. Instead, he expanded it. He said he was going to get government out of our lives. Now is a perfect opportunity to seize an actual occurrence, which we have evidence as unjust. This occurrence concerns an interference with the free-enterprise system, and he won't do anything about it? Also, the president is the chief executive over these regulatory agencies. What do you mean he can't get involved? If he can't, who can?" I was cut short and told that I shouldn't listen to campaign rhetoric.

This really infuriated me. What's wrong with truth in advertising for politicians? They gain many benefits in life at the expense of the public—money, power and prestige. They are selling the public their goods and services. Why is it that they are permitted to deceive and mislead and get away with it?

At least I answered a question I had always been curious about. What if a private citizen called the president with a problem? Would he respond to a group of ordinary citizens? What if the problem concerned national campaign promises? Would he respond? My experience answered these questions with a resounding "no!"

Then, from the ad we got an unexpected phone call from which we were to learn a great deal. This call was from a Washington lobbying law firm. I knew that there were lobbyists, but I did not know the exact details involved or how they went about it. This firm more prominently called itself a public-relations firm. They had seen our ad. They told us that if we were having problems with a regulatory agency, running an ad to solve the problem was not the way to do it. They said they could take care of the problem nicely and quietly for us. I asked how they proposed to do this, since I thought lobbyists only lobbied for Congress. They proceeded to tell me that lobbyists or public-relations firms, as they called them, also handle regulatory agencies.

After more conversations and details, I asked what this little public relations effort would cost me. They said $5,000 down and probably $30,000 overall. I couldn't believe what I was hearing. I told them that I would get back to them.

I decided to hire a private investigator to start investigating the whole matter, including personally investigating those involved.

In our investigation, most of the sources we contacted or who contacted us were informants who wanted to remain anonymous. As publishers, we are honoring that request.

From the ad we also picked up informants within the regulatory agencies themselves. They were curious about the ad, and they were disgusted with the corruption within their own agencies. From our various approaches of investigation into this matter, we learned that Washington in essence, is for sale, and there are a number of ways to buy influence. The most standard and obvious way is campaign contributions to elected officials, which is legal. There is also direct illegal payments to elected officials called bribes. Then there are lobbyists, who must be registered to persuade elected officials how they should vote on certain issues. Those few items are only the tip of the iceberg.

My investigation uncovered the meat of the system for buying government influence, both on the federal and state level. This underground system is where the real money changes hands. Some of it legally, but most of it illegally. Naturally, the whole thing is totally concealed from the public.

Most of the lobbyists in Washington and at the state level are law firms. They call themselves lobbying law firms and many times public-relations firms. These firms go beyond dealing with elected officials. There is a body in Washington considered by some to be more powerful than elected officials. This body is the congressional aides. There are, on the average, about 60 congressional aides for each congressman. Congressmen obviously don't have time to handle every detail of their jobs, and depending upon the congressman, he or she delegates as much work as he or she is unwilling to do. In effect, the office is run by the aides, with whom a citizen will deal 99% of the time. These aides also research legislative bills and have a great deal of influence on how congressmen vote. So a great deal of legal, but unethical lobbying goes on with aides, where the favors are lunches and a host of other perks.

Next comes the public relations with the various government agencies, including both appointees of elected officials and civil service workers. This "legal lobbying," of course, comes in the same manner with lunches and other perks.

There is yet another category which is questionably legal, very immoral and unethical. This one is called buying influence through the jobs program. This is where officials of government departments, especially appointees of elected officials and also civil service workers, work in a department for awhile and give favorable treatment to a certain corporation. In return for this favorable treatment, he is promised a job with the corporation or a job with a law firm that services that corporation at a very lucrative pay. Because a law was recently passed that requires such a government official to sit out a year after he leaves his government duty; he must refrain from working for any corporation with which he has dealt. However, this law can be gotten around very easily, and a year's wait for such a position is no hardship.

Then there are the illegal methods. This is where large-sum bribes are paid directly to congressional aides, appointees of elected officials in government departments, and to civil service workers. It is not as direct as you might think. You can't walk in and hand one of these government officials a bribe. They wouldn't take it. You might be an honest government official who would prosecute them or an honest news media reporter doing a story on them. You have to pay your bribe through a lobbying firm. But it even goes further than that. The lobbying law firm has to employ a personal friend of the influential government official for this to work. A government official is only going to take money from somebody he knows and trusts. We were told that basically what happened to us was that we started out all wrong. We were told that we never were bothered by regulatory agencies before because we were not selling products which competed with vested-interest corporations. We sold horoscopes, commemorative plates, flags, one-shot books, computerized diets, etc. They were one-shot items with a limited life span and really competed with nothing of any big consequence. Now this bread was something different. With this bread and the ad, we unknowingly stepped on the toes of some very influential people and trespassed on a protected market.

First, a housewife inventing a weight-loss product steps on the toes of an arrogant little scientific community, many of whom do not have any creative ability. Not all scientists fall in this category, but there is this certain group which does not like to see innovations that they didn't create or people making money in scientific endeavors.

We also trespassed into the highly protected patent medicine field. This evidently is one of the most powerful, closely knit and influential groups. They have what is called a first-class license in the health field. They especially want to keep prestigious areas like finding cancer cures to themselves. They want to make sure the glamorous curing of this disease comes from their group and from their product line, particularly from an oil-based synthetic drug.

Next, we trespassed into the $5-billion-a-year bread industry. Other companies over the years, smaller baking companies, have been systematically eliminated. Now there are just a handful of major baking companies. The same goes for pharmaceutical companies. Although the total number of pharmaceuticals remains about the same, those with major sales, according to one expert, have dwindled from about 100 in 1960 to about five now.

The baking companies have what you may call a second-class license. They aren't allowed to get into the health field.

So in our informants' minds, there were a multitude of groups that could and probably did send down the order to put us out of business.

Another factor you have with regulatory agencies is that the government hires many young lawyers just out of college. These lawyers come out of the make-believe world of academics, influenced by socialist professors. Many of them just don't like the fact that you are making money. The second type of individual is looking at the government as a stepping stone in his career. If he works for the government for awhile and gets enough notches in his gun (which he gets by the number of businesses he sabotages), then he is considered an effective lawyer who will most likely get a lucrative job in a law firm servicing corporations in his field.

Larger corporations, who have already bought influence, are untouchables, and even if they weren't, they have large law firms and a lot of money to fight in court. The most lucrative victim is a small, viable, visible business with no government influence, with no large law firm, and no money to fight in court. These businesses will succumb quickly, whether the charges against them are valid or not. These regulatory lawyers also are not interested in a very small fly-by-nighter who really didn't ring up that many sales. The next category you deal with in regulatory agencies is the career bureaucrat. He just enjoys showing his power.

And lastly, you do have a certain number of people in regulatory agencies who are honest and who are there to serve the public. However, regulatory actions carried out in the interest of the country and the public are in the minority. A vast majority of government regulatory actions are carried out for the self-serving purpose of vested interest groups.

Many times the majority of workers in a regulatory agency may be honest, but like any other organization controlled by a handful of powerful people, certain agencies have more power than others. The degree of control is also proportional to time. It takes government a great deal of time to evolve to the point where they gain command and control over the lives of the citizens. To make the problem even more complex, the power changes, depending upon who wins elections and who leads regulatory agencies. Much of it has to do with vendettas. For instance, you can go to the Justice Department and turn in a corrupt government official. But that agency probably will not act unless an official in the Justice Department has a vendetta against that particular individual.

We were told that we would not have access to the purchasing-of-government influence system because of the ad we published. Now everyone in the system would be leery of us, for we could be doing investigation work for further publication. We were now considered truly outsiders and renegades.

Next, we discovered something that really drove all of this home. One of our chief competitors had copied the main scheme of the No-Hunger Bread ad, but fulfilled the ad with a honey and bran tablet. This honey and bran tablet, unknown to me, had been on the market before and was produced and marketed by Thompson Laboratories.

This competitor has an attorney who is also an Assistant Attorney General for the Ohio Attorney General. Through some probing, we found that there are hundreds of Assistant Attorney Generals who make $8,000 a year. We couldn't find out if what they do justifies this salary or not.

Although this competitor's ads were changed somewhat to avoid infringing on copyright laws, the ads virtually said the same thing as ours and made the same health claims for fiber. I checked the honey-bran pills sold by Thompson Laboratories. They were sold in retail drug stores. I found them on the shelf with a host of other diet aids. These other diet aids were either pure candy, caffeine pills, diuretic pills, and the relatively new pill, phenylpropanolamine. However, the candy and the honey and bran pill provided legitimacy to our claims that Nancy's Bread is a hunger suppressant. The carbohydrate principle is in the candy and both the carbohydrate and bran principle were in the bran pill. Nancy's Bread was a better product than these because it added several more factors to induce hunger suppression. But the point remained, many of these products had been on the market for 20 years. The FDA had alluded to the fact in its complaint that the bread was not a hunger suppressant. Yet, it possessed several of the qualities of a hunger-suppressant produce which the FDA allowed on the market. As for the fiber claims, it had allowed Thompson to make such claims right in the brochure that accompanied its honey-bran pill in retail stores.

I contacted the FDA and demanded to know why we were being selected for prosecution, and these other products were not. They took the information and said that they would investigate. Nothing to our knowledge was done with Thompson. But they had to do something with our chief competitor. They went through a mock investigation which ended with our competitor's lawyer and an assistant from the Ohio Attorney General's office meeting in Cincinnati, at Simmons' office. The result, our competitor was let go by simply altering his ad somewhat. He was allowed to ship all of his product without interference. He had done two things right. He had sold a product bought and paid for in Washington, and he had influence in the regulatory network through the Ohio Attorney General.

At this time we were still shipping bread in small batch so as not to make it lucrative for the FDA to seize.

Also, after running the Open Letter to President Carter, we made another conference call with Simmons with the same people on the line as before, our New York attorney, our local attorney, my general manager and me. We wanted to see what his reaction was, if there was some way of bringing this to the bargaining table. Upon contacting Mr. Simmons, I could tell he was seething with anger. He said, "Yes," he saw the letter to the President, in fact, he had been in Washington at the time. The lawyers pointed out that we didn't mention FDA's name, and we were still willing to negotiate the matter. We would be willing to do anything to comply with the law and make any adjustments necessary. He restated that he wanted us to stop shipping. I told him we couldn't do that because we had the 30-day FTC rule to contend with, and we had customers who had sent money for the product. We could not afford to return their money, and therefore, we had to give them their product. Seeing as how he would not negotiate with us as to what to do to correct the advertising, we didn't know what to do but keep on shipping. We asked him what would be wrong in shipping all the orders we had so far and enclosing a letter passed by the FDA. The letter would "correct" the advertising and tell the customers that if they felt they had been misled, they were entitled to a full refund. He said absolutely not. He said our only recourse again was to send the people their money back and to get out of the business. We asked him what the status was on the seizure. He admitted that the Open Letter to President Carter had caused a delay in the seizure procedure but that delay was now over and the seizure was proceeding with all due speed.

Looking back on the original ad, it is our belief that we made a tactical error in not mentioning the agency in question. The feedback we got was that this was taken as an indication of our weakness or unwillingness to really follow through with an ad damaging to the FDA.

Meanwhile our 2,000 parcel shipments at a time were not cutting it. There were too many orders, and we were getting complaint letters from furious customers. We had to try something desperate, a calculated risk, to get some of the oldest customers out the door in a bigger chunk. After discussing the matter, we felt there was a good chance that bureaucrats did not work weekends. We knew that they were monitoring our shipments at the UPS office, but the indication we got was that nobody was there on weekends. So the weekend of March 4, 1978, we decided to try to get through with 20,000 parcels of our oldest customers. Our attempt backfired in that they obviously had informants tell them of the shipment. They also must have put pressure on UPS to delay the shipments. For some reason the truck with these parcels did not leave over the weekend as it was supposed to. It sat there until Monday morning.

Simmons seizure request was cleared, but for some bureaucratic reason a court order to seize could not be granted until the Wednesday of that week. Therefore, Simmons had the Ohio Department of Agriculture come in that Monday morning and embargo our shipment. As I mentioned before, state and federal regulatory agencies work hand in hand. They are, in effect, a compromising network.

We were told that Ohio laws for embargo allowed the Ohio Department of Agriculture (ODA) to embargo goods even though they did not have a good reason. But the point was the FDA had to wait until goods went into interstate commerce or until one was shipped across state lines in order for them to seize. The Ohio Department of Agriculture does not have to meet this condition. The ODA could have seized the mix at Colso's when Colso was mixing, but they did not!

Since the Ohio Department of Agriculture embargoed our bread, I wrote a letter to our good governor, James Rhodes, who, for the last decade, has professed to be Ohio's biggest crusader to attract industry and jobs to Ohio. So I wrote him a letter, and I asked him as per his campaign promises regarding bringing industry and jobs to Ohio, would be help our business, which we had planned to launch into a major baking industry in Ohio. Our good governor was very helpful. He sent in return a one-line letter, which acknowledged receipt of our letter. That was it.

On March 9, 1978, the FDA was granted a seizure order. Agents from the FDA U.S. Marshall's office in Cleveland converged on the UPS station in Cleveland and our packaging service plant in Cleveland. They seized 20,000 kits of bread, which totaled 80,000 pounds, plus various other supplies connected with future shipments. Total value of all goods seized was around $200,000.

They coordinated the seizure with television coverage from NBC's affiliate station in Cleveland, WKYC, Channel 3. Cameramen were coordinated to arrive on the scene at the same time as the government officials. U.S. Marshalls posed for the cameras as they got out of the car. The blatant extravaganza of half-truths, out-of-context and distorted facts that Channel 3 put in this news report was then picked up by the rest of the TV stations, local newspapers and put on the wire service across the country. That evening all over the TV our names were smeared, our characters assassinated, our product and our business sabotaged. At first we were in shock after the broadcasts that evening, especially during one broadcast, which showed my wife's picture on the TV screen. My wife and children broke into tears.

As I watched my wife and children in tears and sadness, I vowed that, regardless of whoever was responsible in Washington for this unjust tyrannical act, I would seek them out and legally destroy them if it took me 20 or 30 years. I would hunt them down one by one, as the Jews hunted down the Nazis. This was an atrocity. Nothing more, nothing less. These people I felt were no different than any common war criminal, and this was an act of war.

In fact, in my estimation this matter was even worse, when you consider the fact that there is strong evidence to indicate that people associated with this atrocity were deliberately suppressing cancer cures. This made them no better than mass murderers.

My mother died of cancer at the age of 48 in 1970. It probably was one of the most traumatic experiences in the history of either side of our families. Both sides of the family had an inherited long and healthy life span, and this was a trauma the members had not endured before. Only one who has gone through it can know the agony of watching someone with this hideous disease suffer for months.

Knowing what I knew now made me all the more furious. My mother's doctor gaver her chemotherapy treatments, which were totally ineffective and, in fact, induced pain and symptoms worse than the disease itself. Talk about unsafe and ineffective. Chemotherapy, according to anything I or research investigators have uncovered, is almost totally ineffective against the major malignant forms of cancer. The cancer establishment's claims of success include all cancers, many forms of nonfatal cancers, such as skin cancer, which is not usually fatal. However, the fact is the vast majority of the rally serious forms of malignant cancer are incurable even with today's medical treatments of cutting, burning with radiation, and poisoning the entire body with chemotherapy.

Doctors have to go with what they are given to work with in the way of treatments. If they use other treatments, they are liable for prosecution by this diabolical establishment. I do not know if a cancer establishment was responsible for this bread incident. I just want to make a point that they might have been involved. In an ensuing investigation, we learned in detail just what is going on and what many people call a conspiracy to suppress cancer cures.

In their press releases, the FDA called our bread ordinary whole wheat bread with a little fruit oil in it, which really infuriated us. The bread, of course, is different because of the type of ingredients used, the proportion of ingredients and the preparation. The rising time, cooking temperature and cooking time were vastly different. This was like saying stainless steel was nothing more than iron wtih a little chromium in it.

As far as getting our day in court, the lawyers also revealed that the federal courts are an atrocious place for a citizen to try to get a fair shake when going up against the government. They said, in effect, that Federal judges are not guardians of justice. They are political appointees who can be chosen for a variety of reasons, the least of which is competence. Often they have friends who came up the political ladder with them right in the U.S. Attorney's office. Many of these judges were bureaucrats themselves who worked at federal agencies and were appointed for life. They don't ever have to worry about retribution from the voting public. The whole system is riddled with favoritism and injustice.

The public distrusts the government but views it as an invincible omnipotent force. The reaction we received from the public and our friends was, "Oh my God, what are you going to do? You're dead and buried. The big powerful FDA took action against you. There's nothing you can do." Besides having regulatory agencies and the justice system against us, phone calls came in for interviews from vulture reporters hungry to pick the pieces. One was from a woman from the *Washington Post* who was their consumer advocate. Reporters always say they are going to do a balanced in-depth report. The public doesn't know that 98% of the balanced in-depth reports that you see in the news media were researched with a few minutes of phone calls. They look mainly for things they can take out of context and make half-truths out of innuendos, etc. They always look for the bad. Good news is no news.

The woman from the *Washington Post* was Stephanie Mansfield. She had already made up her mind she was going to do a job on us before she started. You could tell that from her comments and the tone of her voice. She kept asked me what my credentials were to produce such a diet bread. Part of the effectiveness of No-Hunger Bread was the system I invented to use it, the system I had developed when I exhausted all other fad diets developed by doctors. I told her I had researched the system myself and it works. I said the bread allowed me to lose all my weight. I was overweight for 10 years. I have now taken it all off and have kept it off. We have tested it on other people and it's working for them, too. I asked, "What more do you want?"

She said, "You have to be a doctor in order to prove such a thing."

I said, "Doctors are fine, but this particular thing doesn't require a doctor. Besides that's not their area of expertise. Supposed you need someone to jump a six-foot hurdle. So you send somebody to school for four years to learn how to jump hurdles, but he still can't do it. A man comes along who has not been to school, but has taught himself to jump the six-foot hurdle. What are you doing to do? Deny that the second man jumped the hurdle and pretend that the first one did?"

She didn't know what to say to that. She asked me for more details on the bread, probing for something she could use. Then she asked me if I would send her a package of the bread, which I did. Later her "unbiased" story came out. She took the information I gave her and added to it, so it appeared that I was deceiving my customers. She also indicated that because I was not a doctor, the results of the tests done to show that the bread was a hunger suppressant were inaccurate.

I received a call from my Canton lawyer who said that in his last conversation with the attorney handling the case in the Cleveland U.S. Attorney's office, Solomon Oliver, had asked if there was any way that he could get some of the bread. He stated in effect, that he believed it worked.

I said, "What the hell is this? He's prosecuting us, and he doesn't even believe in what he's doing? What is this, a joke?"

We learned that the U.S. Attorney's office in Cleveland had lost a lot of personnel lately and was generally considered undermanned. We learned that a parade of criminals, murderers, rapists, burglars, and drug pushers were being let go because of the U.S. Attorney's office. Dangerous criminals were sent out on the street, but this office spent its time on matters like this—seizing a harmless bread.

We were now starting to experience what is known as the vulture syndrome. In the regulatory network, once one regulatory official finds a victim and makes a kill, all of them come in for a piece of the action. They just want to grab some points, grab some ink in the news media. It started when the Ohio attorney general's office came in to get their piece of the action. They came in and asked us to sign a consent decree, which we promptly refused to do. They said, "All right, look, we'll go back and reword this consent decree so it really says nothing.

It will be meaningless. All it will say is that you have to obey Ohio laws on advertising." Our lawyer said that the consent decree was meaningless, and there was no sense in spending anymore time fighting them. Why don't you just sign it? In talking with the agents from the attorney general's office I said, "I'll sign it with the agreement that you don't publicize it."

So the agreed. We signed the consent decree and sure enough the next day it was publicized. The attorney general needed some ink because there were elections in six months.

After the vulture effect started, we began to get menacing letters from other attorneys general, most prominently from the California attorney general. As per case histories, with the FDA, once they start on you, they don't quit until you are out of business for good.

I held a general meeting with everyone. I said, "I have had it. We are being talked about as though we are convicts. We are on death row, and the most ludicrous part of this whole thing is that we have never even set foot in a courtroom yet." In fact, it wasn't until a few days later that we even received one document of complaint from anyone. All we had so far was a frivolous complaint filed by one of the most corrupt government organizations in existence. We were found guilty by accusation and punished without a fair trial. We did nothing wrong, and I was not going to stand for it. Before planning a strategy of how we were going to fight back, I wanted to reassess the situation and be sure I was right. I looked over the ad that the FDA said was so terrible.

First, you have to write motivational advertising in order to sell anything. Most advertising doesn't work. That's not how most businesses make their money. In a direct-mail business, however, that is your only chance to succeed. A direct-mail companys advertising must work.

Ads, to be effective, must be eye-catching to get through the clutter. They must be exciting and motivational. When a copywriter goes in to write an ad, he does not go in with the thought of deceiving the public.

In order for me to write a good ad, I have to totally believe in the product, and I have to genuinely get excited about it. I then write the ad using tried and proven advertising methods according to a formula. I realize that I can get too exuberant. That's why the ad is turned over to an attorney for legal review and is often altered. That's what happened with this ad: I produced it and took every measure I could think of to make sure it complied with the law. The ad was reviewed by an attorney and I thought it to be within the tolerance level of acceptable advertising and legal requirements. Many other people reviewed the ad, even our local Better Business Bureau. They did not tell me they saw anything wrong with it.

I looked over the ad, taking into account the bread had been seized and all the items that the FDA had dictated. According to their arbitrary decision, yes, the ad could look bad. But then I compared it to ads they allowed to run unmolested, and it became quite obvious this was nothing more than a case of selective prosecution to suppress competition. Following is the No-Hunger Bread ad that precipitated the No-Hunger Bread atrocity.

The point I want to make is this. As I stated earlier, we are all peddlers of something. No group of medical-treatment peddlers has a monopoloy on the human body. The human body is far too complex for any one point of view or philosophy to be effective all of the time. I don't want a surgeon working on me unless he is qualified, and I don't want to buy drugs unless they have been tested. But when they start using this power to eliminate competition and try to centralize the power in a group of people who resemble a deity and we are to blindly believe and obey them without question, then I think it has gone too far.

When you are dealing with the human body, and the incredible number of variables that are involved, you will never find any one thing that works all the time. At most what you have are beliefs and philosophies. Terminal diseases such as cancer cause the most unbearable suffering and the most destructive consequences both physiologically and psychologically to entire families. An overwhelming majority of the population we have polled, including myself, feel that they do not want a disease that represents such a challenge in degree and difficulty to cure to be left to one point of view or in the hands of a certain small clique of power-hungry egomaniacs.

In researching this matter, we have found articles that report that certain scientists were willing to shoot anybody who came up with a cure for cancer before they did and said the person who comes up with a cancer cure had better go hide in the farthest corner of the earth. Just what the hell is going on here and what is this world coming to with this kind of attitude? This phenomenon repeats itself over and over again in research centers across the country, as I experienced working for a research center of a major corporation. Pure jealousy reigns supreme.

After the seizure a surprising thing happened. Instead of the public being ready to crucify us as I anticipated and I am sure our adversaries anticipated, the reaction was just the opposite. They didn't care what the FDA and news media said. They wanted their bread. Call after call and letter after letter said, "You tell those sons-of-bitches to butt out. We want our bread; we know what they stand for." Immediately when the news broke, many people actually came up to our door and asked if they could get the bread before the government seized any more. The FDA and media consumer advocates have almost no credibility with the American public anymore.

We held a meeting with our lawyers to determine what we had to do next. They said the government may seize your goods automatically, but you do have a right to go into court to get them released. Sounds just, but it's not. This procedure could take up to six months. By that time the food is either spoiled or you are out of business. I said, "Well, you will at least have to try. I've got 130,000 people out there who have given their money and do not have a product. I am responsible for those people and I intend to carry through with my responsibility."

The said, "Well, look it's not your fault. Your best deal right now is just to bankrupt the company."

I said, "It is not in my nature to bankrupt the company and stick customers and creditors for their money. I plan to deliver the bread."

So the lawyers set out to research the case to get our bread freed. They said there was no use to try to ship any more because the FDA could seize continuously. We researched the case and came up with what we felt were very good arguments. We had a case we felt we could win, if we could get it quickly into court and out so that we would not have the defeating aspect of having the food spoil and incur losses from customers. They felt such case histories as the Ayds court case showed that there was a case law precedent in this matter. The FDA's other allegations, that we made health claims through implication by citing the benefits of a high-fiber diet, were stretched interpretations that would not hold up in court.

Our attorneys got together with FDA lawyers from Washington in Cleveland. They presented their case. They came back in a state of shock. The New York lawyer said he had never witnessed anything like it in his professional career. He said they simply threw the Ayds case out and said the judge was wrong.

Negotiations proceeded further, and then it was learned that the FDA had an ace in the hole. They didn't really have a good case against us, except for the fact that Colso ordered one of the ingredients with a slight preservative in it. Labeling on the package said, "No preservatives." In our meetings with Colso, we had emphatically told them, "No preservatives, because this is an all-natural food." They had ordered a dry butter, which constituted only 3% of the mix, with a preservative in it. There was about 1 ½% of this preservative, which made the entire preservative content of the mixture infinitesimal and insignificant. But this was what the FDA was going to hang its hat on, and legally it was clear-cut. Our lawyers determined with that one aspect we could not win the case in court.

Without this preservative factor, we might have had a chance because advertising law contains sections that are totally ambiguous and subjective. The most ambiguous section gives a bureaucrat total freedom to arbitrarily invent charges. This section states that advertising must be written so that the dumbest person in the world would not be misled. A major study of TV advertising shows that 90% of the population misunderstands advertisements on TV.

To bring into focus what I am trying to put across here is an example of how a bureaucrat can twist a story and distort nearly any advertisement. Try to recall the cleanest ad you have seen. Many would pick the Coca-Cola commercials. Right? Now here's what a bureaucrat could do with those ads if he wanted to. Here is a fictitious press release issued by the FDA after it seized 10 million gallons of Coca-Cola:

The FDA today seized 10 million gallons of Coca-Cola. Spokesman Wayne Pines said that Coca-Cola's ads were deceptive and that they grossly misrepresent the product and fail to point out many harmful side effects. The charges state that Coca-Cola is nothing more than a sugared, carbonated soft drink that extracts from the cola nut for flavor. The caffeine from the cola nut is a drug that alters body chemistry and can be dangerous in many situations, especially to pregnant women and to heart patients, as it constricts arteries. Also, the carbonated water and sugar promote tooth decay. These points are not brought out in Coca-Cola's advertising. It was stated that Coca-Cola's ads falsely imply that upon drinking carbonated soft drinks a person would gain social acceptance to "in groups" and the young generation. The ads also implied that the drink would create a euphoric effect with a hallucination of parties and gala events springing up around you. Pine said Coca-Cola must produce extensive advertising that would grant a refund to everybody who drank Coca-Cola in the past 10 years, if they felt they had been misled by these ads. Coca-Cola might not be marketed again, because the false impression would last in much of the public's mind. The FDA stated that, if the problems were resolved, upon their arbitrary decision Coca-Cola might be allowed to remain in business if its advertising would state the following:

Coca-Cola is a sugared, carbonated soft drink with flavoring from the cola nut. It contains caffeine, which constricts the arteries and could be dangerous to certain individuals. The sugar and carbonation also promote tooth decay. The soft drink does not quench thirst, because the sugar content causes more absorption of water, and, in fact has the tendancy to make one thirstier. However, Coca-Cola does taste good. So, if you wish to purchase it for that purpose only, we will sell it to you.

This fictitious situation depicts the absurdity of that section of advertising law which says, "The dumbest person in the world cannot misunderstand." A bureaucrat can arbitrarily say that you implied things, depending upon his imagination. We monitored countless other weight-loss product ads, and we could have built a case against any of them. One product, Figurines, produced by Pillsbury, has a slender woman singing and eating a Figurine and saying that she got sweet revenge on dieting. We had over 35 people review the ad and all 35 said they interpreted the ad to mean that Figurines were a sweet tasting, specially developed candy-like substance that had the ability to suppress appetite, or possibly they had some other mysterious eleent that caused one to lose weight. These people got the impression that Figurines had these qualities, yet was still lower in calories than most food. They were totally misled. Would you believe Figurines contain over 150 calories per ounce? Higher, or as high, as most candy bars. What they really are is a candy bar with nutritional supplements of vitamins. You could get the same by taking vitamin pills and eating a candy bar.

We reviewed similar ads for "diet aids," which were nothing more than vitamin pills and protein supplements. But the ads are designed to imply that you could eat all the food you wanted. The ad showed women carrying trays of food through the kitchen for a midafternoon get-together, implying that with this aid you could eat all the food you wanted.

The FDA was putting pressure on us to get us to belly up. The word came back from informants, no more ads. In fact, this was a common cry among many different informants, who were totally unrelated. No more ads. Play the game. Don't' make waves. Get out of the diet business, but you can continue in other forms of business.

Also, during this time, the FDA was doing other things to try to terrorize us. In conversations with us and with our lawyers, it would drop hints of filing criminal charges, which it had no intention of doing, and which would be unlikely to hold up in a court of law. During this period, because we quit advertising, we had to lay off employees. It would contact these ex-employees for interrogation and imply to them that we were in a lot of trouble.

The FDA put a lot of pressure on our legal counsel also to, "Control your client." This coupled with the fact that our lawyers felt confused and beaten in the case law presentation, which they felt we should have won, caused them to be moody. I was preparing to run a second ad, which would name the FDA, and there were second thoughts on both sides.

First, as I mentioned earlier in the book, the legal profession has mixed emotions about the federal bureaucracy. Lawyers have a legitimate concern for their clients, but it's also hard for them to fully dislike the federal bureaucracy in light of the fact that it creates so much work for the legal profession. Considering what seemed to be the futileness of our position, they began rationalizing what the FDA had done. They started calling some members of the U.S. Attorney's office who work for the FDA, overworked and underpaid civil servants who were probably mad that they made $15,000 per year, and I was making a lot of money. With regard to selective prosecution, they said, using an analogy, "You can't stop everybody. If the speed limit is 55 mph and you are going 56, he has a right to cite you. Their action could be taken in many quarters as simply attempting to gain compliance with the law." At this time I decided to take charge of the situation and put everyone in his place.

I said, "This country was founded on the belief that the individual citizen has the right to life, liberty, and the pursuit of happiness. Most importantly in this country a person can start an enterprise without asking permission from the government. Through this enterprise, an individual can let his ambition and ingenuity take him as far as he wants to go, as long as he does not infringe upon the rights of others. Government is supposed to be by the people and for the people.

"I am a taxpayer, citizen and an entrepreneur. I am the star of the show here. You guys are the supporting cast, both you and the government. I represent what every little guy working in a factory or office is led to believe he has the right to do. That is, if he ever wants to get out of there, he has the option to start his own business.

"To put this whole thing in a better perspective so you can understand the injustice, negligence, and abuse of power that took place here, let me describe what should have happened in this case.

"First of all, the relationship between you and I and a government official is similar to the relationship between a customer and a businessman. It is not as though the government is God and you and I are only people. It is not that the government is the parent and you and I are children. The government is not royalty and you and I are not subjects.

"There are certain laws that are essential for the welfare of the country and its citizens. These laws need to be enforced and civil servants should be entrusted with authority and respect to carry out that enforcement. Not worship, mind you, respect. Secondly, they are not little $15,000-a-year, poverty-stricken people. These people make $100,000-$300,000 a year or more in the higher levels of bureaucracy. When you add on your fringes, I would hate to know what they make. I'm pretty sure that they make more than 90% of the citizens they govern. We are paying them a good buck, and we want our money's worth.

"We expect them to be helpful, friendly, prompt, and objective in their enforcement. We also expect them to prioritize their activity, to enforce laws against those whose noncompliance costs us, the citizens, the most money. If they would do that, they would start with price-fixing, bribing of government officials for big contracts, and monopoly attempts, etc. We expect them to do everything with the general welfare of the country in mind. They should keep in mind the fact that we are also tax-paying citizens who deserve fair and courteous treatment. I would think a regulatory agency would go all out to have a program designed so that citizens would know the law to avoid innocent violations. If they feel that a law has been violated, they would first find out if it was an innocent or intentional violation and see if the problem could be remedied as expediently and inexpensively as possible. We would expect thm to hire only honest, fair, friendly, and competent people. We would expect enforcement action to be taken reluctantly and only as a last resort, when no other measure would correct damage to the public, or if the citizen who violated the law was totally uncooperative and found to be one who violated the law deliberately and with malicious intent.

"Getting back to our specific case, what should have happened was that when I asked for a set of guidelines, I should have been provided advertising and sanitation guidelines. They should have told me if I made health claims, I would have to fill out a new-drug application. Until it was granted, I could not advertise and make such health claims. That would have eliminated the problem right here.

"Let's go one step further. Maybe they don't have these guidelines. If in their opinion I had already marketed a food product that violated a law, then they should have come out as early as possible and told me to stop, to minimize my losses and the theoretical damage to the public. They didn't. They could have done that the second day after the first ad ran, but they didn't. Next, they should have determined if my theoretical violation of the law was innocent or intentional. If it was innocent, the most expedient way should have been to correct the problem. This was obviously what they allowed others to do in the past, specifically, to change their advertising or at the very least to mail corrective advertising along with the fulfillment packages, giving the customer a chance for a refund.

"If they felt they had to press charges, I would expect that they would have to file suit like anybody else and prove their case in court before a jury of my peers in a fair trial.

"But that's not what happened. I was deliberately refused help at the beginning. They deliberately let me advertise and order ingredients to the greatest extent possible to create the most damage. They deliberately withheld the fact that they were going to take enforcement action. They deliberately lied when I asked them if they were going to take enforcement action.

"They then misused and abused powers granted to them by law to punish me and sabotage my business by deliberately denying me due process of law and a fair trial. All during this time they were unhelpful and uncooperative.

"Getting back to the speeding-ticket analogy, it wasn't a case of me going 56 miles per hour in a 55-mile-per-hour zone and being ticketed by an honest enforcement official for not complying with the law.

"What really happened, going along with this analogy, was that I drove into a new territory and saw a sign that said 'speed limit'. However, no numbers were posted, just a bunch of fine print. I got out of the car and looked at the fine print, and it was ambiguous. I suspected it was intentional. I saw one of the local constables sitting by the side of the road. I told him I didn't understand the speed-limit sign, and I asked him what the speed limit was. He said, 'Just use your own judgment. It's too hard to explain.' So I reasoned that since the speed limit was 55 miles an hour on just about every highway in the country, it was probably the speed limit here, so I drove 55 miles per hour. However, other people were flying past me at 80 or 90 miles per hour. Shortly the constable pulled up behind me with red lights flashing, while people were still buzzing by at 80 and 90 miles per hour. He said, 'You just violated the law. The speed limit is 54 miles per hour today.'

"I asked, 'How do you know that?'

"He said, 'It's the law. Between the hours of high noon and one o'clock in the summertime, the speed limit is 54 miles per hour.'

"He summoned another government car. The car pulled up and two thugs jumped out and proceeded to beat me up and smash my car with a sledgehammer. I laid there on the pavement looking up at the other people driving by at 80 and 90 miles an hour. They winked and gave the high sign, and the government officials winked and gave the high sign back. It didn't take me long to figure out that the purpose behind all of this was that certain people in this territory wanted the road to themselves.

"Now, with that reorientation, let's have an understanding here. Entrepreneurs create wealth. The government is supporting people like yourself who do not provide the meal ticket for the rest of society and its institutions, from schools on down the line. If you don't believe it, all you have to do is go look through history books and see how quick a town becomes a ghost town after the businesses leave. I am an entrepreneur. I pay your salary. I pay those government officials who work for the FDA's salary, and I expect a little more respect than I have been getting, or I'm going to get rid of both of you. You I can get rid of immediately by firing, and I can get rid of them, too, only it's going to take me a while longer. At this point nobody cares about those 130,000 people out there, except me. You guys act like this is a game, and many times like it's a joke.

"Instead of bureaucratic convenience, let's start talking about the citizen's convenience. Life is a constant dilemma choosing between the lesser of two evils. Are we going to sacrifice the freedom and economic welfare of the country to gain bureaucratic convenience? It's about time they start making laws for our convenience, not the convenience of the bureaucrats.

"I know everybody accused of violating the law says he is innocent. But let's take into consideration many times they may be right, unless you are naive enough to believe that no government official ever took enforcement action unjustly for personal or fraternal gain, or unless you are naive enough to believe that there are no criminals in government. The government has the highest percentage of criminals in society. This is no longer a game, nor is it funny. What they did is an at of war. I consider these people war criminals, and I consider anybody involved with them as accessories. Vested-interest corporations, elected official appointees and civil service workers, U.S. Attorney's office, marshalls those private sectors who benefited from storing the bread, the Federal judge who granted the seizure order are all involved."

From this time on a different tone was set. We had a major meeting strategy session. Out of these sessions we tried to determine exactly what had transpired, for what reason, and strategically what we were going to do about it.

It was a general conclusion that what happened originated from more than one source and for multiple reasons. One, without question, from our review of case histories is that there is a conspiracy to suppress competition in the health business and especially in the cancer area because it would represent such historic fame and prestige for the individual or organization who cured the disease. This cancer and health area is so well-guarded, people are so hyper, that even though our bread ad in no way intended to imply that the bread had anything to do with curing cancer, it was taken that way by these paranoid groups.

Second, we competed in other business areas which may be of less influence, but nonetheless still have some power. These would be weight-loss aids and the bread industry. Third, we have the unelected bureaucracy itself who wants to grow and eventually have dictatorial powers. These individuals are supported by many influential powers from the private sector, but they are still looking out for number one. They want to flaunt their power, show this newcomer who's boss. Fourth, there are members in any bureaucratic organization, especially new lawyers out of law school, who are trying to make names for themselves, or who are trying to stabilize their positions. Our attorney said, "Frankly, there are too many lawyers. They need work, and they are looking for advancement. This is one of the reasons why you are seeing a flood of regulatory activity and a flood of litigation, even in the private sector among private businesses." Fifth, bureaucracies have to justify their existence. They need to get into the news media in front of the people and Congress, especially those members of Congress who appropriate their budgets. Last, you have bureaucrats, such as Simmons, who appear to think that they are the government.

The question was brought up as to, "Did we aggravate the situation?" Looking back, the answer was "no." Just the opposite occurred. I did treat the FDA like royalty. We rolled out the red carpet for those people.

When we called Simmons, I was on the end of a string of frustrations trying to get this bread out the door. I was trying to get it done dealing with Runyan, snowstorms, and everything else you could imagine. I called Simmons, with whom I had cooperated in every way, shape, and form and learned that, all the while, he was letting me dig my own grave with the purchasing of advertising and ordering ingredients.

Everybody concluded that it was true that there was no way all this could have transpired simply because we aggravated it. This was already definitely preplanned long before. As a taxpayer we were entitled to better treatment.

One attorney said, "These guys hear that all the time—that I'm a taxpayer and I pay your salary."

And I said, "Maybe it's about time these ignoramuses start to understand that there is something to it then. We are the taxpayers and we do pay their salaries."

I then asked, "Do we have a lawsuit here?" The attorney said, "Of course, you do, anybody can file a suit. The trouble is you are fighting deep pockets. Even if you sued Simmons individually, the government most assuredly would pick up his case, and you would be fighting a lot of money."

"All right, let's take first things first. First we've got to get the bread to these people and keep this company surviving. It may take us a number of years, but we will deal with those responsible later."

We kept getting the message, "No more ads." I was more convinced my theory is right. Rats don't like the light. They want to remain faceless, but they also think they are invincible and immune from retribution. The bureaucracy, except in very rare cases, is not accountable for its actions to anyone, so this just might be something that pierces this mythical invincibility veil.

But our New York attorney, who dealt with the federal bureaucracy many times in the past, said, "If you do a second ad, there is one danger that you are going to make yourself susceptible to."

I asked, "To what?"

"There exists an unwritten code for suborganization among fellow regulatory agencies called the retaliatory network. Anyone, individual or company threatening the close little fraternity of the federal regulatory agencies or civil service workers will be blacklisted and hit-listed. If the particular agency you attack would not look prudent carrying on a continuing regulatory campaign against you, the retaliatory network will initiate action through other regulatory agencies."

I said, "Look, all of business is a calculated risk. As I said, anything man-made can be dealt with. I don't give a damn whether you call it a retaliatory network or what."

The lawyer also said, "You are going to have to alter the policy that you set out of maintaining a low profile."

I agreed. "From everything I've seen so far and the conclusions I have reached from our investigation at this point, I don't think maintaining a low profile is a valid policy anymore. For some reason, for the past three years regulatory activity has increased exponentially. We aren't the only ones being victimized. For whatever reason, too many lawyers etc., it's here. I also tend to think it's because any government institution or organization takes about 40 years to fully blossom. I think we are seeing the full-fledged results of the New Deal communism."

I related, "I don't want to sound like a witch-hunter, and I know communism is a distasteful word since McCarthy's days, but what else are we going to call it. Look at communism dogma and policies. The first thing they do when they take over is shoot down free enterprise. That is, a guy, instead of starting a business on his own has to ask the government's permission. Only established, vested-interest businesses 'in the party' are allowed to exist. That is what we have here. With more agencies being created and gaining in power, there are a large percentage of businesses where you now have to ask an unelected bureaucrat for permission to go into business. On his arbitrary decision alone, he can delay you to the point where it destroys your venture. In the communist state you have a handful of unelected bureaucrats who live high on the hog and dictate to the rest of the population who exist in a state of semi-poverty. This is nothing more than enslavement, and that's what we have here. Unelected bureaucrats with dictatorial powers who run the country and favor a handful of vested-interest businesses!"

I said, "The next thing a communist government does is eliminate advertising. Advertising is unacceptable to totalitarian governments and to monopolistic organizations because it gives the newcomer a chance to quickly launch a different product, a different approach to problems, or different ideas. Also it throws things out of control. Bureaucrats like things totally under control. They like to allocate everything. So, in effect, what these guys are trying to do is shut off advertising by making advertising innocuous. Advertising has to be written like a legal document per the guidelines put forth in their idealistic academic world. They forget that motivational advertising is one of the reasons this country became so prosperous."

I went on, "I am, therefore, saying right now I don't think there is any place to hide, and, in the future, it is going to get worse. Besides, why should I have to hide? If I want to create an empire, or become popular, that is my inalienable right according to the Constitution.

"Also, in regard to our policy of rolling out the red carpet for any bureaucrats, I don't think that's applicable anymore. As I alluded to before, we are not dealing with nice people. These people are ruthless. They aren't people, they are humanoids with no imagination, sense of humor or sense of decency."

As one attorney pointed out, you can't classify them all like that. I'm talking about the hard-core group that is growing. I know not all government officials are like that. I have friends and relatives who used to work for the government and some of them work for the government right now. They are not like that. I am saying the hard-core element that we are dealing with come under the above description. This is a no-holds-barred war, and they are the enemy. We have several big aces in the hole on our side. One, the public is overwhelmingly on our side, and, if you talk to congressmen, they don't like what the FDA does either, which leads me to this question. If the public doesn't want the FDA and Congress doesn't want the FDA, who does want the FDA, and why is it still in existence in its present format? Why isn't it being dissolved and a new administration formed from scratch with different policies and different people to protect the public from harmful drugs and unsanitary foods?

One attorney observed, "Well, that's campaign rhetoric. You are dealing with vested interests here. Congress is well paid, even though members may not like the FDA, there is a paid-for agreement to keep them in their present structure."

I concurred, "That's quite obvious. But the second ace in the hole we have is that we have nothing more to lose. They do. We are dealing with big corporations, multi-billion dollar concerns, major media networks with influence, and billions of dollars in sales to protect and bureaucrats with lucrative, secure jobs depending upon how well they propagate their propaganda. They have a lot to lose by getting into a mudslinging contest with us."

Also, I still believe that the path-of-least-resistance principle holds. These people want something quick and dirty. They don't want somebody that's going to give them a hassle or put up a fight. They need "points" with Congress and the public to be scored quickly.

Another member at the meeting said, "Do you think our ads naming the FDA will be taken as unpatriotic?" I thought it was a very remote possibility. According to the public opinion we received, the public is fed up with the government. This is the land of free enterprise. American people will not accept a totalitarian government, which is what the New Deal is and what this country has been evolving into.

On the contrary, I think we are patriots and will be looked upon as such. This is the land of free enterprise and that's what the Constitution dictates. This unelected bureaucracy, which is communistic in nature, was spawned clandestinely and against the will of the people. They don't want it. The federal bureaucracy, with its socialistic nature and totalitarian approach, is not truly American. They are aliens. I think it is our job as citizens to expose them and get rid of them. Not to sound hokey, but look at it this way. All the soldiers in all the wars the United States has been engaged in, for the most part, believed that they were fighting for freedom. Granted, many times they were misled, but they still thought they were. Many men fought and died to supposedly stop communism from taking over from the outside. To let communism take over from within would mean that they all died for nothing. I think it's time to realize that there are people in our government who want to take away our freedom and enslave us. Even though you don't like the task as citizens, it is your duty to defeat, or at least stand up to, those totalitarian entities when they engage in an offensive against you.

With much more deliberation, a final counteroffensive strategy was launched. It would consist of: (1) publicity, which we are very good at, much better than the bureaucrats; (2) an all-out extensive and detailed investigation to determine exactly what happened, who was involved, and the nature and extent of the conspiracy, if there was one; and, (3) we would publicize the information we obtained. We would push for legislation to correct the matter even though this is a very long-term item. We would pressure the bureaucracy from within. We would dog and harass those bureaucrats involved for 20 years, if necessary, and campaign for their dismissal. We would create a defense prosecution legislation trust, for which we would solicit other businessmen with the concept that this was a landmark case. If we could prosecute these bureaucrats by suing them individually, winning would be a staggering defeat for this tyranny. We would also include in our list of publicity all congressmen, all federal judges, and all of the news media. Even though a significant number of them are corrupt, it is hard to believe that they are all corrupt. At least we can keep the good ones informed, or possibly organize them. We will get into politics hot and heavy, in fact, form a political division. Fund raising is the key. This was our other ace in the hole that the bureaucracy should have considered when they attacked us. Although we may not have money personally to match theirs, we certainly do have the capabilities, the talent, and the expertise to raise large amounts of money. I could raise money to match the budget of individual agencies, but money isn't the only thing. You have to know how to use it. And we would get a lot more mileage out of our money than they would.

I did not know what other factors were involved in this atrocity, but I was bound and determined to find out. My retaliatory efforts started with a second ad. This time two full pages, which I ran both in the *Washington Star* and in local papers near my home. The total cost for this ad in all the papers was $18,000. In it I named the FDA. The second full-page ad ran on March 12, 1978.

One day shortly after the second ad ran, I came home and my wife called to me from the upstairs that there was somebody on the phone for me. She was crying and visibly upset. When I came upstairs, she was lying on the bed sobbing. I thought, "What the hell is wrong now?" I picked up the phone and it was my general manager, Jim. He said he had received a phone call from one of our most reliable informants, one with definite contacts in high places in government. He said that the informant did not come out and say it directly, but made a strong innuendo that for running that ad we were going to be assassinated. So it's gone this far. This was the end product of the American dream, of a housewife's accidentally inventing a unique product in her own kitchen, and her husband setting up a business to sell the product in the All-American way. The family, the product, and the business are savagely maligned through media smear. They sabotage the business, the product is seized, and how they are going to assassinate us.

I hung up the phone and tried to comfort my wife, who was mostly concerned for the kids. And from that concern she said, "Let's just give it up, it's gone too far."

I declared, "We can't. History shows you cannot appease tyranny. It only gets worse. It's like trying to put out a fire with gasoline. If we give up now, our kids are going to have to live in a world with much more danger, suppression, and discomfort. Besides, what would they think of us if we let somebody do this to us. I am not going to let somebody walk all over me like this and get away with it."

I contacted the informant and asked for the details. He made mention that the Mafia might be involved. Ever since I've been in business, the Mafia has always been responsible for something. They are supposed to be behind drugs, but any cop will tell you anymore it is a widely scattered operation. Smaller people run down to Florida and get drugs and bring them back for sale. People even think I'm a member of the Mafia. I don't even care if there is a Mafia. It is also a man-made organization and not invincible.

I further related, "Maybe some of these federal bureaucrats watch too many Elliot Ness movies. I don't care what they call themselves, Mafia, federal government agents, whatever, they all have one thing in common—you shoot them in the head and they die. Now, unless they have figured out a way to become God or Superman, they are also vulnerable to the same threats they are perpetrating on me!"

I abhor violence and would not break the law, but if we are in a situation where the federal government is now in the business of assassinating citizens who speak out against them, and other government agencies are not going to protect us, we no longer have law and order. It is then civil war, and I said we will handle it accordingly. Weapons and mercenaries are for sale. All the government does is tax the citizen and purchase them. Also, there are a few secrets of advance weaponry that are not for sale. Should anyone attempt any violence on me or any member of my family, retaliation will be swift and sure as death and taxes.

I added, "Now you take that message back to those who told you that they might assassinate us."

I don't know if the message was ever delivered, or if our phones really were tapped, and they heard the conversation. But after that phone call, or possibly because of our second ad, or a combination of both, the pressure really subsided. The rats had run for their holes.

After that I set up a retaliatory trust in the event something happened to me. I allocated money so that others could pick up with the retaliation. All information gathered from our investigation would be available to them including information about the most respected powerful individuals behind the aggression. In all, everybody would be hit, from the soldiers who carried out the aggression, all the way to the top. At that time I made provisions to have my own private security force. I would only count on these systems in the event that we were actually hit with violence and as a last resort. I do not believe in violence as the way to solve problems. I think you need force, but you can use force without violence.

It became apparent that we are dealing with vigilantes and terror-ists. A small group of power hungry crazies were evidently taking the law into their own hands, providing their own version of the old lynch mobs. No wonder the public response fro the second ad was over-whelmingly on our side. I received hundreds of letters from citizens agreeing with me and telling me similar stories of how the FDA, FTC, and various agencies have acted out of control!

In the haggling over the letter, almost another month went by, and we still weren't settled. There were still 130,000 people who had sent money and not received their product. Complaint letters were mount-ing and I was getting frantic. Again, as negotiations stalled and other duties and clients called, the lawyers became inaccessible. Again, we had to get back to negotiating and be the responsible party concerned about the customers.

Finally, in the latter stages of the negotiations, after it had gone on for some time, the FDA also became hard to reach. I finally received a call from the New York attorney and he said, "Look, what I am read-ing between the lines with the FDA lawyers, which I think is what they have been saying right from the very beginning, is that they want out of this thing in the worst way. They just don't know how to do it. The trouble is this letter you are going to mail to the customers. If it goes out with their approval, it then becomes their responsibility and leaves them open to criticism. Maybe a higher-up or somebody in the pharmaceutical business is against this and may throw it back in their face. They just don't want to be responsible for this letter, and I think they are going to tell us to just go ahead and mail the damn thing. I don't think they are going to interfere."

I said, "Fine, then let's mail it. Let's keep in mind that we probably still have a viable product here. Let's not give them any chance to change their mind and come back and seize. We cannot, of course, do too much, because they can arbitrarily seize. But we can make them look bad if they do seize again, if we are very prudent in mailing out this letter.

So we wrote a correction letter, which in effect said that we make no health claims for the bread and that there was a slight trace of pre-servative in it. We mailed the letter out to the list and waited with a great deal of apprehension for the returns. We estimated after waiting many months that if all of them accepted the letter and felt they were not deceived, then the most we could hope for would be close to a 75% return. This is because 25% of them moved or forgot what the whole incident was about. Unfortunately, that was just about our cash differential situation. The max we could afford was about a 40% refund.

The first few days the returns came in and what a relief. The response was well over 70%. The people wanted the bread—all felt that they were not deceived. All the deception and misleading advertising claims were nothing more than a purposely fabricated creation of the FDA to try to put us out of business. We had another big weapon in our pocket for the eventual court showdown with the FDA.

Now we initiated plans to put the bread back on the market. But, before I did that I wanted to make sure that they had nothing to hang their hat on. It was their stand that the tests for the hunger-curbing properties of the bread were not valid, because the people we chose as test subjects were employees of companies who did business with us. They still said it was an invalid test, even when we told them that the employees had no idea that the bread was our bread, and they were just as objective as randomly picked subjects.

I was a psychology major in college and mathematics was my minor. I had a very good knowledge of statistics and testing. There were no really feasible independent test sources available in the U.S. We would have to construct a test that would be irrefutable, according to well-established testing principles. For test subjects we had an independent employment agency select people at random. I then hired two notary publics to supervise the tests, to document and monitor every minute of it. Then we enlisted the services of a psychological statistics professor from my alma mater, the University of Akron, to analyze and sanction the test results.

What were the results of the test? They were even better than before. The object of the test was to prove that the Nancy's special Formula Bread: 1. was not ordinary whole wheat bread in that it had appetite curbing qualities superior to ordinary bread. It had already been demonstrated by many university studies concerning bread and weight loss that whole wheat bread is one of the best appetite curbing foods there is, which proved that Nancy's Special Formula Bread is indeed unique and does have special appetite curbing properties. 2. We wanted to test for how many hours the bread curbed appetite over ordinary whole wheat bread, too. This kind of testing would have called for a great deal more money and time than we had.

Already this test was costing us in excess of $15,000. In order to find out if there was a valid difference between the appetite satisfaction between the two breads, we would have had to call each subject on the hour.

Used in the test as a placebo was the whole wheat bread of our good friends, ITT Continental Bakery, Wonder 100% whole Wheat Bread. I put in the test hours because I knew from the other tests that there was a significant difference. Each test subject was given bread to eat on alternate days. They came in the next day, and they were asked which one satisfied their appetite best and for how long. This was repeated alternating Nancy's Special Formula Bread with Wonder's 100% Whole Wheat Bread for a period of six days. And then a final questionnaire was issued for them to recapitulate the whole test and put down as a final answer which one satisfied their appetite best. In alternate days they had eaten Nancy's Special Formula Bread three times and Wonder 100% Whole Wheat Bread three times. They were instructed not to eat in the mornings and to go as long as they could without eating.

Results were spectacular. Nancy's Special Formula Bread was chosen almost four to one over Wonder 100% Whole Wheat Bread, and the results were so significant that they exceeded the probability of sampling error by six times. Even without structuring the test for the testing of hours of hunger satisfaction, the difference in the hours showed that there could hav been only a 10% chance of error, which means there was a 90% chance that they were significant. It is desirable to have less than 5% error for standard accepted methods of testing.

During this period of time, I had completed writing my book *7 Steps to Freedom* and we had it typeset and printed. How, I will never know, but it was selling well and filling in the money gap. But it was still not quite enough to overcome the money loss. In all the loss included goods that were seized, the refunds we unjustly had to make, the legal fees, the time, the money spent on counter advertising, and the extra people required to carry on the fight. We lost close to $1.5 million, or over 50% of our total sales. This was devastating, since our company, like many others, had a bottom line of a 6% profit. This would be like penalizing a company like Exxon or General Motors one-half of their $80-billion-a-year sales, or penalizing them $40 billion for theoretical over-promotion in advertising. The action by the FDA was tantamount to executing somebody for jaywalking.

Even though we had plastered the FDA with publicity, vultures from the news media still trickled in. They left the bread alone, since we have received all the notoriety, they were trying to make a name for themselves. Our new product, the book *7 Steps to Freedom*, was regarded by real professionals in the direct-marketing industry as the best book ever published on direct marketing. Many businessmen thought it was the best entrepreneurial book ever published by any person in business. It was beyond reproach.

We were secure in that thought, too, but I fell victim to two reporters who misrepresented themselves. One reporter was from the Dallas Times Herald. He flew in from Dallas, Texas, and misrepresented himself as a person, "doing a story on mail order." He implied this paper had admired the book and what we had done, and he was going to do a promotional story on us. What he had in mind to do from the very start was a hatchet job. A distorted half-truth story, which portrayed us as outlaws on the fringe of justice. The other reporter was from the Detroit Free Press. The two reporters came in almost simultaneously, so I did both stories before I saw what they had in mind. In both cases we were smeared on the front pages of these newspapers, two of the biggest in the country.

To counteract these tactics in the future, I followed a certain plan, which I recommend to all entrepreneurs. If contacted by a reporter who wants to do a "balanced story," I would tell the, "Fine, but we are going to be sure that it is a balanced story." I will do the story, because I haven't nothing to hide, but I do want to make sure it's a balanced story. You must sign a contract before you interview me that I have the right to see the final story and have equal time and position to rebut anything you say. Now you can say anything you want, only it's your side against my side. I can't think of anything fairer than that. Guess what? After that nobody wanted to do a story. It sin o guarantee, but if you don't give a guy an interview, he has a very weak story and usually will not do one on you. It is unlikely you will ever have a good story done on you, because it has been repeated often enough, "good news is no news."

I recall one conversation with another reporter. She asked, "In assessing your ad on the bread, why all the hype?"

I observed, "That takes a lot of guts coming from somebody in your business. You mislead the public into believing you are putting out a true cross section of the news, when actually you are only putting gout all the bad things that have happened. You are leading people to believe the world is on the verge of coming to an end. This causes depression and, in extreme instances, can cause suicide. But you don't care, do you? It's all right for you to take money from the public and give them a product which is misleading. How many of your stories are recklessly prepared, contain fudged facts, and , in some instances, are even staged?" I have used this argument other times with other unscrupulous reporters, an they usually don't want to talk any more.

In another case with a reporter, I decided to have some fun. Upon finding out that he might get an interview, he was ecstatic, because I assume many of them knew I wasn't granting them without the contract. I said, "No, I'm in a good mood today, I'll give you one without the contract. Not only that, this is really your lucky day. I'm really going to give you the inside, confidential information of the behind-the-scenes of what happened with No-Hunger Bread." He was really salivating at this point. I said, "You are really going to get the truth. Why I did it and the whole bit. The whole master plan." Naturally he told me to go right ahead.

"Well look," I began, "If you can go back on our record, most people thought of us as a very honesty company in the eight years I had been in business prior to the No-Hunger Bread incident. We had never had any regulatory action involving our company, but overnight it happened."

He said, "What happened?"

I explained, "Well, in the last part of 1977, I contracted what they call latent Black Bartosis. You see, I became the bad guy; I deliberately set out to fleece the public. Now you have to understand that this Black Bartosis might be a plan of nature. If it were not for us bad guys, they wouldn't know who you good guys were."

"But this Black Bartosis really brings on a lot of complex syndromes. This disease really causes you to act irrational. Just because the FDA seized $200,000 worth of my product, splattered my name all over the paper, assassinated my character, allowed other people to do what I was being punished for, I got mad. I don't know what came over me, but I am seeing a psychiatrist to see if it can be cured." At this point, he quickly terminated his conversation and hung up. Funny, I looked for his story, and I never saw it.

It took about four weeks to ship all of the bread, and all the while we waited on pins and needles to see if the FDA was going to seize again. Finally, the last package went out. Lo and behold, no seizures.

From my case history with lawyers who work with the FDA, I knew that what we did was the impossible. They usually seize a company's goods until they go out of business. Certainly no one thought they would let us mail the correction letter to the customer. All the customers received their product and about 30 of them were reordering bread.

In July of 1978, we held a press conference to announce the results of the test and the fact that the bread was no back on the market. Everyone in the media was stunned. NBC's affiliate in Cleveland, Channel 3, WKYC, was dumbfounded. The major TV stations and local news media covered the press conference and the reports we got were excellent, except from Channel 3's, of course. Even though we told them the test was not constructed to determine the significance of difference between hours of appetite satisfaction, they played up that one point in their newscast.

It was not time to launch an offensive against NBC. Evidently, major media news networks also think they are immune to retaliation when they victimize innocent people with their hatchet-job stories. The first thing we did was run an ad against them, which describes their involvement in the No-Hunger Bread incident and their shoddy reporting. The ad ran in the *Cleveland Plain Dealer*, one of the nation's largest newspapers and Ohio's largest newspaper, which is right in their hometown. We also ran ti in our hometown, Canton, Ohio.

Evidently, Channel 3 did not believe that newspapers would run such an ad. There was a litter deliberation on the *Plain Dealer's* part, but the advertising manager got back to us and said the publisher looked at it and said, "Well, they are customers of ours, it did happen and they have a right to free speech."

Of course, there are friends between various news media and we know that Channel 3 got wind of the ad and probably saw it before it went to press. That night I received harassing phone calls from voices with a newsroom background, who tried to imply another hatched story was being done on me. Various innuendos were made over the phone, that they really had the scoop on me, and I had better not run any more ads as I had done in the past.

The ad ran that day and we watched the Channel 3's 6 o'clock news, the same news team that had reported on the Ho-Hunger Bread. We wanted to see their reaction to public humiliation.

The nice guys that they are, they had the woman member of the anchor team do most of the talking during the newscast. During the telecast she mispronounced and stumbled over many words. At the end of the telecast, thinking she was off camera, she hit her desk with her fist and let out a loud sigh. They finally knew how it felt to be on the receiving end of a smear story.

The next phase of counterattack was our initial lawsuit. Overall I felt we had three causes of action. One was against NBC for libel and defamation of character. One against Colso for negligence in putting the preservative in the bread mix against our orders, and thirdly, an overall conspiracy suit to put us out of business, involving all parties, FDA, Ohio Department of Agriculture, Colso, NBC and the Attorney General's office.

Our attorneys felt that our most powerful cases were in this order: 1) the negligence suit against Colso, 2) the conspiracy suit, 3) the libel and defamation of character suit.

Libel and defamation of character suit against NBC was difficult because: 1) it is hard to sue the news media with their protections, and 2) in Ohio you must show damages. My attorneys scrutinized both Betty Furness's report and that of the Cleveland affiliate, WKYC, Channel 3. They felt Betty Furness had gone right up to the line of libel, but her report was probably heavily reviewed by legal counsel, and they felt the case was borderline. But upon reviewing reports from Channel 3, they felt we had a possible libel and defamation of character suit.

Our main concern at this point, however, was to get the bread back on the market, because we definitely felt we had a viable product, and it served my original intention of establishing a high-volume, repeat-sale necessity product. Our main concern here was to insure we stopped the aggression from the so-called consumer protection network, or better put, the competition suppression network. We felt that the FDA had been checked, but we weren't sure about Channel 3. After our full-page ad ran against them, they were completely mum, but we couldn't take the chance that they would not come out again with more publicity, so for insurance, we filed the libel suit against WKYC-TV, NBC, Channel 3 in Cleveland.

When we were researching the suit before we filed it, we had determined that we had fulfilled the financial damage requirement for winning the case. However, upon laying out the exact details for trial, it was found that the researcher, who had collected all the letters for refund requests that could be directly attributed to WKYC-TV in Cleveland, had mistakenly confused that with all of NBC. The researcher had all the refund letters for NBC indeed, but it was in regard to Betty Furness's nationwide broadcast. When we looked through the whole pile, we could not find one refund request or complaint relating to

Channel 3's broadcast. As we had discovered before, the news media has such low credibility with the public that they affect only an infinitesimal percentage of the viewing audience. Betty Furness's telecast, which went nationwide to millions, in the viewing audience did generate hundreds of complaints. From this we could have shown financial damages and, taking into account the apathy factor, parlayed that into lost sales, because it created an element of confusion. However, these few hundred letters in view of the fact that she is heard by millions of people means her credibility is almost insignificant. That's what happened in the case from Channel 3. From their viewing audience in northeastern Ohio, which consists of hundreds of thousands of people, we did not get even one complaint.

With no financial damages, we had to drop the suit against WKYC Channel 3. It was agreed we would drop the suit without prejudice. They wanted us to drop the suit to free them of any ramifications of falsified broadcasting against us. In fact, earlier they had even indicated that they would be willing to pay us a small amount of money to get out from under any liability involving our ensuing investigations. We told them no, that this was just an initial suit to protect what we felt was a viable product. The more serious charges of conspiracy would remain intact and under no condition, unless the claim was in excess of millions of dollars, would we ever accept such an offer to let them off the hook.

During this period of time we also took our documentation of what had transpired regarding the Colso overcharge to the FBI. We felt that the circumstances around this overcharge, and the involvement of government officials, were causes for investigation. We gathered our documentation concerning this particular aspect of the case, complete with witness testimony.

I made an appointment with our local FBI office in Canton. What happened at the FBI office, I think, is of interest to everyone, especially middle-class people, like ourselves. The middle class typically is sheltered from real-life experiences. Both my general manager, Jim and I are lower-middle-class families. We lived in a rough ethnic end of town, but our parents were hard working and provided well for their families. They worked their way up the class ladder, and, in time we became more typically bourgeois.

As young children, we were in close contact with the real world of the street, the law of the jungle and physical survival. However, as the years wore on and the families became more affluent, we settled more into the classical sheltered world of the middle class. The real world is fed to us through laundered information. The middle class gets it in the classroom in school, from the movies, and on TV. This information is well-processed, and when it comes out, it in no way resembles the real world.

As Jim and I were riding to our appointment at the FBI office, we reflected on this matter. We only saw the FBI on the TV, in movies, and heard about it in school. The FBI was definitely the most popular and glamorous government enforcement agency in existence. Was it really the all-fair, just, and all-knowing omnipotent organization as it was portrayed in the movies and on TV?

We arrived at the Federal Office Building in Canton for our appointment. We held our meeting in one of the interrogation rooms, as branch offices of the FBI are fairly small. It appeared this one consisted of at most two to three offices. We engaged in preliminary small talk with the agent. It was quite evident that he was into their TV image. He wanted to impress us with his ability to give us more inside scoop than those TV episodes. He revealed that they don't have agents flying around the country, such as you see on the FBI show on TV. Usually just a phone call to each town where FBI offices exist is just as adequate to get a job done.

As we got int the delineation of what had transpired, you could see that he already knew of the incident and was kind of upset that we were accusing on eof his fraternity brothers of some irregularities. He even started getting defensive about them. He asked, "Do you have any hard proof that a bribe took place?"

I explained, "If we had hard proof, I wouldn't be here. I'd be turning it over to a prosecutor. The sign on the door says Federal Bureau of Investigation. I have probably cause for an investigation, and you get the hard proof. You certainly have to admit that we have just cause for being suspicious." He went on further with his defensive remarks. Like any other person in the news media or any government official that we had talked to, he took on the God composure. If anybody in the government accused you of anything, they must be right. It was the God complex all over again. They were all-good, all-knowing and infallible.

I remarked, "Let me ask you this question. Does the government have some kind of secret test or some kind of secret way that makes all people who work for it, all-good, all-knowing, totally honest, infallible, and incapable of any criminal action? Will you at least grant me this? Has there ever been any hard evidence in the past of corruption in government?" This, of course, was a facetious statement.

He replied, "Of course."

"So you grant me there could, in fact be a great deal of corruption in government?"

He said, "Yes."

"Okay," I declared. "Then we have established that it is more probably that anyone would like to believe that in dealing with a government agency you are going to run into a corrupt official, or a group of corrupt officials. Then your attitude about this is that if the government accused us of something, we must be guilty and that our accusations that the government may be guilty of corruption have to be totally baseless. That is not a valid posture."

At this point he didn't want to talk about it any more. He said he would fill out the report about our allegations, but he did not make the final decision. The final decision is made at the regional U.S. Attorney's office. The more you get into this thing, the more you find that they are all fraternity brothers, and , even worse, they usually all tie together at one power source. The same office that had recklessly, irresponsibly and unjustly helped the FDA to damage our company and our reputation for a self-serving gain was now going to decide whether it should investigate itself.

We had been told earlier by our private investigators before we went to talk to the FBI that we would get no cooperation. Many of these private investigators were former FBI agents, and I talked to three or four different ones, and they all said the same thing. "The bureau, as they call it, had really gone to hell in the last 10 years." But hearsay and seeing for yourself are two different things. After our meeting we were totally disillusioned. Jim and I both looked at each other and had the same thought on our minds. The FBI used to be our heroes. But we were big boys now and logically knew better. But we still had that feeling you get when you find out there is no Santa Claus.

Months went by after we submitted our complaint to the FBI and we heard nothing. Finally, I called the U.S. Attorney's office and managed to track down the U.S. Attorney in charge of the case. He said that it had been determined that there was no basis for our allegations. He was very indignant. He said, "What's the matter with you? These are serious charges."

I said, "Serious crimes usually do carry serious charges."

I asked him how he went about making his determination that our allegations were groundless. He gave the standard comeback of government officials nowadays. He said, "I don't have to tell you anything. I don't work for you; I work for the government."

I said, "That's funny, I thought that as a taxpayer and citizen the government worked for me. You are a government official. You also work for me. Who do you work for then?" After a few moments of his babbling, I said, "Look, it's obvious you aren't going to do anything about it, and I'm not going to waste my time in talking to another useless government official."

We next submitted the incident to our two senators and congressmen. They included Senator John Glenn, Democrat of Ohio, and Senator Howard Metzenbaum, Democrat, Ohio and Representative Ralph Regula, Republican, Ohio. The congressmen all had the same standard comeback. We can't do anything about regulatory agencies. I told them, "You are my government representatives. This is government by representation. If I can't go to you, who can I go to? Don't try to shirk responsibility. You can do something. You just don't want to."

What the congressmen did was take my letters and forward them to the government agency in question. The government agency wrote back some nonsensical babble, which, in effect, restated a few superficial facts, such as PCA advertised the bread, the FDA determined that the advertising violated the Food, Drug, and Cosmetic Act, and the bread was seized. I called back and said, "What kind of action is this? You are making no attempt to investigate this matter. All I am asking for is an investigation and a fair trial. I'm not asking you to going and take action against them without finding out first if there is anything to my charges. Is it too much to ask for an investigation? I have evidence that will lead any rational human being to the conclusion that there were irregularities that took place." Upon pinning them in a corner like this, they usually went into their line of rhetoric that they were only one person in congress and that they couldn't really affect this one situation that much.

Coincidentally, during this period of time there was an incident involving homeowners in the southern part of Canton. Many homes had been built in flood control areas and easement controlled by the Army Corps of Engineers. The Corps neglected to tell the people before they built the houses that by a remote chance they might need this area at some theoretical point in time for the purpose of flood control and they would have to tear down their house and move out. This was truly an unjust action on the part of that Army Corps of Engineers and negligence on top of that. People had a right to complain. However, the point of the matter was, they took their case to our congressmen, and our congressmen went to bat for them. They arranged committees, offered to create new legislation, and made public statements against the Army Corps of Engineers. Why? Because it was a nice, safe issue. Homeowners are as safe as motherhood and apple pie. They didn't want to dirty their hands with the businessman. After all, we are the only ones who put food and clothing in those very homes. We didn't deserve any consideration. It didn't mean anything that this bread incident not only thwarted a possible major industry, but laid people off and threatened the basic freedoms that are the foundation of our country, mainly, that of free enterprise. They threatened the very thing that produces high quality products, low prices, and competition.

After our confrontation with our congressmen, we investigated their voting records. Glenn and Metzenbaum are two ultraliberals, two of the worst senators with regard to voting for free enterprise. The National Federation of Independent Businessmen, the biggest and most respected small-business organization in the country, had determined that Glenn and Metzenbaum each voted against small business 70 percent of the time. Only a few other senators in the country were worse. We did find Regula had a plus. He voted for small business almost 90 percent of the time. Regula was, therefore, half good but was a gutless wonder when it came to servicing you with regard to government injustices.

We had gone through just about every elected government official and government agent whom we paid for the service of protecting us from injustice. We were refused from top to bottom, starting with the president down to the lower bureaucratic agencies. We were not only refused but treated rudely and told by many that they didn't even have to give us the reason why they would not help us. Where on earth did the government ever develop this attitude?

The attitude of the regulatory agencies went even further. Not only were they unfriendly, unhelpful, and arrogant, but they were malicious. It's amazing, people whom you pay to perform services for you not only refuse to help you, but they actually look for ways to hurt you.

As evidenced by the homeowners versus the Army Corps of Engineers' case, bureaucrats will help you if they have something to gain for themselves. However in our case, for some reason, we carried a stigma. Even though we had never set foot in a court of law, we had been accused of the lowest, most dastardly deed, putting out misleading, documented advertising, or over-promoting with documented advertising. The phony consumerism movement, which started in the early '60s, had everybody conditioned that this was truly the worst sin you could commit, mainly because it was the one most prosecuted by the "consumer protection system." Why? Because it is the easiest to prosecute. The advertising laws are nebulous and with documented advertising you have your proof before you in black and white. But is it the worst sin? There are others that are much worse, but are bought and paid for and much more difficult to prosecute. Contrary to a popular belief created by the "consumer protection network," misleading documented advertising is insignificant compared to other illegal methods that fleece the consumer out of money every year. You see, they haven't told you about the other seven methods that are used to fleece the public to a much, much greater degree. I call these the true secrets of success. I will list them in order by the estimated extent to which they take money right out of the consumer's pocket.

Price-fixing and monopolies. Contrary to popular belief, government spending is not the number one cause of inflation. Price-fixing is. Whenever a group of businesses get together and control a critical commodity that is needed for survival, you are going to have artificially high prices that do not reflect the marketplace. These critical commodities then force up all other prices.

Competition, as everyone knows, is the number one element needed for the production of high-quality products at reasonable prices. When you eliminate competition, you immediately have the reverse, shoddy products and runaway inflation.

Bribery. Bribery is used when a purchasing agent, key officer of a corporation or government official takes a bribe to pay a higher price for a product or service instead of picking products or services on the basis of the lowest bid and highest quality. This also contributes to inflation and shoddy products. As everyone knows, one of the biggest markets for bribery is among government officials.

Misleading verbal sales pitches. This is by far where the most deception takes place and the biggest frauds are carried out. And these are the most damaging frauds, because it's hard to defraud somebody out of a lot of money using low-pressure methods from documented advertising.

The old bait and switch trick. This means advertising your cheapest, lowest-quality product at a below-cost price and then switching the consumer to a higher-cost product after he comes in the store.

Fraudulently charging for services or merchandise not rendered. This can be done in many ways by many businesses, such as professionals charging for hours they never put in, repairmen charging for hours and parts they never put in, etc.

Recommending and performing unnecessary work or services. Examples of this are recommending and performing unnecessary medical treatment, unnecessary repair to cars and homes, etc.

Running a sweatshop. Trapping individuals and paying them far below the worth of the work they are performing or having planned personnel turnover so that people are let go when significant raises or benefits would come due.

There are many other secrets to success, and as you can see, the public has been grossly misled by the consumer advocate hucksters. These hucksters would have you believe that deceptive documented advertising is the cause of most economic woes and nothing could be further from the truth. To go even further, they would have you believe that the worst culprits of all are people in direct-mail or mail-order as they call it. To give you a better perspective of that, if you took all mail-order sales of all the companies in the United States, it would not even total one third of all the sales of the nation's largest oil company, Exxon. Even though Exxon is the number one oil company in sales, it represents a fraction of the total sales of the oil industry alone. Although direct-mail represents 11 percent of all consumable merchandise sold, when you look at it with respect to the gross national product, which represents all goods and services sold, the number is infinitesimal.

From another perspective, direct-mail and mail-order companies usually sell products that are not vital necessities. People purchase them from their disposable income, and people do have a choice whether they want to buy them or not. It is not a case of getting fleeced for a vital commodity you must have for existence and being unable to do anything about it. As you can see, our good old consumer advocates who crusade against and denounce deceiving the public have engaged in a little public deception of their own over the past 20 years.

Almost every individual is guilty of a little deception. Loafing on the job. Not paying for goods received. Cheating on income taxes. Most people are honest, as mentioned before; few of us are intentionally dishonest. We've always got a rationalization when we do stray a little bit. Maybe the best way to put it is that 90% of the people are honest 90% of the time. "There is a little bit of larceny in all of us."

It can also be said that we were guilty of deception and that we were rationalizing our position. I held many meetings on the subject to try to objectively determine if that was the case. Before I went ahead I wanted to make sure I was right. I poured over the facts and came up with an objective opinion. After numerous meetings with a substantial number of objective reviewers, in summary, this was the conclusion reached by almost everyone.

Yes, technically you could say that we violated the law. Advertising law is extremely ambiguous and unworkable. But if we did violate the law, we did it innocently. What stands out in this case is the selectiveness of prosecution, the inequitable treatment relative to similar cases, the punishment which did not fit the violation, the deliberate denial of due process of law, and lastly, the overtones of the underlying motivation of the regulatory network with regard to suppression of competition.

We were soon to get many more examples of just how selectively the regulatory network does prosecute. It was surfacing more and more how important this issue was and why it is mandatory today that a law should be drafted against this unethical practice. Selective prosecution shakes the very foundation of the law and order.

If the FDA came down on every corporation or individual equally in similar instances, I would say, "Well, they are hard-nosed about it, but at least they are fair, and that's the law, and I'll adapt accordingly. It's just like adjusting to a referee at a basketball game. You might find a referee that calls them very close, which is fine, as long as he calls them close for both teams. A lot of coaches might not like referees who call fouls closely and might not agree with them in principle, but they do respect them if they are consistent. Consistency is important. It gives credibility, predictability and allows one to adjust to rules and regulations, but that is hardly what is happening in the regulatory network.

We were going to become even more infuriated about this matter. We were ready to launch the bread back onto the market by picking up where we left off in the direct-mail media first.

We were going to go back to our ROP media.

Our competition selling bran pills and PPA had found out through various methods how to do the ROP system and unknown to us had been running it hot and heavy for the past six months. They had been let off the hook scott free with almost identical ads. They had run almost the entire ROP circulation hard and heavy with an ad almost identical to the bread.

When we started to roll out the bread again, the ROP media market was totally depleted and the ads bombed. At this point I was livid. But there was still more to come.

My first book, 7 Steps to Freedom, had been running for a period of time and was doing well. We had now discovered that two individuals in California had copied our 7 Steps to Freedom full-page newspaper ad word for word, except for wherever "Ohio man" appeared and changed it to "California man". They even used my pictures and the pictures of my family. They were running these ads in newspapers, keeping the money and not giving the customers any product, a blatant fraud. I quickly phoned the California Attorney General's office, another U.S. Postal Inspection Service. I told him we had an emergency, and we had better stop these thieves before they skipped the country with the money. Astonishingly, they were nonchalant about the whole thing. I called them back repeatedly on the issue and to our knowledge they did nothing about it.

I called the California attorney general's office specifically and chewed them out from one end to the other. We asked them how dare they give us a hassle on legitimate products like our bread where there was a question as to whether we were overpromoting, and yet they did nothing about a real crime like this.

It was becoming more and more apparent that there is a very small spectrum of people that the Consumer Protection Network prosecutes—small, viable, visible businesses with no influence in the government. The real thieves in the higher echelon with influence are let go, and the small thieves, the one bureaucrat called small potatoes, are given a low-priority status, because you don't get as big a feather in your cap for such a prosecution.

It had become obvious that the highest point of susceptibility to devastating regulatory action for a small business comes to that point when they are very visible, yet have no government influence, relatively little money to fight in court, and no large legal staff. This susceptibility really increased when a company trespassed on a protected territory of a vested-interest corporation. Now the reason for the incredibly swift and unjustly severe action by the Consumer Protection Network with regard to our diet bread became quite understandable.

A bureaucrat trying to justify his existence or a new lawyer trying to make a name for himself has a very small spectrum of companies with which to work. A substantial number of viable companies have a vested interest in the government and are listed as untouchable. Other large companies have formidable law firms and funds to fight in court. They also carry influence with the news media because of advertising dollars. A small thief brings no glory. But when you are a new, viable, visible company with no government influence, or litigation resources, you look like a trapped chicken to a hungry fox to the Consumer Protection Network.

What you must do to become a permanent, viable, major business in the United States

We had prepared a new bread ad to launch the retail sales. The New York attorney decided it would be a good idea to go on a goodwill mission to Cincinnati to talk to Mr. Simmons, to show that we made an effort to review the new ad with him. It was decided at the last minute that it would be best if I did not go down. So, the New York attorney and my general manager, Jim, met each other in Cincinnati to attend the meeting that had been prearranged with Mr. Simmons.

Jim drove home from the meeting that evening and came into the office the following morning. Everybody who knows Jim would say he is a friendly, easy-going individual who likes just about everyone. When he came in that morning, he was almost frothing at the mouth. He said, "You think I'm mad now, you should have seen me coming home last night. I will never go to such a meeting again and be treated like that by anyone."

It seems that the New York lawyer had given Jim instructions before the meeting to simply sit there and say nothing when Mr. Simmons started ranting on. Jim described the meeting as follows:

"We went into a federal building where we received a security badge. We went up a certain number of floors to where the FDA offices are located. Everything was waxed and cleaned to an excessive degree. When we got to Mr. Simmons' office, his secretary met us and gave us instructions on how the introductions would take place, the way you would if you were meeting the King of England or someone noble. She said Mr. Simmons would first introduce his subordinates in the meeting and then you would introduce yourself. His office was large and plush and looked like that of a major corporation president. Simmons, himself, made a bad appearance. Not so much his natural looks, but the way he groomed and carried himself. He was short, stocky, with a close-cut crew cut and big ears.

"During the entire meeting, Simmons was obstinate to any effort at diplomacy. I don't understand how the government can be so irresponsible to put a man like that in that position."

Jim was right. There was something seriously wrong with the federal government putting people like this in these positions.

It was now October 1978, and the U.S. Attorney's office was now bugging us to do something about the 80,000 pounds of bread that had been seized. To date it had been sitting in frozen cold storage and a decision had to be made on it. It was costing a great deal of money each day to store it. The government was getting a little nervous because I would assume it would come out of the U.S. Attorney's department budget, if they could not get us to pay.

The came to us with a proposal that was ridiculous. We were to sign one of their consent decrees that said we blatantly violated the law and would not market the bread anymore. Then the bread was going to be destroyed.

We argued, "Why does the bread have to be destroyed? There is nothing wrong with the bread itself. The only thing wrong, as you claim, is the packaging. Really, the only significant thing wrong with the packaging is that it doesn't mention that there is a slight preservative in it. That could even be hand stamped on." None of this, of course, was acceptable. The bread had to be destroyed.

The haggling back and forth continued into November, and all of a sudden we received a notice. A federal judge, William K. Thomas, had gone ahead and let the U.S. Attorney have a hearing on the disposition of the bread without our presence, and he had given the order for the bread to be destroyed. This was ridiculous. First of all, the lawyers couldn't figure out how they pulled it off without us being there. Secondly, there was no need to destroy 80,000 pounds of harmless bread. It was still perfectly good because it had been frozen. Remember, this was enough bread to feed about 80,000 people for a week or give a nourishing, filling meal to 1.2 million people. Just by adding water it would make over 100,000 pounds of bread, which converts to about 2 million slices.

We then came up with a great idea. Since the government was so obstinate about simply letting us repackage the bread for obvious vindictive reasons, they surely would let us give the bread to the needy, which we were willing to do. So we made an urgent emergency communication with Judge Thomas and told him we would be willing to do anything, pay all the expenses, repackage the bread if necessary, and give it to either a local orphanage, the Salvation Army or the Red Cross. When our lawyers contacted the judge, he thought that it sounded like an excellent idea. So we prepared the manpower to repackage the bread in bulk bags with proper labeling and give them to the most needy charity.

However, a few days later we received a letter from Judge Thomas. This gutless wonder must have been persuaded into backing out of the plan by the FDA and the U.S. Attorney's office.

This was indeed another low point, another significant disillusionment concerning the humanity of the federal government. There simply wasn't any.

This especially put my wife and me in a state of depression. Destroying that bread was like destroying part of us. If we could have given it to the needy, at least we would have felt that it would have helped somebody and served some purpose. But to senselessly and unnecessarily destroy enough bread to feed 1.2 million people for absolutely no good reason was beyond my comprehension or the comprehension of anybody who was associated with us at the time.

I said, "I guarantee you there will be no media coverage of this event, but I for one am going to document it." I hired a photographer and investigator to track down where the bread was going to be taken and how it was going to be destroyed.

They found it was going to be taken to the Euclid Landfill in Euclid, Ohio, and bulldozed under. I arranged for the photographer to be there to take the pictures of the bread being destroyed. On that day trucks were loaded at Sheriff's cold storage in Cleveland hauled to the Euclid Landfill.

But guess who else was there taking pictures. It was Sue Morgan, FDA agent for Mr. Simmons. Mr. Simmons must have wanted pictures of the bread being destroyed for a trophy.

While our photographer was taking his pictures, the owner of the landfill came storming over and told the security guards to throw our photographer off the premises. He was ranting that we were taking these pictures to smear all over the front page of the *Plain Dealer*. So the photographer went off the land and used a telephoto lens to finish taking the pictures which can be seen below and on the following page.

We waited for media coverage, but not one individual from the media showed up. They say the news is full of half-truths; well, it may have been at one time, but that is past the boards. I would have to estimate you now see only 10% of the truth on the news.

At this point in time at our company, we discussed what to do about James C. Simmons, the FDA's main perpetrator of the No-Hunger Bread atrocity. Although we had already embarrassed him within the federal government and likely hurt his career, we felt that was not enough punishment for so vile an act as he committed.

However, due to the fact that we were so economically strapped and would have to face yet another corrupt government agency in yet a new war (this will be discussed shortly), we decided to wait to give Mr. Simmons his due until we had the resources to do so.

The depletion of the market for Nancy's Bread due to the perceived easier-to-use over-the-counter diet pills made selling the bread mixture or the bread loaves impossible. This was because there was such a small markup.

I think came up with the idea of selling the recipe in printed form.

So I created sales generation systems to sell the bread recipe which turned out to be successful. In a few months we were selling over 30,000 bread recipes a month, and customers were deliriously happy about the bread. We were inundated with letters from customers who said they were losing weight painlessly, and many said they were never able to lose weight with any other product before. Here are just a few of the letters.

"I never thought in my whole life I could ever be thankful enough to shout about saying I am on a bread recipe and diet. And believe me, what a bread recipe and diet. I started it on July 22. I was then 155 pounds. I now weigh 145 pounds. To me that is terrific." –Terri Lorenzo, Edgerton, Ohio

"I have lost 50 pounds and I do not want to gain it back. Your bread recipe and diet sure worked well. And now that I have removed the weight I wanted to, I need your help in keeping it under control. Please let me know if I can change my food preferences in a little and get another bread recipe and diet." –Raymond Matthews, Silver Spring, Maryland

"My daughter is so satisfied with her bread recipe and diet and has, to date, lost a total of 25 pounds since beginning your bread recipe and diet. She looks very well and does not have any flab whatsoever. We are quite satisfied and pleased with

her results and tell everyone about what a fine program you have." Mrs. Phillip Donohue, Los Angeles, California

"I am so pleased with the bread recipe and diet you prepared for me. I have lost 13 pounds in two weeks. Many people have asked me where they can get an application. Could you send me about 20 of them so that I can give them to my friends?" –Juanita Pringle, Greenbelt, Maryland

"I just wanted you to know that I have never been so pleased with myself as I am right now. When I started the bread recipe and diet, I weighed 161 and today I weight 120, just one pound more than I weighed in November, 1945, when I got out of the service! I have tried other diets, even took pills under doctors' instructions, but nothing worked as well as the computer diet has worked. I have taken in my clothes so many times that it is much easier to start new. When I buy anything new, I can usually take a size 8 or at the most a size 10." –Loretta Ferguson, Vernon, Connecticut.

So there we were making money again, the customers were happy, and we were safely and pleasantly helping to relieve the public of the serious health problem of obesity. It was good for us, good for the customers, and good for the country, but it was not good for the patent-medicine industry which perceived it was losing sales on its patent-medicine prescription and over-the-counter diet pills, which not only did not work but were harmful to the user's health.

But the patent-medicine industry couldn't use the FDA because we weren't selling an actual food product this time. The FDA cannot regulate printed material. Also, after the thrashing we gave it, it would be unlikely that it would even try. So it used another then-corrupt government agency who could put a good and valid printed product off the market – the United States Postal Service. The U.S. Postal Service at this point, in large part due to us, is a much-improved government agency. But at that time it was one of the most tyrannical and unconstitutional government agencies that existed. It still has unconstitutional powers, but at the present time the management team of the USPS seems to be much more ethical. But keep in mind as you read the following what the U.S. Postal Services can do to you if another corrupt management team gets in power again.

The U.S. Postal Service law department contacted us that it was investigating us and wanted us to stop marketing the Nancy's Bread recipe. Of course, it couldn't find anything wrong with the promotions or the product. But after a great deal of far-reaching effort, it did come up with a ridiculous charge on which to file a civil suit against us. It said that one of the diet programs that we recommended along with the bread recipe, according to its "medical experts," did not have enough daily calorie intake to be a safe diet. This was, of course, ridiculous because the diet was designed to provide adequate protein and other key nutrients, and the required calories would come from the lost fat.

But it simply wanted an excuse to put the Nancy's Bread recipe off the market. This certainly added more evidence to what our sources were telling us about the conspiracy about the federal government to put natural-health remedies on the market in favor of patent-medicine health remedies. Again the reason is patent medicines can be, as the term implies, "patented;" therefore, they can be controlled by a handful of people and marked up 10 to 100 times. A natural-health remedy cannot be patented, controlled by a few people and, on average, can only be marked up 20-50%.

The U.S. Postal Service filed a civil suit against us on the Nancy's Bread recipe and then filed another civil suit against a sequel to my *7 Seven Steps to Freedom* book which was published in 1982 titled *SuperBiz*. *SuperBiz* contained an expose of the No-Hunger Bread atrocity. After that it would monitor our company and wait for any new product to come out and invent a false charge and file a civil suit against that product.

The USPS obviously thought it could defeat us by simply stripping away our economic resources to fight back as we did against the FDA. It would soon find out that it was wrong. I created so many net profit generation systems in such a short period of time that there was no way that the USPS could keep filing civil suits without becoming apparent that its intention was not to protect the consumer, but it had a conspiracy to put us out of business.

We launched a full-scale lethal counterattack against not only the U.S. Postal Service as an agency but also the individual culprits in the postal inspection service, the law department, and the judicial officer department who were perpetrating these unlawful acts.

Most of this counteroffensive went along the same lines as the counteroffensive against the FDA, so I will not go into detail here as to what all transpired.

Our counteroffensive included broadcast and print publication expose ads. But this time we also included direct-mail that went to reporters in all the major news media across the country, to Congress, to the direct-marketing industry, and right into the neighborhoods of the individuals in the U.S. Postal Service who were perpetrating these unlawful acts. We also picked one of the frivolous civil suits it filed and took the U.S. Postal Service all the way through the legal mill, all the way to the U.S. Supreme Court. If there is any thing a bureaucrat hates it's work. We made the litigation super-voluminous in detail to create the maximum work for the involved U.S. Postal Service officials.

Of course, we did not win the case because of civil service laws under which the U.S. Postal Service operates are unconstitutional and constitute mock justice. But in the process we did find a major chink in the armor that threatened to destroy the unconstitutional system. This chink in the armor was that, through our litigation discovery and investigation, we found that in the history of the U.S. Postal Service's administrative court. Through these unconstitutional laws the U.S. Postal Service administrative court is the main court where all defendants must go. You can then appeal to the regular federal court system. This is usually an effort in futility. But, the discovery of the fact that the U.S. Postal Service administrative court was a mock court did pose as a serious threat. This point was cast off in our appeals because we did not bring it up in the administrative court proceedings. We did not find this mock-court factor until the administrative court process was completed. We only found it after we started the appeals process.

But in our exposes, we did point this out. This point was looked upon with great interest by the direct-marketing industry.

At the end of this war, we won a substantial victory. The U.S. Postal Service no longer bothered us. The U.S. Postal Service administrative court for the first time in history was now letting defendants win. And many of the culprits who perpetrated the frivolous lawsuits against or company were either demoted or fired. The key expose that was the main weapon in defeating the U.S. Postal Service in its corrupt defensive against our company is shown below.

Here is the letter and expose on U.S. Postal Service regulatory corruption we mailed to our Congressman, with copies to all of Congress, the entire direct-marketing industry, and the news media across the nation.

To Whom It May Concern:

This letter is an urgent request for your affirmative action on three immediate threats to the viability of The Suarez Corporation and nearly all other direct marketing companies.

Also enclosed is an update on information that we presented to you, on one of these threats, a few months ago. The enclosed, updated information presents evidence of serious improper activity in the United States Postal Service – improprieties of the nature of those going on in the EDA Generic Drug Division and in HUD.

Enclosed is more hard evidence that the U.S. Postal Service Law Enforcement Departments carry out selective prosecution and mock justice. This investigation shows a definite double standard in regulatory enforcement one for the top 100 largest direct marketing companies and another standard for small and medium-size direct marketing companies. The investigation also shows that the small and medium size companies that are prosecuted are put through a mock justice system in which the United States Postal Service wins 100% of the time.

The updated study shows, with even greater certainty, that over the past eight years, not one of the long-established, top 100 direct marketing companies has ever been prosecuted for anything, even though there is enclosed proof that they mail the same type of promotions for which small and medium size companies were prosecuted. And, a number of the top 100 direct marketing companies have been prosecuted by states' attorneys general, and one is amongst the top 5 complaint generators for the Better Business Bureau and has an unsatisfactory BBB rating. Yet, with all of this, none of the long-established, top 100 has had a regulatory action brought by the U.S. Postal Service within at least the past eight years.

These improprieties in the U.S. Postal Service are no small matter. The mails are the most critical form of communication in our nation. The mails are also a major trade medium and a critical cog in all of commerce. The U.S. Postal Service already has dangerous police state powers with which they can stop the communications and trade of any individual or organization in the U.S. without even the semblance of a fair trial. Although the misuse and abuse of this power appears to be mostly limited to the direct marketing industry at this point, it could easily be expanded to just about any other field of human endeavor in the United States. The U.S. Postal Service has already censored books published by certain companies in the direct marketing industry and could censor all communication if they wished. Anyone who has used the mails in any way, even in small part, concerning any endeavor, is subject to the police state powers of the U.S. Postal Service.

Also enclosed are pertinent documents concerning The Suarez Corporation's recent encounter with the mock justice system associated with the U.S. Postal Service. In 1985, we were falsely accused by the U.S. Postal Service of mailing a deceptive promotion for an exceptional product we produced, which provided a free report on how a citizen could find out if they had money coming from states' unclaimed funds departments and an optional report for $19 that showed citizens how to find out if they had other benefits coming from government of which they were not properly informed.

When we alerted you to this mock justice system by the U.S. Postal Service in the past, you informed us that we must first go through the court system before you could do anything about it. Well, we have gone through the court system, if you could call it a court system.

We went through the entire farce of the U.S. Postal Service Administrative Court in which no one from the private sector has ever won, and then appealed the case through federal court all the way to the supreme court. All of this took nearly five years, cost us nearly a half a million dollars in direct our-of-pocket costs, at least another half a million dollars in internal cost and millions of dollars in lost sales.

To summarize the procedure briefly, a U.S. Postal Service Civil Service employee, or group of employees from the Postal Inspection Service and Law Department, can make a false accusation against a private sector company. This false accusation is then first rubber-stamped by the federal court system in order to get temporary restraining orders and preliminary injunctions. The Postal Service does not need to prove anything to get these TROs and preliminary injunctions. The victim is then taken into the U.S. Postal Service's Administrative Court where, again, another U.S. Postal Service employee who masquerades as a judge rubber-stamps the false accusations after a number of weeks of mock ritual. The postal service employee "judge" then issues a cease and desist order and all the orders for the victim's product are returned and the victim is prohibited from ever mailing the promotion again. When the victim appeals this administrative court decision in the federal courts, he again finds that this mock decision is rubber-stamped by the federal courts and that the higher courts will not even hear an appeal.

So, we have now gone through the entire mock court system, and we now have hard evidence that we have a political problem. As our congressmen, we want you to correct this political problem.

Also, we have other serious government threats to our business. Postal rates are now increasing 100% faster than inflation and there is a massive offensive for an interstate sales tax.

Therefore, specifically, what we are asking for and what we are, in fact, demanding is the following:

1. Sponsor legislation amending 39 USCA Section 3007 which currently allows the Postal Service to obtain a temporary restraining order and preliminary injunction pursuant to rule 65 of the Federal Rules of Civil Procedure merely upon a showing of probably cause. The burden of proof should be the same for the Postal Service as it is for any other party, i.e., "...it clearly appears from specific facts shown by affidavit or by verified complaint that immediate and irreparable injury, loss, or damage will result to the applicant..." A probably cause standard is very nebulous and arbitrary in light of the consequences which befall a mailer in the event a temporary restraining order and preliminary injunction is ordered, i.e., having its incoming mail detained pending the conclusion of the statutory proceeding and any appeal therefrom. The legislation you could sponsor should amend 39 USCA Section 3007 so that upon the Postal Service's belief that probable cause exists that 39 USCA Section 3005 or 3006 has been violated, the Postal Service may seek a temporary restraining order and preliminary injunction pursuant to the standards which such orders are granted under the federal rules of civil procedure.

2. Sponsor a companion bill in the House of Representatives of the United States mirroring S. B. 594 cited as the "Administrative Law Judge Corpse Act." The passage and enactment of such legislation would create significant improvements in the ability of an accused party obtaining a fair and impartial hearing. It is also anticipated that the practice of selective enforcement would be eliminated.

3. Co-sponsor H. R. 1147, introduced by Representative Phillip M. Crane (R.-IL), which would privatize the Postal Service. This legislation proposes to transfer all Postal Service property to a corporation which satisfies certain requirements including that the corporation is not a department, agency or establishment of the United States. The bill provides for postal employees to be justly compensated in the form of issued securities in the new corporation and for comparable retirement benefits. It would also establish rate setting authority and an interim Postal Privatization Commission to carry out transitional programs.

4. Convince Representative William Ford Peren (D-MI), (Chairman of the Postal Office and Civil Service Committee), to have the government accounting office initiate and conduct a thorough investigation

of the Postal Inspection Service and Consumer Protection Division Law Department to expose and terminate the practice of selective enforcement.

Ralph, our company faces a life or death situation in this matter. We cannot be spending millions of dollars on new promotions and products to create hundreds and even thousands of future jobs in the community if we are going to have the sword hanging over our heads that at any time a civil service worker can invent a false charge against our company and automatically punish us by putting that product off the market, knowing that no proof in an impartial court is needed and that there is a 100% chance that their accusation will be upheld in the mock court system. Also, it will do us no good to invent great products and create great sales promotions for these products when we cannot mail them to prospects because the postage is too high and to have any chance of making a profit. And, it makes no sense to do any of the above if, after all is said and done, all of our profits will be taken by use taxes and other taxes.

You are our main federal representative. On top of that, since we are staunch Republicans, Senators Glenn and Metzenbaum are not going to help us. We have no where else to turn.

Ralph, today I want to inform you that although it's the last thing in the world I would want to do, if you do not provide us with major, affirmative and effective help on this matter, we're going to have to use our resources to get a representative in office who will. I am sorry, but we have no other choice in the matter.

I would like to have a personal meeting with you on this serious matter at our corporate headquarters as soon as possible. Please let me know when I can have this meeting.

Sincerely,

Benjamin D. Suarez, President

The Suarez Corporation, Chairman

The United States Citizens Association

Enclosure – details on this regulatory corruption problems.

BDS/ag

This expose was included with the aforementioned letter

A SPECIAL REPORT ON SELECTIVE PROSECUTION

AND MOCK JUSTICE BEING CARRIED OUT BY

THE UNITED STATES POSTAL SERVICE

A special report produced in a joint effort by the investigative reporting department of American Community Magazines, a division of The

Suarez Corporation, and the United States Citizens Association, a nonprofit citizens organization which was founded by The Suarez Corporation

BRIEF: This investigation found a definite double standard in The U.S. Postal Service consumer regulatory enforcement. Small mail-order companies face excessive, letter-of-the-law enforcement and a rigged court system, but large, long-established mail-order companies are NEVER prosecuted even though a significant number engage in mail fraud according to USPS standards for small companies. Small and "fringe" mail-order companies experience extremely excessive enforcement action—about 3,000 were prosecuted over the past eight years. Not one of the top 100 long-established mail-order companies has ever had any type of USPS enforcement action in the past eight years even though many send out mailings, numbering in the hundreds of millions, that are arguably more deceptive than mailings for which small mail-order companies were prosecuted and severely punished. Also, state attorneys general have prosecuted a number of these top-100 companies, and one of the top 100-companies is amongst the top-five complaint generators with the Better Business Bureau and has an unsatisfactory rating. The USPS administrative court is rigged – the USPS wins 100% of the time. The U.S. federal court system is also rigged in the USPS's favor – the USPS wins virtually 100% of the time in temporary restraining orders (TROs), injunctions, and appeal suits on USPS administrative court decisions. It was also found that the USPS definitely has a top-priority enforcement target of products that compete in the apparent protected market territories of health and finance.

An ongoing eight-year investigation by The Suarez Corporation and the United States Citizens Association (USCA) has revealed that the United States Postal Service (USPS) law enforcement departments, for the most part, do not operate in the public interest.

This investigation determined the following:
THE USPS ENGAGED IN DISCRIMINATION IN CONSUMER LAW ENFORCEMENT, DOES NOT PROSECUTE THE BIGGEST AND WORST OFFENDERS IN MAIL FRAUD AND ENGAGES IN MOCK JUSTICE.

Over the past eight years, and likely as far back as the USPS has existed, not one major, established company or organization has been prosecuted civilly or criminally for mail fraud. (We define a major established company or organization as one that has sales exceeding $100 million per year for a sustained period of over seven years.) Yet the investigation clearly showed that many of these corporations and organizations mail hundreds of millions of direct-mail solicitations per year that are arguably fraudulent and, in fact, worse than similar promotions for which small and medium size companies and organizations were prosecuted.

The United States Postal Service prosecutes exclusively small- and medium-sized companies and new start-ups. They also prosecute what is known in regulatory circles as the "fringe" companies. These area companies that have just started to make substantial sales in the range of three to 100 million dollars per year but are not really strong financially, have no influence, and are naïve. These companies, because of their medium size, garner notoriety for the USPS.

The USPS prosecutes mail fraud under both criminal and civil statutes. But prosecution under the civil statues, 39 USC Sec. 3005 and 3007, allows the USPS to deal severe punishment without even the semblance of a fair trial. Therefore, most of the abuse comes from prosecutions under the civil statutes.

Here are findings of this investigation of the USPS prosecutions under the civil statutes.

The law enforcement activity of the USPS falls under three mail departments:
1. The Postal Inspection Service
2. The Law Department
3. The Judicial Officer Department

USCA attorneys reviewed approximately 3,000 cases, which were all cases filed between 1981-1988, by the USPS under USC Title 39 Sec. 3005 and 3007. USCA has also compiled and analyzed numerous direct mail promotions, sent to consumers from 1985 to 1988, which brought no enforcement action. From this study the USCA has been able to establish a pattern of whom the Law Department and the Postal Inspection Service prosecute, whom they do not prosecute, and their priorities in enforcement action.

Here are the types of prosecutions carried out by the USPS.

TYPE 1 – Justifiable prosecution of actual mail fraud by fringe and small companies.

TYPE 2 – Unwarranted prosecution of fringe companies in order to gain notoriety.

TYPE 3 – Unwarranted prosecution of small and new start-up companies in order to meet quotas.

TYPE 4 – Unwarranted prosecution of fringe and small companies that are competing with special interests who have apparently influenced the USPS.

TYPE 5 – Unwarranted prosecution of companies that sell products that cause the government to work and/or lose money.

TYPE 6 – Unwarranted prosecution of companies that publish negative material on the government.

Most of the USPS prosecutions appear to be justified (Type 1). But a large percentage are not justified (Types 2-6).

Here is the System Used in Prosecutions
Under 39 USC Sec. 3005 and 3007

STEP 1 – Most of the time the decision by the USPS to initiate an investigation for possible enforcement action originates from a pattern of consumer complaints. But in a substantial number of cases, investigations start when there are no consumer complaints. The USPS Postal Inspection Service and the Law Department have certain products categorized as "red flags" which, from our observation based on a pattern of facts, exist for no other purpose than to restrict competition to favored special interests (type 4 prosecution). When the direct-mail solicitation, print of TV promotion for this product is observed by any number of research and monitor personnel in the USPS, an alert memo is passed on to the power figures and the USPS law enforcement departments.

Also it appears investigations are initiated at the request of influential persons in government and in the private sector.

STEP 2 – Pending results of an investigation, a decision is made by the power figures in the USPS law enforcement departments to prosecute the target company. Most of the time they intend to put the product off the market and the company out of business.

STEP 3 – A strategic plan is formulated for the prosecution of the target company, a plan which includes law department research and soliciting the services of "experts" on the subject, who are usually incompetent people who have been unsuccessful in their chosen field of endeavor but who do have degrees and other honors (which do not really qualify them as truly effective experts in their fields). Many times these paid witnesses testify on a continuing basis for the postal service and are readily available.

In most cases enforcement action by the USPS is warranted. But, in many unwarranted enforcement actions, the targeted product is usually as good, and most of the time much better, than the products being marketed by the favored special interest. Also in these unwarranted action cases, the promotion for these products contains nothing false, either by inclusion or by omission. Therefore, the USPS has to invent a charge. Since there is nothing false in the promotion, the USPS will say "it is misleading." The USPS knows full well that 20%-30% of people are confused by any type of communication, be it a book, movie, newscast or advertisement. Studies have shown this conclusively. Such a charge could be made about any effective advertisement.

Such a trumped-up charge sometimes initially looks like it may have substance, but it is unlikely the case could be won in front of an impartial judge or jury. The USPS knows it does not have to worry about that. It will file the charge under the civil statutes which guarantee it a mock justice system, which is 100% in its favor. The USPS won't have to worry about impartial judges or juries of the defendant's peers.

Again, the USPS's intent many times is not to work in the public interest. The intent is to put a product or service that competes with the favored special interest off the market, or to reach its quotas, or to punish a company for exercising freedom of speech, or to gain publicity for the USPS.

STEP 4 – A threatening correspondence is mailed to the target company's chief operating officer or statutory agent, which outlines the intended prosecution by the USPS and demands that the company sign a "consent decree," which will put the product off the market and likely the company out of business. These consent decrees, sometimes called consent decree judgments, are just that – judgments that are agreed to by the target company and have the same force of law as though a judgment were made in the court. The only difference is that the defendant does not admit any guilt but does agree to cease and desist doing whatever it is to which the USPS objects.

STEP 5 – A USPS law enforcement official, usually a postal inspector, many times accompanied by a law department official, will call for a meeting with the target company's chief executive or attorneys. In this meeting, a signing of the consent decree is demanded along with voluntarily allowing the USPS to hold all orders for the product that are still left to come in. Many times the USPS will also demand a refunding of money to the people that have already ordered the product. If the company agrees to this, usually no further action is taken, but the company has its product taken off the market and usually will go out of business because it has already spent advertising dollars and inventory for the product and thus will have no revenue to meet these expenses.

STEP 6 – If at this point the company refuses to cooperate or refuses to allow the post office to hold future orders while the consent decree is being negotiated, the USPS will file for a temporary restraining order (TRO), followed by a preliminary injunction in the district federal court of the target company's state, an action which will force the holding of the orders for the product by the local post office.

In these TRO and preliminary injunction hearings, the USPS does not have to prove anything. It does not have to prove that anyone was actually deceived. It only has to show "probable cause" that the promotion for the product theoretically MAY be deceptive or the product theoretically MAY be injurious. Also, the target company's attorneys are at a great disadvantage at the TRO hearing, because they only get a few days, at the most, in which to prepare while the USPS has been preparing its case for weeks.

Virtually no one has ever won a TRO or preliminary injunction case with the USPS because the statute and case law governing this proceeding is blatantly unjust and in favor of the USPS, and federal judges are blatantly biased in favor of the USPS. The USPS wins virtually 100% of the time. (There appears to be only one exceptional case where the USPS lost a preliminary injunction case in a Wisconsin federal court.)

In these proceedings, the federal judge is openly biased in favor of the USPS. Attorneys say that the judge has no choice in the case because of the statutes and previous case law. But if such were the case, computers could decide these cases, not judges. In the cases we have witnessed, the postal service had presented no compelling proof whatsoever of their charges in order to get TROs and preliminary injunctions.

But the federal judges will make their decision as follows. Their opinion will totally ignore the defendant's witnesses no matter how good they are. They will simply give credence only to the USPS's witnesses, citing such suggestive things as, "They made a good appearance and conducted themselves well." They will then simply invent a far-reaching reason that the USPS is granted a TRO or preliminary injunction.

STEP 7 – The temporary restraining order (TRO) and preliminary injunction are granted virtually 100% of the time and all of the victim's mail (the orders for the product that are at the post office and orders to come), is seized – permanently. There is no chance that the victim will win if he carries out the court fight against the USPS.

Therefore, at this point, most defendants who are small and medium companies and new start-ups will be faced with the fact that the revenue from this product will be totally cut off. In nearly all cases, this product will be the company's main source of revenue and, in most cases, it will be their only source of revenue. Furthermore, they will have no more income. Therefore, they will have no more money even to fight in court should they desire.

STEP 8 – Many times, the USPS will issue news releases when it files this civil suit and also after it "wins" a TRO and a preliminary injunction. Therefore, three times the victim's name will be smeared in the news media, in front of business colleagues and in front of friends and relatives.

At this point many times the victim will face loss of credit, key business colleagues and suppliers. He or she will be portrayed in the community as some kind of criminal who has had a fair trial in front of a jury of his or her peers and an impartial judge and has been convicted of a felony.

No one can accurately calculate monetarily how much is lost by the company or the principals in the company through character assassination, which comes about when the news of a TRO and preliminary injunction hits the local media. Also, there is incalculable emotional damage done to the employees of the company in question. Morale falters, and key employees are sometimes lost even though the product in question may be a good one and the company has done nothing wrong.

Remember, the only action the victim was guilty of was introducing to the market a better product than was being offered by favored special interests of the USPS or exercising his or her right to free speech.

To this point (the time period usually involves 4 – 6 weeks) all this has cost the victim $5,000 - $10,000 in legal fees; $10,000 - $20,000 in internal costs for the company's part in fighting the case; and usually hundreds of thousands to millions of dollars in lost sales.

Not to mention the total disruption of business.

STEP 9 – At this juncture, most victims sign a consent decree which takes the product off the market and, most of the time, puts them out of business.

STEP 10 – For the few victims who have the money to go on, a worse scenario of injustice awaits them far beyond what they could possibly imagine. In order to keep fighting in "court," the victim must appear as a "respondent" in the USPS administrative "court." Here, postal employees act as judges and are even more blatantly biased than the federal court judges. They don't try to dignify this unjust system by calling the victims "defendants," and the postal employees who act as "judges" wear suits, not black robes.

STEP 11 – At this point, the victim usually must pay a huge retainer to the law firm that will defend the company. To fight a case in this administrative court costs $50,000 to $300,000.

STEP 12 – The victim must now use up much more internal costs in order to help the attorneys prepare the case. A conservative estimate of this cost would be around $200,000.

STEP 13 – The administrative court will take its good old time before hearing the case, and it's likely not to be heard for three months.

STEP 14 – When the case is heard, the victims and their attorneys must travel to Washington and stay there for the duration of the case, which usually lasts a week but which could last several weeks or more.

STEP 15 – In the USPS administrative "court" hearing, the victim will experience abomination of justice and unethical practices.

USPS attorneys will fabricate and engage in what we have observed as unethical practices such as trying to intimidate the victim or the victim's witnesses into saying they had admitted guilt to USPS officials before the hearing. They use the threat that if the victim does not tell the "truth," (that is, what they want said) the victim will be liable for perjury and criminal charge. They also will tell the victim's attorneys that they are not going to introduce certain evidence, and then they will surprisingly introduce it anyway. Just about anything is admissible in this court – hearsay and so on – with much more leniency given to the Postal Service but not the respondent when the respondent presents such evidence.

Do not be surprised to find a "judge" that is openly partial to the USPS to the point where USPS attorneys will sneer and snicker at the victim and their counsel because they know that no matter how good a case the victim's counsel presents, the USPS will win.

It is not that the USPS has great attorneys; it does not. It is just that the deck is stacked in the USPS favor. The USPS uses witnesses who are paid to say anything. If the USPS brings in consumer witnesses, it usually solicits for these witnesses and brings in cranks and chronic complainers.

STEP 16 – After the administrative hearing is over, the victim will have to wait three to six months for a decision from the administrative "judge."

But the USPS will already know the outcome before it is rendered. In this administrative "court," the USPS wins 100% of the time, even with the fact that USPS attorneys just go through the motions and use poor and paid witnesses.

STEP 17 – The decision is then officially rendered by the USPS administrative "judge." Not only will it be in favor of the USPS, but the USPS will usually win all counts. The decision will be blatantly one-sided, with little chance for attorneys to even have grounds for appeal. (There has been a recent exception where a company did win some points but lost the case. We believe this exception occurred because the USPS was aware of the USCA investigation.)

Also, contrary to the propaganda published about the USPS civil procedure, one cannot then go into federal court and get a fair trial. One can sue the USPS in federal court and try to get the case overturned, but if the administrative "judge" has not made a technical error, which in most cases they will be sure that they haven't, one really has no legal basis for an appeal. Even if there was an error, the federal court system is also biased in favor of the USPS. Therefore, the railroad job is absolute and sure. There was one exception in which a victim won in such an appeal suit, but then the victory was overturned in the appellate court. Again, the USPS wins virtually 100% of the time.

To this point, the elapsed time is ten months with $100,000 to $350,000 in legal fees, $150,000 in internal costs, and hundreds of thousands to millions of dollars in revenues from lost product sales.

STEP 18 –At this point, if the victims still have the resources to sue the USPS on the administrative "court" decision in federal court, they are in for yet more expense and blatant injustice. This suit will cost $10,000 to $20,000 and take six to twelve months.

And again, not only will the USPS win, but the decision that the judge will render will be 100% in favor the USPS, therefore, giving the victim absolutely no chance for further appeal.

Again, many times news releases will make the victims appear as though they were criminals who were tried and convicted in a real court of law with a fair trial and a jury of their peers.

STEP 19 – Any future appeals to higher courts are even more fruitless. Appeals to higher courts, and eventually the Supreme Court, will take another two years and an additional $100,000. This will bring the grand total in lost monies and time to anywhere from $200,000 to $450,000 in legal fees; to over $200,000 in internal costs; and again hundreds of thousands to millions of dollars in lost sales; and to over four years of wasted time.

What a victim is likely to encounter in higher appeals courts is a panel of judges who already have their minds made up and refuse to consider the argument that the administrative court is inherently unconstitutional unless this issue was raised before the administrative court. In other words, unless one has swallowed one's suicide pill before the administrative court (by bringing up the point that the administrative court is rigged), the federal appellate courts don't want to hear it.

However, the above point may be the Achilles' heel in this USPS administrative court scam. This Achilles' heel is the fact that the unconstitutional USPS administrative court has never been challenged in regular federal court. The USPS administrative court system can be exposed as being unconstitutional thus forcing the federal courts to recognize it. All it would take is for one respondent to assert before the USPS administrative court that his/her due process rights are being violated because the USPS administrative hearing is inherently fraught with conflict of interest, e.g., the administrative law judge is under the auspices of the very agency over which he is presiding. While this argument will most certainly fail before the USPS administrative law judge and surely doom the case there, it will protect the record, thus on appeal the federal courts will have to confront and rule on this matter.

Here is an analysis of USPS Postal Dockets (1981-1988), made to determine if a double standard of law enforcement is used by the USPS.

The purpose of this analysis was to examine whether any of the top-100 mail-order companies (rated by sales volume), have been the subject of regulatory action by the USPS during subject years.

A page-by-page examination of the postal dockets over this eight-year period revealed only one case where one of the top-100 mailers was the subject of a USPS regulatory action. And this company was not a long-established company but a relative newcomer. The name of this company is one with which many are familiar: Poole's.

Otherwise, there was only one other case which might involve a top-100 company. It involved Triangle Industries Marketing Research Institute, an engineering wholesaler out of Beverly Hills, California. This company might be Triangle Industries; however, this is doubtful since Triangle Industries' direct-mailing activities are related to magazine subscriptions, and the USPS charge had nothing to do with such.

Although not a top-100 company, General Nutrition Corp. had at least ten actions brought against them in 1984 for false representation concerning the sale of various diet products. This company is rated No. 207 in the top 250. In each case a consent decree was entered into.

Additionally, further evidence of USPS selective enforcement and favoritism is demonstrated by the fact that the New York State attorney general's office was left without assistance or interest of the USPS to investigate, prosecute or settle matters with Times Inc., Home Shopping Network and CVN Cos. No action was taken against these companies by the USPS, but yet the New York attorney general found cause to prosecute these top-100 companies.

Also, one of the top-100 companies is amongst the top-five complaint generators for the Better Business Bureau and has an unsatisfactory rating.

Overall, 1987 U.S. mail-order sales and contributions amounted to approximately $148.71 billion. Of this total, consumer mail-order sales accounted for approximately $70 billion; business mail-order sales amounted to $42 billion; and charitable mail order totaled $37 billion. The top-100 mail-order companies account for $39,922,400,000 and/or approximately 27% of total sales and just over 50% of all consumer sales.

Review of Samples of Deceptive and Misleading Mailings

The U.S. Postal Service charged that IHS (International Home Shopping) violated postal laws by mailing a promotion involving unclaimed funds. In fabricated, nit-picking charges that would tax the imagination, the Postal Service claimed that this promotion was deceptive because it misled the addressee into believing that the promotion came from a government agency, that the addressee was deceived into believing they had unclaimed funds coming, and that the addressee had to pay to receive these unclaimed funds. In fact, the promotion stated clearly that it was from International Home Shopping and was not affiliated with a government agency; that IHS did not know if the addressee in particular had unclaimed funds coming; and, in fact, the unclaimed funds report was given away free, while an optional report on other government benefits was available for a fee at their discretion.

The promotion generated no consumer complaints and, in fact, the customers were well-satisfied with the reports that they received. The only problem that the promotion did cause was that the states had to work and refund money to citizens that was rightfully theirs. (The states willfully, albeit inadequately, publicize unclaimed funds information and the names of those due unclaimed funds because the states use the unclaimed funds' monies on state expenditures.)

The review of deceptive promotions by certain top-100 companies was based upon samplings of deceptive/misleading mailings assembled from mid-1987 through 1988 by USCA investigators.

The few current promotions that are reviewed here consist of sweepstakes run by American Express, Funk & Wagnalls, Hosiery Corporation of America, and Time In. publishers of *Working Women, Sports Illustrated,* and *McCalls.*

1. American Express (20th-largest rated company). The product was being sold was a subscription to *Travel and Leisure* magazine. The teaser used is a free issue to the magazine for one month, but by accepting the free offer consumers obligated themselves to accept the additional issues with the right to cancel after the first month. In order to cancel after the first month, they must use a cancellation number, and it is unlikely the consumers will retain it. Again, confusing sweepstakes rules are utilized, including pasting stamps on different forms. The non-order blank is provided, but it is in an awkward place and can be easily overlooked. The only reference to it is at the end of the promotion letter.

2. Funk & Wagnalls. Their parent is Field Publications. They are the 43rd largest mail-order company. They use a teaser of a free atlas; however, one can only get the freebie if one agrees to a trial subscription, which is contained on the sweepstakes entry form.

3. Hosiery Corporation of America. The product is hosiery. The teaser is a 10-cent check made out to the consumers which will entitle them to buy one pair of hosiery. The window envelope shows a check, and one does not realize that it is for only 10 cents until one opens it up. By using the 10-cent check to buy the "free pair of hose." One is entered into the sweepstakes, which triggers the shipment of four more pairs, sent approximately every 4-5 weeks, for the cost of $2.79 a pair plus postage/handling. Consumers are told that they can cancel at any time and that there is no obligation to buy.

4. Time Inc. (Publishers of *Working Women, Sports Illustrated* and *McCalls*). They are the third-largest mail-order company. All of their promotions use a teaser window envelope, indicating that the consumer is guaranteed or will be paid a large sum of money. After opening the envelope, consumers find that they must return a winning number in order to be guaranteed such payment. The promotion then contains an abundance of glitzy prizes, which can

be won by entering the sweepstakes and that the consumer may obtain one free issue of the particular magazine by completing a form marked "Sweepstakes Entry." The promotion is designed to compel the consumer to try a free issue thereby obligating himself to further issues. It also requires the consumer to take some sort of affirmative action in order to cancel the subscription. In all of these Time Inc. promotions, the ability or opportunity to just enter the sweepstakes is very unclear and almost hidden.

The USCA believes that the largest mail-order companies referenced herein arguably engage in deceptive, misleading, or fraudulent mailings. However, if these companies were instead small companies and engaged in the same mailings, the postal service would most certainly prosecute these companies for mail fraud.

It is apparent that the top-100 mail-order companies have escaped for the past eight years the wrath of USPS regulatory enforcement. This has occurred despite the fact that many top-100 mail-order companies engage in questionable and arguably misleading and deceptive promotions by using teasers and sweepstakes that are arguably deceptive, misleading, confusing, and obligatory. At the same time, while some smaller or fringe companies engage in the same type of promotions, many have been the subject of USPS regulatory enforcement actions!

The USPS should enforce the law in a nondiscriminatory, equitable manner. But they do not. It's time to ask the question, Why?

How do certain top-100 direct-marketing companies obtain such favoritism from the USPS? Considering the recently found FDA and HUD corruption, the USCA is conducting further investigations to find out. We think the justice department should also investigate the U.S. Postal Service.

Returning now to the next set of events. Our company was now on its feet again from another major victory over a corrupt government agency. We then turned our attention to finishing the job on the FDA and, in particular, James C. Simmons, the main culprit in the No-Hunger Bread atrocity.

Two of the initial tactics against Mr. Simmons were to hire private investigators to search out what they could find on Simmons and simultaneously to make an expose letter to all of the food and drug companies that were under his Cincinnati region office. A copy of the letter starts below. These two efforts indeed revealed misconduct by Simmons as follows:

1) Simmons is held in low esteem by the vast majority of the Cincinnati office FDA employees, and many regard him as an unfit supervisor and public official.

2) Many of Simmons' employees were outraged by the Nancy's Bread atrocity and indicated that it was widely held that the actions taken at Simmons' direction were excessive, unnecessary and a waste of taxpayers' money.

3) In the late '70s and early '80s, Simmons exercised a double standard with respect to regulatory enforcement with excessive enforcement action against small companies and little to no action taken against large companies. Several employees indicated that Simmons was wined and dined by large food and drug companies under his jurisdiction.

4) During the late '80s, Simmons had engaged in almost no regulatory enforcement action, even though certain companies under his jurisdiction apparently violate regulations that threaten the health and safety of the public.

5) Simmons is a tyrant who carries out Gestapo-like tactics against his employees, including suspected wiretaps.

6) Simmons engages in racial discrimination as evidenced by the huge increase in EEOC complaints during his tenure as district staff director.

Here is the letter we mailed from one predecessor organization to the Better Government Bureau. It was called the USCA. (United States Citizens Association):

To Whom It May Concern:

We have reason to believe that there are certain high-ranking officials in the FDA who are not working in the public interest and are not fit to deal with the public.

One such official, who is the subject of this letter, is James C. Simmons, Director of the FDA, Cincinnati regional office.

We have reason to believe that Mr. Simmons engages in discriminatory enforcement of FDA regulations, takes excessive and unwarranted regulatory actions, and is malicious in carrying out enforcement against companies that are selected for enforcement action.

In carrying out such actions, Mr. Simmons misuses FDA seizure laws which are meant for the seizure of dangerous and harmful products. Mr. Simmons misuses these laws against safe and harmless products in order to destroy and/or punish certain companies he personally does not favor without the target company being provided a fair trial. Mr. Simmons also conducts himself in a manner that provokes and antagonizes executives of those companies who are victims of this activity.

The USCA is a non-profit citizens organization which exists to promote the interests of U.S. citizens. One of the divisions of the USCA is an investigative division which also compiles complaints from citizens concerning government agencies and government officials.

The USCA has received complaints from a number of private corporations under the authority of the FDA Cincinnati regional office which claimed that Mr. Simmons took unjustified action against their companies. Here is a brief summary of one of these complaints involving Mr. Simmons.

In 1978 one company tried to market a very good diet bread but were neophytes in marketing food products. They asked for rules and guidelines from Mr. Simmons office, but none were provided. After they started marketing the bread and were receiving tens of thousands of orders, Mr. Simmons sent two agents to their office under the false pretenses of "routine checks." The company specifically asked these agents if anything was wrong, and if there was, they would be glad to be cooperative. But all during their encounter, which took several weeks, Mr. Simmons' agents repeatedly said that nothing was wrong and all they were doing was a routine check.

All the while Mr. Simmons' Agents were gathering information that would allow the FDA to seize the inventory of the diet bread. Mr. Simmons' intentions, which he deliberately did not disclose, were to seize as much of the diet bread as possible to put the company out of business.

The seizure by the FDA was then carried out. During the seizure, Mr. Simmons coordinated television coverage to humiliate and assassinate the character of the executives of the company. We know at this time, that Mr. Simmons did not have any consumer complaints, and therefore, we suspect he had complaints from competitors in the synthetic drug business because this diet bread was selling well and posed a competitive threat to a new synthetic patent diet pill which was introduced to the market at the same time.

But even worse, after the diet bread was seized, which amounted to 20,000 4-lb. cartons, (80,000 pounds, of mix, enough to make 112,000 pounds of bread by adding water, enough to feed 1,200,000 people) the company offered to take on the expense of distributing the seized bread to those people who were going hungry in Ohio, Mr. Simmons saw to it that they were not allowed to do this.

Although the FDA complained about the advertising for the diet bread, the real legal basis for the seizure was the following which was ridiculous. Inadvertently, one of the ingredients suppliers of a minor ingredient had put a preservative in that ingredient. But this preservative in the entire bread mix would have amounted to an ineffectual trace. The bread was perfectly good and harmless.

Mr. Simmons saw to it that the bread was destroyed and plowed under in a landfill in Euclid, Ohio. To make matters even worse, he had one of his agents go up to the Euclid landfill and take pictures of the bread being plowed under. The only reason we could see that Mr. Simmons would want such pictures would be so that he could gloat over such a matter, which certainly has to reflect a cruel and malicious nature.

We do not feel Mr. Simmons acted in the interest of the public or acted as a fit government administrator for the following reasons. The seizure of this diet bread was totally unnecessary and unwarranted. If Mr. Simmons was only trying to gain compliance with FDA regulations, and really did not have a malicious intent, he would have simply made it known at the beginning to the company that the label and marketing of the bread did not meet his approval. The company, from the start, demonstrated that they wanted to comply with regulations and would be cooperative in doing so. If Mr. Simmons had made his intentions known earlier, the company would have not produced and packaged a large amount of the bread under the labeling that did not meet Mr. Simmons' approval and would have made changes to the advertising. The changes could have been made early and thus inexpensively to meet with the approval of Mr. Simmons.

Secondly, after a large amount of the bread had been packaged, it is well documented that in other such cases large companies were allowed to sell out mislabeled packages and correct the labeling when new packages were printed.

Lastly, there was certainly no reason beyond the stretch of anyone's imagination why Mr. Simmons would not allow enough bread to feed over 1.2 million people to be provided to the hungry people in Ohio rather than needlessly destroying it.

We do not feel that this is the way a good government official should behave. Amongst other things, Mr. Simmons' antagonistic, cruel and malicious behavior is bad for the public image of the federal government. This incident left deep scars and has turned many employees of this company against the federal government.

Along with other antagonizing comments Mr. Simmons made to company executives, he said the following: "Get out of the business." "People like me are the real power in government, not elected officials." "If you do not do as I say and get out of the business, I will have your product seized and have television cameras and reporters there."

We could not believe that 10 years later Mr. Simmons is still in his position and apparently still carrying on activities that are not in the public interest. Therefore, the USCA is taking efforts to find out the full extent of Mr. Simmons' activities against private corporations under his authority in an effort to get Mr. Simmons removed from his position.

Therefore, we are mailing these letters to all private corporations under Mr. Simmons' jurisdiction to confirm to what extent he is carrying on these activities on an ongoing manner. We are also making this letter available in the office where Mr. Simmons works to find out if he has discussed such matters with his employees.

If you have any such information that Mr. Simmons is not conducting himself in the public interest, please contact the USCA. The full story regarding the diet bread incident is enclosed for your information.

Sincerely yours,

/s/ Frank Seaton
Frank Seaton
Investigator
The United States
Citizens Association
FS/mld
Enclosure

We then documented the misconduct information that we found on Mr. Simmons into expose material and mailed it to all the top administrators in the FDA and Mr. Simmons' employees there at his Cincinnati office. We received many responses from Simmons' employees confirming to us what an unfit government official he was. They also reported to us that a short time after we mailed the letter to all of his employees, Simmons called all of the employees to a large conference room to defend against the expose. They said in that meeting that

Simmons was so visibly shaken that he was trembling uncontrollably and was virtually unable to speak.

Regarding what the FDA administrators did with Mr. Simmons: It is virtually impossible to fire a civil-service worker in the federal government. We were told what they usually do if an unfit government official is an administrator is to deprive him of bonus money and not promote him. As we last checked in late 1993, Simmons was still at his original position at the Cincinnati office and obviously had not received a promotion to a higher administrative job in over 15 years, since he took that position in 1977.

The following details our fight with Washington State Attorney General Ken Eikenberry, who filed a frivolous lawsuit against us and tried to smear our good name.

At the beginning of his gubernatorial campaign in the spring of 1992, Ken Eikenberry was considered the runaway favorite to win the governor's race. Eikenberry held large, seeming insurmountable leads over all other candidates. He had been re-elected as attorney general three times by wide margins, had previously held political office in the state legislature, and had headed the Washington State Republican party in the '70s. He was the only candidate with statewide name recognition.

Five years before his gubernatorial run, Eikenberry siphoned over $100 million of public money into the attorney general's office, so he could institute lawsuits that would bolster his career – even though they were not in the public interest. This was ostensibly done to further his campaign for governor. He increased spending at five times the rate of inflation. It appears that he hired over three times the number of personnel needed in an attorney general's office for a state that size in order to build an in-house campaign team. His overall budget of $52 million per year was over two and a half times that of attorneys general budgets for similarly sized states.

In order to get free publicity, Eikenberry filed hundreds of apparently baseless civil lawsuits against Washington State businesses and companies across the nation, including Proctor and Gamble here in Ohio.

But in late 1991, the bully finally picked on the wrong guy. Eikenberry filed a false and frivolous lawsuit against our Lindenwold Fine Jewelers division, a national jewelry retailer of both fine jewelry and high-quality synthetic gem jewelry. Eikenberry's main target in the suit was an advertisement for cubic zirconia diamond simulant jewelry, called "CZ" jewelry. It appears Eikenberry had special plans for this particular lawsuit. It appears he was going to team up with TV reporter Herb Weisbaum of KIRO-TV, a CBS affiliate in Seattle, Washington. The plan was to blow this petty civil suit out of proportion, to get a national news story, to launch his gubernatorial campaign. Weisbaum did run a preliminary story in December, 1991, which contained certain falsities in order to preview the "big story." This report got national coverage on the "CBS This Morning" show.

However, unknown to Eikenberry, Lindenwold was only one of 13 divisions of The Suarez Corporation, now Suarez Corporation Industries. He did not know we were a widely diversified marketing and communications company. Unfortunately for Eikenberry, one of the other divisions was Campaign Services, one of the best and most advanced political service bureaus in the nation. Also unknown to Eikenberry was the fact the owner and president of Suarez Corporation Industries, yours truly, is highly regarding as one of the leading marketing experts in the nation.

An investigation of Eikenberry by Suarez Corporation Industries revealed his pattern of self-serving and special-interest-serving actions. It was determined by Suarez Corporation Industries investigators that Eikenberry was perhaps one of the worst and most destructive politicians in the country. He was about to ascend to a state governorship, which influences national politics and is considered the next step to the presidency. At this point, we decided that it was in the public interest to take action to defeat Eikenberry on behalf of businesses across the nation and the 100,000 customers the company had in Washington.

A well-designed political strategy was developed in early 1992, utilizing the company's high-tech political expertise. The strategy called for crippling Eikenberry's fund-raising campaign with an initial attack in May, 1992, and then finishing him off in the Republican primary with a second attack, just before the elections in the fall of 1992. The strategic campaign against Eikenberry called for well-targeted, effective political ads using the media of television, radio, newspapers, direct-mail, and telemarketing.

The campaign against Eikenberry worked beyond expectations. The May 1992 attack severely damaged Eikenberry's fund-raising, to the point where after the attack, his opponents were raising $5 for every $1 Eikenberry raised. The initial attack also drastically cut Eikenberry's lead in the polls, which had been as much as two to one over his nearest opponent. Eikenberry's lead continued to drop throughout the summer.

After the second attack in August of 1992, Eikenberry fell to second in the Republican primary race behind Sid Morrison, a member of the U.S. House of Representatives from east Washington. Eikenberry would have lost the Republican primary in September, had it not been for an 11th-hour near miracle. A week before the primary, the National Rifle Association, which had a vendetta against front-runner Morrison for voting in favor of the Brady Bill, ran nearly a million dollar's worth of television advertising slamming Morrison and promoting Eikenberry. Eikenberry barely squeaked out a primary victory with less than one percent of the vote.

In a vindictive retaliation for the Suarez campaign against him, Eikenberry filed another frivolous civil suit against the corporation during the summer of 1992. As part of the proceedings, Eikenberry obtained over 100,000 names and addresses of Lindenwold customers in the State of Washington, and mailed a letter to many, perhaps all, of these customers denouncing Lindenwold and telling the customers that he was going to stop Lindenwold from doing business in Washington. The letter backfired.

Eikenberry found that Lindenwold's customers were highly satisfied and that the company was offering them the highest-quality jewelry at the best prices in the nation. Eikenberry's letter resulted in a barrage of angry responses from Lindenwold customers, rebuking Eikenberry for his unwanted interference and unjust attack on a reputable company. Most customers were angered because they were looking forward to doing much of their Christmas shopping from Lindenwold's catalog, and Eikenberry's actions threatened a major inconvenience. This letter cost Eikenberry an additional substantial number of votes.

On November 3, 1992, Eikenberry was defeated in the general election by Mike Lowry, a candidate who had never held a state office, by 53% to 47%.

But the problems were not yet over for Weisbaum and CBS. Suarez Corporation Industries filed a lawsuit against Weisbaum and CBS for broadcasting a malicious reckless and false story that defamed us. The lawsuit sought $25 million in damages.

Again, counter-offensive tactics are not going to help you if you have done something truly wrong. They were successful for us because in these unjust regulatory actions, we were innocent of any wrongdoing.

As a result of the effective counter-offensives that we carried out against federal regulatory corruption, we have not had one case of unjust regulatory action on the federal level since 1985.

At the state level, all direct-marketing businesses are harassed by the criminal element in the state attorneys general offices numerous times per year. Ever since our successful counteroffensive against the unscrupulous attorney general, Ken Eikenberry, we have not had one incident of unjust regulatory action from any state attorney general.

This is an edited excerpt from the book *7 Steps to Freedom II* by Benjamin D. Suarez. To read the rest of the story please purchase the book by contacting the Suarez Corporation at: www.suarez.com.

For the "No-Hunger Bread" type recipe, go to www.naturalcures.com.

How to Find a Health-care Practitioner Who Doesn't Use Drugs and Surgery

The most important thing you can do if you want to prevent and cure illness and disease without drugs and surgery is to take personal responsibility for your health! Truly, the miracle for every illness and disease, and virtually every problem you will ever experience in your life, is to take personal responsibility. You need to know that the government is not going to take care of you. Your friends are not going to take care of you. Your family does not have the responsibility to take care of you. Your boss does not have the responsibility to take care of you. Society is not going to take care of you. No one is coming to the rescue.

If you want to live a happy, successful life the number one most important thing you could ever do is to take personal responsibility for everything that happens in your life. You cannot have victim mentality. You can't have "oh, poor me" mentality. You can't have "everything bad happens to me" mentality. You need to take charge of your life. You need to be the leader in your own life first. You need to take 100 percent personal responsibility. When you do, you will see absolutely miraculous changes in your life. I am in the process of writing a book called *The Five-Minute Miracle*. In this book I talk about how in just five minutes a person's life can completely change if they simply take personal responsibility. I point out and show all the facts backing up the statement that everything that's wrong in your life you are the cause of.

That is hard for most people to understand because they want to point the finger at society, the government, the weather, the situation, their living conditions, their parents, and everything else around them. They want to believe that they are not the cause of what is happening in their life. This is untrue. You are the "cause" of everything that happens in your life. Most people live a life totally at the "affect" of everything that goes on around them. Most people live a life like a ship on the high seas without a rudder and without an engine, simply going wherever the wind blows and wherever the tide takes them. Most people live a life believing they have no control over what happens in their life; that all the situations around them are in control of their life. This is not true. You are 100 percent in control of your life and your destiny. When you wake up and apply "The Five-Minute Miracle," which is taking personal responsibility, everything in your life changes for the better!

In relation to health, the first thing you must do is take responsibility for finding natural cures for your disease. It is your responsibility to find the CAUSE of your disease. It is your responsibility to investigate and seek out the answers. It is your responsibility to find the solutions. Many people see miraculous cures in their health when they simply wake up one morning and make the decision that they are going to beat their disease, and they are going to find the cause and the cure. I've seen people simply make that decision and within days their disease is cured. It seems miraculous, but the fact is once they made up their mind, once they made the DECISION that they were going to beat the disease, their own mind and belief cured the disease!

I believe the first, most important thing you can do is take personal responsibility and make the decision that you are going to find the cause and cure for your disease. In order to do this, in my opinion, the first thing you must do is seek out licensed health-care practitioners to help you achieve this goal. I believe it is vital that you get treated by licensed health-care practitioners and do not attempt to treat yourself. I, myself, know huge amounts of information when it comes to the cause and curing of illness and disease. I believe I know a lot about preventing disease. However, I still go and seek the advice and opinions of licensed health-care practitioners on a REGULAR BASIS! I do this to prevent disease, gain more knowledge, and get other people's insights and viewpoints. I do not believe I'm the smartest guy in the world. I do believe that two heads are better than one. If you truly want to prevent disease, and if you truly want to cure disease, it is vital that you seek advice from licensed health-care practitioners. It is equally important that you do not look at these people as gods or "all-knowing." It is important that you seek several opinions and understand that you are only getting OPINIONS. You must gather the information yourself, listen to the various opinions, review the various viewpoints, and you make the decision of the course of action that YOU feel most comfortable with. Remember, it's your body, it's your health, it's your life. You take charge and take responsibility.

In order to help you find a licensed health-care practitioner you can go to www.naturalcures.com. On my Web site I will be listing thousands of licensed health-care practitioners from all around the world. It is my intention to also have these individual health-care practitioners and clinics reviewed so that you can see what other people have experienced when they were treated by these licensed health-care practitioners or clinics. You can also go to your local Yellow Pages and look under naturopath, chiropractor, massage therapist, colon therapist, oriental medicine, homeopathy, acupuncture, holistic medicine, or any of the other modalities that are in the "natural health care" arena. I am also providing here a list of some references that could be helpful. This certainly is not a complete list, but a good starting point. Even if you are not sick or experiencing any negative symptoms, I would strongly encourage you to see several licensed health-care practitioners now! It is better to prevent disease than to worry about trying to cure it once you have it.

Acupressure
www.acupressure.com

Acupuncture
www.acupuncture.com
www.medicalacupuncture.org
www.aaom.org
www.nccaom.org
www.tai.edu

Alexander Technique
www.alexandertech.com

Alphabiotics
www.alphabiotics.biz

Aromatherapy
www.naha.org
www.pacificinstituteofaromatherapy.com

Asthma
www.sorvinoasthmafound.org

Aston Patterning
www.aston-patterning.com

Ayurvedic Medicine
www.ayurveda.com

Bioenergetic Bodywork
www.bioenergetic-therapy.com

Biological Dentistry
www.biologicaldentistry.org
www.holisticdental.org
www.nihadc.com

Bowen Therapy Technique
www.bowendirectory.com

www.boweninfo.com

Callahan Technique
www.tftrx.com

Cancer
www.centurywellness.com

Candida Cleansing
www.lifeforceplan.com

Chelation Therapy
www.abct.info
www.acam.org
www.centurywellness.com

Chiropractic
www.10ac.com
www.amerchiro.org
International Chiropractors Association
www.chiropractic.org
www.worldchiropracticalliance.org

Colon Therapy
www.i-act.org

Craniosacral Therapy
www.upledger.com

Detoxification and Cleansing
www.wecarespa.com
www.hippocratesinst.com

Drug Rehab
www.narcanon.net

Energetic Rebalancing
www.energeticmatrix.com
www.energeticbalancing.us

Feldenkrais
www.feldenkrais.com

Gentle Wind Project
www.gentlewindproject.org

Hakomi
www.hakomiinstitute.com

Healing Touch
www.healingtouch.net

Hellerwork
www.hellerwork.com

Herbal Medicine
www.herbalgram.org
www.ahpa.org

Homeopathic Medicine
www.homeopathyusa.org
www.homeopathyhome.com
www.homeopathic.com
www.homeopathic.org
www.homeopathy.org

Iridology
www.iridologyassn.org

Kinesiology
www.ask-us.org
www.icak.com
www.uskinesiologyinstitute.com

Magnetic Field Therapy
www.naam-heart.lle.org
www.polarpowermagnets.com

Massage Therapy
www.abmp.com
www.amtamassage.org
www.aobta.org

Music Therapy, Sound Therapy
www.musictherapy.org
www.soundlistening.com

Naturopathic Doctors
www.naturopathic.org
www.calnd.org
www.findnd.com
www.hanp.net

Neuro-Emotional Technique
www.NetMindBody.com

Organic Information
www.organic-center.org
www.organicconsumers.org
www.ota.com

Orthomolecular Medicine
www.orthomed.org

Osteopathic Medicine
www.academyofosteopathy.org
www.holisticmedicine.org
www.cranialacademy.com

Reflexology
www.reflexology-usa.net
www.reflexology-usa.org

Reiki
www.reiki.org

Rolfing
www.rolf.org

Rosen Method
www.rosenmethod.org

Sunlight Therapy
www.solarhealing.com
www.sungazing.com

Total Integration Therapy
www.livingfreedom.net
www.touch4health.com

Trager Approach
www.trager.com

The medical clinic that I recommend and that I personally visit is:

Dr. Bruce Fong
Sierra Integrative Medical Center
380 Brinkby Avenue
Reno, NV 89509
775-838-5388
www.centurywellness.com

Other Helpful Web sites

www.dreammoods.com/commondreams
www.drrathresearch.org
www.tolifeonline.com
www.therealessentials.com
www.themeatrix.com
www.eatwellguide.org
www.davidwolfe.com
www.sunfood.net
www.lifeforceplan.com
www.mercola.com
www.thetruthaboutsplenda.com
www.healthfreedom.net

www.naturalcures.com
www.thewhistleblower.com
www.kevinfightsback.com
www.wolfclinic.com
www.whatthebleep.com
www.thecorporation.com
www.corporatewatch.org
www.personsinc.org
www.prwatch.org
www.tvnewslies.org
www.www.foxbghsuit.com.

About the Author

Kevin Trudeau is fast becoming the nation's foremost consumer advocate. Knowing from firsthand experience the power of greed, Kevin pled guilty to felonies in his youth and spent almost two years in prison realizing that "the love of money" is the root of all evil. Kevin then reprioritized his life. His new business and personal mission statement became, "We positively impact the whole person." Today Kevin is known as one of the great American success stories. He is regarded as one of the most prolific business leaders in America building a $2 billion global business empire. What makes this most amazing is that Kevin has no formalized education; no family connections; started with no money; never received any venture capital, loans, or financing; no government grants; and ran all of his businesses profitably out of cash flow. *The Wall Street Journal* called him "a marketing guru." *The Chicago Sun-Times* called him "the infomercial king." Having been attacked and sued in three continents, Kevin knows from personal experience how big business and government try to debunk individuals who promote products that could hurt the profits of the giant multinational corporations. Today Kevin spends most of his time spearheading www.naturalcures.com, the Web site that promotes education about natural healing therapies; and the www.thewhistlebl ower.com, the Web site that exposes corporate and government abuse and corruption. Kevin is actively pursuing lawsuits against the individuals, corporations, and government agencies that take advantage of the average consumer. He is also dedicated to the formation of various foundations to pursue these goals and has donated much of his fortune for that purpose. Kevin is available for personal appearances,

571

seminars, and book signings on a limited basis. Call 800-931-4721 for more information. If outside the U.S.A., please call 847-850-1476 if you would like more information on personal appearances or seminars by Kevin Trudeau, or to order books, or to subscribe to Kevin Trudeau's Natural Cures Monthly Newsletter.

Kevin loves comments from readers. Send correspondence to Kevin Trudeau in care of: Alliance Publishing Group, Inc. P.O. Box 207, Elk Grove Village, IL 60009.

AUTHORS WANTED!

Alliance Publishing Group wants to publish your book! This is an unprecedented opportunity for authors who cannot get published because their books are too controversial or because they as authors who are not well known. Alliance Publishing Group, founded by Kevin Trudeau, is interested in your manuscript and potentially publishing your work. If you are an author who has written a book, or has a concept of a book, please contact us. Subjects include corporate and government corruption, health, nutrition, anti-aging, or any information on natural cures. Please send your manuscript or book proposal to:

Alliance Publishing Group
P.O. Box 207
Elk Grove Village, IL 60009

LOSE 30 POUNDS IN 30 DAYS!

The Weight-loss Secrets They Don't Want You To Know About

BY KEVIN TRUDEAU

ORDER KEVIN'S NEWEST BOOK ON CD

Quantity	Book or CD Title	Price (each)	Total Price
	Lose 30 Pounds in 30 Days: The Weight Loss Secrets They Don't Want You to Know About	$20	
		Shipping	$4.95
	Add 8.75% sales tax for IL residents		
	Grand Total		

Call 847-403-7497

Name:_____

Address:_____

City_____State_____Zip_____

Make checks payable to: Natural Cures, Inc.

Visa/MC #._____Exp. Date_____

Signature_____

Mail to: Natural Cures, Inc.
            P.O. Box 92271
            Elk Grove Village, IL 60009

Order

"*Natural Cures They Don't Want You to Know About*"

at 50% Off!

Buy 10 of these Natural Cures books for friends and family for only $15 each (plus S&H) .

Limited time offer!

Call 847-403-7497 to order

Subscribe to "Kevin Trudeau's Natural Cures Monthly Newsletter"

The only unbiased health newsletter in the world! Kevin accepts no advertising and sells no products. Get health information and new natural cures discoveries not available anywhere else. Your subscription is vital and necessary for the fulfillment of the mission!

Only $5.95 per Month!

Call 847-403-7497 to order

What People Are Saying About This Book

I had heart problems, high blood pressure, and high cholesterol. I was on all kinds of pills that didn't seem to make any difference. After I read Kevin Trudeau's book, I decided to go holistic and found a new doctor. Now I am off all the pills, my blood pressure seems fine, and my cholesterol seems to be within normal ranges. Yesterday I went to a heart doctor, and he gave me a clean bill of health. No drugs were used. If you are interested in doing things naturally, that's the way to go.

—TK, Jackson, Mississippi

I ordered the book the minute I saw the show on TV. There are so many things the book touched on that I suspected my whole life. I immediately read the parts about being fat, why Americans are fat, and how to lose weight without ever having to worry about it the rest of your life. I also followed the different liver cleansing recommendations, and in two months I lost 45 pounds just from the tips in the book. I'm 52 years old and nothing's ever worked before. I've bought all the diet products and gone to all the different clubs. But the one thing that no one ever told me was in this book. It's the biggest breakthrough ever, and nobody knows about it. It's just as the book said: the diet industry is making a lot of money off of us. The fitness clubs and the manufacturers of nutritional supplements make millions of dollars this way—why would they want to help us lose weight? They'd rather pay people to cover up the information. It makes sense. Everything in the book makes sense. The book reveals a different kind of approach to weight loss—it actually gets to the core of the problem and gets rid of the underlying fat, which is a result of yeast in the body. I'd read and tried everything, and I'd gotten nowhere until I read this book. It's an amazing book.

—*BS, Seattle, Washington*

I can't say enough about this book. We read it last Thanksgiving on our way to see some folks in South Carolina. We talked about it on the airplane all the way down there, and everybody was listening to us. We just can't quit talking about this book. It has changed our way of thinking and our way of eating, and it is so simple to read. Anybody could read this book and benefit from it. We certainly have. No words can describe how much the book has changed mine and my husband's lives. I suffer from headaches and allergies all the time, and just after we got this book my husband was diagnosed with a terminal disease. Now we're seeing awesome results. I preach the book all the time—I've given it to my boss, my boss's twin sister, everybody in my office. It's amazing how the American public is kept in the dark. I was reading Kevin Trudeau's newsletter about the hazards of beef, and while my husband was on the road I read it to him over the phone. We were both so mad about it. I never dreamed that I could ever be free from allergies, and I can tell you this book is a life changer.

—*CB, La Marque, Texas*

The book was great—it really opened my eyes. I liked it so much I bought copies for my kids and the book on tape for one of my sons. I have told many people about this book. I've lent the book to my cousins and friends and recommend that they buy it. It is worth the money. They will learn how to take care of their bodies without drugs.

—*RM, Wilmington, Delaware*

The book has changed our lifestyles completely—the way we think and the way we eat. It's had a very positive impact on our life. Two weeks after starting to read chapter 6, the whole family began to feel happier and healthier. We haven't been to a doctor in more than a year. Ever since I saw the show in September I started to make some changes. I say: Try it, you've got nothing to lose.

—*DB, Baltimore, Maryland*

I have followed about half of the recommendations in chapter 6. Now I don't feel pain anymore, and I can sleep at night. I had tremendous arthritis on one side of my body from the hip down, and I'd been in pain for about four years. I refused to take painkillers such as Vioxx; I would use topical ointment, but I would not take anything orally. When I read the book, I started drinking the "magic juices," switching to organic products, and did just about everything mentioned. Now I can go out for walks—even my daughter doesn't believe it. I've found that you can feel better in life. I'm almost 77, and I have never felt this good.

—DA, Norwood, Massachusetts

◇◇◇

This book is amazing! A friend highly recommended it to me, and I've been thrilled with it. What really spoke to me was the way the drug industry makes so much money by keeping people in an unhealthy state. I also identified with the cleansing process outlined in the book and actually went through one of the cleanses. Although I started off the cleanse being about 70 pounds overweight, I only intended to clean out my body. But the weight that I lost, combined with the absence of headaches, has gotten me really excited about the power of natural alternatives. Getting up at 6 o'clock in the morning is not the chore that it used to be, and I no longer want to take a nap in the afternoon. I am a new person, and it's really exciting. I've made some changes in my eating habits and so forth, but I'm not limited to two or three items a day. This book is refreshing, brutally honest, and truthful. If you are interested in improving your health, this book is a must read. I have recommended it to family members because they are important to me and I want them to have their health back. You've got to read it.

—*JC, Boulder, Colorado*

I read the book and listened to it on CD, and then my husband and I started following its recommendations, trying to do as much as we could to be healthy. I try to eat more healthy things and to eliminate as many toxins from my body as possible. My skin seems more radiant and vibrant; I do seem healthier, and I have more energy. I agree with Kevin Trudeau completely that we need to get off of prescription drugs. I recommend the book to all my friends and family because it is very important to get the word out: you don't need to be a slave to prescription drugs, and you don't need surgery, particularly since the disease ends up coming back anyway. Instead you need to change your lifestyle and your diet. We need to educate the public about the food additives that poison the body, making you feel really bad and giving you problems that you wouldn't otherwise have.

—*TK, Wheeling, Illinois*

◇◇◇

Since reading the book, I have switched to organic foods, vegetables, dairy products—everything I can get my hands on around here that's organic. And over the past few months I've noticed a difference: the types of ailments and illnesses I get, such as colds or arthritic problems, are of very short duration and are much less severe than before. Right now I am recovering from a back injury; I have not used a single over-the-counter drug, yet my back has gotten better more quickly. For many years I had been duped by a low-fat diet that didn't lower my cholesterol. In fact, my triglycerides went off the scale while I was following that diet. Then I tried low-carb diets, with their artificial sweeteners and so forth, not realizing that I was poisoning myself the whole time. Of course, those did not work, either. Not only do I recommend the book to my family and friends, but being in the health care profession I've also recommended it to my colleagues. My family and I are throwing out the stuff in our cabinets and cupboards to make room for the new types of foods we are eating. We are also cleaning out our medicine cabinet.

—*BD, Jevierville, Tennessee*

The book has helped me to better educate my patients on the importance of the body's pH; I use the pH strips in my office and give them to patients to take home with them. Then we start to establish a better alkaline state with coral calcium, more vegetables, and other things mentioned in the book.

Reading it helped me understand this process much more efficiently. It's an excellent book, and I'd recommend it to anybody. I have already recommended it to my son, a chiropractor in practice with me. He's been reading it and is excited about it, too. When you read the book, you become enthusiastic about doing different things that you hadn't thought of before. Anyone who reads it will be better off health-wise.

—Dr. JMN, Alexandria, Virginia

When I read the book, I learned a lot of information that I hadn't heard about, such as the way drug companies operate and how the government allows them to get away with it. I have been practicing natural cures for more than thirty years, ever since I saw my uncle die from misdiagnosis—first he lost one leg and then the other leg, and still he eventually died—so I knew that there was a better way. The book shows how to eliminate toxins and keep the body pure and free of poison, and it also suggests foods to eat to help the body get stronger and replenish itself. I recommend the book to everybody. When I teach Tai Chi, I tell students about some of the things I've read in the book, such as how to keep your body a little purer, what to eat, what not to eat. I also refer students to the book because it explains a lot of ways in which drug companies try to hide information that could help us cure our bodies instead of prolonging illness.

—TL, Schaumburg, Illinois

◇◇◇

I watched the television program about the book, and it touched on so many subjects that were personal to me. Number one is cancer. I lost my mom to cancer when she was only fifty years old. Since I'm now forty-two, I'd have only eight more years to live if I followed in her footsteps. But I want to live a long, healthy life, and that's basically why I bought the book. When I started reading that a cure for cancer had been known for many years, I burst into tears. I knew that there had to be a cure, and I knew also that there had to be some kind of cover-up. Because of it, I lost somebody who was my best friend and who was very important to me. And I lost her needlessly. She could still be here today, sharing all our joys and sorrows, but because of the lack of information, she's not. And the treatments that are available are simply sadistic. Another motivation for buying the book was my diagnosis of "chronic fatigue syndrome." After reading the book, I changed my diet and began to have more energy. I just feel better now. I drink only filtered water—it's amazing how little changes can make you feel so much better from day to day. I had been on lots of diet programs that didn't work for me. Supposedly on one diet you could choose whatever you wanted to eat, and you just had to count the calories in the foods you were eating. But that didn't work, because there were so many things I was eating that were actually making me hungry. The book also discusses in depth the subject of aspartame, which I was consuming in massive quantities and which was causing me to have headaches.

Doctors would tell me that the headaches were brought on by stress and that there was nothing I could do about them. This went on for years. Since reading the part of the book about aspartame, I have avoided aspartame and have not had any headaches. To me, that in itself makes the book worth a million bucks. I couldn't stop reading it. As soon as I opened the book—it took me only two nights to read the whole thing—I began to highlight certain areas of importance and took notes. I bought the book for three other people whom I knew it would benefit. This book is unbelievable. What's amazing to me is how people give me a hard time about wanting to be healthier and wanting to eat all natural and organic foods, as though it's a big scam.

—*SZ, Buffalo, New York*